Classics in Media Theory

This comprehensive collection introduces and contextualizes media studies' most influential texts and thinkers, from early 20th century mass communication to the first stages of digital culture in the 21st century.

The volume brings together influential theories about media, mediation and communication, as well as the relationships between media, culture and society. Each chapter presents a close reading of a classic text, written by a contemporary media studies scholar. Each contributor presents a summary of this text, relates it to the traditions of ideas in media studies and highlights its contemporary relevance. The text explores the core theoretical traditions of media studies: in particular, cultural studies, mass communication research, medium theory and critical theory, helping students gain a better understanding of how media studies has developed under shifting historical conditions and giving them the tools to analyse their contemporary situation.

This is essential reading for students of media and communication and adjacent fields such as journalism studies, sociology and cultural studies.

Stina Bengtsson is Professor of Media and Communication Studies at Södertörn University. Her research covers media audiences, practices and ethics, and how people coexist with media technologies in everyday life. She has published several books and articles in journals such as *Communication Theory*, *Media, Culture and Society* and *Journalism*.

Staffan Ericson is Associate Professor of Media and Communication Studies at Södertörn University. He has previously co-edited special sections in the *International Journal of Communications* and *Media, War and Conflict*. He is currently a participant in the project *A Sea of Data: Mediated Temporalities of the Baltic Sea*.

Fredrik Stiernstedt is Professor of Media and Communication Studies at Södertörn University. His research covers media industries, media policy, media history and media trust. Recent publications include *Prison Media: Incarceration and the Infrastructures of Work and Technology* (with Anne Kaun) and *The Future of the Nordic Media Model: A Digital Media Welfare State?* (with Peter Jakobsson and Johan Lindell).

"The risks of amnesia in media debates are huge, as we deal with the headlong rush of AI. But this outstanding collection reminds us of the deep roots media and communications studies has in the 20th century's sociology, psychology and cultural theory classics. Twenty-eight helpful explanatory essays unpack those texts in illuminating ways and give today's students all the context they need for understanding the latest media developments in a well-grounded way."

Nick Couldry, *London School of Economics and Political Science, UK*

"Summarizing a milky way of stellar contributions to media and communication research and situating each contribution in wider disciplinary and inter-disciplinary universes, *Classics in Media Theory* provides an essential companion and complement to the textbooks that commonly guide introductory courses in the field."

Klaus Bruhn Jensen, *University of Copenhagen, Denmark*

"This valuable resource for professors and students provides elegant pedagogical translations of theoretical texts that have become conceptual pillars of Media and Communication Studies. Written with care, contemporary sensitivity and empathy for the newcomers to the discipline, the chapters compellingly demonstrate the abiding relevance of these works to the exploration and understanding of our current media world."

Maria Bakardjieva, *University of Calgary, Canada*

Classics in Media Theory

Edited by
Stina Bengtsson, Staffan Ericson and Fredrik Stiernstedt

LONDON AND NEW YORK

Designed cover image: Sensay / Getty Images

First published 2024
by Routledge
4 Park Square, Milton Park, Abingdon, Oxon OX14 4RN

and by Routledge
605 Third Avenue, New York, NY 10158

Routledge is an imprint of the Taylor & Francis Group, an informa business

© 2024 selection and editorial matter, Stina Bengtsson, Staffan Ericson and
Fredrik Stiernstedt; individual chapters, the contributors

The right of Stina Bengtsson, Staffan Ericson and Fredrik Stiernstedt to be
identified as the authors of the editorial material, and of the authors for their
individual chapters, has been asserted in accordance with sections 77 and 78 of
the Copyright, Designs and Patents Act 1988.

All rights reserved. No part of this book may be reprinted or reproduced or
utilised in any form or by any electronic, mechanical, or other means, now
known or hereafter invented, including photocopying and recording, or in any
information storage or retrieval system, without permission in writing from
the publishers.

Trademark notice: Product or corporate names may be trademarks or
registered trademarks, and are used only for identification and explanation
without intent to infringe.

British Library Cataloguing-in-Publication Data
A catalogue record for this book is available from the British Library

Library of Congress Cataloging-in-Publication Data
Names: Bengtsson, Stina, 1971- editor. | Ericson, Staffan, editor. | Stiernstedt,
Fredrik, editor.
Title: Classics in media theory / edited by Stina Bengtsson, Staffan Ericson and
Fredrik Stiernstedt.
Description: Abingdon, Oxon ; New York, NY : Routledge, 2024. |
Includes bibliographical references and index.
Identifiers: LCCN 2023054736 (print) | LCCN 2023054737 (ebook) |
ISBN 9781032557960 (hardback) | ISBN 9781032557953 (paperback) |
ISBN 9781003432272 (ebook)
Subjects: LCSH: Mass media--Study and teaching. | Mass media--Philosophy.
Classification: LCC P91.3 C49 2024 (print) | LCC P91.3 (ebook) |
DDC 302.23071--dc23/eng/20240401
LC record available at https://lccn.loc.gov/2023054736
LC ebook record available at https://lccn.loc.gov/2023054737

ISBN: 978-1-032-55796-0 (hbk)
ISBN: 978-1-032-55795-3 (pbk)
ISBN: 978-1-003-43227-2 (ebk)

DOI: 10.4324/9781003432272

Typeset in Sabon
by Taylor & Francis Books

Contents

List of figures		viii
List of contributors		ix
	Introduction	1
	STINA BENGTSSON, STAFFAN ERICSON, AND FREDRIK STIERNSTEDT	
1	Walter Benjamin (1936) "The Work of Art in the Age of Mechanical Reproduction"	9
	LINUS ANDERSSON	
2	Herta Herzog (1941) 'On Borrowed Experience'	24
	JONAS ANDERSSON SCHWARZ	
3	Max Horkheimer and Theodor Adorno (1947) 'The Culture Industry: Enlightenment as Mass Deception'	39
	SVEN-OLOV WALLENSTEIN	
4	Paul F. Lazarsfeld and Robert K. Merton (1948) 'Mass Communication, Popular Taste and Organised Social Action'	53
	SVEN ROSS	
5	Claude Shannon and Warren Weaver (1949) *The Mathematical Theory of Communication*	70
	HEIKE GRAF	
6	Erving Goffman (1959) *The Presentation of Self in Everyday Life*	84
	ESPEN YTREBERG	
7	Jürgen Habermas (1962) *The Structural Transformation of the Public Sphere: An Inquiry into a Category of Bourgeois Society*	96
	ANNE KAUN	
8	Marshall McLuhan (1967) *The Medium Is the Massage*	111
	INGRID FORSLER	

vi *Contents*

9   Michel Foucault (1971) *The Order of Discourse*   125
    ANNIKA EGAN SJÖLANDER

10 Jean Baudrillard (1971) 'Requiem for the Media'   139
    GÖRAN BOLIN

11 Stuart Hall (1973) 'Encoding and Decoding'   151
    JOHAN FORNÄS

12 Raymond Williams (1974) *Television: Technology and Cultural
    Form*   166
    STAFFAN ERICSON

13 James Carey (1975) "A Cultural Approach to Communication"   183
    LARS LUNDGREN

14 Laura Mulvey (1975) 'Visual Pleasure and Narrative Cinema'   196
    SOFIA JOHANSSON

15 Dallas Smythe (1977) "Communications: Blindspot of Western
    Marxism"   211
    FREDRIK STIERNSTEDT

16 Gaye Tuchman (1978) *Making News: A Study in the Construction
    of Reality*   227
    ANNA ROOSVALL

17 Pierre Bourdieu (1979) *Distinction*   242
    JOHAN LINDELL

18 Elizabeth L. Eisenstein (1979) *The Printing Press as an Agent of
    Change*   256
    MARIE CRONQVIST AND KAJSA WEBER

19 Roland Barthes (1980) *Camera Lucida*   268
    PATRIK ÅKER

20 Benedict Anderson (1983) *Imagined Communities*   284
    PER STÅHLBERG

21 Frederic Jameson (1984) 'Postmodernism, or the Cultural Logic of
    Late Capitalism'   297
    ANDERS BURMAN AND MAGNUS RODELL

22 Janice Radway (1984) *Reading the Romance*   310
    STINA BENGTSSON

Contents vii

23 Neil Postman (1985) *Amusing Ourselves to Death* 322
   MICHAEL FORSMAN

24 Friedrich Kittler (1985) *Discourse Networks 1800/1900* 335
   OTTO FISCHER

25 Daniel Dayan and Elihu Katz (1992) *Media Events: The Live Broadcasting of History* 345
   JOHANNA SUMIALA

26 N. Katherine Hayles (1999) *How We Became Posthuman* 358
   JESPER OLSSON

27 John Durham Peters (1999) *Speaking into the Air* 372
   JOHAN FREDRIKZON

28 Lev Manovich (2001) *The Language of New Media* 390
   PETER JAKOBSSON

   Index 403

Figures

5.1	Transmission model (Shannon 1949, p. 34)	73
5.2	Circular communication model	79
7.1	Adapted from Habermas' original publication in English translation (1989, p. 30)	101
11.1	'Encoding and Decoding' (Hall, 1973/1980: 130, after Hall, 1973/2007: 388)	153

Contributors

Patrik Åker is Associate Professor of Media and Communication Studies at Södertörn University. He has written about a wide range of topics from photography, visual communication, journalism, music streaming, historical perspectives on media, to the relationships between media and spatiality.

Linus Andersson is Associate Professor in Media and Communication Studies at Halmstad University, Sweden. His scholarly contributions encompass a diverse range of subjects, including alternative and activist media, media literacy, and critical thinking. Currently, his research is focused on examining disinformation and conspiracy theories within the context of digital media culture.

Jonas Andersson Schwarz is Associate Professor of Media and Communication Studies at Södertörn University. He is primarily interested in digitalization, everyday life, and social structures – especially the ways in which platforms and datafication relate to civic issues, governance, epistemology, and media ecology.

Göran Bolin is Professor of Media and Communication Studies at Södertörn University. He is the author of *Value and the Media: Cultural Production and Consumption in Digital Markets* (Ashgate, 2011), *Media Generations: Experience, Identity and Mediatised Social Change* (Routledge, 2016) and *Managing Meaning in Ukraine: Information, Communication and Narration since the Euromaidan Revolution* (MIT Press, 2023).

Anders Burman is Professor of History of Ideas at Södertörn University. Three of his main research areas are the history of ideas in education, modern political intellectual history, and the thought of Hannah Arendt. He has written, edited, or co-edited some forty books, including a monograph on the history of democracy and the anthology *Hegelian Marxism: The Uses of Hegel's Philosophy in Marxist Theory from Georg Lukács to Slavoj Žižek* (co-edited with Anders Bartonek).

Marie Cronqvist is Professor of Modern History in the Department of Culture and Society at Linköping University. Her research covers media history and Cold War culture. She is the main coordinator of the Entangled Media

x *List of contributors*

Histories (EMHIS) research network and vice-chair of the ECREA Communication History Section.

Otto Fischer is Professor of Rhetoric at Uppsala University. He is one of the founders of the book series *Library of Media History*. In his research he focuses on the relationship between media and emotions, mainly in 18th-century German and Scandinavian Literature.

Johan Fornäs is Professor Emeritus of Media and Communication Studies at Södertörn University. Based on critical hermeneutics and cultural studies, his publications explore issues of identity and interpretation, for example, in *Cultural Theory and Late Modernity* (1995); *In Garageland* (1995); *Consuming Media* (2007); *Signifying Europe* (2012); *Capitalism* (2013) and *Defending Culture* (2017).

Ingrid Forsler is a Senior Lecturer of Media and Communication Studies at Södertörn University. She has a background in arts and media education and her research interests include imaginaries about media in educational contexts and how they are expected to transform learning.

Michael Forsman is Professor of Media and Communication Studies at Södertörn University. His research concerns media, children and youth, media literacy, and the digitalization of education.

Johan Fredrikzon is a postdoctoral fellow at the Division of History of Science, Technology and Environment, KTH Royal Institute of Technology and a visiting scholar at the University of California, Berkeley (2022–2024). His current project is a history of artificial intelligence (AI) from the perspective of errors and mistakes.

Heike Graf is Professor of Media and Communication Studies at Södertörn University. Her research interests are in the areas of environmental communication, migration, ethnic diversity in newsrooms and media practices. In particular, she makes use of systems theory as it was developed by Niklas Luhmann.

Peter Jakobsson is Associate Professor of Media and Communications Studies at Uppsala University. He has published research on a wide range of topics, including the digital media industry and digital infrastructures; media systems and the media welfare state; social class and the media; and trust and distrust in the news media.

Sofia Johansson is Associate Professor of Media and Communication Studies at Södertörn University. Her research interests range from the analysis of different forms of popular culture to news and digital media, with a focus on media audiences. She has published on topics including tabloid journalism, celebrity culture, online sociality, music streaming and young people and digital news.

Anne Kaun is Professor of Media and Communication Studies at Södertörn University, and a Wallenberg Academy Fellow studying the democratic implications of automated decision-making, artificial intelligence, and digitalization more generally.

Johan Lindell is Associate Professor of Media and Communication Studies at the Department of Informatics and Media, Uppsala University. His research focuses on media use and social inequality, fields of cultural production, and media systems.

Lars Lundgren is Associate Professor of Media and Communication Studies at Södertörn University. He is the author of *No Heavenly Bodies: A History of Satellite Communications Infrastructure* (with Christine Evans) and has been published in journals such as *Media History*, the *European Journal of Cultural Studies*, and the *International Journal of Communication*.

Jesper Olsson Professor of Literature at Uppsala University. His research focuses on literature, art and media ecologies. Currently he writes on literary techno-ecologies and older sound recordings of poetry. His latest book publication is the short essay "Postdigital Literature" (2022).

Magnus Rodell is Associate Professor of History of Ideas at Södertörn University. His research interests include nationalism, national identity, monuments, commemorations, cultural memory, cultural theory, material culture, and place.

Anna Roosvall is Professor of Media and Communication Studies at Stockholm University. She studies climate journalism, cultural journalism, activism, and "artivism" through a lens of justice and democratic theory and how the nature-culture, culture-politics, and national-transnational continuums are imagined among journalists and activists.

Sven Ross is Senior Lecturer of Media Studies. His main research field is the representation and audience reception of social class on television, using both quantitative and qualitative methods. His main theoretical contribution has been a discussion and development of Stuart Hall's encoding/decoding model.

Annika Egan Sjölander is Professor and Chair in Media and Communication Studies at Umeå University. Her research concerns communication *for* sustainable societies in the Anthropocene, focused on developing our understanding of the democratic role of media and communication in complex decision-making processes and societal transformations.

Per Ståhlberg is a media anthropologist and Associate Professor of Media and Communication Studies at Södertörn University. His research interests include professional cultures and meaning management in India and Eastern Europe. Among his publications is *Managing Meaning in Ukraine: Information, Communication and Narration since the Euromaidan Revolution* (with Göran Bolin, MIT Press, 2023).

xii *List of contributors*

Johanna Sumiala is Professor of Media and Communication Studies at the University of Helsinki. She is Visiting Senior Research Fellow at LSE, London, and Visiting Professor at the University of Bath. Her publications on media events, death and ritual include *Media and Ritual* (Routledge, 2013), *Hybrid Media Events* (Emerald, 2018) and *Mediated Death* (Polity, 2021).

Sven-Olov Wallenstein is Professor of Philosophy at Södertörn University and editor-in-chief of *Site Zones*. Recent publications include *Critical Theory: Past, Present Future* (ed. with Anders Bartonek, 2021) and *Spacing Philosophy: Lyotard and the Idea of the Exhibition* (2019, with Daniel Birnbaum).

Kajsa Weber is Associate Professor of History at Lund University. Her research focuses on early modern print as well as digitization and historical scholarship. She is the coordinator of the research platform DigitalHistory@Lund and member of the steering committee of Lund Center for the History of Knowledge.

Espen Ytreberg is Professor of Media Studies at the University of Oslo. He researches media history, media, and communications theory, and also writes literary nonfiction. Latest academic book publications: *A Social History of the Media*, 4th edition (Polity, 2020, with Peter Burke) and *Media and Events in History* (Polity, 2022).

Introduction

Stina Bengtsson, Staffan Ericson, and Fredrik Stiernstedt

One of the editors of this book was once a participant in a seminar with a famous French sociologist. The professor gave advice about projects and research ideas to the researchers and doctoral students that were participating. Then, someone asked the question of how best to understand one's contemporaries and contemporary society. Perhaps the person asking the question had expected an answer about innovative research methods or about which social phenomena could say the most about the times we live in. But the sociologist had other advice. He said: stop following the noise of the news, turn off your feeds, and use the time you earn to re-read sociology's classic texts. There was silence in the room. Would the way to understand the society of the 21st century go via texts written at the end of the 19th century, by people like Karl Marx, Émile Durkheim, Max Weber, and Georg Simmel?

This anthology can be said to be based on a related idea: anyone who wants to understand today's media society has much to gain by returning to earlier analyses, theories, and ideas – to what could be called the "tradition of ideas" of media studies. For students, teachers, and researchers in media and communication studies, such a thought can probably be perceived as even more drastic than it did for the audience of the French sociologist. Turning off the contemporary media noise – isn't this precisely the subject's object of study? Looking backwards – isn't the subject justified by the assumption that society is constantly being reshaped by new media technologies? And which would these "classical" texts be? Can the subject really show any equivalents to the foundational texts of a subject like sociology? Should we even bother to point them out? Isn't the maintenance of a disciplinary "canon" something that characterizes a research field that is self-absorbed, conservative, and narrow?

The editors of this anthology think that contemporary media studies can have a lot to gain by following the French sociologist's advice. By continuing to consider the contemporary media landscape through the questions that have previously been asked and ways of thinking about media that have developed in previous media cultures and societies, we think that we can be helped to deepen our understanding of what is happening today.

DOI: 10.4324/9781003432272-1

2 Bengtsson, Ericson, and Stiernstedt

What is a tradition of ideas?

Traditions of ideas do not, of course, float freely in the air, but are formulated and summarized in books and other texts written by specific people. Also in media studies, references are made repeatedly to texts that are assumed to represent the approach of a certain research tradition, the explanatory power of a certain theory, the potential of a certain method, and so on. During the course of an education within media studies, for example, most students will at some point come across a reference to a shorter text entitled "Encoding/Decoding", written in the 1970s by the author Stuart Hall. For the student who wants to go straight to the source, the text is easy to locate: it can be found in many readers in media studies and cultural theory that have been published since the 1980s and it circulates in various versions online. The topic of the text also seems immediately relevant for media studies and for ongoing discussions within the field: the text presents a model of the role that television, and in a broader sense, mass communication have played in circulating meaningful messages, from encoding to decoding, as well as a proposal for how we can classify variations in the reception of such messages.

Of course, Hall was far from alone in thinking about and writing about television and communication in the 1970s. So why exactly has his text – originally an internal research report, addressed to staff at the Centre for Contemporary Cultural Studies in Birmingham, England – survived into the 21st-century curricula? Why are some texts canonized and others not?

An answer to that question, which at first glance may seem unproblematic, is that it is the strongest texts, the most convincing analyses and theories that prove to last over time. In the marketplace of ideas, where researchers and intellectuals operate, quality is what counts. On closer reflection, however, such an assumption seems unlikely to be true. Some canonized texts are far from complete; on the contrary, they can be obscurely written, contradictory, thin on empirical evidence (several of the texts discussed in this book, including Hall's, exhibit such characteristics). As research in the sociology of science has been able to show, it is often completely different factors than quality that have controlled the spread and influence of a certain work: the network and social background of the author, the internal logic of the discipline, timing, luck – many factors seem to be able to make a certain work canonized and another forgotten. Not least, a critical understanding of power and privilege seems to be absolutely necessary for the understanding of how intellectual traditions are formed. Also, the canonical texts of media studies turn out to be strikingly often written from a privileged position: by people from certain countries and language areas (the USA and Great Britain), and by people of a certain gender (men) and ethnicity/race (white). (It is significant that many readers of "Encoding/Decoding" reacted with surprise when they first saw a picture of the author: Stuart Hall was black, of Jamaican/British background.)

It is such insights that can lead to the conclusion that discerning a canon is at best pointless, at worst harmful. One should therefore not publish books like

Introduction 3

this one and perhaps avoid talking about "traditions of ideas" at all. One problem with such an attitude is that traditions of ideas actually exist. They may reflect unjust power relations, we might agree with them or not, but their effects will not dissolve by themselves. If we want to criticize them (and the conditions by which they have been selected), we should also be familiar with them. Also: to the extent that a canon has been created by human actors engaging in an intellectual discussion, it may also be open for transformation, through continued conversation. New, or previously forgotten, works may be added. Dated and overrated works may be taken out. A book of this kind therefore simultaneously becomes an entry in the discussion about what a canon is, and a proposal about how it could be changed, within the framework of the broad, messy, and sluggish conversation that is the nature of scientific knowledge production and research.

In this book, it is the *traditions* of thought or theory that are at the centre, alongside the selected, canonized, texts. Theoretical traditions are ways of thinking that bring together groups of people at a certain time, in a special context and who are interested in similar phenomena, ask similar questions, or work methodically in a similar way. Our ambition is therefore to highlight the collective dimension of scientific thinking, in ways that may not be transparent when we encounter individual, canonized texts, one by one. On the other hand, the individual text may present us with special opportunities; to approach such collective ways of thinking "at work", to engage pedagogically with more general issues of "academic literacy" (the varying genres of scientific writing, the effects of context and historical distance).

Why read "classic" texts?

During the last fifty years or so, canon has been a contested concept. In the Anglo-American world, debate flared up (again) in the 1990s, after Harold Bloom's *The Western Canon: The Books and School of the Ages* in the early 1990s (Bloom 1994). This debate has often revolved around questions of representation: who is or is not included in the list of canonized thinkers and texts (and what does it mean for our understanding of the world)? The scope of this critique has been to widen the breadth of canonized voices (Backe 2015) by including marginalized groups in the construction of a canon. More recently, Willems (2022) suggest challenging the uses of history in canonical texts, as an attempt to uncover them as "the institutionalized standardization and normalization of whiteness (and maleness)" (Baugh-Harris and Wanzer-Serrano 2018 p. 338, quoted in Willems 2022 p. 3) rather than as markers of "intellectual quality and interest" (Katz et al. 2022 pp. 4–5, quoted in Willems 2022 p. 3). In the German-speaking world there is currently a vivid debate which orbits around the nature of the literary canon itself and "the mechanisms through which it is formed, and the powers by which it is maintained, eventually arriving, in many cases, at the underlying question of what 'literature' is". In this questioning, particularly new media may play a pivotal role (Backe 2015 p. 2).

4 *Bengtsson, Ericson, and Stiernstedt*

The selection of texts for this book do reflect some themes of this debate. While it does not explore the question of what "literature" is, it does raise issues of definition of a medium, in ways which may provoke previous demarcations. While it does not seek to replace the intellectual traditions that usually are put forward as the basis of media studies, it does try to include new perspectives in the plethora of voices which has traditionally represented it, in scholarly literature. This means including not only more female voices, but also texts originally emanating from the outside of an Anglophone, academic context, in particular the intellectual tradition of continental Europe. This is not predominantly an attempt to rethink the centre in relation to the periphery, but rather a way to provide students with a richer and more varied toolbox for analytically thinking about, and approaching, the contemporary media landscape.

Familiarity with the shifting phases of such a "messy conversation" is an important prerequisite for in-depth knowledge of a scientific field, such as media and communication studies. This is something that an education in media studies should provide to its students. A characteristic that is often found in "canonized" or "classic" texts is precisely that they have been formulated in relation to such a conversation. Stuart Hall's text, for example, can hardly be said to have delivered any innovative discoveries about what happens when we watch TV. Rather, his proposed model of communication was shaped by a desire to distance himself from how *other* traditions had tended to imagine TV viewing and communication more broadly. Hall's understanding of these earlier traditions was in turn based on a number of individual texts: many of the intellectuals of the 20th century had felt distaste for the mass culture of their time, but it was especially Adorno's and Horkheimer's criticism from the 1940s that had taken hold. Many had proposed models of communication, but especially Shannon and Weaver had developed the information theory. Many had speculated about the social effects of the mass media, but Lazarsfeld and Merton in particular were believed to summarize the view of the social sciences. Hall seemed to find weaknesses in the assumptions of all these traditions, but also ways to get around them, by connecting to other intellectual traditions: in particular the semiotic paradigm that had been developed by, among others, Roland Barthes. If we assume that Hall's text constitutes a foundational text for media studies, then it turns out to be built up by its relationship to a number of other texts, and not least, traditions of thought. The fact that several of the texts that Hall once railed against are also included in the present anthology indicates another quality of "classic" texts: they simply seem to be "good to think with", even if, or perhaps precisely because, we do not at all agree with the authors' theses. They may tickle our "sociological imagination", as C. Wright Mills put it, even though, or perhaps precisely because, the world the text depicts is now distant. They may demonstrate ways of understanding, in Raymond Williams's formulation, the "technique and cultural form" of a medium, even though, or perhaps precisely because, the medium in question has long since changed its guise.

Introduction 5

Rather than fixing an immutable list of texts and treat them as museal objects, the idea behind this book has been to facilitate an inventory or a repository of texts, filled with tools that may have continued value for our navigation within the contemporary media landscape. Like other navigational tools (maps and compasses for example), they can help us see where we came from and where we are: which paths remain open, which have previously proved impassable, which questions remain worth exploring, which ones are no longer worth trying. Not least we can get help in distinguishing what is "new" in our media landscape, and what is not. The media industries' own representatives – those who want to sell new products and services or justify their own importance – often tend to emphasize precisely what is new and volatile with "new media". It is easy to be persuaded by this rhetoric. At the same time, it is necessary, for those who want to study the media from a scientific perspective, to try to distance themselves from the hype that can surround phenomena in the field. Often the degree of change can be smaller than we first thought. Something might have changed on the surface, while the basic patterns and structures, and the most important questions and concerns raised by them, remain constant. So, readers of this book will for example discover that although the monopoly-like companies that control social and digital network media – such as Facebook and Google – are "new" actors in the field, their power can be understood in the extension of the political economy that Dallas Smythe analyzed in the 1970s. And, although today's "influencers" are a phenomenon that has arisen in symbiosis with the digital network media, their activities and position are reminiscent of the so-called two-stage hypothesis, a theory of media effects via personal influence, which was developed by media researchers in the 1940s. And despite the fact that gender equality and feminist theorizing have developed and spread in society since the 1970s, we can still use Laura Mulvey's thoughts on a "male gaze" to understand how gender is constructed in the media today.

This is not to say that the storehouse of classic texts would be one filled up with eternal truths. All the traditions of media studies are anchored in a historical context. They have been formulated in relation to the "big questions" of their time, to the research trends and media technologies of their time. Theodor W. Adorno's impression of the emerging mass media was, for example, marked by fascism's grip on Europe and Stalinism in the Soviet Union during the 1940s. Raymond Williams' writing develops in relation to British class society and the growing cultural dominance of the United States, and to development of the public service media in the post-war welfare society. Friedrich Kittler and Katherine Hayles formulate their theories in relation to the arrival of digital technology, and the aftermath of the Cold War. If we learn to read classical texts in such a historicizing way, we can also gain a more nuanced understanding of the possibilities and limitations for our own knowledge and how it develops. What in our time has shaped our thoughts about media and communication? Where are our own blind spots, the hidden prerequisites of our own theories?

We may also discover a new dimension in a classical text, which may not have been visible to its author. If we think about our own cellars or attics at home, it's

6 *Bengtsson, Ericson, and Stiernstedt*

often like this: when we pick out an old forgotten piece of furniture or a flower vase, we will most likely see it in a different way than when we once placed it there. Maybe because we have changed, or because the context is different; the inherited curtains fit better in the living room now, with the new sofa. This is sometimes also the case with texts and traditions of ideas. Walter Benjamin's text about the work of art in the age of reproduction, for example, gained new explanatory power for new generations with digitization, almost 70 years after it was written. When the technology magazine *Wired* named Marshall McLuhan its "patron saint" around the turn of the millennium, it was because his writings from the 1960s already seemed to say what should be said about the Internet era. When the distance between the past and the present is experienced as so frictionless in a text, prophetic gifts are readily attributed to the individual author. But we might as well ask ourselves what it is, in our own time, that has made these particular texts so readable, while others appear so distant.

Principles of selection, uses of the book

Considered as a repository, the tradition of ideas in media studies is exceptionally large and messy. After all, the field has emerged from different scientific disciplines, and the chapters in this book also provide samples of completely different, sometimes incompatible approaches and methods: immanent criticism, phenomenological reflection, mathematical and statistical analysis, philosophical speculation, empirical observation, and more. The authors of the texts discussed have been schooled in subjects as diverse as comparative literature, philosophy, sociology, history, political science, linguistics, mathematics, economics and so on. Very few, if any, of these texts have been formulated within the framework of a media studies discipline. Hall's text is one of those which, in retrospect, can more explicitly be said to raise one of the core issues of media studies. In many other texts, the effects of the media have come to be revealed by authors with completely different agendas: Benedict Anderson wanted to illuminate the nation as an imagined community, Jürgen Habermas the emergence of the modern public sphere, Pierre Bourdieu the sociology of taste, Erving Goffman the conditions of human interaction, and many others. Such texts, of course, give an indication of how profound the media have affected modern social life (and theory formation). Their continued relevance within an established discipline of media and communication research also suggests, paradoxically, continued risks with so-called "media centrism". According to a motto from the 1970s, the center of media research should lie "outside the media themselves", a perspective that has gained strong momentum during the last decade's oft-repeated motto of a "non-media-centric" media studies.

Against this background, establishing a selection of relevant texts representing a tradition of ideas within media studies is, of course, a daunting task. In this case, the book's selection has taken place in dialogue – and negotiation – with the participating authors. The editorship has thus been more collective

Introduction 7

than is usually the case with anthologies and textbooks. However, a common point of departure has been that the book should include what are usually perceived as central parts of media and communication research (or, internationally, "media studies"). At least in Scandinavian and Anglo-Saxon textbooks and curricula, there is now a relative agreement on which traditions are part of the discipline's root system: this includes at least sociological mass communication research, critical theory, cultural studies, and medium theory. At the same time, we have not shied away from rearranging the storage a little, for example by choosing texts other than those that usually represent these traditions, or by supplementing the repertoire with newly added currents of thought (media archaeology, posthumanism).

The final selection turns out to cover a period of just under 70 years, from 1936 (Walter Benjamin's essay "The Work of Art in the Age of Mechanical Reproduction") to 2001 (Lev Manovich's book *The Language of New Media*). This was not an obvious choice. Questions about media and communication have of course been discussed before the year 1936. Among the very earliest written texts found in Western cultural history, by ancient philosophers such as Heraclitus (5th century BC), Plato (4th century BC) and Aristotle (4th century BC), we may recognize a series of questions that we could today call media theoretical (see, for example, Holt 2014). In both the Old and New Testaments of the Bible – books written during a time period of approximately 1500 years, from the 15th century BC to approximately AD 100 – there is material for a history of ideas in communication (see, for instance, Durham Peters 1999, Simonson 2010). However, our selection has, like the usual self-understanding of the discipline, placed the emphasis on the (mass) media of the 20th century, up to and including the arrival of digital media.

Each chapter in the anthology is an original contribution and deals with one classic text. Each author has been instructed to place the text in its historical and scholarly context, to present a close reading of its central content, and to discuss its relevance today. The articles are intended to offer support for the students' own reading of the original texts, not to replace such readings. If the anthology was merely to be used as such a shortcut – a source of second-hand notes, for re-use in examinations – its intended value would largely be lost. But our approach also assumes that the classical texts can be complicated and that reading them can offer considerable resistance. Often, we miss the context that was given at the time when the text was first published: with what other texts the author took issue, was inspired by, or engaged in polemics against; to which major and dominant contemporary questions the author related; to which historical phenomena the text refers and relates. Added to this is the fact that the language and presentation may be archaic and foreign, that theoretical concepts may be taken for granted and not explained, and that the unwritten rules of the relevant genre – manifesto, research review, philosophical essay, peer review article – may be unfamiliar to the reader. Our ambition has hence been for the chapters in this book to provide support in ways of approaching different types of scholarly texts.

8 *Bengtsson, Ericson, and Stiernstedt*

The texts have been organized chronologically, according to the year of publication of the original text. However, the idea has not been that the book should be read consecutively, from cover to cover. Rather, different original texts and articles may be used in different occasions – during introductory and method courses, or for thematic deepening in the writing of a thesis. The discipline of media studies may be the main subject of education, but students and researchers in related subjects, who are looking for an overview of the field, may also find this selection useful. Our hope is that the anthology will in this way become a resource which – like the traditions of ideas themselves – continuously deepens the understanding of our contemporary and future media landscape.

References

Backe, H. J. (2015). The literary canon in the age of new media. *Poetics Today*, 36(1–2), 1–31.

Bloom, H. (1994). *The Western canon: the books and school of the ages.* New York: Harcourt Brace.

Hall, S. (1973/2007). Encoding and decoding in the television discourse. In A. Gray, J. Campbell, M. Erickson, S. Hanson & H. Wood (Eds., 2007), *CCCS selected working papers: Volume 2* (pp. 386–398). Routledge.

Holt, K. (2014). Mediekritik bortom medierna: Om filosofi som mediekritisk resurs [Media criticism beyond the media. About philosophy as a media critical resource]. In F. Stiernstedt (ed, 2014) *Mediekritik* [*Media criticism*] (pp. 23–37). Lund: Studentlitteratur.

Katz, E., Peters, J. D., Liebes, T., & Orloff, A. (2002). *Canonic texts in media research. Are there any? Should there be any? How about these?* Polity Press.

Peters, J.D. (1999). *Speaking into the air: a history of the idea of communication.* Chicago, Ill.: University of Chicago Press.

Simonson, P. (2010). *Refiguring mass communication: a history.* Urbana: University of Illinois Press.

Willems, W. (2023). The reproduction of canonical silences: re-reading Habermas in the context of slavery and the slave trade. *Communication, Culture & Critique*, 16(1), 17–24.

1 Walter Benjamin (1936) "The Work of Art in the Age of Mechanical Reproduction"

Linus Andersson

Introduction

In 2022, *The Manual*, a lifestyle magazine, published an article titled "Why Vinyl Records Are Making a Comeback in 2022." The author highlights a significant observation, stating that "This year, [...] marks the first instance in over a generation where sales of physical vinyl records have exceeded those of CDs" (John, 2022). The renaissance of what was previously deemed an obsolete analogue format has become evident.

Over the span of 30 years, the landscape of recorded music and music consumption underwent significant transformations characterized by technological innovation, legal disputes, and shifts in consumption patterns. The early 1980s witnessed the emergence of the compact disc (CD) as a novel medium for storing and playing music. In contrast to analogue gramophone records that reproduced sound through physical tracks, CDs stored audio digitally. This digital conversion enabled greater data storage efficiency, packing more information into a smaller space. For instance, while a vinyl record required both sides of a 12", diameter disc to accommodate music, a CD could house the same content on just one side of a 4.7" disc. Notably, the shift to digital format eliminated the auditory disturbances caused by dust or scratches on vinyl surfaces, leading to an overall enhancement in sound quality (even though vinyl enthusiasts claim the opposite). The industry benefited substantially from this transition, as CDs were cheaper to produce and stock, and their superior audio quality allowed them to be sold at higher prices. This format shift also spurred music enthusiasts all over the world to repurchase albums – they already owned in vinyl – in the new CD format. The peak of CD sales occurred around the year 2000. However, this move towards digitization set the record industry on a trajectory that would eventually reshape the entire economic fabric of the music business.

The digitization of recorded music meant a detachment from its traditional delivery system (Jenkins, 2006). In the analogue era, the symbolic content (that is, the music) was inherently linked to its physical manifestation (the grooves etched onto the disc) (Gendron, 1986). Hence, digital music stored on CDs could easily be stored as files on electronic devices like hard drives or USB

DOI: 10.4324/9781003432272-2

10 *Linus Andersson*

sticks. In contrast to prior methods of music reproduction, copies of digital files retained their fidelity, mirroring the original content and presenting identical sound. As computers became ubiquitous, software for compressing and playing music files became widespread. Record collections moved into the computer, and soon, internet connections became efficient enough for users to share music files. Suddenly, it was possible to listen to recorded music without paying for it.

The first music file-sharing service, *Napster*, was introduced in 1999, only to shut down in 2001 due to a court order prompted by legal action from the music industry and prominent artists such as Metallica. The lawsuit accused Napster of distributing copyrighted material without authorization. However, alternative platforms and technologies soon filled the void left by Napster, facilitating the finding and sharing of music files. Notably, The Pirate Bay, a BitTorrent tracker, gained considerable prominence in this domain. Managed by three Swedes, it situated Sweden at the epicentre of the clash between the global film and music sectors and illicit file sharing, a phenomenon that boasted millions of users in Sweden alone.

The issue of file sharing during the 2000s carried substantial political implications. Swedish Prime Minister Fredrik Reinfeldt encapsulated this sentiment in a televised debate on October 14, 2008, stating, "While we believe that copyrights should be protected, we are not willing to criminalize an entire generation of young people." The early controversies sparked by digitization climaxed in a high-profile trial against The Pirate Bay, paralleled by the emergence of the Pirate Party – a political party that secured representation in the 2009 EU elections. This party's formation reflected the potent political dynamics generated by the digital paradigm shift.

In response to industry efforts to curtail file-sharing activities, a network of activists called *The Pirate Bureau* (Piratbyrån) released a compilation of writings addressing topics such as file sharing, copyright, and internet policy (Kaarto & Fleischer, 2005). The closing chapter of the anthology is an essay titled "The Work of Art in the Age of Digital Reproduction," introduced with the following statement: "This text is a remix of 'The Work of Art in the Age of Mechanical Reproduction,' published by Walter Benjamin in 1936. Single words have been replaced to clarify that the analysis, now as then, is about file sharing" (Kaarto & Fleischer, 2005: 149).

What was it that made internet activists of the 21st century turn to Benjamin's 70-year-old essay for arguments to bolster their stance in the file-sharing dispute? Indeed, the activists in *The Pirate Bureau* are not alone in using Benjamin's essay to address a contemporary problem. A cursory Google search reveals a plethora of similar intertextual references in various contexts:

The Work of Art in the Age of Biocybernetic Reproduction
The Text in the Age of Digital Reproduction
Drone Warfare: War in the Age of Digital Reproduction
Grading In The Age Of Mechanical Reproduction
Love in the Age of Mechanical Reproduction
Virginia Woolf in the Age of Mechanical Reproduction

Walter Benjamin (1936) 11

This chapter aims to introduce, contextualize, and problematize the essay "The Work of Art in the Age of Mechanical Reproduction" (Benjamin, 2007/1936). Walter Benjamin (1892–1940), a German literary scholar and cultural critic, was active in the early 20th century and formulated his theoretical perspectives in close alignment with the critical theory of the Frankfurt School (see Chapter 3 in this volume). Additionally, his contributions have been recognized as a precursor to various other intellectual currents explored within this book. These encompass the critical inquiry advanced in cultural studies and the Birmingham School (see Chapters 11 and 12 in this volume), the media philosophies advanced by Marshall McLuhan (see Chapter 8 in this volume) and Friedrich Kittler (see Chapter 24 in this volume), and the postmodern turn epitomized by Jean Baudrillard's work on symbolic exchange, consumption, and simulation (see Chapter 10 in this volume).

The text and its author

Walter Benjamin is commonly depicted as an academic outsider whose life story is intertwined with a sombre period in European history. He was part of the cohort of left-leaning intellectuals active in Europe during the interwar era, a time marked by extreme political polarization. With the ascent of the Nazi regime in 1933, his native Germany swiftly disintegrated from a fragile democracy to an authoritarian single-party rule. As a Marxist and a Jew, Benjamin recognized the impossibility of remaining in Germany, leading him to spend his last years in exile in Paris. By August 1940, as German forces occupied France, he secured an entry visa to the United States with assistance from Max Horkheimer. However, en route to crossing the Atlantic, Benjamin encountered delays at the Spanish border. Fearing capture by the Gestapo, he tragically took his own life on the night of September 27 in the Spanish village of Port Bou.

Few of Benjamin's contributions to the philosophy of history, art, literary theory, and critical cultural studies were published as completed academic works. His production consists primarily of essays, commentaries, critiques, fragments, and unfinished drafts (most prominent is the so-called "arcades-project" about the history of modern culture, viewed from the perspective of 19th-century Paris, a draft that has become hugely influential for cultural studies). Benjamin's path diverged from traditional academia as he pursued an intellectual journey beyond its confines. Instead of becoming a conventional university lecturer or professor, he carved a niche for himself as a freelance writer, critic, essayist, and journalist. This choice imbues his texts with a distinct openness and uniqueness, deviating from the confines of structured academic prose. "The Work of Art in the Age of Mechanical Reproduction" embodies this spirit. Classified as an "essay," it exhibits a more relaxed structure compared to the rigidity of academic writing. Consequently, readers must approach it with particular attention. Unlike contemporary scientific articles, which tend to present one or two themes in a methodical manner, Benjamin's essay expresses ambiguity, oscillating between historical and analytical arguments while introducing numerous interrelated themes.

12 *Linus Andersson*

Due to its fragmented, occasionally incomplete, and open-ended nature, Walter Benjamin's oeuvre has prompted an extensive body of secondary literature. This phenomenon has persisted since his writings were initially introduced to a wider audience in the mid-1950s, mainly through the efforts of friends like Theodor Adorno and Hannah Arendt. Consequently, his writings have evoked a diverse array of interpretations. Various traditions and disciplines have asserted connections to Benjamin, including various strains of Marxism, theologians, cultural critics, literary scholars, historians, and philosophers (Bolz & van Reijen, 1994: 92; Caygill, 1997: x).

A misunderstood text?

"The Work of Art in the Age of Mechanical Reproduction" is often hailed as Walter Benjamin's most influential and, concurrently, his most misunderstood piece of writing (Caygill, 1997: 81). How, then, can this text be subject to misunderstanding?

One example of a misunderstanding could involve interpreting the essay's title as a lamentation for the demise of fine arts – believing that contemporary mass production and consumption of cultural products have obliterated the essence of art. Rather, the text strives to elucidate how new media have contributed to a fresh perspective on the notion of art, necessitating a reassessment of art history and established values. In this light, the essay can be read as a facet of Walter Benjamin's life-long project to construct a materialist (Marxist) theory of art (Kang, 2014: 102). It seeks to present a conceptual framework that challenges conventional notions like "creative power," "genius," and "eternal value," supplanting them with concepts impervious to exploitation by fascist ideologies.

Another prevalent misconception involves overstating Walter Benjamin's enthusiasm for new media and popular culture. The essay is frequently juxtaposed with Horkheimer and Adorno's work on the culture industry (Horkheimer & Adorno, 1997/1944) or Adorno's pieces on the fetish character of popular music (Adorno, 1982/1938; Adorno, 1989). In this comparison, Benjamin is often cast as an optimistic interpreter of the liberating potential of new media and popular culture, positioned in contrast to Theodor Adorno's pessimism (as seen in Moore, 2009: 197 ff; Scannell, 2003; or Chapter 3 in this volume). While Adorno identifies a standardized industry producing mindless commodities consumed by a passive, alienated public, Benjamin perceives technology's potential to empower individuals, enabling consumers to evolve into active culture producers. However, as Chapter 3 of this volume illustrates, much unites Benjamin and Adorno, and their ideas evolved in close dialogue. They both believe that the separation between art and everyday life is a significant tragedy of modernity, despite having divergent viewpoints on the potential and circumstances for their reconciliation.

Lastly, it is worth noting that Benjamin's essay exists in three different versions. The version under discussion here is the one known as "Zweite Fassung," the second revised German edition, which was translated into English and

Walter Benjamin (1936) 13

published in the volume *Illuminations*, edited by Hannah Arendt (Benjamin, 2007/1936). This version comprises fifteen chapters, a preface, and an epilogue.

In the subsequent sections, Benjamin's essay is delineated based on three core themes: technology, aesthetics, and politics. Although these themes are intertwined within the essay, they are presented separately here for clarity. The conclusion also provides examples illustrating how this text has been scrutinized and contemporized.

Technology

The importance of technological innovations tends to be both exaggerated and underestimated. "This changes everything!" states the advertisements, but what is assumed to change and in what way is rarely clear from the onset. The tools we develop to overcome bodily limitations, sustain life, assist our memory, or maintain social connections may push the boundaries of what we imagine or take for granted. However, such processes are complex and difficult to understand.

Benjamin opens his text with a preface that alludes to Karl Marx's exploration of the capitalist mode of production. Marx claimed that the mechanisms generating value within the system would eventually erode the conditions necessary for this very value creation. As Benjamin describes it, Marx's inquiry possessed "prognostic value" (Benjamin, 2007/1936: 217), enabling forecasts about the system's evolution – akin to meteorologists predicting future weather conditions based on present observations. Unlike numerous 19th-century socialists who envisioned ideals of a socialist utopia, Marx's commentary on the future did not necessitate prophetic insight; a comprehensive analysis of existing circumstances sufficed. This approach is known as "immanent critique": a well-crafted, critical examination of the contemporary state, including its inherent tensions and contradictions, offers insights into potential future developments. It is evident that this attribute is also what has made Benjamin's essay a classic; its observations and contemplations on technological advancement remain pertinent nearly a century after its first publication.

During the 19th century, Europe witnessed the ascent of bourgeois society, which exhibited a profound preoccupation with technological breakthroughs such as the steam engine, the railroad, and extensive industrialization. This period was steeped in a fervent belief in technological determinism (see Chapters 12 and 24 in this volume), fostering the conviction that novel machinery would propel societal progress. A pertinent quote from "The Communist Manifesto," authored by Marx and Engels, encapsulates this fascination:

> Subjection of nature's forces to man, machinery, application of chemistry to industry and agriculture, steam-navigation, railways, electric telegraphs, clearing of whole continents for cultivation, canalisation of rivers, whole populations conjured out of the ground – what earlier Century had even a presentiment that such productive forces slumbered in the lap of social labour?
>
> (Marx & Engels, 1990/1848)

14   *Linus Andersson*

Benjamin notes that it took half a century before it was possible to see how the change in the productive forces described by Marx had come to impact the field of culture. Based on this observation, the essay aims to analyse the consequences of how we define, understand, and relate to art and culture.

Reproduction

An apparent transformation in the domain of cultural creation is the advent of mechanical reproduction. Technologies like photography, film, and the press facilitated the mass production of symbolic artifacts. In the initial chapter of his essay, Benjamin highlights the historical context of artwork reproduction. He mentions how aspiring artists learned by emulating their mentors and sometimes even participated in producing and disseminating their master's creations. Additionally, the practice of forging has existed throughout history. Irrespective of the intent, such reproductions required labour comparable to the act of creation itself; duplicating a painting demanded a similar or even greater effort and skill than crafting the original piece. However, technical reproduction introduced a new dimension: the capacity to mass-produce works of art and artistic objects. The photograph is noteworthy in this context as it represents the first instance where the human hand has been "freed [...] of the most important artistic functions which henceforth devolved only upon the eye looking into a lens" (Benjamin, 2007/1936: 219). Photographic reproduction operates with the swiftness of the eye, capturing all that lies before the lens.

Two manifestations of this technique caught Benjamin's interest: the reproduction of existing works of art and images and art forms entirely based on reproduction, such as photography and film.

Reproduction of art

In the initial segment of Benjamin's exploration concerning the significance of reproduction technology for artworks, he addresses the themes of visibility and accessibility. A reproduction of an artwork generated through technical processes differs from an imitation, as the concern of counterfeiting becomes inconsequential in technical reproduction. Reproductions of paintings by artists like Picasso or Dali displayed in places such as a dentist's waiting room are unlikely to be misconstrued for the originals; instead, they serve as a reminder of the originals' existence. Technical reproduction exhibits greater autonomy compared to manual replication; it can "put the copy of the original into situations which would be out of reach for the original itself" (Benjamin, 2007/1936: 220). Reproductions enable us to experience artworks in ways that were previously unattainable. The photograph, for instance, can emphasize facets of the artwork discernible solely to the camera's lens, altering the image through cropping and thereby transforming its meaning. Artworks can now come to meet its observers, as seen in the instance of reproductions displayed in waiting rooms. Some of Benjamin's interpreters, such as Scannell (2003) and Moore (2009), perceive this accessibility as having a democratizing potential. Reproduction allows a broader audience to access experiences and knowledge once restricted to privileged elites. In essence, reproduction facilitated mass consumption within the realm of culture.

Film

A pivotal aspect of Benjamin's essay delves into how the medium of film has introduced novel avenues for perceiving reality. "The characteristics of the film," writes Benjamin, "lie not only in the manner in which man presents himself to mechanical equipment but also in the manner in which, by means of this apparatus, man can represent his environment" (Benjamin, 2007/1936: 235). This passage can be seen as a precursor to contemporary discussions on mediatization. Since Benjamin's era, an array of techniques for perceiving reality has arisen to the extent that some propose our reality could be described as a mediated construction (Couldry & Hepp, 2017). Benjamin draws a parallel to psychoanalysis, which furnishes tools for deepening the comprehension of everyday life's nuances: a slip of the tongue, for instance, ceases to be a mere verbal error, instead revealing subconscious desires. The significance of film technology's capacity to "stretch" time and space (via techniques like zooming and slow motion) lies not predominantly in enhancing our understanding of things we have already seen but rather in "focusing on hidden details of familiar objects." Benjamin labels this aspect of visibility, unearthed by the camera, as "unconscious optics" (Benjamin, 2007/1936: 237). Much like psychoanalysis made the realm of the unconscious accessible, photography unveils the hidden visual realm.

A central theme in the initial theorizing on film revolved around its "shock effect." Rapidly unfolding moving images scarcely grant viewers ample time to apprehend the occurrences, which stands in stark contrast to how we engage with paintings:

> Let us compare the screen on which a film unfolds with the canvas of a painting. The painting invites the spectator to contemplation; before it the spectator can abandon himself to his associations. Before the movie frame he cannot do so. No sooner has his eye grasped a scene than it is already changed.
>
> (Benjamin, 2007/1936: 238)

Critics who met this whirlwind of impressions with skepticism stressed the corporeal nature of the film experience, emphasizing its call for emotional reactions, a trait often linked to "lower" or primal responses. New media technology often gets interpreted through the lens of "immediacy" (Bolter & Grusin, 1999), where audiences establish direct contact with the depicted content. This connection endures in film genres like horror, splatter, and pornography. However, feelings of fear, disgust, or excitement triggered by aesthetic

16　*Linus Andersson*

stimuli are seldom viewed as indicators of artistic merit. On the contrary, it frequently takes years for what is initially perceived as a pure effect to be assessed and appreciated in terms of artistic value (as with the canonization of horror films like *The Texas Chainsaw Massacre*). Benjamin underscores this by stating, "Clearly, this is at bottom the same ancient lament that the masses seek distraction whereas art demands concentration from the spectator" (Benjamin, 2007/1936: 239).

Benjamin illustrates the emergence, decline, and occasional resurgence of various historical art forms like tragedy, epic, and tableau. However, only one art form has exhibited continuity across human history: architecture. Over time, the fundamental requirement for shelter has driven the evolution of methods that merge immediate functionality with visual communication. Buildings serve practical purposes while also being objects of observation. Film introduces an art form that fosters analogous modes of observation. Comparable to famous painting reproductions in a dentist's office, it encourages communal diversion rather than individual rumination.

Aesthetics

Beyond its contemplation of technology, Walter Benjamin's essay contributes to a theory of media aesthetics. However, it is vital to underscore that aesthetics here does not pertain to a theory exclusive to the fine arts but aligns more closely with the Greek root term "aisthesis" (Bolz & van Reijen, 1994: 92). This refers to techniques that present novel modes of perceiving reality, wherein specific aspects of reality are accessible solely with the assistance of technical instruments (such as x-rays, microscopes, television). Simultaneously, as highlighted in the preceding section, the essay also explores the transformation of fine arts when they encounter new technology.

Cult value and exhibition value

What distinguishes a work of art from a utility item? Is it that it has no direct practical use? Or is it that it invites reflection and contemplation? An interpretation suggests that artworks encompass a significance beyond what is found in ordinary objects. Benjamin illustrates how artworks, like Orthodox Christian icons, originally held roles in worship and rituals. This nearly mystical quality is termed the "cult value" of art by Benjamin. Reproduction renders artworks accessible, enabling encounters with viewers. However, through this accessibility, a transformation occurs: "Even the most perfect reproduction of a work of art is lacking in one element: its presence in time and space, its unique existence at the place where it happens to be" (Benjamin, 2007/1936: 220).

An artwork possesses a uniqueness that eludes replication, unlike its reproduction, a quality that cannot be fully captured in the reproduced version. To address this phenomenon, Benjamin introduces the concept of the "aura."

A comparable approach to this line of thought can be found by drawing parallels to Marx's concept of value (Marx, 1867: 31 f.). According to Marx, an item's value stems from its capacity to satisfy a particular need, referred to in Marxist terms as its use value. Additionally, an item's value lies in its potential to be traded for other goods in the market, known as its exchange value. Use value and exchange value are mutually exclusive and unable to be realized simultaneously (that is, a shirt cannot be worn and sold at the same time).

Just as a commodity's use value and exchange value cannot be actualized simultaneously, a similar dichotomy exists between an artwork's cult value and the exhibition value. Being uniquely tied to a specific "Here and Now" is incompatible with being universally accessible to everyone, anytime and anywhere. New media technology has, however, enabled heightened accessibility, necessitating a fresh approach to defining and comprehending art.

Aura, authenticity, and a new aesthetic gaze

The reproduction of a work of art does not diminish its meaning, but it erodes its authority and distinctive essence – its aura.

> [T]he technique of reproduction detaches the reproduced object from the domain of tradition. By making many reproductions it substitutes a plurality of copies for a unique existence. And in permitting the reproduction to meet the beholder or listener in his own particular situation, it reactivates the object reproduced.
>
> (Benjamin, 2007/1936: 221)

According to Benjamin, the elevated significance of authenticity, originality, and aura in Western culture is primarily attributed to technical limitations rather than enduring aesthetic values. The uniqueness and authenticity of a work of art were celebrated due to the absence of alternative forms of aesthetic engagement. The art forms facilitated by reproduction technology demanded a fresh model and conceptual framework for aisthesis. In lieu of contemplation, there is distraction, the "scattering" of attention.

The tension between Benjamin's and Adorno's viewpoints on "mass culture" resurfaces here. In an exchange of letters, they explore the parallels between Benjamin's essay and Adorno's rejoinder titled "On the Fetish Character of Music" (Adorno, 1982). Benjamin writes:

> In my essay I tried to articulate positive moments as clearly as you managed to articulate negative ones. Consequently, I see strengths in your study at points where mine was weak. Your analysis of the psychological types produced by industry and your representation of their mode of production are most felicitous. [...] I see more and more clearly that the launching of the sound film must be regarded as an operation of the cinema industry designed to break the revolutionary primacy of the silent film, which

18   *Linus Andersson*

generated reactions that were hard to control and hence politically dangerous. An analysis of the sound film would constitute a critique of contemporary art which would provide a dialectical mediation between your views and mine.

(Benjamin, 2010: 153)

Adorno's exploration of popular music also delves into a shift in perception, underscoring how the culture industry influences and controls this ability, in his case, the act of listening to popular music. As artworks evolve into commodities, the connection between the observer and the work becomes objectified. In a renowned excerpt, Adorno explains how a concertgoer at a Toscanini concert worships the money he [sic] paid for the ticket rather than appreciating the music (1982: 279). Adorno contends that cultural industry products present a distorted, illusory authenticity, while for Benjamin, the matter of authenticity has become outdated.

Politics

In the cited letter to Adorno, Benjamin notes that silent films were "politically dangerous" due to their resistance to control. This comment highlighted a political facet of the artwork that demanded safeguarding. The 19th century witnessed the emergence of an aesthetic ideal in response to industrialism and technological advancement. Characterized by romanticism, it championed an outlook where art stood separate from history: life is transient, while art is enduring. The 19th-century aesthetic movement advocated for artistic autonomy, epitomized in the maxim "l'art pour l'art," or art for art's sake. Within this framework, a genuine artwork maintains autonomy, unaffected by external influences, societal shifts, or the passage of time. Benjamin asserts that this impervious concept of art from the 19th century lacks relevance in the new era. Viewing technical reproduction's impact on artworks, one can discern that they became susceptible to historical influence.

It is, among other things, this line of reasoning that introduces a political dimension to Benjamin's analysis:

> But the instant the criterion of authenticity ceases to be applicable to artistic production, the total function of art is reversed. Instead of being based on ritual, it begins to be based on another practice – politics.
>
> (Benjamin, 2007/1936: 224)

In contrast to artworks that prompt contemplation, the era of reproduction gives rise to works that necessitate the viewer's assimilation. These works no longer retain their pristine detachment from their original historical setting; instead, they actively impact and are influenced by the world surrounding them. This phenomenon became palpable in Benjamin's time.

Politics and art

One of the most frequently cited passages in the essay is the concluding sentence of the afterword: "This is the situation of politics which Fascism is rendering aesthetic. Communism responds by politicizing art" (Benjamin, 2007/1936: 242).

The concept of aestheticization of politics is easily comprehensible. During Benjamin's time of writing, Germany and Italy were under dictatorships characterized by dramatic spectacles, where political institutions were supplanted by mass gatherings and exhibitions glorifying metaphysical ideals like determination, courage, beauty, and strength – epitomized in Leni Riefenstahl's films *Triumph of the Will* and *Olympia*. Citizenship transformed from having constitutional rights and obligations to embodying the correct "worldview" or "sentiment" for the nation, party, or people. This notion of aestheticized politics resurfaces in the analysis of contemporary populism and authoritarian tendencies, notably visible in internet memes employed by the American alt-right movement (Woods & Hahner, 2019).

The politicization of art is a readily identifiable theme that continues to be relevant today. Popular culture, in particular, frequently faces allegations of being "woke," infused with identity politics, political correctness, and social justice ideologies. In a June 25, 2021, interview on Real Time with Bill Maher, renowned filmmaker Quentin Tarantino expressed his concerns about this trend, which he perceived in Hollywood: "Especially this past year, ideology has become more important than art. It's like ideology trumps art. Ideology trumps individual effort. Ideology trumps good. Ideology trumps entertaining."

This perspective on the interplay between politics and aesthetics also invites a critical analysis of concepts rooted in the aesthetic of the "disinterested gaze." This notion reappears in Jürgen Habermas' (1989) depiction of the re-feudalization of the public sphere, Guy Debord's (2021) "society of the spectacle," Baudrillard's (1985) examination of the "silence of the masses," and ideas like "post-politics." When traditional political institutions falter and fail to serve as genuine platforms for meaningful discourse, alternative public spheres become essential. Cultural spaces, for instance, can gain importance for democratic conversations. Berthold Brecht, a German playwright and writer closely connected to Benjamin, stands as a significant figure in the realm of politicized art. Brecht's influence on 20th-century drama was profound, not only due to his plays like *The Threepenny Opera, Mother Courage and Her Children*, and *The Good Person of Szechwan*, becoming cornerstones of modern theatre, but also for his introduction of epic theatre – a style that broke away from the bourgeois naturalist theatre of the 19th century. To put it simply, 19th-century theatre aimed to captivate the audience's complete engagement and make them forget they were watching a performance.

In contrast, Brecht, driven by political motives, advocated for a theatre that openly acknowledged its performative nature. Addressing the audience directly and challenging spectators, his intention was to rouse them from their passive

20 *Linus Andersson*

comfort within the theatre and prompt active involvement. This stylistic approach has also been embraced in film and television fiction (Nichols, 2010).

The age of extremes

During the interwar period, Europe grappled with stark divisions: communism gained momentum with the rise of the Bolsheviks in Russia and the establishment of the Soviet Union, while fascism and Nazism emerged in Italy, Spain, and Germany. The prevalent liberal democracy that now characterizes Western Europe was scarcely present. Given the intense political polarization of the time, it is logical that an essay on art would also delve into political considerations.

For contemporary readers, the essay's political terminology may appear outdated. Since the collapse of the Soviet Union and the fall of the Berlin Wall, socialism has been seen by few as a viable political option. Similarly, fascism has been reduced to an insult or a stereotype in action movies. However, during Benjamin's time, fascism held genuine political influence in Europe. Given its metaphysical mysticism, fascism is challenging to define as a political ideology, and there are substantial differences among the major movements labelled as fascist. For instance, Nazism rejected modernism, while Italian fascism embraced and glorified it (Eco, 1995). Despite this inherent ideological ambiguity, fascism utilized culture as a form of politics in various ways.

This historical experience and context also mean that a discussion about the aestheticization of politics versus the politicization of art, as suggested by Benjamin, risks being reduced to two political projects – fascism and communism. However, it is crucial to note that beyond this historical framework, Benjamin also elucidates how new media provide novel avenues for perceiving and comprehending reality and generate fresh modes of human existence, along with their associated potentials and constraints for the individual (Kang, 2014). Benjamin underscores that these emergent possibilities inherently hold political significance as they redefine the demarcations between the private and public domains and illuminate the dynamics of power.

Problematization

Walter Benjamin's essay holds a significant place in both media studies and 20th-century cultural theory. Its enduring influence has sparked inspiration and continues to do so. However, the practical applicability of its conceptual framework in contemporary media research is subject to scrutiny. Benjamin's concepts like "cult value," "exhibition value," authenticity, and "aura" resonate intuitively, yet establishing empirical evidence for their existence can be challenging. This parallels the concept of "mediatization," which captures everyday experiences but has prompted ongoing debates within media research about its scientific utility (e.g., Deacon & Stanyer, 2014).

The rhetorical style in Benjamin's essay can sometimes overshadow its complex arguments, potentially reducing intricate relationships to simplified slogans. The essay's manifesto-like tone, possibly contributing to it being misunderstood (Caygill, 1997), resonates with its political intent. It appears to present a choice between politicized art and aestheticized politics associated with totalitarianism, which may overlook post-war aspirations for democratic education through mass media. These include the American endeavor to nurture a "democratic personality" founded on liberalism, individualism, and consumerism (Turner, 2014), as well as European efforts to organize broadcasting based on public service principles and the mass media's contribution to the public good (see Chapter 12 in this volume).

In hindsight, as a product of technical reproduction, film did not result in the disappearance of the aura. Instead, movie stars, and subsequently rock stars and pop artists, became surrounded by a distinctive aura. Following World War II, existentialists revived authenticity as a philosophical ideal embraced by artists and popular culture. The concept of being authentic and genuine in artistic expression was a concern for Ingmar Bergman and Kurt Cobain alike. Even when works of art are created as reproductions, the issue of authenticity can still arise, as can be seen in the case of the works of Andy Warhol, an icon in the realm of pop art. Beginning in the 1960s, Warhol used mass production techniques such as silk screen printing to create paintings depicting celebrities and stock items of consumer culture. Today, these original prints hold a status similar to paintings canonized throughout art history, in contrast to their original ephemeral presentation. There have even been controversies within the art world on how to distinguish between genuine and fake copies of Warhol's work (Levy & Scott-Clark, 2010).

In considering the relevance of Benjamin's analysis in today's context, we can examine the ongoing public discourse about social media, screen time, and the growing "tech-lash." Critics contend that social media detracts from our attention span and hinders our ability to focus (Forsler, Guyard & Andersson, forthcoming). Drawing from cognitive science and neuropsychology, these critics portray digital technology as a source of distraction, which is commonly assumed to be negative. However, Benjamin's perspective offers an alternative lens on these concerns: perhaps distraction is not a problem but rather a novel mode of perception emerging. This viewpoint challenges the popular notion that our brains are ill-equipped to process the wealth of stimuli presented by digital media, reminiscent of the scepticism expressed about film a century ago.

Summary

Benjamin's essay can be succinctly encapsulated through four pairs of concepts that embody the themes he explores. The first pair involves the interplay between the original and the copy. Technical reproduction enhances accessibility to the original while introducing new art forms that challenge the copy-original distinction. This leads to the second distinction, highlighting the shift from cult value to exhibition value, as reproduction emphasizes exhibition value over cult value. The third distinction concerns two modes of engagement:

22 Linus Andersson

contemplation, individual and focused before an artwork, and distraction, collective and linked to mass consumption. Lastly, the essay juxtaposes aestheticized politics, favouring emotional response, with politicized art, utilizing art for social critique and alternative formulation.

References

Adorno, T.W. (1989). *Introduction to the Sociology of Music*. New York: Continuum.

Adorno, T.W. (1982/1938). On the Fetish-Character in Music and the Regression of Listening, in Arato, A. & Gebhardt, E. (eds.). *The Essential Frankfurt School Reader*. New York: Continuum. 270–299.

Baudrillard, J. (1985). The Masses: The Implosion of the Social in the Media. *New Literary History*, 16(3), 577–589.

Benjamin, W. (2007/1936). The Work of Art in the Age of Mechanical Reproduction, in Arendt, H. (ed.). *Illuminations*, translated by Harry Zohn, from the 1936 essay. Schocken Books, 1969. 217–253.

Benjamin, W. (2010). Reply, in Adorno, T.W., Benjamin, W., Bloch, E., Brecht, B., Lukács, G., & Jameson, F. (eds.) *Aesthetics and Politics* (New ed.). London: Verso. 146–154.

Bolter, J. D. & Grusin, R. (1999). *Remediation: Understanding New Media*. Cambridge, MA: MIT Press.

Bolz, N.W. & Reijen, W.V. (1994). *Walter Benjamin: en introduktion*. [Walter Benjamin: An Introduction] Göteborg: Daidalos.

Caygill, H. (1997). *Walter Benjamin: The Colour of Experience*. London: Routledge.

Couldry, N. & Hepp, A. (2017). *The Mediated Construction of Reality*. Cambridge, UK: Polity Press.

Deacon, D. & Stanyer, J. (2014). Mediatization: Key Concept or Conceptual Bandwagon? *Media, Culture & Society*, 36(7), 1032–1044.

Debord, G. (2021). *The Society of the Spectacle*. Critical Editions.

Eco, U. (1995). Ur-Fascism. *New York Review of Books*. June 22, 1995.

Forsler, I., Guyard, C. & Andersson, L. (forthcoming). Detoxing the Brain: Understanding Digital Backlash in the Context of the Media Effects Tradition, in Syvertsen, T., Fast, K., Karlsen, F. & Kaun, A. (eds.). *The Digital Backlash*. Nordicom.

Gendron, B. (1986). Theodor Adorno Meets the Cadillacs, in *Studies in Entertainment: Critical Approaches to Mass Culture*. Indiana University. 18–38.

Habermas, J. (1989). *The Structural Transformation of the Public Sphere: An Inquiry into a Category of Bourgeois Society*. Cambridge: Polity Press.

Horkheimer, M. & Adorno, T. W. (1997/1944). *Dialectic of Enlightenment*. (Vol. 15). Verso.

Jenkins, H. (2006). *Convergence Culture: Where Old and New Media Collide*. New York: New York University Press.

John, S. (2022, January 4). Why Vinyl Records Are Making a Comeback in 2022. *The Manual*. https://www.themanual.com/culture/why-vinyl-is-coming-back/.

Kaarto, M. & Fleischer, R. (eds.) (2005). *Copy me: samlade texter från Piratbyrån*. [Copy Me: Collected Texts from the Pirate Bureau] Stockholm: Roh-nin.

Kang, J. (2014). *Walter Benjamin and the Media*. London: Polity.

Levy, A. & Scott-Clark, C. (2010). Warhol's Box of Tricks. *The Guardian*. August 21, 2010. https://www.theguardian.com/artanddesign/2010/aug/21/warhol-brillo-boxes-scandal-fraud.

Maher, B. (2021,June 25). Real Time with Bill Maher. *HBO*.

Marx, K. (2015/1867). *Capital: A Critique of Political Economy*. (Vol. 1). Arkose Press.

Marx, K. & Engels, F. (1990/1848). *Manifesto of the Communist Party*. London: Lawrence & Wishart.

Moore, R. (2009). *Sells Like Teen Spirit: Music, Youth Culture, and Social Crisis*. New York: New York University Press.

Nichols, B. (2010). *Engaging Cinema*. W.W. Norton & Company.

Scannell, P. (2003). Benjamin Contextualized: On "The Work of Art in the Age of Mechanical Reproduction", in Katz, E. (ed.). *Canonic Texts in Media Research: Are There Any? Should There Be? How About These?*Cambridge: Polity Press. 74–89.

Turner, F. (2014). *The Democratic Surround: Multimedia & American Liberalism from World War II to the Psychedelic Sixties*. Chicago: The University of Chicago Press.

Woods, H.S. & Hahner, L.A. (2019). *Make America Meme Again: The Rhetoric of the Alt-right*. New York: Peter Lang.

2 Herta Herzog (1941) 'On Borrowed Experience'

Jonas Andersson Schwarz

Introduction

Mad Men is a popular American TV series that depicts the rise of the advertising industry in New York in the 1960s. The main protagonist, Don Draper, is a kind of heroic yet tragic adman who undergoes a series of trials that can be seen as typical of the emergence of the modern mass-consumer society. In the very first episode, 'Smoke Gets in Your Eyes', the viewers meet Greta Guttman, a serious scientist with a German accent and statement eyeglasses, who convinces Don Draper and the other employees of the Sterling Cooper advertising agency that people smoke cigarettes because they are actually motivated by their death drive:

> **Dr. Greta Guttman:** *Before the war, when I studied with Edler in Vienna, we postulated that what Freud called the 'death wish' is as powerful in life as those for sexual reproduction and physical sustenance.*
> **Don Draper:** *Freud, you say. What agency is he with?*

This argument hardly convinces the fictional advertising men of the TV show – but, in the context of this chapter, Guttman herself is highly interesting. As it turns out, the TV show's advertising theorist is probably based on a real scientist.

Herta Herzog (1910–2010) is known in media research for founding the approach known as the 'uses and gratifications' (U&G) model, which places great emphasis on respondents' own explanations and justifications for their uses of different types of media. Herzog is historically relevant as both one of the first female media researchers and – like many of her peers – part of the wave of German-speaking intellectual émigrés who were forced to flee fascism and migrate to the United States. Unlike many of her peers with the same academic pedigree, however, Herzog later established a life in the service of the expansionist post-war capitalism at that time, as a research manager at one of America's leading advertising agencies. As part of her work at McCann Erickson, Herzog – like the fictional Guttman – was a key co-creator of the mass-consumerist ideology that many people live under today. Trained not only in psychology but also (paradoxically, one might think) in the radical social

DOI: 10.4324/9781003432272-3

theories formulated by the likes of Theodor Adorno and Max Horkheimer, she played an instrumental role in introducing novel theories about society and new civic ideals to American society.

Much like her mentor and life partner Paul Lazarsfeld, Herzog managed to synthesise critical theory with applied research and to merge this theoretical and empirical apparatus with the modern American practices of marketing and communications. As a result, consumerism and market logics were strengthened rather than weakened. Capitalist techniques for exercising power were refined, the consequences of which are still evident today. Here lies a major contradiction: under the auspices of consumer ideology, the idealistic and radically anti-capitalist impulse that had been so central to critical theory soon became re-appropriated. In practice, critical theory came to have radically different applications than thinkers like Horkheimer and Adorno could have anticipated (see Chapter 3 in this volume).

More specifically, Herzog contributed two important elements to media research – one methodological and the other theoretical. She was one of the first to combine qualitative and quantitative methods and thereby developed a very effective methodological approach – a kind of 'triangulation' of methods in which the blind spots of one method are illuminated by the other method, allowing the different methods to balance each other. In addition, she established a theoretical model that was ahead of its time in many ways: Herzog stipulated that media users are, at their core, active, rational beings who are generally capable of choosing and justifying their own consumption habits. When she formulated this assumption in the early 1940s, it served as a novel complement to the linear transmission model of communication (see Chapter 5 in this volume). In many respects, her contribution also served as an antithesis to one of the implicit assumptions of early critical theory: namely, that the mass media would pacify and alienate the media audience.

'On Borrowed Experience': administrative and critical research

What makes 'On Borrowed Experience' (1941) the most significant article in Herzog's oeuvre is that it is one of the first research articles to ask questions about the *listeners' personal uses for and advantages from* listening to the radio. In other words, her study asks questions about the audience's motivations – and does so with considerable sensitivity to the interpretative, qualitative element involved. In this work, Herzog examines so-called 'daytime serials'. These were serialised radio plays, for which the term 'soap operas' was already established at the time: light drama in serial form, aimed at housewives. These were traditionally broadcast during the day and were often centred on family life and love stories. As Lawrence Levine once remarked, radio soap operas exhibited that which is marvellous in the context of rather ordinary life: 'People could relate to daytime serials in terms of their own existence; they could see themselves in them' (Levine, 1992: 1382).

26   Jonas Andersson Schwarz

Herzog's study was based on in-depth interviews with 100 American women. She notes that it was only a preparatory, relatively speculative analysis, as the conclusions drawn from it came to form the basis of the hypotheses in her later publication, 'What Do We Really Know About Daytime Serial Listeners?' (Herzog, 1944). Nevertheless, in this preparatory study, she already manages to clearly show how the female respondents used the radio programmes as a guide to their own daily lives. Most of the respondents were housewives, and all were avid listeners of radio soap operas; the study can therefore be said to be one of the first studies of fandom within a particular media culture. Her results show how radio listeners actively project the narratives of radio soap operas onto their own lives, using the different narratives as ways of dealing with personal problems and other everyday challenges. She identifies three types of personal exchange from the respondents' descriptions of what they received from the soap operas:

1   An outlet for inner feelings;
2   Daydreaming and wishful thinking;
3   Ethical and emotional guidelines and life lessons.

Her text is notably specific and detailed in its account of the specific moral dilemmas that the radio programmes raised for the listeners; thus, it serves as a precursor to the reception studies of women's culture that later emerged in the 1980s, when researchers such as Ien Ang, Dorothy Hobson, Janice Winship and Janice Radway (see Chapter 22 in this volume) conducted more detailed explorations of what Herzog had demonstrated so much earlier. Tamar Liebes (2005: 370) has pointed out that Herzog elevates the theme of feminised, allegedly 'simple' popular culture to a worthy research object in its own right as she pays attention to what media audiences have to say. At the same time, Herzog makes informed assumptions about her respondents' subconscious choices and needs in a manner similar to those of more critical scholars of the later 20th century. Liebes also argues that Herzog's exposition runs 'closer' to the media audiences' own life-worlds in many ways than Ang's and Radway's studies do, as these later authors place more emphasis on the media texts than Herzog does.

Herzog's study precedes contemporary cultural studies in that she identifies ethical guidelines for media use; in other words, she is motivated by normative concerns. Such normative concern is often emphasised in today's interpretative, qualitatively oriented, ideology-critical research – and Herzog, too, is careful to identify such aspects:

> These listeners do not have a 'personal' interest in the stories in the sense that they want to identify with, or escape into, the content of the stories. They use the stories chiefly as a means to demonstrate to themselves or some of their co-listeners that they were right in predicting the outcome.
>
> (Herzog, 1941: 81)

The narrative logic that the listeners are responsive to is primarily one of ethical/moral issues, involving judgements about which fictional character is more 'deserving' of failure or success. The constructedness of fiction is also exposed: many of the listeners, Herzog explains (1941: 82), would not accept the soap opera narratives outright, as if they were substitutes for the flow of everyday life. At the same time, many of the listeners noted that the narratives did help them to better adapt to the world they themselves lived in.

Stories give more meaning to reality and make everyday life less boring. By providing guidance on how to act in difficult situations, stories can make reality seem less threatening and can help the listener navigate and categorise her own world. In effect, radio programmes become like alien worlds that listeners enter into for a while – often with many lessons learned. Herzog shows how listeners *take the time* to actively *engage* with these constructed media worlds.

In Katz and Lazarsfeld's famous volume, *Personal Influence* (1955), the researchers formulate a so-called 'two-step' hypothesis of the social dissemination of knowledge. In their study, all the respondents are women; however, as respondents, they are presented in a genderless fashion as representatives of the entire population (Douglas, 2006). It could be argued that, in this way, Katz and Lazarsfeld serve to obscure the role of gender in media use. On the other hand, Herzog lets the women speak *as women*, although she never goes as far as to link her results to explicit gender theory. Rather, her main theoretical framework remains grounded in mid-century psychology.

It was Lazarsfeld (1941) who identified two branches of media research: 'administrative' and 'critical'. Later, Katz and Katz (2016) argued that these alleged branches were related and partially overlapped from the very beginning. Herzog's research manages to navigate both branches. In the few studies she published under her own name (1940, 1941, 1944, 1946), it is clear how Herzog mixes structurally inclined and almost industry-oriented insights with more psychologising attempts to understand the media audiences' own motivations, expectations and dreams. For example, in 'Radio – The First Post-War Year' (1946), she answers a series of questions about a still relatively new medium: how is radio production organised and financed? How is the industry developing? Who are the players in audience measurement and how are they developing? What is the demographic, economic and geographical composition of the radio audience? In 'What Do We Really Know About Daytime Serial Listeners?' (1944), she makes it clear that, in order to understand a medium, researchers must gain a systematic understanding of the media content (i.e. programming) along with a comparative understanding of users versus non-users – and a closer, deeper familiarity with the various kinds of satisfaction users actually seek from using the medium. She then validates her research questions by testing a series of hypotheses against several rather extensive survey studies.[1]

Herzog's work embodies a fundamental assumption of U&G research: namely, that the psychological and social attributes of individuals and groups – including personality, interests, values, needs, relationships with the environment and social roles – underlie and shape media use. This assumption is

28 Jonas Andersson Schwarz

congruent with contemporary efforts that particularly emphasise the role of *gratification* in mundane uses of the mass media (e.g. Cantril, 1942), as well as with later texts (e.g. Katz et al., 1973; Lundberg & Hultén, 1968).

Herzog's work was overlooked for several decades. As the chapter on Lazarsfeld and Merton in this volume shows (see Chapter 4 in this volume), Merton has often been credited with the invention of the focus group interview method, even though it is more reasonable to view this method as a collective product that was gradually worked out by the trio of Herzog, Lazarsfeld and Merton. Several contemporary media scholars (Klaus & Seethaler, 2016a) have observed that Herzog had taken important steps on the path towards more interpretive audience research as early as in 1941. She brought a dimension of critical questioning to an otherwise descriptively oriented, functionalist research field by using subjective interpretation to observe a contradiction in the housewives' statements: on the one hand, radio soaps were said to *fail* to fulfil the potential for women's emancipation; on the other hand, they did offer *opportunities for recovery and recognition* (Katz & Katz, 2016).

A historical opportunity for women media researchers

How are we to understand the historical situation of women in the United States at the time of the Second World War? Douglas (2006) has argued that it was a time of transition. In the United States, as in several other countries, the enlistment of men in the war effort meant that women had to enter the labour market and (temporarily) do the jobs that men normally did. This contributed to a normalisation of women as labourers. Nevertheless, the strictness of gender policy in bourgeois society remained, and a stasis of norms, rules and beliefs was upheld. As a result, women – despite often doing at least as good a job as their male counterparts – did not always receive the appreciation and respect they should reasonably be expected to have received, at least when seen from the more egalitarian perspective of our time (Douglas, 2006).

The Princeton Research Institute, the University of Newark's Office of Radio Research and Columbia University's Bureau of Applied Social Research: in all of these places, Lazarsfeld was a key organiser and had rows of knowledgeable staff members assisting him, including some 50 women, ranging from assistant managers to research assistants, secretaries and interviewers. Of these, Herzog was the most prominent. Of course, these female collaborators would have had their own experiences of media life and their own familiarity with other women, including friends and acquaintances as well as respondents. Rowland and Simonson (2014: 4) have argued that such experiences implicitly contributed to the Columbia School's strengths in the study of everyday media use.

Herzog distinguished herself early on as one of the key contributors to the famous 'Invasion from Mars' study conducted by Hadley Cantril under the auspices of the Princeton Institute (1940). The object of this study was the famous radio dramatisation of the *War of the Worlds* broadcast on Halloween 1938, which set off panic in many of its listeners. Of the estimated 6 million

Herta Herzog (1941) 29

Americans who listened, the researchers found that a quarter seemed to have believed the radio programme's fake news story about an ongoing invasion from space. However, the majority of these panicked listeners appeared to think that the invasion was not from Mars but was a conventional military invasion from Germany. The researchers' explanation was that the listeners had a latent fear of Germany because Hitler was in power and the Munich Agreement[2] was fresh in their minds. Herzog was one of the people who conducted the qualitative follow-up interviews with respondents about why they panicked.

Thus, Herzog made her career not only in a turbulent period of world history but also in the midst of an important transition period for media research. This becomes especially clear when noting how marginalised her research became in the historiography that formed in the wake of Princeton's Office of Radio Research. Although Herzog established innovative methods such as the focus group interview, established social scientists such as Robert Merton were the ones who became famous by being credited with these innovations. Even though she was an independent professional, many of Herzog's achievements were generally mentioned as a subordinate complement to those of her more famous husband, Paul Lazarsfeld. The term 'the Matilda effect', coined by Rossiter (1993), refers to the tendency in historiography to exclude or downplay the achievements of female scholars. It is interesting to wonder how Herzog herself would have related to this all-too-common tendency. In the interviews she gave towards the end of her life, Herzog seemed fairly unconcerned about her lack of recognition, although she took pains to emphasise that she had actually established important terms and methods such as the focus group method and the concept of 'image' in marketing. Herzog avowedly held that she was not a feminist and that gender had never played a role in her professional life (Herzog, 1994). After a long career in advertising, she returned to audience research at an old age in the 1980s and published 'Decoding "Dallas"' (1987) – a reception study in which German respondents were asked how they interpreted *Dallas*, an American TV soap opera that was very popular at the time.

New media, new need for knowledge, new methods

The United States was already a media society before the Second World War, as Shearon Lowery and Melvin De Fleur (1995: 93) observe in their overview of the emergence of mass-communication research. At that time, there were nearly 2,000 daily newspapers and thousands of other periodicals in the United States. New media such as film and radio were monumentally popular and rapidly expanding. Radio was established in the 1920s; by the time of the Second World War, there was a system of hundreds of radio stations interconnected in national networks. Within a few decades, the United States had gone from a society in which virtually only print media existed to a society that could justifiably be called a multimedia society. The war had not hit the American economy as hard as the European economies, so this already vibrant media

30   *Jonas Andersson Schwarz*

society continued to flourish during and after the war. The advertising industry that had emerged during the expansive 1920s through the efforts of innovators such as Edward Bernays slowed down during the war and then took off, setting the terms of the American entertainment and media industry until the emergence of the Internet at the turn of the millennium. Herzog was instrumental in establishing what Vance Packard (1957) identified as 'motivational research', which still forms the basis of marketing and propaganda today.

It is clear that, due to such rapid changes, there was very little empirical knowledge in the beginning on how audiences oriented themselves in this abundance, why different kinds of media content appealed to some audiences more and to others less, what media audiences' attention was directed to and why, and whether some media audiences were active while others were passive. What needs and desires were met by media use, and how were audiences actually affected? Until around 1940, very few studies had been conducted in this area, and those early studies that had been carried out, such as the Payne Fund studies on the role and impact of film, had several shortcomings (Lowery & De Fleur, 1995: 382).

In many ways, the story of Herta Herzog is the same as that of many other Germanophone social science scholars and of how their life of exile in the United States became a veritable springboard to something greater. At home in Europe, Lazarsfeld and his colleagues had developed new methods and theories on opinion formation and media effects; however, these were undeveloped in many respects. Although philosophically well-read, these social scientists did not shun quantitative methods. On the contrary, the survey method had been established even before the Second World War, and both Herzog and Lazarsfeld came to place great emphasis on quantitative approaches. After all, surveys and audience measurements can effectively quantify audience perceptions. Still, the couple heeded the risk of oversimplifying and even missing fundamental issues – often those relating to motivations and associations. Stanton and Lazarsfeld went on to experiment with makeshift electrical measuring devices designed to gauge audience reactions, although Theodor Adorno famously dismissed this method, holding that such trinkets would give grotesquely simplified pictures of social life. One of Adorno's main objections was that the devices could not demonstrate whether the measured opinions were in fact products of commercial marketing, rather than genuine expressions of subjective feelings and opinions.

It was to compensate for the shortcomings of such quantitative methods that Herzog came to develop important complements. She was one of the first to synthesise different methods into a coherent picture of radio listening and newspaper reading as meaningful practices in people's everyday lives. Later in her career, Herzog pioneered associative survey methods, in which respondents were asked to draw different products and talk about them while drawing – including the now famous Rorschach test, in which respondents are shown random spot patterns and asked to describe what they see (Klaus & Seethaler, 2016a: 18). In addition, she was one of the key authors of the marketing theory distinction between brand 'image', 'profile' and 'identity'. In the latter half of

Herta Herzog (1941) 31

her career, at the McCann advertising agency, Herzog proposed that brands are seen by audiences as 'images' and that this overall 'image' of the brand can be understood as the sum of the impressions the customer receives from a variety of sources, which in turn generates a 'brand personality' that the audience as a whole tends to agree on but to which individual people may have different attitudes (Herzog, 1963, in Klaus & Seethaler, 2016a: 20). This is a semiotic concept that now seems so well-established that few people might reflect on its origins. As a sociological concept, the notion of the brand was later popularised by influential marketing and management theorists such as Keller (1993) and Kotler et al. (1996). [3] This idea of brand 'images' and 'identities' can be criticised for often being part and parcel of a rather superficial view of the world. Nevertheless, in an interview (Klaus & Seethaler, 2016a: 137), Herzog pointed out that her original use of the term actually referred to Freud's concept of *Imago* (also the name of an influential journal, founded in 1912), a profound psychological term that was central to Carl Gustav Jung's work as well. Contemporary scholars such as Featherstone (2017) and Klaus and Seethaler (2016b) have emphasised Alfred Adler's role in the post-war emergence of psychological theories of image-making and desire (more detail on this is provided below), as such components make up integral parts of the apparatus of advertising. Arguably, understanding this genealogy is even more urgent in our time, as environmental factors have made expansionist consumerism no longer as tenable as it was thought to be in Herzog's time.

In the context of this article, however, it is more important to focus on Herzog's role as a mass-communication researcher. Her choice to interview radio listeners – rather than simply analysing the radio content – gave the listeners a voice and opened up the possibility of analysing their descriptions of the medium and what they did with the medium, as opposed to simply making assumptions about the effects of the medium, which was common in media research at the time.

While Herzog's conception of the active audience had already crystallised during the 1930s (Klaus & Seethaler, 2016b: 242), Kleining (2016: 132–133) posits that it is very likely that the subsequent development of the focus group interview was partly a result of the war effort, since Herzog was asked to study the psychological and social effects of propaganda as part of her employment at the Bureau for Applied Social Research during the war (also see Merton & Kendall, 1946: 542). Unable to study the direct effects of propaganda, the researchers recruited Eastern European immigrants in New York in order to create small test groups, expose them to radio programmes and observe their reactions. The researchers called this method 'focused interviews' and the groups 'focused groups'. The first studies reportedly took place in 1942. Robert Merton was one of the more prominent leaders of the project but did not participate to the same extent as Herzog in the actual design and implementation of the studies; his interest was more theoretical, and he later published manuals teaching the method in question (Merton et al., 1956), in which Herzog is mentioned on only one page. In this passage (1956: 5), it is striking how

32   Jonas Andersson Schwarz

Herzog's role is relegated to the periphery. At the same time, it is important to note that, the year after Herzog and Merton developed the method, Herzog left the Bureau of Applied Social Research to become the Head of Copy Research at the McCann Erickson advertising agency. While her move from academia to the advertising industry probably did not cause any bad blood – she remained friends with her old research colleagues, although she did divorce Lazarsfeld in 1945 – her exit may have caused Merton to believe that she was not particularly eager to have her name in the academic annals. In addition to the fact that she was a woman and that Merton was in a managerial position, Herzog's active departure from the academy may have contributed to Merton feeling justified in effectively erasing her from academic historiography.

The uses and gratifications model: the emergence of a new theoretical perspective

By the late 1960s, U&G theory – often referred to as just 'U&G' or 'the functional approach' – was already an extensive and widely established subfield within the larger field of media and communications studies (Lundberg & Hultén, 1968: 32), with some of the earliest studies emerging during the 1920s (1968: 37). Borrowing from psychology, sociology, anthropology, political science, journalism and cultural history, this type of approach aims to shed light on structural conditions and provide in-depth studies of the process and effects of mass communication. Lundberg and Hultén (1968) note that the U&G model can be considered a specific branch of mass-communication research that aims to shed light on 'the receivers and their role in the transmission process [...], primarily, how the receiving individuals experience and utilise the carriers of mass communication called mass media' (1968: 32). Studies like that of Blumler and McQuail (1968) were considered innovative at the time because they clearly broke with the transmission model (see Chapter 5 in this volume) that had long been the norm in media studies and established the idea that audiences are goal oriented (McQuail et al., 1972).

Nevertheless, this research approach should not be seen as a coherent model in the conventional sense, Lundberg and Hultén continue, as it is not constructed from a limited number of well-defined factors or elements whose interrelationships have been specified and whose context has been clearly delineated. Rather, this usage model should be viewed as a rubric for applied research that emphasises the role of recipients in the communication process and stipulates that individuals are selective in their media use and act according to their perceived desires and needs. A key research interest in this subfield is to identify the functions that users perceive media to have for them.

The idea of imagined *functions* that media are assumed to have for people was also established by Merton (1957) and is directly linked to that period's enthusiasm for system theories and cybernetic ideas about how different elements have different functions in dynamic systems. From this perspective, it follows that societies and individuals can be thought of as consisting of

Herta Herzog (1941) 33

different systems. This way of imagining the world had direct effects on the media research of the time (see Chapter 4 in this volume). With respect to Herzog's research, it is notable that, while Herzog actually uses interpretive methods and emphasises, for example, ritual and individual psychological explanations for different people's media choices, her immediate successors largely replaced this focus with an interest in what Merton referred to as 'observable objective consequences' (Lundberg & Hultén, 1968: 42).

As a result, the U&G model has been criticised, especially since the emergence of critical cultural studies in the 1960s and 1970s (see Chapters 11 and 22 in this volume). For example, David Morley (1980/1999: 132) notes that the U&G model quickly became more about psychology than sociology: while its early studies (i. e., Herzog's research; Berelson, 1949; Waples et al., 1940; Warner & Henry, 1948) were indeed concerned with specific media content and specific media audiences, much of the subsequent U&G research looked for underlying psychological structures without giving sufficient weight to, for example, time, place, and linguistic, cultural and demographic specificity. Examples of the latter, more orthodox application of the usage model include works by Bailyn (1959) and Pearlin (1959), whose studies' lack of contextualisation was also criticised at the time (De Fleur, 1966, in Lundberg & Hultén, 1968: 41–42). Much of this research has been summarised by Klapper (1960).

In this more functionalist mode, U&G research carries the risk of evoking an all-too-optimistic picture in which the mass media – as a set of systems – act in response to simple supply-and-demand calculations in which media users themselves are perceived as being capable of determining what is good for them, in terms of needs and desires. In this picture, the media therefore fulfils a democratic potential, as everyone is assumed to use these media because they 'get something out of them'.

In the early 1970s, the U&G model was in an expansive phase, with scholars such as Blumler and McQuail (1968), McQuail et al. (1972) and Katz et al. (1973) consolidating the model into a field of its own. At the same time, the myth of freedom of choice in media provision was strongly challenged, most notably by Elliott (1974), who noted that, although media audiences do choose, they do so from a predefined range of selection. It is true that this range has increased many times over since the mid-to-late 20th century, but the same principle still applies today. Moreover, in practice, the absolute majority of users will make similar, norm-driven choices – in other words, 'dominant readings', as Stuart Hall called it (Morley, 1980/1999: 132; see also Chapter 11 in this volume).

Does anyone really know herself well enough to determine what she actually receives from, say, a television programme? When asked, can a person honestly and comprehensively identify her own various motives and/or incentives for consuming different media? Can the person really identify all the possible reasons that might exist? As for the possible reasons she explicitly identifies – will she even remember them all? Gantz (1996) is one of many who have criticised the U&G model for being dependent on the questions asked and the settings and conditions for these questions to be answerable. All too often, the questionnaire determines what reasons respondents can give when asked about gratifications. Regardless of how exhaustive the lists are, writes Schrøder (1999: 41), there will always be possible personal experiences that are *not* included. This issue undermines the validity of such studies, as the researcher can never be sure that the results adequately depict the real phenomena that are intended to be described.

Thus, in the decades following Katz et al. (1973), it became clear that such problems multiply as overly narrow understandings of the U&G model continue to be applied. The methods in question tend to be:

- Behaviourist (based on overly simple stimulus-response models);
- Reductionist (tending to summarise rich experiences in overly simple and unambiguous categories);
- Instrumental (making it too easy to draw hasty normative interpretations);
- Confirmatory (carrying the risk that the results say whatever the researcher prefers them to say and – in the case of commissioned research – what the commissioner prefers them to say);
- Lacking in validity (involving empirical accounts that rely on individuals' self-reporting of their perceived motives, which hardly ensures that the questions are adequate and the answers valid);
- Individual centred (in which the ontology of the research risks being based on an imagined, transactional 'economic man').

So, how vital is the U&G model today? To begin with, since the arrival of the Internet and, more specifically, social media, the notion of 'active use' has become almost a default way of imagining civic interaction with various media. From the very outset, Internet media has rested on the stipulation that audiences are primarily 'users', and it is rare to see Internet media users being described as 'passive'. It is only secondly that people are considered to be viewers, listeners, readers, players and so on, depending on the nature of the service in question. One could go so far as to see different interfaces as primarily technical systems that contain individuals in different scripted behaviours, and to perceive that the communicative functions only take place when these first conditions are fulfilled.[4] In order to access streaming media, one must begin by becoming a user of the service in question – this is the basic premise. It is questionable whether it is at all possible to participate in today's digital media society without being a user of technical systems.

In a similar vein, there seems to have been a shift in the public perception of media use. 'Mass communication' is often associated with passivity, whereas today's media are 'social' and 'interactive' – and thus primarily associated with activity. Here, the 'couch potatoes' of the late 20th century form a sharp contrast with the constantly clicking, playing, messaging, sharing and selecting smartphone users of the early 21st century. Thus, it is not surprising that many people seem to take the core beliefs of the U&G model for granted – so much

Herta Herzog (1941) 35

so that media students today are drawn to this particular model because it seems to confirm their own sense of participation, empowerment, agency and choice. However, this chapter shows that the model is far from problem-free, due to the many blind spots, simplifications and overestimations of the research approach in question.

Herzog's legacy

Let us return to the *Mad Men* episode this chapter began with. The observant viewer is struck by a number of ingenious details; for example, the initials 'G. G.' are a reference to Herta Herzog's initials. The fictional Edler could be Karl Bühler, who was Herzog's teacher in Vienna, although he is much more likely to be Alfred Adler, whose interpretation of Freud was very influential in the United States at the time. Russell Jacoby (1996) has argued that Adlerian psychotherapy glosses over the treatment of neurosis and instead seeks to cushion the more aspirational aspects of the self and ease people's conformity to capitalist society. Lisa Featherstone (2017: 102–137) contends that this was a perfect intellectual match for the real Herta Herzog, as she rose to fame in top executive roles at a very real advertising agency – McCann Erickson – throughout the late 1940s, 50s and 60s. By the 1960s, Freud's theories had become hot topics of conversation among the coastal jet-set in the United States. As early as in the 1920s, Edward Bernays – the originator of the modern concept of public relations – had been deeply influenced by Freud and translated his psychodynamic theories into instrumental techniques for mass persuasion. Bernays' interest was hardly unexpected, as he was Freud's nephew.

Perhaps Herzog's legacy has been considered to be weaker in media research than in the world of advertising and marketing, where her development of the focus group interview as a method, along with the concept of 'brand image' and her years at the helm of McCann Erickson, qualify her as a celebrated advertising woman. Much like Mary Wells-Lawrence, the mastermind behind the famous 1977 'I Love NY' advertising campaign, or Jane Maas, a copywriter at the advertising agency Ogilvy & Mather who co-authored the classic *How to Advertise* (Roman et al., 1976), Herzog could be placed within a pantheon of pioneering advertisers and female role models. That said, Elisabeth Klaus (Klaus & Seethaler, 2016a: 33–34) criticises the fictional portrayal of Herzog in *Mad Men*, as the dramatisation makes Herzog appear to be much more inhibited – both theoretically and methodologically – than she actually was.

Let us consider the notion of the *active* media user, who makes informed choices. Is this an idealistic figure? I would argue that, since the subject's capacity to discern and resist ideological interpellation is implicit in critical theory, this theory is built on the possibility of rational civic agency – or even activity. Herzog took this hopeful image of active media users and tested how and in which ways their personal considerations of media use held up empirically. In contrast with critical theory, however, she later translated her empirical understanding of different behavioural aspects of media use into actionable

36 *Jonas Andersson Schwarz*

business insights. This may have been controversial to some; in many ways, what Herzog did was to make use of the critical thinking emphasised by Adorno and Lazarsfeld, applying this analytical work to serve the persuasive, behavioural machinery of capitalism. Taken together with the simple observation that Herzog was a woman, could this explain in part why Herzog later became overlooked in mass-communication research? Hopefully, the summary presented in this chapter can serve to illuminate this blind spot.

Notes

1 Two surveys with around 5,000 respondents each (US-wide and Iowa samples), one survey with 1,500 respondents (Ohio), and another smaller study in three US cities.
2 In this agreement, which took place a year before the outbreak of war in 1939, Hitler was supposed to settle for a ceded territory in what was then Czechoslovakia, whereupon British Prime Minister Neville Chamberlain thought he had 'appeased' Nazi Germany and uttered the fateful words 'peace for our time'.
3 Keller (1993) was careful to identify 'brand image' as the invention of both Herzog (1963) and Newman (1957).
4 Consider, for example, that social media offers interfaces that are, on the one hand, rigid and regimented 'choice architectures' (Münscher et al., 2015), yet, on the other hand, veritable mixers of media content, serving different patterns of media use. In audience research, this is sometimes theorised through the concept of 'media repertoires' (Hasebrink & Domeyer, 2012), as people combine and interrelate with media in ways that become meaningful to the media users themselves. Different communicative functions are blended in social media users' newsfeeds (Gillespie, 2018: 40–44), yet the interfaces are clearly steering the users in various directions. Moreover, the interfaces follow strict technical standards and rules that all users must conform to (the 'micro-level' digital platform logic, according to Andersson Schwarz, 2017).

References

Andersson Schwarz, J. (2017). Platform logic: An interdisciplinary approach to the platform-based economy. *Policy & Internet*, 9(4), 374–394.

Bailyn, L. (1959). Mass media and children: A study of exposure habits and cognitive effects. *Psychological Monographs*, 73, 1–48.

Berelson, B. (1949). What missing the newspaper means. In Paul F. Lazarsfeld & Frank N. Stanton (Eds.), *Communications research 1948–1949* (pp. 111–129). Harper & Brothers.

Blumler, J. G., & McQuail, D. (1968). *Television in politics: Its uses and influence.* Faber & Faber.

Cantril, H. (1940). *The invasion from Mars: A study in the psychology of panic.* Princeton University Press.

Cantril, H. (1942). Professor quiz: A gratification study. In Paul F.Lazarsfeld & Frank N.Stanton (Eds.), *Radio research 1941* (pp. 34–45). Duell, Sloan & Pearce.

De Fleur, M. L. (1966). *Theories of mass communication.* David McKay.

Douglas, S. (2006). Personal influence and the bracketing of women's history. *Annals of the American Academy*, 608, 41–50.

Elliott, P. (1974). Uses and gratifications research: A critique and a sociological alternative. In J. G. Blumler & E. Katz (Eds.), *The uses of mass communications: Current perspectives on gratifications research* (pp. 249–268). Sage.

Featherstone, L. (2017). *Divining desire: Focus groups and the culture of consultation*. OR Books.

Gantz, W. (1996). An examination of the range and salience of gratifications associated with entertainment programming. *Journal of Behavioral and Social Sciences*, 1, 11–48.

Gillespie, T. (2018). *Custodians of the Internet: Platforms, content moderation, and the hidden decisions that shape social media*. Yale University Press.

Hasebrink, U., & Domeyer, H. (2012). Media repertoires as patterns of behaviour and as meaningful practices: A multimethod approach to media use in converging media environments. *Participations: Journal of Audience & Reception Studies*, 9(2), 757–779.

Herzog, H. (1940). Professor quiz: A gratification study. In Paul F. Lazarsfeld & Frank N. Stanton (Eds.), *Radio and the printed page* (pp. 64–93). Duell, Sloan & Pearce.

Herzog, H. (1941). On borrowed experience: An analysis of listening to daytime sketches. *Studies in Philosophy and Social Science*, 9(1), 65–95.

Herzog, H. (1944). What do we really know about daytime serial listeners? In Paul F. Lazarsfeld & Frank N. Stanton (Eds.), *Radio research 1942–1943* (pp. 2–23). Sage.

Herzog, H. (1946). Radio – The first post-war year. *Public Opinion Quarterly*, 10(3), 297–313.

Herzog, H. (1963). Behavioral science concepts for analyzing the consumer. In P. Bliss (Ed.), *Marketing and the behavioral sciences* (pp. 76–86). Allyn & Bacon.

Herzog Massing, H. (1987). Decoding 'Dallas': Comparing American and German viewers. In A. A. Berger (Ed.), *Television in society* (pp. 95–102). Transaction.

Herzog, H. (1994). *Letter to Elisabeth M. Perse, 12* September [obtained as a proxy copy via Wayback Machine, Dec. 24, 2022]. Outofthequestion.org. https://web.archive.org/web/20220401000000*/http://outofthequestion.org/userfiles/file/Herta%20Herzog%20(Sept%2012%201994%20to%20Elisabeth%20Perse).pdf.

Jacoby, R. (1996). *Social amnesia: A critique of contemporary psychology*. Transaction.

Katz, E., Blumler, J. G., & Gurevitch, M. (1973). Uses and gratifications research. *Public Opinion Quarterly*, 37(4), 509–523.

Katz, E., & Katz, R. (2016). Revisiting the origin of the administrative versus critical research debate. *Journal of Information Policy*, 6, 4–12.

Katz, E., & Lazarsfeld, P. F. (1955). *Personal influence*. Free Press.

Keller, K. L. (1993). Conceptualising, measuring, and managing customer-based brand equity. *Journal of Marketing*, 57(1), 1–22.

Klapper, J. (1960). *The effects of mass communication*. Free Press.

Klaus, E., & Seethaler, J. (Eds.) (2016a). *What do we really know about Herta Herzog?* Peter Lang.

Klaus, E., & Seethaler, J. (2016b). Crossing the borders: Herta Herzog's work in communication and marketing research. In P. Simonson & D. W. Park (Eds.), *The international history of communication study* (pp. 237–255). Routledge.

Kleining, G. (2016). The discovery process in Herta Herzog's research on radio daytime serials—with an appendix on the invention of the focus group. In E.Klaus & J. Seethaler (Eds.), *What do we really know about Herta Herzog?* (pp. 117–135). Peter Lang.

Kotler, P., Armstrong, G., Saunders, J., & Wong, V. (1996). *Principles of marketing*. Prentice Hall.

Lazarsfeld, P. (1941). Remarks on administrative and critical communications research. *Studies in Philosophy and Social Science*, IX(1), 3–20.

Levine, L. W. (1992). The folklore of industrial society: Popular culture and its audiences. *American Historical Review*, 97(5), 1369–1399.

38 *Jonas Andersson Schwarz*

Liebes, T. (2005). Viewing and reviewing the audience: Fashions in communications research. In J. Curran & M. Gurevitch (Eds.), *Mass media and society* (4th ed.) (pp. 356–374). Hodder Arnold.

Lowery, S., & De Fleur, M. (1995). *Milestones in mass communication research: Media effects* (3rd ed.). Longman.

Lundberg, D., & Hultén, O. (1968). *Individen och massmedia* [*The Individual and the Mass Media*]. Norstedts.

McQuail, D., Blumler, J. G., & Brown, J. R. (1972). The television audience: A revised perspective. In D. McQuail (Ed.), *Sociology of mass communications* (pp. 135–165). Penguin.

Merton, R. K. (1957). *Social theory and social structure*. Free Press.

Merton, R. K., Fiske, M., & Kendall, P. L. (1956). *The focused interview*. Free Press.

Merton, R. K., & Kendall, P. L. (1946). The focused interview. *American Journal of Sociology*, 51(6), 541–557.

Morley, D. (1980/1999). The nationwide audience: Structure and decoding. In D. Morley & C. Brunsdon (Eds.), *The Nationwide Television Studies* (pp. 117–301). Routledge.

Münscher, R., Vetter, M., & Scheuerle, T. (2015). A review and taxonomy of choice architecture techniques. *Journal of Behavioral Decision Making*, 29, 511–524.

Newman, J. W. (1957, Nov-Dec). New insight, new progress for marketing. *Harvard Business Review*, 35, 95–102.

Packard, V. (1957). *The hidden persuaders* (new ed. 1967). Penguin.

Pearlin, L. J. (1959). Social and personal stress and escape television viewing. *Public Opinion Quarterly*, 23, 255–259.

Roman, K., Maas, J., & Nisenholtz, M. (1976). *How to advertise: What works, what doesn't—and why*. St Martin's Press.

Rossiter M. W. (1993). The Matthew/Matilda effect in science. *Social Studies of Science*, 23(2), 325–341.

Rowland, A. L., & Simonson, P. (2014). The founding mothers of communication research: Toward a history of a gendered assemblage. *Critical Studies in Media Communication*, 31(1): 3–26. doi:10.1080/15295036.2013.849355.

Schrøder, K. C. (1999). The best of both worlds? Media audience research between rival paradigms. In P. Alasuutari (Ed.), *Rethinking the media audience: The new agenda* (pp. 38–68). Sage.

Waples, D., Berelson, B., & Bradshaw, F. R. (1940). *What reading does to people: A summary of evidence on the social effects of reading and a statement of problems for research*. University of Chicago Press.

Warner, W. L., & W. E. Henry (1948). The radio daytime serial: A symbolic analysis. *Genetic Psychology Monographs*, 37, 3–71.

3 Max Horkheimer and Theodor Adorno (1947) 'The Culture Industry: Enlightenment as Mass Deception'

Sven-Olov Wallenstein

Introduction

The chapter 'The Culture Industry: Enlightenment as Mass Deception' in *The Dialectic of Enlightenment* (1947/2002) is one of Horkheimer and Adorno's most cited texts and has produced a continually proliferating critical debate (see Kellner, 2002). Horkheimer and Adorno's analysis tends to give a one-sided picture of popular culture, but there are many reasons to perceive nuances in this reading. First, the context must be noted: the book was written by German academics in exile in the United States, at a time when the authors feared that fascism would be victorious on the other side of the Atlantic as in Germany of that time. The sombre quality pervading the book is thus marked by the historical situation and, in order to assess the book's claims about the culture industry in a productive fashion, it is necessary to view them in relation to Adorno's later writings, which include many new perspectives.

Second, Adorno's early texts already contain elements of a more complex dialectical rendering of the relation between mass culture and what he refers to as 'autonomous art'. This is notably hinted at in his discussion with Benjamin on the latter's 'The Work of Art in the Age of Mechanical Reproduction', to which the chapter 'The Culture Industry' in *The Dialectic of Enlightenment* constitutes a further response, even though Benjamin's name is never mentioned (with his suicide in 1940 as a likely reason for the omission of any polemics).

This theme is also at the centre of Adorno's late writings, such as in his unfinished final work *Aesthetic Theory* (1970/1997), where the dialectic of high and low, as well as the autonomy of art, is shown to be a function of social organisation. In these late writings, the largely negative view of the culture industry becomes part of an analysis of the 'administered world' – that is, the bureaucracy of late capitalism – in which cultural production tends to have a stabilising function. Moreover, while autonomous art and its capacity for resistance are too conditioned by the social order, they cannot be reduced to it.

The debate with Benjamin

Benjamin's artwork essay, written between 1934 and 1935 in Paris,[1] takes as its starting point the new forces of production in film and photography and their

DOI: 10.4324/9781003432272-4

40 Sven-Olov Wallenstein

capacity to undo inherited conceptions of the creator-genius and the immemorial values and secrets of art (see Chapter 1 in this volume). Such ideas, Benjamin writes, not only underpin an outdated theory of art but also – when transposed to the social sphere – support fascist politics, and this political aim must be borne in mind when reading the text. As indicated by the original title of Benjamin's work, *Reproduzierbarkeit* (Reproducibility), the issue is not reproduction but reproducibility. For film and photography, technological reproducibility belongs to the objects themselves and does not befall them as an external accident. In technological reproducibility, the sense of the 'here and now' – of the work's uniqueness and authenticity, of what Benjamin calls its 'aura' – dissolves. This dissolution releases the object from tradition, in a way that at first appears to be destructive but is in fact the progressive moment.[2] Benjamin goes so far as to speak – brutally – of a 'liquidation [*Liquidierung*] of the traditional value of the cultural heritage' (Benjamin, 1936/1969: 221) that liberates us from the weight of the past, above all in cinema. Shakespeare, Rembrandt and Beethoven have all appeared on the screen, causing them to lose their sacrosanct status.

This loss of value in turn brings about a shift in our perception. If the aura, as Benjamin suggests, is a sense of distance that does not disappear regardless of how close we get, then its destruction draws things closer to us; we learn to see the similarity in things, and artworks become adjusted to mass consumption. The connection between the artwork and religion and cult is severed. As an example, Benjamin refers to the poet Stéphane Mallarmé and his idea that the world ultimately exists in order to become a book, *Le Livre*; thus, the world itself is replaced by what Benjamin, somewhat enigmatically, calls 'exhibition value' (Benjamin 1936/1969: 226).[3]

All attempts to inject cult values into photography and film are therefore deemed to be reactionary, including on the level of form, since they aspire to seal new artistic forces of production in old relations of production based on a contemplative attitude. Against this, Benjamin pits the distancing produced by the apparatus in film, which allows for a transformed spectatorial position: the viewers test the actor and only project themselves into the events on the screen through the apparatus, just as the actor's performance is broken up into discrete parts, forcing the actor to observe her actions from the outside. This places film in opposition to theatre (which may seem slightly odd, since Benjamin's observations actually draw on his discussions of Brecht's theory of 'epic theatre'; see the essays in Benjamin, 1930/1998) where the self-presence of the actor is the key. The cult of 'personality' – the 'star' system – is the precise countermove to this loss of aura, as proposed by the capitalist production system, against which Benjamin marshals the utopian claim (possibly derived from Sergei Eisenstein) that everyone has the right to be filmed. Similarly, the difference between writers and readers is gradually obliterated in the press as well as in avantgarde literary experiments, to the effect that the debate over form versus content must be rethought based on the author as 'producer' (Benjamin, 1934/1998).

Here, there is also a new relation to science. The traditional painter relates to the filmmaker as the magician does to the surgeon: the first employs magic charm and *actio in distans* to release the inner essence of the object, while the second penetrates the object and decomposes it in a series of analytical operations. The new analysis of movement and social space made possible in cinema actually renders it analogous to psychoanalysis, and Benjamin famously speaks of an 'optical unconscious' – 'The camera introduces us to the optical unconscious (*Optisch-Unbewußten*) as does psychoanalysis to unconscious impulses' (Benjamin, 1936/1969: 227, trans. modified) – in which the seemingly marginal slips in our discourse are brought to attention. This gives rise to an attitude of testing instead of immersion, and the model Benjamin gives is that of a famous image: a group of boys selling newspapers, while leaning over their bicycles to analyse the last race of the Tour de France with great expertise.

This quality makes the new media more accessible to a mass audience. A painting has never been the focus of a mass experience; it remains locked within the orbit of a single individual and his contemplative stance in front of the work, such that its very phenomenology seems to perpetuate the status of the religious fetish. The new works, on the other hand, should be experienced while in a form of 'distraction' (*Zerstreutheit*) (Benjamin, 1936/1969: 247–249), rather than in a contemplative attitude. This distraction, Benjamin claims, has long been predominant in architecture, which focuses on an impure and tactile experience instead of a purely optical one, and on the insertion of the work into a social praxis from which it can never be detached as an isolated item for aesthetic contemplation. The new art, Benjamin says, arises immediately out of – and reflects back on – the urban masses; in this respect, it has a direct political significance.

This makes the new media not only into a highly efficient political instrument but also (in what is the most risky and tenuous point in his argument) into an instrument whose very technological structure seems to render it inherently progressive. This is why Benjamin displays such a surprising confidence in the final section of his text, where he claims that, when fascism seeks to aestheticise politics and finally to understand the destruction of humankind as an auratic phenomenon, Communism responds by politicising art, as if the success of such a displacement would be somehow guaranteed by the very structure of media. This politicising of art takes place by way of the new progressive technologies in their instrumentality, whereas the fascist aestheticisation tales place by means of an interpretation of society based on 19th century aestheticism and its rejection of technology.

Adorno responds in a famous letter dated March 18, 1936. Against the immediate revocation of the artwork's use value, he proposes that the reification inherent in traditional artwork – its separation from the immediacy of life – should not be seen just as a loss or deprivation, but more fundamentally as a necessary condition for its capacity to resist society and attain a certain transcendence in relation to the actual world, which is the very precondition for its capacity to acts as a *critique*. It is just as 'bourgeois', Adorno claims, to deny

42   Sven-Olov Wallenstein

the reification of the subject in cinema (the aura of the theatre actor that disappears in the technical dimension of montage), as it is naïve and too hasty – 'it would border on anarchism', Adorno says (Adorno & Benjamin, 1999: 129) – to deny the reification of the autonomous work in favour of an immediate use, that is, an art that would lay claim to direct invention in the praxis of life. Indeed, Adorno also expresses an essential disenchantment with the aesthetic moment that occurs through the advance of technique; however, the difference between Adorno's and Benjamin's perspectives is that this disenchantment must be understood precisely as an *artistic* technique, in terms of the immanent laws of construction for the work itself. Mallarmé's poetic materialism, which shows that poetry is made of words, and Schönberg's 12-tone method of composing, which imposes a seemingly foreign set of objective parameters on the composer's subjectivity, dissolve the traditional idea of creation as a mystical act much more efficiently than the practices of the feuilleton writer or the industrial division of labour in the movies, whose disenchanting effects Adorno considers to be vastly exaggerated. Benjamin's remarks on the distancing of the moviegoer seem equally misguided to Adorno: rather than emancipation, they signal bourgeois sadism and an influx of barbarism. Certain of Benjamin's terms, such as 'test', are congealed concepts, hiding the fact that film in general is highly auratic, infantile and realistic. Chaplin is not revolutionary; instead, he appeals to sadistic impulses and makes us comply with real violence.

'I cannot express my feelings about the entire piece more clearly than by telling you how much I would like to see a study of Mallarmé precisely as a counter-point to this essay' (Adorno & Benjamin, 1999: 128), says Adorno, meaning that it is only when *l'art pour l'art* is seen as essentially related to popular art, as its *precise and determined other*, that it is possible to understand the dialectical totality as a contradictory whole. The aura is broken down just as much in autonomous work as it is in the art of mass consumption, albeit because of an inner, formal development in the first case and because of external demands in the second. Reification is neither simply a loss nor a gain *but both of them at once*. The two extremes of autonomous and popular art touch each other, but only if they are credited with the same dialectical value, whereas Benjamin appears to simply reject one of them as if it were, in Adorno's expression, 'counter-revolutionary' (Adorno & Benjamin, 1999: 128). Moreover, Adorno continues, it would be a bourgeois or a proletarian romanticism – but in both cases a romanticism – to opt exclusively for one of the two versions. In a famous and oft-cited phrase, Adorno summarises his critique of Benjamin's dream of directly transforming art to life when he claims that both the respective works of the avantgarde and mass culture 'bear the stigmata of capitalism, both contain elements of change […] Both are torn halves of an integral freedom, to which, however, they do not add up' (*Beide tragen die Wundmale des Kapitalismus, beide enthalten Elemente der Veränderung* […] *beide sind die auseinandergerissenen Hälften der ganzen Freiheit, die doch aus ihnen nicht sich zusammenaddieren lässt*) (Adorno & Benjamin, 1999: 130). The true is not the whole but the *whole as differing from itself*, split in two halves that can just as little be reconciled as one of them can be simply discarded.

Max Horkheimer and Theodor Adorno (1947) 43

Adorno's letter is thus a defence of autonomous artwork, although it is by no means a simplistic one. By following Adorno's references to music, it can be seen that Adorno views artwork as being caught up in technology and eventually becoming a planned work, which threatens to undo its own status as work in the end, along with subjective impulses – a problem that Adorno would diagnose a decade later in his *Philosophy of New Music* (1949/2006). In this sense, autonomy is not an answer but a problem that must be continually faced anew.

The regression of listening

A large part of Adorno's writings is dedicated to music. In his essay on jazz, written in the same year as his letter to Benjamin (Adorno, 1936/1997), Adorno develops his ideas in relation to popular music of the time. His knowledge of jazz was limited at the time (see Okiji, 2018; Paddison, 1996), and the fact that his judgements still stand in later writings (Adorno, 1953/1981) indicates that Adorno never took the time to deepen it in any significant sense. However, his true interest lay in other forms of music, ranging from Beethoven to the second Vienna School (Schönberg, Anton Webern and Alvan Berg) and their legacy in the post-war avantgarde. In the same way that focusing solely on Horkheimer and Adorno's chapter on the culture industry gives a skewed picture of Adorno's sociology of culture, reading Adorno's philosophy of music with the jazz essay as a grid (it constitutes less than 1% of his writings on music) deprives the philosophy of its substance. Furthermore, it should be noted that the sharp division between popular and advanced music that can sometimes be seen in Adorno's earlier writings is not his final word. On the contrary, transgressing this difference can be done in many ways while preserving the dialectical tension between the 'torn halves', as is shown in Adorno's later writings, where he undertakes a revision of the history of modernism in light of the impasses of the post-war development (e.g. in Adorno's (1960/1996) monograph on Mahler).

Notwithstanding the weak contextual underpinning of Adorno's early jazz essay, as well as the absence of proper musical analyses, a set of basic ideas emerges in this work that would be developed in subsequent texts and would have important bearings on his other writings on music. First and foremost, there is the idea of subjectivity and freedom that, for Adorno in jazz, is rendered as a caricature in the apparent spontaneity of the soloist, which in the end is only ornamental and signals subjection to the mythical collective (later, in *Philosophy of New Music*, Adorno would detect similar moves in Stravinsky). What is at stake is an adaptive virtuosity, for instance in the syncopated rhythm whose irregularities only confirm the underlying structure, and which Adorno perceives to be analogous to the individual's illusory freedom in capitalism.

Similarly, the conjuring up of archaic impulses, bodily acting out and ecstasy is only a taming of excess and a subjection to the commodity: a repetition of the new and disruptive that ends up in an eternal recurrence of the same. The temporal unfolding in music from Beethoven onward is replaced by repetitive

44 Sven-Olov Wallenstein

spatial forms without development – in this too, similar to Stravinsky and, to some extent, to certain aspects of 12-tone music. Adorno deciphers false freedom and false excess as castration anxiety and, when the listener is encouraged to dance instead of listening, this cancels the distance and reflexivity that music has conquered in bourgeois society in favour of a repressive desublimation – that is, a partial lifting of repression that only strengthens it, leaving everything as it was before.

In a subsequent text, 'On the Fetish-Character in Music and the Regression in Listening' (1938/2002), these themes are developed to include both popular and serious music. In a letter to Benjamin from February 1, 1939 (Adorno & Benjamin, 1999: 305), Adorno notes that the text records his initial encounter with America, and this context is important. After arriving in the United States, Adorno's first employment was in a radio research project at Princeton in 1938, where he was appointed director of the section on 'programming'. The project lasted for 2 years until its financing dried up; in this period, Adorno developed a sharp criticism of the pervasive empirical-sociological method that leans heavily on standardised question sheets and renders any deeper analysis of the social conditions of listening impossible. In addition, he found himself in conflict with the project leader, Paul Lazarsfeld (see Chapter 4 in this volume), who had already formulated the ambition in terms of market surveys 3 years earlier: to provide 'knowledge by means of which to forecast and control consumer behavior' (Kornhauser & Lazarsfeld, 1935: 4).

In his letter to Benjamin, Adorno regrets that the text was written too quickly and contains too many jeremiads. Nevertheless, it provides a more developed analysis of the status of subjectivity under monopoly capitalism than the jazz essay. The first claim is that the concept of taste, which otherwise would be at the centre of discussions of programming, becomes irrelevant, since there no longer exists an autonomous subject capable of choosing. The standardisation of music is just as much a standardisation of the subject and its preferences, and both become increasingly dependent on the commodity form. What triggers choice is no longer appreciation; in this aspect, Adorno perceives an ironic similarity to contemporary serious music, which also eschews pleasure but aims for recognition – which in turn is rejected in autonomous art, where estrangement is the fundamental feature. And yet, the process of commodification empties out the latter, the works gradually lose the (negated) meaning that they aspire to, while light music no longer entertains in the proper sense but only fills out 'the pockets of silence that develop between people molded by work, work and undemanding docility' (Adorno, 1938/2002: 280). Fetishism and regression encompass all spheres of music, and they shape the modern subject and a particular form of listening (to which Adorno would later return in a more detailed way; see Adorno (1962/1989)). Listening is always a cultural practice, which Adorno often sets in opposition to theories as different as phenomenology and naturalist objectivism: what we hear is never nature but always a result of historical mediation, which takes on a new form in the culture industry.

Adorno underlines that this should not be construed as moralising psychological remarks on the slackening of character or the decadence of modern subjectivism, nor as a lament against the predominance of immediate sensuousness; the sensuous dimension was by no means impossible to integrate in autonomous music, as is shown by Mozart. What appears in the regression of listening is not a newly won freedom from conventions but instead an intensified subjection to them; if there is a power of resistance today, it would rather lie in asceticism.

As in his 1936 letter to Benjamin, Adorno once more stresses the dialectical nature of the relation between autonomous and entertainment. The different spheres of music do not form a continuum from high to low but rather form a contradictory totality. However, the contradiction, which is the truth of totality, is obscured by the subsumption of the different moments in consumption: classical works all become 'standards', and we admire stars and technical virtuosity, 'the voice' and finally the instruments themselves, with the Stradivarius as the ultimate fetish.

In *Capital*, Marx stresses the claim that fetishism is not a psychological concept but belongs objectively to the commodity as such. Adorno applies this to a particular sphere, where it has specific features. In the end, what the consumer worships is not an idol, but quite simply the money spent on the ticket to the concert with Toscanini (to get 'value for money'); not because of any misunderstanding that ought to be corrected, but because of the structure that contemporary listening imposes on the subject. The value extracted is an experience that can in turn become an exchange value, which produces an infantilisation – an atomistic mode of listening that looks for highlights or mistakes to book and add together.

Atomism is not just dissolution, however; it also produces new capacities, such as those in sports, although, in the end – with an obvious reference to Benjamin's 'distraction' – these amount to a form of 'deconcentration' (*Dekonzentration*) (Adorno, 1938/2002: 305) that occurs at the expense of a perception of the totality as a structured whole of interlocking parts. The focus is shifted from structure to timbre, instrumental acrobatics and other features that belong to the domain of affects and impulses and that may give the listener a sense that normalcy is exceeded, whereas it is in fact reinforced. This is the form of expertise displayed by Benjamin's newspaper boys: one looks for details and extraordinary achievements, which in turn produces a rage against everything that is old and outmoded – even things recently praised by the expert, but which now appear 'corny'. Time and history are negated in favour of a timeless present that claims to be new, yet only revolves around itself.

The culture industry

One of the crucial claims in the analysis proposed in *The Dialectic of Enlightenment*, directed against various conservative cultural historians and critics who in modernity perceive only dissolution, is that we do not find ourselves amidst a chaos of styles and forms caused by the levelling of

46   *Sven-Olov Wallenstein*

'anything goes'; rather, we are within a pervasive form that holds sway over culture in its integrality – the total power of capital that produces false identity. This is what is meant by the term 'industry': what we see is not disorder but a mass production of culture that is wholly rationalised and draws on the most advanced technology available. The opposition to Benjamin is clear: Adorno rejects the idea that technological innovations as such would bring about progressive changes; in the culture industry, they simply allow for a more pervasive and rational exertion of power and control of behaviour.

This standardisation is not to be understood as a strict uniformity but as a process of differentiation in which everything has its standard and level, in order to preserve the illusion of competition and choice without which the subjects' acceptance could not be had. In it, the effective possibility of choice is reduced and subsequently recast into the form of an individual taste that miraculously always finds something that responds to its preferences. Consumption now becomes a process to be steered by research groups, as Lazarsfeld proposed without further ado, and individual responses appear as statistical phenomena.

Horkheimer and Adorno borrow the concept of 'schematism' from Kant, where it denotes a hidden but indispensable function in the subject that welds together concepts and intuitions to a coherent experience. Schematism is now prefigured outside the subject: its task is to piece together clichés, so the viewer will always know how the film ends. The interest is therefore displaced from the totality of the work to its technical details and special effects, which was in some way already the case in romanticism and in its insurgence against the schemas of classicism. Today, however, the deviations are integrated into a new totality in which pre-set mechanisms of identification and recognition usurp the role of fantasy.

At the same time, there is a dialectical relation to advanced art here as well, in that both obey a logic organised by prohibitions, albeit of a different nature. If advanced art shuns repetition, recognition and redundancy and wants to attain an autonomous language character (which is a paradox that eventually severs the link to language and ends up in a rationalised system that eradicates meaning; see Adorno 1955/2002), the culture industry prohibits that which would irrevocably shatter recognition. It aspires to a sense of the natural, precisely to conceal that it is a jargon – none of which excludes, but in fact calls for, virtuosity: 'But the true masters, as both producers and reproducers, are those who speak the jargon with the same free-and-easy relish as if it were the language it has long since silenced' (Horkheimer & Adorno, 1947/2002: 101). In the end, the difference between authenticity and artifice is obliterated, the tension disappears, and what remains is only a diffuse identity.

This in turn sheds light on earlier styles and their enforced unity: significant art has always offered a resistance to integration, expressing 'the chaotic expression of suffering' (Horkheimer & Adorno, 1947/2002: 103). Later, in *Negative Dialectics*, Adorno defines this as the very task of philosophy, as such: 'The need to lend a voice to suffering is a condition for all truth' (Adorno, 1966/ 1990: 17f). Distrust of unity and of style as imposed from above thus belongs to

Max Horkheimer and Theodor Adorno (1947) 47

authentic art as well as to philosophy, precisely as an expression of social injustice and suffering – and not just because of purely formal considerations.

In this sense, artworks always contains a promise. In their very existence, and not necessarily in their content, they suggest that everything could be different. And yet the promise is also a mirage: it can never be fulfilled, since art, by stepping out of the society on which it always depends, turns into an ideology by setting up a merely apparent world that claims to be a higher and truer reality. In his posthumous work *Aesthetic Theory*, Adorno summarises this predicament: 'Aesthetic experience is that of something spirit may find neither in the world nor in itself; it is possibility promised by its impossibility. Art is the ever broken promise of happiness' (Adorno, 1970/2004: 135f). In the administered world of late capitalism, however, the promise is silenced by being reduced to culture, which pits culture against itself: 'To speak about culture always went against the grain of culture' (Horkheimer & Adorno, 1947/2002: 103).

This levelling is in fact what is produced by the advanced liberalism that is accused of lacking style: everything is acceptable if it does not disturb the established order. It would be misleading, Adorno writes, to blame this on an absence of culture or an assumed 'cultural lag' that would characterise America. On the contrary, it was pre-fascist Europe with its institutional remains of an authoritarian feudal culture that was lagging behind modern capitalism, while this moment of historical non-synchronicity provided art with a latitude that is disappearing today.

This does not mean that the tension between mass culture and art would simply have vanished; Horkheimer and Adorno once more return to the claims put forward earlier in Adorno's letter to Benjamin:

> The split between them is itself the truth: it expresses at least the negativity of the culture which is the sum of both spheres. The antithesis can be reconciled least of all by absorbing light art into serious or vice versa. That, however, is what the culture industry attempts.
>
> (Horkheimer & Adorno, 1947/2002: 107f)

In the false reconciliation, entertainment becomes the principal category. But entertainment does not entertain; it rather prolongs work and fulfils a compensatory function in which the subject only experiences afterimages of the work process. Leisure turns into a production of experiences that only superficially appear to be relaxing, while intensifying anxiety underneath. Its function is dressage, that we eventually accept the order of things by way of an inverted sadism, finding satisfaction in the repetitive cruelties of animated cartoons: 'Donald Duck in the cartoons and the unfortunate victim in real life receive their beating so that the spectators can accustom themselves to theirs' (Horkheimer & Adorno, 1947/2002: 110).

The culture industry robs the subjects precisely of what it promises them. It would be wrong to say that it builds on sublimation; on the contrary, it is overflowing with fantasies, not least erotic. However, it suppresses them at the

48 *Sven-Olov Wallenstein*

very moment when the desired object is exposed, while advanced art, in its ban on images, provides fantasy with a movement that transcends the taboo: 'Works of art are ascetic and shameless; the culture industry is pornographic and prudish' (Horkheimer & Adorno, 1947/2002: 111). Laughter has a similar function, and it tends to conceal any underlying fear; it compensates for missed happiness and betrays it. To laugh at something is to laugh it away, to repress proper satisfaction. In this way, laughter cleanses the affects and shows the truth about Aristotle's *katharsis*, the 'purification' of our feelings of fear and compassion that was once ascribed to Greek tragedy. Whoever is amused is playing along: entertainment makes us forget suffering and the idea that resistance is possible; it relieves us of the negativity of thought.

For the individual, the poverty of life is compensated by the dream of winning, itself statistically almost impossible, and one will have to enjoy the happiness of others in the absence of one's own. The old work ethic, telling you that toil brings reward, is transformed into the fantasy of the minimal chance: the idea that anyone can be chosen is a substitute for the fact that no one is. Chance and planning converge, and everyone is replaceable; but one must believe in the power of chance to be able to fall in line. The outsider, the one who starves and freezes, is branded as a crook, on the other hand – but, in the end, even tragedy can be absorbed by order and can become a calculated moment in the way of the world, corroborating that it is run by destiny.

This is why the individual, in what seems like a society of total individualism, actually becomes a pseudo-individual: 'Pseudoindividuality is a condition for apprehending and detoxifying tragedy: only because individuals are none but mere intersections of universal tendencies is it possible to reabsorb them smoothly into the universal' (Horkheimer & Adorno, 1947/2002: 125). Bourgeois society abolishes and affirms the individual at the same time, by way of its rich array of pre-set choices, consumption objects, prefabricated fantasies and dreams, all of which promise the satisfaction and happiness that is always denied. To consume is to exist, but no object delivers on its promise.

This generalised consumption brings about a shift from use value to exchange value. Instead of pleasure, what is attained is social status within a differentiation where everything can be substituted and nothing exists for its own sake. This affects artworks as well: commodification penetrates their interiority and turns them into fetishes, in the process rendering the fetishism of the object world invisible:

> For consumers, the use value of art, its essence, is a fetish, and the fetish – the social valuation, which they mistake for the merit of work of art – becomes its only use value, the only quality they enjoy. In this way the commodity character of art disintegrates just as it is fully realised.
>
> (Horkheimer & Adorno, 1947/2002: 128)

One of the crucial instruments for this is advertising, which becomes an organising principle in the culture industry to the effect that what is in fact

Max Horkheimer and Theodor Adorno (1947)   49

experienced and consumed is not the things themselves, but signs of their existence, markers for an experience that no one actually has:

> Culture is a paradoxical commodity. It is so completely subject to the law of exchange that it is no longer exchanged; it is so blindly equated with use that it can no longer be used. For this reason it merges with advertisement.
> (Horkheimer & Adorno, 1947/2002: 131)

Commodity fetishism and autonomy

A concept that recurs several times in the discussion above and is hinted at in many of Adorno's writings from the 1930s – as well as playing a tacit role in the analysis of the culture industry, even though it is mentioned only once in the text – is *fetishism*. This term points to crucial features of art's autonomy, its relation to means and relations of production as well as its own immanent technical procedures, and ultimately its claim to a 'truth content' (*Wahrheitsgehalt*) that would be both conditioned by society and set apart from it. While Adorno's analysis of this passes through many stages, I will limit myself here to considering the analysis of fetishism proposed in *Aesthetic Theory*, where the concept is dealt with in a way that draws out its conflicted and even contradictory implications. The concept is never given a sustained treatment, and it is necessary to extract elements of a theory from its many occurrences in shifting contexts that seem to preclude a systematic analysis. Yet, a synoptic overview of Adorno's claims shows them to be distributed along three lines.

First, fetishism is perceived as a *negative* process that obscures true relations and processes, whereas art would have the power to counteract its mystifying force; fetishism belongs to the logic of commodities and, if it enters art, it is as a destructive force. Second, fetishism appears as a fundamentally *ambivalent* phenomenon, in being both that which art must fight against and its inescapable condition; there is no art that is not caught up in commodification, and the task must be to fight it from within. Third, as a way of interlacing the first two claims, fetishism is not just a negative albeit unavoidable external condition of art in the administered world; it is also, and more fundamentally, the *condition of possibility for its truth content*. It is the rigidifying power of aesthetic objectification that gives art its necessary distance to society. The good and the bad are not external to each other; rather, they are two sides of the same loop, as it were, so that truth belongs to falsity just as much as falsity to truth.

As a *negative* concept that threatens to overtake art, while the latter still retains the capacity to propose a series of countermoves, fetishism enters into art as the idea of the artwork as a thing that can be possessed, in analogy to the idea of an exploitable property within the psychic economy of the self that can be assessed in terms of a balance sheet that allows stimuli to be added together: 'heard the Ninth Symphony tonight, enjoyed myself so and so much' (Adorno, 1970/2004: 16). Against these forms of fetishism – the intrusion of the commodity as a model for possession and the work's dissolution into stimuli – Adorno

50   *Sven-Olov Wallenstein*

proposes that the 'darkness' of art might be a way to 'cancel the spell that this world casts by the overwhelming force of appearance, the fetish character of the commodity', first and foremost since artworks 'by their very existence [...] postulate the experience of what does not exist and thereby come into conflict with the latter's actual non-existence' (Adorno, 1970/2004: 76).

As an *ambivalent* concept, fetishism denotes something that threatens to overtake the work not only from the outside but to its very mode of existence. If the new becomes a fetish by being drawn into the logic of the commodity, this cannot be dispelled by simply rejecting the latter but must be criticised from within the work; it expresses 'the paradox of all art that is no longer self-evident', that 'something made exists for its own sake' (Adorno, 1970/2004: 29) and, in this sense, it is one with the claim to autonomy. New ways of conceiving works, such as musical notations that rebel against fixation and aspire to create a new latitude and openness in composition and performance practices, are regressive in one sense, Adorno suggests, and their attempts at resuscitating 'neumic-graphic imitations of musical gestures' are 'simply reification of an older level' (Adorno, 1970/2004: 130). Yet, they have a validity in registering how the work suffers from being a thing, from the fetishisation of what in itself is a process: autonomy is a 'rigidification' (*Erstarrung*) that breeds insurgencies, but there is no way back. In a slightly different context, where the issue is the capacity of art to deliver meaning, Adorno notes the theological roots of this conception but underscores that it must not be conflated with revelation, since this would 'amount to the unreflective repetition of its *unavoidable* fetish character on the level of theory' (Adorno, 1970/2004: 139, trans. mod).[4]

The fetishism inherent in autonomy, however, requires that art always be looked at from the outside as well as from the inside, to remind its viewers of its dual character: it is at once autonomy and *fait social*, both of which contain their respective forms of fetishism. In a passage that recalls John Cage, Adorno suggests that his readers think of music piped into a restaurant, where the 'hum of conversation and the rattle of dishes and whatever' (Adorno, 1970/2004: 328) become part of the work; similarly, the positivist aesthetics that he had denounced earlier for their dissolution of the work into consumable stimuli and for being a fetishism of sensory surfaces can just as much be marshalled against the 'fetishisation of artworks that is itself part and parcel of the cultural industry and aesthetic decline'; they also point to the 'dialectical element that no artwork is ever pure' (Adorno, 1970/2004: 347). Fetishism is inevitable, inevitably positive as well as negative, which is why its destructive aspects on one level can be marshalled against those on another; it is a split phenomenon, as it were, ceaselessly mutating into its other and back again.

As the *condition of possibility for truth*, fetishism first sets the work apart from empirical reality, so that simply by virtue of such distance – not because of its actual content – the work stands for something else; through its alienation, it is also something positive, and what is set up as an 'alien and rudimentary fetish that endures in opposition to the subject is the plenipotentiary of the nonalienated' (Adorno, 1970/2004: 149). In the section that develops the

Max Horkheimer and Theodor Adorno (1947) 51

most detailed explication of fetishism (Adorno, 1970/2004: 295–298), subtitled by the German editor as 'Art's double character: *fait social* and autonomy; on the fetish character',[5] Adorno stresses that the modern phenomenon of art's emphatic opposition to society is what gives art a social content, rather than its use of technologies or the empirical stuff that enters into it: art is 'crystallising in itself as something unique to itself' (Adorno, 1970/2004: 296), and its seeming asocial quality is in fact the determinate negation of a determinate society and what gives it a critical distance to reality.

This is why being guilty of fetishism is not in itself disqualifying; nothing is outside of guilt, and the truth content of artworks is predicated upon the fetish character that sets them apart from the empirical world and its instrumentality, to the effect that only what is *useless* can prefigure another *use* beyond the equation of use-exchange value that is the precondition for commodity fetishism. For this reason, the chapter on the culture industry in *The Dialectic of Enlightenment* – despite its dystopian accents and limited horizon – should be read as a part of a larger project to map the potential of art and aesthetics in late capitalism: its limitations and unavoidable impasses in both theory and practice, as well as its potential.

Notes

1 The essay exists in three different versions, printed in *Gesammelte Schriften* (1980), Vol. I/2 (first and third version) and Vol. VII/1 (third version). For a discussion of the differences between these versions and the publication history, cf. the editorial remarks in Vol. VII/2, 661–690.
2 If the decay of the aura in the artwork essay is presented as a positive phenomenon, then other texts from the same period provide a more complex picture, in which a sense of loss and mourning comes to the fore. See, for instance, 'A Short History of Photography' (Benjamin, 1931/1969).
3 In the third version, Benjamin explains the term by referring to the development of cult objects in religion, which become more accessible as they are put on display, and not directly in terms of institutions such as museums: 'With the emancipation of singular artistic practices from the womb of ritual, the opportunities for exhibiting their products increased' (Benjamin, 1980: 358). Benjamin gives the example of a portrait bust vs. a fixed statue of a god, and an easel painting vs. a fresco painting. In modernity, the relation between the two poles (cult value and exhibition value) has been fundamentally reversed, he suggests, and cinema is the art that makes possible the highest and most intense 'confrontation with the archaic phase' (*Urzeit*) of art (Benjamin, 1980).
4 The adjective 'unavoidable' (*unausweichlich*) has unfortunately disappeared from the translation, which somewhat forecloses the argument. Adorno might be read as saying that fetishism *must be*, cannot *not be*, repeated on the level of theory, since it is unavoidable, but that this repetition must be carried out in a reflexive way.
5 The headings are not Adorno's own but have been inserted into the table of contents by the editors, and they greatly facilitate the reader's orientation; in the 2004 Continuum edition cited here, they have unfortunately been omitted.

References

Adorno, T. W. (1936/1997). On jazz (S. Weber & S. Weber, Trans.). In T. W. Adorno (Ed.), *Prisms*. MIT Press.

52 Sven-Olov Wallenstein

Adorno, T. W. (1938/2002). On the fetish-character in music and the regression in listening (R. Leppert, Trans.). In R. Leppert (Ed.), *Adorno on music* (pp. 288–317). University of California Press.

Adorno, T. W. (1949/2006). *Philosophy of new music* (R. Hullot-Kentor, Trans.). University of Minnesota Press.

Adorno, T. W. (1953/1981). Perennial fashion: Jazz (S. Weber, Trans.). In T. W. Adorno, *Prisms* (pp. 119–132). MIT Press.

Adorno, T. W. (1955/2002). The aging of new music (R. Hullot-Kentor & F. Will, Trans.). In R. Leppert (Ed.), *Adorno on music* (pp. 181–202). University of California Press.

Adorno, T. W. (1960/1996). *Mahler: A musical physiognomy* (E. Jephcott, Trans.). University of Chicago Press.

Adorno, T. W. (1962/1989). *Introduction to the sociology of music* (E. B. Ashton, Trans.). Continuum.

Adorno, T. W. (1966/1990). *Negative dialectics* (E. B. Ashton, Trans.). Routledge.

Adorno, T. W. (1970/2004). *Aesthetic theory* (R. Hullot-Kentor, Trans.). Continuum.

Adorno, T. W., & Benjamin, W. (1999). *The complete correspondence 1928–1940* (H. Lonis, Ed.; N. Walker, Trans.). Polity Press.

Benjamin, W. (1930/1998). *Understanding Brecht* (A. Bostock, Trans.). Verso Books.

Benjamin, W. (1931/2005). A little history of photography (R. Livingstone, Trans.). In Michael W. Jennings, Howard Eiland, and Gary Smith (Ed.). *Selected Writings*, vol. 2, part 2, 1931–1934 (507–530). The Belknap Press of Harvard University Press.

Benjamin, W. (1934/1998). The author as producer. In W. Benjamin, *Understanding Brecht* (A. Bostock, Trans.). Verso Books.

Benjamin, W. (1936/1969). The work of art in the age of mechanical reproduction (H. Zohn, Trans.). In H. Arendt (Ed.), *Illuminations* (pp. 217–253). Schocken Books.

Benjamin, W. (1980). *Gesammelte Schriften* (R. Tiedemann & H. Schweppenhäuser, Eds.). Suhrkamp.

Horkheimer, M., & Adorno, T. W. (1947/2002). *Dialectic of enlightenment: Philosophical fragments* (E. Jephcott, Trans.). Stanford University Press.

Kellner, D. (2002). Theodor W. Adorno and the dialectics of mass culture. In N. Gibson & A. Rubin (Eds.), *Adorno: A critical reader* (pp. 86–109). Blackwell.

Kornhauser, A. W., & Lazarsfeld, P. (1935). *The techniques of market research from the standpoint of a psychologist* (Institute of Management Series). American Management Association.

Okiji, F. (2018). *Jazz as critique: Adorno and black expression revisited*. Stanford University Press.

Paddison, M. (1996). *Adorno, modernism and mass culture: Essays on critical theory and music*. Kahn and Everill.

4 Paul F. Lazarsfeld and Robert K. Merton (1948) 'Mass Communication, Popular Taste and Organised Social Action'

Sven Ross

Introduction

A central question in media research is how mass media influence people and society. The history of media effects research has often been described as a narrative structured into three or four periods characterised by different accounts of the strength and type of the media's influence on people and society (O'Neill, 2011). A long-established view holds that research – and the general understanding in society – at the beginning of the 20th century regarding the influence of the media was dominated by ideas about the powerful and simple effects of mass media on people. Terms such as the 'hypodermic needle model' and 'magic bullet theory' are often used with reference to this period. The continuation of this scenario is usually that media research in the United States took a big step forward during the late 1930s and early 1940s, when the view of the media's effects became more complex. The developing approach at this time was that the media have relatively limited effects that are modified by social and individual factors, and that the media generally reinforce rather than change existing attitudes (Klapper, 1960).

This historiography has been problematised and criticised for being too simplistic (Neuman & Guggenheim, 2011; Perse & Lambe, 2016); nevertheless, the intention in this chapter is not primarily to revise the historiography. Instead, the aim is to present, contextualise and discuss a classic article written by two scholars at the forefront of the developments of the 1940s: Paul F. Lazarsfeld and Robert K. Merton. Lazarsfeld is usually viewed as a leading representative of what later came to be known as 'the dominant paradigm' or 'mainstream' in media research – that is, research based on a generally empiricist scientific approach analysing media content and effects, primarily (but not exclusively) using quantitative methods. This approach is usually attributed to a liberal-pluralist view of society, which is, in practice, an acceptance of the prevailing social structure of the Western world.

In this chapter, I will present and discuss the article 'Mass Communication, Popular Taste and Organised Social Action', both as an interesting text *per se* and in relation to the debate on the dominant paradigm and perspectives on media effects. I will give examples of the article's influence and relate it to Lazarsfeld's extensive research production, as well as briefly discuss the

DOI: 10.4324/9781003432272-5

54 Sven Ross

criticism that has been levelled at this kind of media research. First, I briefly present the two authors of the article, to provide some background to the text.

Paul F. Lazarsfeld: a pioneer in American media research

Paul Felix Lazarsfeld (1901–1976) was born and raised in a secular Jewish family in Vienna at the beginning of the 20th century. His mother was a prominent psychologist, his father a lawyer, and their home was often visited by Vienna's leading intellectuals. An active socialist in his youth, Lazarsfeld studied psychology after high school but then earned a doctorate in mathematics in 1925 (which he later used in his research career). He earned his living first as a high school teacher and subsequently by starting an independent research agency, Wirtschaftspsychologische Forschungsstelle (Economic Psychology Research Centre) (Jerabek, 2001, 2017; Lazarsfeld, 1969). Lazarsfeld and his young colleagues, who were also socialists (including Marie Jahoda, Hans Zeisel and Herta Herzog), conducted voter surveys to find out how to win elections, although they mainly undertook market research for companies to finance the research agency. The agency was formally independent of the university but had a board of distinguished professors (Neurath, 1998). Lazarsfeld later used this model of research organisation in the United States. Jahoda, Zeisel and Lazarsfeld jointly conducted an important and extensive case study of how people were affected by unemployment in the village of Marienthal in Austria (Jahoda et al., 1933/1972). The study was received positively because of its innovative use of the 'sociography' method, among other things. It was a field study that used both qualitative and quantitative methods to understand daily life in a village where almost everyone was unemployed.

This led to Lazarsfeld receiving a Rockefeller Fellowship, prompting a move to the United States in the fall of 1933. When his scholarship expired, it was impossible for him to return to Europe because of the authoritarian political developments that had occurred in Austria, where the Socialist Party was banned in 1934 (Lazarsfeld, 1969). Lazarsfeld's fellowship was extended for one year, after which he started a new research bureau in Newark, USA, to analyse questionnaires financed by the National Youth Administration. His experience with audience research also helped him obtain a position in a new radio research project at Princeton University. Lazarsfeld still conducted most of his empirical analysis at his own research bureau, which was relocated to New York in 1938 and was loosely associated with Columbia University (Neurath, 1998). Herta Herzog (see Chapter 2 in this volume) was one of Lazarsfeld's assistants at that time (becoming his second wife in 1935).

Lazarsfeld became a saviour for Columbia University, as its social sciences faculty had been in trouble for several decades (Merton, 1998). In 1941, he was appointed professor of sociology at Columbia University at the same time as Robert Merton. This was a compromise between two informal wings at the institution, 'the theoretical' and 'the empirical'. A power struggle between the two scholars was expected; instead, the 'theorist' (Merton) and the 'empiricist'

Paul F. Lazarsfeld and Robert K. Merton (1948) 55

(Lazarsfeld) soon became collaborators and good friends. This was the beginning of many years of productive collaboration and friendship.

In 1944, the radio research agency was transformed into the Bureau of Applied Social Research, which established Columbia as a leading American institution for sociology and mass-communication research. Lazarsfeld's career rapidly ascended, partly due to his solid statistical methodological competence and familiarity with European social theory and partly because he was a skilled organiser. He applied the same working method that he had developed at his first research bureau in Vienna, including hiring students as research assistants and training them in practical research work. Lazarsfeld was also adept at finding funders; this, too, he had learned in Vienna due to the necessity of doing market research for companies to fund the research agency. At the same time, he focused on addressing social science research questions, often using the same data.

A very productive period now began. Lazarsfeld had earlier organised innovative data collection in connection with the 1940 presidential election for what is considered one of the first panel studies; that is, the same sample was interviewed several times – over a period of 6 months, in this case. This made it possible to study changes (and the absence of change) in opinion in detail. Which voters switched positions during the campaign and, if so, when? This data resulted in the epochal voter study *The People's Choice: How the voter makes up his mind in a presidential campaign* (Lazarsfeld et al., 1944/1948). The study showed, among other things, that most voters tended to stick with their early choice: fewer than 10% chose a different candidate from the one they had intended to vote for six months earlier. This is one of the studies most often cited in support of the thesis of the media's limited effects. However, Lazarsfeld et al. (1944/1948) argued that the lack of voter change was in itself a kind of media campaign effect, as the campaign kept most of the voters' intentions in place.

An unexpected finding of this study was that, in follow-up interviews with people who had switched parties, the researchers were told that it was often because of conversations with other people that they had changed their minds and not because of media influence. This led to the first formulation of the so-called two-step hypothesis – the theory that the media often exert influence through dissemination via direct contact with other people. This hypothesis was then explored more extensively in the project that culminated in the book *Personal Influence: The part played by people in the flow of mass communications* (Katz & Lazarsfeld, 1955). Lazarsfeld gradually moved on to work on the development of quantitative sociological analysis methods, becoming a pioneer of latent structure analysis. By then, he had already left a decisive mark on US media research and sociology. His influence was not restricted to theory and methodology; he also played an important role as a teacher and organiser, and many of his students became influential in sociology and media research departments.

56 *Sven Ross*

Robert K. Merton: sociology's concept developer

Robert King Merton (1910–2003), the son of Russian Jewish immigrants, grew up in one of the poorer neighbourhoods of Philadelphia but was able to attain a successful academic career in sociology via scholarships. He started studying sociology at Temple University in Philadelphia and completed his PhD at Harvard. Merton's PhD dissertation was a pioneering work in the sociology of science that analysed the relationship between religion and the rise of modern scientific thought. After a few years at Tulane University in Louisiana, Merton came to Columbia University at the same time as Lazarsfeld. As mentioned earlier, Merton and Lazarsfeld had a long and productive collaboration, although they seldom published together. 'Mass Communication, Popular Taste and Organised Social Action' is one of only a few co-written papers. However, the two scholars discussed research and organisation-related issues almost every day during the 1940s, often for several hours a day.

Merton is better known as a sociologist than as a media researcher. Nevertheless, he undertook several empirical media studies in the 1940s, in addition to the more theoretical article that is the focus of this text (Simonson, 2005). One of these, titled *Mass Persuasion: The Social Psychology of a War Bond Drive* (Merton et al., 1946), introduced the qualitative method of the 'focused interview', which received its first detailed presentation 10 years later (Merton et al., 1956; see Chapter 2 in this volume for a discussion of Herzog's role in this). In addition, Merton conducted one of the first empirical studies of the relatively new two-step flow theory (Merton, 1949). He also exerted informal influence through his daily conversations with his colleague Lazarsfeld at Columbia University (Lazarsfeld, 1975; Merton, 1998). Merton's contribution to the article 'Mass Communication, Popular Taste and Organised Social Action' was decisive, as will be discussed below.

Within sociology, Merton is best known for his skill in formulating useful theoretical concepts that have been widely used by other researchers; examples include 'self-fulfilling prophesies', 'unanticipated consequences of action', 'reference groups', 'theories of middle range' and more. One of his most influential contributions to modern sociology, the further development of functionalist theory, is a key part of 'Mass Communication, Popular Taste and Organised Social Action'. Functionalism is often considered to be a defining characteristic of the so-called dominant paradigm in sociology. The functionalist analysis model in American sociology – at least in Talcott Parsons' version – assumed that societies consist of social systems held together by subsystems that fulfil various functions, and that the entire system is held together by certain basic values. Merton developed the functionalist theory in a more complex direction, in part by introducing the concept of 'dysfunction'. According to Merton, it is not obvious that a subsystem has a positive function for all actors in the system, or even for the whole system, just because it exists. A subsystem can be dysfunctional – that is, it can have negative consequences for the system – and still exist (Merton, 1957, p. 51). The subsystem can still be

Paul F. Lazarsfeld and Robert K. Merton (1948)   57

preserved, for example, because it is advantageous for certain other subsystems. The concept of dysfunction then reappears in 'Mass Communication, Popular Taste and Organised Social Action'.

The article: 'Mass Communication, Popular Taste and Organised Social Action'

This text was originally published in 1948 in an anthology, *The Communication of Ideas* (Bryson, 1948). The starting point was a lecture given by Lazarsfeld in 1947 as part of a lecture series at the Hebrew Theological Seminar in New York, arranged by director Lyman Bryson. Lazarsfeld himself commented on how the article came about:

> My presentation was a combination of two earlier speeches which had been published by then and which were sequential summaries of the Bureau's work on the effect of mass media. The transcript of this new speech was, as usual, unprintable, and I asked Merton to make it suitable for publication. When I got the text back from him, my own ideas were put into fluent English and occasionally enriched by references to classical writers I had probably never heard of. But he had included a four-page section called 'Some Social Functions of the Mass Media'. It contained Merton's own analytical reflections, and therefore I felt that the article should be published jointly.
>
> (Lazarsfeld, 1975, p. 52)

Thus, Robert Merton became a co-author. By the following year, the article had been reprinted in Wilbur Schramm's anthology *Mass Communications* (Schramm, 1949), which gave the text greater exposure. It has since been reprinted several times (e.g. in Duffy & Turow, 2009; Marris & Thornham, 1999; Peters & Simonson, 2004; Rosenberg & White, 1957; Schramm & Roberts, 1971).

The authors begin the article by noting that the influence of mass media has become a widely debated issue in society: 'Many are alarmed by the ubiquity and potential power of the mass media' (Lazarsfeld & Merton, 1948, p. 95). According to the authors, many people have an almost magical belief in the power of the media. Although this belief seems somewhat exaggerated, they say, it points to something that should be taken more seriously: changing types of social control exerted by powerful actors in society who can manipulate their audience using propaganda techniques (1948, p. 96). In a democratic society such as the United States, violent methods are not used. Instead, those who want to control public opinion use other methods, such as 'mass persuasion' through radio programmes and advertisements, to maintain the social and economic status quo (1948, p. 96f). Another question that many people wonder about, according to the authors, concerns the negative influence of popular culture on the cultural taste of its audience. This was a common theme in the discussion of mass culture in the early 20th century.

58   Sven Ross

Overall, the authors conclude that there is some basis for these concerns; they also point out that research has provided only incomplete answers to these questions so far. To go further, they ask three new questions (1948, p. 98):

1   What do we know about the effects of the media's existence itself?
2   What are the effects of media ownership structure and organisation in the United States?
3   What do we know about the effects of specific types of media content, in relation to the possibility of using the media for social purposes?

The first question, on the effects of the media's existence itself, feels modern. It is essentially the same question asked in current research on society's mediatisation, even though the authors do not primarily see it from a media technology perspective. Here, Lazarsfeld and Merton point out that research cannot provide a clear answer, while making a preliminary judgement that the media's impact is often overestimated: 'Granted, for a moment, that the mass media play a comparatively minor role in shaping our society' (1948, p. 99). Even though 'huge audiences' are reached through the media, their impact may not be proportionally large, according to the authors. Here, we can see an example of the limited effects thesis.

Lazarsfeld and Merton go on to ask why so many people are concerned, if the authors are right that the effects of the media's existence are not really that dramatic (1948, p. 99). They suggest that there is an 'unwitting' psychological mechanism that explains this concern. Through industrialisation and the transformation of working life, the public has more free time and can therefore consume more popular culture. The fact that most people choose simple entertainment instead of sophisticated culture is seen by some observers as indicative of the deterioration of culture. In addition, many people are concerned that popular culture has a negative influence on the audience and its cultural tastes.

Next, Merton's main contribution to the discussion is introduced, regarding the social function of the media, while the discussion continues to address the possible effects of the mere existence of the media. This is done by presenting three possible functions of mass media. It is the presentation of these three functions that has inspired and influenced other media researchers from different theoretical traditions.

The first function is *status conferral*. According to the authors, the media give status to people, organisations and social movements (1948, p. 101). Because certain people appear a great deal in the media, the public assumes that these people are important in some way. Here, a certain circularity is assumed: 'If you really matter, you will be at the focus of mass attention and, if you *are* at the focus of mass attention, then surely you must really matter' (1948, p. 102).

The second social function is *the maintenance of social norms*. By exposing behaviour that violates widespread norms (even if the behaviour is not illegal), the media uphold certain principles. The authors believe that people overlook certain deviations from general morality (e.g. prostitution and corruption) as

Paul F. Lazarsfeld and Robert K. Merton (1948) 59

long as they take place under the radar; however, when these acts are publicised, sanctions are required.

The third function is the *narcotising dysfunction* of the media. Here, 'dysfunction' refers to a phenomenon or subsystem that has *negative* effects on a larger system (Merton, 1957, p. 51). 'The narcotising dysfunction of the media' thus refers to how the modern media can give citizens the feeling that they are being enlightened and responsible citizens just by following news media and factual programmes. This can give people a feeling that they understand the world while doing nothing actively to make society better (except perhaps, today, clicking *like* or *dislike* in social media). According to Lazarsfeld and Merton, this function is dysfunctional because it should be in the interest of modern societies to have active citizens rather than politically passive ones (1957, p. 105). The significant amount of time devoted to media consumption, for example, is in itself a certain obstacle to social and political engagement. Lazarsfeld and Merton then state that this narcotising dysfunction can hardly be doubted, although more research is needed to verify its prevalence.

It could be argued here that, from the perspective of a dominant elite, this narcotising dysfunction could be seen as a positive function rather than a dysfunction. People in power may think that it is good (for them) if most people are politically passive. This is a recurring theme in Marxist theories of hegemony.

Lazarsfeld and Merton then go on to discuss the structure of the media in terms of ownership and organisation. What role does this structure play in the media's impact on society? The social effects can vary depending on whether the media constitute a privately controlled for-profit system or a state-controlled one (Lazarsfeld & Merton, 1948, p. 106f). The authors begin by stating that mass media in the United States, for the most part, are privately owned and profit oriented, which is not entirely the case in many other countries; as examples, they give England and the Soviet Union, where radio broadcasting is controlled by the state. A central factor in the United States is that it is primarily the advertisers – not the readers or listeners – that finance the media: 'And, all intent aside, he who pays the piper generally calls the tune' (1948, p. 107). Here, the authors sound more like political-economic media theorists and Marxists than defenders of the current order. The media are said to contribute to maintaining 'the current social and economic system' because they are supported by business interests. The media repeat messages that confirm the prevailing social structure, which 'emphasises the duty to accept'. It is not just *what* the media say that matters but what they *don't* say. The media 'effectively restrain the cogent development of a genuinely critical outlook' (1948, p. 107). The occasional socially critical messages that are conveyed are said to be drowned in the huge amount of commercial entertainment.

The subsequent section on cultural taste is somewhat patronising towards popular culture, especially towards the part of it aimed at women. The authors try to understand the reason for this 'generally known low level of popular taste'. Lazarsfeld and Merton try to provide a kind of demographic explanation

60 *Sven Ross*

for this. Broadly speaking, they assume that it was a smaller social stratum – 'a selected aristocratic elite' (1948, p. 109) – that essentially made up 'the cultural audience' in the past; in modern society, however, thanks to education and the rise of the mass media, cultural consumption has become accessible to broad populations. Their conclusion is that there has not really been a general decline in cultural taste; rather, the audience has expanded and now includes more people who lack the same educated taste as the former elite audience.

The article concludes with a discussion of the effects of the media regarding the possibility of promoting social goals – or 'propaganda for social purposes', as the authors put it (1948, p. 112) – such as counteracting racial discrimination or promoting knowledge development. They identify three conditions, at least one of which should be met for effective communication regarding social objectives: namely, monopolisation, canalisation rather than changing basic values and supplementation with face-to-face personal contacts.

1 *Monopolisation:* Messages that are widely disseminated in the media while not being met by contradictory messages are likely to have a greater impact than messages that are contradicted by other messages. The authors provide examples from both authoritarian countries and the United States to support this thesis (1948, p. 113).
2 *Canalisation:* Messages based on existing behaviours or attitudes are more effective than those that try to establish new ones (1948, p. 114). Messages that attempt to counter ethnic prejudice have usually been ineffective, as these prejudices are often deeply rooted. The media can thus more easily perpetuate existing values than change them.
3 *Supplementation:* Media messages can be effective in some cases, even though they do not meet the conditions of monopolisation or canalisation; namely, if the media messages are supported by direct personal communication with people trusted by the recipient (1948, p. 115).

If most of these conditions are met, the chances of success are even greater. Lazarsfeld and Merton mention Nazi Germany and the Soviet Union as examples of societies in which monopolistic media messages interacted with extensive campaigns that included meetings, courses and so forth. Nevertheless, all three conditions are rarely simultaneously present in media campaigns in democratic societies, according to the authors (1948, p. 117). First, such campaigns usually need to fight against existing values, and it is expensive to achieve monopoly-like dominance in the media landscape. Combined with the economic structure of the media, this situation results in the mass media 'cementing the social structure' in democratic societies and in the corporate world having a *de facto* 'psychological monopoly' (1948, p. 117). The conditions of the media thus ultimately lead to 'the mass media working for the maintenance of the prevailing social and cultural structure rather than its change' (1948, p. 118).

The article's influence and relevance today

As previously mentioned, 'Mass Communication, Popular Taste and Organised Social Action' has been reprinted in several different anthologies between at least 1949 and 2009. What is striking about the article is that it has been used to support a whole range of theories and media analyses. For example, the text has been cited as a precursor to the agenda-setting theory (Katz, 2001; Perse & Lambe, 2016; Simonson, 1999) and has been linked to cultivation theory (Morgan & Shanahan, 1992) and third-person effect theory (Tal-Or et al., 2009).

Above all, the three 'social functions' have apparently inspired other media researchers. Regarding the media's *status conferral function*, media researcher James B. Lemert tried to specify the idea of status conferral in two studies and tested it experimentally. He found some support for the thesis and modified it as 'credibility conferral' in connection with news delivery (Lemert, 1966, 1969). Simonson (1999) also linked status conferral to the concept of confidence and found support for the process but argued that it is a complex effect that depends on several factors. In addition, Simonson believed that the agenda-setting theory 'can be seen as a footnote' to the idea of status conferral. Katz (2001) also noted this connection. Moreover, the originator of the agenda-setting theory, Maxwell McCombs, has mentioned status conferral as a concept that was incorporated into the agenda-setting theory (McCombs, 2014, p. 57).

Status conferral has also been linked to the representation of different social categories. The feminist media researcher Gaye Tuchman refers to Lazarsfeld and Merton in her oft-cited article on the representation of women in the media. She believed that, through their emphasis on the upper class, 'the women's pages encourage all citizens to imitate the upper class and to chase after high status' (Tuchman, 1978, p. 28). Similar reasoning has often been put forward by feminist researchers as justification for quantitative content analyses of the representation of women and men in the media, which have revealed a recurring pattern of approximately 30% women and 70% men in various types of media. The same type of argument can be made about the skewed representation of social classes found in many content analyses (Morgan & Shanahan, 1992). The dominance of the upper-middle class and the marked underrepresentation of working-class people is a recurring pattern (e.g. Signiorelli, 1984). This partly reflects the status of different classes in society and partly *affects* the status. In today's media climate, the tendency to link status to visibility seems to have accelerated, with many measuring their own status in terms of the number of likes and followers on Instagram or other social media.

Tal-Or et al. (2009) claim that Lazarsfeld and Merton's idea of the media's *norm-enforcing function* can be linked to the third-person effect theory in that the exposure of certain behaviours is important – not because the behaviours themselves are necessarily seen as immoral, but because the media exposure is believed to influence what *other* people think about the matter (2009, p. 100). The idea that the media maintain moral standards may not be original, but Lazarsfeld and Merton's specific description of the process is somewhat unusual. That the public exposure of inappropriate behaviour (e.g. sexual abuse, as in recent years in connection with the #metoo movement) leads to strong reactions provides many examples of this function of the media. The media – including social media – can function as a 'people's court' opposing various violations of norms, such as drug use and the mistreatment of women.

The idea of the media's *narcotising dysfunction* is probably the most original idea in the article, and it has been the starting point for research of slightly different kinds, including work by Tan (1977), Morley (1990), Andacht (2014), Katz (2014), Dozier et al. (2016) and Esitti (2016). As a recurring theme in this research, studies that suggest passivity and lack of engagement on the part of the audience sometimes refer to Lazarsfeld and Merton. Tan (1977) argues that his study of a group that voluntarily abstained from watching TV for a period of time provided some support for Lazarsfeld and Merton's thesis because the respondents' TV viewing appeared to reduce social interaction. Morley (1990) uses the thesis of narcotising dysfunction as a starting point for a discussion of various studies that demonstrate that the news often fails to engage the audience, although he also links the issue to reception research within cultural studies (see Chapter 12 in this volume). The thesis of a narcotising dysfunction has also been linked to today's use of social media. Dozier et al. (2016) uses Lazarsfeld and Merton's concepts to interpret some surprising results in their study of online political activism. Andacht (2014) and Esitti (2016) also use Lazarsfeld and Merton's concepts in analyses linked to social media.

In his study of the history of media research, the Finnish media researcher Veikko Pietilä argues that 'Mass Communication, Popular Taste and Organised Social Action', together with an article by Harold Lasswell from the same year (Lasswell, 1948), marked the beginning of functionalism within media research, through the introduction of the two functions of status conferral and norm preservation, along with narcotising dysfunction (Pietilä, 2005, p. 136). Functionalist thinking was also strong in the 'uses and gratifications' research of the 1960s and 1970s, albeit more at an individual level, as it focused on the functions of media use for the individual.

Lazarsfeld and Merton's third condition for changing media effects, the supplementation of direct human contacts, is partly based on the two-step flow hypothesis, which was first formulated in *The People's Choice* (Lazarsfeld et al., 1944). The theory was later further developed and studied empirically in *Personal Influence* (Katz & Lazarsfeld, 1955). This theory has had a very strong influence on media research (Weimann, 1994), as well as on the practice of advertising and public relations. The two-step hypothesis was systematically adopted relatively early on in information campaigns, marketing and public relations, sometimes under terms such as 'word-of-mouth' and 'buzz marketing'. In recent years, its commercial use has taken a direction that Lazarsfeld and Merton could hardly have dreamt of. With the emergence of the Internet and social media, many opinion leaders have moved to the Internet, and 'influencer' has become a profession (Hund, 2023). Influencers that market products to digital followers for personal gain are certainly very different from the opinion leaders studied in *Personal Influence*, but the link is clear, and some marketing consultants and theorists refer to Katz and Lazarsfeld's research. In terms of communication theory, digitisation and commercialisation have led to various modifications of the two-step model and new ways of categorising opinion leaders, with different types of 'multi-step models' (see, e.g. Katz, 2015; Schäfer & Taddicken, 2015; Uzunoglu & Kip, 2014).

The influence of 'Mass Communication, Popular Taste and Organised Social Action' mainly stems from the set of theoretical ideas presented in the article (particularly the three 'social functions') about how the media can influence people and society – ideas that other researchers have since adopted and used in various ways. In addition, the discussion of the three conditions for effective social influence provides a concise and easy-to-understand description of the theory of limited or conditional effects, which is usually seen as typical of the dominant paradigm.

Criticism of Lazarsfeld and the dominant paradigm

'Mass Communication, Popular Taste and Organised Social Action' has received relatively little, if any, criticism from other media scholars, even though other parts of Lazarsfeld's research were later harshly criticised by scholars with more critical perspectives. The most influential of these critics were the sociologist C. Wright Mills (1959) and the media researcher Todd Gitlin (1974). Mills focused primarily on *The People's Choice*, while Gitlin aimed at *Personal Influence*.

Mills was a colleague of Lazarsfeld's at Columbia and even worked on the data collection for *Personal Influence*. In 1959, Mills published *The Sociological Imagination*, which partly presents Mill's own vision of what sociology should be and partly conveys a harsh critique of Lazarsfeld's view of social research and methods, especially in relation to *The People's Choice*. One of Mill's criticisms is that Lazarsfeld used 'abstracted empiricism': on the one hand, abstracting the studied individuals from their social context; and, on the other hand, not contextualising the voters' intentions in relation to the larger social structure and party apparatuses. In a more nuanced discussion, Bryant (1985) argues that the first criticism missed the mark because *The People's Choice* does in fact contain a description of the local community, while there was more support for the issue of the absent organisational connection. However, it should be noted that Lazarsfeld did include a description – admittedly brief – of the local strength and activity of the Republicans and Democrats (Lazarsfeld et al., 1948, p. 13).

Media researcher Todd Gitlin published a long article in 1974 that contained scathing criticism of Lazarsfeld's research approach in general and of *Personal Influence* in particular (Gitlin, 1974). The article 'Mass Communication, Popular Taste and Organised Social Action' is briefly mentioned there; however, it largely escapes criticism, instead being mentioned as Lazarsfeld's most critical text (1974, p. 222). Gitlin begins his article by arguing that the dominant

64 *Sven Ross*

paradigm is represented by Lazarsfeld and his school's focus on 'specific, measurable, short-term, individual, attitudinal, and behavioural "effects" of media content, and the conclusion that the media are not very important in the formation of public opinion' (1974, p. 207). Gitlin notes that, in *Personal Influence*, Katz and Lazarsfeld do in fact articulate certain reservations by admitting that it would be important to analyse long-term effects; however, this is not enough for Gitlin because the reservations are given too little space in the text (1974, p. 211f).

Gitlin is also critical of Lazarsfeld's and Klapper's emphasis on the reinforcement or preservation of existing attitudes (which also appears in 'Mass Communication, Popular Taste and Organised Social Action') (1974, p. 216). This criticism is somewhat strange because this effect can be viewed as aligning with many Marxist critical analyses of the media's hegemonic preservation of the prevailing social system. However, Gitlin argues that Lazarsfeld avoids the concept of ideology, instead only talking about specific attitudes. Gitlin also points to cases in which sudden changes in audience perceptions and attitudes have taken place when some new phenomenon suddenly becomes known to the audience. Nevertheless, this argument hardly contradicts the arguments made in 'Mass Communication, Popular Taste and Organised Social Action', as long as the new attitudes do not radically contradict the old ones (which is not evident in Gitlin's example).

Gitlin is also critical of the emphasis on consumption effects in *Personal Influence*. Three of the four topics analysed in that book deal with consumption decisions (i.e. the marketing of food and household goods, motion picture selection and fashion consumption), while only one deals with public affairs. To some extent, this was because Lazarsfeld lacked the resources to conduct such a large study without receiving funding from commercial companies. Until 1949, the Bureau of Applied Social Research was only associated with Columbia University and had to partially finance its operations through outside contracts. Another partial explanation could be that Lazarsfeld was generally focused on method development and on what affects people's decision-making in general, in several different areas.

In response to Gitlin's criticism, Katz (2001) later pointed out that Lazarsfeld had published another, longer article in 1948 that dealt with several different types of effects, both short term and long term, at different levels. By distinguishing among four types of units and four types of effects, from immediate response to institutional change, and by combining these two dimensions, a matrix of 16 different effect processes was obtained, which Lazarsfeld went through systematically with examples (Lazarsfeld, 1948). Lazarsfeld thus considered that it was also necessary to study long-term changes at the system level, although he himself in practice chose to concentrate on studies of relatively short-term media effects at the individual level.

While Gitlin made some valid points in his criticism of the method in *Personal Influence*, he attributed to the book a role it did not claim. Katz and Lazarsfeld did not say that all influence was mediated through other people or

Paul F. Lazarsfeld and Robert K. Merton (1948) 65

that media effects were only short term or occurred only at the individual level; they did not say that the two-step hypothesis should be the model for all effect research. Gitlin was right, however, in stating that *Personal Influence* had a major impact in media research and that three of the four influence topics studied were about consumption and only one about current affairs (due to the sponsors). As mentioned earlier, the two-step hypothesis was later instrumentally used in advertising and public relations.

It is worth posing the question how the young Austrian socialist Paul Lazarsfeld turned – at least in the eyes of his critics – into a representative of 'administrative' research in collaboration with capitalist companies. In a late interview, Lazarsfeld said that he was part of a social movement in Vienna, the Social Democratic Party, but did not find anything like this political environment when he came to the United States. Instead, he had to struggle with finding jobs and funding research to make a living and with developing his general research interests (Stehr, 1982). Lazarsfeld used funding from both government sources and private companies in several ways: to fulfil the funders' goals, to support the research bureau and its staff, to train students and to develop communication theories and methods.

Concluding remarks

Is the article 'Mass Communication, Popular Taste and Organised Social Action' an expression of the dominant paradigm, a critical social analysis or both? If the dominant paradigm is defined as consisting of a positivist view of science, a methodology dominated by quantitative methods and (in terms of media influence) a theory of limited effects and a liberal-pluralist view of society, then it is primarily the idea of limited – or, rather, conditional – effects that is expressed in the article. In terms of method, the dominant paradigm is largely (although not exclusively) characterised by quantitative methods. 'Mass Communication, Popular Taste and Organised Social Action' does not contain a single figure, although it does contain summaries of extensive quantitative research, such as research on the three conditions for effective influence regarding social causes. In addition, the article presents theoretical reflections and hypotheses, such as those concerning the three social functions. Thus, the article does not explicitly address methodological issues, even though quantitative surveys form its basis. Both Lazarsfeld and Merton worked with qualitative methods as well as quantitative, albeit not to the same extent (see Lazarsfeld, 1944, 1972; Merton et al., 1956).

If we follow Gitlin and consider the view of limited media effects as being central to the dominant paradigm, then what is the conclusion? Regarding the influence of the media, Lazarsfeld and Merton's article is somewhat contradictory, as the authors themselves point out. First, they say that public concern about the potentially enormous effects of the media is exaggerated; later, they conclude that it is difficult to change people's attitudes through the media, although it is possible through one or more of the three factors of

66 *Sven Ross*

monopolisation, channelling and personal contact. At the same time, Lazarsfeld and Merton point to three possible – and not insignificant – effects that merit further investigation: status conferral, maintenance of norms and narcotising dysfunction. All in all, these arguments paint a complex picture that only partially matches the theory of limited effects.

In addition, the article contains formulations that are not at all aligned with the dominant paradigm. These formulations are more typical of research within political economy and critical theory, including claims about the social-preservation role of the media and the power of the capital-rich media owners. They are also assumptions at the system level rather than at the individual level. Simonson and Weimann (2003, p. 10) emphasise these socially critical formulations in their laudatory article on 'Mass Communication, Popular Taste and Organised Social Action', whose title begins with 'Critical Research at Columbia'. They argue that 'Mass Communication, Popular Taste and Organised Social Action' is an example of how the dividing lines within media research at that time had not been drawn as sharply as was later the case in the 1970s and 1980s. For example, in the late 1930s and early 1940s, a certain amount of collaboration occurred at Columbia University between Lazarsfeld and Horkheimer's group from the Frankfurt School, which moved its institute from Europe to New York in the mid-1930s (Lazarsfeld, 1941, 1975; Wheatland, 2009). The distance between Lazarsfeld and the Frankfurt School later widened (see Lazarsfeld, 1972), as did the gap between 'critical researchers' and 'liberal-pluralist empiricists' with the rise of critical perspectives in the 1970s and 1980s. Although this discussion is still ongoing to some extent, there have been attempts since then to bridge the differences, both methodologically and theoretically (see, e.g. Sjøvaag & Moe, 2009, for a later discussion of these issues).

The most striking thing about Lazarsfeld and Merton's article is its influence on media researchers of very different orientations – both effects researchers and scholars applying more critical approaches. Returning to the question of the article's relevance today, it can be argued that, due to technological development, it is difficult to maintain that the impact of the mere existence of the media is relatively modest. Different types of media, both digital and 'traditional', saturate our everyday life in ways that Lazarsfeld and Merton could hardly have anticipated. Furthermore, their reasoning about popular taste can be viewed as somewhat dated. However, in other respects, their text seems as relevant now as it was then – in some cases, even more relevant now – in terms of status conferral, norm preservation and narcotic dysfunction. In a way, 'Mass Communication, Popular Taste and Organised Social Action' can be viewed as an early attempt to combine quantitative empirical effects research with critical reflections on the media's system-preserving role in society.

References

Andacht, F. (2014). A critical and semiotic approach to the wonderful, horrible life cycle of the *Kony 2012* viral video. *TripleC*, 12(1), 214–237.

Bryant, C. G. A. (1985). *Positivism in social theory and research*. Macmillan.

Bryson, L. (Ed.) (1948). *The communication of ideas*. Harper & Brothers.

Dozier, D. M., Shen, H., Sweetzer, K., & Barker, V. (2016). Demographics and Internet behaviors as predictors of active publics. *Public Relations Review*, 42, 82–90.

Duffy, B. E., & Turow, J. (Eds.) (2009). *Key readings in media today: Mass communication in contexts*. Routledge.

Esitti, S. (2016). Narcotising effect of social media. *Journal of Institute of Social Sciences Cankiri Karatekin University*, 7(1), 1015–1030.

Gitlin, T. (1974). Media sociology: The dominant paradigm. *Theory and Society*, 6, 205–253.

Hund, E. (2023). *The influencer industry: The quest for authenticity on social media*. Princeton University Press.

Jahoda, M., Lazarsfeld, P. F., & Zeisel, H. (1933/1972). *Marienthal. The sociography of an unemployed community*. Tavistock Publications.

Jerabek, H. (2001). Paul Lazarsfeld – The founder of modern empirical sociology: A research biography. *International Journal of Public Opinion Research*, 13(3), 229–244.

Jerabek, H. (2017). *Paul Lazarsfeld and the origins of communications research*. Routledge.

Katz, E. (2001). Lazarsfeld's map of media effects. *International Journal of Public Opinion Research*, 13(3), 270–279.

Katz, E. (2014). Back to the street. When media and opinion leave home. *Mass Communication and Society*, 17, 454–463.

Katz, E. (2015). Where are opinion leaders leading us? *International Journal of Communication*, 9, 1023–1028.

Katz, E., & Lazarsfeld, P. F. (1955). *Personal influence: The part played by people in the flow of mass communications*. The Free Press.

Klapper, J. (1960). *The effects of mass communication*. The Free Press.

Lasswell, H. (1948). The structure and function of communication in society. In L. Bryson (Ed.), *The communication of ideas* (pp. 37–51). Harper.

Lazarsfeld, P. F. (1941). Remarks on administrative and critical communications research. *Studies in Philosophy and Social Science*, 9, 2–16.

Lazarsfeld, P. F. (1944, April). The controversy over detailed interviews – An offer for negotiation. *Public Opinion Quarterly*, 8(1), 38–60.

Lazarsfeld, P. F. (1948). Communication research and the social psychologist. In W. Dennis (Ed.), *Current trends in social psychology* (pp. 218–273). University of Pittsburgh.

Lazarsfeld, P. F. (1969). An episode in the history of social research: A memoir. In D. Fleming & B. Bailyn (Eds.), *The intellectual migration: Europe and America, 1930–1960* (pp. 270–337). Harvard University Press.

Lazarsfeld, P. F. (1972). *Qualitative analysis: Historical and critical essays*. Allyn and Bacon.

Lazarsfeld, P. F. (1975). Working with Merton. In L. A. Coser (Ed.), *The idea of social structure: Papers in honor of Robert K Merton* (pp. 35–66). Harcourt Brace Jovanovich.

Lazarsfeld, P. F., Berelson, B., & Gaudet, H. (1944). *The people's choice: How the voter makes up his mind in a presidential campaign*. Duell, Sloan and Pearce.

Lazarsfeld, P. F., Berelson, B., & Gaudet, H. (1948). *The people's choice: How the voter makes up his mind in a presidential campaign* (2nd ed.). Columbia University Press.

Lazarsfeld, P. F., & Merton, R. K. (1948). Mass communication, popular taste and organised social action. In L. Bryson (Ed.), *The communication of ideas* (pp. 95–118). Harper.

68   Sven Ross

Lemert, J. B. (1966). Two studies of status conferral. *Journalism Quarterly*, 43, 25–33.

Lemert, J. B. (1969) Status conferral and topic scope. *Journal of Communication*, 19, 4–13.

McCombs, M. (2014). *Setting the agenda. The mass media and public opinion* (2nd ed.). Polity Press.

Marris, P., & Thornham, S. (Eds.) (1999). *Media studies: A reader* (2nd ed.). Edinburgh University Press.

Merton, R. K. (1949). Patterns of influence: A study of interpersonal influence and communications behavior in a local community. In P. F. Lazarsfeld & F. Stanton (Eds.), *Communications research 1948–1949* (pp. 180–219). Harper and Brothers.

Merton, R. K. (1957). *Social theory and social structure* (Rev ed.). The Free Press.

Merton, R. K. (1998). Working with Lazarsfeld. In J. Lautman & B.-P. Lécuyer (Eds.), *Paul Lazarsfeld (1901–1976): La sociologie de Vienne à New York* (pp. 163–211). L'Harmattan.

Merton, R. K., Fiske, M., & Curtis, A. (1946). *Mass persuasion: The social psychology of a war bond drive*. Harper & Brothers.

Merton, R. K., Fiske, M., & Kendall, P. L. (1956). *The focused interview*. The Free Press.

Mills, C. W. (1959). *The sociological imagination*. Grove Press.

Morgan, M., & Shanahan, J. (1992). Television viewing and voting 1972–1989. *Electoral Studies*, 11, 3–20.

Morley, D. (1990). The construction of everyday life: Political communication and domestic media. In D. L. Swanson & D. Nimmo (Eds.), *New directions in political communication: A resource book* (pp. 123–146). Sage.

Neuman, W. R., & Guggenheim, L. (2011). The evolution of media effects theory: A six-stage model of cumulative research. *Communication Theory*, 21, 169–196.

Neurath, P. (1998). The life and times of Paul Lazarsfeld. In J. Lautman & B.-P. Lécuyer (Eds.), *Paul Lazarsfeld (1901–1976): La sociologie de Vienne à New York* (pp. 505–518). L'Harmattan.

O'Neill, B. (2011) Media effects in context. In V. Nightingale (Ed.), *Handbook of media audiences* (pp. 320–339). Blackwell.

Perse, E. M., & Lambe, J. L. (2016). *Media effects and society*. Sage.

Peters, J. D., & Simonson, P. (Eds.) (2004). *Mass communication and American social thought: Key texts 1919–1968*. Rowman & Littlefield Publishers.

Pietilä, V. (2005). *On the highway of mass communication studies*. Hampton Press.

Rosenberg, B., & White, D. M. (Eds.) (1957). *Mass culture. The popular arts in America*. The Free Press.

Schramm, W. (Ed.) (1949). *Mass communications: A book of readings*. University of Illinois Press.

Schramm, W., & Roberts, D. F. (Eds.) (1971). *The process and effect of mass communication* (2nd ed.). University of Illinois Press.

Schäfer, M., & Taddicken, M. (2015). Mediatised opinion leaders: New patterns of opinion leadership in new media environments? *International Journal of Communication*, 9, 960–981.

Signiorelli, N. (1984). The demography of the television world. In G. Melischek, K. E. Rosengren & J. Stappers (Eds.), *Cultural indicators: An international symposium* (pp. 137–157). Verlag der Österreichische Akademie der Wissenschaften.

Simonson, P. (1999). Mediated sources of public confidence: Lazarsfeld and Merton revisited. *Journal of Communication*, 49(2), 109–122.

Simonson, P. (2005). The serendipity of Merton's communications research. *International Journal of Public Opinion Research*, 17(3), 277–297.

Simonson, P., & Weimann, G. (2003). Critical research at Columbia: Lazarsfeld's and Merton's 'Mass communication, popular taste and organised social action'. In E. Katz, J. D. Peters, T. Liebes & A. Orloff (Eds.), *Canonic texts in media research* (pp. 12–38). Polity Press.

Sjøvaag, H., & Moe, H. (2009). From fermentation to maturity? Reflections on media and communication studies: An interview with Todd Gitlin, Jostein Gripsrud & Michael Schudson. *International Journal of Communication*, 3, 130–139.

Stehr, N. (1982, August). A conversation with Paul Lazarsfeld. *The American Sociologist*, 17, 150–155.

Tal-Or, N., Tsfati, Y., & Gunther, A. C. (2009). The influence of presumed media influence: Origins and implications of the third-person perception. In R. L. Nabi & M. B. Oliver (Eds.), *The Sage handbook of media processes and effects* (pp. 99–112). Sage.

Tan, A. (1977). Why TV is missed: Functional analysis. *Journal of Broadcasting*, 21(3), 371–380.

Tuchman, G. (1978). Introduction: The symbolic annihilation of women by the mass media. In G. Tuchman, A. K. Daniels & J. Benét (Eds.), *Hearth and home: Images of women in the mass media* (pp. 3–38). Oxford University Press.

Uzunoglu, E., & Kip, S. M. (2014). Brand communication through digital influencers. *International Journal of Information Management*, 34(5), 592–602.

Weimann, G. (1994). *The influentials: People who influence people*. State University of New York Press.

Wheatland, T. (2009). *The Frankfurt School in exile*. University of Minnesota Press.

5 Claude Shannon and Warren Weaver (1949) *The Mathematical Theory of Communication*

Heike Graf

Introduction

Communication issues were a central theme in antiquity, mainly within rhetoric. With the rise of modern science in the 19th century, increased fragmentation and specialisation evolved within the branches of science. Several disciplines within modern science – including both natural and social science – began to take a greater interest in human communication. With the advent of electronic media such as the telegraph, telephone and radio, which allowed simultaneous communication between distant locations, physical presence was no longer required for direct communication, changing the conditions of human communication. These new telecommunication technologies gave rise to new theories and models for understanding modern communication.

Shannon and Weaver's mathematical model of communication excludes questions of meaning in communication processes, focusing instead on technical issues of information transfer. How is it possible that such a theory of communication has become relevant to the humanities and social sciences, fields of research that are particularly interested in how meanings are made by individuals and groups of people? In particular, Shannon and Weaver's theory has gained a foothold and is being further developed in cybernetics, an interdisciplinary theory of communication and control in machines and biological and social systems, as well as in systems theory, a sociological theory for observing and describing communicative contexts (i.e. systems), which is briefly introduced at the end of this chapter.

About the book

In discussions on the history of communication, the mathematical theory of communication is attributed to the two North American mathematicians and engineers Claude Elwood Shannon (1916–2001) and Warren Weaver (1894–1978). In fact, it was Shannon who developed the model based on his studies of technological information transmission and Weaver who later understood it as a model for human communication. Their short book titled *The Mathematical Theory of Communication* (1949) consists of a half-page preface by both

DOI: 10.4324/9781003432272-6

authors, an introductory chapter written by Weaver (about 30 pages) and Shannon's previously published description of the mathematical communication model (about 100 pages). Introducing his own chapter, Weaver writes:

> The mathematical theory of the engineering aspects of communication, as developed chiefly by Claude Shannon at the Bell Telephone Laboratories, admittedly applies in the first instance only to problem A, namely, the technical problem of accuracy of transference of various types of signals from sender to receiver.
>
> (Weaver, 1949/1964, p. 6)

Shannon worked at a telephone company, researching how to best encrypt information in order to facilitate the successful transmission of messages, while Weaver was a research officer and director of the Natural Sciences Division at the Rockefeller Foundation. Shannon worked practically on how to eliminate interference so that the information people wanted to send – for example, by telegraph or telephone – would arrive and be reproduced as accurately as possible. Thus, as Shannon explains, the meaning of the messages did not matter:

> The fundamental problem of communication is that of reproducing at one point either exactly or approximately a message selected at another point. Frequently the messages have meaning; that is, they refer to or are correlated according to some system with certain physical or conceptual entities. These semantic aspects of communication are irrelevant to the engineering problem.
>
> (Shannon, 1949/1964, p. 31)

In 1948, Shannon published the results of his investigations under the title 'A Mathematical Theory of Communication' in the telephone company's own journal, *Bell Systems Technical Journal*. Curiously, it took several years for his fellow engineers to grasp the significance of his discovery. Weaver, however, was impressed: he had previously worked with computer-controlled language translation and saw here a possible way to get closer to that goal. He wanted to give Shannon's article a larger audience; thus, a year later, the joint book *The Mathematical Theory of Communication* was published.

The book contains Weaver's introductory chapter, 'Recent Contributions to the Mathematical Theory of Communication', a shorter version of which had been published in *Scientific American* in 1949, and a reprint of Shannon's earlier article, now titled 'The Mathematical Theory of Communication'. The change in Shannon's previous title from '*a* theory' to '*the* theory' clearly indicates that something ground-breaking is being published, with considerable relevance for a wider audience. Both authors state in the preface that they intend to develop the theory of information management from perspectives other than pure engineering for future research efforts: 'It is intended that subsequent developments in the field will be treated in a projected work dealing with more general aspects of information theory' (Shannon & Weaver, 1949/1964, preface).

72 *Heike Graf*

In the preface, the authors recommend reading Weaver's chapter first, to get a general understanding of the research area, and then delving into the mathematical aspects and formulas. For a social scientist or humanities scholar, Weaver's chapter is easier to understand than Shannon's, as the latter spends several pages developing equations to solve the problems of information transmission in a mathematical way. Still, Weaver's ambition is to clarify what Shannon's basic assumptions can mean for human communication.

The book – and especially Shannon's contribution – has been criticised for dealing only with 'machine communication', which makes its application to human communication very limited (e.g. Craig & Muller, 2007; Mattelart & Mattelart, 1998). Shannon himself made it clear that he was not interested in human communication *per se*, nor in questions about the meaning of content, because machines do not care about that. Weaver, however, believed that Shannon's theory could be applied to human communication and defined the term 'communication' in a broader sense by choosing an inclusive definition:

> The word communication will be used here in a very broad sense to include all of the procedures by which one mind may affect another. This, of course, involves not only written and oral speech, but also music, the pictorial arts, the theatre, the ballet, and in fact all human behavior.
>
> (Weaver, 1949/1964, p. 3)

I will return to this definition later in the chapter.

Shannon and Weaver's communication model

Bringing together Shannon's mathematical model of communication and Weaver's interpretation of it, the book outlines a simple model to explain how communication occurs and can be facilitated. This model (Figure 5.1), which is found in Weaver (1949/1964) and Shannon (1949/1964), became famous and was widely used in early media and communication research; it has also survived in areas such as strategic communication research. At first glance, both Shannon and Weaver treat communication as the transmission of a message, which is still a common concept today. The authors ask: how can mathematical models be used to make communication (e.g. via a telephone) as smooth and efficient as possible? In general, the model shows that communication can be divided into five different components or stages, which can be treated separately. All these components are discussed in terms of mathematical calculations.

According to the authors, communication begins with a source of information, from which a message is formulated and transmitted to a receiver. It may seem obvious that communication takes place in this way and follows such a linear course; however, as will be discussed, it is not in fact obvious at all. The same point is challenged in non-linear models of communication.

Claude Shannon and Warren Weaver (1949) 73

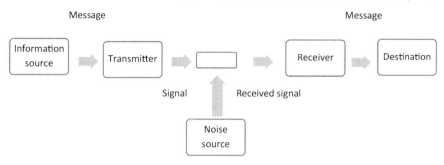

Figure 5.1 Transmission model (Shannon 1949, p. 34)

This description contains recognisable words such as *information, message, sender/transmitter* and *receiver*, all of which are widely used in today's communication literature. When transmitting information, the selected message from an information source is encoded into signals in such a way that it can be sent to a receiver via channels. In this way, the authors distinguish between *information* and *message*.

According to Shannon, a message can be understood as an expression that can take different forms, such as (a) a sequence of letters in a telegram, (b) a voice on a radio or telephone or (c) a voice and moving pictures on television (Shannon, 1949/1964, p. 33). The message is converted into signals to make transmission possible. Shannon's goal was to calculate exactly which signals could be omitted without losing information. In digital systems, a transmitter recodes the amount of information into signals that are sent down a channel to a technical receiver that decodes the signals back into the original message. In other words, the message has reached its destination when it is decoded by a receiver. For the machine that transmits the message, it does not matter what the message is about; everything is encoded into signals that are completely disconnected from the meaning of the message.

The direction of the arrow indicates that this is a one-way, linear model. Communication is a process that moves from a sender/transmitter to a receiver. Anything that can come between the sender and the receiver, that affects the decoding and that is not intended by the sender, is considered to be noise; examples include technical disturbances such as crackling in the telephone line or the delay of sound and image in video transmissions. To manage and minimise these disturbances, Shannon devotes many pages of his text to finding technical solutions using mathematical formulas.

In arguing for a broad perspective of communication, Weaver points to three levels of problems in communication processes. The first is the technical level, which involves how information is transferred from sender to receiver and how smooth and stable the signal is. The second is the semantic level, which is about how accurately the transmitted information conveys the meaning that the sender wanted to convey when the message was sent. The third level concerns

74 *Heike Graf*

the effectiveness of the communication – that is, how effectively the sender succeeds in influencing the behaviour (conduct) of the receiver in the intended direction. 'It may seem unnecessarily narrow', as Weaver points out, to assume that all communication is about influencing others, but 'it is clear that communication either affects conduct or is without any discernible and probable effect at all' (Weaver, 1949/1964, p. 5). Today, we refer to this way of thinking as 'strategic communication', which is a type of communication that aims to influence the recipient in a desirable way. Strategic communication can be found in public relations, advertising, pedagogy, political communication and so forth.

According to Weaver, these three levels (technical, semantic and strategic) overlap. Here, the superiority of the technical level must be considered: the technical can stand alone, while the semantic and strategic need technology to communicate. If the technical is flawed, it affects the semantic and strategic, but the reverse is not true. This supremacy of materiality over content has been a starting point for media theories seeking to address the importance of technology for mediated communication (see Chapters 8 and 24 in this volume).

In summary, Shannon's mathematical communication model, along with Weaver's application of it, offers a simple way of describing communication: the so-called 'transmission model'. This model has become famous because of its simplicity and has been adopted by media and communication researchers. It has also been subjected to criticism for being too simple, as human communication is not one-way. However, I argue that there is more to find in this book that is important for human communication, as I will show below.

What is information?

Shannon has gone down in history as the father of information theory, even though he never used the term himself, calling his model 'communication theory'. Shannon wanted to know how much information can be contained in a message in order to send the maximum amount over a given channel, given the transmission bandwidth. This is also a question of how much of the signal can be left out without information being lost. Therefore, the receiver is already taken into account because the probability that the signal will be received at the destination is calculated. Thus, communication is more than one-way because it includes the receiver; as Weaver claims, a general theory 'will surely have to take into account not only the capacity of the channel but also ... the capacity of the audience' (Weaver, 1949/1964, p. 27). Moreover, in human communication, people give their 'signals' a kind of order in the hope of being understood – or, in other words, to increase the probability of being received/decoded and thereby connected to another human being. '(I)f you overcrowd the capacity of the audience you force a general and inescapable error and confusion' (Weaver, 1949/1964, p. 27). In this theory, the receiver plays an active role and is not a passive entity, as it appears in Figure 5.1 shows.

Shannon was early in using the word 'bit' ('binary digit') to calculate the set of basic units in a message that needs to be encoded for transmission. The word 'bit' stands for a choice between two values: 0 or 1 (yes or no). A bit can take only one of those two values. The encoding of information in zeros and ones subsequently became the basic language used by computers.

At the time, it was radical to think of information as binary choices of ones and zeros. Until then, the transmission of information had only been thought of as something that took place within an electromagnetic field, separate from the various forms of messages through telephone, telegraphy or radio. This technical innovation made it possible to combine different forms of transmission. Nowadays, it does not matter if it is a telephone or radio signal, an image or data traffic, because everything can be converted into zeros and ones.

For Shannon, information is the basic unit that constitutes a message selected from a set of possible messages (Shannon, 1949/1964, p. 31). The concept thus has nothing to do with content or meaning (also see Weaver, 1949/1964, p. 8). Information itself has no meaning: it is only about selection and how to mathematically calculate the selection of possible messages. Information, in Shannon's sense, is thus only a statistical or mathematical question 'that measures freedom of choice' (Weaver, 1949/1964, p. 19). It is also because of freedom of choice that we have to deal with uncertainty, the subject of the next section.

Weaver views Shannon's conceptualisation of information as an important new theory that has more general implications than purely technical ones. He defines information 'as the logarithm of the number of choices' (Weaver, 1949/1964, p. 10), referring to a mathematical function for the number of choices made from a set of different alternatives. Information, Weaver argues, is therefore not about what you say; it is not about content as is usually understood, but rather about what the sender *could* have said (and thus what is possible to say) (Weaver, 1949/1964, p. 9). Information is thus a measure of the freedom of choice a person has in choosing what to express. As mentioned above, the amount of information in a given communication situation is defined by the logarithm of the number of possible choices the sender has in selecting the message. These choices are 'governed by probabilities' (Weaver, 1949/1964, p. 11); the sender could have chosen to send something different. In other words, the sender chooses which message to send among all the possibilities available. However, these 'probabilities [...] are not independent, but [...] at any stage of the process, depend upon the preceding choices' (Weaver, 1949/1964, p. 11).

Thus, Weaver's suggestion is that the use of language can now be understood through mathematics. He gives examples from the English language: 'If the last symbol chosen is "the", then the probability that the next word be an article, or a verb form other than a verbal, is very small' (Weaver, 1949/1964, p. 11). If the idea of information is elaborated as the set of possible choices in a communication situation, then the use of language shows that every statement has a positive side (what is said/shown, etc.) and a negative side (what is not said/shown, etc.). For example, when I say: 'I am drinking coffee', I am also communicating other information: namely, that I am not drinking tea, water or beer; that I am not spilling or vomiting coffee; and that it is me who is drinking coffee, not my husband, daughter, neighbour, and so on. I only have to say

76   *Heike Graf*

these four words and can leave out the others because they are implicit. This is exactly what Shannon calculates when transmitting information. These four words are the basic unit that needs to be transmitted and nothing more.

When we designate one thing in preference to another thing, we ascribe meaning to it. How this is then understood or received is another matter, and Weaver guards against further explanation because '... semantic problems have wide ramifications' (Weaver, 1949/1964, p. 5). However, in order to deal with 'the difficult aspects of meaning', Weaver claims to study the 'influence of context' (Weaver, 1949/1964, p. 28) or the constraints on meaning-making, as he shows with respect to language, which offers a probability of word order. In everyday situations, we need to know the conventional framework in which communication takes place in order to increase the probability of successful communication. For example, we communicate differently in a university seminar than we do with our peers in a pub in order to ensure connectivity in communication.

Entropy and redundancy

To discuss how choices are handled in communication, the authors use the concepts of entropy and redundancy. Entropy is a concept borrowed from thermodynamics that emphasises the various alternatives involved. In the present context, this term refers to the number of possible messages from a source, meaning the myriad choices that can be made in communication. While entropy is a measure of unpredictability, the concept of redundancy refers to the limits and predictability of our communication choices, which can also be called context. The context of watching a movie in a movie theatre sets some limitations on how a person can communicate. Or, to use the example of language again: our free choice is limited by the structure of language, as an inherent redundancy, if we want to be understood. For example, if I want to announce what I am doing right now and write: 'I am sitting at my desk', then my ability to express this is limited because the English language gives me a clear structure. If I mix the letters randomly and write: 'Mis gattomn ta sked', then it is more complicated to find out which letters follow each other (entropy). According to Shannon's definition, the first sentence is information-poor and the second sentence is information-rich. This may sound strange, but it is because the concept of information refers only to possibilities. In the second example, it is difficult to predict which letters will follow each other (there are many more possibilities), while in the first example, the order is given. When we want to clarify our messages in a given context, we use one word over another based on the vocabulary available to us. Freedom of choice is thus limited. However, different genres of language are redundant to varying degrees. For example, the word order and sentence construction that are possible in poetry are not possible in legal texts.

The challenge for engineers is to design a technical system that can cope with entropy – that is, with all the potential messages that a source can offer. One assumption is that choices are likely to be made based on previous choices, as discussed above. This is an assumption that is used in computerised communication today. The advertising we see on our screens is based on the digital traces we leave behind, which are assumed to show our preferences by reflecting the choices that we have made in the past (things we have bought, places we have visited, links we have clicked on, etc.).

To summarise: to both Shannon and Weaver, 'information' in the mathematical model of communication does not refer to specific facts or data. The notion of information is completely divorced from content or meaning and is about the probability of choices made in a situation to increase connectivity. However, as Weaver has shown, this approach is a good starting point for theories of human communication, as he claims:

> The concept of information developed in this theory at first seems disappointing and bizarre – disappointing because it has nothing to do with meaning, and bizarre because it deals not with a single message but rather with the statistical character of a whole ensemble of messages, bizarre also because in these statistical terms the two words *information* and *uncertainty* find themselves to be partners.
>
> (Weaver, 1949/1964, p. 27)

Selection and uncertainty

When you have choices, you have to choose. The concept of choice, or selection, is important to Shannon and Weaver. It is an overarching concept that explains the underlying processes of communication and appears throughout the book. As mentioned earlier, Shannon treats the central question of how to think about selection – that is, choice and freedom of choice in a communication system – in purely mathematical terms. According to Shannon, technology must be open to different options because we do not know in advance what choices will be made: 'The system must be designed to operate for each possible selection, not just the one which will actually be chosen since this is unknown at the time of design' (Shannon, 1949/1964, p. 31).

This requires the system to deal with uncertainty. Shannon tries to find a mathematical solution to this problem by calculating the total number of messages that can be selected and thus ensuring that the communication channels accommodate all these possibilities. This is done with the help of logarithms, so the message can finally be sent in a transmission channel that is adapted to the current type of message. A unit (bit) of information thus indicates what choices the sender has.

This perspective illustrates something that is essential to human communication: the fact that communication is fundamentally about choice and selection. For example, if I want to send a birthday greeting, I can choose from a variety of messages: a standard card by mail or online, or a personalised greeting in a chat group or video call. If I use spoken language, the words 'happy birthday' and

78   *Heike Graf*

'birthday' are most likely to appear. In this way, my choices are limited and depend on the context, culture and structure of the language (redundancy). The central concept of selection, which is the starting point for Shannon and Weaver's approach, highlights something fundamental in human communication that we are not always aware of in everyday life.

Consequently, if information is associated with choice and selection, and we cannot always be sure which selection will be made, then the problem of uncertainty in communication processes arises. This problem is both practical and philosophical and affects both machines and humans. When we have many choices, the environment is information-rich, and we do not know in advance which choices will be made in communication. As new communication technologies are introduced, the amount of information increases. Today, we even talk about 'information overload'. Weaver believes that this development contributes to the fact that uncertainty in communication has increased:

> The greater this freedom of choice, and hence the greater the information, the greater is the uncertainty that the message actually selected is some particular one. Thus greater freedom of choice, greater uncertainty, greater information go hand in hand.
>
> (Weaver, 1949/1964, p. 18/19)

Although Shannon repeatedly emphasises that he only concentrates on the purely technical issues, he also reveals fundamental issues of human communication, in cooperation with Weaver. Human communication is also based on selection and, therefore, needs to handle uncertainty. At the end, Weaver is convinced that the time has now come to include issues of understanding, meaning and context in a theory of communication (Weaver, 1949/1964, p. 27). How and when can a message be understood if uncertainty must be taken into account because senders and receivers act selectively?

Criticism and further development

This approach of putting communication in a central position when explaining actions between machines – which can also be applied to humans – has inspired various disciplines and led to a wave of new research areas. Explaining how to influence people and how to do so more effectively has always been of interest. Harold Dwight Lasswell's (1902–1978) communication model from 1948 is a more verbalised version of Shannon and Weaver's model, stating: who says what through what channel to whom with what effect? (Lasswell, 1948). On the one hand, this means that the sender of the message wants to be able to measure the effect on the recipient. On the other hand, the model makes it possible to think in the following terms: by changing the message or changing the distribution channel, it is possible to change the effect. The process of influence is clearly derived from a linear process that starts with a sender influencing a receiver. Empirically, however, such influence processes are difficult to prove;

there may be a desired effect, but it does not have to occur, as Shannon and Weaver's notion of uncertainty makes clear.

Later academic research has moved away from this concept of one-way communication, focusing instead on the active role of the receiver, which was already present in Shannon and Weaver's approach. This active role has been further developed by abandoning the linear model for a circular model – an idea that originated in cybernetics. Norbert Wiener (1894–1964), who was Shannon's teacher and the father of cybernetics, was interested in how both machines and living organisms process information and closely examined their control mechanisms. In his book *Control and Communication in Machines and Living Organisms* (1948), Wiener introduces the feedback principle, establishing that machines and social systems operate in a circular rather than linear fashion. Management (and thus influence) takes place through self-organising processes, which means that information is processed within systems (i.e. communication contexts) and is not imposed from outside.

This idea was taken up by the anthropologist Gregory Bateson (1904–1980), who emphasised that the external signals we receive are processed internally in our consciousness. In human communication, it is not the transmission of signals that causes an effect; rather, we react to the outside world based on our internal cognitive processes. In other words, it is only possible to receive signals according to an individual's own capabilities, not those of others. The same is true for machines: an analogue radio, for example, cannot receive digital signals. Internal cognitive processes are both closed with respect to their own operations and open to the outside world, such as in a communication situation (Bateson, 1951, p. 186). Based on these concepts, Bateson developed the circular communication model (Figure 5.2).

Viewing communication as a circular process makes the complexity of communication more obvious. Communication is a system based on reciprocity (i.e. mutual influence rather than simple causality). Because it connects the actors involved, a communication system is self-producing. Communication takes place through the relationship between its different components. This meta-discussion is

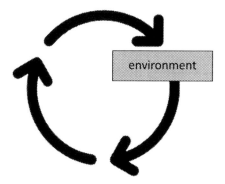

Figure 5.2 Circular communication model

80   *Heike Graf*

detached from meaning and asks only how communication works; nevertheless, it does not exclude the study of meaning in communication.

Bateson points out that the brain also operates in this way, making binary choices, which is related to findings in neurobiology: our most basic cognitive operation is to distinguish one thing from another. Thus, every time we perceive, we are making choices. For example, in a completely dark room, we would not be able to distinguish a person's body from its environment through sight alone. We might be able to hear the person making sounds or feel their body with our sense of touch. In order to perceive, we must be able to differentiate; we must be able to relate one thing to another, such as a body to its environment. This means that information – as the unit of communication – can be understood as *difference*. Later, Bateson (1973) provided an effective and well-known definition of the concept of information, claiming that information is a difference that makes a difference.

Systems theory, as developed by the sociologist Niklas Luhmann (1927– 1998), follows the same path. Information is different for everyone and is therefore linked to an observer. Luhmann emphasises that it is empirically difficult to prove whether one's thoughts have been correctly understood because no human consciousness can communicate directly with another. Since we cannot read each other's thoughts, we only know what is communicated. On the one hand, consciousness is a basic prerequisite for communication; on the other hand, a person's consciousness is inaccessible to other people and is therefore outside the communication system. As empirical evidence of the difference between consciousness and communication, it is possible for us to *think* something other than what we *say*. Luhmann follows Shannon in excluding the question of how one succeeds in conveying the meaning one wants to convey. Accordingly, he defines the concept of information – which is not to be equated with definite facts – by emphasising the importance of selection: 'Information is always a form of surprise in the selection process' (Luhmann, 2002/2013, p. 217).

Luhmann claims that we have not only the freedom to choose but also the compulsion to choose, which he describes using the words 'double contingency'. The term 'double' means that there are at least two parties involved in human communication; therefore, there is a double constraint on choice. It implies that unforeseen events can occur or that attention can shift. While Shannon uses probability calculations for technical systems to achieve a certain degree of security in the reception of information, Luhmann applies this to social processes: we constantly consider what we can and cannot expect in communication. Expectations can either be fulfilled or turned into disappointments. Consequently, according to Luhmann, communication is a selection process consisting of a synthesis of three selections: information, message and understanding. In line with Shannon's work, these three different units stand for themselves to a certain extent and thus have a certain autonomy (Luhmann, 2012). The notion of 'information' is linked to the external world, while the notion of 'message' is linked to the internal operations that determine how information is communicated. Here, Luhmann takes up Shannon and Weaver's distinction between 'information' and 'message'. It is only when information is transformed into a message that we know that communication has been initiated. In Shannon and Weaver's model, communication can only be said to have occurred when the message has reached the receiver; it is not enough for someone to say something. Luhmann agrees, claiming that communication is only complete when the difference between information and message is understood. Luhmann's concept of understanding is also consistent with Shannon's work because it does not depend on semantics: it is only a matter of the receiver noticing and responding to a message. This does not mean that B must have understood what A had in mind. Even the expression 'I don't understand' is a response. Especially with the introduction of communication technologies such as writing, printing and computers, it becomes clear that the information a recipient receives is increasingly disconnected from what the sender had in mind. Therefore, the term 'understanding' generally denotes 'a condition that guarantees that communication can continue' (Luhmann, 2002/2013, p. 219), meaning a possibility to connect with each other.

In this context, meaning comes into play by being defined as a basic pre-requisite for communication; through meaning, communication finds its motivation to continue. However, meaning does not consist of the sender's intention or any factual situation; rather, it is a relationship between the current message and other possibilities (what could have been said), which again refers back to the work of Shannon and Weaver. The meaning of what was selected does not so much lie in the information value of the item itself as it does in the fact that the selected item was chosen in favour of all other possible selections. This approach clearly differs from others, such as critical theory, in which Jürgen Habermas views communication based on semantics as an ideal state that should be char-acterised by consensus and should strive for correct understanding (see Chapter 7 in this volume). Shannon's view of communication does not need to take thoughts into account, which makes it possible to include different types of complex systems, such as machines (i.e. computers, artificial intelligence (AI)) in communication theory. Shannon himself developed the idea of how a machine can be programmed to participate in a game of chess (Shannon, 1950).

Today, humans already have experiences with machines that communicate with us. In many cases, we do not even realise that they are robots. The sociologist Elena Esposito (b. 1960) emphasises that we communicate with machines that do not understand the content of the communication, yet we still communicate with them. While Shannon emphasises that it is not meaning that is transmitted but signals, Esposito pushes the thesis further by claiming that it is not even necessary to understand what the other has intended; communication takes place anyway. Therein lies the success of AI. Thus, machines do not try to understand the content of the communication but interact directly with us (Esposito, 2017, p. 260). 'What algorithms are producing is not the intelligence of people but the informativity of communication' (Esposito, 2022, p. 18).

According to Esposito, communication does not begin with a source, as Shannon and Weaver posited, but with the perspective of the receiver, who can

82 *Heike Graf*

derive information that is different from what the sender had in mind. In relation to Shannon and Weaver, the challenge of the development of AI lies in the fact that the machine acts in an uncertain manner and produces information that neither the machine nor the human being has any knowledge of. Machines can create – and have already created – new ways of selecting and, in doing so, they have produced information that is surprising (Esposito, 2022).

Summary

Shannon and Weaver's mathematical theory is less about what communication is and more about how it occurs and how it is possible, despite its built-in uncertainty. Thus, their theory emphasises the process nature of communication. Shannon and Weaver were the first to draw attention to the vagueness and uncertainty of communication by proposing a theory of the (im)probability of communication (Nassehi, 2019). By not assuming that information has an inherent meaning but only viewing information as the result of a choice, the theory of communication makes it possible to look at meaning-making in a complex way and provides explanations for why information and messages can be understood in different ways. As the father of information theory, Shannon paved the way for modern information processing by establishing that information does not depend on content but on operations, and that meaning depends on the internal conditions of the means of transmission. He still inspires scientists to explain communication between humans and machines, even though the machine does not understand the content of the communication.

Shannon and Weaver offer a general theory that makes it possible to go beyond questions of semantics, meaning, understanding or the connotations of symbols in the communication process. In this way, their book provides a basis for explaining the function of meaning and the conditions and frameworks for meaning-making in a complex communicative context. Thus, their theory of communication is ultimately less about the successful understanding or transmission of a message to a receiver, as communication is usually described, and more about the conditions that enable connectivity possibilities in communication, which take into account the active role of the receiver.

References

Bateson, G. (1951). Information and codification. A philosophical approach. In J. Ruesch & G. Bateson (Eds.), *Communication: The social matrix of psychiatry* (1st ed.) (pp. 168–211). Norton.

Bateson, G. (1973). *Steps to an ecology of mind. Collected essays in anthropology psychiatry, evolution and epistemology*. Paladin Books.

Craig, R. T., & Muller, H. L. (Eds.). (2007). *Theorising communication: Readings across traditions*. Sage.

Esposito, E. (2017). Artificial communication? The production of contingency by algorithms. *Zeitschrift für Soziologie, 46*(4), 249–265.

Esposito, E. (2022). *Artificial communication*. MIT Press.

Lasswell, H. D. (1948). The structure and function of communication in society. In L. Bryson (Ed.), *The communication of ideas* (pp. 37–51). Harper.

Luhmann, N. (2012). *Theory of society* (vols. 1 & 2). Stanford University Press.

Luhmann, N. (2002/2013). *Introduction to systems theory*. Polity Press.

Mattelart, A., & Mattelart, M. (1998). *Theories of communication: A short introduction*. Sage.

Nassehi, A. (2019). *Muster. Theorie der digitalen Gesellschaft*. Beck.

Shannon, C. E. (1949/1964). The mathematical theory of communication. In C. E. Shannon & W. Weaver (Eds.), *The mathematical theory of communication* (pp. 29–125). University of Illinois Press.

Shannon, C. E. (1950). XXII. Programming a computer for playing chess. *The London, Edinburgh, and Dublin Philosophical Magazine and Journal of Science*, 41(314), 256–275.

Shannon, C. E., & Weaver, W. (Eds.) (1949/1964). *The mathematical theory of communication*. University of Illinois Press.

Weaver, W. (1949/1964). Recent contributions to the mathematical theory of communication. In C. E. Shannon & W. Weaver (Eds.), *The mathematical theory of communication* (pp. 3–28). University of Illinois Press.

Wiener, N. (1948). *Cybernetics or control and communication in the animal and the machine*. The Technology Press.

6 Erving Goffman (1959) *The Presentation of Self in Everyday Life*

Espen Ytreberg

Introduction

When someone brings out a camera to photograph us, we often want to correct the way we present ourselves. We try to look good when the picture is taken, more or less consciously, more or less casually. People have reacted in this way since the time of the first amateur photographers. Today's media affordances have expanded our means of self-presentation, such as the use of amateur photos as an important component of our personal profiles on social media. The fact that we display so much of who we are and what we look like on such profile pages has provoked widespread discussion. What version of ourselves are we really conveying to others in this way? Do we reveal too much about who we are as individuals, or do we – on the contrary – present a manipulated version to appear better than we are?

On a fundamental level, these questions concern the relationship between front stage and back stage – terms Goffman used interchangeably with 'front region' and 'back region'. This conceptual pair has become part of the standard vocabulary of media studies. As theoretical concepts, they emanate from Erving Goffman's book *The Presentation of Self in Everyday Life* (1959). This conceptual pair is perhaps the single most important reason why Goffman's book is considered an important text in media studies contexts, even though it does not deal with media directly.

Goffman was a sociologist and one of the greatest thinkers in this field; he has been called the most influential American sociologist of the 20th century (Fine & Manning, 2003). Like the social philosopher Michel Foucault and as a sociologist such as Pierre Bourdieu, Goffman has exerted a largely indirect yet great influence on media studies. His influence is primarily due to his strong skill in observing human relationships and inventing new concepts that are applicable to the analysis of social contexts. Goffman focused on relatively small and everyday phenomena that are easy to miss but still speak volumes about how social life works. Media researcher Joshua Meyrowitz is one of those who has been strongly influenced by Goffman's way of looking at the world: 'He made me aware of things I knew, but did not know that I knew' (Meyrowitz, 1985: 2).

DOI: 10.4324/9781003432272-7

Throughout his writing career, Goffman not only invented a host of influential new concepts but also continually abandoned them in favour of new ones. He likened his concepts to scaffolding, which, after all, 'is there to build other things with and should be erected with a view to taking them down again' (1990: 220). Nevertheless, a theme remained in all of this conceptual invention: Goffman always tended to view human interaction as a form of theatre – a drama with roles and an underlying dramaturgy. This metaphor is clear in concepts such as front stage and back stage and in another central concept from *The Presentation of Self*: 'impression management'. Moreover, the theatre metaphor is the basis for concepts that Goffman developed further on, such as 'ritual' and 'frame'. It is also the basis for the texts that Goffman wrote on the topic of media, which were added in a later phase of his career than *The Presentation of Self* and have received less attention from media researchers (Ytreberg, 2002, 2010). Still, these texts are important for understanding how Goffman thought about media dramaturgy and how his concepts have been used in media research.

What happens when social life is viewed as a spectacle?

The Presentation of Self in Everyday Life is a systematic book that gives a general description of basic social roles and situations found in everyday life. The discussion is therefore at a relatively high level of abstraction, such as when overarching concepts are introduced and explained, although the book also contains numerous examples and concrete illustrations from everyday life. It describes what a 'role' consists of (among other things, which 'façade' it requires), how people enter roles and maintain them through their performances, and how these roles can be questioned and thus be more difficult to master. In a separate chapter, Goffman writes about how roles are played in different ways depending on whether the individual is on or off stage. At the end of the book, he discusses the relationship between the role and the self. Here, he expresses scepticism that there would be such a thing as an underlying and anchoring self that is independent of the roles we play in everyday life. On the contrary, he suggests that this self is itself a social product. For Goffman, people are fundamentally beings who move in and out of different roles in order to live their complex lives together.

The animating idea in Goffman's dramaturgical approach is quite simple: If we take a social situation and apply dramaturgical principles to it, what will we then be able to see and put into words? What happens if, for example, we study a guest being served in a restaurant or a group of passengers on a bus? At first, these kinds of social situations do not seem to have much in common with a stage play, and its participants do not immediately bring actors to mind. None of them have practiced what they are doing, they are not wearing costumes and there is no fictional element. In the case of the bus, it is not even obvious that the situation is a social one, because people usually do not aim to interact with strangers on the bus.

86 *Espen Ytreberg*

A closer look at these two situations, however, reveals that they do have some dramaturgical dimensions. One such dimension is the playing of roles. In everyday language, it is common to talk about how people tend to play certain roles in order to be appropriate and competent in particular situations. The role of waiter is an example. Goffman defines a role as 'the enactment of rights and duties attached to a given status' (1990: 27). Waiters obviously have certain obligations towards their guests; they also have rights, although the latter are not as clear. The waiter places the guests at the tables, controls the rhythm of the meal together with the kitchen and signals when it is time to pay. In short, the waiter exercises control over the dramaturgy of the meal.

As for the duties and rights that come with the role of bus passenger, it is necessary to study them in detail to see them, but they are there. People riding the bus actually follow a fairly strict set of rules in order to fulfil their roles as passengers: they touch each other as little as possible, look at each other only furtively and get on the bus at the stop after the disembarking passengers have disembarked. According to Goffman, we play such roles in everyday performances all the time, since a performance is 'all the activity of a given participant on a given occasion which serves to influence in any way any of the other participants' (1990: 26). In reality, therefore, everything we do in the presence of others has something of a role-playing and performative dimension to it.

At the same time, the others who are present for our little performances in these social situations assume the role of an audience – another metaphor taken from drama. Basically, Goffman says, these others make certain demands on us and we on them, as long as we are together. We must fulfil these requirements – something that tends to make people's appearances in social situations regular and repetitive. In some cases, we play our roles deliberately and perhaps according to a prearranged plan, such as when we give a presentation in a meeting or read a storybook to a child. But Goffman emphasises that role-defined performances do not require us to have an underlying intention for – or awareness of – what is happening. What we do all the time and under all circumstances in social situations is to control others' impressions of us. Knowingly and unknowingly, we constantly do small things to show others that we cooperate and that we are playing our role acceptably.

As in an actual theatre, social situations can be divided into front and back stage – that is, that which happens on the stage and that which takes place in the stage wings or behind the stage altogether. For Goffman, the relationship between them is relative, in that back-stage behaviour is hidden from stage view and therefore can diverge from it: 'A back region or backstage may be defined as a place, relative to a given performance, where the impression fostered by the performance is knowingly contradicted as a matter of course' (1990: 114). In Goffman's well-known description, the restaurant kitchen is a back stage relative to the dining room, the front stage, where waiters and guests interact with each other across the tables. A wall usually serves as a physical boundary and prevents contact between the restaurant's front and back stage. In the kitchen, waiters may behave in a way that would be inappropriate in the serving area.

Erving Goffman (1959)   87

They can swear, joke and make snide remarks about the guests in front of the chefs. In this way, they get a break from the demands that come with performing among the restaurant guests.

It is worth noting that, because the relationship between the front and back stage is relative, one person's back stage can be another person's front stage. The same kitchen where the waiter relaxes can be a stage for the chef's apprentice, who may need to escape to the back alley to find her back stage and a break from her role requirements.

It was through *The Presentation of Self* that the dramaturgical perspective entered the field of social-scientific and humanistic research. However, the basic insight was considerably older. 'All the world's a stage, and all the men and women merely players', wrote William Shakespeare, in his play *As You Like It* (published in 1623). What Goffman did in *The Presentation of Self* was to apply this idea systematically to social situations. However, he did so with a caveat. 'All the world is not, of course, a stage, but the crucial ways in which it isn't are not easy to specify', wrote Goffman with a typically paradoxical formulation (1990: 78). His approach was pragmatic: Goffman perceived that dramaturgical metaphors had significant explanatory power and used this power for analytical purposes.

For a media researcher, it is worth knowing that Goffman's dramaturgical vocabulary had its origins in a previous work on communication. *The Presentation of Self* was a reworking of his doctoral thesis, *Communication Conduct in an Island Community* (1953), which was based on an ethnographic study Goffman had conducted of traditional everyday life on one of the Shetland Islands. In this early work, it is already clear that Goffman regards all performances in social situations as acts of communication. It is always difficult to separate the social from the communicative in Goffman's work.

In his doctoral thesis, Goffman used the sender-message-receiver triad – a theoretical communication framework that was already relatively traditional at the time. With *The Presentation of Self*, Goffman moved on to his more innovative dramaturgical vocabulary. This was the first of a series of conceptual shifts that would characterise his entire career. Time and again, Goffman replaced established concepts with new ones, even when the established ones were his own. Starting in the 1970s, Goffman developed the concept of 'frame' as an overall tool for explaining how people understand social situations. Through this approach, he came to give the dramaturgical metaphor a more limited and specified function within the realm of social interaction. In his main later work, *Frame Analysis* (1986), Goffman used dramaturgical language primarily to describe planned performances before an audience. Theatrical drama was still a central example, as were instances of interpersonal communication such as lectures.

At around the same time, Goffman began to refer to a wide range of examples from the world of media. In *Gender Advertisements* (1979), he contributed to feminist analysis by showing how photographic representations in the popular press of the time were dominated by women performing in front of the

88 *Espen Ytreberg*

camera within the confines of a narrow and conventional repertoire of roles. Goffman carried out his most extensive analysis of mediated performances in his last book, *Forms of Talk* (1981), which contains an essay of over a hundred pages on professional performances on the radio. While *The Presentation of Self* was about the common dramaturgical features of all social performances, whether mediated or interpersonal, Goffman was now interested in how what he called 'dramatic scriptings' in media differed from other forms of communication in important respects. For example, he pointed out that a higher degree of consistency and efficiency in speaking is required of a radio announcer than of a person speaking in more everyday contexts.

Despite his shifts in conceptual vocabulary after *The Presentation of Self*, Goffman believed that he was holding on to the basic approach of thinking of social situations as a form of drama. This approach could be said to become an undercurrent in Goffman's later works, in which he developed other (and often more refined) concepts for analytical purposes. In the introduction to *Forms of Talk*, which deals with spoken language, Goffman comments: 'deeply incorporated into the nature of talk are the fundamental requirements of theatricality' (Goffman, 1981: 4).

Media researchers' uses of Goffman

As already mentioned, Goffman has exerted a wide and extensive influence on other researchers in a number of scholarly disciplines. In sociology, central figures such as Pierre Bourdieu and Anthony Giddens have emphasised Goffman's influence. Goffman's relationship to media and communication theory has even become the subject of a separate monograph (Winkin & Leeds-Hurwitz, 2013). Within media studies, Goffman's concepts and analyses have come to characterise a number of different areas, including the sociolinguistic analysis of media language and mediated social interaction (see e.g. Brand & Scannell, 1991; Ekström, 2012; Lundell, 2010); feminist media research (e.g. Krijnen & van Bauwel, 2015); frame analysis of news and journalism (e.g. Gitlin, 2003; Matthes, 2009); and, not least, research on digital and social media (e.g. Bengtsson, 2016; Ditchfield, 2020; Kilvington, 2021; Marwick & boyd, 2010; Papacharissi, 2002).

In what follows, I first and foremost deal with the media research that has taken up and developed the metaphors of 'front stage' and 'back stage' from *The Presentation of Self*. This dramaturgical pair of concepts has a long history of use in media studies. An early, ambitious and widely cited example is Joshua Meyrowitz's book on television, *No Sense of Place* (1985), in which he combines the ideas of Goffman with those of Marshall McLuhan in an argument that television tears down the walls that separate different social situations in everyday life. Meyrowitz emphasises that the technology of television makes it possible to expose individuals to a degree that makes it impossible for them to hide back stage. Instead, they must develop a behaviour that mixes the formality typical of many stage contexts with the informality and intimacy of being

Erving Goffman (1959) 89

behind the scenes. The result is a performance that is between the back stage and the front stage: a 'middle region behaviour', as Meyrowitz calls it. Thus, Meyrowitz's insights are developed through a processing and further development of Goffman's concepts.

Goffman's work has also been important in the kind of historically oriented media sociology that is interested in how the media have shaped performances and interactions in different ways over time. John B. Thompson's book *The Media and Modernity* (1995) is a media history in which the media's shaping of social life is a key component in a broad narrative of how modern Western society has come to be. In his book, Thompson argues that the development of mass media led to a fragmentation of social situations – an argument that runs counter to Meyrowitz's in many ways. In Thompson's account, mass media do not converge on the 'middle region' but rather produce two separate kinds of back stage: 'production' and 'reception'.

With the rise of digital and social media, media studies' use of Goffman's concepts has gained momentum. His dramaturgical approach aligns well with the forms of performance and social interaction found in computer games and on social media accounts. After all, social media are routinely designed specifically for people to act out certain more or less predefined versions of themselves. The relationships between people can also be affected in this mediated environment. For example, Facebook has played a part in redefining what a 'friend' is.

In social media, both the possibilities of self-presentation and the demands on it seem to expand. Moreover, similarly to electronic media, social media have been shown to feature complex and fluid relationships between front stage and back stage. An example of the latter is the use of mobile phones, which may lead to a person talking in two social situations at the same time – the situation in which the person is physically located and the media context of the phone call. As Richard Ling (2009) has pointed out, the distinction between front and back stage becomes fluid in such situations. In a way, the telephone conversation and the physical social situation function as each other's backdrops. Ling relates the example of a mother who has a conflict with her child on the phone while she herself is out at a restaurant with a colleague. It can be embarrassing for both the mother and the colleague when information leaks out from the front stage of the telephone dispute to the back stage of the restaurant. Here, the use of mobile phones seems to force a kind of communication on two different stages where 'front' conflicts with 'back'.

Those who appear on social media can face similar complexities in commanding their audience. Alice Marwick and danah boyd (2010) have described what they call a 'context collapse' between front and back stage that occurs when the audience on social networks such as Facebook or Instagram includes colleagues, friends, family members and partners. In everyday social situations, we usually interact with these different groups at different times and in different places. However, social media mix them together, making the groups aware of each other. According to Marwick and boyd, this situation has consequences

90   *Espen Ytreberg*

similar to those described by Meyrowitz in the case of television. Speakers must adjust their messages towards a kind of middle ground and hope that they are acceptable to widely varying audiences.

In today's society, pervasive demands on performance can be found not only in the media but also in organisational life, for instance. In a media-saturated world, demands on appearances make themselves felt in many social arenas – including organisational life. In the book *Perform or Else* (2001), John MacKenzie describes how organisations and bureaucracies meet the demands of what international business parlance calls 'performance'. According to MacKenzie, working life has shifted towards putting greater focus on transparency and evaluations. Organisations must demonstrate that they are performing – in a way, not unlike how performers need to show their best side to their audience. Another and related arena for self-presentation in contemporary work life is so-called personal branding, which is based on the idea that a person's individuality can be communicated as if it were a brand for a product.

Yet another contemporary area in which Goffman's work has obvious relevance is that of surveillance (see e.g. Trottier, 2018). The underlying technologies of digital and social media allow the media industries to map users through the automated and algorithm-controlled tracking of their online activities. In some instances, these activities are of an intimate and covert character, in which case it becomes an acute question whether someone is watching or listening. In many ways, the social media world of extended exposure and surveillance matches Goffman's general view of social life quite closely. Social life, as Goffman describes it, can be said to consist of those who are concerned about their performances and those who keep track of them.

Goffman in his time

The Presentation of Self in Everyday Life was primarily written within the framework of interpretive American social research in the middle of the previous century. Several of the most important currents of thought at this time meet in Goffman's work. Goffman was influenced by sociologist Émile Durkheim's functionalism, in the sense that he was always interested in what enabled people to make social situations function so as to aid social cohesion. Goffman's tendency to see society as fundamentally characterised by a common striving towards order ran counter to a critical impulse; nevertheless, such an impulse can also be observed in certain parts of his work. This applies, for example, to *Gender Advertisements*, which focuses on the fundamental contradictions and conflicts of power between genders.

The current of thought known as symbolic interactionism was at least as important to Goffman as his view on society's striving towards order. Within the so-called Chicago school, which would also become an important influence in media studies, researchers became interested in the kinds of everyday social environment that Goffman was working with, such as interactions on city streets and everyday life in institutions. As formulated by George Herbert Mead

Erving Goffman (1959) 91

(2015), symbolic interactionism was concerned with the ways in which individuals make their way in a world made up of linguistic symbols. It is through this shared world of meaning, thought Mead, that we understand life around us as well as ourselves. This idea has a long history. When considering the American perspective on symbolic interactionism it is natural to mention pragmatism and what the philosopher Charles Horton Cooley called the 'looking-glass self' – the idea that our very perception of who we are is formed as we take on our fellow human beings' expectations that we should be someone. 'Others' are the mirror we must look into in order to see ourselves.

The Presentation of Self in Everyday Life has been seen as part of a wider movement in 1950s Anglo-American scholarship towards the dramaturgical (Burke, 1969) and performances and performativity (Austin, 1994). It is also useful to view the book in light of the development of American and other Western societies at this time. Erving Goffman grew up in Canada, in a family of Ukrainian-Jewish descent. His father owned a small shop, which he ran with Goffman's mother (Winkin, 1988). In other words, the family's income came from a type of work in the service industry where the seller's appearance *vis-à-vis* the customer played an important role.

It has been said about this kind of white-collar service work that it involves selling not only a product but also an experience. As in the case of the waiters Goffman wrote about in *The Presentation of Self*, an acceptable role performance is required in order for a salesperson to succeed on the stage that is the shop. In this book, as in most of his works, Goffman focused his analytical attention on service occupations. In the preliminary study for *The Presentation of Self*, the service at the hotel in Shetland where Goffman lived played a central role. Later in his career, he would study doctors and patients in mental hospitals, casino employees and lecturers at universities – as well as professional performers in radio and television, ranging from music presenters to newscasters.

In short, it is helpful to view Goffman's research in the context of how white-collar and service occupations came to dominate Western working life. This process took place around the middle of the 20th century, when capitalist production moved from a focus on commodity production in factories towards what is commonly referred to as a 'service economy'. As the sale of services increased, appearances, performances and role mastery became more economically significant and more generally central to social life. In this historical development lies a possible explanation for why Goffman was so interested in how a performance can contribute to maintaining social control. Goffman tended to portray social situations as quite precarious, with a constant inherent risk of embarrassment and defeat motivating the need for control and negotiation (Scannell, 2007). It is possible to see an anxious salesman type from the 1950s in the United States behind Goffman's general descriptions of social interaction. This type of American white-collar worker has been discussed by the historical sociologist David Riesman, who wrote about the emergence of an 'other-directed' personality (Riesman, 2001). Riesman argues that American middle-class suburban life of the 1960s was characterised by consumption as a

92   Espen Ytreberg

means of social self-assertion, which created people who constantly tried to conform to others in order to have their status and self-worth confirmed.

It is undeniable that Goffman's performers are other-directed in their constant endeavour to adapt to the demands of social situations. Goffman has been criticised for speaking of the American middle class as if it were representative of people in general (Gouldner, 2000). At the same time, however, researchers have been able to use Goffman's terminology to describe social situations that differ from those found in his own works – including mediated ones. Moreover, Goffman may usefully be placed in a historical context that was more about nonconformism than conformity. While further developing the dramaturgical vocabulary from *The Presentation of Self*, Goffman spent most of the 1960s at the University of California at Berkeley. It was a time and place for subcultures: for feminism, civil rights and anti-authoritarian ideologies. This is a relevant context for the part of Goffman's writing that deals with dominance and social deviance. His performers certainly contribute to maintaining order, but the price they have to pay is to adapt to role demands that often appear restrictive and sometimes downright oppressive. This particularly applies to his studies of patients in mental hospitals (Goffman, 1961) and the pictured women in women's magazines. It also speaks to the situation of people who appear on radio and television, who must adapt to strict conformity requirements, according to Goffman.

Media performances and social order

The Presentation of Self in Everyday Life was the first of many works in which Goffman presented social life as a performance – and a rather risky one, at that. Although he emphasised that impression management often occurs unconsciously, it is hardly a coincidence that Goffman later came to write about a wide range of people who are deliberately deceptive in their appearances: con artists, impersonators, gamblers, spies and impostors. He had a tendency to mention those media professionals who appear on radio and television in the same breath, as Goffman tended to associate what they did with something deceptive. Their performances often appeared to be like everyday communication among family or friends, even though it was clear that considerable institutional authority lay behind them.

For Goffman, risk was a basic feature of social life; in the introduction to *The Presentation of Self*, he therefore placed great emphasis on individuals' need to manage that risk, while using the concept of 'management' to describe our constant striving to achieve control. By choosing a concept from organisational and business life, Goffman implied that the communicative work we all undertake in our everyday life is related to the work that a company's or other organisation's manager does to ensure that work is well-ordered, smooth and effective. In the introduction to *The Presentation of Self*, Goffman clearly stated that the dramaturgical perspective was well suited to analysing 'especially the kind of social life that is organised within the physical confines of a building or plant' (1990, unpaginated). In other words, the dramaturgical perspective was particularly relevant to life in organisations and institutions – larger structures characterised by decision-making hierarchies, professions and fixed roles. At the same time, Goffman's work was limited in terms of psychological and individual motives and experiences, which Goffman was inclined to under-value. Thus, for example, his work cannot be used to investigate conflicts between the demands of one's role and the experience of one's deeper self, as Arlie Hochschild (1983) has pointed out.

Viewing Goffman's work as being concerned with the places where actors meet structures reveals a connection between *The Presentation of Self* and Goffman's later work from the 1970s and 1980s, when most of his empirical material came from the media. Relative to today, that time was dominated by mass media that engaged in one-way communication, with senders typically being centralised and hierarchical media organisations. Individuals who per-formed to a broadcast audience from a position of authority – such as hosts, reporters and announcers – did so on behalf of an institution and as its employees. This often brought a degree of formality that made it easy to see how, for example, radio announcers spoke differently to their audience than people spoke to friends or family in an everyday context; that is, the radio announcers' speech was a more disciplined and controlled variant of ordinary speech (Goffman, 1981: 326–327). According to Goffman, radio announcers were merely more noticeably influenced by what essentially rules us all – namely, the need for control. Conversely, Goffman placed much of what is often viewed as typical of mediated communication at the heart of everyday interaction: the importance of planning, the way we assume the role of audience and the very element of dramaturgy.

To make matters more complex, the speech of a radio announcer can often be reminiscent of everyday and informal communication – not only today but also in the era of mass media. According to Goffman, however, informality in the media is an illusion, an imitation of the real thing that has been created in a studio with the help of scripts. In such cases, informality is literally 'written in' and must be activated by professionals specialised in the craft of creating a flow of seemingly fresh talk from such scripts. This illusion is functional, in the sense that it makes the programme fit better into many of the everyday situa-tions of listening to the radio. In an essay on lecturers from *Forms of Talk*, Goffman wrote about how these communication specialists function as a kind of translator between everyday micro-contexts and the power structures of society. They use their performance skills to make institutional messages fit into the social situation of the lecture room, in the same way a person might use a shoehorn to fit into a tight shoe, as Goffman put it (1981: 194).

As previously suggested, it is not easy to position Goffman within established academic schools and traditions. Because he generally worked with everyday social situations and often studied these in great detail, Goffman has been linked to the tradition of microsociology. He has often been considered to have little to say about the macrostructures of society, such as class and ideology,

94 Espen Ytreberg

gender and ethnicity. However, this perspective risks undervaluing Goffman's contribution to understanding all that which makes our everyday interaction regular, ordered and controllable. 'The interaction order' (Goffman, 1983) was Goffman's theme for the speech he gave after being elected president of the American Sociological Association, shortly before his early death from cancer in 1982. Goffman ended that speech by precisely emphasising that everyday interaction is shaped by the forms of order represented by society's institutions and macrostructures. Goffman positioned those who perform in the media exactly at this intersection.

References

Austin, J. L. (1994). *How to do things with words*. Harvard University Press.

Bengtsson, S. (2016). The presentation of self in a virtual world: Working in Second Life. In J. Webster & K. Randle (Eds.), *Virtual workers and the global labour market* (pp. 219–237). Palgrave Macmillan.

Brand, G., & Scannell, P. (1991). Talk, identity and performance: "The Tony Blackburn Show". In P. Scannell (Ed.), *Broadcast talk* (pp. 201–226). Sage.

Burke, K. (1969). *A grammar of motives*. University of California Press.

Ditchfield, H. (2020). Behind the screen of Facebook: Identity construction in the rehearsal stage of online interaction. *New Media & Society*, 22(6), 927–943. https://doi.org/10.1177/1461444819873644.

Ekström, M. (2012). Gaze work in political media interviews. *Discourse & Communication*, 6(3), 249–271. https://doi.org/10.1177/1750481312452200.

Fine, G. A., & Manning, P. (2003). Erving Goffman. In G. Ritzer (Ed.), *The Blackwell companion to major contemporary social theorists* (pp. 457–485). Blackwell.

Fine, G. A., & Smith, G. W. H. (2000). *Erving Goffman* (Sage Masters of Modern Social Thought, vols. 1–4). Sage.

Gitlin, T. (2003). *The whole world is watching: Mass media in the making and unmaking of the new left*. University of California Press.

Goffman, E. (1953). *Communication conduct in an island community* [Unpublished doctoral dissertation]. University of Chicago.

Goffman, E. (1961). *Asylums*. Penguin Books.

Goffman, E. (1970). *Strategic interaction*. Basil Blackwell.

Goffman, E. (1979). *Gender advertisements*. Harvard University Press.

Goffman, E. (1981). *Forms of talk*. University of Pennsylvania Press.

Goffman, E. (1983). The interaction order. *American Sociological Review*, 48, 1–17.

Goffman, E. (1986). *Frame analysis: An essay on the organisation of experience*. Northeastern University Press.

Goffman, E. (1990). *The presentation of self in everyday life*. Penguin Books.

Goffman, E. (2007). *Interaction ritual: Essays in face-to-face behavior*. Transaction Publishers.

Gouldner, A. W. (2000). Other symptoms of the crisis: Goffman's dramaturgy and other new theories. In A. W. Gouldner (Ed.), *The coming crisis of Western sociology* (pp. 378–390). Basic Books.

Hochschild, A. R. (1983). *The managed heart: Commercialisation of human feeling*. University of California Press.

Erving Goffman (1959) 95

Jenkins, R. (2010). The 21st century interaction order. In M. H. Jacobsen (Ed.), *The contemporary Goffman* (pp. 257–274). Routledge.

Kilvington, D. (2021). The virtual stage of hate: Using Goffman's work to conceptualise the motivations for online hate. *Media Culture & Society*, 43(2), 256–272. https://doi.org/10.1177/0163443720972318.

Krijnen, T., & van Bauwel, S. (2015). *Gender and the media: Representing, producing, consuming*. Routledge.

Ling, R. S. (2010). The "Unboothed" Phone: Goffman and the use of mobile communication. In M. H. Jacobsen (Ed.), *The contemporary Goffman* (pp. 275–292). Routledge.

Lundell, Å. K. (2010). The before and after of a political interview on TV. *Journalism*, 11(2), 167–184. https://doi.org/10.1177/1464884909355906.

Marwick, A., & boyd, d. (2010). "I tweet honestly, I tweet passionately": Twitter users, context collapse, and the imagined audience. *New Media & Society*, 13(1), 114–133. https://doi.org/10.1177/1461444810365313.

Matthes, J. (2009). What's in a frame? A content analysis of media framing studies in the world's leading communication journals, 1990–2005. *Journalism and Mass Communication Quarterly*, 86(2), 349–367. https://doi.org/10.1177/107769900908600206.

McKenzie, J. (2001). *Perform or else: From discipline to performance*. Routledge.

Mead, G. H. (2015). *Mind, self & society*. The University of Chicago Press.

Meyrowitz, J. (1985). *No sense of place: The impact of electronic media on social behavior*. Oxford University Press.

Papacharissi, Z. (2002). The presentation of self in virtual life: Characteristics of virtual home pages. *Journalism and Mass Communication Quarterly*, 79(3), 643–660. https://doi.org/10.1177/107769900207900307.

Riesman, D. (2001). *The lonely crowd*. Yale University Press.

Scannell, P. (2007). *Media and communication*. Sage Publications.

Thompson, J. B. (1995). *The media and modernity*. Polity Press.

Trottier, D. (2018). *Social media as surveillance*. Routledge.

Winkin, Y. (1988) Erving Goffman: Portrait du sociologue en jeune homme [Portrait of the sociologist as a young man]. In Y. Winkin (Ed.), *Erving Goffman: Les moments et leurs hommes* (pp. 11–93). Seuil/Minuit.

Winkin, Y., & Leeds-Hurwitz, W. (2013). *Erving Goffman: A critical introduction to media and communication theory*. Peter Lang.

Ytreberg, E. (2002). Erving Goffman as a theorist of the mass media. *Critical Studies in Media Communication*, 19(4), 481–497. https://doi.org/10.1080/07393180216570.

Ytreberg, E. (2010). The question of calculation: Erving Goffman and the pervasive planning of communication. In M. H. Jacobsen (Ed.), *The contemporary Goffman* (pp. 293–312). Routledge.

7 Jürgen Habermas (1962) *The Structural Transformation of the Public Sphere: An Inquiry into a Category of Bourgeois Society*

Anne Kaun

Introduction

The motto of the internet forum Flashback is 'Real freedom of expression'. With 15,000 new posts daily, it is one of the largest and most popular online forums in Sweden (Åkerlund, 2021). Here, tofu recipes, talk about cars, exchanges about experiences with ankle monitoring and tips on how to make your own kombucha are interspersed with a spectrum of political extremes, including misogynistic and xenophobic posts (Askanius et al., 2023). The forum is moderated by a small army of hand-picked moderators and an even more exclusive group of administrators who monitor compliance with the community's rules. It is freedom of speech in real life, pure and simple. Or is it?

Founded in 2000, Flashback became a Swedish expression of the so-called 'participatory culture', which expanded in the mid-2000s on platforms such as Facebook, Twitter and the now almost forgotten Myspace and Friendster. Flashback reflects, in many ways, the tensions that characterise today's media landscape, where audiences become producers and anything can be said without being filtered. At the same time, discussions on the platform are tightly regulated by community rules that are often of unclear origin. Therefore, the question remains: Are such platforms offering a space for genuine discussions and exchanges of arguments, or are they places for radicalisation, fringe publics and polarisation?

Emphasising social media as forms of participatory culture seem quite distant today. Social media platforms are now referred to not as sanctuaries for democracy and open dialogue but rather as either part of a surveillance culture that exploits our creative expressions and social relationships or as places where we display our narcissistic selves in pursuit of likes and shares. While the discussion around social media and participatory culture used to centre on issues such as the tension between low thresholds for participation and the profit motive of platforms, the question today is who should and should not be allowed to appear on social media. Is it dangerous for democracy if conspiracy theories and disinformation are shared? Should White power sympathisers be given space on social media? Should we allow anti-democratic positions as a way to follow the essential principles of liberal democracy? Freedom of

DOI: 10.4324/9781003432272-8

expression is fundamentally about the conditions for democracy and can be particularly linked to its deliberative version, which is based on the exchange and negotiation of rational arguments. The idea that democracy is about deliberation in a public sphere, where the aim is to reach consensus, has, since the 1960s, been mainly associated with the German philosopher Jürgen Habermas. His model and historical analysis of the changes in public life have inspired and underpinned many studies and have contributed to what can best be described as a specific subdivision of media and communication studies, called public sphere theory.

In this chapter, I provide a brief overview of the main arguments of Habermas's conceptualisation of the public sphere, introduce some of the major critiques and revisions of his canonical text and discuss its relevance today.

Overview of *The Structural Transformation of the Public Sphere*

Like many of the theorists with which we familiarise ourselves in this book, Habermas is not a media and communication scholar, but his theories have significantly impacted the subject. Jürgen Habermas was born in Düsseldorf but grew up in a small town in North Rhine-Westphalia. His father was described as a *Mitläufer* [1] during the Nazi regime of the 1930s and 1940s. In this sense, Habermas differs from the first generation of representatives of the so-called 'Frankfurt School', whose most important representatives, Theodor W. Adorno and Max Horkheimer, but also Erich Fromm, Herbert Marcuse and many others, had to flee Nazi Germany because of their left-wing political commitment and their Jewish backgrounds. Habermas studied philosophy, history, psychology, literature and economics at the universities of Göttingen, Zurich and Bonn. In 1956, he joined the Institut für Sozialforschung in Frankfurt as a research assistant to work with Horkheimer and Adorno (who had returned to Germany after the end of WWII), but their collaboration was characterised by conflicts that eventually led Habermas to leave Frankfurt for his habilitation. He later returned to the University of Frankfurt as a professor of philosophy and sociology. However, he declined an invitation to become the director of the Institut für Sozialforschung. Although his relationships with Adorno and Horkheimer were not always harmonious, he is still recognised today as part of the second generation of critical theory.

Early on, Habermas worked as a freelance journalist and often participated in public debates on current political issues. For example, he engaged in debate around the student movement in the 1960s and against conservative legislation in the 1970s. He also reacted critically to the increasing radicalisation of the left in the 1970s. More recently, questions about European integration and the role and future of the EU have become important to Habermas. His social engagement is an important aspect to consider when approaching his key work. Habermas's theorising has always been rooted in the *Lebenswelt*—the world of people's lives—with the ultimate goal of understanding how we can live better and create a reasonable world together. In 2022, he published a collection of

98　*Anne Kaun*

essays and interviews in the book *A New Structural Transformation of the Public Sphere* (*Ein Neuer Strukturwandel der Öffentlichkeit*) (2022), where he clearly adds a critical edge to his earlier reasoning. Drawing on critical scholars, such as Shoshanna Zuboff and Christian Fuchs, he is outspoken and critical of the dominant position of large social media platforms.

Habermas's 1962 book *The Structural Transformation of the Public Sphere* (in German *Strukturwandel der Öffentlichkeit*), which was his habilitation thesis, was translated and published in English in 1989. The English translation led to a renewed interest in the author's work and theories in the international research community. The text is more sociological than his later, more philosophical writings in that Habermas is interested in different social institutions and how they change in interaction with one another and over time. The book is divided into three parts that discuss the (a) emergence, (b) character and (c) dissolution of the bourgeois public sphere. In the concluding chapter, Habermas focuses on the concept of public opinion, which has replaced publicity as the dominant concept and the focus of important social actors, such as politicians. In this book, Habermas combines different traditions of thought, and his analysis spans various disciplines, such as sociology, economics, law, political science and social and cultural history. He uses methods and knowledge from these disciplines to examine the conditions and characteristics of the public sphere, which he argues are closely linked to the idea of a democratic society.

Habermas's way of interweaving different fields, social discussions and different materials, such as legal texts, popular literature and newspaper articles, makes the book a particularly exciting but also difficult reading experience. Habermas's style is sometimes difficult to access, with half-page-long sentences. An anecdote that is often cited in connection with his way of expressing himself is how a student interrupted him during a lecture and asked him to express himself a little more clearly and less convolutedly. Apparently, half the class applauded, while the other half disagreed.

What is the bourgeois public sphere?

What does Habermas mean by the public sphere? The original book from 1962 is a historical review of the emergence and disappearance of the ideal public sphere for a democratic society, it is difficult to separate the definition from the historical narrative that Habermas developed. He takes us from the pre-modern Middle Ages to modern media society, describing worlds of thought and discourse as well as specific places and physical aspects of the public sphere. In one of the central sections, Habermas describes the bourgeois public sphere as follows:

> The bourgeois public sphere may be conceived, above all, as the sphere of private people come together as a public; they soon claimed the public sphere regulated from above against the public authorities themselves, to engage them in a debate over the general rules governing relations in the

basically privatized but publicly relevant sphere of commodity exchange and social labor. The medium of this political confrontation was peculiar and without historical precedent: people's public use of their reason (*öffentliches Räsonnemnt*).

(Habermas, 1989, p. 27)

The kind of public sphere that Habermas analyses can thus be described as a collection of private individuals who discuss and negotiate problems that are of public interest to reach a consensus on how to solve these issues. The resulting public sphere takes on the role previously played by the aristocratic, representative public sphere. It is also in the bourgeois public sphere that a critique and questioning of aristocratic and feudal power structures takes place. The joint decision-making that takes place in the bourgeois public sphere is based on rational discussions and negotiations about common concerns. Things like birth, title or emotional considerations should not—at least in the ideal case—have any impact on the decisions made. According to Habermas, this kind of public sphere emerged during the 19th century in Europe (he studied mainly England, France and Germany) when several major social changes coincided. First, feudal power structures and absolute royal power were dissolved. Second, a new class developed in connection with the rise of capitalism: the bourgeoisie entered the stage of history in the 18th century as a separate and self-conscious class with economic and cultural influence.

The bourgeois avant-garde of the educated middle class learned the art of critical–rational public debate through its contact with the 'elegant world'. This courtly–noble society, to the extent that the modern state apparatus became independent from the monarch's personal sphere, naturally separated itself, in turn, more and more from the court and became its counterpoise in the town.

(Habermas, 1989, p. 30)

The educated citizens of the new, emerging bourgeoisie thus came together to develop and exchange rational arguments. The public sphere in which this took place and whose issues were addressed here was separate from private life or the private sphere, where, among other things, family affairs and financial arrangements were settled. However, to develop rational ideas and arguments, sources of inspiration were needed. Habermas pointed to the roles that newspapers, novels and other cultural expressions that address and reflect social issues played in this process. Various new media forms thus played a decisive role in the development of the liberal public sphere: periodicals and other literary expressions, such as the novel, gathered important information, linked people across time and space and illustrated citizens' individual experiences in a way that made it possible to talk about them. However, this idealisation of the public sphere as a forum for debate created in and through print media was complemented by a material, spatial aspect: the salons and coffee houses where private individuals gathered for discussion.

100   *Anne Kaun*

The 'town' was the life center of civil society, not only economically; in cultural–political contrast to the court, it designated especially an early public sphere in the world of letters whose institutions were the coffee houses, the salons, and the *Tischgesellschaften* (table societies). The heirs of the humanistic–aristocratic society, in their encounter with the bourgeois intellectuals (through sociable discussions that quickly developed into public criticism), built a bridge between the remains of a collapsing form of publicity (the courtly one) and the precursor of a new one: the bourgeois public sphere.

(Habermas, 1989, p. 30)

The liberal public sphere replaced a public sphere that previously existed to represent the ruler's power to the people. The absolute state power used and created publicity or visibility mostly to emphasise and demonstrate power. It was a display of wealth and influence in what were called 'tower parties', which were a kind of performance by the king or aristocrats in front of an audience. The new version of the public sphere fulfilled a new and important function: examining authority through an informed and critical discussion among the bourgeoisie. Thus, Habermas examined a specific public sphere. He was not directly interested in a popular public sphere that would include other kinds of gatherings, such as peasant uprisings, guilds or popular movements (Dahlkvist, 2003). This can be partly explained by the fact that he was interested in a rationality of discussion and reasoning that could be developed in bourgeois forums, such as coffee houses and salons (*Tischgesellschaften, Sprachgesellschaften*), and cultural production (e.g. newspapers and other publications that required a certain level of education to make them available).

The civic public sphere is characterised by three important aspects, as summarised in Figure 7.1. First, the personal status of individual citizens plays no role in participation. Neither the position of power nor economic conditions should affect the importance given to different arguments in the discussion between private individuals. Second, the civic public sphere is a place and a forum where common, shared interests are negotiated. Previously, it had been the privilege and role of the Church and royal power to interpret and define what constituted common problems and how they should be solved. This interpretative power and monopoly were dissolved and displaced with the emergence of the bourgeois public sphere. Third, philosophy, literature and art become important forums for the interpretation of social issues. These are freely circulated and potentially accessible to all. However, they are freed from being part of the publicity for and representation of the Church and the court. As culture became a freely circulated commodity, the public sphere also became accessible to all. Everyone would have the opportunity to participate. This starting point can be seen as somewhat ironic, given how limited participation was: 'everyone' here did not mean everyone in a nation but everyone who belonged to the bourgeois class and who had the time and resources to gather in coffee houses and parlours to indulge in free discussion, which at that time mainly included White men.

Private realm		Spheres of public authority
Civil society (Realm of commodity exchange and social labour)	Public sphere in the political realm	State (realm of the 'police')
	Public sphere in the world of letters (clubs, press)	
Conjugal family's internal space (bourgeois intellectuals)	Market of culture products (town)	Court (courtly–noble society)

Figure 7.1 Adapted from Habermas' original publication in English translation (1989, p. 30)

The three aspects of the civil public sphere are, of course, difficult to achieve, and Habermas's description was perhaps primarily concerned with an ideal that had never been achieved. Not everyone has the opportunity to participate in the same way. It is not always the best argument that convinces, but perhaps how and by whom it is presented, and not everyone has the resources to participate in cultural expressions to develop their opinions and arguments. This is one reason why many argue that Habermas did not investigate an existing bourgeois public sphere; rather, he constructed an ideal type or mixture of different public spheres that may never have existed in reality in the way described above[2].

What conditions allow a bourgeois public sphere to emerge?

Two basic conditions must be fulfilled for the kind of publicness that Habermas described as emerging: a distinction between the private and the public and a certain rationality.

To distinguish between the private and the public, Habermas drew inspiration from Hannah Arendt (1958), whose book *The Human Condition* was published just as Habermas was working on civic publicness and visibility. Arendt analysed the way in which the social (the common) in society arises. Her starting point was the household, which was perceived as a separate sphere for private but also economic life. She described the household as a separate

102 *Anne Kaun*

place where daily needs were managed. This private sphere is pulled into the public sphere as the economy develops into its own system, with a bearing outside of private households. This leads to the fundamental restructuring of economic and political life, as these two hitherto separate and individualised areas are woven together into what is called society. Arendt distinguished between two dimensions of publicness, namely, what she called the space of appearance and the common world. The first dimension—similar to Habermas's bourgeois public sphere—is based on communication and free exchange between citizens negotiating different political positions. The second dimension is the background of this communicative sphere. It includes institutions, artefacts and ways of organising society that separate people from nature but also bring them together in a community. The shared (or common) world is a prerequisite for the political sphere, where people can cooperate to solve political problems together.

In addition to the division between private and public that Habermas drew from Arendt (1958), he pointed to reason and rationality as prerequisites for the bourgeois public sphere. Reason enables rational communication and discussion in the public sphere—a discussion conducted by educated and well-informed individuals. In Habermas's description of the bourgeois public sphere, there is little room for the emotional claims that we are accustomed to in the media today.

How did the bourgeois public sphere come about?

The starting point for Habermas's model of the bourgeois public sphere was the pre-modern public spheres, including the ancient '*bios politikos*'. This political sphere emerged when citizens in the ancient independent city–state gathered in the *agora* (a public meeting place) and participated in collective decision-making. In the ancient city–state, public life was separated from private life, yet they were mutually dependent. Dahlkvist (2003), a political scientist, argued that without women and slaves, who were part of the material production and reproduction of society and who performed their work in the private sphere, there would not have been free and virtuous White men who could reason in *bios politikos*. Willems (2023) provided a similar point by rereading Habermas's concept of the public sphere through a decolonial lens. She asked what it would look like to consider the preconditions of London's coffee houses and newspapers from the perspective of invisible and marginalised groups that provided the necessary infrastructure for these places to emerge. By exploring the silences of established canonical texts, she argued, we can critically engage with and decolonise knowledge (re-)production in a more radical way than considering race another prism of how to make sense of the public sphere (Willems, 2023).

From the ancient public sphere, Habermas derived the idea that a clear distinction between private and public was needed. The polis sphere is then the area of common affairs, and the oikos sphere is where private affairs take place and are negotiated. Departing from the ancient public sphere, Habermas addressed the feudal or aristocratic representative public sphere that emerged in the High Middle Ages (around 1100–1600). This feudal public sphere was characterised by the absolutist state and aristocracy. Here, the distinction between private and public disappeared.

Aristocrats' power was based on both private ownership and their disposal of it. At the same time, they acted as public authorities, creating laws and regulations for the courts. Public life consisted of the ruler presenting themselves to their people in processions, festivities and jousting. The aristocratic public sphere was thus designed to represent, display or demonstrate absolute power to the people. The people were audiences rather than participants in the public sphere.

As ownership and trade changed, the feudal order lost its importance. Trade connected the previously separate courts, while the bourgeoisie, as owners of land and means of production, increasingly gained power and space in society. The bourgeoisie, comprised of merchants, bankers, publishers, owners of manufacturing plants and so on, constituted a novel group that became both the addressee and the counterpart of state power. With the development of trade in goods, the transmission of information on markets, prices, raw materials, and so on, between the various trading centres became increasingly important. Trade and the importance of news transmission thus developed in tandem with each other. As trade spread, nation–states emerged, and they required a centralised state power with tax collection and a bureaucratic system that replaced the more personal and individualised power relations that prevailed under the old private property society (feudalism). With the emergence of the modern state apparatus, the distinction between the private and the public from the ancient era reemerged.

Why did the bourgeois public sphere disappear?

From the middle of the 19th century, an important change took place: the state became increasingly involved in private life. According to Habermas, with the emergence of the welfare state, more and more responsibilities that previously lay within family and private life were transferred to the state. The welfare state regulated citizens' private lives through, for example, various types of social insurance. Social reforms and the provision of support became a way for the state to regulate the lives of private individuals, thereby restricting their freedom, even if it also increased their security. In parallel with the emergence of state welfare institutions, increased centralisation and bureaucratisation meant that public debate was becoming less important and less influential in decision-making and governance processes. At the same time, the economic sector was growing and becoming more independent as capitalism evolved into more advanced forms. Therefore, companies gained power in society and began holding important roles in public life. Habermas quoted German sociologist Hans Paul Bahrdt, who described the process of change as follows:

> The industrial firms build apartments or even help the employee to become a homeowner; they organize concerts and theater performances, offer

104   *Anne Kaun*

continuing education classes; they provide for the elderly, widows and orphans. In other words, a series of functions originally fulfilled by institutions that were public, not only in the legal but also in the sociological sense, are taken over by organizations whose activity is non-public.

(Habermas, 1989, p. 154)

This development also contributed to the shift between the private and public spheres. Additionally, commercial interests were increasingly emerging in the symbolic sphere, which Habermas considered crucial to the deliberative public sphere, namely, the media. With the commercialisation of the media—especially the press—the public sphere was increasingly characterised by profit interests. Habermas argued the following:

On the one hand, to the extent that the press became commercialized, the threshold between the circulation of a commodity and the exchange of communications among the members of a public was leveled; within the private domain, the clear line separating the public sphere from the private [sphere] became blurred. On the other hand, however, to the extent that only certain political guarantees could safeguard the continued independence of its institutions, the public sphere ceased altogether to be exclusively a part of the private domain.

(Habermas, 1989, p. 181)

Regarding commercialisation, the audience developed from a culture-reproducing to a culture-consuming audience. In terms of the commercialisation of media, several researchers have described the increasing spread of tabloid journalism and infotainment formats. Commercialisation was thus often seen as a threat to journalism and, consequently, to democracy. The dominant view was that commercial journalism differed from traditional journalism in content and form. During the 1990s, the number of programmes and channels available increased, and the audience was fragmented as more niche programmes became available. In addition, new formats, such as reality TV (Hill, 2005), were emerging, and political programmes, interviews and debates with politicians were becoming shorter and reduced to so-called 'soundbite journalism' (Esaiasson & Håkansson, 2002; Rinke, 2016). With the emergence of an increasing number of privately owned, profit-driven media channels, the traditional news media also changed: the climate increasingly became one of adapting to what consumers, rather than citizens, wanted.

Habermas described commercialisation as a kind of refeudalisation of the public sphere. By this, he meant that the liberal public sphere reverted to being a representational public sphere, where the performance and display of power were at the centre rather than the exchange and discussion of rational arguments that led to the best solutions to common political problems.

Critical interpretations of the bourgeois public sphere

It was not until the 1980s that translations of *The Structural Transformation of the Public Sphere* allowed Habermas's ideas to spread internationally. The spread among international readers thus came long after Habermas published the book in German, and by then, he had further developed and revised certain ideas, especially in his theory of communicative action (Habermas, 1984; 1992).

However, as early as 1972, Oskar Negt and Alexander Kluge (also active in the Frankfurt School tradition) published an important critique and development of Habermas's theory of the bourgeois public sphere. They emphasised the importance of counter-publics or alternative public spheres and focused particularly on the public spheres of working-class organisations. According to Negt and Kluge (1972), publicness should be understood as a form of organisation of collective and social experience. They tried to develop an idea of publicness in a different social class than that of the bourgeoisie that reflected workers' experiences of a precarious life. They stressed the importance of considering the experience and organisation of workers because they were a majority in society at the time and constituted the class that most crucially contributed to the creation of value in the economy.

An important event in the international reception of Habermas's theory was a seminar at the University of North Carolina in Chapel Hill, USA, organised in 1989 in conjunction with the publication of the English translation. The participants included many key academics, such as Nancy Fraser, Michael Schudson, Nicholas Garnham and Craig Calhoun. During the seminar and in a subsequent edited volume, the participants formulated some of the most important critical engagement with Habermas's theory of the bourgeois public sphere. Nancy Fraser (1992), for example, was critical of the idea that there should be one single public sphere. Rather, she advocated a multiplicity of different publics competing with one another, a kind of pluralism of publics and counter-publics in which different communities emerge. This important critique, especially from a feminist perspective, points out that not everyone was included in the bourgeois public sphere and, in line with Negt and Kluge's (1972) argument, shows that marginalised groups need and create their own spaces and counter-publics where they can develop communities and formulate their interests.

Given the increasingly globalised world of the 1980s, Fraser (1992) also questioned the national character of Habermas's public sphere. She asked whether publics can and should emerge beyond the nation–state while wondering how far the civic public sphere extends. Not all citizens can meet face-to-face to exchange rational arguments and reach consensus. Fraser emphasised the importance of considering transnational publics, diaspora and global exchanges. She also emphasised that the public sphere is not only about consensus but mostly about conflicts, which are often unsolvable, even with rationality and reason (Fraser, 1992).

106 *Anne Kaun*

Another aspect raised was the feminist critique of the distinction between the private and the public. The motto 'the personal is political' expressed the view that the personal experience of, for example, domestic oppression is linked to social and political structures. The phrase was used by the feminist movement in the late 1960s and was an important starting point for politicising private life and making the role of women in maintaining the social order visible through, for example, invisible work in the home. The feminist critique once again emphasised how exclusionary Habermas's ideal public sphere was. It was mainly men who could participate and exchange rational arguments.

At the same conference, Nicholas Garnham (1992) emphasised the role and importance of public service media in large-scale modern societies. This was because it was (at least most of the time) free from commercial coercion and direction. According to Garnham (1992), public service media should be seen as an opportunity to revitalise and maintain the ideal that Habermas argued had existed for a short period before its decline began at the end of the 19th century.

Habermas (1992) revised some aspects of his theory in response to the criticisms made at the conference in the edited volume that was published later on. For example, he focused on new social movements that emerged in the 1960s and 1970s, which, according to him, shaped a new civil society based on grassroots movements that changed the relationship between the state and individual citizens. His earlier conceptualisation of the public and private spheres did not include a civil society of this kind.

The conference and the edited volume thus summarised many criticisms of Habermas's idea of the bourgeois public sphere. Notably, the criticisms came many years after the first publication, and Habermas himself emphasised that his thinking had developed in a different direction.

Another important development was his interest in the philosophy of language. This was already present when he developed the idea of the bourgeois public sphere, as it was based on deliberative and rational dialogue. He developed this thinking further in his comprehensive theory of communicative action (Habermas, 1981/1995a, 1981/1995b). The basic idea was that reason is not something objective or instrumental; rather, it is created and constituted in and through communicative action. Reese-Schäfer (1995) summarised the theory of communicative action as follows: to examine someone else's statement with regard to its truth, its normative accuracy or its veracity, one must first accept these claims as rational and valid (i.e. one must assume that the interlocutor is rational). Testing this statement can lead to negative results. However, the starting point of the exchange has to be, in Habermas's terms, communicative rationality. According to his theory, it is universal; all present and future societies must be measured by it. The basic idea that democratic societies are based on consensus reached through the exchange of rational arguments already characterised Habermas's theory of the bourgeois public sphere, but it was further developed here to theorise modernity as a whole.

A new structural transformation of the public sphere?

The seminar at the University of North Carolina in 1989 included a discussion of whether Habermas's theory of the bourgeois public sphere was still relevant in the 1980s. Today, one can ask whether the idea of a common public sphere still holds, especially considering that the public sphere is mainly mediated and that our media today are highly specialised, niche and increasingly personalised. There is discussion about filter bubbles, the polarisation of public debate and the importance of emotions rather than rational arguments to be convincing. It is said that rational arguments, information and knowledge do not have the same impact as they did before and that we live in an era of post-truth. In the context of this discussion, digital media and especially social media, are often presented as a breeding ground for the new irrationality and hyper-emotionalised public sphere. Can this be seen as an extension of the decay of the deliberative public sphere described by Habermas in the 1960s, or do new media enable new kinds of publics and exchanges?

As happens often, the answer is not a simple yes or no but rather an 'it depends'. Social media, in particular, has been highlighted in the discussion on how the public sphere has changed. In connection with the emergence of social media, the idea of a participatory culture and an ongoing democratisation of the public sphere was formulated. It was not only journalists, politicians and other so-called 'publicity professionals' who were visible but also so-called 'ordinary people' who could easily reach the mediatised public sphere. Jenkins (2006) described this development as participatory culture, which emerges as the means of media production become cheaper and easier to manage. The main idea is that everyone can produce media content and share it free of charge and in a creative way, which is both activating and inspiring. Jenkins (2006) argued that participatory cultures are a kind of popular culture that can be traced back to the 19th century. This idea of content produced and disseminated by laypeople fundamentally characterises social media today; it is their business model. Users pay through their activities and the data collected about them when using digital platforms—data that can be sold or used for marketing purposes. However, is this an example of a deliberative public sphere, as described by Habermas? Is it a place where rational arguments are exchanged to reach a consensus on political issues?

Indeed, Jenkins's (2006) idea of participatory culture is one way of describing the change, namely, as an improvement and democratisation as more people participate. However, many have argued that the positive potential of digital and social media platforms has been exaggerated in much contemporary research and debate (e.g. Iosifidis, 2010) and that they have instead become hypercommercialised echo chambers. The internet and social media are dominated by a few large corporations; instead of a diversity of voices, the powerful few are heard the most. In 2022, Habermas published a collection of recent texts and interviews in which he returned to issues of the public sphere and the relationship between media and democracy, which he had not addressed for

108 *Anne Kaun*

quite some time. In the main text of the collection, he discusses the contemporary media landscape and how the public sphere has changed yet again.

Habermas (2022) noted that we have a greater diversity of media channels. The public sphere is characterised by a larger supply and demand for opinions, arguments and beliefs. Neither the change in media offerings nor the change in audience does necessarily lead to critical and free opinion formation. However, the dissonance of messages and voices means that some media users are retreating to isolated echo chambers with like-minded people. In addition, the new public sphere is characterised by the hypercommercialisation of opinions and positions in the context of platform capitalism. Media platforms build their business models on the extraction of users' data while contributing to surveillance capitalism by tracking us and our social relations. Social media, according to Habermas (2022), leads to the further commercialisation and commodification of our lifeworld or everyday life, while the gatekeeping function of traditional media loses importance as we absorb news in other ways.

An important part of the change is the so-called 'audience turn' (i.e. the greater embedding of the audience in media production). This has contributed to the de-professionalisation of journalism; at the same time, journalism has come to be expected to provide a neutral and apolitical service. Instead of providing in-depth coverage and interpretation of social issues, newsrooms have become centres for data analysis and 'attention management'. For both commercial platforms and traditional media, the main task has become getting consumers' attention. They have simply become part of the attention economy. According to Habermas (2022), social media contribute to the emergence of spontaneously self-regulating and fragmented publics that are separate from the editorial and official public spheres. Within these fragmented publics, interpretations and positions circulate that become self-referential and confirm perceptions that are already dominant among the participants. Communication creates confirmation in small, fragmented groups that perceive their views as universal because they are not subject to counterarguments.

Social media also allows for uncensored communication with an anonymous audience. What emerges from this exchange is neither a public nor a private sphere but an inflated sphere that is similar to what could previously emerge from private correspondence. The participants in such a communicative sphere do not address issues of importance to society as a whole but private issues. Habermas (2022) stated that the entire political system is damaged if the infrastructure of the public sphere turns the attention of citizens away from important social issues that require joint decision-making. This is precisely what has happened, as the public sphere has lost the gatekeeping and agenda-setting function that allowed for a common understanding of societal problems that should be subject to a common solution. He therefore concluded his text with a plea for a media infrastructure that safeguards the inclusive and deliberative character of the public sphere and enables public opinion. He does not see this as a political position but as a constitutional necessity for democracy.

Conclusion

Social media promised to be a place for free dialogue regardless of background and resources, but its nature has changed since it first appeared. According to Habermas, rational arguments about socially important issues should be seen and discussed in public. Traditional journalism, especially in public service, has had this function, but social media platform companies have (to date) largely renounced their role as media and thus their responsibility to the public. Forums like Flashback that promise 'real freedom of expression' have instead come to be dominated by anti-democratic ideas. This does not contribute to the public sphere that Habermas described in 1962; rather, it does the opposite. As we have seen, the debate on the concept of the public sphere is far from over; the idea and the quest for a common public sphere are still alive and are perceived as part of the democratic organisation of society. There is a fairly broad consensus that the public sphere—whether plural or singular, consensus- or conflict-oriented, open and inclusive or separatist and radical counter-public—is an important part of democracy. However, exactly what it should look like and how it should be achieved are the subjects of many different opinions. Perhaps this discussion is like the public sphere itself; it is never complete or finalised. The discussion itself is a way of creating the public sphere by talking about and theorising it both within and outside academia.

Notes

1 *Mitläufer* is a term used to describe Germans that neither took a central position within the Nazi party and movement nor explicitly expressed critique. They rather marched with the mainstream.
2 Figure 7.1 shows that Habermas sees the bourgeois public sphere not as part of the private sphere but as a bridge between the private sphere and the spheres of public power. The public comprises a political public, a literary public and the city as a physical place where discussions take place.

References

Åkerlund, M. (2021). Influence without metrics: Analyzing the impact of far-right users in an online discussion forum. *Social Media+ Society*, 7(2), doi:20563051211008831.
Arendt, H. (1958). *The human condition*. University of Chicago Press.
Askanius, T., Kaun, A., Brock, B., & Larsson, A. (2024, forthcoming). 'Time to abandon Swedish women': Discursive connections between (violent) misogyny and white supremacy in Sweden. *International Journal of Communication*.
Dahlkvist, M. (2003). Inledning till Habermas, J. *Borgerlig offentlighet*. Arkiv förlag.
Esaiasson, P., & Håkansson, N. (2002). *Besked ikväll! Election programmes in Swedish radio and TV*. Stiftelsen Etermedierna i Sverige.
Fraser, N. (1992). Rethinking the public sphere: A contribution to the critique of actually existing democracy. In C. Calhoun (Ed.), *Habermas and the public sphere*. MIT Press, pp. 109–142.
Garnham, N. (1992). The media and the public sphere. In C. Calhoun (Ed.), *Habermas and the public sphere*. MIT Press, pp. 359–376.

110   *Anne Kaun*

Habermas, J. (1981/1995a). *Theory of communicative action. Vol. 1. Action rationality and social rationalisation.* Suhrkamp.

Habermas, J. (1981/1995b). *Theory of communicative action. Vol. 2, Zur Kritik der funktionalis- tischen Vernunft.* Suhrkamp.

Habermas, J. (1984). *Borgerlig offentlighet. Kategorierna 'privat' och 'offentligt' i det moderna samhället.* Archives.

Habermas, J. (1989). *The structural transformation of the public sphere: An inquiry into a category of bourgeois society.* Polity.

Habermas, J. (1992). Further reflections on the public sphere. In C. Calhoun (Ed.), *Habermas and the public sphere.* MIT Press, pp. 421–461.

Habermas, J. (2022). *Ein neuer Strukturwandel der Öffentlichkeit und die deliberative Politik.* Suhrkamp.

Hill, A. (2005). *Reality TV: Audiences and popular factual television.* Routledge.

Iosifidis, P. (2010). The public sphere, social networks and public service media. *Information, Communication & Society,* 14(5), 619–637.

Jenkins, H. (2006). *Fans, bloggers, gamers: Exploring participatory culture.* New York University Press.

Negt, O., & Kluge, A. (1972). *Öffentlichkeit und Erfahrung: Zur Organisationsanalyse von bürgerlicher und proletarischer Öffentlichkeit.* Suhrkamp.

Reese-Schäfer, W. (1995). *Habermas: An introduction.* Daidalos.

Rinke, E. M. (2016). The impact of sound-bite journalism on public argument. *Journal of Communication,* 66(4), 625–645.

Willems, W. (2023). The reproduction of canonical silences: Re-reading Habermas in the context of slavery and the slave trade. *Communication, Culture & Critique,* 16(1), 17–24.

8 Marshall McLuhan (1967) *The Medium Is the Massage*

Ingrid Forsler

Introduction

How can a text like *The Medium Is the Massage* be read? Anyone trained in reading academic texts by looking for the main argument, reading the headings to get a sense of the structure or looking at the reference list to understand the tradition in which it is written will soon realise that such methods are inadequate here. The book, which is subtitled *An Inventory of Effects*, was first published in 1967 and is a collaboration between Marshall McLuhan and designer Quentin Fiore that consists of cartoons, photographs, short texts and typographic experiments. How do you cite such a text? What is the main argument of an image? What methods are used to arrive at the results? Is it research at all?

According to media historian John Durham Peters, the answer to the latter question is *no*: 'One reads McLuhan for sparks, not scholarship' (Peters, 2015: 17). Media researchers keep returning to McLuhan's more academic texts for ideas and inspiration, but his oeuvre includes other productions as well, such as film, television appearances, sound recordings and textbooks. Much of this material was used as reference material in this chapter, as a concretisation of McLuhan's more enigmatic works. The extensive number of popular media productions featuring McLuhan and his ideas suggest that he can be understood not only as an academic but also as an educator and public intellectual. As such, he does not speak only to the scholarly community but also encourages all citizens to consider the relationship between media, humans and society. As Canadian film and media scholar Janine Marchessault (2008) writes, this makes McLuhan an early proponent of what is now referred to as 'media literacy'. This educational bias is particularly evident in *The Medium Is the Massage* (TMIM), which is clearly aimed at a wider audience, while simultaneously constituting a key or guide of sorts to McLuhan's other, perhaps less accessible, work. This chapter will thus approach TMIM primarily as a pedagogical text.

The Medium Is the Massage as an educational text and non-book

Every good teacher knows that the form in which you teach must match the content. A lecture on visual communication should include numerous images,

DOI: 10.4324/9781003432272-9

112 *Ingrid Forsler*

while a lesson on Socratic dialogue is probably best organised as a seminar based on conversation. From this perspective, TMIM can be understood as a way of communicating one of McLuhan's main theses: that the form of a medium is its actual message. Continuing this line of thought, a traditional book can only express linear thinking, while a collage of photographs, drawings and short texts can also demonstrate the effect of different media forms on the human mind. It is said that the original title of the book was 'the medium is the message', but a printing error turned the word *message* into *massage*. According to the story, McLuhan was so delighted by this misprint that he changed the title to 'the medium is the massage'. Whether this is the truth or one of the many myths surrounding McLuhan's life and work is difficult to say, but the present title has been interpreted as a tongue-in-cheek description of how different media process – or 'massage' – our senses.

For lack of a better word, TMIM has hitherto been referred to as a book. Based on McLuhan's definition of a book as a medium that prioritises linear thinking, individualism and contemplation, however, this is not an accurate description. This issue was pointed out by the semiotician Umberto Eco in his critical essay 'Cogito Interruptus' (1967), published later in the same year as TMIM, where he refers to the latter as a 'nonbook' with the argument that TMIM is not self-supporting but must be read in relation to McLuhan's other texts. For Eco, TMIM is merely a kind of illustration or appendix to McLuhan's then most recently published work, *Understanding Media* (1964). 'The trouble', writes Eco (1967: 232), 'is that *The Medium is the Massage*, to be completely understood, needs *Understanding Media* as a code'.

McLuhan himself did not object to this interpretation; he readily admitted that TMIM did not contain any new material but was meant to spark an interest in his other books (McLuhan, 1987: 339). It is also often stated that McLuhan was not particularly involved in the production of the book, with the project being more driven by the designer Quentin Fiore and the project manager Jerome Agel than by McLuhan. This adds a further dimension to the idea of TMIM as a non-book, since books – in addition to being self-supported and linear – are characterised by a clear division of roles between author, illustrator and publisher, which does not apply here. Copyright is also problematised in the text itself in a section that discusses how this idea is linked to the art of printing rather than the art of writing as such. Historically, books were produced by hand in monasteries and for a higher purpose; the idea of intellectual work as private property came later, with the possibility of mass production (McLuhan et al., 1967/2001: 122–123). In other words, the somewhat unclear conditions behind the production of TMIM can be seen as a kind of meta-commentary on the relatively new idea of copyright as related to the mass production of print media.

Instead of a book, TMIM can be regarded as a pedagogical illustration of a more comprehensive theoretical framework, almost like how a teacher uses a slide-show presentation to exemplify perspectives from the literature in a university course. Admittedly, McLuhan is a somewhat eccentric lecturer who

Marshall McLuhan (1967) 113

tends to diverge from the subject and is very fond of poetic metaphors, but he is also an entertaining one. Like Eco, many have described TMIM as a popularised light version of *Understanding Media*, whose first chapter is specifically named 'The medium is the message'. Visual culture researcher Kevin Brooks (2009), however, argues that TMIM – with its focus on consumer culture and media history – also contains elements from McLuhan's earlier works, *The Mechanical Bride: Folklore of Industrial Man* (1951) and *The Gutenberg Galaxy: The Making of Typographic Man* (1962). The next section will discuss the central arguments in TMIM, how they overlap with McLuhan's earlier books and how these texts can be read and used to understand the contemporary media landscape.

You and the media

One way to attract interest in a subject is to depart from the person listening or reading and try to answer the question they might ask themselves, namely: 'why is this relevant to me?'. Thus, in the name of pedagogy, TMIM starts from the reader, who is addressed in the opening chapter entitled 'You', followed by 'Your family', 'Your neighborhood', 'Your education', 'Your job', 'Your government' and 'The others'. The point of zooming out like this is to show how media cannot be isolated from everyday life, as it shapes every part of culture, society and our way of thinking. From this starting point, the rest of the book unfolds in three main sections or arguments:

1. Each media technology is an extension of our senses and prioritises different ways of thinking and understanding the world.
2. Each era in human history is characterised and conditioned by a particular media technology.
3. Therefore, to understand social and cultural change, we should study media as technologies rather than as content.

After a somewhat chronological presentation of these points, the reader is addressed again in the final pages of the book, with the rhetorical question 'and who are you?' (1967/2001: 153). This question is accompanied by an illustration from Lewis Carrol's children's book *Alice in Wonderland* in which Alice – the size of a mouse – meets a hookah-smoking caterpillar who asks this very question: who are you? The answer, which is another quote from Carrol's book, is displayed on the next page, where Alice explains that she cannot answer the question since she has undergone so many changes in just one day. This answer can be read as a summary of the book's main message: namely, that we cannot answer the question of who we are without first understanding the (media) environment in which we find ourselves and how it has developed historically. A catchier summary of this idea can be found on the back cover of the book, printed in capital letters: 'all media work us over completely'. The phrase is repeated a few pages into the book and developed:

114   *Ingrid Forsler*

> All media work us over completely. They are so pervasive in their personal, political, economic, aesthetic, psychological, moral, ethical, and social consequences that they leave no part of us untouched, unaffected, unaltered. The medium is the massage. Any understanding of social and cultural change is impossible without a knowledge of the way media work as environments.
>
> (McLuhan et al., 1967/2001: 26)

This statement might come across as bold. Is the impact of the media on human culture really this fundamental? Today, this passage would no doubt be seen as an example of unreflective technological determinism – the idea that all social change is caused by technology, downplaying human agency. The epithet is pejorative: no one refers to their own research as techno determinist. According to the German media theorist Geoffrey Winthrop-Young (2011: 125), calling others technological determinists is a bit like saying that they are into strangling cute puppies – an adequate reason to reject their arguments without further discussion. When the British cultural theorist Raymond Williams accuses McLuhan of technological determinism in his book *Television – Technology and Cultural Form* (1974) (see Chapter 12 in this volume), it is thus a fundamental criticism of McLuhan's theories, which – according to Williams – completely disregard the social and political aspects of media and media use (Peters, 2017: 18). In this debate, Williams represents a social constructivist stance, in which any effects of technology are viewed as being determined by social processes, not the other way around. Medium theory, the overarching media research tradition to which McLuhan belongs, has also been accused of technological determinism, which might explain why it has sometimes been overshadowed by other, more social constructivist, approaches.

McLuhan and medium theory

The term *medium theory* was first introduced by Joshua Meyrowitz (1995), who considered himself part of this tradition. Meyrowitz uses the term to describe researchers who are interested in the specific properties, or *biases* (Innis, 1951), of a medium and how they enable different kinds of communication, thinking and being. To a certain extent, Meyrowitz agrees with Williams that medium theory underestimates the role of financial and political interests in the historical development of media; however, he also points out that this disregard for the social does not imply a view of people as passive victims of technology. Rather, he argues, it highlights how technology prioritises certain types of content and use over others, which in turn has implications for power structures in society. As the form of a medium becomes more important than its content, this tradition has come to rely on an expanded definition of media that includes not only mass media but also other types of communication technologies such as money, clothing, buildings, transportation systems and electric light.

Marshall McLuhan (1967) 115

Meyrowitz identifies different generations of medium theorists, where the first generation was active from about 1950 to the mid-1980s; apart from McLuhan, he includes the literary scholar Walter Ong and the political economist and fellow Canadian Harold Innis in this generation. These seemingly different scholars were united through their interest in the relationship between social change and the emergence of new communication technologies, often centred around turning points in longer civilisation processes, such as the transition from spoken to written culture, the introduction of monetary economics or the invention of the printing press. It is worth noting that these theorists in 1950s North America were at one such turning point in history, as television replaced print media as the dominant mass medium. The shift from mechanical to electronic media coincided with other social changes such as economic growth, commercialisation, the expansion of school systems and an emerging youth culture. For McLuhan, who was clearly influenced by Innis' theories on how the stability or potential for change in each culture can be traced to its dominant communication technologies, it was television that created the conditions for these changes. For him, the shift from mechanical to electronic media represented a change as profound as the transition from spoken to written culture; more precisely, it represented a return to oral culture.

It may seem counter-intuitive that the increased popularity of television should mean the end of a visual era. 'But isn't television itself a primarily visual medium?' one might ask, just as journalist Eric Norden did in his interview with McLuhan for *Playboy* magazine in 1969. McLuhan replied to the question in his characteristically wordy manner by explaining why the opposite applies: while the misunderstanding that television is an extension of sight is understandable, television is in fact primarily an extension of our tactile senses, or touch. Television, he stated, is a cool medium that requires the viewer to fill in the missing information – unlike the radio or press, which are rich in information and require less involvement from the reader or listener. Television represents a new way of thinking and understanding the world from a more collective viewpoint in comparison with the detached and individualistic approach associated with written culture. The return to an oral culture thus involves exiting the visual or literary world of logic and linearity and entering an acoustic world, where everything happens simultaneously and is experienced through multiple senses. McLuhan concludes that this 'new' oral culture is different from the one that preceded written culture, since electronic media also enable oral communication over large distances, thereby shrinking the world.

In a 1970 lecture, McLuhan returned to the image of *Alice in Wonderland* to describe how revolutionary this change from visual to oral culture really is. Entering the acoustic world means suddenly finding yourself – like Alice – in a world where all the laws of logic seem to be suspended. In this situation, no wonder it is difficult to answer the question of who you are! One way to understand the importance attributed to television as a medium in the mid-20th century is to compare it with our own time, which is similarly characterised by a transition from electronic to digital media, and to reflect on the range of

116 *Ingrid Forsler*

social phenomena attributed to digitalisation in the public debate – from mental illness to world revolutions. Read from a pedagogical perspective, the assertive tone in TMIM can also be understood as a way to catch the interest of the reader. A good teacher knows how to simplify complex ideas and may even exaggerate at times to get a point across. One example of such an exaggeration is the quote above that opens with 'All media work us over completely'. Another is the almost over-explicit illustration of the shift from a visually oriented culture to an oral one on page 121 in the book, which shows a photomontage of a human face whose eye has been replaced by an ear.

The same predilection for exaggeration and provocation regarding the role of technology in culture can be found in the work of the German media theorist Friedrich Kittler (see Chapter 24 in this volume) who, to some extent, continued the legacy of medium theory from the 1980s onwards, although the agency Kittler attributes to technology is far greater than that in McLuhan's 'sophisticated' technological determinism (Williams, cited in Peters, 2017: 18). Kittler would never agree to the idea of media as extensions of humankind; rather, he argues that humans are an extension or consequence of technology (Winthrop-Young, 2011: 122). What unites McLuhan and Kittler, however, is their role as provocateurs in an academic climate in which 'technological determinist' and 'puppy strangler' are equally crude epithets. Both men deliver quotable one-liners to spur academic debate and highlight the dominance of social constructivist perspectives on media. In this sense, McLuhan and his successor Kittler are not only educators but also, as Peters (2017: 24) puts it, *trolls* whose statements should not be interpreted too literally. Kittler is more extreme than McLuhan in his understanding of the power of technology and argues that, since media constitute the very conditions for how we perceive the world, a critical scrutiny of them is impossible; in contrast, McLuhan clearly distinguishes between humans and technology and believes that there are ways to distance ourselves from the media in order to say something about it. In TMIM, this perspective is most evident in the sections dealing with media as invisible environments, where the authors discuss strategies to make visible the effects of media technologies on our senses.

The emperor's new clothes: media as environments and infrastructures

As mentioned in the introduction, one of the main arguments of TMIM is that we are surrounded by media technologies that condition our way of perceiving and being in the world. The way identity is shaped in relation to media is illustrated in the book through the different metamorphoses of Alice in her journey through Wonderland. To describe the elusive nature of the media environments that shape us, the authors use another popular children's story, *The Emperor's New Clothes* by Danish author H.C. Andersen. The story describes how a vain emperor is fooled by two swindlers, who claim they can weave the most beautiful fabric in the world and turn it into stunning clothes. They proceed to tell the emperor that this fabric has magical properties, as it is invisible to anyone who is either stupid or incompetent in their profession. No one in the kingdom dares to say that they cannot see the fabric the swindlers claim to be working on, and the emperor ends up posing naked before his people to show off his new clothes. Since no one in the assembled crowd wants to appear stupid, only a child dares to state the obvious: the emperor is naked!

In TMIM, this story is represented by a cartoon image of the naked emperor and a text that retells the end of the story (1967/2001: 88–89). The reason why the child dares to speak up about it, according to the authors, is that he or she has not yet adapted to the society or environment in which the emperor's words are law and is therefore able to perceive changes in the environment as they occur. For McLuhan, seeing and making visible what others take for granted is associated with the kind of maladjustment that can be found in art, poetry and humour, which often use defamiliarisation to encourage new ways of looking at the ordinary and habitual. The potential of art to make visible environments and their structuring properties, which otherwise tend to escape attention, is well summarised in this quote from TMIM:

> Environments are not passive wrappings, but are, rather, active processes which are invisible. The groundrules, pervasive structure, and overall patterns of environments elude easy perception. Anti-environments, or countersituations made by artists, provide means of direct attention and enable us to see and understand more clearly.
>
> (McLuhan et al., 1967/2001: 68)

The view of art as a kind of eye-opener partly motivates the design of the book, which predominantly consists of visual material and compilations of different types of media content. For a contemporary reader, however, the design of the book also illustrates how the familiar tends to become invisible in an unfortunate way, namely that McLuhan, Fiore and Angel seem blind to the sexism that permeated the culture in which TMIM was written. Throughout the book, fully or partially undressed female bodies appear without any real motivation or to illustrate random quotes, such as when a close-up of a pair of legs dressed in mesh tights and a photograph of a woman in a dress with the word 'love' on it (where the 'o' forms a hole in the fabric that exposes the stomach of the model) are juxtaposed with the text 'When information is brushed against information, the results are startling and effective' (1967/2001: 76–78). Ironically, in *The Mechanical Bride*, McLuhan discusses precisely this issue: that women's bodies are used to market and sell various goods and the importance of critically examining the assumptions – or, the invisible environment – that advertising constitutes. The fact that, just a few years later, women's bodies are used to sell TMIM can be interpreted as an acknowledgement of the motto that it is difficult, if not impossible, to stand completely outside one's own time, regardless of the method of investigation or means of expression.

McLuhan also made other statements that come across as deeply disturbing to a contemporary reader, and feminist media scholar Sarah Sharma describes

118 *Ingrid Forsler*

his texts as 'peppered with frequent misogynistic, racist, and nonsensical commentary' (2022: 3). One of the more disturbing examples is the previously mentioned *Playboy* interview, in which he discusses the indigenous population and black minority of North America as being essentially different from the white population. This can be understood as a symptom of the same issue revealed by the representation of women's bodies in TMIM: in the environment in which McLuhan lived and worked (i.e. North America in the 1960s), both sexism and structural racism were so embedded in the culture that he simply failed to recognise them. Understanding the context in which a text is written and how it is conditioned by the invisible norms of its time is a prerequisite for reading and making sense of older texts. Without letting McLuhan 'off the hook for being a man of his times', Sharma and others have shown that his theories can be used to approach questions of power and politics, even though McLuhan himself was not particularly interested in these questions (Sharma, 2022: 5).

Although the imagery of TMIM – as well as some of the metaphors and contexts associated with McLuhan – has not aged well, the same cannot be said of his interest in media as environments. On the contrary, the shift from electronic to digital media has reinforced the ontological properties of media. Digital media not only serve as transmitters of different messages but also increasingly structure how we perceive the world and organise our social lives. GPS and map services on smart phones have altered how we relate to places, translation apps have transformed how we perceive foreign languages, and the debate on 'screen time' has changed how we understand and structure everyday family life. It is probably even more difficult today than 50 years ago to distinguish the impact of a single medium on our culture or to understand the extent to which media orient our thinking and acting. This difficulty is partly due to the convergence of different media, which makes it hard to talk about television as one medium and the press as another, and there is a renewed interest within contemporary media studies in how media systems constitute invisible environments that underpin and structure our lives. According to a frequently cited definition, such *media infrastructures* are linked to practices, standards and classification systems that are learned and mastered within communities of practice and are invisible until they cease to function (Star & Ruhleder, 1996). Several of these characteristics are discussed in TMIM.

The book begins by discussing how the navigation of media environments – or, what contemporary media researchers would call infrastructures – is something that is learned within a particular community, particularly in professional life. 'Professionalism', the authors write, 'is environmental. [...] The professional tends to classify and to specialise, to accept uncritically the groundrules of the environment' (McLuhan et al., 1967/2001: 93). In contrast, the amateur seems to have the same role as the previously discussed artist, child, or comedian: namely, to make visible what has become so established in the environment that it is taken for granted. Here, the authors point to several interesting indications that are relevant to the contemporary digital media landscape, such as how professional roles are changing and specialising with regard to

Marshall McLuhan (1967)   119

digitalisation and how classifications are becoming increasingly important in our understanding of the world (see e.g. Star & Bowker, 1999). An example of this is the collection and processing of user data from various digital platforms, which is available only to a very limited professional group of data analysts. The categories used to sort and classify data are equally invisible to the ordinary user, although this classification is crucial to how the world is represented through big data.

Later in the book, the authors discuss how media infrastructures and technologies first become visible when they no longer function. Pages 148–149 portray an inverted spread from a New York Times article about a massive power outage that took place in the Northeastern United States in 1965, leaving over 30 million people without electricity for up to half a day. If the blackout had lasted longer, the authors argue, more people would have understood how electrical technologies shape, or 'massage', every aspect of our lives. In comparison, people today might only become aware of how often they use their smart phones when they visit remote areas without wireless coverage.

Scholars in this field often emphasise that infrastructures are based on already-established structures or systems and that, by studying these, it is possible to understand something about contemporary media environments. This concept is associated with the next theme in TMIM: drawing heavily on McLuhan's second book, *The Gutenberg Galaxy* (1962), the authors discuss different communication eras to explore how cultures emerge and change.

The future in the rear-view mirror

A spread in the middle of TMIM shows a collage of a rear-view mirror in front of a windshield. The background is a blurry photograph of what appears to be a highway tunnel with the taillights of another car in front. The rear-view mirror is located on the top of the picture and shows a silhouette drawing of a stagecoach pulled by four horses, with two people in cowboy hats on the coachman's seat (1967/2001: 74–75). The message is clear: we travel towards the future with our eyes fixed on the past, while the past – here represented by a stereotypical image of the 'Wild West' – is constructed in relation to the present.

One consequence of looking backwards, McLuhan argues, is that we tend to use new media technologies in the same way as old ones instead of utilising their medium-specific qualities. 'When faced with a totally new situation, we tend always to attach ourselves to the objects, to the flavor of the most recent past', as stated on the bottom edge of the collage (1967/2001: 75). But to understand new media and their transformative potential, it is necessary to first understand the relationship between older media technologies and the human environments they created. Pages 44–75 of TMIM therefore consist of a super-compressed review of different eras in the history of human communication (Brooks, 2009). This review starts with the transition from oral to written culture and discusses how the alphabet as a technology prioritises the visual at the expense of the auditory. By extension, the development of the alphabet brought

120   *Ingrid Forsler*

a shift from magical and emotional thinking to linear and rational 'step-by-step' thinking. The dominance of vision over other senses also led to a different way of understanding space, which was manifested in art through the central perspective. Whereas oral cultures depict what is known to exist in the world, similar to an X-ray or a child's drawings, artworks in written cultures only show what is visible from a certain viewing position – that is, an individual and distanced perspective on the world. The art of printing strengthened the dominance of the visual and manifested writing and reading as individualised practices. This typographic era was followed by the electronic era, in which TMIM was written. The authors argue that the electronic era is a return to an oral, non-spatial world where everything happens simultaneously. The *audience* of people with unique perspectives formed in the typographic era is here transformed into a *mass*.

The historicising part of TMIM described here contains some of the more innovative design experiments in the book, which both utilise and challenge the format of the book. Here, I return to the analogy of the book as a lecture, where the lecturer chooses to demonstrate the material through a short exercise when the audience starts to lose concentration. The lecture covers what has just been reviewed – namely, how the printed text prioritises individualism and a separation between different forms of knowledge – with express speed. This becomes clear particularly through the medium of the 'lecture' at hand (which is a book in which readers can immerse themselves). To regain the attention of the audience, the lecturer skips to the next slide in the presentation – that is, the next page of the book (1967/2001: 54). The only problem is that this page is impossible to read because its text is mirrored. The reader is then forced to go outside the intimate context of reader/book and involve some additional technology in order to see what the page says. Fiore probably intended for people to find a mirror and read the text there, but contemporary readers can just reach for their smart phones to photograph and then view the mirror image of the page.

This unexpected development in the interactivity of the book illustrates a central thesis in medium theory: namely, that technologies expand what is possible to know and see. In this case, smart phones with built-in cameras – which most people now carry with them wherever they go – offer an expanded perception in which reality is understood as two-dimensional images that can be manipulated at will. Once it becomes possible to read the backwards text, the reader finds that it is a quote from the educator John Dewey, who argues against the division of different forms of knowledge. This in turn points to McLuhan's interest in and his work's relevance to schools and education.

Media in/and education

As well as being a pedagogical text, TMIM contains several sections directly related to schools and education. In the introductory part, which is aimed directly at the reader, this is discussed under the heading 'Your education'. This chapter is a criticism of the gap between the school as an institution and the

Marshall McLuhan (1967) 121

media landscape in which a child is immersed outside school hours. Schools are compared to factories, where teachers break down knowledge into separate subjects and lessons instead of addressing more complex questions. Much of this criticism can be recognised in the current debate on education, which discusses how children should be able to develop 'future competences' in a school culture that is increasingly characterised by goal orientation and assessment (see e.g. Biesta, 2010). The discussion on education is resumed towards the end of the book where, interestingly, readers encounter a line of reasoning similar to the current debate, which contrasts the goal orientation in education with the changing labour market. Young people today do not want *goals* that prepare them for a specific occupation, the authors argue; they want *roles* and tasks that engage them (McLuhan et al., 1967/2001: 100).

McLuhan first discussed the idea of a holistic school and learning outside the classroom in the essay *Classroom without Walls* (1960) which he later developed with his colleagues in the book *City as Classroom* (1977). In these texts, McLuhan argues for a school that interacts with the new media culture and makes use of its technologies instead of treating them as mere disturbances. When teachers become isolated in their classrooms, it increases the distance between school and the reality of children and young people, warns McLuhan. He further points out that this separation is a relatively recent invention and that learning prior to the literacy culture took place mainly outside the classroom through observation and doing, while higher education during the same period was based on the spoken word. The first break came with written language, which was criticised by Socrates on pedagogical grounds because he believed it would impair the memory of students (McLuhan et al., 1967/2001: 113). Printing technology brought the next threat to the school as an institution and the beginning of an individualisation of learning (that is still ongoing), as it allowed students to have their own books instead of receiving all information from the teacher (McLuhan, 1960). Similar to how the printed book went from being a perceived threat to the school to becoming the medium around which learning is organised, McLuhan argues that we should utilise the potential of new communication technologies instead of shutting them out.

At the same time, it is important to note that McLuhan was far from being a technology evangelist; on the contrary, he was deeply pessimistic about the dominance of electronic media at the expense of books. The fact that different media prioritise different forms of knowledge and enable different types of learning is even more developed in the writings of media ecologist Neil Postman, who sharply criticised what he saw as a dismantling of serious education in favour of the superficial knowledge transmission offered by television (see Chapter 23 in this volume). While Postman argues that schools should act as a counterpoint to the surrounding media society by focusing on the written word, critical thinking, and deep knowledge, McLuhan argues that too great of a difference between school and everyday life can, at worst, make school seem meaningless to students. Being thrown from the collectivist and engaging world of television into an environment built entirely around the 'hot' medium of

122 *Ingrid Forsler*

books is too abrupt, McLuhan argues (Norden & McLuhan, 1969). By this, McLuhan did not mean that books should be thrown out of school; he was a trained literary scholar who often used examples and metaphors from literary history to illustrate his theses. Rather, he meant that educators must take electronic media seriously and study not only older art and culture but also contemporary media culture in schools and universities.

Interest in schools and media education is a common thread running through McLuhan's work. As early as 1959, he was commissioned by the US National Association of Educational Broadcasters (NAEB) to write a new media literacy curriculum for secondary schools. Although the curriculum was never used, it formed the basis for *Understanding Media* (1964), which in turn lent much of its material to TMIM (Marchessault, 2008). According to communication researcher and historian David Black, McLuhan's simultaneous interest in pedagogy and his experimentation with different media forms were no coincidence. To begin with, McLuhan viewed learning as an art, which – like other art forms – could provide a kind of anti-environment that makes the invisible appear. Secondly, McLuhan's ideas about how media extend and 'massage' our senses lose their meaning if communicated only through the visual medium of the printed text (Black, 2010). These two characteristics are especially evident in TMIM, making this book a perfect introduction or side reading to McLuhan's other, more academic work.

Concluding summary

My ambition with this chapter was to provide an overview of the arguments raised in TMIM, how the book is structured and how it relates to McLuhan's further production. This chapter suggests that readers should approach TMIM as a pedagogical intervention rather than as a conventional academic text. Although the book was written at a time when television was the dominant medium and home computers had not yet been introduced, there are good reasons to return to this book to understand something about the contemporary media landscape. The main argument of TMIM – that we live through and in media – is even more accurate in today's digital media culture than it was in the electronic culture of yesterday. The relevance of TMIM is also noticeable in media studies, where research areas such as infrastructure research, cultural techniques and media materiality are expanding and gaining increased scholarly interest.

Many have argued that history has proved Marshall McLuhan right when it comes to media development. It is less common to discuss his educational legacy. While it may seem disappointing that the relationship between schools and media has been discussed in almost the same way since the 1960s, McLuhan's wish that media should be studied seriously has undoubtedly come true. If you are reading this book, you are probably studying media at the university level, and the need for media literacy education for children and young people is now emphasised in educational contexts around the world. "Above all and in all and through all, Marshall McLuhan was a teacher" writes Walter Ong

(1981: 129). As such, he offered *new things* to think about, as well as *new ways* of thinking about the familiar. 'New things', in this case, are new media technologies, and 'the familiar' refers to the historically conditioned environments in which media are embedded. The 'new way' of understanding the familiar is to examine it precisely as environments, rather than as independent phenomena whose effects can be studied in isolation. The historical perspectives on media offered by McLuhan make up an important contribution to the field of media literacy by encouraging educators and students to look outside the present to understand more about the relationship between media, culture and society. Another of McLuhan's contributions is the experimental design of TMIM, which can be used as a starting point to advance visual and innovative pedagogies in media education.

References

Biesta, G. (2010). *Good education in an age of measurement: Ethics, politics, democracy.* Paradigm Publishers.

Black, D. (2010). McLuhan the teacher. *ESC: English Studies in Canada*, 36(2), 24–28.

Bowker, G. C., & Star, S. L. (1999). *Sorting things out: Classification and its consequences.* MIT Press.

Brooks, K. (2009). More "seriously visible" reading: McCloud, McLuhan, and the visual language of The Medium Is the Massage. *College Composition and Communication*, 61(1), 217–237.

Eco, U. (1986). Cogito interruptus. In U. Eco & W. Weaver (Eds.), *Travels in hyperreality: Essays.* Harcourt Brace Jovanovich, 221–238.

Innis, H. A. (1951). *The bias of communication.* University of Toronto Press.

Marchessault, J. (2008). McLuhan's pedagogical art. *Flusser Studies*, 6, 1–13.

McLuhan, M. (1951). *The mechanical bride: Folklore of industrial man.* Routledge & Kegan Paul.

McLuhan, M. (1960). Classroom without walls. In E. Carpenter & M. McLuhan (Eds.), *Explorations in communication.* Beacon Press, 1–3.

McLuhan, M. (1962). *The Gutenberg galaxy: The making of typographic man.* Routledge & Kegan Paul.

McLuhan, M. (1964). *Understanding media: The extensions of man.* Routledge.

McLuhan, M. (1970). Living in an acoustic world [Film]. Marshall McLuhan Speaks Special Collection. https://marshallmcluhanspeaks.com/lectures-panels/living-in-an-acoustic-world.

McLuhan, M. (1987). *Letters of Marshall McLuhan.* Toronto: Oxford University Press.

McLuhan, M., Fiore, Q., & Agel, J. (1967/2001). *The medium is the massage: An inventory of effects.* Gingko Press.

McLuhan, M., Hutchon, K., & McLuhan, E. (1977). *City as classroom: Understanding language and media.* Book Society of Canada.

Meyrowitz, J. (1995). Medium theory. In D. Crowley & D. Mitchell (Eds.), *Communication theory today.* Polity Press, 50–77.

Norden, E., & McLuhan, M. (1969, March). The Playboy interview: Marshall McLuhan. *Playboy Magazine.*

Ong, W. (1981). McLuhan as teacher: The future is a thing of the past. *Journal of Communication*, 31(3), 129–135.

124 *Ingrid Forsler*

Peters, J. D. (2015). *The marvelous clouds: Toward a philosophy of elemental media.* The University of Chicago Press.

Peters, J. D. (2017). "You mean my whole fallacy is wrong": On technological determinism, *Representations*, 140(1), 10–26.

Sharma, S. (2022). *Re-understanding media: Feminist extensions of Marshall McLuhan* (1st ed.). Duke University Press.

Star Leight, S., & Ruhleder, K. (1996). Steps toward an ecology of infrastructure: Design and access for large information spaces, *Information Systems Research*, 7(1), 111–134.

Winthrop-Young, G. (2011). *Kittler and the media.* Polity Press.

9 Michel Foucault (1971) *The Order of Discourse*

Annika Egan Sjölander

Introduction

The French philosopher and historian of ideas Michel Foucault (1926–1984) begins his inaugural lecture at the Collège de France in Paris on a December day in 1970 by wishing that he could just have slipped himself surreptitiously into the talk [discours] that he was about to give. But Foucault's wish was not only for that particular instance, but also applied to all those that he should "have to give here, perhaps for many years to come" (Foucault, 1981:51). His difficulty in beginning his speech is linked to a desire to try to escape the weight of the tradition of the institution, or in other words, the ever-compelling order or power of discourse. The title of his lecture, "L'ordre du discours", aptly enough treated this phenomenon, *The Order of Discourse*, and was first published in 1971. In this speech, also a thirty-page paper, Foucault presents the main features of his vision of discourse analysis. It presents the reader with a summary of an entire framework of discourse analysis, including not only theoretical insights, but also practical guidelines regarding how to conduct concrete studies. This is one of the text's great advantages, in addition to being written by the man often referred to as the "father" of discourse analysis.

The global debate of our time regarding the widespread problems caused by climate change, as well as the often controversial proposals regarding society's efforts to counteract these effects, can all be said to belong to the climate discourse. This discourse includes all speech about climate change issues, in both public and private spaces, as well as the practices and institutions that generate and support such speech. While Foucault himself did not experience the post-2007 period, when the problems of climate change were seriously established on society's agenda, his understanding of discourse suggests that climate discourse, like other discourses, though vast, multifaceted and involving numerous actors, nevertheless constitutes a distinctive and delimiting practice. It limits our understanding and knowledge of the phenomenon in question. There are thus always perspectives that do not fit in, views that are discarded before they are even heard. These views are, as a rule, often difficult to discern or detect. However, the Swedish climate activist, Greta Thunberg, when aged just 16, has had a remarkable impact in a brief time on the content of climate change

DOI: 10.4324/9781003432272-10

discourse, not only in Sweden but also globally. Her decision to strike outside the Swedish parliament on Fridays, for the well-being of the climate, has in itself set a precedent for other students, and launched the global movement #FridaysForFuture. Using popular social media sites such as Facebook, former Twitter (now X) and Instagram, has brought together hundreds of thousands of young people, from across the world, who share a concern for the climate, and demand that adults take more action. For this reason, they have joined Greta Thunberg in a school strike, to pressure politicians to act faster to achieve the Paris Agreement's goal of keeping global warming to a maximum of 1.5 degrees Celsius. The exceptional power of Thunberg's advocacy in today's climate discourse, is illustrated by all the crucial meetings which she has addressed, and all the influential individuals and world leaders whom she met in only her first year of campaigning. The UN climate summit COP24 in Poland, the World Economic Forum in Davos, the Pope, the European Parliament in Strasbourg and the British and French parliaments: Thunberg has addressed them all. She has even been nominated for the Nobel Peace Prize. A young person, a child as she called herself then, never could have been invited to the seats of global power, and asked to speak, without extensive media coverage in both traditional and social media. They have generally reported positively on her initiative, and supported her protests with various types of comments about the campaign. Greta Thunberg's extraordinary ability to address, as well as engage, the audiences she has met in her speaking tour is also crucial to her impact. And, nevertheless, the critique she levels on the world of adults is withering. Yet, in the wake of her success, several selected critiques, published in the media and directed at Thunberg as a person, exemplify something Foucault might have called "counter-power". In one example, she is described as mentally disturbed, while a second complains that compulsory schooling is neglected during the strikes.

The notion of discourse

Let us now return to the text of *The Order of Discourse* and the framework of discourse analysis that Foucault outlines for us. To begin with an understanding of discourse itself, it is, as mentioned, a distinctive and delimiting practice, not to mention one with very tangible material consequences. For example, our way of speaking about, and understanding, the problem of climate change has an impact on our actions. A discourse is further understood as all written and spoken phrases or utterances about a certain phenomenon, including the whole practice that produces these statements. Otherwise, in everyday speech, the word discourse is usually used in the sense of conversation, statement and speech. This is true here as well, but, for Foucault, discourse also means something more. It involves an entire arrangement of conversations, statements and speeches about different phenomena and concepts that together form a whole, a discourse. Foucault (1981:52) states bluntly: "We know quite well that we do not have the right to say everything, that we cannot speak of just anything in any circumstances whatever, and that not everyone has the right to speak of anything whatever". Here precisely lies the interest in reflecting on the extraordinary attention paid to Greta Thunberg. Discourses shape our understanding of the world and each other. Discourses also set limits to it. As individuals we cannot completely escape their power however much we wish to do so, not even as researchers. We are inevitably part of discourses, although a certain degree of resistance may be possible. What regulates a discourse, according to Foucault, is a set of rules of exclusion.

The study of discourse, therefore, is not about analysing an abundant stream of words. Discourses, according to Foucault, seek to avoid the appearance of being out of the ordinary. They appear natural and inherent. "Thus discourse is little more than the gleaming of a truth in the process of being born to its own gaze" in Foucault's (1981:66) own words. The discourse easily escapes even the researcher's perceptive gaze. However, that the discourse eludes the analyst should not be interpreted to mean that a researcher must seek to get behind, or beyond, the discourse. There is nothing to be exposed or unlocked. Foucault asserts that no hidden underlying structure exists to be discovered. A discourse's regularity rather appears in its articulations, in the concrete practice. Discourse is shaped by what is before our own eyes. The researcher's archaeological task is to seek to identify the rules shaping statements in such a way that they can be perceived as legitimate and true. What knowledge does the discourse produce? The genealogical task that follows requires an examination of the workings of this process. What conditions enable this situation, this particular order of discourse?

One question, which many ask when they begin work with discourse analysis, regards the boundary of discourse. Is anything beyond or outside of discourse? Here Foucault is somewhat ambiguous. More often than not, he emphasises that we are enclosed within discourses, that we cannot escape their power. Yet, in places, his texts hint at something beyond the discourse, the nature of which is difficult to pin down. Those following Foucault work from both interpretations (Egan Sjölander, 2011). In critical discourse analysis, several scholars also speak of the "non-discursive". The philosophical school known as critical realism, which influenced Norman Fairclough, for example, adopts this approach. Here, the researcher strives to approach the outer limit of discourse, even if it is rarely possible to pass completely beyond it. On the other hand, in discourse theory as formulated by Ernesto Laclau and Chantal Mouffe, reasoning regarding any such a "limit of discourse" is difficult to find. This more radical post-structuralist approach argues instead that we should recognise that such limits are illusions. However, this reasoning is not to be interpreted as meaning that discourses have no material significance. Rather, the point is that even physically tangible phenomena, such as earthquakes, receive meaning and become comprehensible as we use words to describe them. All meaning-making is therefore discursive.

128 *Annika Egan Sjölander*

Discursive control mechanisms

In *The Order of Discourse*, Foucault identifies several common processes, described as "procedures for exclusion" or control mechanisms operating on the content and form of any discourse. He proceeds to describe three external and three internal control mechanisms. These, in turn, are useful guidelines in the study of discourse. The first external control mechanism concerns the forbidden word. Firstly, in every discourse there are taboos, that is, topics, angles and perspectives that must not be mentioned, and which are completely excluded. At first glance, these may be difficult to detect, because these limitations are often normalised. But by wondering what is unsaid in a given context or what ought to have been included in a discussion, you will go a long way. Adopting a historical perspective, along with Foucault, permits the discursive changes over time to make visible what is currently excluded. Comparisons between related discourses can also be a good starting point for analysis vis-à-vis other meaningful comparisons, for example of similar situations or phenomena in other countries, regions, and so on. As regards the climate discourse and the case of Greta Thunberg, a taboo can be said to have been broken since she as a child, in a way far from the ordinary, speaks out and hold adults accountable for the problems they are causing future generations. This perspective was largely invisible in the past, which also shows the changing nature of discourses. Secondly, rituals are created for different occasions, which also cull the actors in a discourse. Any person seeking to participate and contribute to a debate, for example, must be well aware of the situation, as violations are regularly exposed. Thunberg has, as mentioned, done a fine job of decoding rituals in different contexts, and this has contributed to the success of her appearances. The particular customs and practices shaping a specific discourse are subject to analysis, as well as the question of transgressions, that is, when are rituals not observed, and transgressions noticed? The third control mechanism or procedure concerns the space for speech and the privileged subject. Not everyone can assume the right to speak or occupy space. Foucault (1981:52) describes this as "the privileged or exclusive right of the speaking subject". Every discourse includes some individuals who feel they have and are attributed this right, and others who do not. The question for analysis may be: Can we identify these subjects? And further: What similarities and differences exist between privileged subjects and those subordinated to the particular order of discourse? In Thunberg's various appearances, she herself repeatedly describes her choice to speak out on climate change despite being a child, as the only possibility, given the alarming consequences that would follow failure to enact radical change.

The second external control mechanism, raised and discussed by Foucault, is that of division and rejection. He argues that discourses operate on the principle of distinguishing, for example, the true from the false, the sane from the mad, the good from the evil, and the normal from the abnormal. This hierarchical sorting, with a clear superiority and subordination, regulates speech and shapes our understanding of phenomena and the world at large. Such divisions, as well

Michel Foucault (1971)   129

as an either/or mindset that values one while discarding the other, have shaped, according to Foucault, our knowledge for a very long time, and in many areas. Flying and eating meat are two types of actions repeatedly repudiated in climate discourse, since both entail emitting large quantities of carbon dioxide.

The third and final external control mechanism regulating discourse, according to Foucault, is an overarching – his words – "will to truth". This involves the exaltation of the true and the rejection of the false. The will to truth touches something fundamental in our modern culture, shaped since the Enlightenment, in which science has a special place as a "producer of truth". Foucault writes:

> Certainly, when viewed from the level of proposition, on the inside of a discourse, the division between true and false is neither arbitrary nor modifiable nor institutional nor violent. But when we view things on a different scale, when we ask the question of what this will to truth has been and constantly is, across our discourses, this will to truth which has crossed so many centuries of our history; what is, in its very general form, the type of division which governs our will to know (notre volonté de savoir), then what we see taking shape is perhaps something like a system of exclusion, a historical, modifiable and institutionally constraining system.
>
> (Foucault, 1981:54)

The analysis of how the will to truth manifests itself in a discourse can be placed or undertaken on a more general level than the other external control mechanisms, that is, prohibition, division and rejection. Here it is often useful to study the institutional support for the "truth production" of discourse, including its distribution. In modern (western) societies, science has a particularly high status and much power as a producer of truth, but other (knowledge) institutions, which also strive for objectivity, neutrality and independence, are also of importance. Authorities is one example. Journalism another. If we analyse the climate discourse again, science predominates as a producer of truth, supported by other institutions, such as government authorities and the news media.

Alongside these external control mechanisms, there are also various internal procedures for controlling the content and form of discourse, as Foucault indicates. These include the classification, organisation and distribution of meaning-making, and are provided through what Foucault describes as the role of commentary, the author function and the organisation of the discipline (or discourse). Restrictions on discourse are thus not only imposed from the outside, but also exert control from within. Discourses regulate themselves according to Foucault.

The role of commentary in a discourse is, first of all, to recite or reiterate the content of discourse on its own terms. This constitutes nothing less than the familiar in a discourse, the already known which is recited or repeated by the commentary. In this way, the role of commentary in a discourse may seem unimportant, even banal. But this overlooks the fact that the repetition of

130   *Annika Egan Sjölander*

certain views and perspectives simultaneously reinforces them, making them more plausible and seemingly more "true". The moment something is repeated, other views and alternatives fall into oblivion. The role of the commentator in a discourse can easily remain invisible, because it does not seem to offer any perspective of its own, but only puts forward what others have already said. At the same time, Foucault reminds us that the effects of commentary can be significant. Journalists often adopt the role of commentators in various discourses, that is, not taking any position of their own, but only giving voice to others, like politicians or various experts. Government officials, including communications managers, also have a commentator-like role in many issues they address on professional terms. In their exercise of official authority, they must remain neutral and independent, and may not promote their own views. In many ways, the #FridaysForFuture movement's campaign adopts the role of a communications manager in relation to science. Those engaged in the movement rely on its representatives, and strive to put forward the views of climate scientists.

As regards the author function as a mechanism of deletion in a discourse, this function operates within the discourse, as the term itself indicates, and not necessarily as something strictly associated with or reserved for certain individuals. In the essay "What is an author?", Foucault (1998) argues that, by studying a discourse's author function, a researcher can interpret the discursive movements somewhat more easily than if one were to study themes or concepts within a discourse. The author function further contributes to the internal order of a discourse by accounting:

> for the unity of the texts which are placed under his name. He is asked to reveal or at least carry authentification of the hidden meaning which traverses them. He is asked to connect them to his lived experiences, to the real history which saw their birth. The author is what gives the disturbing language of fiction its unities, its nodes of coherence, its insertion in the real.
>
> (Foucault, 1981:58)

At the same time, Foucault (1981:58) stresses that not all discourses necessarily contain the author function, since there are "plenty of discourses which circulate without deriving their meaning or their efficacity from an author to whom they could be attributed". This question must therefore be examined on a case-by-case basis. The author function varies according to what epoch and what type the discourse belongs. However, the individual Greta Thunberg has clearly been assigned an author function in the climate discourse. From the stance of the child, a clear way forward is formulated that concerns the adult world regarding the unfulfilled promises of the Paris Agreement. The author function also signals that the discourse is something that matters.

> ...the fact that the discourse has an author's name, that one can say "this was written by so-and-so" or "so-and-so is its author," shows that this discourse is not ordinary everyday speech that merely comes and goes, not

something that is immediately consumable. On the contrary, it is a speech that must be received in a certain mode and that, in a given culture, must receive a certain status.

(Foucault, 1998:211)

The organisation of disciplines is the third internal control mechanism identified by Foucault that limits the production of meaning in discourse. Having principally studied different sciences, it was natural for him to focus on the organisation of academic disciplines. For those who study other phenomena, the reasoning can instead be transferred, at least in part, to the organisation of the discourse at hand. The mechanisms within a given discourse that Foucault (1981:59) identifies as pivotal are the definition of the object domain, the methods whose use is permitted, and a "corpus of propositions considered to be true" within a given discourse. In an analysis of the organisation of the discipline, or that of a discourse, it is therefore important to try to identify how phenomena are defined and what is said to belong or not, what methods of understanding the phenomenon are accepted or not, and what statements about the phenomenon are regarded as unproblematic, that is, natural or "true". Even for those not studying a scientific discipline, the phenomenon or discourse that interests one also often constitutes, or at least can be related quite easily to, a specific field of knowledge. The discourse also helps to produce so-called truths regarding the phenomenon in question. It is therefore crucial to ask not only how knowledge is produced in the discourse in question, but also what organisation is behind this particular production of meaning. Here, once more, the close interconnection of power and knowledge in Foucault's way of thinking becomes visible. Advocating and defending scientific knowledge and institutions, like in the climate discourse, is fairly unproblematic in many countries like, for example, Sweden, at least if compared to, for instance, the situation in the United States or Australia when climate change is discussed.

The analysis of the external and internal control mechanisms of discourse belongs to an archaeological approach and, according to Foucault, should always be combined with a genealogical investigation. Central to this process is the question of a discourse's conditions of possibility. As a researcher, we should therefore ask ourselves: What makes this discourse possible? On what conditions, terms and preconditions does this discourse rest? This requires an abundance of interpretive work by the individual researcher. The climate discourse example, including the so-called "Greta Thunberg Effect", presupposes, among other things, a mediatised society in which climate change issues are taken seriously, both by decision-makers and the population at large. Science's relatively high status is also key. The same applies to the belief in the ability of individuals to make a difference, and influence major events. The general perception of children as uncorrupted truth tellers also plays a role.

When all this analytical work is done, the elements of discourse analysis which Foucault identifies as the most essential will hopefully have been addressed. In sum, Foucault states that firstly, it is important to question the

132 *Annika Egan Sjölander*

will to truth, secondly, to restore to the discourse its character as an event and thirdly, to lift the sovereignty of the signifier. A discourse's truth effect can then, at least to some extent, be relativised, its contingency be made visible and what is naturalised also be questioned.

The discourse-analytic research programme Foucault outlines, in his inaugural lecture, also contains other interesting concepts useful in the study of discourse and meaning-making processes. Events and series constitute one such pair of concepts that can also help to break up the researcher's habitual patterns of thinking, for example as regards cause and effect. But there are many others. And while it may be impossible even for researchers to escape the power of discourse, we might nevertheless, as Foucault himself describes so well in this text, imagine that the power of discourse analysis can be brought to bear against the otherwise coercive order of discourse. These, in any event, were the thoughts he sowed at that time, and many of the seeds are still germinating.

What is an author?

That Foucault has come to be crowned the "father of discourse analysis" may seem an ironic epithet, as he quarrelled a great deal with our culture's predominant ideas regarding authorship and originality. He questioned how the content and form of texts can be said to have originated in the thoughts and consciousness of individuals (that is to say, geniuses). Foucault (1998) highlighted instead, how the creation and meaning of texts are closely linked to the specific social contexts or concrete contexts from which they emerge. In this sense, Foucault can be said to dismantle or deconstruct the traditional notion of the author as the original source for the meaning of what is written or expressed. The approach he presents instead decouples the authorial subject from the "product", that is, the texts. Foucault speaks of different functions of discourse that produce speech and writing. The author function is thus one such function, which can be taken up by different individuals at different times depending on the situation, conditions and requirements. In philosophical terms, Foucault can be said to criticise the then-prevalent modern notion of the subject, as described in the philosophy of mind, which strongly emphasises the individual's thought and his or her own mental processes in creation. The view of the unique role of the novelist, the scientist and the investigative journalist in relation to their work thus changes. However, Foucault is not alone in offering this alternative perspective. In the late 1960s, the crucial role of contextual factors in meaning-making, was increasingly linked to the whole so-called linguistic turn in the humanities and social sciences. The seminal book, written by Peter Berger and Thomas Luckmann (1991), describing how individuals perceive and their social reality gets shaped, was first published in 1966: *The Social Construction of Reality*. The book coined a now-ubiquitous phrase: the "social construction of reality". This perspective aims to recognise that meaning, for phenomena, is always constructed in relation to the specific historical, cultural, social and economic context from which it emerges. The meaning of X is thus never fixed,

Michel Foucault (1971)   133

as contexts vary (see also Chapter 16 in this volume). To return to Foucault, his extensive historical investigations have shown, in one field after another, how dominant views of different phenomena have varied from time to time. The seemingly normal is thus relative. This applies, for example, to a culture's view of madness or insanity (Foucault, 2001). Another example is views of the body, the healthy and the sick and what should and can be cured, as well as how this is best done (Foucault, 1975). A third example is the view of what is criminal and to be punished in a society, as shown, among other things, by the birth of the modern prison (Foucault, 1991). Foucault's last major work, planned as a six-volume history of sexuality, is a further example.

Foucault's different periods

Foucault's great significance for posterity is palpable. For at least fifty years, he has been among the most widely read thinkers. This "outsider", as he is sometimes termed, manages to capture, fascinate, infuriate and disorient his readers. *The Order of Discourse* (1981) is no exception, though its limited scope, thanks to the nature of a speech, sharpens its focus, and prevents the text itself from being baggy. Foucault's (1972) important preparatory work, in the form of the book, *The Archaeology of Knowledge*, in which he presents his methodological archaeological approach in greater detail, is much more extensive and ornate, as well as ambiguous. This work also developed arguments, for example as regards the central notion of discourse, which Foucault also refers back to and builds on in his inaugural lecture.

A thought that is constantly in motion is otherwise Foucault's hallmark, as is his lively wordplay. Foucault's writing is often divided into different periods, namely the early archaeological and the subsequent genealogical period. The analysis of different systems of knowledge throughout history, conceptualised as episteme, belongs to the initial archaeological phase of Foucault's scholarship. In terms of epistemological perspectives, his approach is described as structuralist here. The idea that each historical epoch is shaped by a dominant regime of knowledge, an episteme, is such a structuralist trait. The archaeology of knowledge also formulates in large part the very essence of the discourse-analytic edifice as it is articulated in *The Order of Discourse*.

Foucault's genealogical studies, carried out and published after *The Order of Discourse*, and which include *Discipline and Punish* (Foucault, 1991), on the birth of the modern prison and originally published in 1975, came to be seen as examples of Foucault as a poststructuralist, or even a postmodernist. Here he consistently applied a social-constructivist approach. By this time, Foucault had also clearly distanced himself from Marxism, which strongly influenced the perspectives of many of his contemporaries, as regards understandings of society and its development.

The Swedish Foucault scholar and sociologist, Mats Beronius (1991:44), describes genealogy as an ambition to "be able to describe the development of a phenomenon or event in order to make it comprehensible in a more everyday sense". Beronius continues:

134   *Annika Egan Sjölander*

> Genealogy is a method that seeks to understand the soil from which, for example, the modern man comes, and in which she lives still. When one is interested in genealogy, one is interested in the structures, practices, institutions or ideas that influence the present. The genealogist asks, not what actually happened in the past, but rather what still lives from that time, and in what particular way is it alive.
>
> (Beronius, 1991:50)

The form of discourse analysis which Foucault describes in *The Order of Discourse* puts forth both an archaeological and a genealogical approach. It is therefore important that researchers use both approaches in their work. As concerns genealogical analysis, it is most important for a researcher to focus on the question of what conditions of possibility are presupposed by any given discourse. Because it is only then, that what is taken for granted in any specific discourse can be relativised. The possibility arises to question what seems normal, including the conditions that must be met for this to be the case. Much of the explosive power of discourse analysis lies precisely here, in showing the changeability, or contingency, of what seems inherent and fixed. Another important element, in any Foucault-inspired discourse analysis, is to wonder what historical ties can be linked to the discourse under study, and/or to the present. What relationships appear to have broken down over time? What possible links are missing? What conditions and phenomena have changed over time, and how? These genealogical reflections are thus made in parallel with, or following, the archaeological excavations of a studied discourse. In the latter, the researcher is engaged in trying to identify how different control mechanisms in a discourse operate.

Power and knowledge

During his later genealogical period, Foucault largely focused on detailed empirical investigations of the modern society's institutions and their emergence, what one might call the discursive practices, including their potential power over the individual. But Foucault was also interested in various forms of counter-power and resistance. Foucault's revolutionary way of conceptualising power is, incidentally, one of his great scholarly contributions. Rather than thinking of power as a property, something that person A has, which he can exercise over person B, Foucault (2000) advocated a position understanding power as relational. Power is present in all relationships and productive, and cannot be understood merely as subordination, something negative. Foucault (1980) also shows in his writings, quite usefully, how closely linked power and knowledge are.

Despite the fact that his conception of power is one of Foucault's lasting imprints on the history of science, he himself, somewhat surprisingly, in an interview with colleagues at the University of California, Berkeley, claimed that, in fact, power and the exercise of power did not really interest him.

Rather, his main interest has always been the subject and its creation. That is, the human or the individual (as distinguished from the collective). This type of query also emerges most clearly in the last, so-called "third" period of Foucault's work, identified by some in his collected scholarly output. The human body is central here, as are all kinds of societal disciplinary powers, to which people are subject due to external as well as internal pressure, such as self-discipline. Science also works in service of this kind of power. Biopolitics, in simple terms the way modern society or the state controls life itself and the human body, including both physical and mental health, is one of the most central objects of study for Foucault. He developed the concepts of biopower and biopolitics, which have been used extensively in his wake, often in conjunction with arguments about governance, or so-called "governmentality". In brief, this concept is applied to describe how we conceive of managing others and ourselves in various contexts. In a seminar, given at the University of Vermont in the United States only two years before his death, Foucault explains regarding knowledge, technologies of the self and the modern man's self-care and control, that:

> My objective for more than 25 years has been to sketch out a history of the different ways in our culture that humans develop knowledge about them-selves: economics, biology, psychiatry, medicine and penology. The main point is not to accept this knowledge at face value but to analyze these so-called sciences as very specific "truth games" related to specific techniques that human beings use to understand themselves.
>
> (Foucault 1988:17–18)

While most descriptions divide Foucault's work into distinct periods, typically an early, archaeological period, followed by a genealogical period, it is easy to discern the common threads running through his entire scholarly output. Thoughts recur and, above all, are deepened and developed with time. At the same time, paradoxically, the richness of his writing belies any attempt at simple categorisation, and the reader is often left with the feeling that the text is ambiguous. This is also the attraction of reading Foucault in the original. *The Order of Discourse*, formulated in the midst of a transitional period, as well as a time when the roof beams of his scientific edifice were largely in place, communicates very much of the "everything" in his scholarly message. Therefore, it is well worth reading.

Foucault's significance

Having familiarised ourselves with the elements of the discourse-analytic research programme outlined by Foucault in his inaugural lecture, as well as with the various phases of his scholarly career, it is now appropriate to briefly summarise his significance for today's social scientists, as well as the humanities at large. This is especially relevant for discourse analysts, but also for media

136 *Annika Egan Sjölander*

and communication scholars more generally. As mentioned, Foucault's success is closely linked to the linguistic turn in the humanities and social sciences. This turn involved an emphasis on the role, and crucial importance, of language in the human perception of reality and the understanding of various phenomena. Thus, communication in different forms, both mediated and interpersonal, drew increasing attention from scholars. Foucault also provided an alternative to historical materialism or Marxism. At the same time, he retained a well-developed conflict perspective in his theoretical work, which remains important. Meaning-making and discourse, per Foucault, are always formed through struggle. Also, they are always imbued with power. Discourse analysis offers research tools to address this constant creation of meaning, and to better understand how our access to the world is shaped and changed in and by discourse. Language is thus not seen as a mere medium: it is precisely in language, in the production of meaning, that struggles are won and lost. The secondary Foucault literature often stresses the applicability of his concepts and approaches. They can be used in concrete empirical analyses. But, as with many other continental thinkers, not least in the French intellectual tradition, his language is colourful, and far from simple. We may learn about methods of scientific analysis, as we do in *The Order of Discourse*, but these are not set out in the form of simple guidelines or concrete handbooks to be followed. An active approach, on the part of discourse analysts, to the framework and interpretive work is assumed when designing specific studies.

For anyone interested in discourse analysis, Foucault's texts are almost unavoidable. In principle all influential discourse analytic thinkers in his wake, including those in media and communications studies, have built on Foucault's contributions in their own work. I am thinking, for example, of the trio of leading critical discourse analysts, namely Norman Fairclough, Teun van Dijk and Ruth Wodak, who shaped this approach from a strong sociolinguistic base. Each of them has also studied concrete media discourses, often on racism, as well as communication in the form of the interaction of individuals in groups, such as conversations between doctors and patients. Media discourse (1995), by the British professor Norman Fairclough, has long been popular course literature in media and communications studies in Europe and elsewhere. It includes a three-dimensional model for discourse analysis that is specially adapted for modern (mass) media, which many students have since used. Text, discursive practice and socio-cultural or social practice are three distinct levels that should all be studied, according to Fairclough. Glancing at Fairclough's definitions of his own core concepts, including discourse, discursive practice and discursive order, he too leans heavily on Foucault.

The post-Marxist discourse theorists Ernesto Laclau and Chantalle Mouffe are another influential pair of scholars actively engaged with Foucault in their work. They have also influenced many media and communications scholars, even if they themselves have not studied media and communications per se. Rather, they have formulated a Foucault-inflected political philosophy that lives on, sowing the seeds for further Foucault interpretations, as well as concrete empirical studies, in media and communications studies and beyond.

Foucault himself was well aware of the power of media and, in time, the implications of (intellectual) celebrity. In 1980, when a *Le Monde* journalist requested a long interview for a Sunday supplement, he accepted. But Foucault also set one non-negotiable condition. He would only accept if he could remain completely anonymous. The readers of the newspaper must not know that it was Foucault who was speaking. The philosopher would appear in disguise. He justified his stance by noting that the intellectual scene is so at the mercy of the media that fame takes precedence over ideas. A thought can no longer be received as such, Foucault argued, and consequently, what is said matters less than who says it (Foucault, 2003).

Criticism of Foucault

Finally, it is important to consider the criticism of Foucault. While his archaeological excavations involved work in the archives, and he focused on the concrete discursive practices in his studies, many fellow historians are critical of Foucault's handling of his sources (Poster, 1982). He is perceived as being overly categorical, of making sweeping conclusions about very long periods of time. Feminist scholars are another group frequently at odds with Foucault's texts. While Foucault proved a valuable partner in formulating cogent arguments about how seemingly inherent categorisations, such as gender, are actually "made", he nevertheless showed a consistent disinterest in gender aspects in his work, for example in the work on the history of sexuality. The misogynist current both baffles and annoys feminist scholars (Ramazanoglu, 1993). The well-known American philosophy professor and justice theorist Nancy Fraser (1989) is also one of them. Another theme, in critiques of Foucault, is what real possibilities for resistance actually exist within or between discourses. What ability does an individual have to act for herself, what is her authority or agency in a given discourse? Foucault's approach, according to some critics, appears overly deterministic and "negative". The limiting functions of discourses simply overshadow the possibilities of counter-power. Foucault has also been accused of being inconsistent in his use of terms or concepts.

During Foucault's early career, before receiving his doctorate, he came to study and work in Sweden. He taught French at Uppsala University, and served as cultural attaché in the same city, at the Maison de France, for several years in the 1950s. His memories of Sweden, however, do not bear witness to a particularly enjoyable experience. Foucault was said to find it cold, and he did not like the bright summer nights. But Foucault did greatly benefit from Uppsala University's library, Carolina Rediviva, with its unique historical archives from the 17th and 18th centuries, containing medical documents from so-called madhouses and poorhouses. His studies there also formed the basis of what would become his thesis in 1961, called *Madness and Civilization: A History of Insanity in the Age of Reason* (Foucault, 2001). However, the defence of this thesis eventually had to be held in France, rather than at Uppsala University itself, upon the advice of the Uppsala's professor of history of ideas, Sten

138 *Annika Egan Sjölander*

Lindroth, who did not approve Foucault's drafted manuscript. Despite this particular discursive order, it is evident that Foucault's historical works are still read and discussed widely with great interest around the world, and not least the essential text *The Order of Discourse*.

References

Berger, P. L. & Luckmann, T. (1991). *The social construction of reality: a treatise in the sociology of knowledge*. London: Penguin.

Beronius, M. (1991). *Genealogi och sociologi. Nietzsche, Foucault och den sociala analysen*. [Geneaology and Sociology. Nietzsche, Foucault and the social analysis.] Stockholm: Brutus Östlings Bokförlag Symposion.

Egan Sjölander, A. (2011). Introduction. In A. Egan Sjölander & J. Gunnarsson Payne (Eds.), *Tracking discourses. Politics, identity and social change* (pp. 13–48). Lund: Nordic Academic Press.

Fairclough, N. (1995). *Media discourse*. London: Edward Arnold.

Foucault, M. (1972). *The archaeology of knowledge and the discourse on language*. New York: Pantheon Books.

Foucault, M. (1975). *The birth of the clinic: an archaeology of medical perception*. New York: Vintage Books.

Foucault, M. (1980). *Power/knowledge: selected interviews and other writings 1972–1977*. (C. Gordon, Ed.). Brighton: Harvester Press.

Foucault, M. (1981). The order of discourse. Inaugural lecture at the Collège de France, given 2 December 1970. In R. Young (Ed.), *Untying the text: a poststructuralist reader* (pp. 48–78). London: Routledge & Kegan Paul.

Foucault, M. (1988). Technologies of the self. In L. H. Martin, H. Gutman & P. H. Hutton (Eds.), *Technologies of the self: a seminar with Michel Foucault* (pp. 16–49). Amherst: University of Massachusetts Press.

Foucault, M. (1991). *Discipline and punish: the birth of the prison*. Harmondsworth: Penguin.

Foucault, M. (1998). What is an author? In M. Foucault, P. Rainbow & J. Faubion (Eds.), *Essential works of Foucault, 1954–1984.: Vol. 2, Aesthetics, method and epistemology* (pp. 205–222). London: Penguin.

Foucault, M. (2000). *Essential works of Foucault 1954–1984.: Vol 3, Power*. London: Penguin Books.

Foucault, M. (2001). *Madness and civilization: a history of insanity in the Age of Reason*. London: Routledge.

Foucault, M. (2003). The masked philosopher. In M. Foucault (Ed.), *Essential works of Foucault 1954–1984.: Vol 1, Ethics* (pp. 321–328). London: Penguin Books.

Fraser, N. (1989). *Unruly practices. Power, discourse and gender in contemporary social theory*. Minnesota: University of Minnesota Press.

Poster, M. (1982). Foucault and history. *Social research*, 49 (1), 116–142.

Ramazanoglu, C. (Ed.) (1993). *Up against Foucault: explorations of some tensions between Foucault and feminism*. London: Routledge.

10 Jean Baudrillard (1971) 'Requiem for the Media'

Göran Bolin

Introduction

In the wake of the 1968 student revolt in Paris, the German philosopher, essayist and cultural critic Hans-Magnus Enzensberger (1970) wrote an oft-quoted text about the democratic potential of the media, with a particular focus on radio and television. Like his compatriot Bertolt Brecht (1932/2000) several decades earlier, Enzensberger had a positive attitude towards the new media and recognised their emancipatory potential. In his article, Enzensberger criticises what he perceives as a prevailing consensus within Marxist-oriented research, which only seems to emphasise the 'new media' of radio and television as parts of an oppressive 'consciousness industry'. Instead, Enzensberger puts forward the inherent revolutionary seeds carried by the media. The radio, he argues, can be used subversively to lend a voice to oppressed groups and liberation movements in the so-called 'Third World', in order to undermine prevailing power relations. However, the media must change organisationally so that those who are only consumers become producers as well; that is, people must change from being receivers to becoming transmitters also.

Baudrillard's article 'Requiem pour les media' (Requiem for the media) (1971) is written in direct response to Enzensberger's article and presents a detailed critique of his arguments. The opening sentence – 'Il n'y a pas de théorie des media' (There is no theory of the media) – is a powerful dismissal of Enzensberger's text, whose title 'Baukasten zu einer Theorie der Medien' (Constituents of a theory of the media) does indeed try to propose basic building blocks of such a theory. Why, then, does Baudrillard think that Enzensberger's text does not contribute to a theory of the media? Before returning to that question, it is important to know the foundations on which Baudrillard's position rests in order to understand said position. In what follows, therefore, I will first give an account of Baudrillard's academic trajectory and the theoretical context within which his thinking should be viewed. I will then explain in more detail the differences between Enzensberger and Baudrillard. Next, I will discuss Baudrillard's media theory from a wider perspective before I account for the relevance of his work for contemporary research. Finally, the article is rounded off with a summary and a reflection on the type of academic dialogue 'Requiem for the Media' exemplifies.

DOI: 10.4324/9781003432272-11

140 *Göran Bolin*

The theoretical context

Baudrillard can be said to have held a special position as an academic. Like Marshall McLuhan (1964), he was an academic celebrity during his lifetime, being known far outside the academic field and figuring in popular fiction. In the film *The Matrix* (1999), for example, which problematises our perception of reality, the protagonist Neo uses a copy of Baudrillard's book *Simulacra and Simulations* (1981/1994) as a hiding place for money and data disks. However, the attention he was given did not seem to impress Baudrillard himself, as was evident from interviews in which he was asked to comment on the film (e.g. in a widely distributed interview in the French weekly *Le Nouvel Observateur* in 2003/2004). Baudrillard's followers in academia are numerous, and there are journals such as the *International Journal of Baudrillard Studies* that are entirely devoted to this theorist.

Baudrillard's academic biography provides some keys to the reading of 'Requiem for the media'. Baudrillard began his academic career by studying German literature at the Sorbonne in Paris, where he also devoted himself to writing literary criticism and translating German authors such as Bertolt Brecht, Karl Marx and Peter Weiss. Eventually, Baudrillard became interested in sociology and received his doctorate in 1968. At that time, he had just moved to the newly founded branch of the Sorbonne, Paris X Nanterre, which was located in one of the suburbs of Paris. The University of Nanterre had a reputation for being radical; it played a central role in the student uprisings of May 1968 – an event that, together with an in-depth knowledge of the German discussion of media, power and liberation, clearly coloured Baudrillard's discussion of communication in 'Requiem for the Media'.

In addition to these purely biographical circumstances, it is important to understand Baudrillard's theoretical background in linguistics, anthropology, political economy and Marxism, from which he received inspiration. Above all, Baudrillard takes the idea of symbolic exchange (*échange symbolique*) as a normative point of departure when he evaluates the communicative shortcomings of the electronic media. This idea of symbolic exchange originates in the anthropological theory of gift economies that stemmed from the work of Marcel Mauss (1925/1990). Like his uncle, Émile Durkheim, Mauss sought to analyse what binds a society together. Mauss highlighted the 'gift' as an integrating institution in primitive societies. By giving someone a gift, the giver not only hands over a thing but also creates a social bond between the giver and the receiver. The recipient of a gift is in debt to the giver and, by repaying the gift, the relationship of debt is equalised and the social bond is confirmed. The return gift must be somewhat more exclusive in relation to the original gift, in order for a reciprocal bond between giver and receiver to arise. An overly lavish gift creates a power relationship and is, in fact, rather an aggressive symbolic act. This action is most aggressive when the giver presents a gift while knowing the recipient will be unable to reciprocate it. In such cases, the gift takes the form of humiliation.

Gift economies are thus symbolic economies that regulate social relations. They are important in archaic societies with a low degree of formalised social structure and working divisions, but their principles of reciprocity remain in modern societies. When we go to a birthday party, we consider what kind of present we received from the person celebrating on our last birthday. If we help a neighbour with something, we expect to receive help ourselves when we need it. In this way, the principle of the gift lives on in modern societies, even if it lacks the same strong integrative significance it has held in non-formalised social formations.

Baudrillard's influences include a rereading of Marx and a modification of the latter's theory of value. Marx (1867/1976) distinguished between the use value and exchange value of an object as follows: all things that are manufactured and can be of use have use value; however, some things also have exchange value, in that they can render a price in a market by someone being willing to pay for the item with money or by exchanging it for something. The object is then transformed into a commodity. Both the use and the exchange values arise in production, through the combination of raw materials and labour. However, not all production results in exchange value. In the world of education, such as in schools or kindergartens, an enormous production of objects takes place as children make drawings and handicrafts. However, although the picture frame that pleases a grandparent as a Christmas present certainly has great personal value for the one receiving the gift (and acts as an integrator by strengthening family ties between generations), it usually cannot be sold in a market. It has use value but not exchange value.

For Baudrillard, this distinction between use value and exchange value is insufficient in modern, media-saturated societies. Therefore, he launched the concept of 'sign value' as a complement to the political economy's concepts of use and exchange value. In doing so, he was inspired by economists such as John Kenneth Galbraith (1958), who pointed to the increased importance of advertising for value-creating processes and noted how advertising thereby triggered a need for traditional economic theories to be modified. Following this viewpoint, Baudrillard believed that the process of commodity circulation had undergone a fundamental change, in which the symbolic dimensions of goods had become dominant over their functional aspects (i.e. their use values).

Like his compatriot Louis Althusser (1970/1971), Baudrillard proposed an alternative relationship between society's base and superstructure, attributing to the latter a greater importance than it was given by Marx, who preferred to view the superstructure as a reflection of power relations in the material social base. The reason for Marx's preference, Baudrillard believed, was that Marx's economic analysis of the commodity circulation process was based on the production of material goods, whereas the goods produced in an information society increasingly lack material substance, or their value is dominated by their design qualities. These thoughts were developed by Baudrillard in his PhD thesis, which he presented in 1968 as *Le système des objets* (Baudrillard, 1968). This thesis was examined by a remarkably distinguished examination

142   *Göran Bolin*

committee consisting of Henri Lefebvre, Pierre Bourdieu and, in particular, the semiotician Roland Barthes. An illustrative example of the significance of the sign in the context of consumption is that consumers today buy goods not just for their functionality but also for the connotations they activate. American cars, argued Baudrillard, were appreciated for their large tail fins, which connote 'speed' or 'victory over space'. These cars were bought not because they were fast but because they connoted speed, thereby conferring on their owner the status of being a person with a fast car – as well as all the lifestyle markers and distinctions that followed with such an evaluation (Baudrillard, 1968: 83f.). Another area in which design qualities overshadow the functional qualities of goods is in fashion. Here, Baudrillard was strongly influenced by Barthes' (1967/ 1990) semiotic analyses of the fashion system. In fashion, and especially in haute couture, the functionality of clothes – whether it be to warm or shield the body – is clearly subordinated to peoples' stylistic preferences, and the elevated stars of fashion are those who shape clothes through their design work – a specific form of signifying practice.

Baudrillard's update of political economy theory is thus adapted to a society that is increasingly built around signs and in which the economic system is a semiotic system of exchanges, correspondences and power relations. Today's society is driven by signifying practices, in which the communicator, the designer and the lobbyist – and why not the influencer? – assume the role of the hero, rather than the engineer of industrial society.

The criticism of Enzensberger

Like Marshall McLuhan, Enzensberger was focused on the new media as technologies. The two scholars also differed in many areas: Enzensberger was somewhat critical of McLuhan's associative analytical style, which he called 'confused' and accused of consisting of 'undigested observations' that caused McLuhan's theory to become apolitical (Enzensberger, 1970: 29). In contrast, Enzensberger aimed to bring forward a possible emancipatory use of the new media, among which he included not only the mass media of radio and television but also other media already available among the population at that time, such as video, tape recorders, cameras, 8-mm film cameras and computers. In these media, Enzensberger saw opportunities for people to organise themselves in alternative forms. It is thus no coincidence that Enzensberger has been a central point of reference for research on alternative media (e.g. Atton, 2002).

However, Baudrillard does not deal with the technical limitations and possibilities of the medium in exactly the same way as either McLuhan or Enzensberger (or Brecht). McLuhan (1964), with his slogan 'the medium is the message', emphasises the importance of technology on a societal level, where the fact that television exists and has the ability to distribute content has far greater societal implications than what content is being spread, whereas Enzensberger focuses on the significance of the organisational dimension of the media. In comparison, Baudrillard focuses on the medium as a technological

Jean Baudrillard (1971)   143

channel that acts as the carrier of the signs and frames the code within which people meet in communicative exchange. Through this, Baudrillard also differs from all these predecessors, above all Brecht and Enzensberger. Radical politics, the latter argue, require real communication, and radio and television are (in their eyes) means of communication that can be used in an emancipatory way, if only radical forces such as the labour movement or protesting students can gain access to them and can control the messages distributed under self-selected organisational forms. Against this optimism, Baudrillard argues that control over the means of production does not matter. The technology itself counteracts the symbolic exchange that would make real communication between people possible. It is therefore not a critique of political economy in the traditional sense that social analysis requires, not an analysis of production relations *vis-à-vis* the material objects that is needed, but a critique of the political economy of the sign system itself.

For Baudrillard (1971/1981), Enzensberger's approach is therefore flawed; the communicative limitations of broadcast media are not rooted in control over the means of production or organisational form; rather, they involve media's properties as mediators of symbolic content. The problem with broadcast media is that they cannot establish a reciprocal relationship between the transmitter (giver) and the receiver, since there is no possibility for the latter to respond (to 'return the gift'). A symbolic exchange is never established and is left unfinished. Using Althusser's terminology, it could be said that the interpellation staged by broadcast media – the way in which they address their recipients – places the latter in a position where no answers are possible. The act of communication remains unfinished, and the spectators find themselves interpellated in a position they cannot change, subject to a communicative power that places the spectator in an inferior position. The media do not engage in communication, argues Baudrillard: they 'stage non-communication' (1971/1981: 169).

The basis for Baudrillard's criticism of broadcast media is Baudrillard's specific view of communication as an exchange – as dialogue and reciprocity. The radicalness of his view lies in his insistence that what falls outside this ideal state of symbolic exchange is non-communication – or, as he develops in his later writings, only a simulation of communication:

> What characterises the mass media is that they are opposed to mediation, intransitive, that they fabricate non-communication – if one accepts the definition of communication as an exchange, as a reciprocal space for speech and response, and thus for *responsibility*. In other words, if one defines it as anything else than the simple emission/reception of information.
>
> (Baudrillard, 1985: 577)

This quote well illustrates Baudrillard's view on communication as a communal ritual rather than a pure transmission of information (see Chapter 13). As a consequence, however, all forms of mediated communication become a simulation of the real act of communication, since mediation always affects that which is mediated.

144 *Göran Bolin*

The concept of simulation holds a particular position in Baudrillard's thinking and must be understood in relation to the symbolic order and the sign relationships that (he argues) organise society. This symbolic order must also be understood within a historical perspective, where each epoch is characterised by specific sign relationships and where the sign of each epoch is successively detached from its referent – that is, what the sign refers to. Here, Baudrillard is clearly influenced by Roland Barthes' (1967/1990) in-depth and methodologically rigorous study of the fashion system as a set of interrelated signs; it was no coincidence, after all, that Barthes was one of the examiners of Baudrillard's thesis.

Baudrillard's influences also include Walter Benjamin's analysis of the mechanical reproduction techniques of photography and film (see Chapter 1 in this volume). In his essay on the work of art in the age of mechanical reproduction, Benjamin (1936/1977) points out how the aura of a work of art – its 'Here and Now' – is obliterated by the emergence of copies. Before the advent of photography, questions about copies of art were about the degree of fidelity to the original or about forgeries; in contrast, the question of the original becomes completely meaningless for a photograph. A photograph has no original in that sense.

Baudrillard bases his media theory on a distinction between symbolic exchange (real communication) and the semiotic – that is, the simulation of communication staged by the media. Following Benjamin, he holds that the techniques of reproduction from photography onwards (i.e. film, the Internet) transform or translate the symbolic exchange from 'lived form' to 'sign form' – a representation that causes us to consume the world as signs. In this increasingly sign-saturated world, Baudrillard argues, we live surrounded by signs in the 'desert of the real' (Baudrillard, 1981/1994).

In the book *Simulacra and Simulation* (1981/1994), Baudrillard describes three states of simulacra linked to different historical phases (or orders): in a pre-modern era, images have a referent that exists in reality. In this phase, the relationship between representation and referent is obvious: no one would mistake Leonardo da Vinci's famous painting the *Mona Lisa* for the real woman who was the model for the painting (Lisa del Giocondo). With photography, this relationship changes. The photograph bears a very real – iconic – relation to its referent: the light reflected by a portrayed human (e.g. in the famous photograph of Che Guevara by the photographer Alberto Korda) leaves its imprint on light-sensitive celluloid film and thus creates a relation to its depicted object. With this arises the conflation of representation and person that the French painter René Magritte ironically commented on with his famous painting *Ceci n'est pas une pipe* (This is not a pipe) – a naturalistic painting that, of course, *is* not a pipe but *represents* a pipe. The point is that we, as spectators of the work of art, know that a common answer to the question 'What is this?' would receive the answer 'A pipe', just as someone could hold up Korda's portrait and say: 'This is Che Guevara'.

Baudrillard argues that the third stage of simulacra occurs in the age of late capitalism (see Chapter 21 in this volume). Here, Baudrillard believes, the power of the sign has suppressed the referent. Baudrillard makes an analogy between a map and what the map seeks to depict, pointing out that the map precedes reality: that we perceive reality through the map. A contemporary example can be provided by the Bulgarian-American media researcher Nadia Kaneva (2018), who, using Baudrillard's conceptual apparatus, has studied so-called nation branding campaigns – that is, the kind of branding campaign where a country (often one with a short history of independence, such as those formed after the breakup of Yugoslavia in the early 1990s) is trying to 'put itself on the map'. The point of these activities is to present a positive and attractive image of the nation-state to an external audience of international politicians, foreign investors and tourists. Through such a manoeuvre, the country hopes to attract an inflow of foreign investment capital, increase its inflow of tourists and achieve wider political recognition. This example illustrates how the map – that is, the representation of the country in question (in Kaneva's case, Kosovo) – becomes a prescriptive image of the country, based on marketing techniques and a set of signs that point to various supposedly attractive qualities. Such a campaign is thus a matter of strategic communication aimed at 'brand building' and image management. How the outside world perceives the country in question becomes more important than what the country is actually like; that is, the sign for the country (the map) becomes more important than the referent.

Baudrillard's theory of mediatisation

Over the past couple of decades, a discussion has arisen about the mediatisation of culture and society (see e.g. Lundby, 2014). Several researchers claim to have introduced this theoretical approach (e.g. Asp, 1990); however, this perspective is already present in Baudrillard's article 'Requiem pour les media' (1971), although he discusses it most fully in his book *L'échange symbolique et la mort* (Baudrillard, 1976), later translated into English as *Symbolic Exchange and Death* (Baudrillard, 1976/1993). In connection with a discussion of the work of Benjamin (1936/1977) and McLuhan (1964), Baudrillard suggests the concept of 'mediatised information' (*l'information médiatisée*), arguing that a contemporary object 'no longer has anything to do with yesterday's object, any more than "mediatised" information has with the "reality" of facts' (Baudrillard, 1976/1993: 63) – or, in the French original: '*n'a plus rien à voir avec l'objet antérieur, pas plus que l'information médiatisée avec une 'realité' des faits*' (Baudrillard, 1976: 98). For Baudrillard, this is due to the fact that all information is a result of selection; for example, in broadcast media, it is an edited series consisting of isolated sections from reality, where the camera angle, lighting and choice of sequences structure the outside world for the viewers. Importantly, Baudrillard's perception of the selection of information should also be seen as a consequence of his theory of simulacra: according to Baudrillard, mediatised information precedes every fact about reality; it leaves its mark on reality and is thus also part of the 'real' world.

146 *Göran Bolin*

Baudrillard's view of mediatisation differs markedly from other European approaches to this process. Where most scholars emphasise the influence of media institutions on other spheres of society (above all, how journalism as an institution affects politics), Baudrillard emphasises the governing power of technology and the semiotic system or 'code' that makes symbolic exchange impossible and creates a simulation of communication. Although Baudrillard was one of the first scholars to use the concept of mediatisation (see also Averbeck-Lietz, 2014), his specific 'techno-semiotic' approach has not won any large following (Bolin, 2023) – at least, not in comparison with the institutional perspective on mediatisation (e.g. Hjarvard, 2013) or the socio-cultural approach to mediatisation that is usually set up as an alternative to the institutional perspective (see e.g. Hepp & Krotz, 2014; Jansson, 2018). The institutional perspective generally bases its analyses on a shorter time horizon that extends no further back than the middle of the 20th century and provides a more causal explanatory model that reveals the influence of the media on other institutions based on an internal 'media logic' (Altheide & Snow, 1979). Researchers within the socio-cultural mediatisation approach take a wider view of the mediatisation process, engaging with meaning-making practices and their textual imprint within the framework of a longer history of human communication. This involves viewing the media environment as a surrounding world within which both individuals and institutions act. In that sense, the cultural perspective can be said to include the Baudrillardian perspective and its presentation of the media as semiotic systems of meaningful signs, although the cultural perspective is inherently more constructivist compared with Baudrillard's hyper-structuralism.

The distinctions between the institutionalist and the socio-culturalist approaches are mainly visible with a focus on European research. However, there has long been a vivid discussion of mediatisation processes in Latin America, and the relation between these perspectives has been highlighted in the last couple of years (see, e.g. Scolari et al., 2021). It is worth noting that technological and semiotic approaches are much more common in the Latin American discussion, among researchers such as Eliseo Verón (2014) and Mario Carlón (2020). Although these Latin American scholars seldom refer to Baudrillard explicitly, many have been trained in the same French contexts as Baudrillard and were students of the same semioticians and structuralists in the 1960s and 70s, which makes their approaches very similar to Baudrillard's; in fact, such approaches can be described as a mixture of the techno-semiotic and the socio-culturalist approaches.

Contemporary implications

Baudrillard's and Enzensberger's texts focus on the then relatively young medium of television. But what relevance do their ideas have today, in a world of interactive, personal and mobile media? What about the digital, personal, mobile and social media we surround ourselves with today – are they not dialogical? Our opportunities to express ourselves in the contemporary media landscape are seemingly endless, as each social media user is both a producer and a consumer of communication, albeit not at exactly the same time. How does this change Baudrillard's theory?

Baudrillard would probably say that, yes, many more people have been given the means to communicate. However, by analogy with the futility of taking over television companies, regardless of how progressive or benevolent the taker-over is, Baudrillard would point out that, although many are broadcasting, is anyone listening? Moreover, even if someone listens, can this someone answer? Is there really a genuine opportunity for symbolic exchange in social media? Is there room for both giving and receiving? Baudrillard would probably be sceptical. As William Merrin (2005: 25) has pointed out, the so-called dialogical functions of digital media only reinforce the illusion of exchange and more effectively hide the fact that the media simulate communication, while in fact they stage non-communication.

Another area where Baudrillard's theory is applicable concerns the increased computerisation and datafication of society that we are facing in the technologically highly developed parts of the world – the era Shoshana Zuboff calls the 'age of surveillance capitalism' (Zuboff, 2019). However, in order to do so, it is necessary to adjust Baudrillard's theory somewhat. Paradoxically, despite his criticism of Marx, Baudrillard could not free himself from the material production process and the material and tangible goods that he theorised. Baudrillard was stuck in a world that ultimately produced goods with a material basis, such as a car or a piece of clothing. Curiously, he had very little to say about the goods that are completely free of such qualities, such as purely digital goods or commodities. In fact, today's objects are increasingly commodities for which we pay large sums, but which have no materiality in the sense that they can be touched, put in a pocket or hung in a wardrobe (Bolin, 2011: 20). Computer programs and pieces of information are examples of such 'intangible' items. In an earlier context, I have discussed four such goods that do not exist outside of their digital form: the audience commodity, the format, the brand and computer traffic (Bolin, 2014). I will highlight one of these here: namely, the audience commodity – the product that is packaged and sold by the media industry to advertisers and others with an interest in addressing specific target groups of consumers or citizens (see Chapter 15 in this volume).

First, a distinction must be made between the audience as a statistical aggregate of various sociological and/or behavioural variables and the social subjects who use media. It is the former that constitutes the audience commodity, or – in the marketing language of the digital age – the 'digital consumer'. The social subjects who use media are, of course, contradictory individuals who act in unpredictable ways; capricious and largely uncontrollable. The digital consumer, on the other hand, consists of a statistically verified and highly predictable usage pattern, to which advertising and other offers can be directed. It is around this commodity that the commercial media industries are centred.

148 *Göran Bolin*

But what does this have to do with Baudrillard? Well, the digital consumer is what Baudrillard would call a 'simulacrum' – a map or representation that has no referent in 'reality'. It is a unity constructed as a combination of signs, drawn from a multitude of individuals' actions, but which cannot be traced back to any single individual of flesh and blood. Like Magritte's depicted pipe, the digital consumer is a representation of a behavioural pattern, often without indications of social factors such as gender, age and education; it is based more on factors such as the IP address of the computer or mobile used, geographical coordinates at the time of use, type of activity (e.g. a Google search), time of activity, context (e.g. other searches) and so on. Nevertheless, this commodity has real effects on how the market and the media industries act – what decisions are made, what media recommendations we are provided with and what consequences these have for us as very real social subjects who use the media and means of communication. We live, so to speak, enclosed in the consequences of the signs on which the audience commodity are constructed.

Conclusion

Baudrillard's requiem for electronic media was written in direct response to Enzensberger's article, which in turn intervened in the discussion among Brecht, McLuhan, Benjamin and the Frankfurt School. This series of responses could be described as an advanced and somewhat wordy Twitter or Facebook thread, where the authors respond to each other's arguments, modify, reject and offer alternative positions. This form of intellectual exchange, once common in continental Europe, has largely disappeared from academic conversation today, at least in the form that Enzensberger and Baudrillard engaged in. It is found, however, in the similar discussion between Adorno and Benjamin (see Chapter 3 in this volume) or in some of Marx's various writings. For example, *The Poverty of Philosophy* (Marx, 1847/1975) was written as a long 'Answer to the "Philosophy of Poverty" by M. Proudhon', as the subtitle clearly marks. Today, these conversations are held in other arenas – at research conferences and on blogs, in addition to the digital deliberations on social media. Perhaps Baudrillard would view these conference discussions precisely as a return to symbolic exchange – an interpersonal act of communication between co-present communicating subjects that is not disturbed by technological aids as channels of communicative exchange.

References

Altheide, D. L., & Snow, R. P. (1979). *Media logic.* Sage.
Althusser, L. (1970/1971). Ideology and ideological state apparatuses (Notes towards an investigation). In *Lenin and philosophy and other essays* (pp. 121–176). Monthly Review Press.
Asp, K. (1990). Medialisation, media logic and mediarchy. *Nordicom Review*, 11(2), 47–50.
Atton, C. (2002). *Alternative media.* Sage.

Jean Baudrillard (1971)   149

Averbeck-Lietz, S. (2014). Understanding mediatisation in "First Modernity": Sociological classics and their perspectives on mediated and mediatised societies. In K. Lundby (Ed.), *Mediatisation of communication: Handbooks of communication science* (pp. 109–130). De Gruyter Mouton.

Barthes, R. (1967/1990). *The fashion system*. University of California Press.

Baudrillard, J. (1968). *Le système des objets* [The system of objects]. Gallimard.

Baudrillard, J. (1971). Requiem pour les media [Requiem for the media]. *Utopie*, 4, 35–51.

Baudrillard, J. (1971/1981). Requiem for the media. In *For a critique of the political economy of the sign* (C. Levin, Trans.) (pp. 164–184). Telos.

Baudrillard, J. (1976/1993). *Symbolic exchange and death*. Sage.

Baudrillard, J. (1981/1994). *Simulacra and simulation*. University of Michigan Press.

Baudrillard, J. (1985). The masses: The implosion of the social in the media. *New Literary History*, 16(3), 577–589.

Benjamin, W. (1936/1977). The work of art in the age of mechanical reproduction. In: J. Curran, M. Gurevitch, & J. Wollacott (Eds.), *Mass communication and society* (pp. 384–408). Edward Arnold.

Bolin, G. (2011). *Value and the media: Cultural production and consumption in digital markets*. Ashgate.

Bolin, G. (2014). Institution, technology, world: Relationships between the media, culture and society. In K. Lundby (Ed.), *Mediatisation of communication* (pp. 175–197). De Gruyter Mouton.

Bolin, G. (forthcoming 2024). Communicative AI and techno-semiotic mediatisation: Understanding the communicative role of the machine. *Human-Machine Communication*, 7.

Brecht, B. (1932/2000). The radio as a communications apparatus. In M. Silberman (Ed.), *Bertolt Brecht on Film and Radio* (pp. 41–48). Methuen.

Carlón, M. (2020). *Circulación del sentido y construcción de colectivos: en una Sociedad hipermediatisada* [Circulation of meaning and construction of collectives: In a hypermediatised society]. Nueva Editorial Universitaria – UNSL.

Enzensberger, H.-M. (1970). Constituents of a theory of the media. *New Left Review*, 64, 13–36.

Galbraith, J. K. (1958). *The affluent society*. Hamish Hamilton.

Hepp, A., & Krotz, F. (2014). *Mediatised worlds: Culture and society in a media age*. Palgrave Macmillan.

Hjarvard, S. (2013). *The mediatisation of culture and society*. Routledge.

Jansson, A. (2018). *Mediatisation and mobile lives: A critical approach*. Routledge.

Kaneva, N. (2018). Simulation nations: Nation brands and Baudrillard's theory of media. *European Journal of Cultural Studies*, 21(5), 631–648.

Lundby, K. (Ed.) (2014). *Mediatisation of communication*. De Gruyter Mouton.

Marx, K. (1847/1975). *The poverty of philosophy. Answer to "The Philosophy of Poverty" by M. Proudhon*. Progress Publishers.

Marx, K. (1867/1976). *Capital. A critique of political economy* (vol. 1). Penguin Books.

Mauss, M. (1925/1990). *The gift: The form and reason for exchange in archaic societies*. Routledge.

McLuhan, M. (1964). *Understanding media: The extensions of man*. McGraw Hill.

Merrin, W. (2005). *Baudrillard and the media*. Polity.

Scolari, C. A., Fernandez, J. L., & Rodriguez-Amat, J. R. (Eds.) (2021). *Mediatisation(s): Theoretical conversations between Europe and Latin America*. Intellect.

Verón, E. (2014). Mediatisation theory: A semio-anthropological perspective and some of its consequences. *Matrises*, 8(1), 1–8.

Zuboff, S. (2019). *The age of surveillance capitalism: The fight for a human future at the new frontier of power*. Public Affairs.

11 Stuart Hall (1973) 'Encoding and Decoding'

Johan Fornäs

Introduction

Stuart Hall's 'Encoding and Decoding' (1973) has gained enormous importance as the provider of a critical cultural perspective on media, power and meaning: how power relations develop when media are used in acts of communication to create meanings that shape the social world. First, this chapter will focus on Hall's text itself: what it says and how it argues. The chapter then continues to describe the development and major works of the text's author. In a third step, the text will be related to how the entire field of cultural studies has grown and developed – especially in the United Kingdom, where Hall was a key unifying figure. Finally, the strengths and limitations of the text will be discussed, and how it enriches the understanding of how media and culture are intertwined. This chapter develops ideas from Fornäs (1995, 2014, 2017) and Fornäs et al. (2007).

The text: 'Encoding and Decoding'

In 1973, Stuart Hall's 'Encoding and Decoding in the Television Discourse' was published as a stencilled paper from the Centre for Contemporary Cultural Studies (CCCS) in Birmingham, where Hall was the director. A revised version, simply entitled 'Encoding/Decoding', was published in 1980 and has been since then a central reference in the borderland between media studies and cultural studies. The two versions differ on several minor points; the most widespread text from 1980 will be focused on here.

Hall presented an alternative view that broke with the linear effect models of mass-communication research, such as that of Shannon and Weaver (1948/1949) (see Chapter 5 in this volume), in which communication was described as a kind of pipe mail where the sender creates a meaningful text that is transported to the receiver for unpacking and interpretation, with the goal of faithfully recreating the intended meaning. Instead of such rectilinear models of transmission, Hall wanted to capture the complexity of the processes by which media audiences and users interpret media texts and give them meaning. In reception, the meaning of the text is reconstructed on the basis of contextual factors that are specific to different situations and groups of viewers. (The

DOI: 10.4324/9781003432272-12

152   *Johan Fornäs*

concept could be described just as well using readers or listeners, but Hall mostly exemplifies with television.) This results in opportunities for misunderstanding and lack of communication; it also gives recipients the chance to produce alternative interpretations of the media content that subtly or radically differ from those of the producers. Hall's article makes his argument in four steps.

(1) First, Hall polemicises against traditional mass-communication research. He notes that communication processes have four interconnected stages or moments: production, circulation, distribution/consumption (later equated with reception) and reproduction. Here, Hall refers to Karl Marx, who offered in *Grundrisse* (1939/1993) a complex analysis of the capitalist commodity form in terms of a dialectical interaction between production, distribution (transport), circulation (exchange through buying and selling) and consumption. Hall had worked with Marx's commodity analysis in another context; here, however, only a brief hint is offered before focusing on the relationship between producers/senders and consumers/receivers. (In the original 1973 version of Hall's text, Marx's concepts were not included at all – they were added in later editions. Instead, Hall began that version by emphasising that his semiotic-linguistic foundation combines the analysis of symbolic structures with social and political perspectives.)

Hall emphasises that the four moments of the communication process do not fully coincide but are only loosely connected to each other, allowing for asymmetry between the encoded and decoded meaning structures. They are not identical or strictly causally linked, but more temporarily 'articulated'. Here, 'articulation' is both about expression and joining: in it, otherwise separate elements are brought together in a specific context, such as the tongue and teeth in linguistic pronunciation, or the truck and trailer of an 'articulated lorry'. Hall borrowed the concept of articulation from the political theorist Antonio Gramsci, the linguist Ferdinand de Saussure and the structuralist Louis Althusser in order to abandon ideas of deterministic causal relationships and allow different constellations to produce different results in the creation of meaning and knowledge. In Hall's analysis, articulation means that something is expressed linguistically at the same time as different meaning contents in a certain situation are linked to a concept – not as a logical necessity but through political and ideological struggles.

(2) Hall's point is that, when communication processes bring these moments together, a discursive power struggle arises between different interests. This cannot be understood from a linear view, in which a finished message is transported from producer to audience. Thus, in the second step, Hall introduces a semiotic conceptual apparatus that – in a lucid visual figure – describes media production as 'encoding' and reception as 'decoding'. This does not refer to binary data codes, but rather to semiotic or cultural codes such as rules for how to use specific languages, genres or forms of expression. The moments of encoding and decoding are relatively independent from each other and can lead to very different results. The producer assigns meaning to the media text based on certain frameworks of knowledge, relations of production and technical

Stuart Hall (1973)   153

infrastructures. The viewer interprets the same text in a different context and from a different subjective perspective. Therefore, the encoded sentence may differ from the one decoded by the audience. Communication is no automatic transmission but is based on textual interpretation, in which codes in the form of language and other traditional rules for the use of symbols are applied. Such a decoding is never unequivocal; rather, it opens up the possibility of several different perspectives.

The famous flowchart shown in Figure 11.1 is primarily designed for mass communication through television, radio or newspapers, where the products (i.e. the programmes or texts) are produced by an editorial office or some other form of collective institution and then disseminated to a wide audience. It is less suitable for more interactive social media with more diffuse boundaries between producers and audiences. As shown in the figure, the producers create the media text and give it meanings based on their own cultural, social and technical contexts. When the audiences receive the media text, they make their own interpretations, based on their situations, experiences, needs and interests. (The first version in 1973 includes a dashed feedback loop from right to left at the bottom of the figure, suggesting that viewers' interpretations of media texts affect their way of thinking and acting, which in turn has effects on the contexts of future media production. That complication was deleted in the 1980 version.)

The figure both resembles and differs from traditional communication models. The linear flow implied by the arrows from left to right feels familiar, with the media text (e.g. a television programme) as a mediating link between the sender and receiver. In similar models, an individual producer and consumer are usually included as the start and end points of the process; here, they are not explicitly visible but are rather assumed to be embedded in a more collective constellation. Neither is the mediation of the media over time and space explicitly stated; rather, it is assumed to be integrated into the 'programme'

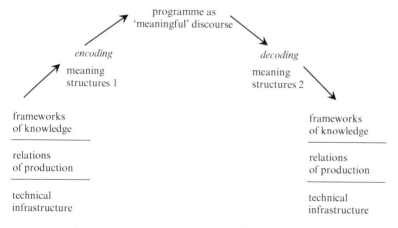

Figure 11.1 'Encoding and Decoding' (Hall, 1973/1980: 130, after Hall, 1973/2007: 388)

154 *Johan Fornäs*

stage. Instead, the figure focuses on the context-dependent interpretation processes, which are otherwise often overlooked as self-evident when mass-communication research tends to describe recipients as passive victims of the media's supremacy. This is an important aspect of Hall's *cultural* perspective on communication, since culture has to do with meaning-making practices. The fact that Hall puts quotation marks around 'meaningful' may be because the whole point is that the programme is not really full of meaning on its own but is given meaning in its meeting with the viewers, so that perhaps one might speak of 'meaning-inviting', if that were not such a clumsy expression.

(3) In the third part, Hall confronts other influences and ideas. (In Hall's first version, the model is applied to the television genre of 'Westerns'.) Hall combines linguistic semiotics with Marxist and structuralist ideology theory. Concepts such as code, icon, realism, representation, denotation and connotation are taken from semioticians such as Charles Sanders Peirce, Umberto Eco and Roland Barthes (see Chapter 18 in this volume). Based on Louis Althusser's structuralist Marxism, seasoned with Antonio Gramsci's political theory, concepts such as ideology and hegemony, relative autonomy and determination are discussed. Hall shows how dominance relationships and interpretive options interact in the world of television, and how power relationships in production influence but never completely determine the meaning content of the media text or the interpretation made by audience members. There must be '*some* degree of reciprocity between encoding and decoding moments' for there to be communication at all, but this correspondence is 'not given but constructed' as a result of 'an articulation between two distinct moments' (Hall, 1973/1980: 136). Media texts are anchored in dominant ideological power relations but are still open for critical action.

(4) In the fourth step, Hall constructs three main hypothetical positions in which encoding and decoding can relate to each other. In the *dominant-hegemonic position* or code, the viewer interprets the text based on the same frames of reference that the producers used when encoding, and thus approves the ideologies that they codified. In the *negotiated position*, compromises are made so that the meaning content encoded by the sender is partly accepted and partly adjusted, based on the viewer's interests and experiences. Finally, there is a purely *oppositional position*, where the interpretation goes against the grain and totally rejects the dominant discourse. The sender's intention is often to make the receivers interpret the content of the text in the same way as the sender, so that the dominant interpretation is reproduced; in practice, however, the viewers can always construct partially different or even opposite meanings in reading the media text.

This model can be illustrated by a fictitious television programme about the tangible problems of integrating a growing stream of refugees. The producers agree with public opinion and the parliament majority that this is a problem that needs to be addressed through restrictions on immigration, and the interviews and reports contained in the programme seek to support this dominant interpretation of the situation from different perspectives, although there are different opinions about whom to blame, how big the problem is or how to fix it. Viewer A fully agrees with this approach and – like the programme makers and the majority of politicians – is concerned about the situation. Viewer B knows and likes many, nice immigrants. She thinks that the programme is too alarmistic and believes that, while several of its statements and claims are valid, others are misleading. The fears should therefore neither be neglected nor exaggerated by a total stop of immigration. Only a certain reduction of the stream of asylum seekers is needed for the integration processes to work better. Viewer C is strongly against the whole image that the programme offers and believes that immigration actually benefits the receiving country. She rejects all the programme's main arguments and interprets them as an expression of a prevailing fear-mongering and nationalist ideology. Although these three positions are not illustrated in Hall's figure, he makes clear in his text that there are different receivers, each situated within their own contextual factors, who interpret any media text differently. Some are close to the preferred meaning indicated by the encoding on the left of the figure; others are oppositional and can be thought to be further to the right in the figure.

Hall's model inserts a semiotic paradigm into a social framework and can be used in both textual analysis and ethnography. Hall describes the communication process as consisting of mutually relatively autonomous steps that influence each other but always leave a certain leeway – a 'polysemic' ambiguity. Ideology is not about any direct transmission of messages from media producers to the audience, with predetermined effects. The encoding and decoding of meanings are relatively independent of each other. Mediated by the reading of the media text itself, the encoding affects the decoding but cannot determine its outcome. The producers prefer and intend certain interpretations, and power relations cause their preferred interpretations to be normally reproduced, but critical media users can always question them through alternative interpretations, based on their conditions. At the time, this eye-opening insight defied prevailing beliefs in both conventional and critical mass-communication research. Hall summed up a *cultural* perspective on the media in a communication model where media users in conflicts of interpretation can make critical counter-interpretations and modifications, which means that the results of media use must be investigated empirically and cannot simply be deduced from production studies or textual analysis.

The theorist: Stuart Hall

Stuart Hall was born in 1932 in Kingston, Jamaica. He came from a mixed-race family; his darker skinned father was United Fruit's Jamaican chief financial officer, while his mother had British roots. Hall receive a classical English education and became involved in Jamaica's struggle for independence at the same time. In 1951, he came to England to study at Oxford University. In 1959–1962, he was the first editor of the political theory journal *New Left Review*, in the spirit of a non-dogmatic 'Marxism without guarantees'. Hall worked as a

156   *Johan Fornäs*

teacher and editor in London from 1961 until his move to Birmingham in 1964, where he became a researcher at the then newly formed Centre for Contemporary Cultural Studies (CCCS) and served as its director in 1968–1979. The CCCS (which was closed down by Birmingham University in 2002) won international acclaim for developing a productive environment – with small resources – in which students and faculty organised study groups and published stencils and anthologies that came to leave deep traces in the political history of cultural studies. Then, as a sociology professor at the Open University from 1979, Hall continued to cross boundaries between schools of thought and disciplines – as well as between research, arts and politics – in his teaching, writing and speaking right up until his death in 2014.

Hall's early texts in *The Popular Arts* (1964) and *Resistance through Rituals* (1975/1977) focused on the media, popular culture and youth culture. Based on ideas from the Chicago school of criminology and sociology, among other things, British research on youth subcultures studied youth styles as a form of ritual resistance or culturalised politics. This had a wide impact, not just in UK universities but also internationally, as well as in political debate and social work outside the universities. With his colleagues, Hall further published several anthologies on other political and social issues, including *Policing the Crisis* (1978/2013) and *New Times* (1989). Inspired by leftist theorists such as Antonio Gramsci, Louis Althusser, Michel Foucault, Ernesto Laclau and Chantal Mouffe, he sought to understand media power as dynamic and contested rather than as a fixed and predetermined structure. Until his last lines in *After Neoliberalism?* (2013: 17), Hall emphasised that the dominant neoliberal ideology is never secure but always contains fissures that open opportunities for resistance. In books such as *Questions of Cultural Identity* (1996), he engaged with postcolonial issues of migration, multiculturalism, racism and ethnicity. This was part of a general and highly influential thematisation of how identities are fragmented, dynamic and constructed in social interaction, which was also applied to gender and sexuality.

Media and communication studies is one of the fields where Hall's work has gained the strongest entry into basic literature. Perhaps that field was young enough to approve of such a critical intervention, while older disciplines tended to close their doors to oppositional and hard-to-categorise newcomers such as cultural studies. Hall never actually earned a PhD, and his fame is not based on any single theoretical monograph or empirical investigation. Instead, in a series of political and educational articles, anthologies and interviews, he pointed out ways forward and wrestled with current themes and issues. Hall worked collectively with others in courses, media, conferences and exhibitions. He united qualities not often seen together in one person, which made him a highly communicative researcher with the ability to initiate collective learning processes and dialogic interventions. On the one hand, he had something to *say*, to communicate. He not only analysed, interpreted and theorised but also served as both a critical and a supportive guide, gathering scattered perspectives into one convincing direction in the political theory debate. Cultural studies must intervene in everyday life and not build closed castles of introverted theorising in thin air. Hall always had a key focus on power – not as a metaphysical essence but as a concrete social practice – in relation to resistance but also to meaning and identity. On the other hand, with his combinatorial and communicative talent, Hall managed more than many others to *listen* and convey other people's thoughts. He broadened the field of cultural research by curiously taking previously despised 'low' phenomena seriously, such as popular culture, multicultural media culture and working-class culture. At the same time, he bridged and brought together otherwise separate perspectives and allowed them to be productively refracted against each other, as for instance with dynamic cultural history and structuralist semiotics, or with lived experience and critical discourse analysis (e.g. Hall, 1980a, 1997).

The tradition: British cultural studies

Hall was at the forefront of transforming British cultural studies from the local 'Birmingham school' into a global field. Interdisciplinary studies of culture and society have been conducted in many different contexts, such as in the sociology of culture (including the seminal work of Pierre Bourdieu) and in the critical theory of the Frankfurt School (cf. Chapters 3 and 17 in this volume). But cultural studies became a key concept through the Birmingham researchers, including Hall. This began in the 1950s, with groundbreaking books such as Richard Hoggart's *The Uses of Literacy* (1957/1990) and Raymond Williams' *Culture and Society 1780–1950* (1958/1968), which formulated fundamental questions about how art, culture and media relate to politics, power and social relations. The next step was the founding of the CCCS in Birmingham in 1964, which established a progressive and creative meeting place for forward-thinking younger researchers and students. A third step was taken in the 1970s, when a series of working groups published thematic stencils and anthologies that soon became classic texts in the field and made the Birmingham School an increasingly globally renowned hub for critical cultural research.

This burgeoning intellectual movement became a relatively accessible entry site for younger scholars from non-traditional backgrounds. British universities and colleges grew rapidly in the 1960s, providing growing space for students without wealthy or well-educated parents. Young women, working-class children and people with colonial roots (like Hall) brought with them a more critical perspective on academic knowledge; they were also more open to 'low' or transgressive themes such as popular culture, everyday life or social movements. In addition to their academic practice, they were often involved in public education, cultural life and politics. They were a generation of 'inside outsiders', with one foot in the academy and one outside, thereby equipped with an embodied understanding of what class, gender and ethnicity meant in the production of knowledge. Cultural studies thus contributed to a self-reflexive modernisation of social and cultural research.

158   Johan Fornäs

What was meant by 'culture' varied in the 1960s. Sometimes it indicated studies from a societal perspective of aesthetic phenomena, from fiction to youth subcultures. But more often the goal was to apply a certain perspective to almost anything: studies of a cultural kind rather than studies of cultural objects. Such cultural studies focused on the creation of meaning and thus built bridges between the aesthetic and the anthropological concept of culture: defined by the arts or by life forms ('a whole way of life', to use Hall's mentor Raymond Williams' famous phrase). The hermeneutic or semiotic definition of culture as meaning-making or 'signifying practice' developed gradually, until – in his last book, *Culture* (1981: 12 f. and 207 ff.) – Williams viewed modern societies as so complex that the gap between culture and nature, as well as the notion of 'whole ways of life', was no longer relevant or useful. If culture is meaning-making practice and media are techniques used in this communicative meaning-making, then cultural studies and media studies must have much in common. Since Hall's text gained circulation in 1980, there has indeed been an extensive overlap between these two fields of knowledge. Overviewing the history of the field of cultural studies, Hall (1980b: 117) emphasised that the media theme was a central focus within CCCS from the very beginning; the same applies globally today to most environments where cultural studies thrive.

In many ways, the encoding/decoding model was typical of this new inter-disciplinary tradition of ideas, which brought together humanities and social science perspectives in various contexts on aesthetics and politics, textual interpretation and lived experience, actors and structures. This bridge-building caused cultural studies to be perceived differently in different disciplines. In the social sciences, the result has been an increased interest in the form and meaning of texts; in the aesthetic disciplines, it has fuelled a contextualisation that relates texts to everyday practices, social institutions, political processes and epoch-specific 'structures of feeling' (Raymond Williams' concept; see Chapter 12 in this volume).

The field of British cultural studies shares many features with the German critical theory of the so-called Frankfurt School. Both examine issues of meaning and power at the intersection of culture and society. Both were inspired by libertarian and undogmatic interpretations of Marx, striving not to regard cultural phenomena as direct reflections of prevailing material productive forces or social relations of power and production. However, the Frankfurt School's use of the concept of 'mass' was emphatically questioned by the majority of cultural studies scholars at the time, in stark opposition to Horkheimer and Adorno's (1944/2002) portrayal of the media as a totalitarian machine that dupes the masses and neutralises all attempts at resistance (see Chapter 3 in this volume). Hall's thesis about the relatively independent decoding of media texts and the possibility of several different oppositional approaches links to that polemic; it also targeted those proponents of mainstream mass-communication research that view media effects as a linear result of media producers' manipulation of passively receptive audiences.

Cultural studies scholars also criticised deterministic approaches to technological development (see Chapters 8 and 13 in this volume). New technologies interact with other social conditions in unpredictable ways. In area after area, there are open processes of struggle and negotiation between different actors and positions, which compete with each other for interpretive prerogative. The balance of power can always shift; thus, empirical studies are required to determine which tendencies have the upper hand in each situation. This is why the model of encoding and decoding emphasises frameworks of knowledge, relations of production and technical infrastructure as key contexts for how media users make meaning.

In a commentary, Hall (1980b: 117 f.) summarises how the proponents of British cultural studies broke with the prevailing paradigms dominated by American empirical mass-communication research: (1) They broke with the behaviourist idea that media content has effects that directly affect people, where certain stimuli give rise to precise responses, in order to examine the more complex ideological roles of media instead. (2) They broke with the view of media texts as transparent and unambiguous carriers of messages and meaning, in order to pay more attention to the form and structure of the content. (3) They broke with the view of the media audience as passive and homogeneous to instead study multiple forms of active reception and media use. (4) Finally, they re-actualised questions about dominant ideological representations.

Hall's model was applied and developed in a series of empirical reception studies, not least by David Morley (1980, 1986), who – together with Charlotte Brunsdon – further developed the differentiated view of the media audience in a reception analysis of the British Broadcasting Corporation (BBC)'s news programme *Nationwide*. Morley (1980: 167) emphasised that each media text has a varying range of interpretive possibilities – a polysemy or ambiguity – which is not infinite or completely open but limited by the power relations in which the texts are inscribed. Different groups, such as different classes, tend to interpret media in different ways; there are also individual variations based on the experiences of each media user. This is where the idea of repertoires of decoding strategies came in handy. The model is a well-established reference in the rich Scandinavian and Dutch traditions of reception studies (e.g. Ien Ang, 1991; Joke Hermes, 1995; Ingegerd Rydin, 1996; Sofia Johansson, 2007).

After the first seminal texts of the 1950s, the foundation of the CCCS in 1964 and the wider impact of the British canon in the 1970s, a fourth step was taken in the development of cultural studies around 1980, in the form of a rapid spread and internal differentiation of the field. This had three transformative results:

(1) First, there was a *geopolitical spread*. Even before the CCCS, interdisciplinary cultural research had been conducted in many parts of the world. Still, when the developments in Birmingham gained wide fame, such approaches became visible as a (more-or-less) unified field that other directions could connect to or distance themselves from. British cultural studies became a magnetic pole that influenced culture-oriented media researchers globally (a) to take 'low' and despised everyday phenomena seriously and (b) to pay attention to the

160 *Johan Fornäs*

contradictions of media use. For example, Jürgen Habermas (1992: 439) found reason – with reference to Hall's text and to the work of Morley (1986) – to reassess his earlier Adorno-influenced pessimistic view of the media as a unitary instrument of power, in favour of a recognition that media have both authoritarian and emancipatory potentials (see Chapter 7 in this volume).

With research projects, publications, centres, educational programmes and networks, cultural studies offered an interdisciplinary meeting place with simultaneously critical, reflexive and bridge-building functions: a borderland for dialogues between different disciplines and other interdisciplinary fields (Bennett, 1998). There, powerful mainstream ideas within research – as well as in politics and everyday life – were questioned; there was an ongoing critical reflection on the role of academic knowledge in society, and doors were opened for new dialogues, interactions and combinations.

(2) Second, in the working texts from the CCCS during the 1970s and 1980s, a *theoretical pluralisation* can be discerned in the form of an increasingly diverse mixture of references, theories and methodologies. With names such as Jean Baudrillard, Jacques Derrida and Michel Foucault, poststructuralism, deconstruction and discourse analysis gave new impulses to established conceptual and cultural-historical or structuralist-semiotic approaches. Some scholars connected to Pierre Bourdieu's cultural sociology, others to psychoanalytic theories from Jacques Lacan and Julia Kristeva. A free-spirited new thinking arose in these intellectual crossroads, along with internal conflicts, such as between those who favoured advanced theorising and those who advocated a return to the empirical basis of experienced reality through ethnography, in order to avoid losing their footing in the daring cross-currents of thought.

In several countries, the British cultural studies tradition interacted with other currents in cultural research. The different regional conditions and contexts for applying this perspective gave researchers in different parts of the world the opportunity to refine and develop different aspects of cultural studies. In the United States, for example, the work of James Carey (1975/1992) and Janice Radway (1984) aligned strikingly with Hall's thinking and, in that context, cultural studies developed a North American variety through cross-fertilisation with other traditions, such as pragmatism and symbolic interactionism (see Chapters 13 and 22 in this volume). In the Nordic countries, Latin America and East Asia, the gaps between critical theory and cultural studies were not nearly as deep as they were in the United Kingdom and the United States. In Sweden, for instance, a corresponding interaction was visible with broader youth culture research, ethnology, cultural sociology and social history.

(3) Third, a *critical intersectionality* evolved – a wider diversity of critical perspectives that strengthened yet competed with each other. The emphasis on class differences was striking at first. The pioneers often had a working-class background and worked not only in universities but also in adult education. There was a particular interest in working-class experiences and living conditions, as well as in the broad popular culture – particularly youth culture – where British subcultural analysis became internationally famous. It was not

only the working class but also women and non-whites that began to make inroads into the world of research, putting gender, sexuality, ethnicity, race and nationality onto the agenda. Feminist and postcolonial perspectives quickly gained ground, as exemplified by Angela McRobbie and Paul Gilroy. Furthermore, when the field of cultural studies expanded, even more voices came in from other parts of the world, with Janice Radway as an example (see Chapter 22 in this volume). Radway had never heard of British cultural studies when she got her breakthrough in 1984, but her work had strong similarities to what Hall was doing and was therefore quickly incorporated into the cultural studies canon.

In sum, these various dimensions of pluralisation contributed to enriching the field of cultural studies while simultaneously making it difficult to define and delimit. A great number of theories were adopted, although their originators did not always identify with this field. It is therefore impossible to draw any strict boundaries around the crossroads of cultural studies. There is no obvious core of theories or methodologies; rather, those in the field tend to take a critical yet communicative approach that is based more on open networks than on any strict canon. Bridge building makes the contours of thought vaguer, in that the omnivorous hunger for new combinations allows different sub-currents to pull in different directions.

Amid this diversity, however, some common threads are needed: central values that justify the field's existence and make it worth maintaining. Questions of meaning, power and identity are often emphasised as key concepts, such as in the statutes of the Association for Cultural Studies (ACS):

> By the term cultural studies we refer to the inter- and trans-disciplinary study of and intervention into the relations between cultural practices and the social relations and organisation of power. Cultural studies researches and theorises cultural practices and forms, and their effects, by placing them into the contexts of relations in which they emerge, through which they circulate and into which they are appropriated. Cultural studies focuses on the production and reproduction of such relations and on the agencies which enable or resist them.
>
> (www.cultstud.org)

This undeniably fits well with Hall's text.

The interpretations: critical remarks

'Encoding and Decoding' highlights the possibility for each media text to be interpreted in different ways by different users and in different contexts. In the same manner, even Hall's text opens up differently to different types of readers. Some critical reflections may be useful here. For example, Hall initially refers to Marx and suggests that communication processes combine four elements: 'production, circulation, distribution/consumption, reproduction', but that thread is never really explored. Marx's model is based on capitalist commodity

162   *Johan Fornäs*

production and is therefore best suited for commercial mass communication, where production and consumption are strictly separated. But is it equally valid for public service or for interactive social media? Does the commodity form apply to all modern mediated communication?

Morley (1992: 120 f.) highlights three other problems in Hall's model. First, the producer's intentions are mixed up with the meaning of the text. Even the expression 'preferred meaning' suggests a desire and will on the part of the sender, while more advanced reception theories emphasise that the meaning of texts cannot be reduced to such intentions but is created in the encounter between texts and readers. Does the preferred meaning reside with the author, in the text or with the reader? Second, despite its critical ambitions, the model has too many similarities with previous linear communication models in which meaning is transported from sender to receiver. Third, decoding actually consists of several different interconnected processes – in particular, the model confuses understanding with agreement. To understand what a media text says is to reproduce its meaning, but this does not have to mean that the recipient agrees with what the text expresses.

Hall himself realised Morley's first objection: the unclear dividing line between a media text's dominant or 'preferred meaning' in the encoding, the media user's dominant interpretation or 'preferred reading' of it in the decoding, and the dominant ideology of society at large (Pillai, 1992: 222, 231 f.; Hall, 1994: 261 f.). There is no a priori equivalence between these three. Anyone who decodes a media text in an oppositional way does not necessarily go against the prevailing ideology, nor can the possible audience reactions be limited to just the three that Hall mentions.

Swedish media researcher Sven Ross (2011) addresses a related ambiguity regarding the three strategies for media interpretation. Not all media texts encode society's dominant ideology; some are critical or even oppositional to this prevailing order. The question, then, is whether an interpretation that affirms the dominant ideology should be classified as dominant or oppositional. Anyone who is positive about a critical television programme is, conversely, affirming the oppositional text but in opposition to the social power. Ross suggests that both encoding and decoding can be divided into dominant, negotiated and oppositional, resulting in a complicated square with nine possible fields.

Hall's article aimed to exchange the transmission model of communication for an articulation model that emphasises the ongoing processes and struggles in which meaning is created. The model was part of a polemic against traditional empirical ('positivist') methods for content analysis and effect studies (Hall, 1994: 253 f.) (cf. Chapters 5 and 13 in this volume). It was intended to break with the idea of media content as a fixed meaning in a message that is transmitted from the sender (who creates an unambiguous text) to the receiver (who then unpacks it and recreates its true meaning). In such a linear communication model, the meaning of the media text is self-evident, and the only question is whether the recipient understands it or not. In contrast, the encoding/decoding model describes the text as a complex structure of meanings that is negotiated in interaction between people and media texts and between producers and consumers. Because the meaning is not fixed and given in advance, the interpretation leaves openings for ideological and political struggles, for power and resistance.

Hall (1994: 268) claimed to have a basic hermeneutic view. He could therefore have connected to how Hans-Georg Gadamer (1960/1989), Paul Ricoeur (1969/1974) and the literary tradition of German and American 'reception theory' described meaning as being made and changed through constant conflicts of interpretation in the encounter between texts and readers (see Chapter 22 in this volume). Instead, Hall was stuck with semiotics, and his figure ended up being closer to the transmission view than he intended. The terms 'encoding' and 'decoding' can be associated with some kind of cipher, where the sender inserts a sentence into the text that the receiver then reproduces. Hall's stated intention was rather to show that 'decoding' is a meaning-making practice and thus also a production process rather than a consumptive deciphering of a specific meaning of the content. Many communication models let arrows symbolise transmission or influence. However, it is important to think about what each arrow means: the transmission of media texts or of meaningful content? A chronological sequence or a causal influence? Hall's fourth arrow continues to the right, in the same direction as the previous ones, contributing to the impression of a trans-mission-based chain of effect – a transfer of meaningful media content from sender to receiver – even though that was not the intention at all. Could the arrow have run in the exact opposite direction? Even if media use affects the context of the reception, Hall's text is primarily about how contexts cause dif-ferent audience groups to interpret the same media content in different ways, which might have been conveyed better by an arrow in the opposite direction.

Although Hall's text thus raises certain questions, it undoubtedly deserves its central place as a classic text in media and communication theory. Hall sum-marised the semiotic communication view in British cultural studies and anchored the conflict-filled processes of media text reception in cultural, social and technical contexts. His work paved the way for empirical ethnographic research that methodologically and theoretically united social science and the humanities. The idea of articulation between the moments and the three decoding strategies gained great importance for audience and reception research, enabling a refined cultural perspective that could better break with the prevailing mechan-ical-influence models in cultural industry criticism, mass-communication research and technological deterministic information theory. 'Encoding and Decoding' stood on the threshold of this development, which rapidly led to an acceptance that media are interpreted in different ways. This text grappled in inspiring ways with important questions of identity, power and meaning that remain highly relevant in media studies, as well as in everyday media life.

References

Ang, I. (1991). *Desperately seeking the audience*. Routledge.
Bennett, T. (1998). Cultural studies: A reluctant discipline. *Cultural Studies*, 12(4), 528–545.

164 Johan Fornäs

Carey, J. W. (1975/1992). A cultural approach to communication. In J. W. Carey (Ed.), *Communication as culture: Essays on media and society* (pp. 13–36). Routledge.

Fornäs, J. (1995). *Cultural theory and late modernity.* Sage.

Fornäs, J. (2014). Stuart Hall's dialogic interventions. *Inter-Asia Cultural Studies, 15*(2), 186–190.

Fornäs, J. (2017). *Defending culture: Conceptual foundations and contemporary debate.* Palgrave Macmillan.

Fornäs, J., Becker, K., Bjurström, E., & Ganetz, H. (2007). *Consuming media: Communication, shopping and everyday life.* Berg. sh.diva-portal.org/smash/record.jsf?pid=diva2%3A360136&dswid=5072

Gadamer, H.-G. (1960/1989). *Truth and method* (2nd ed.). Sheed and Ward.

Habermas, J. (1992). Further reflections on the public sphere. In C. Calhoun (Ed.), *Habermas and the public sphere* (pp. 421–461). The MIT Press.

Hall, S. (1973/2007). Encoding and decoding in the television discourse. In A. Gray, J. Campbell, M. Erickson, S. Hanson & H. Wood (Eds., 2007), *CCCS selected working papers: Volume 2* (pp. 386–398). Routledge.

Hall, S. (1973/1980). Encoding/decoding. In S. Hall, D. Hobson, A. Lowe & P. Willis (Eds., 1980), *Culture, media, language* (pp. 128–138). Hutchinson.

Hall, S. (1980a). Cultural studies: Two paradigms. *Media, culture and society, 2*(1), 57–72.

Hall, S. (1980b). Introduction to media studies at the centre. In S. Hall, D. Hobson, A. Lowe & P. Willis (Eds.), *Culture, media, language* (pp. 117–121). Hutchinson.

Hall, S. (1994). Reflections upon the encoding/decoding model: An interview with Stuart Hall. In J. Cruz & J. Lewis (Eds.), *Viewing, reading, listening: Audiences and cultural reception* (pp. 253–274). Westview Press.

Hall, S. (Ed.) (1997). *Representation: Cultural representations and signifying practices.* Sage/The Open University.

Hall, S., Critcher, C., Jefferson, T., Clarke, J., & Roberts, B. (1978/2013). *Policing the crisis: Mugging, the state, and law and order* (2nd ed.). Palgrave Macmillan.

Hall, S., & du Gay, P. (Eds.) (1996). *Questions of cultural identity.* Sage.

Hall, S., & Jacques, M. (Eds.) (1989). *New times: The changing face of politics in the 1990s.* Lawrence & Wishart.

Hall, S., & Jefferson, T. (Eds.) (1975/1977). *Resistance through rituals: Youth subcultures in post-war Britain.* Hutchinson.

Hall, S., Massey, D., & Rustin, M. (2013). *After neoliberalism? The Kilburn manifesto.* Soundings.

Hall, S., & Whannel, P. (1964). *The popular arts.* Hutchinson Educational.

Hermes, J. (1995). *Reading women's magazines: An analysis of everyday media use.* Polity Press.

Hoggart, R. (1957/1990). *The uses of literacy.* Penguin.

Horkheimer, M., & Adorno, T. W. (1944/2002). *Dialectic of enlightenment: Philosophical fragments.* Stanford University Press.

Johansson, S. (2007). *Reading tabloids: Tabloid newspapers and their readers.* Södertörns högskola. urn:nbn:se:sh:diva-1600

Marx, K. ([1858]1939/1993). *Grundrisse: Foundations of the critique of political economy.* Penguin Books/New Left Review.

Morley, D. (1980). *The "nationwide" audience: Structure and decoding.* British Film Institute.

Morley, D. (1986). *Family television.* Comedia.

Morley, D. (1992). *Television, audiences and cultural studies.* Routledge.

Pillai, P. (1992). Rereading Stuart Hall's encoding/decoding model. *Communication Theory, 2*(3), 221–233.

Radway, J. (1984). *Reading the romance: Women, patriarchy, and popular literature.* University of North Carolina Press.

Ricoeur, P. (1969/1974). *The conflict of interpretations: Essays in hermeneutics.* Northwestern University Press.

Ross, S. (2011). *The encoding/decoding model revisited.* International Communication Association Conference. urn.kb.se/resolve?urn=urn:nbn:se:su:diva-71460

Rydin, I. (1996). *Making sense of TV-narratives: Children's readings of a fairy tale.* Tema Barn.

Shannon, C. E., & Weaver, W. (1948/1949). *The mathematical theory of communication.* University of Illinois Press.

Williams, R. (1958/1968). *Culture and society 1780–1950.* Penguin.

Williams, R. (1981). *Culture.* Fontana Press.

12 Raymond Williams (1974) *Television: Technology and Cultural Form*

Staffan Ericson

Introduction

The year is 2006, and Swedish television is celebrating 50 years on the air with a gala that is being broadcasted live from Stockholm. Early in the program, the singer Tommy Körberg performs a delicate ballad written for the occasion, with a theme that emerges in the first lines of the lyrics: "Everything must change, nothing will remain … In the silent passage of time, no, nothing remains." The chorus continues with a reminder: "But there are things on this earth to be trusted. Such as, the clouds will give us rain, the sun has its course, and the birds their song."

It may seem odd to celebrate a historical anniversary with a song about the constant erasure of the past. Yet, this performance seems to demonstrate that something does "remain." A large screen behind the singers and musicians on stage shows sequences of historical, moving images (which are displayed in full-screen format on the TV broadcast). In total, there are some fifty sequences, five to ten seconds long; most seem immediately familiar, and some are even iconic. While Körberg sings about the passage of time, the screen shows:

- Bombers flying in over unknown territory (perhaps the Balkans?)
- The face of a child, crying desperately
- Nelson Mandela and his wife walking in a crowd, making the victory sign
- Neil Armstrong and Buzz Aldrin walking on the surface of the moon
- Children playing on one side of a wall while soldiers guard the other side
- A soldier jumping over barbed wire in Berlin
- The Swedish King and Queen announcing their upcoming wedding
- Planes dropping bombs over Vietnam
- A badly burned and naked Vietnamese girl running along a country road
- Charles and Diana getting married
- The wreck of the boat *Estonia* at the bottom of the Baltic Sea
- ABBA winning the Eurovision Song Contest in Brighton
- The opera singer Birgit Nilsson in a crowd of admirers
- Arafat, Clinton, and Rabin shaking hands at Camp David
- The Beatles being welcomed by fans at a Swedish airport

DOI: 10.4324/9781003432272-13

Raymond Williams (1974)   167

- The models Twiggy and Mary Quaint in 1960s hairstyles
- A stranded Russian submarine, the U 137, being towed out of Swedish waters
- Riots in central Stockholm in the 1960s during the "battle of the elms"
- Boris Yeltsin with a Russian flag and soldiers, in front of a damaged government building
- The cold-war spy Wennerström being led out of a Swedish courtroom
- A plane landing in the Red Square in Moscow
- John F. Kennedy's funeral, with his young son saluting
- The final scenes of the first season of the Swedish version of *Survivor*, announcing the winner
- Olof Palme giving a speech
- The skyscrapers at the Word Trade Center collapsing
- Hippie youths dancing in a meadow (perhaps Woodstock?)
- A monk in flames, seated on a city street
- A Swedish demonstration against the war in Vietnam
- An injured child being carried away by a man (a war zone, perhaps in the Middle East?)
- Khrushchev and Castro shaking hands
- Swedish cars switching sides from left- to right-handed traffic
- An international demonstration against nuclear tests
- A tsunami wave hitting a beach in Thailand
- A prisoner staring into the camera through barbed wire (maybe Srebrenica?)
- Rockets launching and detonating (perhaps nuclear tests in Korea?)
- The group Roxette performing for an enthusiastic audience
- The JAS *Gripen*, a Swedish fighter aircraft, crashing on a runway during its test flight
- Gunnar Myrdal, Eyvind Johnson, and Harry Martinson receiving the Nobel Prize
- Swedish Foreign Minister Anna Lindh giving an uninhibited laugh
- UN Secretary-General Dag Hammarskjöld smiling among people at an airport
- Newspaper headlines announcing the crash of Hammarskjöld's airplane
- Astrid Lindgren, the children's books' author, with a flower wreath in her hair
- A crying child with severe facial injuries
- The Chernobyl nuclear reactor after its meltdown, filmed from the air
- Groups of people sitting on the remains of the Berlin Wall
- Princess Victoria inaugurating a bridge between Öland and the Swedish mainland

In written form, this compilation seems chaotic—or, on second thought, offensive. Within seconds, the viewers are transported from the grave of the *Estonia*'s passengers at the bottom of the sea to ABBA's Eurovision triumph; from the collapse of skyscrapers during the terrorist attack in New York to young people dancing in the meadows of Woodstock; and from a revered writer of children's books to a child in severe pain. How are viewers supposed to relate

168 Staffan Ericson

to these images? Each individual segment displays a slice of reality, but their interconnection remains surreal. There is no chronological order to these events, nor any narrative logic to form a story with a beginning, middle, and end. Even if some kind of connection can be glimpsed between sequences— whether thematization, montage, or repetition—it dissolves with the next sequence. Or, if this stream corresponds to some kind of inner monologue, as in "subjective realism," there is no way of knowing who it belongs to. If anything, the organization is that of a random generator.

Nonetheless, whoever edited this stream of images had little need to worry about confusing or offending the viewers, as we are sufficiently accustomed to accepting such a stream as a festive moment in primetime entertainment. We are accustomed to such streams not only in terms of their *content* (here, the individual segments draw heavily on classic "media events"; see Chapter 25 in this volume) but also in terms of the *form* in which they are presented. This point may be said to confirm Raymond Williams' main idea about the specificity of television, as formulated in *Television: Technology and Cultural Form*:

> In all developed broadcasting systems the characteristic organization, and therefore the characteristic experience, is one of sequence or flow. The phenomenon, of planned flow, is perhaps the defining characteristic of broadcasting, simultaneously as a technology and as a cultural form.
>
> (Williams 1974/1990: 87)

Television as flow

It is also this form, according to Williams, that represents the significant novelty of television and radio.

> In all communication systems before broadcasting media, the essential items were discrete. A book or pamphlet was taken and read as a specific item. A meeting occurred at a particular time and place. A play was performed in a particular theater at a set hour. The difference in broadcasting media is not that these events, or events resembling them, are available inside the home, by the operation of a switch. It is that the real program that is offered is a sequence of these and other similar events, which are the available in a single dimension and in a single operation.
>
> (Williams 1974/1990: 87)

It is this unifying "dimension"—"the central television experience: the fact of flow" (Williams 1974/1990: 95)—that allows us to describe an evening spent as "watching TV," rather than as watching one or more programs. It is our familiarity with this "single operation" that glosses over the awkwardness of juxtaposing images of real death (on a beach in Thailand, at the bottom of the Baltic sea) with images of entertainment (on a beach in *Survivor*, on a Eurovision stage in Brighton). It is this "fact" that makes sense of an apparently chaotic series of segments, accompanied by a song about the passage of time, as a fitting celebration of the anniversary of television; for being in the midst of the flow of television is both to be *live* (where "everything changes, nothing remains") and to have access to collective memory (to something we can "trust," like the passage of the sun or the singing of birds).

A form of organization that is so ubiquitous, so present in our everyday lives, runs the risk of being invisible, like water is to fish. Williams claims to have discovered the flow of television in a moment of confusion, when the normal suddenly appeared alien. The most frequently quoted passage in Williams' book, which has been identified as the origin of modern television theory (Gripsrud 1998), describes how the Englishman gets lost when watching TV in an American hotel room in 1970:

> One night in Miami, still dazed from a week on an Atlantic liner, I began watching a film and at first had some difficulty adjusting to a much greater frequency of commercial 'breaks'. Yet this was a minor problem compared to what eventually happened. Two other films, which were due to be shown on the same channel on other nights, began to be inserted as trailers. A crime in San Francisco (the subject of the original film) began to operate in an extraordinary counterpoint not only with the deodorant and cereal commercials but with a romance in Paris and the eruption of a prehistoric monster who laid waste New York. Moreover, this was sequence in a new sense. Even in commercial British television there is a visual signal – the residual sign of an interval – before and after the commercial sequences, and 'programme' trailers only occur between 'programmes'. Here there was something quite different, since the transitions from film to commercial and from film A to film B and C were in effect unmarked. There is in any case enough similarity between certain kinds of films, and between several kinds of film and the 'situation' commercials which often consciously imitate them, to make a sequence of this kind a very difficult experience to interpret. I can still not be sure what I took from that whole flow. I believe I registered some incidents as happening in the wrong film, and some characters in the commercials as involved in the film episodes, in what came to seem – for all the occasional bizarre disparities – a single irresponsible flow of images and feelings.
>
> (Williams 1974/1990: 91–92)

As indicated in this quotation, Williams' confusion is geographically determined. His flow theory is one of several theories published on media and culture during the 20th century that contrast American commerce with European cultural heritage (e.g., Adorno's analysis of the culture industry or Baudrillard's analysis of the postmodern; see Chapters 3 and 10 in this volume). Like many media critics in the 1970s, Williams is inclined to see the global development of television as a direct result of "the expansion of the American communication system"—an "operation" rooted in the U.S. military and media industry, aimed

170 *Staffan Ericson*

to "penetrate" the broadcasting systems of all available states (Williams 1974/ 1990: 39). A contemporary traveler who turns on the TV in a foreign hotel room today—be it an American, European, or Asian—is probably less likely to suffer the kind of culture shock experienced by Williams in Miami. Few would need the support of linguistic information, marked pauses, or visual cues to distinguish the trailer from the commercial or the film. Anyone with a standard subscription at home should be familiar with how sequences may be organized into 24-hour streams, primetime, or seasons. In retrospect, this fact can be said to confirm another of Williams' points: Planned flow has a homogenizing effect. Its form tends to undermine differences between commercial and public service systems, national and global channels, fact and entertainment, and sequence and program. Of course, the fact that Williams seems to have gotten this right does not mean that his flow theory retains its full explanatory value in the present day.

A "modern classic"?

When a Swedish publisher chose to publish a translation of *Television: Technology and Cultural Form* for a series of "Modern Classics" in 2001, this 1974 text landed in an alien environment. According to the common periodization, the book was written during the era of national mass communication (ca. 1955–1985), when broadcast media had few and highly regulated producers, limited frequencies, and a relative scarcity of content. As a result, audiences were large and could be simultaneously addressed. Those days are long gone. The subsequent phase, which Williams clearly saw coming, was one of a multi-channel universe, characterized by the deregulation of broadcast media, an abundance of content via satellite and cable, a multitude of producers, and audiences spread over space and time: *narrowcasting* rather than *broadcasting*. Around the turn of the millennium, the threshold of the Internet era was clearly visible, triggering dramatic declarations of the death of television from both media industry and media scholars. The remaining fragments of that era now seem to scatter over a new landscape, identified through keywords such as *convergence, connectivity, platforms, prosumers*, and *digitization*. So why would anyone—and media and communication scholars in particular—want to return to a theory of 1970s television?

For some, the authority of the author's name would be sufficient. Raymond Williams, who died in 1988, has held a firm position in the canon of media and communication studies since the 1960s, at least. In the last decade, there have been signs of an intensified interest in his work, with the publication of new biographies (Smith 2008), new compilations of original works (e.g., Williams 1958/2014), and secondary literature (e.g., the interview book *Politics and Letters*, 1979/2015, which outlines the full breadth of Williams' interests, including fictional and dramatic work and engagement in politics and education, in addition to academic writing). Within media studies, Williams' position is primarily outlined in a trilogy of books published between the late 1950s and the early 1960s: *Culture and Society* (1958), *The Long Revolution* (1961), and *Communications* (1962). In retrospect, these books are widely held to provide road maps for cultural studies as an academic field and for studying media within this field. A decade later, Williams' book on television opened up a new academic subfield, that of *television studies*. It should be noted that the attribution of canonic status to Williams' books may appear to contradict some of the aspiration of his earlier works. According to these, a self-imposed focus on "the best that has been thought and said" is what characterizes an "ideal" version of culture, set to preserve absolute and timeless values, through "selective traditions" (Williams 1961/2001: 66). Instead, Williams aims to open up a path for the study of culture as "a whole way of life" (Williams 1958: 18). In addition, if and when the study of television achieves the status of a specific academic field, this would risk obscuring precisely the sort of connections that Williams wants to make visible—connections between technology, education, society, and history, in "the flow of meanings and values of a specific culture" (Williams 1974/1990: 118).

Another type of justification might ignore both the individual author and the academic canon, but argue that the relevance of Williams' theory has been largely confirmed by recent media developments. Indeed, the rumor of the death of the medium of television seems to have been somewhat exaggerated. In the early decades of the 21st century, there has been ample evidence of the unifying power of television in times of crisis and social change (e.g., terrorist attacks, natural disasters, revolutions, and presidential elections). Streaming services such as Netflix, HBO, Hulu, Disney, and Viaplay have been claimed to initiate a "new golden age" for the home delivery of drama and sports. If anything, the practice of YouTube viewing seems to confirm that the television segment may be more important than the program, as already noted by Williams. Devices that bear little resemblance to the classic television set in the living room at first glance, such as tablets, laptops, and smartphones, are still being used to "remediate" (Bolter & Grusin 2000) content produced for and by television. Moreover, the connection between television and such devices should perhaps be understood precisely through the logic that Williams used to explain the record-breaking spread of the television set in 20th century living rooms: its adaptation to an "at once mobile and home-centered way of living" (Williams 1974/1990: 26). If so, there may also be a connection between these and much earlier devices that were also related to television, according to Williams: not only the radio but also gramophones, cars, cameras, and household appliances. Williams likes to point out such hidden historical continuities. A Swedish reader may be particularly intrigued by how Williams inserts the late 1890s dream-plays of Swedish author August Strindberg's into television history:

> Indeed it is one of the most striking examples of the complicated relationships between new forms of experience and new kinds of technology that Strindberg was experimenting with moving dramatic images in the same decade in which, in quite another environment, the pioneers of motion

172 *Staffan Ericson*

pictures were inventing some of the technological means that would eventually make this kind of dramatic imagery possible and in the end even commonplace.

(Williams 1974/1990: 56–57)

Williams' willingness to go beyond the context of his own era and to his medium of choice may invite the reader to connect to experiences of the contemporary media landscape. Could mobile privatization be at the root of today's broadbands, Wi-Fi networks, and smart phones? Is today's smart home an extension of the TV set's "window to the world," and thus of Strindberg's attempt to break out of the closed room of naturalistic theater? Is today's extended viewing of TV series a continuation of the desire for "dramatic simulation," in which Williams saw one of the most pervasive effects of television, according to the lecture that installed him as a professor at Cambridge in 1974?

Till the eyes tire, millions of us watch the shadows of shadows and find them substance; watch scenes, situations, actions, exchanges, crises. The slice of life, once the project of naturalistic drama, is now a voluntary, habitual, internal rhythm; the flow of action and acting, of representation and performance, raised to a new convention, that of a basic need.

(Williams 1975/1989: 5)

The status of Williams' book as a "classic" in media theory is partly due to how it opens up a path for this sort of self-reflective, contextualizing reading. Ultimately, every reader is faced with the question that Williams once directed toward television: How do we historicize media?

Williams the historian

"It is often said that television has altered our world" (Williams 1974/1990: 9). William opens his book with this sentence. He then immediately adds that such a statement could just as well be made about the car or the atomic bomb (a prime example of today could be the Internet). Such statements often sound obvious but may turn out to involve inexhaustibly complex issues. Nevertheless, Williams claims, such issues are not to be regarded as "abstract": "They form an increasingly important part of our social and cultural discussions, and they are always decided in practice, by real and actual decisions" (Williams 1974/1990: 10).

The first task Williams approaches in *Television* is a semantic dissection of the claim that "television has altered our world." He identifies nine possible meanings, more than half of which are classified as expressions of "*technological determinism*" (emphasis original, Williams 1974/1990: 13). These all assume that a technology has been invented as the result of an internal research process, and that the main effects of this invention are to be recognized in terms of historical and societal progress, and in the setting of conditions that "create the modern world" (Williams 1974/1990: 13). Without television, the argument usually goes, certain events would never have occurred. The remaining meanings are classified by Williams as *"symptomatic technology"* (emphasis original, Williams 1974/1990: 13). These, too, assume that the technology has emerged from internal processes, but its effects are instead perceived as the byproduct of a societal change that is "in any case occurring or about to occur" (Williams 1974/1990: 13). If this latter group of meanings were to be illustrated using the traditions discussed in this volume, a "symptomatic" tendency might be sensed in, for example, Lazarsfeld and Merton's view of media effects and popular taste (see Chapter 4 in this volume), Habermas' view of media and democracy (see Chapter 7 in this volume), or Jameson's view of postmodern aesthetics (see Chapter 21 in this volume). In such cases, the alleged change (i.e., the reorganization of mass society, the decay of the public sphere, or the cultural logic of late capitalism) is somehow assumed to be "occurring anyway," with or without the support of new media technologies. As for technological determinism, it would be difficult to find *any* tradition that voluntarily embraces the term. Its main function, for Williams and for many other critics of 20th century media theory, seems to be to reveal a flaw in the way *others* think (cf. Durham Peters 2017).

Readers of *Television* eventually realize that Williams perceives this flaw in the works of Marshall McLuhan. This criticism has often been repeated against so-called medium theory, both in its classical version—as represented by not only McLuhan (see Chapter 8 in this volume) but also Harold Innis and Neil Postman (see Chapter 23 in this volume)—and in its more recent variations, such as the "media archaeology" inspired by Friedrich Kittler (see Chapter 24 in this volume). In the introduction to *Television*, Williams offers no references to specific scholars or traditions but simply notes that an overwhelming proportion of the most common assumptions about television—in research, industry, or media policy—are either techno-deterministic or symptomatic. To Williams, both types of assumptions are misguided. And they make the same mistake: They isolate and abstract the technology from its surrounding society and thereby obscure how certain technologies emerge in relation to "known social needs, purposes and practices" (Williams 1974/1990: 14).

So, what would the alternative be? At first glance, *Television*'s disposition and headings do not reveal a drastic break from approaches used in the standard literature of media studies. The first two chapters sketch a background, in terms of the technology, social history, and institutions of the medium. Williams then presents an inventory of its types of content and how these have taken over and/or developed from previously known formats (i.e., news, drama, education, sport, advertising, etc.) or created new ones (i.e., the documentary drama, feature, debate, sequential comedy, etc.). In the middle section of the book, chapter 4, Williams presents an original, comparative study of "flows" in British and American television, which is divided into three levels: from *long-range* (programming; the organization of schedules) to *middle-range* (the integration of separate titles, programs, and sequences) to *close-range* (the detailed sequences of words and images). Chapter 5 then deals with the question of the effects of television, while chapter 6, the final chapter, highlights expected developments and their possible alternatives.

174 *Staffan Ericson*

The concepts and passages that have proven to be most influential—namely, those on flow, mobile privatization, and Williams' night in Miami—emerge gradually, particularly in the fourth, analytical chapter, and are delivered without much fanfare. A second reading confirms that they follow organically from a vision of culture and history that guides the book from the very first page—a vision that was gradually developed in the three books Williams wrote a decade earlier. This vision is succinctly expressed in the opening chapter of the second of these books, *The Long Revolution*:

> Our whole way of life, from the shape of our societies to the organization and content of education, and from the structure of the family to the status of art and entertainment, is being profoundly affected by the progress and interaction of democracy and industry, and by the extension of communications. This deeper cultural revolution is a large part of our most significant living experience, and it is interpreted and indeed fought out, in very complex ways, in the world of art and ideas. It is when we try to correlate change of this kind with the changes covered by the disciplines of politics, economics, and communications that we discover some of the most difficult but also some of the most human questions.
>
> (Williams 1961/2001: 12)

Thus, it is *processes of change* within a modern society that attract William's interest, and only those that may be related to a *life experience* that is socially shared. If we "isolate" or "abstract" different aspects of such change—such as art from entertainment, politics from economics, or education from technology—we risk breaking the connections in which Williams claims to find a "continuity of experience"; the links between individual and social experience. Consequently, the cultural theory advocated by Williams is to be devoted to "the study of the relations between elements in a whole way of life" (1961/2001: 63). "Communications" (Williams 1962) will hold a prominent place in such studies—not in terms of some "secondary" process in which information is transferred, but as the primary process by which people and societies share experience.

With this program in mind, Williams was more or less obliged to write a book about television. It was there, if anywhere, that modern society communicated with itself; there, if anywhere, that experiences of the world were shared, in a process involving all kinds of forces and interests (technical, political, economic, aesthetic, etc.). And, by the time William discovers the flow on that evening in Miami, he has identified a pattern—an organization—that could reveal the interrelationship among these forces and interests, and a possible connection between "technology," "cultural form," and shared experience.

So, when Williams turns to television, it is not under the assumption that this technology has "caused" a deeper cultural revolution. It could just as well be argued that the development of this technology was "caused by" the ways in which a revolution had already shaped "our whole way of life." The flows of television appeared because mobility, change, and variation characterized the modern experience of life. Moreover, the specific uses of broadcasting media (public and regulated production but private and home-based consumption) appeared because of specific demands raised by this social experience:

> Socially, this complex is characterized by two apparently paradoxical yet deeply interrelated tendencies of modern urban industrial living: on the one hand mobility, on the other hand the more apparently self-sufficient family home. The earlier period of public technology, best exemplified by the railways and street lighting, was being replaced by a kind of technology for which no satisfactory name has yet been found: that which served an at once mobile and home-centered way of living: a form of *mobile privatization*. Broadcasting media in its applied form was a social product of this distinctive tendency.
>
> (Emphasis original, Williams 1974/1990: 26)

The sort of "tendency" or "complex" that Williams refers to here might be understood as the "zeitgeist." But Williams seems to be reaching for a more distinct phenomenon, resembling his adaption of the term "structure of feeling" in his 1950s studies of film and modern drama. This term originally referred to the intersection of lived experience, dramatic conventions, and means of communication that could be registered in works of art, particularly during times of change, and particularly in the work of pioneering artists such as Strindberg. In *The Long Revolution*, Williams expands the scope of this term: It now refers to "a very deep and very wide possession, in all actual communities, precisely because it is on it that communication depends" (1961/2001: 65). Thus, the sort of articulation of historical totality that may be manifested in emerging structures of feeling is no longer limited to a "work of art as a whole." Rather, it runs through all social and cultural practices, constituting "the particular living result of all elements in the general organization" (1961/2001: 64). Twelve years later, in *Television*, Williams introduces the notions of "flow" and "mobile privatization" to perform this task; that is, to correlate changes in ideas and conventions to changes in politics, social organization, and communications. *Television* may in fact be Williams' most consistent attempt to apply the program of *The Long Revolution* in the realm of media.

Williams the media theorist

So, how does Williams' work relate to other traditions of media studies? As a constructor of theory, Williams is something of a solo artist. The reader is offered few actual references; when they do come, they tend to be critical, at times, unnecessarily dismissive. In *Television*, Williams explicitly contrasts his approach with two alternatives: sociological mass communication research and McLuhan's medium theory.

In his early works, Williams had identified a guiding principle in Marx's historical materialism: Any cultural analysis should start from the existing

176   *Staffan Ericson*

relations of production. However, Williams could not recognize the modern world as described by 20th century Marxists, especially the Frankfurt School: "A dying culture, and ignorant masses, are not what I have known and see" (Williams 1958/2014: 7). The experience of culture as "ordinary" and "common" is rooted in Williams' upbringing in the British working class, and he finds little reason to revise it after entering the world of Oxford and Cambridge.

At the same time, the overall picture of modern culture that gradually emerges in *Television*—that of an "irresponsible flow" that obliterates all differences and of a standard that stems from "the expansion of the American communication system"—does not seem dramatically different from, for example, Adorno's critique of the culture industry (see Chapter 3 in this volume). Williams' description of how television handles debate and discussion—"a public process, at the level of response and interrogation, is *represented* for us by the television intermediaries" (emphasis original, Williams 1974/1990: 52)—may be reminiscent of a later version of the Frankfurt School's media critique: Jürgen Habermas' description of the demise of the public sphere (see Chapter 7 in this volume). It remains unclear whether Williams read Habermas' book on this topic from 1962, which did in fact refer to Williams' *Culture and Society* from 1958. As a realist and materialist, Williams takes issue with television's "attempts to represent public opinion" or, in his words, to "*simulate a representation by their own criteria*" (original emphasis, Williams 1974/1990: 53). His recurrent complaint of how television seems to stand in for reality may touch on themes later associated with Jean Baudrillard and postmodernism (see Chapter 10 in this volume). In one of his final texts, Williams notes how British television's coverage of the Falklands War in 1982 simultaneously establishes and erases a sense of distance from the real events in the war zone. To Williams, the experts commenting on the course of the war engage in what seems like an extended build-up to a football game, expecting "at least something to happen, according to the usual rhythms of television" (Williams 1989: 14). About a decade later, Baudrillard (1995) suggests that the Gulf War did not really "take place" outside of the screens of CNN.

While Baudrillard drew some inspiration from McLuhan, Williams' rejection of the latter's ideas—which he found "ludicrous" (Williams 1974/1990: 153)—is probably one of the lasting influences of *Television*. Its readers may note that the author makes little effort to provide a comprehensive picture of the object under attack; we are never told which of McLuhan's texts is being referred to, in what precise sense these would qualify as expressions of "formalism" and "determinism," and why, if so, these positions are so offensive. Upon a more sympathetic reading, it does seem possible to relate basic ideas in *Television*— such as the exposure of the flow as the "technology and cultural form" of a single medium, in relation to its social and cultural environment—to some of McLuhan's basic themes: namely, that "the medium is the message," and that the primary "effect" of the media should be sought in their organization of time, space, and "ecology" (see Chapters 8 and 23 in this volume).

Raymond Williams (1974)   177

To further complicate things, Williams' affiliation with his assumed home turf of British cultural studies does not appear to be fully consistent. This research field has often declared a special interest in popular, "low" cultural forms, as opposed to the "high" tradition, or the artistic avant-garde. Williams, however, is more than happy to write about Coleridge, Ibsen, Brecht, and Ingmar Bergman, long after having acknowledged how "the selective tradition" of the humanities may exclude lived culture. In *Culture and Society* and *The Long Revolution*, William's aim is hardly to *abandon* the high tradition, for the cultivation of an alternative garden; rather, he aims to *re-interpret* it, in order to reveal its connection to that "deeper cultural revolution." Moreover, the field of cultural studies is supposed to advocate the empirical study of the reception processes of real users, in contrast to the text-based analysis commonly practiced within the aesthetic humanities. Williams, however, continues to read texts, with a keen eye for the sort of social analysis that engaged Marxists such as Georg Lukacs, Benjamin, and Adorno: Williams, too, expects the social determination of texts to register in cultural "forms," rather than in "content."

Williams claimed to be surprised when his colleagues in the humanities saw his growing interest in film, television, and the press as a switch in academic subject, from literature/drama to media sociology. To him, the connections were already there: between a television commercial and the early techniques of surrealism, or between depictions of a private life in a 1960s sitcom and the confinement of experience in Chekhov. As for the methods of sociological mass communication research, Williams did not hesitate to present some of his results in *Television* in the form of quantitative tables. But he remains puzzled; firstly, by how human intention tends to be hijacked by the formulas of media sociology—"who says what, how, to whom, with what effect" (Harold Lasswell) does not say enough about the *purposes* of communication. In his own analyses of texts and technologies, Williams finds it notoriously difficult to orient without an identifiable source or a human need. Thus, in contrast to both techno-deterministic and symptom-technical interpretations, Williams wants to "restore *intention*" (emphasis original, Williams 1974/1990: 14) to the study of television. As technologies emerge and develop with "certain purposes and practices already in mind," their effects should be seen as "direct," rather than marginal or symptomatic. In mobile privatization, a collectively experienced structure of feeling, Williams sees the sort of human need that both shapes and is shaped by technology, indicating "at once an intention and an effect of a particular social order" (Williams 1974/1990: 128).

Secondly, Williams found it hard to stomach the kind of abstraction that allowed sociological study to equate television audiences with the masses. He stated his view as early as in *Culture and Society* (1958: 289): "Masses are other people. There are in fact no masses, there are only ways of seeing people as masses." This may be another of Williams' more enduring imprints on media studies in general: By the mid-1990s, the prefix "mass" had all but disappeared from book titles and course descriptions within the discipline. *Television* displays how Williams' intention was not just to avoid the devaluation attached to

178   Staffan Ericson

this prefix; he perceived limitations in the way in which standard questions of mass communication research—concerning the "effects" in terms of violence, socialization, and so forth—had "abstracted" and normalized a series of assumptions: When and why is violence legitimate, and in whose interest are we socialized? According to Williams, a "real" sociology of communication should be directed at the historical process and cultural order in which the normalization of such assumptions *was* an "effect." Furthermore, social sciences' preoccupation with objective "methods" tended to obscure a range of important qualities such as understanding, evaluation, and empathy, which Williams viewed as contributing to, or counteracting, the social relations within which communication systems would operate.

To replace the masses as the assumed recipients of television, Williams basically offered … himself. Four years prior to writing *Television*, Williams took on the task of television critic for the BBC's magazine *The Listener*. His reviews reveal the presence of an essentially open but deeply ambivalent viewer. Williams repeatedly notes the impact of an overall "flow" in the experience of viewing, yet his assessments are almost exclusively about programs (understandably so, as the genre of criticism is firmly rooted in cultural forms that attend to separate items). He avoids the conventional divisions between "serious" and "entertaining" programs but distinguishes those that "look like someone has successfully meant something by making them, not just placed them in a market" (Williams 1989: 129). This criterion results in rough verdicts of some of the BBC's prestigious programs (i.e., cultural magazines and avant-garde TV drama) but works out well for live football and Monty Python sketches. Overall, Williams shows few signs of a symptom that has characterized many intellectuals' takes on television: the desire to identify a generally "low" quality within television, in order to affirm the value of something "high" outside of it. As a specialist in modern drama, Williams is convinced that television currently shows not only the most but also the best. A soap opera such as *Coronation Street* is undervalued in its depiction of "people regularly and connectedly known; the development of a life situation":

> If we look at it that way round, and stop despising TV serials, we might get to a position in which the facts of connection and consequence could be written as experience, rather than as a plot-calculation.
>
> (Williams 1989: 83)

When Williams is disappointed by what he sees, it is usually from the vantage point of a value system that is partly realist and partly modernist. In terms of representing society, the medium is fundamentally flawed: "Nobody would believe there are 56 million people in England: we hear and see so few of them" (Williams 1989: 42). Furthermore, the realness of what and who we do get to see is fundamentally deceptive:

> Television is so good when it presents real events that it gains a power which it then abuses: nominally, to set up an anteroom, beside everything

Raymond Williams (1974) 179

that is happening – a budget, a cup final, an election, a horse-race – but actually making the anteroom the arena, the reaction the event, and the commentators the real agents.

(Williams 1989: 97)

If you expect this window on the world to represent *contemporary* life, you are in for more disappointment. According to Williams, television is a deeply nostalgic medium. In the early 1970s, the median time of the output of British television was estimated to be circa 1925. "What sort of society is it," Williams asks, "in which the newest technology carries the oldest messages?" (Williams 1989: 87). On television, the past is mostly "sad" and "vanishing" (Williams 1989: 72), "all art and buildings" (Williams 1989: 58), while the present is "muddled and hateful" (Williams 1989: 72), "all people and confusion" (Williams 1989: 58).

To realize its true potential as technology, television should show us places we have never seen, events we could not even imagine, causing us "to be moved, abruptly, to a quite different view point ... a brief transcendence, in the power of a new way of seeing" (Williams 1989: 48). In contrast, the "modernism" of television is dedicated to style and worn-out clichés:

Nothing flows, nowadays, so well as an Oxo commercial, a genteel art film, an elderly commentator's reminiscences of history. In this kind of work, where form is everything, we see dissolves of sun-lit woods and revolutionary crowds and waves breaking and mouths opening and rockets and streaming hair.

(Williams 1989: 53)

At one point in *Television*, Williams tries to describe the form of a type of content that would represent "television itself" (Williams 1974/1990: 76 f). To close in on the "primary process of technology" (Williams 1974/1990: 77), Williams simply suggests that we turn off the sound. Watching the flow of images in silence is an "experience of visual mobility," of "contrast of angles," which he finds "surprising" and often "very beautiful." Significantly, the only people who tend to share his experience, Williams notes, are painters. By switching the sound off, Williams effectively distances his experience from the discursive dimension in which many other scholars (cf. Morse 1985, Scannell 1991) have found the most insistent aspect of television's communicative process: the stream of direct address and interpellations coming from voices and faces in the box; the standing invitation to an interaction or dialogue that will remain one-sided or "para-social" (Horton & Wohl 1956).

As a theorist, what Williams tends to *seek* in television is the sort of cultural form that would organize a "real" historical process, a totality, "a whole way of life." Such a medium might have the potential to integrate our culture. But what Williams actually tends to *see* on television, as a viewer (in his reviews and in *Television*), is rather the inauthentic integration of art, life, history, and society; the maelstroms of an "irresponsible flow."

180 *Staffan Ericson*

After television

Back in the 1970s, Williams used the geographical distance between two television systems—British and American—to highlight general patterns in television as a technology and cultural form. In our time, we may use the historical distance between Williams' world and our own to measure the outcome of some of his predictions. In techno-material terms, Williams predicted the imminent arrival of portable videophones, large flat screens, and high-definition television as early as in 1974. In all cases, their broader impact turned out to be delayed until the late 2000s (Apple launched its iPhone in 2007; CRT-TVs effectively disappeared from the market around 2008; in 2010, HDTV broadcasting more or less became the European standard). By that time, their arrival was basically thought of as the result of *digitalization*, a sort of framing Williams might find techno-deterministic. Ironically, in 1974, Williams also predicted that McLuhan's ideas on media would soon be forgotten. With digitalization, their relevance apparently grew. Nevertheless, while Williams' book never touches on the analog/digital distinction, it has been claimed that his cultural materialist framework remains highly relevant to our understanding of the digital media landscape (cf. Fuchs 2017).

A contemporary reader might have the strongest sense of recognition when Williams penetrates to the deepest, most detailed level of analysis, such as when he focuses on the words and images in the news flow of American television:

> Over much of the actual news reporting there is a sense of hurried blur. The pace and style of the newscast take some priority over the items in it /.../ the flow of hurried items establishes a sense of the world: of surprising and miscellaneous events coming in, tumbling over each other, from all sides /.../: "today…today…today…now…fast…today…or tomorrow… don't miss it…today…coming out…today…today…at this moment… today…now…."
>
> (Williams 1974/1990: 116 f)

By now, the continuous tabulation of a live "flow" of events has been organized as updates on 24-hour channels such as CNN and the instantaneous connections of digital networks. In recent decades, the growing importance of speed and the expansion of an eternal "now" have been recurrent themes in cultural theory, as raised by postmodernists such as Fredric Jameson and Jean Baudrillard (who also tend to illustrate their analysis with television), sociologists such as Hartmut Rosa (2013), and historians such as Francois Hartog (2015). In particular, the latter's declaration of "presentism" as the new "regime of historicity" contains formulations that could well have appeared in Williams' descriptions of the temporality of television: "a permanent, elusive, almost immobile now" (Hartog 2015: 17); "since it has neither past nor future, this now fabricates daily the past and the future it needs, through its choice of the immediate" (Hartog 2015: 113).

Perhaps Williams' analysis of television as flow can be viewed as anticipating a wider spread of presentism, as a "structure of feeling"—much like Strindberg's drama, in his time, anticipated the movement of images. Williams might have appreciated such a comparison: His lifelong interest in artists such as Strindberg, Chekhov, and Brecht was clearly based on their ability to articulate cultural transformations. In Williams' case, the method of articulation is not primarily artistic, nor, it might be claimed, strictly scientific. Rather, it emerges from the persistent effort to historicize—here, with television as example—the connections between a technology, its social context, and its cultural form (and vice versa). By the end of *Television*, readers may be more or less convinced that the key to understanding this medium resides in "flow" and "mobile privatization." But we can hardly question the author's intention, stressed in the last sentence of the book, to contribute to the sort of "information, analysis, education, discussion" that will serve us in "decision" and "action" on urgent matters. In this, media and communication studies have much to learn from Williams' book, even after the last TV has been turned off.

References

Baudrillard, Jean (1995), *The Gulf War Did Not Take Place*, Bloomington: Indiana University Press.

Bolter, Jay, Richard Grusin (2000), *Remediation. Understanding New Media*, Cambridge, Mass.: MIT Press.

Durham Peters, John (2017), "You mean my whole fallacy is wrong": On technological determinism, *Representations*, 140 (Fall), 10–26.

Fuchs, Christian (2017), Raymond Williams' communicative materialism, *European Journal of Cultural Studies*, 20 (6). https://doi.org/10.1177/1367549417732998.

Gripsrud, Jostein (1998), Television, broadcasting, flow: Key metaphors in TV theory. In *The Television Studies Book*, Christine Geraghty, David Lusted (eds.), London: Arnold.

Hartog, Francois (2015), *Regimes of Historicity. Presentism and Experiences of Time*, New York: Columbia University Press.

Horton, Donald, Richard Wohl (1956), Mass communication and para-social interaction, *Psychiatry: Journal for the Study of Interpersonal Processes*, 19, 215–229.

Morse, Margaret (1985), Talk, talk, talk. The space of discourse in TV news, sportscasts, talk shows and advertising, *Screen*, 26 (2), 2–17.

Rosa, Hartmut (2013), *Social Acceleration. A New Theory on Modernity*, New York: Columbia University Press.

Scannell, Paddy (ed.) (1991), *Broadcast Talk*, London & New York: Sage.

Smith, Dai (2008), *Raymond Williams: A Warrior's Tale*, Cardigan: Parthian Books.

Williams, Raymond (1958), *Culture and Society, 1780–1950*, London: Chatto & Windus.

Williams, Raymond (1958/2014), Culture is ordinary. In *Raymond Williams on Culture & Society: Essential Writings*, J. McGuigan (ed.), London: Sage Publishing.

Williams, Raymond (1961/2001), *The Long Revolution*, Ontario: Broadway Press.

Williams, Raymond (1962), *Communications. Britain in the Sixties*, London: Penguin.

Williams, Raymond (1974/1990), *Television: Technology and Cultural Form*, London: Routledge.

182 *Staffan Ericson*

Williams, Raymond (1975/1989), *Drama in a Dramatised Society: An Inaugural Lecture*, Cambridge: Cambridge University Press, reprinted in Raymond Williams, 1989.

Williams, Raymond (1979/2015), *Politics and Letters: Interviews with the New Left Review*, London: Verso.

Williams, Raymond (1989), *Raymond Williams on Television*, London: Routledge.

13 James Carey (1975) "A Cultural Approach to Communication"

Lars Lundgren

Introduction

About thirty years after it was originally published in 1975, James Carey was asked if he would change anything if he had the chance to revisit his classic essay, "A Cultural Approach to Communication." Carey retorted in his characteristic rhetorical style: "It was necessary to write such things at the time to try to clear some space in the academy so other things could be done." (James W. Carey, in Grossberg 2006b: 199). His essays are often based on the elegant historicization and contextualization of the phenomenon under discussion, while always keeping an eye on the present. Accordingly, he began his response by noting that in the mid-1970s it was necessary to formulate the key arguments of the essay. He felt stifled by the climate of American communication research at the time, and considered it almost impossible to engage in studies of culture and communication based on the humanities. In December 2004, however, when Lawrence Grossberg asked the question, he no longer saw it as necessary to write an essay such as "A Cultural Approach to Communication" because what was being called for in the essay had by then become integral to academic research into communication.

Apart from the collection of essays *Communication as Culture: Essays on Media and Society*, in which "A Cultural Approach to Communication" constitutes the first chapter, Carey never published a book-length study. Instead, he published a large number of articles and essays covering an impressively wide range of topics. Carey's writing was by no means limited to questions of the role of Cultural Studies in the academy, which engaged him in the 1970s, but spanned a very wide area, ranging from advertising and journalism to technology and democracy—not least the role of the university in democratic societies. He rarely engaged in his own empirical studies and investigations. Instead, as in "A Cultural Approach to Communication," his texts were frequently based on readings of influential authors and scholars. These readings often served a specific purpose, not least because he used them to position himself against what he perceived as problematic perspectives on communication. Perhaps most famous, and challenged, is Carey's characterization of Walter Lippmann as an elitist by contrasting him with the, according to Carey, more democratically

DOI: 10.4324/9781003432272-14

184 *Lars Lundgren*

oriented John Dewey, who, as we will see, was important for the development of Carey's own thinking about communication.[1]

In the introduction to "A Cultural Approach to Communication," Carey already warns against casually citing classic authors, as doing so more often than not obscures the complexity of their work. Today, Carey is just such a classic author whose texts are quoted routinely, and whose nuances and complexity often get lost. This chapter looks at an essay of Carey's that is among his most influential and often cited, sometimes almost ritualistically. What is the essence of this essay? How has it been interpreted and used in media and communication studies? What is the relevance of the essay today, and how can Carey's ideas be used to understand contemporary debates in media and communication?

Before returning to "A Cultural Approach to Communication," however, we turn to Carey's childhood and early university years, which provide important background for understanding his project.

From Rhode Island to Illinois

James W. Carey was born in 1934 in Providence, Rhode Island on the east coast of the United States. His upbringing in a working-class Irish Catholic neighborhood differed markedly from a traditional academic background. At an early age he was diagnosed with a heart ailment, prompting his doctor to prescribe rest, and, as a result, Carey did not attend school until he was fourteen. He thus spent his early childhood being home-schooled for a mere hour a week. Instead, Carey received his education in a completely different environment. By talking to the neighborhood's priests, unemployed, and retirees, he gained insights that are reflected in most of his academic work, in which conversation is always central:

> It was a wonderful life. I wasn't educated in the technical sense so there were things I had to learn rather late. But in terms of understanding the immediacies of economics and history, of learning by direct experience how communities are put together, how people behave, what they're interested in, learning the commonsense wisdom of people, it's a tremendous way to learn.
> (James W. Carey, cited in Munson & Warren 1997: xxii)

Had it not been for the heart condition, Carey's future would most likely have been either in the military or in a nearby textile mill. Instead, he was enrolled in a high school secretarial program. His aptitude for reading was soon discovered, especially in English and history, and despite his very limited schooling, he was awarded a scholarship to study at the University of Rhode Island in Kingston. There he earned a bachelor's degree in business administration in 1957, and shortly thereafter underwent a pair of surgeries that corrected his heart condition. His heart, which had most tangibly provided Carey with an unconventional education, was no longer a threat, and he could move on to the environment where he would earn both his master's and doctoral degrees, the University of Illinois at Urbana-Champaign.

The University of Illinois was key to the development of American communication research, not least through Wilbur Schramm who founded the Institute of Communication Research. At the Institute, quantitatively oriented behavioral scientists such as Charles Osgood coexisted with critical Marxists such as Dallas Smythe (see Chapter 15 in this volume) and Herbert Schiller. Although the Institute was an eclectic environment where the emerging science of communication could take many forms, Carey could not quite find a role there. Osgood and his colleagues advocated a strongly positivist view of science dominated by quantitative research, which Carey more or less openly despised. The fact that Carey did not work more closely with Smythe and Schiller and the other Marxists at the Institute had a more personal explanation, as he could not accept what he perceived as an authoritarian and almost Stalinist Marxism. Looking back to his time at Illinois, Carey described Herbert Schiller as a "bourgeois Marxist; a particularly unattractive example of the breed who speaks of fiery rebellion and lets other people go out and take risks and clean up the aftermath but doesn't take any risk himself" (Carey in Grossberg 2006a: 24). Carey's description of Schiller is not flattering, nor is it particularly accurate. However, it reflects how Carey, in the early 2000s, still viewed his position at the Institute, and why it was necessary for him to carve out his own academic niche.

It is not difficult to see why Carey distanced himself from the quantitative behavioral science that was as far removed from the informal schooling of his childhood as one could get, and how his relationship with Marxist scholars was shaped by a working-class background that did not quite resonate with or relate to the petty-bourgeois Marxism he saw in Schiller, for example. It is in light of his upbringing that Carey as a young scholar found himself caught between a dogmatic quantitative view of science and an equally dogmatic Marxism, and one can understand the opening quotation of this chapter, in which Carey states that it was necessary to create space for a different kind of science.

For Carey, the answer was what he came to call Cultural Studies.[2] He had begun using the term in the mid-1960s as a description, a label, for the proseminar he organized at the Institute of Communication Research. However, it was only with "A Cultural Approach to Communication" and another influential essay, "Communication and Culture," also published in 1975, that he began to seriously outline what eventually became known as Cultural Studies. He was inspired by Max Weber's *Kulturwissenschaft* but later explained that the term science (*wissenschaft*) was reserved for the positivists at the Institute, and that they would never allow it to be used for the kind of research Carey represented.

Elements and key arguments of the essay

"A Cultural Approach to Communication" opens with a secretive and anonymous reference: "When I decided a few years ago to read seriously the

186   *Lars Lundgren*

literature on communications, a wise man suggested that I begin with John Dewey" (Carey 1975/1989: 13). The man with the good advice later turned out to be Carey's colleague Jay Jensen, and the choice to make Dewey the portal figure in the essay was crucial to how Carey developed his argument (Pooley 2016: 10). The essay is divided into two parts. In the first, Carey first introduces what he has become best known for: the distinction between the transmission and ritual views of communication. The second part of the essay points to the power of adopting a ritual view of communication, and how this can lay the groundwork for a more nuanced and viable field of communication research.

In the first pages of the essay, Carey presents his own reading of Dewey, noting that not only was he fascinated by communication—"of all things communication is the most wonderful" (Dewey 1938: 385)—but also that he emphasized that "[s]ociety exists not only by transmission, by communication," but also "in communication" (Dewey 1916: 5). Emphasizing this shift in preposition points out that communication can be understood as, on one hand, the transmission of messages in space and, on the other, as the glue that binds people and society together. This dichotomization is the basis for presenting two approaches to communication, the transmission view and the ritual view. It is important to emphasize that Carey's interest focuses on how communication has been conceptualized and what views have been used to understand communication, something he identifies by tracing different historical forms of thinking about communication. The idea of communication as transmission focuses on information sent and transferred between people separated in space, while the ritual perspective emphasizes communication as a means of maintaining communities over time. For Carey, the difference between the transmission and ritual views of communication is expressed through the practices associated with each approach. The transmission view considers communication as information to be transmitted, broadcast, and conveyed, often for the purpose of persuasion and control, while the ritual view considers communication as an act of participation, cohesion, and community. As a consequence, the distinction emphasizes the spatiality of transmission and the temporality of ritual.

> A ritual view of communication is directed not toward the extension of messages in space but toward the maintenance of society in time; not the act of imparting information but the representation of shared beliefs.
>
> (Carey 1975/1989: 18)

Carey's words seem to position the two views as mutually exclusive, as if dictated by *either/or*—either communication is seen as the transmission of messages in space or communication is seen as the maintenance of communities over time. The dichotomy between transmission and ritual is a powerful rhetorical figure that Carey also emphasizes in several other texts. However, just a few pages after defining the ritual perspective in the above quotation, he notes that "[n]either of these counterposed views of communication necessarily denies what the other affirms" (Carey 1975/1989: 21). In the conversation with

Lawrence Grossberg, Carey also recognized that his "own forms of binary thinking get in the way. I certainly did not intend that reading" (Grossberg 2006b: 200). However, he could have easily avoided this misunderstanding, this binary thinking, by pointing to Harold A. Innis, who was one of Carey's early teachers. Long historical perspectives as well as communication as extension in space or the maintenance of societies over time are figures of thought very close to what Innis called "the bias of communication," whereby Innis avoided the polarization by emphasizing the importance of what he called communicative equilibrium (Innis 1951). For Innis, the key to the survival of an empire was to find a balance between communication as bridging space and communication aimed at maintaining cultures and traditions over time. Given this, it is surprising that Innis is not mentioned even once in the essay, although opportunities to do so are definitely there.

Carey never considered the two views as mutually exclusive and emphasized that they would always be intertwined. It is in the context of this argument that Dewey re-enters the narrative of the essay, and Carey argues that the strength of Dewey's work is precisely the effort to bridge the gap between transmission and ritual.

The first part of the essay ends by noting that the tension between the transmission and ritual views not only represents different approaches to communication, but also corresponds to different historical periods, technologies, and social types (Carey 1975/1989: 22). This idea may also be derived from Innis who, in his book *Empire and Communications* (Innis 1950), devotes himself to a detailed study of different historical empires, from Egypt to the British Commonwealth, and the characteristics of their communication systems. In "A Cultural Approach to Communication," however, Carey does not point to any particular historical period, other than by referring to his own experience and entry into academia.

Furthermore, he notes that the transmission view has dominated American communication research since the 1920s, perhaps especially at the University of Illinois, not least through functionalism and behavioral science, which, according to Carey, had by then reached a dead end: "It could no longer go forward without disastrous intellectual and social consequences" (Carey 1975/1989: 23). From Carey's point of view, these traditions were overly characterized by preconceived truths and stagnant intellectual development. To avoid these devastating consequences and better utilize the tension between transmission and ritual, Carey suggests that the study of communication should shift its focus toward biology, theology, anthropology, and literary studies. There, Carey argues, one would find the fertile ground needed to better understand the role of communication in society.

The core of "A Cultural Approach to Communication" is Carey's historically based thesis that the view of communication has been dominated by two different perspectives: communication as the transmission of messages in space for the purpose of exercising control, and communication as the maintenance of societies over time through creating common values and belief systems. The

188   *Lars Lundgren*

second part of the present essay deals, as mentioned, with Carey's proposal for how the ritual perspective can be translated into the study of communication.

The USA and Europe

"A Cultural Approach to Communication" articulates an almost exclusively American story, and a quick reading of it gives an almost provincial impression. According to the essay, it is the American academic departments that have come to be dominated by a transmission view, and the solution to this problem is to be found above all in Dewey and his successors in the Chicago School, with qualitatively oriented sociologists such as George Herbert Mead, Charles Horton Cooley, and Robert Park, and later also Erving Goffman (see Chapter 6 in this volume). It is the American experience that underpins Carey's tracing of the history of the transmission view: the experience of moving, of being transported, from Europe to America, of building railways and telegraph lines as a means of overcoming and controlling a vast continent. Carey does note in passing that it is only by turning to the European academy and its intellectual legacy that a better understanding of communication as ritual and culture can be achieved, but this call is not followed up later in the essay except in its very last pages, where the British cultural studies scholar Raymond Williams (see Chapter 12 in this volume) becomes part of the story.

The fact that the starting point and anchoring should be in the USA is telling and must be read in relation to his second essay from 1975, published in the collection *Communication as Culture: Essays on Media and Society* under the title "Mass Communication and Cultural Studies." This essay first appeared as a review essay of anthropologist Clifford Geertz's influential book *The Interpretation of Cultures*. The review essay was entitled "Communication and Culture," and was revised and published at least twice before being published in *Communication as Culture.* [3]

Several arguments and passages of the review essay are almost identical to those in "A Cultural Approach to Communication." However, "Mass Communication and Cultural Studies" situates the discussion in a European context and as having intellectual roots in the European tradition. The anthropologist Geertz was indeed American, working mainly at the University of Chicago and at Princeton, but in his review essay *of The Interpretation of Cultures*, Carey noted that Geertz's book was "an avenue through which important European scholarship can enter the United States" (Carey 1975: 174).

It was through Geertz that the American academy could come into contact with a European intellectual tradition, and not least the Cultural Studies that emerged there in the post-war period through writers such as Stuart Hall and Raymond Williams (see Chapters 11 and 12 in this volume). In "Mass Communication and Cultural Studies," it is Geertz's epistemological contribution that comes to the fore, and how it enables an interpretive science. Through Geertz, Carey formulates the goal of scientific activity as:

to understand the meanings that others have placed on experience, to build up a veridical record of what has been said at other times, in other places, and in other ways; to enlarge the human conversation by comprehending what others are saying. Though modest, the inability to engage in this conversation is the imperative failure of the modern social sciences. Not understanding their subjects—that unfortunate word—they do not converse with them so much as impose meanings on them.

(Carey 1975: 188–189)

That Carey was attracted to Geertz's pursuit of conversation, of making meaning together, is not difficult to understand given the role of conversation in his upbringing and early education. It is through engagement with other people that historically grounded and interpretive scholarship can be developed.

"Mass Communication and Cultural Studies" also provides the reader with a somewhat different explanation of the dichotomy between the transmission and ritual perspectives on communication, which is now charged with a geographical meaning. Carey now points to how American communication research is locked into the transmission view while European cultural studies embraces the ritual view. It is from this perspective that Carey emphasizes the value of the European intellectual tradition and how it can revitalize American communication research. The differences and similarities between "A Cultural Approach to Communication" and "Mass Communication and Cultural Studies" illustrate how Carey drew on his various predecessors to make similar arguments, while at the same time slightly shifting the focus of the argument. In the first essay, it was John Dewey who simultaneously helped Carey to formulate the problem and, through his successors at the Chicago School, to remedy it. In the second essay, however, it was through Geertz and his connection to the European academy that Carey articulated his argument, although both essays ultimately serve the same purpose.

Transmission and ritual: view or model?

The second part of "A Cultural Approach to Communication" begins with Carey presenting his own definition of communication, which he believes is "of some intellectual power and scope: communication is a symbolic process whereby reality is produced, maintained, repaired, and transformed" (Carey 1975/1989: 23). Here, then, the essay departs from tracing and discussing the historical roots that gave rise to the two perspectives on communication to a definition that points to a model for understanding communication as such. Based on this definition, Carey sets himself the task of trying to make sense of the symbolic production of reality. To do so, he argues, we must first break down some of our preconceived assumptions that come from what can be described as common sense. One such assumption is that there is a reality independent of us, which we then approach and make sense of with more or less precise descriptions. Carey notes that this is a problematic and reductive

190 *Lars Lundgren*

understanding of the world, and provides an example from a very concrete everyday situation—a primary school child learning to walk to school by himself. As a first option, the child can be offered a map, with his own house and school drawn on it, as well as important landmarks such as buildings and intersections to help orient the child. The map can have varying degrees of precision and detail, but regardless of this, its purpose is to make the route between home and school comprehensible. Carey then points out that there are other ways to convey the way home. A song could orient the child ("first you turn to the left, then you turn to the right") and would be easily memorized. A third option would be to teach the child a dance that guides his movements through space and imitates the way home. Carey's point is that space can be represented in various symbolic forms, by signs on a piece of paper, by sound or movement, and that these forms allow us to represent a reality that is not present. However, the symbolic representations are not just an image of an external reality but are also co-creators of that reality: "We first produce the world by symbolic work and then take up residence in the world we have produced" (Carey 1975/1989: 30). In the footnote immediately following this quotation, Carey notes that we do not just produce one world; rather, as the phenomenologist Alfred Schütz has noted, there are multiple realities (Carey 1975/1989: 35, note 7). Carey notes that, although he lacks the space to further problematize this matter, it strengthens his criticism of so-called effects research that fails to take this into account.

If we understand the role of communication in society in the way Carey suggests, the transmission view is not enough: it cannot form the basis of a model that helps us to understand and analyze these processes because it reduces the multifaceted complexity of communication (Carey 1975/1989: 32). It is also with this observation the essay moves from exposing two different approaches to communication to asking whether they can form the basis of a model for analyzing communication. While the first part of "A Cultural Approach to Communication" was mainly concerned with a ritual *perspective* on communication, Carey devotes the final pages of the essay to discussing the ritual *model* as the basis for an interpretive communication research.

Carey emphasizes that the transmission perspective on communication is not limited to (American) academia, but that it characterizes the view of communication found in society at large. He does this by returning to the story of the child finding his way to school, and the common view of the map as a simplification, a reduction of the infinite detail of reality. In this way, maps are made comprehensible for a specific purpose: a map intended to help a child find his way to school does not need to contain detailed information on topographical conditions, for example, whereas this may be crucial for a runner who wants to perform well in a race. It is precisely by reducing the amount of information about reality that maps become useful for specific purposes. Carey's point is that different maps thus produce different realities. This means that our symbols are not just representations of reality, but are representations *for* reality: when we create a map, it does not just depict reality, but it creates a specific version of reality by emphasizing certain details and suppressing others (Carey 1975/1989: 29).

The double meaning of the human use of symbols, that is, that they both describe and create reality, has particularly interesting implications for the study of communication. It is ironic, Carey notes, that the study of communication is often concerned with communication about communication, with his own essay being one of many examples of this. But it also means that the models we use to understand communication have precisely this double meaning: "Models of communication are, then, not merely representation of communication but representations *for* communication ... Our models of communication, consequently, create what we disingenuously pretend they merely describe" (Carey 1975/1989: 32). The consequences, as Carey points out earlier in the essay, are disastrous. He argues that there is an obsessive commitment to the transmission view of communication and that this leads to our communication models being almost exclusively about power and control from an essentially political perspective. Here we come full circle, and what the introduction to the essay calls the transmission and ritual perspectives, based on a historical investigation of the origins and meaning of the concepts, in the second part of the essay, instead become more applied models. The elegance of "A Cultural Approach to Communication" is precisely this turn: that it is only through a ritual view of communication that the dominance and effects of the transmission perspective can be understood.

It is not only our understanding of communication that has come to be characterized by the transmission perspective. The resulting focus on communication as bridging space, as a tool for power and control, means that important aspects of human communication are overlooked. Society also consists of aesthetic experiences, religious ideas, values, and emotions, which are better understood from a ritual perspective. Carey draws on Raymond Williams (see Chapter 12 in this volume), who emphasizes how our lives are shaped by our experience of society as a whole that emerges through communication. Understanding this requires a model of ritual that reveals how our reality is constructed, shared, modified, and maintained (Carey 1975/1989: 33). "A Cultural Approach to Communication" concludes by arguing that the value of the ritual model goes beyond merely developing a better understanding of communication, but is a necessary tool for restoring and revitalizing a shared culture.

Conclusion

Carey stated in the interview quoted at the beginning of this chapter that it was no longer necessary to write an essay such as "A Cultural Approach to Communication." The cultural approach to communication suggested by Carey is by no means as marginalized now as it was in the 1970s. What is the relevance of the essay today, then? Why should we read "A Cultural Approach to Communication" and what does Carey's thinking tell us about today's media landscape? Is it merely a historical document that captures a crucial period in the history of American media and communication studies? Or can it still illuminate a kind of underlying complexity in our contemporary studies of culture and communication (Carey 1975/1989: 14)?

192 *Lars Lundgren*

Carey was, of course, quite right that the essay had outlived its role as a polemic advocating a more interpretive tradition in communication studies—the space he said he needed to create in the mid-1970s is now well established. The divide that Carey identified has recently been problematized and questioned. It has been argued that the divide has resulted in a kind of vacuum in the study of communication, and that communication studies has become blind to the many ways in which the two perspectives are often interwoven (Lundgren 2008; Packer 2006; Sterne 2006).

In a highly influential book, *Media Events: The Live Broadcasting of History* (1992) by Elihu Katz and Daniel Dayan, ritual plays a more concrete role in analyzing the role of communication in society (see Chapter 25 in this volume). At the center of Dayan and Katz's analysis is the media event, a specific genre of broadcast television. The meaning of the media event varies from case to case, of course, but the authors emphasize that these cases are always regarded as historical, as milestones, or the start of a new era. The role of the media event is to attract and bring together large audiences, nationally and globally, and often they are seen as a reconciling force in society.

Although Carey is not mentioned or cited in the book, it is hard not to be reminded of the ritual model's emphasis on shared experiences and the role of communication in maintaining communities over time. In the introduction to *Media Events*, Dayan and Katz explain that they follow a Durkheimian spirit in considering the creation of a sense of belonging and participation. But they also point to televised events, that is, broadcasts that gather large audiences, serve as ceremonies, and highlight shared values, and here the absence of Carey seems somewhat odd. Although Carey would share the view of media events as ceremonial, he would also argue that even everyday viewing is surrounded by ritualization, as has been emphasized in many studies of television (Bolin & Forsman 2002; Brunsdson 1978; Morley 1980).

Furthermore, when Dayan and Katz argue for the importance of paying attention to and studying media events, they emphasize that it is through media events that the full potential of electronic media is realized (Dayan & Katz 1992: 15). This formulation is strongly reminiscent of Carey's argument for the ritual model, in which he pointed out that it is only by adopting a ritual perspective on communication that its complexity can be revealed.

There are, of course, crucial differences between how Carey understood the ritual perspective on communication, and how Dayan and Katz use the ritual perspective to analyze media events. One crucial difference is Carey's emphasis on ritual as something ubiquitous in our communication, while the media event is well delimited in both time and space. However, they share the seemingly simple but important conclusion that the complexity of communication can only be understood if we also study it from a ritual perspective.

As we have seen, "A Cultural Approach to Communication" outlines, although self-admittedly somewhat crudely, two main perspectives that have historically dominated our understanding of communication. Fittingly, toward the end of his career and in the years following his death, various works have been published concerning Carey's intellectual legacy and how it can be understood and used in contemporary communication studies (Munson & Warren 1997; Packer & Robertson 2006; Pooley 2016).

Carey's interest in the intellectual history of communication, in how it can be understood from the perspectives of transmission and ritual, has very much lived on. An important example of this is *Speaking into the Air: A History of the Idea of Communication* (1999), in which John Durham Peters illustrates how the intellectual history of the concept of communication can be understood through the relationship between dissemination, on one hand, and dialogue, on the other (see Chapter 27 in this volume). The former treats communication as the dissemination of information in space, which Peters traces to the Bible and Jesus' sermons to his disciples, while dialogue is instead found in Plato and is characterized by face-to-face communication. It is difficult not to see the parallels with Carey, even though the conceptual apparatus differs. When Peters talks about dissemination, Carey talks about diffusion, and when Peters talks about dialog, Carey talks about ritual.

There are, of course, crucial differences between Carey's and Peters' thinking about communication, the latter being much more appreciative and forgiving of the transmission perspective. But the example shows that Carey's understanding of communication is not only fruitful in relation to 20th century American academia but can actually provide a basis for understanding the longer history of the concept and study of communication. Perhaps this is the greatest contribution of what Carey saw as a necessary intervention in 1975. While the distinction between transmission and ritual may have been the result of his own binary thinking, ultimately obscuring his point, it nevertheless paved the way for a more nuanced intellectual history of the field of media and communications.

Notes

1 For an interesting discussion of what has been called the Lippman–Dewey debate, see Jansen (2008, 2009), Rakow (2018), and Schudson (2008, 2016). Carey's work has been addressed in two anthologies: *James Carey: A Critical Reader* (1997), edited by Eve Stryker Munson and Catherine A. Warren, and *Thinking with James Carey* (2006), edited by Jeremy Packer and Craig Robertson. In *James Carey and Communication Research* (2016), Jefferson Pooley, Carey's last graduate student, provides an in-depth account of Carey's work and a detailed analysis of his intellectual influences and of the debates that he was engaged in. The book includes an excellent chapter on "A Cultural Approach to Communication," including its origins and wide-reaching influence.

2 It is worth noting that the history as well as meaning of the notion of cultural studies differs between the North American and European traditions.

3 Much of Carey's writing emerged in this way, with arguments being worked out in one essay and then transformed, rearranged, and developed in another. Jefferson Pooley's book *James W. Carey and Communication Research* (2016) provides an excellent account of how his essays, and thinking, shifted and developed over time.

194   Lars Lundgren

References

Bolin, G. & Forsman, M. (2002). *Bingolotto. Produktion, reception, text.* [Bingolotto: Production, reception, text]. Mediestudier vid Södertörns högskola.

Brunsdon, C. (1978). *Everyday Television—Nationwide*. British Film Institute.

Carey, J.W. (1975/1989). "A Cultural Approach to Communication," in Carey, J.W. (1989). *Communication as Culture: Essays on Media and Society* (pp. 13–36). Unwin Hyman.

Carey, J.W. (1975). "Communication and culture. Review essay of Clifford Geertz," [Geertz, The Interpretation of Cultures], *Communication Research*, 2 (2): 173–191.

Carey, J.W. (1989). *Communication as Culture: Essays on Media and Society*. Unwin Hyman.

Dayan, D. & Katz, E. (1992). *Media Events: The Live Broadcasting of History*. Harvard University Press.

Dewey, J. (1916). *Democracy and Education*. Macmillan.

Grossberg, L. (2006a). "From New England to Illinois: The Invention of (American) Cultural Studies. James Carey in conversation with Lawrence Grossberg, Part 1," in Packer, J. & Robertson, C. (eds.) *Thinking with James Carey. Essays on Communications, Transportation, History* (pp. 11–28). Peter Lang.

Grossberg, L. (2006b). "Configurations of Culture, History, and Politics. James Carey in conversation with Lawrence Grossberg, Part 2," in Packer, J. & Robertson, C. (eds.). *Thinking with James Carey. Essays on Communications, Transportation, History* (pp. 199–225). Peter Lang.

Innis, H.A. (1950). *Empire and Communications*. Clarendon Press.

Innis, H.A. (1951). *The Bias of Communication*. University of Toronto Press.

Jansen, S.C. (2008). "Walter Lippmann, Straw Man of Communication History," in Park, D.W. & Pooley, J. (eds.) *The History of Media and Communication Research: Contested Memories* (pp. 71–112). Peter Lang.

Jansen, S.C. (2009). "Phantom Conflict: Lippmann, Dewey, and the Fate of the Public in Modern Society," *Communication and Critical/Cultural Studies*, 6 (3): 221–245.

Lundgren, L. (2008). *Culture and Transmission: The Technological and Cultural Reach of International Syndicated Radio*. Doctoral Diss. Stockholm: Stockholm University.

Morley, D. (1980). *The "Nationwide" Audience: Structure and Decoding*. British Film Institute.

Munson, E.S. & Warren, C.A. (eds.) (1997). *James Carey: A Critical Reader*. University of Minnesota Press.

Packer, J. (2006). "Rethinking Dependency: New Relations of Transportation and Communication," in Packer, J. & Robertson, C. (eds.) *Thinking with James Carey. Essays on Communications, Transportation, History* (pp. 79–100). Peter Lang.

Packer, J. & Robertson, C. (eds.) (2006). *Thinking with James Carey. Essays on Communications, Transportation, History*. Peter Lang.

Peters, J.D. (1999). *Speaking into the Air: A History of the Idea of Communication*. The University of Chicago Press.

Pooley, J. (2016). *James W. Carey and Communication Research*. Peter Lang.

Rakow, L.F. (2018). "*Family Feud: Who's Still Fighting about Dewey and Lippmann?*" *Javnost – The Public*, 25 (1–2): 75–82.

Schudson, M. (2008). "The 'Lippmann-Dewey Debate' and the Invention of Walter Lippmann as an Anti-Democrat 1986–1996," *International Journal of Communication*, 2: 1031–1042.

Schudson, M. (2016). "*Walter Lippmann's Ghost. An Interview with Michael Schudson*," *Mass Communication and Society*, 19 (3): 221–229.

Sterne, J. (2006). "Transportation and Communication: Together as You've Always Wanted Them," in Packer, J. & Robertson, C. (eds.) (2006). *Thinking with James Carey. Essays on Communications, Transportation, History* (pp. 117–135). Peter Lang.

14 Laura Mulvey (1975) 'Visual Pleasure and Narrative Cinema'

Sofia Johansson

Introduction

It is late evening in a run-down part of Hollywood, Los Angeles. The traffic roars, while the sound of sirens echoes in the background. In a lacklustre hotel room, an alarm bell rings, waking a young, beautiful woman. The camera zooms in on her half-naked body, still in bed. It lingers on her bottom, dressed in black lace panties; then, as she turns around to switch off the alarm, it slowly sweeps across her belly and the rest of her upper body. A shadow covers the woman's face and, as she gets dressed, only parts of her body are kept in focus: bust, wrists, legs and eyes.

The depicted scene is taken from the famous opening sequence of the Hollywood film *Pretty Woman* (1990), in which the American actor Julia Roberts plays a prostitute engaging in a love affair with a rich businessman. *Pretty Woman*, a hugely successful romantic comedy in its time, still manages to cast a spell on new audiences due to its timeless Cinderella narrative. Yet, it quickly drew criticism for its light-hearted way of portraying prostitution, as well as for objectifying the female character in scenes such as the one described here by portraying her primarily as an object of desire. In the latter aspect, this movie can be said to follow a long tradition in Hollywood cinema, with similar examples easily found today.

It is probably not unusual for young scholars of film and media to ponder over why certain visual codes seem so resilient in mediated narratives about men and women: why male and female bodies keep being portrayed in a particular way in Hollywood films, fashion photography and advertising, for example, or why certain products, such as cars and online games, are often marketed with the help of lightly clad female models. It is, however, difficult to develop an extensive theoretical discussion on the meaning and framing of the gaze without referring to the British film scholar Laura Mulvey, who first became famous for an essay titled 'Visual Pleasure and Narrative Cinema', published in the journal *Screen* in 1975. This essay, which has since been translated into several languages, focuses on how classic Hollywood cinema from a particular time period reflected gendered power structures by incorporating the audience into what Mulvey calls 'the male gaze'. Drawing on psychoanalytical theory for

DOI: 10.4324/9781003432272-15

Laura Mulvey (1975) 197

her argumentation, Mulvey points to how the spectator – via the positioning of the camera, the editing and the structure of the narrative – is placed in a 'male' viewer position, with implications for the interpretation of the content.

A simple Google search for 'Laura Mulvey' at the time of the writing of this chapter yielded 440,000 hits, with information about the author's life and works available in the public domain. Those who are interested can, for example, read about how Mulvey, who is currently professor of Film Studies at Birkbeck, University of London, has also worked as an avantgarde filmmaker outside of her long academic career. The number of search hits can be seen as one (albeit superficial) testament to the undisputed cultural influence Mulvey has gained, granting her a reach far beyond the academic sphere. Today, 'Visual Pleasure and Narrative Cinema' is required reading for many film and media students around the world, inspiring young feminists and new filmmakers alike.

A child of its time

The link to feminism's second wave

Although the notion of the male gaze continues to fascinate new generations, 'Visual Pleasure and Narrative Cinema' may come across as a somewhat difficult text to navigate for the contemporary reader, as it relies on a dense conceptual framework and a use of language that may be less familiar to the reader of today. Thus, to receive as much from the essay as possible, it is valuable to know something about its origins. Here, the 'second-wave' feminism of the 1960s and 1970s, which came to play an influential role in the arts and in other social and cultural arenas in UK universities, acts as an important backdrop. While the feminists of the first wave fought for suffrage and equality before the law, the second wave brought a broader range of issues involving economic and social equality into focus, including the right to fair pay, workplace equality, the sharing of domestic responsibilities and women's right to make decisions involving their bodies.

Even if the idea of distinct 'waves' of feminism can be questioned (see Thornham & Weissman, 2013) it is possible to point to certain characteristics that defined the women's movement of that time. In retrospect, British film and media scholar Christine Geraghty, a contemporary of Mulvey, describes the feminist circles of the 1970s as being based in part on utopian ideals while also being united and politically oriented: 'a feminism which was radical, passionate, politicised and collectively organised' (2013: 12). The collectivism described by Geraghty was exemplified by the women's reading groups that flourished at the time, some with links to universities or other established organisations and others consisting of friends who met to discuss books or copied texts (2013: 11–15). Mulvey, who graduated from St Hilda's College at Oxford University in 1963, participated in a so-called Women's Liberation reading group in the early 1970s, whose members would read texts by male theorists such as Friedrich Engels, Claude Lévi-Strauss and Sigmund Freud in

198 Sofia Johansson

order to discuss family life and the role of women in society. She later empha-sised this reading group and the feminist context as key to the development of her essay (Mulvey et al., 2015: 68).

A vital feature of 'second-wave' feminism was its insistence on viewing the personal experience of women as part of the overall political struggle for change, as reflected in the popular slogan 'the personal is political'. As part of this effort, the female body came to be perceived as a political site of struggle, something that Mulvey describes as a partial explanation for her interest in the way it was visually represented:

> ...the early days of the Women's Liberation Movement had established a kind of politics that centred on the female body as a site of struggle – a struggle for reproductive rights and health (abortion/freely available con-traception) and women's demands to define their own sexuality. By exten-sion, we came to examine the representations of the female body as its own form of politics.
>
> (Mulvey et al., 2015: 70)

Aside from stimulating debates about sexuality, reproductive rights and access to contraceptives, the notion of the female body as political, then, led to dis-cussion about its mediated representation.

Psychoanalysis and film theory

While Mulvey's essay is anchored in 'second-wave' feminism, it is also shaped by an intellectual heritage that relies heavily on psychoanalysis. As mentioned earlier, Freud was one of the authors discussed in Mulvey's reading circle, whose members found his ideas about human psychology especially useful for deepening their understanding of the patriarchal structures that they felt per-meated their society and that – with the aid of Freud's thinking – could be understood as part of a collective subconscious (Mulvey et al., 2015: 69). When writing 'Visual Pleasure and Narrative Cinema', Mulvey was inspired by French psychoanalyst Jacques Lacan, who introduced influential re-readings of Freud in the 1950s and 1960s. In fact, it was Mulvey's ability to combine these psycho-analytical perspectives with a feminist media analysis that can be said to have added such explosive power to her essay. Certainly, analysing how women were represented within popular culture was not a completely novel endeavour: for instance, in the early 1970s, British author and art historian John Berger received critical acclaim for his *Ways of Seeing* (1972/2008), a BBC documentary and subsequent book about Western art and culture, in which Berger pays attention to the recurring function of the female body as an erotic object. Still, Mulvey found a particularly fruitful theoretical model for explaining this phe-nomenon, with a specific focus on film.

Without underestimating Mulvey's originality, it is worth noting that her interest in psychoanalysis and film as an ideological instrument was intimately linked to prominent intellectual currents of the time. Similarly, film theory had become an expanding area of analysis, with the British journal *Screen* a major arena for discussion and scholarship. *Screen*'s contributors drew on elements of psychoanalysis, Marxism and semiotics, among other influences, to shed light on the form, content and potential influence of different films and television programmes. They emphasised such media forms as multidimensional 'texts' that were capable of ideologically positioning the viewer – 'the spectator' – and often provided vigorous critiques of conventional films and programmes (see Easthope, 1993/2013: 8–14; Rushton & Bettyson, 2010: 5–6, 52–69; Turner, 2003: 85–88).

Thus, it is no coincidence that this was the forum in which 'Visual Pleasure and Narrative Cinema' was published. Mulvey has described suffering from severe writer's block after her graduation from Oxford. A couple of years before the publication of her famous essay, Mulvey presented it as a paper at a conference in the French Department at the University of Wisconsin. Aided by *Screen*'s editor, Ben Brewster, she spent a great deal of effort perfecting the content and form of the essay before its publication. This meticulous attention devoted to the actual structure and form of the text – something that is perhaps less common in academic writing today – can be understood as an expression of the porous boundaries between film theory and filmmaking and artistic creation at the time, with Mulvey herself having a foot in both camps (Mulvey et al., 2015: 74).

'Visual Pleasure and Narrative Cinema' in brief

Hollywood cinema, change and rebellion

What is 'Visual Pleasure and Narrative Cinema' about? In this relatively short 13-page essay, which is divided into four main parts, not much space is actually devoted to the empirical material. The title alludes to the classic form of Hollywood film that Mulvey is interested in, which had its heyday during the 1930s–1950s and continued until the mid-1960s. This is the period in which the Hollywood 'star system' was established – a time when iconic film stars such as Greta Garbo, Clark Gable and Marilyn Monroe were able to draw huge cinema audiences (see Dyer, 1979/2008, 1986/2004). Mulvey argues that this period gave rise to a kind of filmmaking that – despite its varied expression – was based on a certain formal *mise-en-scène* that shaped the viewing in specific ways, which she views as a reflection of the ideological premises that Hollywood was part of (1975: 7). In the empirical analysis, she provides pertinent illustrations from the film production of director Josef von Sternberg, who made a series of cherished films with the actor Marlene Dietrich in the 1930s, and from the work of Alfred Hitchcock, with his famous films *Rear Window* (1954), *Vertigo* (1958) and *Marnie* (1964).

In the introduction, Mulvey states that the starting point of the essay is 'the way film reflects, reveals and even plays on the straight, socially established

200 Sofia Johansson

interpretations of sexual difference which controls images, erotic ways of looking, and spectacle' (1975: 6). At the same time, she makes clear that her ambition is part of a comprehensive challenge to the 'magic' possessed by the film industry. In the 1970s, the economic and technical conditions for film production had changed, not least through the introduction of portable 16 mm cameras, which paved the way for film productions without big budgets or access to Hollywood studios. Hollywood cinema and its successors were challenged by avantgarde and alternative film production, with young, radical filmmakers questioning the content and aesthetic conventions of classical narrative cinema. Mulvey aligns with this process: 'It is helpful to understand what the cinema has been, how its magic has worked in the past, while attempting a theory and a practice which will challenge this cinema of the past' (1975: 6). Thus, it is not only the feminist element that is brought to the fore in the essay's introduction but also the way in which it is part of a wider intellectual and artistic critique.

'Visual Pleasure and Narrative Cinema' is undoubtedly written in a rebellious, polemic spirit, clearly coloured by 'second-wave' feminism and contemporary intellectual currents.[1] For example, psychoanalysis is described as 'a weapon' with the potential to reveal 'how the unconscious of the patriarchal society has structured film form' (1975: 6), while the situation of women is described as oppressive and frustrating under 'the phallocentric order' (1975: 7). Mulvey's radical approach is evident both in her choice of words and in the analytical positioning of the text, which show her overall intention to, as she puts it, 'destroy' film's very beauty and pleasure: 'It is said that analysing pleasure, or beauty, will destroy it. That is the intention of this article' (1975: 8). Mulvey's aspiration, just like that of her fellow sisters in the women's movement of the time, is thus to instigate change, and her contribution is to point out how the cinema's ability to create a pleasurable viewing experience is interlinked with repressive social and cultural structures.

Behind the pleasurable viewing

Even though 'Visual Pleasure and Narrative Cinema' is often taken as an example of an analysis of representation in media texts, much of it deals with the experience of viewing – that is, the mechanisms behind the viewer's orientation towards the media content. Mulvey argues that there are several ways in which films offer the viewer pleasure, one of which stems from the desire to watch someone else. She uses the term *scopophilia*, which Freud considered to be part of the sex drive, in which pleasure is obtained by viewing others through a curious and controlling gaze. According to Freud's way of thinking, scopophilia can be observed early on in children's voyeuristic activities, such as wanting to see 'forbidden' body parts, and continues to exist in adults as a basis for erotic pleasure. Based on Freud's ideas, Mulvey notes that, in its most extreme form, scopophilia can be perpetuated in some individuals, such as in voyeuristic 'peeping toms', as a perverse obsession with viewing others in a controlling way as sexual objects. She also argues that conventional cinema confirms and reinforces this scopophilic tendency in the spectator. Although what is shown on the film screen is clearly there on display and, in that sense, is hardly something that the spectator 'sneaks a peek at', Mulvey points to how the film's narrative and composition build up a 'hermetically sealed world' (1975: 9) that plays out independently of the spectator. Along with the darkness in the auditorium, which contrasts with the brilliance of the screen, and the positioning of the spectators in the auditorium, this setup contributes to the experience of peeking into a private world.

In addition to this element of pleasurable viewing, Mulvey identifies another central component, which she describes as cinema's *narcissistic aspect* (1975: 9). Here, she relies on Lacan's idea of the 'mirror stage' as a stage in human self-development, where the small child's discovery of its mirror image and subsequent understanding of this as an 'ideal self' forms the basis for later self-understanding and identification with others. In the same way that the mirror evokes an idealised self-reflection, Mulvey argues that film contributes to an experience of fusion with the image on the screen, through an anthropomorphic, human-centred narrative and imagery, as well as through the glamorous stars who personify ordinary people. By making us temporarily forget ourselves and allowing us to become absorbed in the film's story and characters, a film allows for a 'temporary loss of ego while simultaneously reinforcing the ego' (1975: 10), providing a reminder of the mirror stage in early self-formation.

Mulvey thus refers to two seemingly contradictory aspects involved in the pleasure of viewing. On the one hand, it relates to the erotic desire to view someone else as an object, which stems from the sexual drive and requires a separation between the spectator subject and the film's object. On the other hand, it stems from an identification of the 'self' with what is shown on the screen, which, conversely, means that the distinctions between the audience and the characters in the film world are temporarily dissolved. According to Mulvey, this tension between libido and ego within conventional film narration is handled by means of a simultaneous affirmation, allowing the spectator to identify with one character while erotically watching another.

The male gaze

For this to be possible, however, a strict division is required between an active 'male gaze' and the 'woman' as the passive recipient of this gaze. Under the heading 'Woman as Image, Man as Bearer of the Look', Mulvey underlines how filmic conventions in this respect coincide with wider traditions in popular culture, such as pin-ups, striptease and revues. Mulvey notes that women in these contexts have come to connote what she refers to as 'to-be-looked-at-ness' (1975: 11), which naturally applies to the context of classic Hollywood cinema. In the latter context, Mulvey points out how female characters fulfil the function of an erotic object on two levels: firstly, for the male characters within the film's narrative; and, secondly, for the viewers, whose eyes are drawn to the

202 Sofia Johansson

visually striking woman on the screen. This type of eroticism, she argues, can manifest in different ways; for example, it can involve a preoccupation with a fragmented body – such as Marlene Dietrich's legs or Greta Garbo's face – which contributes to a kind of flatness in the representation of the woman as an iconic image rather than as a nuanced, fully formed character.

In a similar way, Mulvey points to an active/passive heterosexual division in films' narrative, in which the male characters drive the narrative forward while the female ones instead inspire the film's hero to act in different ways. In her analysis, the male character – due to 'the principles of the ruling ideology and the physical structures that back it up' – cannot bear 'the burden of sexual objectification' (1975: 12) and hence emerges as the active component of the narrative. Likewise, the male protagonist is the one with whom the spectator identifies, as the action of the narrative is built up around him. Mulvey suggests that identification with the male character is reinforced by camera techniques (especially deep focus), camera movements determined by the action of the protagonist and editing. Through these techniques, the viewer's gaze becomes aligned with the male protagonist's perspective:

> As the spectator identifies with the main male protagonist, he projects his look on to that of his like, his screen surrogate, so that the power of the male protagonist as he controls events coincides with the active power of the erotic look, both giving a satisfying sense of omnipotence.
>
> (1975: 12)

In this way, the viewer's experience is inevitably drawn into a gendered order, relating to the power to act and the power to see.

Yet, based on her psychoanalytic framework, Mulvey emphasises that, at the same time as the woman functions as an erotic object, she equally signals an underlying threat to the order of power created by the film, in that the woman simultaneously represents an unconscious fear of 'castration'. Mulvey borrows this term from Freud's theory of the 'castration complex', which, according to Freud, represents men's unconscious and primal fear, tied to the mother, of being deprived of the male genitalia – or, by extension, its symbolic attachment to normality and dominance. Based on this idea, Mulvey asserts that 'the woman as icon, displayed for the gaze and enjoyment of men' at the same time 'always threatens to evoke the anxiety it [the woman] originally signified' (1975: 13). In cinema, Mulvey continues, the male unconscious can deal with this dilemma by 'demystifying' the woman, 'examining' or devaluing her, punishing and rescuing her, or taking the edge off the threat she represents by creating a reification in the form of an exalted fetish, such as through an intense focus on the object's physical beauty. With respect to rescuing the woman, the dynamics of the film may also include elements of sadism, in which the female character is broken down or saved by a male hero. This sadism would derive from the unconscious fears associated with the mother figure and the accompanying threat to the 'phallic' order.

After discussing several films as representative of these processes, with Hitchcock as a particularly illustrative example, Mulvey summarises her argument by highlighting how film as a media genre has unique opportunities to create a complex interaction between different gazes. She describes how three different gazes are associated with film: the gaze of the camera, the gaze of the audience and the gaze of the characters. However, Mulvey contends that the latter takes superiority within conventional film, due to its illusionistic claim to reality, which contributes to maintaining 'the neurotic needs of the male ego' (1975: 18). Finally, to break this illusion – making the readers of the essay (and the spectators of film) aware of the mechanisms that lie behind the pleasure associated with conventional film – is to be understood as a 'blow' against traditional film conventions. Although this is not mentioned in the text, it is easy to make a comparison between the essay's final compelling point about the need to demystify cinematic conventions and the emphasis within psycho-analysis of the liberating potential in bringing the unconscious to the surface, as part of the process towards self-understanding.[2]

In Mulvey's footsteps

The influence within and outside of the academy

'Visual Pleasure and Narrative Cinema' has been described as a 'founding moment' in the history of feminist film theory (Bergstrom & Doane, 1989: 7). It paved the way for the development of feminist film and media theory, as well as for the later queer and masculinity studies. In the UK, Mulvey's essay had an immediate impact, drawing a response from several writers in the very next issue of *Screen*, in which Mulvey's arguments were at once critiqued and redeveloped (see Thornham, 2015: 883). Similarly, her thoughts were incorporated into the British tradition of cultural studies, as its focus gradually broadened from the study of class and power in media and popular culture to studies of youth culture, gender, identity and media audiences (see Chapter 11 in this volume). In the same way, this essay has come to be included in the canon of academic literature on film, gender and the media in many countries outside of the English-language sphere, and it has equally gained influence in academic subjects such as art history, philosophy, literature and aesthetics.

While it is important to remember that Mulvey discusses film (and, moreover, a certain type of feature film from a specific historical period), it is clear that 'Visual Pleasure and Narrative Cinema' is considered to be relevant to the understanding of other media as well, not least television production (see Boyle 2015a: 880). In fact, Mulvey's idea of the male gaze and its objectification of women seems to be the part of the essay that has gained the most attention – not only in connection to film but also in relation to a range of different media and popular cultural expressions and in terms of art and visual culture more generally. For instance, her emphasis on the gaze as shaped by culture and ideology has been used to illuminate the relationship between ways of seeing

204 *Sofia Johansson*

and image and imagery on a more comprehensive level, in order to understand the relationship between the viewer and the image within art (Steorn, 2013).

Another area in which Mulvey's relevance is obvious is in feminist and alternative film production, where her collaborations with Peter Wollen contribute to films applying a feminist imagery and narrative. Their best-known work, the avantgarde film *Riddles of the Sphinx* (1977), was released in a DVD version in 2013, in line with a renewed interest in making feature films based on alternative and more considered approaches towards gender and representation. Similarly, the theory of the male gaze – sometimes in a simplified or even banal version – has undoubtedly come to resonate in contexts independent of universities and colleges, influencing contemporary phenomena as varied as feminist-oriented advertising, protests against the objectification of women in public spaces, the #MeToo social movement and body-positive activism on social media. Bearing this influence in mind, it must be stated that 'Visual Pleasure and Narrative Cinema' is one of the (few) theoretical works in film and media studies that have managed to significantly inspire an audience outside of the academy, becoming a persistent point of reference for a wide range of adherers.

Critical voices

Criticism against 'Visual Pleasure and Narrative Cinema' touches on several issues. Of these, an important issue concerns the role and pleasure of the female audience. In Mulvey's analysis, the viewer – regardless of biological sex – appears to be powerless against the conventions that determine the gaze and construct it as male. Men *and* women look at objectified women. 'The female spectator' thus became the subject of debate early on, as film scholars such as Mary Ann Doane (1982, 1987) and Jackie Stacey (1994) developed theories about the female viewer, which were addressed by Mulvey as well on several occasions (1981, 2004, 2015a). In this discussion, the possibility of a subversive, sceptical viewing was gradually emphasised, with the idea that the (female) audience has the potential to reject or resist the visual and narrative structures of conventional film:

> Mulvey's dark and suffocating analysis of patriarchal cinema has lost ground to a more confident and empowering approach which foregrounds the possibilities of 'subversive', that is a non-patriarchal mode, of female spectatorship.
>
> (van Zoonen, 1994: 97)

As exemplified in Liesbet van Zoonen's critique of Mulvey, the notion of the subversive spectator – who may view and enjoy conventional Hollywood film while still being critical of it – is seen by some feminist thinkers as liberating and hopeful. Such a belief in audiences' interpretative abilities is reflected in, and can be seen as linked to, a strand of empirical reception research that emerged within media and cultural studies in the 1980s. Partly in response to Stuart Hall's thoughts on encoding/decoding, this research emphasised the agency of audiences and how people's interpretations of different kinds of media are shaped by everyday contexts (see Chapter 11 in this volume). The chapter about Janice Radway (Chapter 22 in this volume) discusses a famous example of this kind of reception research, which can partially be viewed as a polemical response to theorists' emphasis of textual analysis as the preferred method to explain the influence of media content. Within reception research, studying the audience up close was at that time considered to be crucial in understanding how people experience and interpret media in their everyday life; therefore, the theoretical viewer position central to the work of Mulvey and other writers in *Screen* was often rejected.

'Visual Pleasure and Narrative Cinema' has thus been critiqued for ignoring the perspective of the female spectator and for not taking actual audiences into account. Moreover, other scholars have questioned the notion of 'male' and 'female' as static categories, while highlighting the apparent lack of discussion on how race, ethnicity or alternative sexualities function within the structure of the gaze. For example, in a discussion on images and different kinds of gazes, the Swedish art historian Patrik Steorn attempted to re-evaluate Mulvey's way of associating activity and passivity with male and female viewing positions, respectively, arguing for a greater openness to more ambivalent ways of watching images:

> If the desire to see has been split between the active/masculine and the passive/feminine, then what happens to women who fiercely caress a portrayed body with their eyes or male posers eager to please a viewer's gaze? Not to mention all the ambivalent, androgynous, and ambiguous bodies that charm and attract gazes both seduced and horrified.
>
> (Steorn, 2013: 59, author's translation)

Here, Steorn puts his finger on an obvious ambiguity concerning visual culture and the viewing positions invited by it. At the same time, it can be pointed out again that 'Visual Pleasure and Narrative Cinema' solely examines a certain type of film from a period in the history of cinema that was notably subject to the moral censorship of the so-called Hays Code, which prohibited representations of homosexuality, among other restrictions. Yet, taken as a whole, the critical scrutiny of this essay highlights the complex structure and desires of the gaze.

The male gaze today

Relevance in a transformed media landscape

More than 40 years after 'Visual Pleasure and Narrative Cinema' was published, it is worth considering whether the text has anything significant to say to readers of today. Before the essay's 40th anniversary in 2015, a number of

206 Sofia Johansson

retrospectives were published that highlighted the essay's iconic status, while discussing how it can be understood in relation to the development of feminism and our changed society and media landscape. In her book *Death 24x a Second: Stillness and the Moving Image* (2006), Mulvey herself has explored the role that new media technologies play in the experience of film, emphasising the viewer's expanded opportunities to control a film's images and stories. In a retrospective article in the journal *Sight & Sound*, Mulvey describes this book as partly written to 'underline the irrelevance of "Visual Pleasure and Narrative Cinema" to contemporary modes of scholarship' (2015b: 50), due to the essay's link to a specific historical period both in the history of film and in the development of feminist film and media theory.

When Mulvey wrote her essay, the latter was in its infancy. Today, questions about gender and representation are often standard points of discussion in media education and research, as well as – at least in many democracies – constituting an important part of the broader public discourse about the media's role in society. Of course, these questions have hardly escaped the producers and creators of media content, exemplified for instance by the application of the Bechdel test[3] in the film industry, while social movements such as #MeToo and the Women's March have illustrated a continued commitment to feminism's core issues of equality and autonomy. Likewise, within popular culture, the broader challenge of feminism has long been reflected in the gradual rejection of gender stereotypes, with an arguably more varied register of femininity and masculinity at the audience's disposal in mainstream film and television today. In music, popular female artists such as Beyoncé and Taylor Swift are often highlighted as strong role models, whereas the major streaming services that are significant new actors in film and television production boast novel genre categorisations in the style of 'Women who own the white screen', reflecting how some elements of feminist media analysis have been usurped by mainstream popular culture. At the same time, digitisation and social media have introduced previously unthinkable opportunities for users to produce and distribute their own media content, paving the way for further diversity of visual styles and narratives in popular cultural forums.

What do these developments mean for the current understanding of Mulvey's essay? From time to time, the idea is put forward that feminism – partly due to the changes mentioned above – is no longer needed: that equality has already largely been achieved, and that those political demands of the 'second wavers' in particular should now be regarded as outdated, at least in part. 'Postfeminism' is a somewhat fuzzy term that is sometimes used to describe such an outlook; it has also been applied to forms of popular culture that appear to be based on earlier feminist lines of thought but simultaneously reject them.[4] Oft-cited examples of this phenomenon include the television series *Sex and the City* (1998–2004) and the pop group *Spice Girls*. These popular cultural products highlight strong female characters while simultaneously playing on a conventionally 'sexy' or girlish femininity; thematically, they revolve around individualism, heterosexual romance or consumerism. A distinctive feature of postfeminist media content seems to be this precise ambivalence in relation to the male gaze, which is encouraged and rejected at the same time.

Permanence and change

Despite the cultural and technological changes transforming film and popular culture, it is not difficult to find contemporary media texts that could be relatively seamlessly incorporated into Mulvey's analysis. The woman as embodying 'to-be-looked-at-ness' undoubtedly remains as a major component in advertising, fashion, film, pop music and other popular media genres, in which female celebrities often assume a visually appealing and erotic performativity that is seemingly intended for the male gaze, not unlike the glamorous stars of classic Hollywood film. Reality television also provides a few examples, such as *Ex on the Beach* or *Paradise Hotel*, in which the representation of both the male and female body broadly follows conventional patterns. Moreover, certain computer games and virtual worlds undoubtedly seem to illustrate some of the arguments presented in 'Visual Pleasure and Narrative Cinema'. Apart from such obvious examples of more stereotypical representations of gendered bodies and narratives, popular television genres such as the CSI genre and Nordic Noir have also been problematised based on Mulvey's thoughts on the 'sadistic' element of the male gaze, with fictional images of tortured and mutilated female bodies being seen as part of a symbolic violence (McCabe, 2015).

As mentioned earlier, many opposing tendencies can also be found in the current multitude of films and television series now available at the touch of a button, even if such examples often concern ambiguous productions that invite analyses from different perspectives. For example, Lena Dunham's celebrated television series *Girls* (2012–2017) seemed to respond to a quest for greater variety in television's portrayal of women's physicality and sexuality; however, it can also be seen as a continuation of a postfeminist prioritisation of the representation of a predominantly white middle class (Nash & Whelehan, 2017; cf. Schreiber, 2015). Recent popular mainstream film and television productions, such as the Hollywood film *Barbie* (2023) or HBO Max's series *And Just Like That...* (2021–), have been described as similarly contradictory expressions of feminism in popular culture.

Here, a final reflection should be made on today's opportunities for multifaceted (self)representation as offered by digital spaces, which can equally reinforce and erode the structure of the gaze that Mulvey describes. What visual conventions dominate among the selfies and influencers in social media feeds, and why? What happens to the viewing experience – and the gaze that is affirmed – when it is the users themselves handling the camera and telling the story of their lives? A transforming media landscape raises a series of new questions, in which digital media offer a multifaceted area for the continued analysis of visual pleasure and representation.

Conclusion

It is interesting to note, in conclusion, that Mulvey initially imagined her essay to be 'ephemeral' and to have a transitory significance, as she envisioned a new

208 *Sofia Johansson*

kind of film and popular culture replacing old conventions (1989/2009: xxvii). That did not turn out to be the case. As this chapter has shown, Mulvey's thinking has had a lasting influence, and there are countless examples of current media content that seem to maintain the order of the gaze that she identifies in classic Hollywood film, even though new technology and societal developments have reshaped the media landscape overall. At the same time, the essay has not been left unchallenged. Critical questions have been raised about the female spectator, the ambiguous nature of visual culture, the pleasure – and perhaps power – that is potentially involved in being the object of the gaze, and the omission of a discussion of non-normative sexuality and identity.

Certainly, the radicalism that pervades Mulvey's text, with arguments derived from the 1970s feminist demands for women's liberation and the categorical idea of a 'struggle' between the sexes, can be perceived as belonging to the past in some ways. As postfeminists would like to assert, perhaps the battle Mulvey engaged in has already been won, at least in part. At the same time, societal and media contexts are changeable, and it is all too easy – based on an academic and Western context – to take freedoms and opportunities for granted. With ongoing debates about the reduction of women's rights in some democracies, and with the continuation of strong patriarchal structures in many societies across the world, it is arguable that the representation of women's – and equally men's – bodies can still be seen as part of wider political questions that lack simple answers.

Hollywood film is not as simple as it may initially seem, either, and it does not always lend itself to a clear analysis. In the closing scene of *Pretty Woman*, Julia Roberts' character gets the last line. After being 'rescued' by her lover (Richard Gere), who promises economic security *and* true love, she answers without hesitation to the question of what happens now: 'she rescues him right back'. What Mulvey would have said about this change of perspective, we do not know. But perhaps 'Visual Pleasure and Narrative Cinema' can contribute to sharpening the viewer's own gaze, for a clearer vision of the media and images that surround us today.

Notes

1 See Mandy Merck's (2007) discussion on the essay's function as a manifesto.
2 This emphasis on breaking the 'illusionistic claims to reality' overlaps with the German playwright Berthold Brecht's ideas about the need to highlight theatrical constructs in order to stimulate critical thinking in the audience.
3 A test originating in popular culture that is sometimes used to assess a film's overall portrayal of women.
4 Postfeminism is also sometimes understood as a further development of earlier feminist thought, albeit with a focus on individual liberty, identity creation and freedom of choice. See e.g. McRobbie (2009) and Gill (2007, 2016) for overviews.

References

Bergstrom, J., & Doane, M. A. (1989). The female spectator: Contexts and directions. *Camera Obscura*, 7(2–3), 5–27.

Boyle, K. (2015a). Introduction: Visual pleasure and narrative cinema at forty. *Feminist Media Studies*, 15(5), 880–881.

Boyle, K. (2015b). Not waving...Agitating?: "Visual Pleasure and Narrative Cinema," the second wave, and me. *Feminist Media Studies*, 15(5), 885–888.

Doane, M. A. (1982). Film and the masquerade: Theorising the female spectator. *Screen*, 23(3–4), 74–88.

Doane, M. A. (1987). *The desire to desire: The woman's film of the 1940s*. Indiana University Press.

Dyer, R. (1979/2008). *Stars*. British Film Institute.

Dyer, R. (1986/2004). *Heavenly bodies: Film stars and society*. Routledge.

Easthope, A. (Ed.) (1993/2013). *Contemporary film theory*. Routledge.

Geraghty, C. (2013). The BFI Women and Film Study Group 1976–? In H. Thornham & E. Weissman (Eds.), *Renewing feminisms: Radical narratives, fantasies and futures in media studies* (pp. 11–27). I.B. Tauris.

Gill, R. (2007). Postfeminist media culture: Elements of a sensibility. *European Journal of Cultural Studies*, 10(2), 147–166.

Gill, R. (2016). Post-postfeminism? New feminist visibilities in postfeminist times. *Feminist Media Studies*, 16(4), 610–630.

McCabe, J. (2015). Disconnected heroines, icy intelligence: Reframing feminism(s) and feminist identities at the borders involving the isolated female TV detective in Scandinavian-Noir. In L. Mulvey & A. Backman Rogers (Eds.), *Feminisms: Diversity, difference and multiplicity in contemporary film cultures* (pp. 29–43). Amsterdam University Press.

McHugh, K., & Sobchack, V. (2004). Beyond the gaze: Recent approaches to film feminisms. *Signs*, 30(1), 1205–1207.

McRobbie, A. (2009). *The aftermath of feminism: Gender, culture and social change*. Sage.

Merck, M. (2007). Mulvey's manifesto. *Camera Obscura*, 22(3), 1–23.

Mulvey, L. (1975). Visual pleasure and narrative cinema. *Screen*, 16(8), 6–8.

Mulvey, L. (1981). Afterthoughts on "Visual pleasure and narrative cinema" inspired by "Duel in the sun". *The Journal of Cinema and Media*, 15(17), 12–15.

Mulvey, L. (1989/2009). *Visual and other pleasures*. Palgrave Macmillan.

Mulvey, L. (2004). Looking at the past from the present: Rethinking feminist film theory of the 1970s. *Signs*, 30(1), 1286–1292.

Mulvey, L. (2006). *Death 24x a second: Stillness and the moving image*. Reaktion Books.

Mulvey, L. (2015a). Introduction: 1970s feminist film theory and the obsolescent object. In L. Mulvey & A. Backman Rogers (Eds.), *Feminisms: Diversity, difference and multiplicity in contemporary film cultures* (pp. 17–26). Amsterdam University Press.

Mulvey, L. (2015b). The pleasure principle. *Sight & Sound*, 25(6), 50–51.

Mulvey, L., Backman Rogers, A., & van den Oever, A. (2015). Feminist film studies 40 years after "Visual pleasure and narrative cinema", a triologue. *European Journal of Media Studies*, 4(1), 67–79.

Nash, M., & Whelehan, I. (Eds.) (2017). *Reading Lena Dunham's Girls: Feminism, postfeminism, authenticity and gendered performance in contemporary television*. Palgrave Macmillan.

Rushton, R., & Bettinson, G. (2010). *What is film theory? An introduction to contemporary debates*. Open University Press.

Schreiber, M. (2015). *American postfeminist cinema: Women, romance and contemporary culture*. Edinburgh University Press.

Stacey, J. (1994). *Star gazing: Hollywood cinema and female spectatorship*. Routledge.

210 *Sofia Johansson*

Steorn, P. (2013). Blickens erotiska fostran. *Tidskrift för genusvetenskap*, 4, 58–62.

Thornham, H., & Weissman, E. (2013). Introduction: Renewing-retooling feminisms. In H. Thornman & E. Weissman (Eds.), *Renewing feminisms: Radical narratives, fantasies and futures in media studies* (pp. 1–11). I.B. Tauris.

Thornham, S. (2015). On "Visual pleasure and narrative cinema". *Feminist Media Studies*, 15(5), 881–884.

Turner, G. (2003). *British cultural studies: An introduction* (3rd ed.). Routledge.

van Zoonen, L. (1994). *Feminist media studies*. Sage.

15 Dallas Smythe (1977) "Communications: Blindspot of Western Marxism"

Fredrik Stiernstedt

Introduction

In 1974, Dallas Smythe became irritated with an old friend. That friend was Harry Magdoff, and both men were prominent figures within critical social theory and policy debates in the United States at that time. In the mid-70s, Smythe had invited his friend to hold a guest lecture for Smythe's students. The topic was supposed to be on Marxist theory in relation to communications. Smythe, however, was not satisfied with the result, as Magdoff did not address the topic of communications at all. In a 90-minute lecture, Magdoff did not even mention the word "communication," according to Smythe, who described how this specific incident gave him an idea: He wanted to write an article on how communication was a failing of Marxism (Lent 1995: 39).

And so, he did, titling the piece "Communications: Blindspot of Western Marxism." The piece was published in 1977 and spurred an intense debate. The legacy of Smythe's article and the thoughts presented in it continues to be discussed within the field of media and communication studies and still holds great influence. Current developments such as digitalization and platformization have increased the relevance of the "Blindspot" article and renewed a critical discussion on its use in understanding contemporary media development.

The main question that Smythe poses is: What economic function for capital is served by the media? Or, more bluntly: What is the point of communications within a capitalist economic system? Smythe wanted to find a "materialist" answer to this question. For him, and from a Marxist viewpoint, this made it necessary to shift focus to the commodity form of the media and ask: What are the commodities produced by the media? Smythe's position was that most previous work on the media viewed things such as "messages," "information," "images," and "meaning"—or, from a more critical perspective, "propaganda" and "manipulation"—as the commodities of the media. This, he contended was an idealist view that only deals with the "*superficial* appearances" (Smythe 1977: 2, emphasis in original) of the media and not their deeper, materialist, reality. What Smythe aimed for was to slash through this jungle and find a solid materialist answer to the question: "What is the commodity form of mass-produced, advertiser-supported communications under monopoly capitalism?"

DOI: 10.4324/9781003432272-16

212   *Fredrik Stiernstedt*

(Smythe 1977: 3). The answer he provides is that this commodity is the audience. Media content—such as television programs—is the "bribe" or "free lunch" that we receive in order for media companies to obtain our attention and our time—time spent with the media that they then sell as a commodity. Hence, according to Smythe, consuming media is a form of "work"; as he puts it, "off-the-job worktime" (ibid.). Just like "on-the-job worktime," consuming media produces commodities that generate economic surplus value for the owners of the means of production (or, in this case, the means of communication). Smythe summarizes his argument as follows:

> What do advertisers buy with their advertising expenditures? [...] I suggest that what they buy are the services of audiences with predictable specifications who will pay attention in predictable numbers and at particular times to particular means of communication (TV, radio, newspapers, magazines, billboards, and third-class mail). As collectives these audiences are commodities.
>
> (Smythe 1977: 4)

While this is the main point in Smythe's text—and the one that has received the most attention, in the form of both acclaim and harsh criticism—he also contends that the mass media simultaneously produce audiences that are prepared to be dutiful consumers. For Smythe, media content—both editorial and commercial—has the ideological functions of seeking to get people to "buy commodities and pay tax" and to promote values that generally favor the capitalist system and status quo (Smythe 1974/1994: 251–253, see also Fuchs 2012: 696). He therefore picks up the concept of media and communications as a "Consciousness Industry" (Smythe 1981: 5) from the German media critic Hans-Magnus Enzensberger (see Chapter 10 in this volume) and views this industry as a powerful institution in modern societies that both legitimizes and directs the development of the social system.

In the following, I will discuss Smythe's argument in more detail, along with the so-called "Blindspot debate" that his article spurred and the theoretical developments and critiques it has generated. I will also give an overview of the renewed discussion on Smythe's work in the light of contemporary developments such as digitalization and platformization. First, however, I will provide some background and context to Smythe, his work, and the tradition of the "critical political economy of the media" that Smythe's work represents.

Smythe as a critical media researcher

Dallas Smythe was born in Canada but grew up in California in the United States. His academic life began as an economist. During the 1930s, Smythe wrote a dissertation on public transportation in California, within the subject of economic history. Thus, Smythe had a focus on the relationship and interplay between economy and communication from the very beginning of his studies. At the end of the 1930s, he came to work in Washington as a bureaucrat during the period in the United States that was characterized by "the new deal." This was President Franklin D. Roosevelt's progressive reform program, which was based on Keynesian economic ideals and somewhat resembled European and social democratic models of welfare and economic policy. During this period, many young and promising academics with progressive views were recruited to Washington, to help plan and implement Roosevelt's reform program. Smythe was one of them.

Shortly after World War II ended, he left Washington and returned to academia. By that time, the political winds had also begun to turn in Washington, and the progressive economic policy was being toned down, starting in 1945 under President Truman. However, Smythe's experiences from his time in Washington—especially from the period 1943–1948, when he was chief economist for the important Federal Communication Commission (FCC)—would have a decisive impact on his scholarly work in the coming decades. In fact, Smythe was interested in—and engaged in—issues of media politics and policy throughout his life. As Bill Melody has pointed out, Smythe was involved in "almost every major policy development in broadcasting and telecommunication in the United States and Canada during this period [1930s to 1980s] and in many international developments as well" (Melody 1994: 1). Smythe constantly returned to questions about how political and democratic means of control could be used to regulate and create conditions for the media that would make the media contribute to a more reasonable world and to human development, instead of just contributing to legitimizing the status quo or reproducing the current unequal social system. He considered that media and communication hold promise for "realizing the potential of humanity on this Earth" and "liberating human creativity"—and, with his research, Smythe wanted to play a part in this realization and liberation. Melody, who worked with Smythe, summarized Smythe's work as follows:

> For Smythe, the primary purpose of research was to develop knowledge that would be applied in policies and practices to improve the human condition, especially for the disenfranchised and powerless. His emphasis on action and implementation has left us with a large volume of unpublished papers. Although a prodigious researcher, he was always more concerned with researching the new issues that lay ahead than writing up all his completed work for formal publication.
>
> (Melody 1994: 1)

Such an approach is also typical of the scholars operating within the tradition in which Smythe is often placed: critical political economy. As Smythe put it, "The whole point of independent research is to examine critically the major institutions of society so as to better understand their contradictions and limitations, as a platform for *changing* them" (emphasis added).

214   *Fredrik Stiernstedt*

Political economy is a scientific tradition with a long history. It was formed as a separate field of knowledge in the aftermath of the Enlightenment and in connection with the industrial revolution in the 19th century. Its "founding fathers" are thinkers such as Adam Smith, John Stuart Mill, and Karl Marx. The task of political economy is to analyze and understand how the production and control of society's resources were organized, while simultaneously determining the best and most morally satisfying way of organizing social life. Media researcher Vincent Mosco has defined critical political economy as meaning "the study of social relations, particularly the power relations, that mutually constitute the production, distribution and consumption of resources" (Mosco 2009: 2). In today's capitalist society, this means that the focus of said analyses will be on this specific capitalist economic system. The critical political economy of media and communication involves asking questions about the role played by media and communication systems in creating and maintaining power over production; examples include the role of the telegraph in the rise of capitalism or the impact of new media technologies on power relations in the workplace. It also involves examining how media and communication systems are shaped by political and economic structures. Here, examples include how American political and economic interests contributed to the emergence of the platform society we live in; what interests control who has access to resources such as digital infrastructures; and how the media contribute to maintaining social inequality, such as through the images of and stories about society the media convey.

The starting point of critical political economy of the media is thus that media and communication can best be analyzed within the context of the historical development of economic and political structures. It is the "system character" of the media that is at the center of this tradition and that can be said to give this perspective the characteristics of focusing on *structures* over individuals and on *economics* and *production* over content and meaning.

A basic idea within this tradition is that society is permeated by contradictions and that the capitalist system not only produces but also accelerates these contradictions. This contradictory nature of capitalist society is also what enables change. The opposition between labor and capital was fundamental to Karl Marx's analysis of political economy in the 19th century. Industrialization fundamentally changed society, as the industrialists' pursuit of profit created new forms of wage labor and accumulated a large number of workers in urban factories. While this was a prerequisite for efficient profit maximization, it also created opportunities for workers to organize and make demands of their employers. In Marx's analysis, the structural conflicts between labor and capital (i.e., their contradictory interests) drove societal development. Similar dynamics exist in the area of media and communication, where, for example, new digital technologies create greater opportunities for people to share things with each other, spread thoughts and opinions, and organize themselves to improve society, on the one hand, while simultaneously creating new opportunities to monitor, control, and exploit people on the other. For a critical researcher like

Dallas Smythe, it is of the utmost importance to identify such central structural contradictions and examine how they can contribute to change in society. This is done by drawing attention to these contradictions and making them the subject of political struggle. For example, toward the end of his life, Smythe spoke a great deal about the contradiction between economic growth and ecological sustainability, which remains of great importance in today's political discussions. When Smythe and the Vietnamese professor Tran van Dinh wrote an article in 1983 in which they tried to define the task of critical research, they described it as follows:

> By critical researchable problems we mean how to reshape or invent institutions to meet the collective needs of the relevant social community. [...] By critical tools, we refer to historical, materialist analysis of the contradictory process in the real world. [...] By critical ideology, we refer to the linking of critical researchable problems and critical tools with interpretations that involve radical changes in the established order.
>
> (Smythe & Dinh 1983: 118)

For Smythe, "communication was essential for understanding the economy, and political economy was essential to understanding communication processes" (Melody 1994: 2). Today's media development presents us with the challenge of understanding again how politics, economics, culture, and media are connected. What interests control society's communication resources? How is control over communication resources created and maintained? What are the effects of the way in which communication resources are organized? What could an alternative order look like? And how can forces for change be mobilized? These are, in a sense, timeless questions, and they were questions that Smythe worked with. His work can spur us to ask them anew in relation to an ever-changing (media) world.

Smythe's work

In Smythe's research, there were two main tracks or themes. One was about technology and technology's contradictory character. Although technologies are developed by people, they often seem to assume a reified form, such that we perceive—and are made to perceive—that technology is something that simply exists and to which humans must "adapt." On the contrary, Smythe wrote, "technology [is] itself a political thing" (Smythe 1974/1994: 256). By that, he meant that "technology is the fruit of social systems, embodies their consciousness, values and policies and tends to reproduce them wherever it is carried" (ibid.).

Smythe also pointed out that the notion that technology is not political but "apolitical" is in itself a political statement. In particular, he showed how this notion was often propagated by those holding significant power in society, in what he called a "technocratic adventurism" (ibid.). Smythe turned strongly

216 Fredrik Stiernstedt

against so-called technological determinism and theorists such as his contemporary Marshall McLuhan, whom he believed was an apologist who would "dissolve the reality of communications under the *appearance* of the 'medium'" (Smythe 1977: 3, emphasis in original). A famous article of Smythe's has the telling title "Needs before tools," and much of Smythe's work was concentrated on examining the conditions for—and being involved in developing—institutional arrangements in which human needs, expressed through democratic processes, were allowed to set the framework for development.

The second track or theme in Smythe's work concerned the power of the mass media over thinking and opinion formation. Control over information in society was central to Smythe, as "the basis of political power" (Smythe 1974/1994: 254). Smythe often used the term "monopoly capitalist" to describe modern society. By this term, he meant the situation that arose in the West during the middle of the 20th century, in which a small number of large companies gained increasing importance and power, as the pluralistic competition between a multitude of actors that had characterized earlier stages of the development of capitalism had played out its role. What is the role of the media in such a society, and what are the consequences of the ways in which media and communication are organized within this monopoly capitalist society? To a large extent, Smythe argued, the function of the media in this society is to legitimize the prevailing order. Therefore, the media will describe reality in such a way that society appears to be natural and reasonable. Politics, business life, and human relationships will be portrayed in a way that benefits the system we live in—and its masters. Smythe writes:

> The function of the mass media in the monopoly capitalist context, to summarize, is to set the agenda which best serves the interests of the capitalist system.
>
> (Smythe 1974/1994: 253)

This is not a unique or entirely new insight, and this thinking can be recognized from several of the theorists presented in this book. As mentioned earlier, Smythe, in this respect, uses the concept of "Consciousness Industries," which he borrowed from Hans-Magnus Enzensberger (see Chapter 10 in this volume), to describe this function of the media. Moreover, Smythe's analysis of the ideological role of media in a capitalist society does not differ all that much from the perspectives developed in semiotics, critical theory, and the works of (for example) Horkheimer and Adorno (see Chapter 3 in this volume).

If the main question was "What function does the media play in the (monopoly) capitalist system," then Smythe wanted to develop the answer to this question further. The media do not only have purely ideological functions; there is also, argued Smythe, a *materialistic* answer to the question of what function the media have in a capitalist system. It is this question that Smythe tackles in the text that was the basis for the so-called "Blindspot debate," and it is to this text that we now turn our attention.

The "Blindspot"

The starting point of Smythe's article is the polemical assumption that there is no critical (Marxist) theory of communication. The "Blindspot" he wants to address is thus the blind spot of the Marxist tradition. According to Smythe, Marxism should "comprehend man as a message system- and symbol-using animal as well as a working animal" (Smythe 1974/1994: 258). Smythe thought that a critical (Marxist) media theory would follow from a critical theory of communication. It was thus with the question of communication that such a theory would begin and from which a media theory would "flow inevitably" (ibid.). A Marxist critical theory of communication must, Smythe argues, begin with the question of "commodity exchange":

> Money and communications are closely intermeshed [...] Both are media of exchange, both are storehouses of value, and both present standards of deferred settlements of accounts. Perhaps most importantly, in light of information theory and cybernetics, both are concerned with the exchange of information and confer power through the political control of information.
>
> (Smythe 1974/1994: 259)

Therefore, Smythe is deeply critical of linear communication models (see Chapter 5 in this volume). Communication is not about transport—to Smythe, that is a misleading metaphor—but about exchange.

Smythe worked on the question of a general (Marxist) theory of communication throughout his life but never published any major or more comprehensive work in this area. However, the article in focus here is a piece of the puzzle of such a theory, and it is against this background—that is, the idea of a general Marxist theory of communication—that Smythe's text should be understood.

Smythe begins his article by stating: "The first question [we] should ask about mass communications systems is *what economic function for capital do they serve*" (Smythe 1977: 1, emphasis in original). To address this question, Smythe then asks a further question: "What is the commodity form produced by modern mass media?" He notes that most people seem to agree that the goods of the media are their texts (in the broadest sense); that is, the content produced by the media industries. That, says Smythe, is not a complete answer to the question. Instead, he argues, it is necessary to consider the main commodity form produced by modern mass media as "audiences and readerships" (Smythe 1977: 3). Smythe imagines that the content of the media, such as newspaper articles or TV programs, is the compensation (i.e., "bribe") that the media gives to people in order for them to gather around the advertisement. It is the advertising that creates an inflow of money to the media industries, as the audience is packaged and sold, as a commodity, to the advertisers. Smythe asks: "What do advertisers buy with their advertising expenditures? As hardnosed businessmen they are not paying for advertising for nothing, nor from

218   *Fredrik Stiernstedt*

altruism." What they buy is "the services of audiences with predictable specifications who will pay attention in predictable numbers and at particular times to particular means of communication (TV, radio, newspapers, magazines, billboards, and third-class mail). As collectives these audiences are commodities" (Smythe 1977: 4). The audience becomes a commodity because it has a price on a market, it is produced and sold, and work is required to produce it. For Smythe, the time we spend watching advertising is a form of work, and he points out how basically all non-sleep time in a capitalist society is work time. This is a line of thought that has been widely discussed and has been met with resistance from other researchers, which I will return to below.

As Smythe writes a few years later in his book *Dependency Road*, the reason the advertisers buy the audience commodity is because "they perform a valuable service for the advertisers" (Smythe 1981: 8). Advertisers obtain three things from this product, says Smythe. First, the audiences work by "marketing consumer goods and services to themselves." Second, they learn to "vote for one candidate (or issue) or another in the political arena." And third, they "learn and reaffirm belief in the rightness of their politico-economic system" (Smythe 1981: 9).

The role of the audience—or the audience commodity—is thus not only economic but also ideological. As can be noted, only the first point above deals specifically with the direct economic role of audiences as commodities. As early as in his article from 1977, Smythe is clear that he does not perceive that those who are mainly interested in the media's "agenda setting function" (Smythe 1977: 5) are wrong, or that an ideology-critical analysis of the media as a "Consciousness Industry" is uninteresting; however, according to Smythe, such an analysis must also be related to a materialistic analysis of the media's role in the economic system. The media thus create this commodity—the audience commodity—which is required for an advanced capitalist society to function, and which is bought and consumed by advertisers. Audience commodities increase sales and speed up the circulation of goods in society and thereby contribute to companies' profits. But Smythe's argument goes further than that, by connecting the economic, social, and cultural dimensions of communication and consumption. For example, Smythe writes:

> The end product of the giant corporations in the consumer goods and services sector is consumer goods and services. The audiences produced by the mass media are only part of the means to the sale of that end product. But at the larger, systemic level, people, working via audiences to market goods and services to themselves, and their consciousness ultimately are the *systemic* end product: *they* are produced by the system ready to buy consumer goods and to pay taxes and to work in their alienating jobs in order to continue buying tomorrow.
>
> (Smythe 1981: 13, emphasis in original)

Simply put, what the media creates is consumers, as both an economic and a social product. The audience is a commodity that can be sold, bought, and consumed; moreover, as Smythe points out, the work that goes into producing this commodity creates

> a particular kind of human nature or consciousness, focusing its energies on the consumption of commodities, which Eric Fromm called *homo consumens*—people who live and work to perpetuate the capitalist system built on the commoditization of life [...] People with this nature exist primarily to serve the system; the system is *not* under their control, serving them.
>
> (Smythe 1981: 9, emphasis in original)

This, then, is Smythe's answer to the question he opens his text with: What is the media's "function for capital"?

The debate

Smythe's reasoning quickly attracted criticism and debate. His article was published in the *Canadian Journal of Political and Social Theory*; in the same journal, the British media scholar Graham Murdock published a reply entitled "Blindspots about Western Marxism: A reply to Dallas Smythe." While Murdock is prepared to agree with much of what Smythe writes, he is also critical of Smythe's article. The first point of Murdock's criticism is that he believes that Smythe does not give a fair picture of the so-called "Western Marxism," or the critical media research that is conducted in Europe. Smythe polemically opens his text by sweepingly claiming that all Marxist and critical research is only interested in the ideological functions of media and communication—that is, in their content and not their materialistic dimensions; in other words, their more fundamental role in a capitalist economy. That is not true, says Murdock, who points to how several authors, such as the British scholar Raymond Williams (see Chapter 12 in this volume) have in fact tried to integrate the materialistic, cultural, and "ideological" dimensions in their analyses. Murdock believes that this is Smythe's own "blind spot"—that Smythe does not see or understand the value of the European critical tradition. Murdock believes that this tradition already contains much of what Smythe calls for, arguing that

> a critical engagement with western Marxism is still indispensable to the development of a comprehensive and convincing Marxist analysis of mass communications. Not least; this is because the central topics of western Marxism are precisely those which were left underdeveloped in the work of Marx and of classical Marxism: the nature of the modern capitalist state; the role of ideology in reproducing class relations; the problematic position of intellectuals; and the formation of consciousness in conditions of mass consumption. Smythe acknowledges the continuing importance and centrality of these issues and itemises them as areas requiring further development at the

220 *Fredrik Stiernstedt*

very end of his essay. Yet paradoxically he turns his back on the rich sources of insight and conceptualisation offered by European Marxism.

(Murdock 1978: 110)

Furthermore, in his reply to Smythe, Murdock highlights the value of the ideology-critical (European) tradition and tries to explain why "Western Marxism" has focused on issues of culture, consciousness, and ideology to such a degree. In some forms of critical theory and Marxist analysis, culture and media have only been seen as "reflections" of more real, material conditions. Murdock points to how "Western Marxism" has instead shown that there is a "relative autonomy of ideological production and the complexity of its internal dynamics" (Murdock 1978: 117). The media and the texts of cultural industries are not mere reflections or products of the way in which the relations of production in society are organized—for example, they do not always, exclusively, and necessarily favor the interests of the elite; they have a much more complex role than that. Media can be both ideological and counter-ideological—even at the same time (see Chapters 11 and 22 in this volume). It is also obvious, says Murdock, that questions of meaning, culture, and consciousness have become increasingly central in the power conflicts that exist in society. What has happened, he writes, is a change in "the texture of social conflict" (Murdock 1978: 10) in society. It is therefore no coincidence that critical scholars who want to try to understand and criticize the contemporary world will turn their interest toward such questions. This shift in social conflict is in itself a result of the development of capitalism and the emergence of a society characterized by mass consumption and democracy. Murdock also emphasizes that the development after World War II brought conflicts other than those between "labor and capital" into focus. In particular, decolonization has contributed to bringing the issues of ethnicity and racism onto the political and scholarly agenda in a new way, and the same applies to feminist issues, in which "self-determination, political liberation and cultural autonomy" (Murdock 1978: 117) have become increasingly central. If the struggle of the early 20th century focused on political rights and material distribution, then the post-war period was characterized by questions of cultural rights and cultural struggle. According to Murdock, Smythe seems to lack an understanding of the shifts in social conflicts over these periods of time.

In addition to this objection, Murdock criticizes the substance of Smythe's argument. The most important of Murdock's objections concerns the scope of Smythe's thesis that the main role of the media in a capitalist society is to produce audience commodities. Murdock points out that not all media are primarily dependent on advertisers for their finances; for example, popular music, cinema, and comics are not. These media are completely invisible in Smythe's analysis, says Murdock. Other examples include the "public media" or "community media" that are run completely without profit interest. If Smythe claims to answer the question of what the mass media's role in capitalism is, his argument becomes too narrow and seems to be primarily about the press and commercial radio and television. Related to this problem is the question of the role of the state. In a way, it is strange that Smythe says so little about the state, given his own experience as a government official dealing with media and communication matters, as well as his lifelong interest in media regulation and legislation. A full understanding of the role of communications and the mass media in capitalist society must also include some idea of what the relationship between the state and capital looks like. For example, the privatization and deregulation of the media—which lead to increased commercialization—are a political issue. Moreover, political decisions set the framework and conditions for the commercial media's opportunities to act in society. According to Murdock, the ways in which the state and capital relate to each other—sometimes in cooperation and sometimes in opposition—must also be conceptualized in a Marxist, critical theory of the media.

However, Murdock was not the only scholar who reacted to Smythe's text. The ensuing discussion was long-lasting and continues to the present day. An important objection to Smythe was raised early on and concerns the question of what it is exactly that is produced by the media industries when they produce an "audience" (as a commodity). Smythe appears to accept that the statistics collected by ratings industries are an accurate reflection of the real audience—that is, the individuals who watch a TV program or listen to a radio program. Of course, this is not actually true, as was pointed out early on by Eileen Meehan (1984) and Richard Maxwell (1991). It is not the audience itself that is a commodity and is sold; rather, what is sold are the audience statistics created through the provision of the rating industries, which do not necessarily have much to do with the real individuals who use the media (see Chapter 10 in this volume).

This fact touches on another central objection to Smythe's article: What are audiences doing when they use the media? Is it really a kind of work or, more specifically, labor? This question is important, because a cornerstone of the Marxist economic theory that Smythe starts from is that value can only be created through labor. But can media consumption really be equated with wage labor? The compensation received by the audience is the content they get when they consume, for example, TV programs. The salary we usually get for selling our time to employers is money—a universal medium with which we can acquire other necessities of life, such as food, clothing, a home, and so on. No one can live by watching TV, as the compensation we receive (entertainment, information, entertainment, etc.) cannot be exchanged for other goods (Bolin 2005: 297). Media use also lacks other dimensions of wage labor in modern society: necessity and coercion. Although people are formally free to sell themselves on the labor market or not, it is practically impossible for the vast majority of individuals in modern societies to survive without participating in wage labor. Furthermore, the contract we make with employers when we sell our labor time means that we relinquish control over our own time, and submit to a certain compulsion: Whoever bought our labor time now has the right to tell us what to do, and we are obliged to obey. However, the dimensions of

222 *Fredrik Stiernstedt*

necessity and compulsion are missing in the majority of all media use. Some scholars have argued that there is an implicit "compulsion" or necessity to media use, and that users are "under the ideological control of capitalists that possess control over the means of communication" (Fuchs 2012: 704). Hence, we are "forced" to use the services of the media and communication industries in order to maintain social contacts, stay informed about what is happening, and—in some cases—cope with our professional life (ibid.). Although there is a grain of truth in such statements, the comparison of media use with wage labor cannot be said to be entirely satisfactory. Perhaps it is more reasonable to assume that it is not the audience who works to create the product (the audience commodity) that the media sells on the advertising market; rather, it is statisticians and other personnel who are employed and perform paid work in the industries that create ratings, as pointed out by Göran Bolin (2011), among others. This may appear to be a minor objection, but it is a matter of considerable importance. Basically, the interpretation of media use (as labor, or not) is about how we view the individual and society—and how we understand capitalism as a political-economic system. For Smythe, "all non-sleeping time under capitalism [...] is work time" (Smythe 1977: 6). During the day, we work in companies and organizations (salaried work) and, in our so-called "free time," we work at "reproductive labor"—that is, renewing and developing the "product" we sell on the wage labor market (e.g., through recreational activities and rest, or by gaining new skills). Through the media and communication industries, some of this reproductive labor (e.g., when we relax by watching TV) is transformed into a form of productive labor, as our viewing contributes to the creation of a commodity (the audience commodity) that can be sold on the market, creating added profit for the media and communication companies. But is it a reasonable assumption that all the time we do not spend sleeping is a kind of work time? Is it really the case that everything humans do only contributes to reproducing and reinforcing the capitalist system? Reality appears to be more complex and contradictory than that. Moreover, are there no areas of freedom outside of the capitalist system, which Smythe portrays as almost totalitarian? What about resistance, or activities that are completely devoid of economic (or other) utility and value? What about individual agency? British media scholar David Hesmondhalgh summarizes this criticism:

> The underlying but underdeveloped normative position is that all the time we spend under capitalism contributes to a vast negative machine called capitalism; nothing escapes this system. No work or leisure seems, by this account, to be any more meaningful than any other. It is unclear whether Smythe is demanding payment for the unpaid labour of audiences; and in fact it is unclear to me why he does not include payment for sleep in his demands, given that this too seems to involve the reproduction of labour power.
>
> (Hesmondhalgh 2010: 280)

Such objections and problematizations of Smythe's text do not change the fact that Smythe's short and polemical article from 1977 must be said to be a "classic" text in the field of media studies—precisely because it led to an intensive and sometimes fierce debate and discussion. This text has become a reference point and engaged writers for nearly 50 years, and its relevance has not diminished but has rather increased over the years. As Janet Wasko points out, "with the increasing spread of privatized, advertiser-supported media, the audience commodity concept has been accepted by many political economists, as well as other theorists" (Wasko 2005: 29). Above all, the rise of digital platform media—and the new business models they entail—has given new energy to the discussion on the audience commodity, as discussed below.

Smythe's text stimulates discussion because, despite its flaws and shortcomings, it reveals something important and turns our understanding of the media upside down in a thought-provoking way. Most people probably think of media and communication as a matter of messages, content, and texts, as you can see just by flipping through the chapters in this book. For many critical researchers, the media can be perceived as a kind of "Consciousness Industry" that imparts and gives something to the audience; that is, the media teaches us things and socializes us in certain ways of thinking about the world and seeing reality from certain perspectives. But, as Sut Jhally (2018) puts it, this is "conceptualized upside down." Smythe tries to reverse the reasoning: What if we do not think of the media as giving us something but as taking something from us? Jhally writes:

> It [the media] is not characterized primarily by what it puts into you—messages—but by what it takes out: value. Not ideology that it installs in you. That's obviously what it does. But the organization of mass media is around what it takes out of you. That's the same way as in the factory [or in working life more generally]. Value is drawn, and surplus value is drawn, from workers, the same way—how do you explain that?
>
> (Jhally 2018: 8)

The strength of Smythe's article is perhaps not that it fully answers the question of how to explain value extraction in the media but rather that it turns the perspective on its head and opens up discussion about this issue.

Smythe's relevance in today's digital media landscape

Developments in the media and communication industries in recent decades have increased scholarly interest in Smythe's work and in the whole discussion of the audience commodity (McGuigan & Manzerolle 2014). Aside from the ever-increasing deregulation and commercialization of the media, as pointed out in the quote by Wasko earlier, it is digitization above all that has given rise to this renewed interest. Thus, Smythe's work is being used and built upon in many contemporary studies (for a recent contribution see McGuigan 2023). The

224   *Fredrik Stiernstedt*

reason for the resurgence of interest in Smythe's work is mainly due to an increasing public awareness of three consequences of digital media:

First, they have allowed for the unprecedented and in-depth monitoring and control of media users and media use. Audience statistics no longer need to be created using social science methods such as surveys and media diaries, or estimated by monitoring a limited sample of the population electronically (such as through so-called "people meters"). Digital environments and platforms allow for a more direct monitoring of users' activity, as well as a greater opportunity to adapt advertising and media content to suit users' displayed "interests" and "behaviors" in these digital environments. Thus, for example, Christian Fuchs (2012) believes that Smythe's idea that "all non-sleeping time under capitalism is work time" (Smythe 1977: 6) has gained renewed relevance, writing that: "we can say that life has become a factory, factory life" (Fuchs 2012: 716).

Second, digital media have made ad-based business models increasingly important to the media industries. Admittedly, there are still numerous subscription-based services, such as streaming services of various kinds. But a large part of the digital economy is driven by advertising and marketing, directly or indirectly, which are in turn based on renewed and deepened opportunities to follow consumer behavior on digital platforms. Everything we do in digital environments leaves traces, or information about us as users; thus, we produce ourselves as a commodity (an audience commodity) that can be sold to advertisers. However, just as in the discussion around Smythe's original formulations on the work of the media audience, it can be argued that the productive work is not so much done by users as by "employees, engineers, researchers, and much other kinds of professionals that produce statistics, interfaces and algorithms that make possible the constitution of the commodity audience" (Bolaño & Vieira 2015: 58). Of course, this is true; nevertheless, we can compare the value creation that takes place on digital platforms with the value creation in working life by asking: What workers in this case are able to stop production? What group could strike in a meaningful way? Christian Fuchs (2012) asks a similar question, pointing out that—although the employees of relevant companies have some opportunity to create production losses, such as by refusing to develop new services and applications—only "users and clients" have the opportunity to "bring production to a standstill" by refusing to participate in digital networks (Fuchs 2012: 64; see also Dolber 2016: 751).

Third, digitization has meant not only that the media audience "consumes" content produced by media companies but that their own creative production takes on an ever greater importance for the new digital media companies. Platforms such as YouTube or TikTok are largely based on content that is *de facto* produced by "audiences"—that is by the users themselves. The American media economist Philip Napoli writes:

> The notion of the work of the audience, which may have been a bit more tenuous when the work being monetized was isolated to media consumption, becomes more concrete in an environment in which the creative work

of the audience is an increasingly important source of economic value for the media organizations.

(Napoli 2011: 511)

When researchers have studied and analyzed these changes, many have turned to Smythe and to the discussion of the audience commodity and of the "work" that media users perform—work that creates profits for media and communication companies. As a result, the whole so-called "Blindspot debate" has been given a new lease of life in recent years, illustrating how the meaning and influence of classic texts can vary over time, and how concepts can gain new relevance as reality changes.

References

Bolaño, C. R., & Vieira, E. S. (2015). The political economy of the internet: Social networking sites and a reply to Fuchs. *Television & New Media*, 16 (1): 52–61.

Bolin, G. (2005). Notes from inside the factory: The production and consumption of signs and sign value in media industries. *Social Semiotics*, 15 (3): 289–306.

Bolin, G. (2011). *Value and the media: Cultural production and consumption in digital markets*. Farnham: Ashgate.

Dolber, B. (2016). Blindspots and blurred lines: Dallas Smythe, the audience commodity, and the transformation of labor in the digital age. *Sociology Compass*, 10 (9): 747–755.

Fuchs, C. (2012). Dallas Smythe today–The audience commodity, the digital labour debate, Marxist political economy and critical theory. Prolegomena to a digital labour theory of value. *tripleC*, 10 (2): 692–740.

Hesmondhalgh, D. (2010). User-generated content, free labour and the cultural industries. *ephemera*, 10 (3/4): 267–284.

Jhally, S. (2018). Dallas Smythe Award Keynote Lecture. *Democratic Communiqué*, 28 (1): 1–12.

Lent, J. A. (ed.) (1995). *A different road taken: Profiles in critical communication*. Boulder, Colorado: Westview.

Mansell, R. (1995). Against the flow: The peculiar opportunity of social scientists. In: Lent, J. A. (ed.), *A different road taken: Profiles in critical communication*. Boulder, Colorado: Westview, pp. 43–67.

Maxwell, R. (1991). The image is gold: Value, the audience commodity, and fetishism. *Journal of Film and Video*, 43 (1–2): 29–45.

McGuigan, L., & Manzerolle, V. (eds.) (2014). *The audience commodity in a digital age: Revisiting a critical theory of commercial media*. New York, NY: Peter Lang Publishing, Inc.

McGuigan, L. (2023). *Selling the American people: Advertising, optimization, and the origins of Adtech*. Cambridge, Mass.: MIT Press.

Meehan, E. R. (1984). Ratings and the institutional approach: A third answer to the commodity question. *Critical Studies in Mass Communication*, 1 (2): 216–225.

Melody, B. (1994). Dallas Smythe: Pioneer in the political economy of communications. In: Smythe, D. W. & Guback, T. H. (eds.), *Counterclockwise: Perspectives on communication*. Boulder: Westview Press, pp. 1–7.

Mosco, V. (2009). *The political economy of communication*. London: SAGE.

226 Fredrik Stiernstedt

Murdock, G. (1978). Blindspots about western Marxism: A reply to Dallas Smythe. *Canadian Journal of Political and Social Theory*, 2 (2): 109–115.

Napoli, P. M. (2011). *Audience evolution: New technologies and the transformation of media audiences*. New York: Columbia University Press.

Smythe, D. W. (1974/1994). The role of mass media and popular culture in defining development. In: Smythe, D. W. & Guback, T. H. (eds.), *Counterclockwise: Perspectives on communication*. Boulder: Westview Press, pp. 247–262.

Smythe, D. W. (1977). Communications: Blindspot of western Marxism. *Canadian Journal of Political and Social Theory*, 1 (3): 1–27.

Smythe, D. W. (1981). *Dependency road: Communications, capitalism, consciousness, and Canada*. Norwood, NJ: Ablex.

Smythe, D. W. & Van Dinh, T. (1983). On critical and administrative research: A new critical analysis. *Journal of Communication*, 33 (3): 117–127.

Smythe, D. W. (1987,April 20) Freedom is the act of resisting necessity, response to L. R. Sussman. ICASIETAR, Montreal, 10.

Wasko, J. (2005). Studying the political economy of media and information. *Comunicação e Sociedade*, 7: 25–48.

16 Gaye Tuchman (1978) *Making News: A Study in the Construction of Reality*

Anna Roosvall

Introduction

This is a view on our view on the world. How is our view on the world created, through words, and not least through work — newswork?[1] And how is newswork created through our view on the world? It all starts with a metaphor: news is a window on the world. As such, news is transparent and invites us to see the world rather than tries to, or happens to, obscure it. How wonderful! At the same time the window, news, has a frame. It can consist of several separated panes, can be more or less opaque, and it always obstructs or at least limits potential multiplicities of views — large chunks of reality — as much as it offers them. The window provides certain angles and renders others impossible. How…disappointing. Or what a curious conundrum; what an interesting practical and theoretical challenge!

Gaye Tuchman's window metaphor in the introduction to her 1978 book *Making News: A Study in the Construction of Reality* immediately drew me in when I read it as an undergraduate student. The tensions between the open character of the see-through window and the limiting features of the frame, as well as between the subtitle's "construction" and "reality", are indeed compelling. The structure of the book, and the scientific methods used to build it, contain a similarly compelling duality. The book deals with the frame of news — something which has later come to be associated with content and textual analysis — via ethnographic studies of the *making of* news, including interviews and observations.

Making News killed the previously dominant metaphor of news being able to *mirror* the events of the world. While this idea — that news reflects events, places and people — still lives on in everyday speech, it has since the publication of Tuchman's book lost its place as a relevant hypothesis in the social sciences, and more specifically in media sociology, Tuchman's main area of work at the time.

Gaye Tuchman, born in 1943, is an American sociologist, whose work is focused on the sociology of media and culture, of gender, and of higher education. Tuchman has mainly been based at the University of Connecticut, USA, where she was professor in Sociology, and later became emerita. She has had

DOI: 10.4324/9781003432272-17

228   *Anna Roosvall*

visiting positions at, among other places, Stanford, where she was visiting professor of feminist studies and sociology, and the University of Iowa, where she was based at the School of Journalism. Her media focus is thus combined with a journalism focus. In *Making News* she identifies herself as an interpretive sociologist — that is, not a positivist one.

Among Tuchman's other notable works, the chapter "The symbolic annihilation of women", included in *Hearth and Home: Images of Women in the Mass Media*, which Tuchman co-edited with Arlene K. Daniels and James W. Benét (1978), also stands out as extremely relevant in media studies of the 21st century. Tuchman, moreover, contributed to changing dominant views on objectivity through the article "Objectivity as strategic ritual" (1972).

Why should we keep reading *Making News*, then? Tuchman's classic is not only still referred to explicitly in many central texts in the broad field of media and journalism studies, but is also implicitly present in the reasoning in a vast array of others. It constitutes a key part of the foundation upon which these subsequent texts are built: a theory of knowledge and of the construction of reality in which news and media play important roles. The book also inspires methodologically: in order to understand the news as constructed, we have to study the people who make it, how their work is organized into routines, and how their core values are linked to their everyday practices.

Tuchman's language still permeates the word choices in media studies. What is media studies without framing, without facticity, without the pondering on how construction and reality co-exist, and without lessons that could only have been learned from the combination of the long-term ethnography and the theoretical creativity and clarity of Tuchman? This chapter elaborates on all of these aspects, but first it is necessary to set the scene in which the book appeared, and offer a brief overview of the subjects and perspectives tackled in each of the chapters in *Making News*. This is followed by three sections covering "From mirroring to constructing reality", "Processes: News work is theory in practice", and "Processing: News and/as knowledge theory". Ultimately, there is a concluding discussion. Given this chapter's aim to present and discuss *Making News* as an example of a classic in media theory, focus lies on the more theoretical parts of Tuchman's book, but also on how Tuchman intricately connects extensive empirical work and theory building throughout the book.

The time and the reception

Making News was published in 1978. It was Cold War times and the Democrat Jimmy Carter was president in the USA, where Tuchman was based. Neutron bomb tests, and protests, took place around the globe, and among other notable international developments, there were upheavals in Iran, South Africa invaded Angola, and Spain became a democracy following four decades of dictatorship (*On This Day*, n.d.). All of these events were part of processes that had been brewing for a long time and thus coincided not just with the publication of Tuchman's book, but also with the preceding field work she had done.

1978 was also the year when the Hollywood film *The Deer Hunter*, featuring Meryl Streep among others, premiered. Its Vietnam War drama — played out in Vietnam as well as in the USA after the American soldiers had returned — covers the most intense time of US involvement in the war. Like the previously mentioned international developments, the Vietnam War corresponds with the period of Tuchman's ethnographic work at US news organizations (1966–1976). In fact, it was partly Tuchman's concern about the Vietnam War that prompted her to start studying news in 1966 (Tuchman, 1978a: ix).

The National Women's Movement, NOW, had been founded the same year. Together with the general women's movement, it constitutes an important subject in the book, and illustrates the challenges for (certain) NGOs to enter a very traditional news culture. Given Tuchman's gender and feminist focus, and the academic context in which that focus was formed, it is also notable that 1978 saw the first female head of a US university, Hannah H. Gray in Chicago (*On This Day*, n.d.). In media technology news, the first unsolicited bulk commercial e-mail — spam — was sent to all ARPANET addresses on the West Coast of the USA in 1978. It was then to be twenty years until e-mail would become a regular thing. Times were different. And similar. As we shall see, significant traits of the journalistic experiences accounted for in Tuchman's work, as well as the theories that were formed in *Making News*, have remained topical.

What notable works on the theory of news had been published shortly before *Making News*, then? A decade or so had passed since Galtung and Ruge's 1965 article on the structure of foreign news, which introduced the notion of newsworthiness. It had spurred research into the concept of "news value" that was blossoming when *Making News* came about, and which permeates discussions in the book. Furthermore, MacCombs and Shaw (1972) had relatively recently introduced agenda-setting theory, and frame analysis had been established and spread through Erving Goffman's 1974 book with the same name (for more on Goffman's earlier work, see Chapter 6 in this volume).

The Glasgow University Media Group was concurrently an important player on the media sociology scene. In *Making News* there are numerous references to their then forthcoming book, which is referred to as *Bad News Vol. II*, but later known as *More Bad News* (1980). *Bad News* had been published in 1976. Furthermore, Michael Schudson's *Discovering the News: A Social History of American Newspapers* came out the same year as *Making News* (1978). Like Schudson, Tuchman focuses on the USA, and specifically pinpoints "Americans" as the recipients of news on the first line of chapter 1. Americans thus constitute the implied readership. Tuchman's book would, however, come to travel the world, and its metaphors and general ideas would come to be applied in many different national and international contexts.

When the book first arrived, it was indeed well received. A review in *Social Forces* concludes: "[The book] charts the conceptual development of current scholarship in the construction of a theory of news. It also reconfirms Tuchman's place as one of the major pioneers in that effort" (Robinson & Sahin, 1981: 1341–1342). The authors appreciate Tuchman's empirical as well as

230   *Anna Roosvall*

theoretical contribution. They especially hail the theorizing of news as frame and as construction, but also criticize Tuchman for leaving no room for conflict in news organizations, and for advocating too hard for the idea of news as a means "not to know". On the whole, the reviewers declare the book an important contribution to the sociology of mass communication.

A review in *Perspective* (later: *Perspectives on political science*) starts: "Gaye Tuchman's *Making News* is not the sort of book about the media that political scientists are likely to read...", and ends with the conclusion that students concerned with news in the political system *should* read it (Mead, 1979). The reviewer considers the book's consistent link between the theoretical foundation and the observations its greatest strength, and finds that the argument's theoretical significance is clear throughout. From the perspective of political science, the book's organizational thesis is seen as more useful than its sociology of knowledge. In contrast to this, a reviewer in *Sociology of Work and Occupations* (Cantor, 1980) appreciates its contribution to the sociology of knowledge the most, together with the elaboration on the construction of reality, and declares the book a seminal work in these areas.

What should we take away from these reviews, apart from how they tend to appreciate themes and theories that are closest to the journals they were published in (Sociology/Political Science)? Theoretically speaking, a core lesson is that when you read media theory, it is always sensible to look for how it is anchored in broader paradigms of the social sciences and humanities. In the case of *Making News*, we find not just theories about news, but theories of phenomenology, the social construction of reality, and knowledge, as formulated by Berger and Luckmann (1966), Schutz (1967), and Goffman (1974), and as rethought and reformulated by Tuchman herself.

The book at a glance

The introductory chapter, "News as Frame", naturally sets the scene for the rest of the book, sketching two main themes: (1) the act of making news is the act of constructing reality, and (2) journalistic professionalism serves organizational interests by reaffirming the institutional process in which newswork is embedded. Tuchman moreover details the field sites of her ethnographic work: a television station, a newspaper, a press room, and multiple sites where newswork and NGO work centred on the women's movement happened.

The second and third chapters develop theories on *the news net*, a news construction system, in relation to space and time. In chapter 2 the newswork and content aspects of the news net are discussed in relation to news values and geographical scale. This is further developed in chapter 3, in which the social organization of time is added. Tuchman clarifies how this creates certain *types* of news. It appears clearly here that Tuchman is interested in human thinking, how it creates categories, or rather *typifications*, and how these processes construct reality.

Chapter 4 is devoted to professionalism and the flexibility that is allowed in the midst of time and space constraints. What stands out here is how a very concrete and detailed account of the organization of work in relation to news sources embeds a theory of knowledge. Subsequently, in chapter 5 Tuchman argues that news sources and facts constitute each other. This is clarified by the work of the news net, and how these processes ultimately create a *web of facticity* intended to uphold the credibility of news.

Chapter 6, "Representation and the news narrative", focuses on content. In this endeavour, Tuchman places not only news films under the sociological microscope, including choices of shots and narrative structure, but also the constitution of the role of reporters in television news. Chapter 7 merges the discussion of how occurrences can (or cannot) be transformed into events — and thus into traditional news — with an investigation of news about, and media strategies applied by, the women's movement, a movement that had a hard time getting into the media even though what went on around it at this time was politically major.

Chapters 8, 9, and 10 emphasize historical, philosophical, and theoretical aspects. In chapter 8 Tuchman establishes a centuries-long historical framework for her ten-year period of empirical studies, detailing previous mappings and discussions of the emergence of the objectivity ideal in news and the public/private distinction in society (Dahlgren, 1977; Schudson, 1978). This lays the ground for a discussion of freedom of speech and news as ideology. The ideology theme also permeates the following chapters. In chapter 9 Tuchman goes through the theoretical concepts that have been central to the ethnographic investigations (e.g. Berger & Luckmann, 1966; Goffman, 1974; Schutz, 1967). Here, we find theorizing on what happens when the outcome of newswork meets readers, how people make sense of news as part of and as a constructor of reality, and how the questioning of the truth and reality of certain news stories does not stand in the way of a view on news as real and true overall. Finally, the aim of chapter 10 is to assess news as ideology and knowledge. This is achieved through reviewing critique in recent philosophy of science and sociological theory. It broadens the news-related theory of knowledge to concern other areas, summarizes the idea of news as legitimator of the status quo, and in the very last pages returns to the practice of telling a story.

While discussing what news stories are, the book itself is full of stories, drawn from the many interviews and how these are connected to news output and to theory. Barbie Zelizer (2004) describes in fact Tuchman's newsroom ethnographies as "realist tales". These realist tales are in Tuchman's book put in dialogue with theories of newsworthiness, frames, public/private, objectivity, ideology, and knowledge, and from this dialogue, a deepened and rooted theory of knowledge, including how knowledge interacts with ideology, is developed.

From mirroring to constructing reality

Was the mirror metaphor really killed by Tuchman, as stated at the beginning of this chapter, and in that case — how was it done? In order to elaborate on this, we need first to take into consideration the historical and continued

232   *Anna Roosvall*

significance of the mirror metaphor in news. *The Daily Mirror* is a traditional newspaper name. Variations of it appear in diverse countries and languages, the most famous perhaps being the German publication *Der Spiegel*. Public service media remits in turn may include formulations such that the media in question should "mirror" society and its diversity. The mirror metaphor is for instance used over 30 times in the Swedish government's terms and conditions for public service media 2020–2025, where a special section is called "The mirroring task is central" (riksdagen.se). Moreover, objectivity is still an ideal in news media and journalism, even though Tuchman (1972) concluded it mainly functions as a strategic ritual evoked in order to protect newsworkers from risks of their trade, like libel (for more on communication as ritual, see Chapter 13 in this volume, about James Carey's work). Part of objectivity is neutrality. The mirror image connects to this since it is supposedly a neutral reflection of the original in front of it, while paintings, for instance, are generally not. Even photographs are not neutral renderings since the "in front of it" part is, in comparison to the mirror, more obviously constructed through choice of angle, width, clarity, and so on, much like the window *frame* metaphor Tuchman suggests for news. The emphasis on frame rather than window is important here, as the window otherwise expresses, like the mirror, what Theodore L. Glasser (1996) calls journalism's "glassy essence" (borrowing a phrase from Rorty, 1979). This essence encompasses several metaphors for journalism, expressing both what it supposedly is and what it ought to be: a right and morally good see-through channel of simple transmission, directly connected to and corresponding to the world outside, accurately representing it, principally not constructing anything.

Reality is above all associated with the non-constructed, natural, genuine, true, non-created. It is generally understood as "the state of things as they are, rather than as they are imagined to be" (Cambridge dictionary). The thought of reality being constructed may in view of this appear as counterintuitive, even provocative, to media and communication students. It speaks against a common sense which builds on the idea that if something happens, it is a, or even *the*, simple truth. Then, suddenly, I may as a media studies teacher get to witness students having light bulb moments when they so to speak leave "the natural attitude" (where we live before we enter philosophy — or phenomenology) (Schutz, 1967) and ponder upon choices made in representations of the world, in news texts and images ("terrorist"/"freedom fighter", event/process, active voice/passive voice, whose voice…?). And I may remember when I had such light bulb moments myself, in the wake of Tuchman's (and Schutz's) theories. A key contribution of Tuchman's work is in this regard that the mirror metaphor is not killed through a comparison of the original occurrence and how it is described in the newspaper or on news film. Her explication barely has anything to do with that. Instead, it is done through a detailing and theorizing of the process of what happens in between — that is, of aspects of newswork and the epistemology that accompanies it.

General constructionist claims often take the passive form, declaring that *something is socially constructed*, but they could also be presented as an active two-part relation: something (someone) socially constructs something. What (who) constructs, then? Too little attention has been paid to distinguishing agents of construction, writes Mallon (2019). Tuchman has some suggestions. These are not as simple as "journalists", or "newspaper owners"; rather, identifying agents of construction in newswork requires us to think about collective professional agency within the structure, and structural agency in the multi-faceted processes of constructing news. The next section delves into these processes and discusses newswork as theory in practice.

Processes: News work is theory in practice

The act of categorizing is an act of theorizing, writes Tuchman (1978a: 205), and she exemplifies this by showing how diverse events — "different strikes, shortened work hours, a conspiracy case" — have been categorized as types of unrest through their juxtaposition in a news article, as analyzed by the Glasgow University Media Group (1976). Similarly, the women's movement became hard news only when it appeared as a threat to social stability — also a type of unrest (Tuchman, 1978a: 184). Categorization happens throughout the newswork process. It has parallels in science, where classification comes from theoretical understandings of the world in question. Tuchman is more interested in how categories emerge and overlap than what they are. She has an interest in epistemological thinking *in* the process of working and *as* the process of working — how it creates categories, how it constructs reality.

The news net and the web of facticity

A basic categorization in newswork concerns news vs. non-news. Or rather, it concerns what occurrences can become events and thereby be further transformed into news stories. One determining factor, encompassing many determining factors, is *the news net*. The news net is thrown out over the world, over pieces of the world. Some parts necessarily seep through; this is the logic and function of a net. It will catch some fish, but not others. It *aims to* catch some fish, but not others. The net in question is constituted through aspects of time and space, such as the rhythm of newswork and the placement of reporters, the sum of which simultaneously derive from and determine the work. It builds on newswork tradition and (re-)creates newswork tradition in a self-fulfilling process. While the news net has a tendency to make ahistorical news *in terms of its content*, the net itself is dependent on history, on what has been understood to be newsworthy before — for instance, which sources have been used and can provide legitimacy, which organizations need to be monitored and which can seep through the net. Drawing on Dahlgren (1977), Tuchman (1978a: 164) concludes that by maintaining an artificial distinction between public and private, news media allow private institutions not to make the news, while

234 *Anna Roosvall*

focus remains on the public sector. At the same time, newswork tends to prioritize individuals as sources (Tuchman, 1978a: 134). This has generally constituted an obstacle to collective social movements, as shown in one of Tuchman's case studies: the women's movement. Overall, through the logics and practices of the news net, some things are bound to end up on the feature page or become non-news, both of which happened to occurrences regarding the women's movement at the time of Tuchman's investigations, a time when the movement was thriving to a degree that it could have been expected to become major news.

Facticity is another important term in Tuchman's vocabulary of news and knowledge theory. The form of news is overloaded with norms that connote this. On a basic level news media can claim facticity via certain film shots of places and buildings. While this facticity is constructed, news *seems not to* arrange time and space, but just tape or retell happenings — the buildings and places are irrefutably there, in real life. Hence news (film) comes out as presenting facts, not interpretations. More specifically a *web of facticity* creates events: "[e]vents are concretely embedded in the web of facticity, the who, what, when, where, why and how of the traditional news lead" (Tuchman, 1978a: 134). Events, but not issues, can easily be transformed into news stories. Issues are grounded in *analytic explanations of the everyday world* as a socially experienced structure and go beyond a focus on the individual that comes with events (and later in the process with news). Tuchman (1978a: 134) takes institutional racism as an example: it goes beyond the individual, requires a deep analysis, and thus does not work well with the event/story logic. Issues can, however, become facts through the web of facticity. This web is created by fleshing out one supposed fact with a large number of supposed facts, which together become (appear as) self-validating; by cross-reference they mutually validate each other (Tuchman, 1978a: 86–87). This may lead to the avoidance of challenging the legitimacy of offices that hold centralized information — if they and their facts were to be challenged, the news net becomes dismantled, and thus newswork, and in the end news legitimacy, may be dismantled.

Framing

Everyday life is seen by Tuchman (1978a: 206–208) as a field of action, where some actors have greater power to reproduce social meaning; newsworkers are such actors. Imposing a *frame* on an occurrence enables journalists to recognize facts and build facticity (Tuchman, 1978a: 88). Tuchman applies, as mentioned, an ethnographic approach to frames; this has largely been abandoned by later framing analyses. Christian Baden (2020: 229) notes in his chapter "Framing the News" in *The Handbook of Journalism Studies*: "since Gaye Tuchman's (1978a) seminal study on *Making News*, what happens between journalists' discovery of specific, source-sponsored frames, and the publication of specific news frames, has fallen somewhat into neglect". However, Baden (2020: 240) writes that the field of news framing has begun to return to its Tuchmanesque origin, studying framing as "a key journalistic accomplishment, embedded

Gaye Tuchman (1978) 235

within a multifaceted, interactive, and reflexive process", and trying to understand "the workings of journalism in its ever-changing environment".

Tuchman's frame analysis draws in parts on Goffman's (1974) ethnomethodological approach and its rationale of exploring how people make sense of everyday life. This leads to a discussion of how strips of everyday occurrences are sorted by newsworkers and become news (Tuchman, 1978a: 210). In this process, newswork is "attuned to specific understandings of social reality"; newswork thus "finds" certain strips of reality and prioritizes certain understandings of reality through its construction (Tuchman, 1978a: 216). Hence, the search for the frame and the frame are actually the same, says Tuchman (1978a: 103); they cannot be separated, nor understood without each other. If you want to understand existing frames in news output you should therefore look for how they are searched for in newswork, and if you want to understand the search for frames you should look at how frames come out in/as news output. You can say that frames pre-exist in occurrences, in that they find occurrences, impart a character on them, and thus they become events and subsequently stories (Tuchman, 1978a: 193). So, in a sense, news makes events, not the other way around. There is a clear connection between practice and content in this understanding of framing (see Baden, 2020).

Framing theory in Tuchman's version is intertwined with her broader take on power-knowledge relationships. Drawing on field work, interviews, and theorizing she concludes that the media narrows frames where alternatives could appear. In the end this practice of framing becomes a way of promoting the existing social hierarchy.

Processing: News and/as knowledge theory

At the beginning of this chapter, I asked how our view of the world is created. I could have asked how our *knowledge* of the world is created. Knowledge, Tuchman (1978a: 177) writes, is situational. This means that what you see and learn depends not only on where the metaphorical window is placed, how it is framed, and how you as a viewer are placed in relation to it, but also *when* the viewing happens. Knowledge is furthermore not only re-ported (brought back, see Schudson, 2003) this way, but your pre-existing knowledge is at the same time applied in the process of determining the wheres and the whens of the outlooks. In order to understand this, analysis of the outlooks needs to be combined with some introspection regarding the lookers, and in the case of making news, specifically regarding those who construct and mediate the news. The importance of newswork in the construction of reality has been discussed in the previous sections. Here, this thesis is further developed with a view to Tuchman's take on knowledge, ideology and how (imagined) audiences and publics relate to news.

News knowledge work and/as discourse practice

News records social reality while also being a product of it (Tuchman, 1978a: 189). Political press conferences are obvious examples of this; news records the

236 *Anna Roosvall*

press conference and is concurrently being constructed by it. News stories more generally help shape public definitions of what goes on by "selectively attributing to them specific details" (Tuchman, 1978a: 190). These notions of a dialectical relationship between news/language and society, and of the highlighting of choices made in representation (the selectivity) are reminiscent of the critical discourse analysis (CDA) tradition that came to grow strong in media studies following the linguistic turn, which built on Foucault (see also Chapter 9 in this book) as well as the linguistics tradition going back to Ferdinand de Saussure. CDA is concerned with, among other things, what is understood as deviant vs. the norm, which also has been a key focus in media and cultural studies of representation in the tradition of Stuart Hall (1997, se Chapter 11 for Hall's theory of encoding/decoding). Tuchman (1978a: 184) writes that norms are defined by newsworkers as they use, invoke, and apply them. Newsworkers' impact on norms is augmented by the fact that as social organizations attempt to get into the media, they may reaffirm the media's role as legitimator (Tuchman: 1978a: 206). Another way of legitimating is to treat, as Tuchman (1978a: 180) says, what ought to be explained "as fact or assumption", which is similar to what in CDA approaches is discussed as "naturalization".

A main difference between the CDA tradition and Tuchman's constructionist approach is, however, that when Fairclough (1995) and other Media CDA proponents speak of the importance of the production aspect of communication (as part of discourse practice), they may access discourse practice *indirectly* through the texts. Tuchman, however, focuses *directly* on production as such, as part of discourse practice proper. In the case of *Making News*, the grounds for analysis are constituted by a ten-year period of field work in diverse news organizations, including interviews with journalists, editors, and women who were engaged in the women's movement. The width and depth of this analysis exposes the indispensable contribution of the analysis of discourse practice proper.

Knowledge and ideology are socially embedded, people produce and reproduce institutions that hold power and reproduce power as social resource (Tuchman, 1978a: 215); this, as part of discourse practice, concerns media institutions as well as others. "By identifying centralized sources of information as legitimated social institutions..." and identifying these with facts "...newsworkers create and control controversy; they contain dissent" (Tuchman, 1978a: 210–211). Knowledge is hence controlled through construction. An aspect of this that is seldom discussed but that is highlighted by Tuchman as well as by the CDA tradition is *what is not said*. According to Tuchman (1978a: 179), what is not said or done distinguishes between ideology and knowledge: ideology can be characterized as a means *not* to know; hence ideology prevents (some) knowledge. She points out that in this regard the right to know — which is protected in the Universal Declaration of Human Rights, specifically in article 19 where the right to information is stated — comes out as the right to know *certain* broadcast or published facts but missing alternative views (Tuchman, 1978a: 174).

News knowledge theory as general knowledge theory: News (theory) and academia

Tuchman (1978a: 215) says that while it seems trite to observe that knowledge is power, this is not only a dogma of society; it also rules newswork. She exemplifies this with a discussion about how knowledge appears in news vs. academia. I will here detail four aspects of this: *reaffirmation of the social order, objectification, reflexivity,* and *attitudes towards the analytic.*

Power may be realized through the dissemination of some knowledge and suppression of other; at times this has to do with *reaffirmation of the social order.* In both newspapers and television, professional practice limits access to radical views for consumers of news, and hence limits audiences' potential use of media as socio-political resources (Tuchman, 1978a: 176). Kunelius and Reunanen (2012) trace back to Tuchman (1978a) a steady line of research and theorizing that has underlined the insufficient nature of the effort of journalistic professionalism to represent the lifeworld perspective of the people against systemic forces and vocabularies. Catching her approach in one sentence, Tuchman herself writes:

> Through its dispersion of the news net, its typifications, the claimed professionalism of newsworkers, the mutual constitution of fact and source, the representational forms of the news narrative, the claim to first amendment rights of both private property and professionalism — through all these phenomena, objectified as constraints or as resources — news legitimates the status quo.
>
> (1978a: 215–216)

Here, reaffirmation of the social order (status quo) is combined with *objectification* of social phenomena. As Berger and Luckmann (1966, see Tuchman, 1978a: 214) note, social phenomena may become facts through reification, which is essentially a form of objectification. The demand for fact (Tuchman, 1978a: 82) is, however, slightly different in news than in philosophy and science. In the case of news, we have seen that social movements are not likely to make the news unless they adjust to the order of the establishment and as part of this, to the order of the media organizations. Concurrently they may be objectified in and through this adjustment, be treated as a thing (e.g. "the migrant", who in turn can be subsumed in the term "migration"), and have words transformed into quotes that are reified in the news making process (Tuchman, 1978a: 195–96). In the university's case this can happen to phenomena, persons, and actions in courses as well as in research and scientific articles (Tuchman, 1978a: 216–17). Think, for instance, about the occasional objectification of "the media" in media studies (you may not have to look far) and of how researchers may objectify research subjects into research objects.

Drawing on Giddens (1976), Tuchman (1978a: 202) touches on objectification as well as *reflexivity* when she discusses how diverse academic branches

238   *Anna Roosvall*

understand and apply the relationship between researcher and society in terms of a subject-subject relationship between researcher and society in Tuchman's and other interpretive sociologists' work, and a subject–object one in positivist science. This means there is a difference in how researchers view society, informants, and knowledge (Tuchman, 1978a: 206). In the subject-subject case a double hermeneutic (Giddens, 1976) is at play, which means among other things that human reflexivity already takes place before the academic social analysis. What you study is not just an object, but something that is part of reflexive processes beyond yourself. Tuchman (1978a: 203–204) proposes that newsworkers also may apply a subject-subject approach, for instance through how they in their theoretical newswork draw on pretheoretic activities of sources, and draw on facts gleaned from sources when they organize their work with the aim of gaining knowledge. However, as *some* social theory objectifies individuals as members of groups, robbing them of the power to create new meanings subjectively (Tuchman, 1978a: 206), news does, as we have seen, the same. Thus, through the news construction process the pretheoretic may be robbed of its actions and its reflexivity.

Reflexivity and *attitudes towards the analytic* interact in diverse ways in academia and news. Both interpretive and positivist research apply an analytic mode, although to different degrees. News, more specifically, is a social resource whose construction limits an analytical understanding of contemporary life and as such limits *some* knowledge (Tuchman, 1978a: 215). On the side of this lack of analysis, Tuchman finds a lack of reflection among newsworkers. News professionals have claims to reproduce true accounts of social life but as they do not reflect on their own methods, they are not accurate. This approach to self-reflection constitutes a difference between newsworkers and academics (Tuchman, 1978a: 209). If newsworkers would question the traditions of and the basis for their work they could reevaluate why some events are bound to become soft news or non-news; there is a need for reflecting on the journalistic method (Tuchman, 1978a: 215). Here, news can follow in the footsteps of interpretive approaches to research (if conducted thoroughly). And we as readers, writers, students, researchers, can note that Tuchman's method — how it is combined with her thinking about journalistic method (and academic method), as well as what she reveals about it in philosophical-theoretical terms — is rare, and contributes significantly to media and journalism studies. Essentially it is all about how we retrieve — and not least how we understand — knowledge.

Closing discussion: Where is *Making News*? What is *Making News*?

Making News: A Study in the Social Construction of Reality, as well as Tuchman's iconic "Objectivity as Strategic Ritual" article, appear to be most commonly referred to in journalism studies overviews, seminal texts, and journals (see, e.g. Baden, 2020; Wahl-Jorgensen, 2013; and Zelizer, 2004).[2] In an overview and analysis of "the sociology of news paradigm" in the journal *Journalism Studies*, Kunelius and Waisbord (2023) find this subfield still relevant both theoretically and in terms of its rich empirical studies, even given the huge transformations that have taken place in the journalism industry and in the ways in which publics engage with news in the 21st century. The authors discern three field-defining claims: (1) journalists make news, (2) news is made for journalists, and (3) news reproduces the dominant hegemony/ideology (2023: 5). Tuchman relates to all of these areas in *Making News*, and her book is indeed a significant reference in Kunelius and Waisbord's account (specifically credited on points 1 and 2). The authors also acknowledge the influence of Berger and Luckmann (1966) and Schutz (e.g. 1962) on several works in this area. These phenomenological theories are applied in several subfields of the broader media studies field, including mediatization literature beyond journalism and news (see, e.g. Bengtsson, et al., 2020). Between, on the one side, Schutz's *The Problem of Social Reality* (1962) and *The Phenomenology of the Social World* (1967), as well as Berger and Luckmann's *The Social Construction of Reality* (1966), and, on the other side, Couldry and Hepp's *The Mediated Construction of Reality* (2016), in which the authors discuss deep mediatization, we find Tuchman's *Making News: A Study in the Construction of Reality* (1978a), referencing the same texts by Schutz, and Berger and Luckmann, as Couldry and Hepp do. While Tuchman (1978a: 211) above all exposes how the media is dependent on the hegemonic knowledge structure and ideology of society, which is *not* reminiscent of mediatization, she also notes that newsworkers and organizations work to impose a uniform rhythm of processing on occurrences. This points, together with her long-term field work, towards mediatization theory and research. She furthermore writes that news "not only defines and redefines, constitutes and reconstitutes social meanings; it also defines and redefines, constitutes and reconstitutes ways of doing things — existing processes in existing institutions" (Tuchman, 1978a: 196). While this is not mediatization theory as such — it could not be at that time — it constitutes an early capture of some of the mediatization related dynamics to come in media, society, and research.

Tuchman ultimately shows that we need to study work in order to understand ideas, and ideas in order to understand work. Her own work seems overall to have had more long-term impact on the idea of news as an epistemological issue than on ideas about news production as such, or on practice studies, something which also characterizes *Making News*. While Mark Deuze deems Tuchman's research seminal in his book *Media Work* (2007), he notes that it does not fit well with a more recent journalism culture where the dogma is "flexible production/.../and an all-consuming shift of responsibility and accountability toward the individual". A core trait of Tuchman's writing is, however, that her concrete empirical findings, whether still relevant or not in the editing room, become pertinent theoretically and have a longer life in this form — for instance, regarding knowledge production beyond the technology- and economy-sensitive details (e.g., Tuchman, 1978a: 149). A significant practical-theoretical contribution of *Making News* is the weaving together of time and space into an indissoluble yet analytically clear framework: news net-web

240 *Anna Roosvall*

of facticity-frame-construction-knowledge-ideology. Through this framework, Tuchman explores the complex idea of news and the epistemology behind it. Working along scales like the expected-unexpected and known-new, both of which concern time and space, news is indeed a complex curiosity. It is remarkable that such a complicated and confusing phenomenon as news should have such a prominent position when it comes to determining or at least negotiating the what, who, when, where, and why of knowledge in and on the world. A key to entering this universe of ideas is to read media theory classics that juxtapose the terms construction and reality. Many of us who cannot stop thinking about this dynamic follow in the footsteps of Tuchman, whether we know it or not.

Notes

1 I follow Tuchman's way of writing "newswork"/"newsworker", rather than news work(er).
2 *A Handbook in Media and Communication Research* (Ed. Bruhn Jensen, 2002) featured a chapter by Tuchman: "Production of news". In later editions there is no Tuchman chapter. Her work is in the 2020 edition credited mainly in a chapter on methodology. The objectivity article appears more often than *Making News* (and more often than the chapter "The symbolic annihilation of women") (Tuchman, 1978b).

References

Baden, C. (2020). Framing the news. In Wahl-Jorgensen, K. & Hanitzsch, T. (Eds.), *The Handbook of Journalism Studies* (pp. 229–245). Abingdon: Routledge.

Bengtsson, S., Fast, K., Jansson, A. & Lindell, J. (2020). Media and basic desires: An approach to measuring the mediatization of daily human life. *Communications*, 46 (2), 275–296.

Berger P. & Luckmann T. (1966). *The Social Construction of Reality*. London: Penguin.

Cambridge Dictionary (n.d.). Reality. Retrieved at: https://dictionary.cambridge.org/dictionary/english/reality (accessed 20 September 2023).

Cantor, M.G. (1980). Book review: Gaye Tuchman, Making News: A Study in the Construction of Reality. The Free Press, New York, 1978. *Sociology of Work and Occupations*, 7 (4), 503–506. https://doi.org/10.1177/073088848000700406.

Couldry, N. & Hepp, A. (2016). *The Mediated Construction of Reality*. Cambridge: Polity Press.

Dahlgren, P. (1977). *Network TV News and The Corporate State: The Subordinate Consciousness of the Citizen-Viewer*. New York: City University of New York.

Deuze, M. (2007). *Media Work*. Cambridge/Malden: Polity Press.

Fairclough, N. (1995). *Media Discourse*. London: Sage.

Galtung, J. & Ruge, M.H. (1965). The structure of foreign news. *Journal of Peace Research*, 2 (1), 64–91.

Giddens, A. (1976). *New Rules of Sociological Method*. New York: Basic Books.

Glasgow University Media Group (1976). Bad news. *Theory and Society*, 3 (Fall): 339–363.

Glasgow University Media Group (1980). *More Bad News*. London: Routledge.

Glasser, T.L. (1996). Journalism's glassy essence. *Journalism & Mass Communication Quarterly*, 73 (4), 784–786. DOI: https://doi.org/10.1177/107769909607300402.

Goffman, E. (1974). *Frame Analysis*. Cambridge: Harvard University Press.

Hall, S. (Ed.) (1997). *Representation: Cultural Representations and Signifying Practices*. London: Sage.

Jensen, K.B. (Ed.) (2002/2020). *A Handbook of Media and Communication Research: Qualitative and Quantitative Methodologies*. London: Routledge.

Kunelius, R. & Reunanen, E. (2012). The medium of the media: Journalism, politics and the theory of "mediatisation". *Javnost The Public*, 19, 5–24.

Kunelius, R. & Waisbord, S. (2023). The legacy of the sociology of news paradigm: Continuities, changes, and ironies. *Journalism Studies*. Published online: 11 April 2023. DOI: doi:10.1080/1461670X.2023.2192296.

On This Day (n.d.). Historical events in 1978. *Onthisday.com*. Retrieved at: https://www.onthisday.com/events/date/1978 (accessed 8 September 2023).

Rorty, R. (1979). *Philosophy and the Mirror of Nature*. Princeton: Princeton University Press.

Mallon, R. (2019). Naturalistic Approaches to Social Construction. In Edward N. Zalta (Ed.), *The Stanford Encyclopedia of Philosophy*. Retrieved at: https://plato.stanford.edu/archives/spr2019/entries/social-construction-naturalistic/ (accessed 9 October 2023).

MacCombs, M.E. & Shaw, D.L. (1972). The agenda-setting function of mass media, *The Public Opinion Quarterly*, 36 (2), 176–187.

Mead, T.D. (1979). Book review. Tuchman, Gaye. Making News: A Study in the Construction of Reality. United States: Politics and Public Policy. *Perspective*, 8 (5), 88–91. DOI: doi:10.1080/00483494.1979.10740496.

Riksdagen.se (2018). Proposition 2018/19:136. Ett modernt public service nära publiken – villkor 2020–2025. Retrieved at: https://www.riksdagen.se/sv/dokument-och-lagar/dokument/proposition/ett-modernt-public-service-nara-publiken–_H603136/html/ (accessed 5 October 2023).

Robinson, J.P. & Sahin, H. (1981). Book review. Making News: A Study in the Construction of Reality. by Gaye Tuchman. *Social Forces*, 59 (4), 1341–1342.

Schudson, M. (1978). *Discovering the News: A Social History of American Newspapers*. New York: Basic Books.

Schudson, M. (2003). *The Sociology of News*. New York: W.W. Norton.

Schutz, A. (1962). *Collected Papers Volume I: The Problem with Reality*. The Hague: M. Nijhoff.

Schutz, A. (1967). *The Phenomenology of the Social World*. Evanston III: North Western University Press.

Tuchman, G. (1972). Objectivity as strategic ritual. *American Journal of Sociology*, 77 (January), 660–679.

Tuchman, G. (1978a). *Making News: A Study in the Construction of Reality*. New York: Free Press.

Tuchman, G. (1978b). Introduction: The symbolic annihilation of women by the mass media. In G. Tuchman, A. K. Daniels & J. Benét (Eds.), *Hearth and home: Images of women in the mass media* (pp. 3–38). Oxford University Press.

Tuchman, G., Daniels, A.K. & Benét, J.W. (Eds.) (1978). *Hearth and Home: Images of Women in the Mass Media*. New York: Oxford University Press.

Tuchman, G. (2002). Production of news. In Jensen, K.B. (Ed.), *Handbook of Media and Communication Research: Qualitative and Quantitative Methodologies* (pp. 78–90). London: Routledge.

Wahl-Jorgensen, K. (2013). The strategic ritual of emotionality: A case study of Pulitzer Prize-winning articles. *Journalism*, 14 (1), 129–145. DOI: https://doi.org/10.1177/1464884912448918.

Zelizer, B. (2004). *Taking Journalism Seriously*. New York: Sage.

17 Pierre Bourdieu (1979) *Distinction*

Johan Lindell

Introduction

The French sociologist Pierre Bourdieu (1930–2002) cannot easily be placed within any established tradition of media and communication theory, such as cultural studies, medium theory or political economy (Benson, 1999). It is nonetheless perfectly possible to study media and communication with the help of Bourdieu's cultural sociology (Lindell, forthcoming). Bourdieu's work has had a notable and growing influence on the field of media and communication studies, particularly on researchers concerned with digital inequality and media use and on scholars interested in uncovering the culture, norms and practices in fields of media production such as journalism. As this chapter shows, conducting Bourdieu-inspired media and communication research implies in-depth analysis of the social contexts in which the media are embedded and where communication takes place. For a Bourdieu-inspired media researcher, the social dynamics that characterise these contexts are at least as important as the media themselves. People's use of media, or a newsroom's production of journalism, is understood in relation to the social field in which it takes place. The focus is on the power dynamics that characterise these fields, the status positions held by media users or cultural producers and how these positions have come to shape attitudes and practices.

Bourdieu's *La Distinction* provides part of the foundation for a unique social scientific approach that has had a lasting and growing impact on media and communication studies. My purpose in this chapter is to introduce the sociology of culture that Bourdieu developed, which was only adopted in its entirety outside France after his death (Savage & Silva, 2013; Rosenlund, 2015). This kind of sociology – particularly as it is encountered in *La Distinction* – consists of both a theory of the nature of social life and a specific method for how best to approach society and various social fields.

Bourdieu's starting point was a dissatisfaction with contemporary social science, so I begin this chapter by positioning Bourdieu in relation to the overarching currents of thought against which he took issue. I then turn to Bourdieu's main conceptual apparatus: field-capital-habitus. *La Distinction* is one of Bourdieu's most important books because it mobilises his entire

DOI: 10.4324/9781003432272-18

Pierre Bourdieu (1979) 243

conceptual apparatus and its associated method (i.e. correspondence analysis) to shed light on the relationship between class and culture in French society. After delving into the central arguments of *La Distinction*, discussing its craft and looking at common critical objections, I turn to examples of contemporary media and communication research that have been inspired by Bourdieu.

Pierre Bourdieu's middle ground

Pierre Bourdieu began his academic career in philosophy but conducted his first empirical studies as an anthropologist in Algeria in the 1950s. However, most of his career was devoted to sociology. In 1981, he was appointed professor of sociology at the prestigious Collège de France, a position he held until his death in 2002. Thus, Bourdieu was active as a researcher and academic in the second half of the 20th century. That was a time characterised by conflict between different perspectives in the social sciences, which Bourdieu was quick to engage in.

In post-war France, there was a divide in the social sciences between critically oriented neo-Marxists on the one hand and positivists on the other (Coulangeon & Duval, 2015). If Theodor Adorno's and Max Horkheimer's critique of mass culture and the culture industries serve as an example of the first camp, then Lazarsfeld's innovative measurements of the effects of mass communication (often funded by the US industry and military) serve to illustrate the second camp (see Chapters 3 and 4 in this volume). Although the opposition between certain strands of critical theory and more empirically driven quantitative research is not as pronounced today, it still persists.

Another epistemological battle that had a lasting influence on Bourdieu was that between what he referred to as 'subjectivism' and 'objectivism' (Bourdieu, 1989).[1] Phenomenologists, ethnomethodologists and philosophers such as Jean-Paul Sartre, who set out in different ways to describe the world as experienced by social agents and who put focus on the free, creative will and agency of humans, can be contrasted to those who instead emphasised the moulding force of objective structures in society (Brubaker, 1985). 'Objectivists' such as Karl Marx, Friedrich Engels, Émile Durkheim and Louis Althusser differed on many levels, but they shared a view of individuals as the products of the historical and social contexts in which they find themselves. At the heart of the opposition between objectivism and subjectivism is the question of what degree of human agency and autonomy people have in relation to the social structures we are bound up in.

Bourdieu drew inspiration from and built his sociology upon all these camps, while simultaneously being deeply critical of them. He was thus neither a Marxist nor an empiricist à la Lazarsfeld; neither a 'subjectivist' nor an 'objectivist'. In the last chapter of *La Distinction*, Bourdieu quotes the author Karl Kraus to emphasise his own middle way: 'If I have to choose the lesser of two evils, I choose neither' (Bourdieu, 1984: 466). Thus, Bourdieu's sociology, which includes the conceptual triad of field-capital-habitus, aimed to find a way between prevailing epistemological conflicts in the social sciences (Bourdieu &

244 *Johan Lindell*

Wacquant, 1992). Bourdieu wanted to mark out a path for the social sciences that avoided both the non-reflexive, positivist measurement of society and works marked by 'scholastic illusions' that lacked systematic empirical grounding (Bourdieu, 2000; Bourdieu & Wacquant, 1992). At the same time, he sought to create a sociology that took into account people's experiences, understandings and representations of the social world (the so-called subjective realm) along with the social structures that shape and are shaped by these perceptions (the objective realm). In the next section, I centre on Bourdieu's position and how it navigates between the oppositions described thus far.

Bourdieu in brief: field-capital-habitus

Bourdieu shared Karl Marx's (1818–1883) concern with relations of power and how they are upheld in modern societies – that is, he had an interest in inequality and social class. According to Bourdieu, the study of class and power must always be based on systematic observations of society and its actors. Here, he draws much inspiration from another pioneering sociologist, Max Weber (1864–1920), who emphasised the importance of understanding social class positions beyond the distribution of material assets in society. Bourdieu thus breaks with Marx, who approached social class primarily in terms of people's role and position in the mode of production, according to which the vast majority of the population are wage workers who are positioned in an antagonistic relationship with a small minority of capitalists. By contrast, in understanding social class position as a person's access to material *and* symbolic resources, Bourdieu expands the scope of class analysis. *Economic capital* consists of money and other material assets. *Cultural capital* includes all symbolic assets that endow their holders with prestige, such as university degrees and various awards and titles. Cultural capital also exists in an embodied form, such as in knowing how to conduct oneself in a 'proper' or 'correct' manner, or having grown up in 'natural' proximity to elevated and 'fine' culture. *Social capital*, in turn, consists of an individual's network of contacts.[2]

The possession of these resources is what defines a person's position in different *social fields* (Bourdieu, 1986). A field can be defined as a social context in which specific – often unspoken – rules apply, where 'players' participate in struggles for positions. Fields can be described as social microcosms that are governed by their own logics to some extent; accordingly, they are relatively autonomous in relation to each other. Bourdieu studied the educational field, the academic field and the field of cultural production, among others. In the context of this volume, Bourdieu's work can be applied to media fields, such as the journalistic field. It can be seen that journalists are positioned based on their access to field-specific capital – that is, resources that all players recognise the value of. Winning a journalistic award, earning a degree in journalism from a prestigious university, being employed in a well-established and prominent newsroom and reporting on 'real' or 'hard' news such as politics and economics constitute symbolic – that is, field-specific – capital in this field. They give their holders prestige, influence and status (Hovden, 2008). Importantly, a whole society or an entire nation can also be understood as a field, which is exactly how Bourdieu approaches French society in *Distinction*. In Bourdieu's perspective, society should be approached as a social space in which people are positioned on the basis of their access to different forms of capital. With the concepts of field and capital, Bourdieu describes *objective* conditions that characterise social life. I now turn to how these conditions relate to the 'subjective realm' of agency and practice.

Different living conditions and circumstances, which vary in the sense that they are characterised by different access to capital, constitute environments in which people form attitudes, values and behaviours. For instance, children growing up with well-educated parents holding high positions in the labour market tend to have a more extensive map of opportunities compared with children growing up in social conditions deprived of capital. This is manifested, in the fact that the children of university-educated parents tend to surpass working-class children in educational attainments without having superior cognitive abilities (Morris et al., 2016). Bourdieu emphasises that social conditions and backgrounds shape the ways in which we orient ourselves in the social world and how well we fit into different social situations and spaces. The children of working-class parents do not enjoy the same proximity to the educational field as the children of middle-class parents, who are often more at ease in the educational system. In other words, how we manoeuvre in the social world – what we feel we can and should do and what we consider good or bad – cannot be understood without taking into account *objective* conditions and circumstances, such as our social conditionings and backgrounds; that is, our access to capital. The notion of *habitus* captures this phenomenon. Habitus is the socially shaped system of perception and classification from which we make choices and form preferences. It can be understood as a social and moral compass that cannot be disconnected from its origin in objective conditions such as the family and the specific fields in which we are embedded.

With the concept of habitus (which should always be understood in relation to field and capital), Bourdieu argues – in line with 'subjectivism' – that people enjoy a certain freedom of action, or agency: our lives are not predetermined by our family background and social position. Indeed, working-class children do not always end up in working-class professions. However, in line with 'objectivism', Bourdieu emphasises that the choices we make in life tend to correspond to our position in society and in other fields (Bourdieu, 2000); for example, children from working-class backgrounds are overrepresented in vocational education. Bourdieu was thus a sociologist who emphasised social reproduction and stability over change and upheaval (although, it should be noted, accounts of social change are also embedded in his theoretical apparatus). This approach resonates with American sociologist C. Wright Mill's (2000) emphasis on the interplay between self and world, biography and history, and individual and society, and with Anthony Giddens's (1984) structuration theory. Bourdieu distinguishes himself from these related approaches in

246   *Johan Lindell*

that he and his colleagues developed a specific method to test, refine and develop his conceptual framework. *La Distinction* is an example of this method.

La Distinction

La Distinction, Bourdieu's magnum opus, spans over 600 pages. After its publication in French in 1979, it has been translated into 12 languages (including English, in 1984). *La Distinction* remains Bourdieu's most cited work (Sapiro, 2015). This success may seem somewhat strange, since the book 'is very French', as Bourdieu himself states in an opening passage. One explanation of the international success of the book is that it opens the door to a sociological world that gives the reader insight into the relationship between social class, lifestyles and culture consumption. Bourdieu takes on the task of studying different social spaces, with a particular focus on the whole of French society, using complex statistical analyses, ethnographic observations and interviews, newspaper clippings, photographs and the theoretical concepts he spent his career developing.

As a reader might guess from the book's subtitle, *A Social Critique of the Judgement of Taste*, *La Distinction* does away with the idea that 'good taste' is inherent. For Bourdieu, taste – as manifested in political opinions, media habits, home furnishings, sporting interests, music preferences and other leisure pursuits – comprises a tool through which groups distinguish themselves from others and thereby 'legitimise social differences' (Bourdieu, 1984: 7). We are reminded of such social differences every time we find ourselves looking down on someone's manner of dressing, dialect, hobbies or movie preferences – and, conversely, when someone shows contempt for our own tastes and interests or when we feel 'out of place'. Different living conditions, defined by access to capital, function as small social fields in which people become socialised into different taste palettes. By extension, this means that lifestyles, cultural practices and preferences tend to reflect people's class positions and living conditions. Culture is a source of power play.

People who grew up with highly educated parents and hundreds or thousands of books on their bookshelves, and who pursued studies at a university later in life, are more prone than others to report a taste for things such as cultural journalism, so-called 'quality news', jazz and classical music (Lindell, 2018). People from such (cultural) middle-class circumstances do not tend to enjoy institutionalised and canonised culture, because they are more sophisticated than others by nature. They are drawn to these types of cultural expression because they have grown up with a proximity to them, and because they have moved and are moving in fields where this particular taste and lifestyle are held in high regard or even taken for granted. In other words, they have a habitus that is configured to be attracted to certain cultural expressions and to disregard – or have a distaste for – others. A different relationship to the social world may be found in a person who grew up with working-class parents, in a home where ornaments rather than books filled the bookshelves, and where weekends were devoted to watching television rather than attending art exhibitions. In this region of the social space, the so-called 'fine arts' and 'legitimate' culture tend to be approached with scepticism; rather than being described as interesting, beautiful or thought-provoking, the opera, modern art and culture debates in the newspaper may be described as difficult, pretentious or simply 'not for the likes of us' (Bourdieu, 1984: 471).

Bourdieu's point is that there is no objective right or wrong approach to culture. Rather, the people in the examples above reproduce their social positions through the ways in which they relate to various cultural goods. Some groups are better equipped, through their habitus, to navigate the fine arts and other 'legitimate' forms of culture. For others, this kind of culture is viewed as thoroughly alien. *La Distinction* offers a number of examples. One of the clearest, which teases out the difference between the 'aesthetic gaze' of people rich in cultural capital and the more functional approach to art found in the working class, is disclosed in a segment of the book where people are asked to describe a photograph depicting the scarred hands of an old woman. While the working-class respondents described the photograph with words like 'it was a strange way to take a photo' or 'she must have worked hard', the more culturally initiated middle-class observers focused on the deeper meanings of the photograph: 'A very beautiful photo. It is a symbol of work. It reminds me of Flaubert's maid' (Bourdieu, 1984: 44–45).

Many who read *La Distinction* will remember the puzzling maps of the relationships between different lifestyles and social class positions. In one passage, the reader is confronted with a two-dimensional space of social positions; projected onto it are various lifestyles and tastes (Bourdieu, 1984: 128–129). At the top of the space are individuals with high volumes of capital – they have high salaries and high levels of education, and tend to have grown up in relatively privileged social conditions. At the bottom are individuals relatively deprived of both economic and cultural capital. To one side of the space are individuals whose assets are primarily made up of cultural capital; to the other are people who mainly have economic capital at their disposal. This map touches on and revises a well-established notion about class structures in modern societies: the idea that social hierarchy and stratification could be understood and described as a ladder, with the working class located at the bottom, the middle class in the middle and the upper class at the very top. For Bourdieu, this metaphor is problematic because it only captures people's *volume* of capital (where the working class has the least and the upper class the most). By taking into account *what* people's social resources consist of (primarily either cultural or economic capital), Bourdieu advances a new, multidimensional approach to class society. The metaphor of the ladder is replaced with the map – or, the social space.

The social space is not just a theoretical construct. Those who have read *La Distinction* may recall the notion of the social space and the complex figures representing this idea, but fewer know that these maps are the results of a number of statistical analyses. This is where the empiricist Bourdieu comes in.

248 *Johan Lindell*

Using correspondence analysis, an exploratory statistical method developed by Jean-Paul Benzécri in the 1960s and 1970s, Bourdieu and his team of researchers were able to empirically scrutinise the notion of fields, finding that people in different positions (in terms of the volume and composition of their capital) tend to reinforce the norms and logics of fields in their practices and everyday position-takings (through habitus). In his final lecture at the Collège de France, Bourdieu argued that 'Those who know the principles of multiple correspondence analysis (MCA) will grasp the affinity between this method of mathematical analysis and thinking in terms of fields' (Bourdieu in Lebaron & Le Roux, 2018: 503). Several correspondence analyses of survey data led to the conclusion that the French class society was built on the principles of capital volume (i.e. having little or much capital) and capital composition (referring to the difference between people whose capital portfolios primarily consist of either cultural or economic capital) (Bourdieu, 1984; see also Lebaron, 2009; de Saint Martin, 2015). This insight makes it possible for researchers today to talk about different factions within the main social classes, such as the difference between a cultural and an economic middle class (e.g. Flemmen et al., 2017; Lindell, 2018).

As hinted at above, correspondence analyses representing the social space do not only describe the class structure of modern societies. This method also offers the possibility of studying where in the social space different attributes, identities, preferences (e.g. taste/distaste for heavy metal music or international news coverage), practices (e.g. tennis, second-hand shopping and TikTok) and so on fall out. In other words, it is possible to study in detail the relationship between *objective* conditions in terms of access to different forms of capital and *subjective* orientations in terms of lifestyles, choices and values. The result of these analyses – and one of Bourdieu's main points in *La Distinction* – is that taste and lifestyle hierarchies tend to follow social hierarchies. This means, for example, that the taste for recognised and 'legitimate' culture is most common among affluent individuals, especially among those who possess a high level of cultural capital. In contrast, the working class, which is defined by its low levels of capital and whose lack of cultural capital is particularly prominent, is more likely to *not* have an opinion on various cultural goods or to dislike what the 'cultural elite' likes. Bourdieu concludes that there is a statistical overlap, or homology, between social space and the range of cultural goods and practices available in a society at a given time (what Bourdieu refers to as the 'space of lifestyles').

With *La Distinction*, Bourdieu shows that practices and preferences that are usually framed as individual peculiarities can be understood in terms of a broader 'objective' structure. Everyday practices including hobbies, Spotify lists, diets and so on, which appear to stem from altogether individual traits and personal choice, must be understood as being bound up in social regularities and linked to the structure of the social space. Bourdieu's argument is that we tend to reproduce our social positions in society through our taste and lifestyle, including our media practices. The objective conditions – upbringing, level of education, profession and so on – give rise to a subjective moral and cultural compass, a habitus, that pushes us to orient ourselves in social life in a way that corresponds to our position in society. Already privileged people reinforce their position and status by adopting 'good' taste. The resistance sometimes found in capital-poor segments of the population – the feeling that one does not understand opera and modern art, or that politics are 'not for me' – usually leads these social groups to cement their already subordinate position in society (see also Willis, 2017). The social order reproduces itself in an ongoing movement between the 'objective' and the 'subjective' – that is, between social structure (the social space) and practice (habitus). *La Distinction* shows how this is expressed in the world of culture, taste and lifestyles.

Criticism of Bourdieu and *La Distinction*

The fact that *La Distinction* has been translated into 12 languages and is still widely used and cited indicates that it has been well received by the research community. This does not, however, mean that the book has not been criticised. Common criticisms are that (1) Bourdieu reduces people to status-hungry players in fields whose practices and preferences are little more than the extension of their class positions; (2) the description of the relationship between social class and culture is tied to 1960s and 1970s France and thus has no bearing on other places or times; and (3) the language is unnecessarily convoluted, which is ironic, since Bourdieu approached sociology as a 'martial art' to be deployed to uncover instances of symbolic violence (e.g. in revealing how we tend to 'misrecognise' – that is, fail to identify – the arbitrary nature of cultural legitimacy) and thus to combat social inequality (Bourdieu & Wacquant, 1992).

Critics who accuse Bourdieu of reducing people's life choices, tastes and practices to their social positions tend to misunderstand his intention with the conceptual triad of field-capital-habitus. These critics accuse Bourdieu of being the kind of mechanistic 'objectivist' he himself criticised. Through habitus, people are inclined, more or less consciously, to make choices that coincide with their position in a field. That the order of a field or social space has a tendency to be maintained by individuals' socially shaped actions and values is not only a theoretical assumption but also an empirical observation and statistical tendency. However, this tendency can be broken (here, a key notion for Bourdieu is reflexivity). Habitus is not a destiny or a fate, writes Bourdieu (Bourdieu & Wacquant, 1992: 133) – an observation highlighted by the fact that empirical analyses do not always provide clear-cut relations between social class and lifestyles (or 'strong' statistical correlations). Another, and related, critical point has been made by one of Bourdieu's collaborators, the prominent sociologist Luc Boltanski. Boltanski (cited in de Saint Martin, 2015) argues that Bourdieu placed too much explanatory power in habitus. There are other characteristics and attributes beyond class and habitus that shape our orientation in the social world, such as age and generational belonging. This is evident in media research that identifies generation-specific (rather than class-specific) attitudes and patterns of media use (Bolin, 2017).

250 *Johan Lindell*

The second point questions Bourdieu's relevance beyond France in the 1960s and 1970s. Here, a leading figure is US-based sociologist Richard A. Peterson (1992), who argues that the traditional 'elite arts activities' no longer function as dividers between the culturally initiated class factions and those less well-off. According to those who advocate what has come to be known as the omnivore thesis, the privileged classes have become cultural omnivores rather than snobs. There are two problems with how proponents of the omnivore thesis critique Bourdieu. First, they tend to miss the argument on the 'aesthetic gaze' through which Bourdieu paints the picture of the cultural middle class's tendency to appreciate the 'beauty' across a variety of ('high' and 'low') cultural goods. Cultural omnivorousness is thus embedded in and part of Bourdieu's theory (Lizardo & Skiles, 2015). Secondly, critics fail to appreciate that Bourdieu's point was that fields are subject to (slow) transformation over time. Bourdieu was careful to emphasise that an analysis of the social space and the distribution of lifestyles therein only provides a snapshot of ongoing struggles over the legitimate lifestyle (Bourdieu, 1984: 249). Exactly what constitutes cultural capital or 'legitimate' culture will vary over time and space. Thus, if sociologists do not find the same 'French' divisions in the contemporary United States or China, this does not suggest that cultural capital and hierarchies based on symbolic resources do not exist in these societies. Therefore, any Bourdieusian study must deal with questions of what generates status and which lifestyles are the 'legitimate' ones as being open-ended. The strength of Bourdieu's conceptual framework and method is found in their openness and emphasis on always exploring what is going on in different fields.

The final criticism concerns the complexity of Bourdieu's prose. There is no doubt that it is often difficult to engage with Bourdieu's texts. Drawing on the work of philosopher Gaston Bachelard (1884–1962), one of Bourdieu's most important arguments about the practical craft of social science is that it must break with everyday understandings if it is to succeed in reaching beyond what is taken for granted in layman understandings and producing a sociologically rich understanding of the phenomenon at hand. Such a break may require a 'new language' or concepts that risk being perceived as complicated or impenetrable, precisely because they break with or oppose the reader's everyday understanding. While readers may find Bourdieu's writings, including *La Distinction*, difficult to penetrate, they will hopefully have arrived at a new way of looking at the world after finishing the book.

In terms of how *La Distinction* and Bourdieu's sociology in general have been received by the research community, it is clear that the concepts of field, capital and habitus have become staples throughout the social sciences, including media and communication studies. Problematically, however, Bourdieu is often used fragmentally, and the overall holistic epistemology and its theoretical and methodological presuppositions are ignored. For instance, there are countless studies of how 'cultural capital' shapes X, Y or Z. Such studies often leave out other forms of capital and the relationship between them, and fail to account for the field that is being studied, the habitus of the agents and their history and

Pierre Bourdieu (1979) 251

trajectory in the social space. This reductionism largely stems from the fact that it took a relatively long time for correspondence analysis, with its relational and multifaceted approach to the social world, to be used outside France (Savage & Silva, 2013).

Bourdieu in media and communication studies: some examples

Television preferences, news consumption patterns, cinematic preferences and tastes in music vary significantly between social classes. Journalism and media production take place, so to speak, in fields where unique characteristics and unspoken rules define what is possible and what is not. It is thus clear that, with Bourdieu, media researchers today can study the consumption and use of media and the institutionalised production of media (Lindell, forthcoming). Although not as common, largely due to certain epistemological incongruencies between textual analysis and Bourdieu's field theory (Lindell, forthcoming), it is also possible to rely on Bourdieu in the study of media texts, discourse and representation (Dodd, 2021; Sayer, 2018). Bourdieu, however, was not a media scholar. His only book that explicitly focused on media, *On Television* (1998), was a short, inflammatory opinion piece on French television journalism's failure to provide deep analysis and the subsequent negative impact this field had on other fields (not least the academic field). Thus, rather than *On Television*, a media researcher's best tools are found in Bourdieu's broader sociology discussed above. Bourdieu's work can be used to shed light on topical questions facing media researchers today: how does social inequality relate to differences in how social classes access information and relate to journalism? Under what social circumstances does media production take place? How does rapid technological innovation such as artificial intelligence (AI) and smart chatbots change the logics of the practice and distribution of capital within, for instance, the educational field or the journalistic field? How do agents and stakeholders in different fields think about media policy, and which field and which agents have the final say in matters of media regulation? How are different groups represented in the media? How are power and status expressed on social media?

In following the outline and focus of *La Distinction*, media researchers have focused on class-specific patterns in media consumption (Lindell, 2018) and public connection (Hovden, 2023). Here, it is important to note that a Bourdieusian approach to media use requires a break with the 'media-centric' tendency to understand people merely as 'media users' or as members of an audience. In relying on Bourdieu's perspective, we are forced to take into account the fact that people are actors in various fields that are endowed with particular relations of power and hierarchies. We are also encouraged to go beyond disciplinary boundaries and study, for example, media consumption in relation to other lifestyles, thereby providing a deeper and more contextualised understanding of media use in the broader space of lifestyles.

Media researchers have also found Bourdieu's sociology useful in studying media and cultural production (Hesmondhalgh, 2006; Lindell et al., 2020). In

252   *Johan Lindell*

terms of media production, research focusing on the field of journalism has a prominent place, thanks to Benson and Neveu's *Bourdieu and the Journalistic Field* (2005) in particular. Today, research on journalism is crowded with Bourdieusian analyses, including comprehensive studies of the journalistic field as a social microcosm (Hovden, 2008), participant observations to understand the work of a newsroom (Schultz, 2007) and studies on the interplay between actors in the journalistic field and the tech-field from which new competencies and norms are imported (Lindblom et al., 2022).

Given the above discussion on the tendency to ignore or downplay Bourdieu's broader epistemological project, as well as the coherent whole composed of the conceptual triad of field-capital-habitus, media and communication scholars who turn to Bourdieu – whether out of an interest in consumption, production or media texts and discourse – should deal with the following questions (see Bourdieu & Wacquant, 1992: 104–105):

- Which field is being studied? What is the relation of this field to other fields? What is the culture of this field? What struggles are taking place?
- What causes unity and division in the field? Which capitals are recognised as valuable, and what is the distribution of these capitals in the field?
- Who are the actors in the field, what is their habitus, and how does it affect their approach?

Following these points is no easy task. Working with Bourdieu in a fruitful way requires a great deal from the researcher, in terms of understanding both theory and different methods. It also places high demands on the data material used. For example, using correspondence analysis – which was the central method used in *La Distinction* and key in the endeavour to promote a multidimensional understanding of social class and cultural distinctions – presupposes not only that we measure many media and culture consumption variables but also that a number of measures of cultural, economic and social capital are available (Rosenlund, 2015). It is thus crucial for the Bourdieusian approach to guide the research design from the outset, rather than being added to spice things up in the later stages of the research process.

Conclusion

In this chapter, I have summarised the main features of Pierre Bourdieu's sociology and how they manifest in *La Distinction: Critique sociale du jugement*. Bourdieu has contributed greatly to modern social science. In media and communication research, his work has been a major source of inspiration since the 1980s, largely thanks to the English translation of *Distinction* and to a special issue of the journal *Media, Culture & Society* (Volume 2, Issue 3). However, compared with disciplines such as sociology and pedagogy, media studies has been slow to embrace the full research agenda offered by Bourdieu. Nevertheless, interest in Bourdieu has deepened in the last decade, not least in journalism research and research on digital inequality. If the reader takes away three things from this text, I hope they are the following: (1) a general understanding of Bourdieu's sociology and the position he adopts in relation to other prominent ideas about the nature of society and its actors, (2) a basic orientation in the conceptual apparatus of field-capital-habitus, and (3) ideas on how these can be fruitfully applied to understand the dynamics of contemporary societies and their media landscapes.

On a broader level, Bourdieu – and *La Distinction* in particular – offers a pertinent toolkit for analytically approaching the deepening inequality that characterises today's societies. Time and again, research on the cultural and symbolic dimensions of class society has demonstrated the viability of Bourdieu's perspective. While it is no exaggeration to say that media permeate our everyday lives, we cannot rely on 'media-centric' models that ignore the fact that media and communication are bound to social contexts with specific power relations. This is where *La Distinction* remains a key reference for media and communication scholars.

Notes

1 Bourdieu bundles structuralism, network analysis, macroeconomics and semiotics under the epithet 'objectivism'. These perspectives have in common a view of society 'from above', a perspective which, according to Bourdieu, makes them unable to take into account people's creation of meaning, life-worlds and everyday life. In contrast to 'objectivism', Bourdieu positions 'subjectivism', which instead studies society 'from below'. This mode of thinking permeates ethnomethodology, phenomenology, conversation analysis and ethnography, which (according to Bourdieu) instead fail to understand society as a whole and take into account causal relationships (Bourdieu, 1989; Sallaz, 2018).
2 Sometimes, symbolic capital is also mentioned as a separate, fourth form of capital. This is a bit misleading, because symbolic capital 'is not a separate form of capital but rather what all capital becomes when it is misrecognised as capital' (Bourdieu, 2000: 242).

References

Benson, R. (1999). Field theory in comparative context: A new paradigm for media studies. *Theory and Society*, 28(3), 463–498.
Benson, R., & Neveu, E. (Eds.) (2005). *Bourdieu and the journalistic field*. Polity.
Bolin, G. (2017). *Media generations: Experience, identity and mediatised social change*. Routledge.
Bourdieu, P. (1984). *Distinction: A social critique of the judgement of taste*. Routledge.
Bourdieu, P. (1986). The forms of capital. In J. G. Richardson (Ed.), *Handbook of theory and research for the sociology of education* (pp. 241–258). Greenwood Press.
Bourdieu, P. (1989). Social space and symbolic power. *Sociological Theory*, 7(1), 14–25.
Bourdieu, P. (1990). *The logic of practice*. Stanford University Press.
Bourdieu, P. (1998). *On television and journalism*. Pluto Press.
Bourdieu, P. (2000). *Pascalian meditations*. Polity.
Bourdieu, P., & Wacquant, L. (1992). *An invitation to reflexive sociology*. Polity.
Brubaker, R. (1985). Rethinking classical theory: The sociological vision of Pierre Bourdieu. *Theory & Society*, 14(6), 745–775.

254 *Johan Lindell*

Coulangeon, P., & Duval, J. (2015). Introduction. In P. Coulangeon & J. Duval (Eds.), *The Routledge companion to Bourdieu's Distinction* (pp. 1–12). Routledge.

de Saint Martin, M. (2015). From "Anatomie du gout" to *La Distinction*: Attempting to construct the social space: Some markers for the history of research. In P. Coulangeon & J. Duval (Eds.), *The Routledge companion to Bourdieu's Distinction* (pp. 15–28). Routledge.

Dodd, B. (2021). A feel for the frame: Towards a Bourdieusian frame analysis. *Poetics*, 84, doi:101482.

Flemmen, M., Jarness, V., & Rosenlund, L. (2017). Social space and cultural class divisions: The forms of capital and contemporary lifestyle differentiation. *British Journal of Sociology*, 69(1), 124–153.

Giddens, A. (1984). *The constitution of society: Outline of the theory of structuration*. The University of California Press.

Hesmondhalgh, D. (2006). Bourdieu, the media and cultural production. *Media, Culture & Society*, 28(2), 211–231.

Hovden, J. F. (2008). *Profane and sacred: A study of the Norwegian journalistic field*. [Unpublished doctoral dissertation]. University of Bergen.

Hovden, J. F. (2023). Worlds apart. On class structuration of citizens' political and public attention and engagement in an egalitarian society. *European Journal of Cultural and Political Sociology*, 10(2), 209–232.

Lebaron, F. (2009). How Bourdieu "quantified" Bourdieu: The geometric modeling of data. In K. Robson & C. Sanders (Eds.), *Quantifying theory: Pierre Bourdieu* (*pp.* 11–29). Springer.

Lebaron, F., & Le Roux, B. (2018). Bourdieu and geometric data analysis. In T. Medvetz & J. J. Sallaz (Eds.), *The Oxford handbook of Pierre Bourdieu* (pp. 503–511). Oxford University Press.

Lindblom, T., Lindell, J., & Gidlund, K. (2022). Digitalising the journalistic field: Journalists' views on changes in journalistic autonomy, capital and habitus. *Digital Journalism*, 1–20. https://doi.org/10.1080/21670811.2022.2062406.

Lindell, J. (2018). Distinction recapped: Digital news repertoires in the class structure. *New Media & Society*, 20(8), 3029–3049.

Lindell, J. (forthcoming). *Bourdieusian Media Studies*. Routledge.

Lindell, J., Jakobsson, P., & Stiernstedt, F. (2020). The field of television production: Genesis, structure and position-takings. *Poetics*, 80, doi:101432.

Lizardo, O., & Skiles, L. (2015). After omnivorousness: Is Bourdieu still relevant? In L. Hanquinet & M. Savage (Eds.), *Handbook of the sociology of arts and culture* (pp. 90–103). Routledge.

Mills, C. W. (2000). *The sociological imagination*. Oxford University Press.

Morris, T., Dorling, D., & Smith, D. (2016). How well can we predict educational outcomes? Examining the roles of cognitive ability and social position in educational attainment. *Contemporary Social Science*, 11(2–3), 154–168.

Peterson, R. A. (1992). Understanding audience segmentation: From elite and mass to omnivore and univore. *Poetics*, 21, 243–258.

Rosenlund, L. (2015). Working with *Distinction*: Scandinavian experiences. In P. Coulangeon & J. Duval (Eds.), *The Routledge companion to Bourdieu's Distinction* (pp. 157–186). Routledge.

Sallaz, J. J. (2018). Is a Bourdieusian ethnography possible? In T. Medvetz & J. J. Sallaz (Eds.), *The Oxford handbook of Pierre Bourdieu* (pp. 481–502). Oxford University Press.

Sapiro, G. (2015). The international career of *Distinction*. In P. Coulangeon & J. Duval (Eds.), *The Routledge companion to Bourdieu's Distinction* (pp. 29–42). Routledge.

Savage, M., & Silva, E. B. (2013). Field analysis in cultural sociology. *Cultural Sociology*, 7(2), 111–126.

Sayer, R. A. (2018). Bourdieu: Ally or foe of discourse analysis? In R. Wodak & B. Forchtner (Eds.), *Handbook of language and politics* (pp. 109–121). Routledge.

Schultz, I. (2007). The journalistic gut feeling: Journalistic doxa, news habitus and orthodox news values. *Journalism Practice*, 1(2), 190–207.

Willis, P. (2017). *Learning to labour: How working class kids get working class jobs*. Routledge.

18 Elizabeth L. Eisenstein (1979) *The Printing Press as an Agent of Change*

Marie Cronqvist and Kajsa Weber

Introduction

Questions of media transitions, media shifts, and media change are central to media and communication studies as a field of scholarly inquiry. Today's transition from print to digital formats has undoubtedly provoked a renewed discussion of the relationship between oral culture, scribal culture, print culture, and digital culture. It remains a point of departure for most media and communication historians that the technological and epistemological aspects of today's digital transition should be analyzed in the light of previous historical periods of intense and rapid change.

One of these key transition periods was the advent of print technology. In its first century, beginning around 1450, the reproduction of European written texts was, quite literally, on the move from the copyist's desk to the printer's workshop. Handwritten scrolls and manuscripts were replaced by printed materials due to the introduction of movable type. The standardization, mass dissemination, and preservation of the printed text meant that people all over Europe – at least the literate elite – had access to and read the same thing. While the age of the scribe was an age of scarcity, the printing press introduced an opportunity for mass distribution of texts, and with this came new opportunities to spread information and knowledge. Print meant the accumulation, preservation, and circulation of knowledge and thus it came to have a major impact on large processes such as Renaissance thinking, the Lutheran Reformation, and later the Enlightenment and the Scientific Revolution.

No one has been more important for our understanding of this key historical transition and the way it has been framed and discussed than Elizabeth Lewisohn Eisenstein. Her two-volume work *The Printing Press as an Agent of Change: Communications and Cultural Transformations in Early-Modern Europe* (henceforth PPAC), published in 1979 and covering some impressive 750 pages, still retains its firm position in the personal library of every book and media historian. The book has been translated into many languages and remains in print to this day. An abridged version entitled *The Printing Revolution in Early Modern Europe* was published in 1983. In this later version, apart from summarizing some of her key empirical findings, Eisenstein also

DOI: 10.4324/9781003432272-19

placed an even firmer emphasis on discussing the social and cultural developments that were sparked by print as a new communication technology in the early modern era. By placing the word "revolution" in the title of the 1983 book, print's foundational break with the previous communication system of medieval scribes was highlighted.

The intellectual stamina and fearlessness of Eisenstein, visible on the pages of PPAC, probably had their roots in her upbringing. Born in New York in 1923 and raised by a progressive mother, she received scholarly training from an early age at a time when that was still highly uncommon. She graduated from Harvard in the mid-1940s and moved to Washington DC where she made slow advances in her academic career while at the same time being a 1950s housewife and mother. Later she went on to a lectureship at American University and finally a professorship at the University of Michigan in 1975. But already in 1969, she articulated her main thesis on the printing revolution as an "epoch-making event" in an 80-page article in the renowned journal *Past & Present* (Eisenstein 1969).

In the 1970s and 1980s, Eisenstein had no problems placing herself in dialogue with the most influential cultural theorists and communication scholars of her time, such as Harold Innis and Marshall McLuhan and later Walter Ong and Jack Goody (Innis 1950; McLuhan 1964; Ong 1982; Goody 1986). Working with PPAC, Eisenstein's main intellectual sparring partner was undoubtedly McLuhan. In stark contrast to the grand gestures and enchanting theories of the latter – presented particularly in the book *The Gutenberg Galaxy: The Making of Typographic Man* (1962) – Eisenstein remained on the ground. A trained historian, she drew her conclusions from a cogent amount of rigorously and systematically collected historical data and, most importantly, a meticulous reading of previous empirical research. To Eisenstein, context was king, and her own densely contextualized synthesis of previous scholarship on the printing press is impressively comprehensive. While recognizing many merits of McLuhan's thinking, she nevertheless took issue with him on the matter of message versus medium, pleading that the content of printed materials and the form of the printing press as a technological innovation were equally important matters to keep in mind when attempting to grasp the historical influence of print on society.

The outline of the book

In short, PPAC traces the impact of the early printing press on the sociocultural system in which it was embedded. While stressing the innovative aspects of this new communication technology, Eisenstein argues with some force for the need to look at print in relation to the fifteenth-century wider social, political, and economic context. The three concepts in her main title reveal her key interests: printing press technology, historical agency, and temporal change. Of these three, historical agency is no less important than the other two. Technological innovation itself does not drive history, Eisenstein argues, but history is put in

258 *Marie Cronqvist and Kajsa Weber*

motion by people. Changes come about by active agency, and a myriad of agents fill the pages of PPAC: print shopkeepers, clergymen, capitalists, scholars, political elites, and many others. All furthered their interests, businesses, and ideas utilizing the printing press.

While spanning the whole first century of the printing press, Eisenstein locates what she calls "the advent of print" between 1460 and 1480, a rather precise period when the print shops quickly grew from a rare to a common feature of continental European cities. Being a social historian, Eisenstein is mainly interested in the proliferation and effects of the early print shops on the sociocultural, sociotechnical, and socioeconomic system. A true force of economic change, the print shops were capitalist and competitive enterprises. They stimulated the development and introduction of new techniques, skills, and occupations, and they were centred on the commodification of printed paper.

The print shops themselves were noisy and crowded urban spaces where new professionals engaged in working with different techniques of woodcuts, engravings, and etchings. Their importance was however far from merely a matter of technology. The print shops coordinated the city networks of knowledge, directly linking the worlds of university scholars, the scholastic work of clergymen, and early modern state bureaucracy. A general trait of medieval scribal culture had been its fundamental difficulties in preserving and disseminating knowledge as the bulk of manuscripts were unstandardized, fragmented, and scattered all over Europe. The introduction of print and the uniform duplication thus laid the foundation for a transnational circulation of key texts, a "Republic of Letters" characterizing the early modern European book trade (see also Goodman 1994).

Eisenstein's book is divided into three parts. The first part focuses on the main changes that print introduced in relation to the previous medieval manuscript culture of scribes. In the early beginning, the changes were not, Eisenstein argues, primarily a matter of knowledge content, as print indeed handled the same texts as those produced by scribes. However, due to the possibility of multiplying these texts, a series of other structural and infrastructural changes came about. Here, she elaborates on some "features of print" that she holds essential to understanding how print became an agent of change: dissemination; standardization; reorganizing and cataloguing knowledge and data; data collection, corruption, and improvement of text; preservation; and finally, amplification and reinforcement.

- *Dissemination.* After the advent of print, books and other printed items became more readily available and affordable, which had a range of consequences. The broad dissemination meant that more individuals could access text, but also that those who already consumed books had access to many more. Furthermore, the fact that scholars could access larger quantities of books increased their opportunities to consult and compare different texts, which also stimulated a demand for further dissemination of printed materials.

- *Standardization.* For the first time in European history, it was now possible to produce hundreds of identical and fixed copies, something that had been unthinkable for medieval university faculties. Despite standardization, maps, charts, and other printed items presented production difficulties for the early print shops, which struggled with many printer defects. And, as texts were standardized and mass disseminated, so indeed were errors and inaccuracies. The so-called errata list was born, a list located at the end of the book containing emendations and mistakes generated in the printing process. The printed text may have been a significant improvement compared to the manuscript, but contemporary printers still struggled with how to "fix" the text and protect it from corruption.
- *Reorganizing and cataloguing knowledge and data.* Printers developed different cataloguing practices and devices to assist the reader (and presumably consumer) of a book when orienting themselves in the printed text. The title page is perhaps the most visible and familiar invention, but here are also other organizing tools such as running heads, pagination, and indices. Such devices helped bibliographers to rationalize, codify, catalogue, and systematize the printed knowledge of their time and create whole systems of cross-referencing, citation, and indexing.
- *Data collection, corruption, and improvement of text.* Printing increased the transparency of text reproduction for both consumers and producers. At the same time, there was a rapid accumulation of data calling for more charts, indices, diagrams, and tables. New editions of any given text competed on the book market with previous editions, and printers constantly tried to improve their product to attract new customers. Improvement in editing and text design quickly evolved and became standard, as no one wanted to be left behind and lose their market share. Numerous examples from the sixteenth century show how editors and authors strived to complement and enrich their work in new editions. At the same time, contemporary critics were constantly grumbling over how the printing press corrupted the text, for instance the incompetence of printers, correctors or the use of types and images printed so often that they lost their sharpness, leading to a blurry result.
- *Preservation.* "Typographical fixity is a basic prerequisite for the rapid advancement of learning", Eisenstein states (PPAC 1979: 113). Medieval manuscripts were always unique, alone bearing the knowledge that was captured within. Copying by hand was the only way of reproducing the knowledge, but it was constantly a source of mistakes and corruption. Copied versions would always bear some variation in relation to the original. The single document was also exposed to other dangers such as weather, fire, and thieves. Thus, that knowledge after printing could be duplicated and, in this, securely preserved presented opportunities to debate the content of a given text, a feature that, according to Eisenstein, introduced progressive and cumulative change.

260 *Marie Cronqvist and Kajsa Weber*

- *Amplification and reinforcement.* Finally, among the features of print, Eisenstein also points to how typographical culture tended to amplify and augment cliches and stereotypes. When printed materials proliferated, so did the reinforcement of shared references in the shape of narratives, anecdotes, tropes, and symbols. In translations, these fixed references also easily transcended national borders. The word cliche is itself typographic jargon for the technical reproduction of a stereotype, with its roots in the early modern era.

In the second and third parts of PPAC, after having established the features of print, Eisenstein considerably broadens the perspective. Here, she puts forward the argument that the Renaissance revival and its dissemination of ancient classical texts and ideas, as well as the Protestant movement by Martin Luther and the Scientific Revolution, were all conditioned by the printing press and not only facilitated by it. For the Protestant Reformation, print played a crucial role as printing made it possible to disseminate religious texts and pamphlets in vernacular languages. The wide circulation of Reformation pamphlets in the 1520s made it almost impossible for the Church to stifle what was considered heresy. Without print, Eisenstein holds, the Reformation would probably only be a parenthesis in European intellectual history. It affected early modern readership as it allowed ordinary people to access information of various kinds, also – as in the case of early Enlightenment thinking – through clandestine networks of information that challenged both conceived wisdom and censorship.

In the early stages of what has been called the Scientific Revolution, print spurred a set of changes within scientific inquiry that helped to synchronize existing knowledge, systematically compare texts and images, and enhance the use of common methodologies and practices. This helped to foster not only the rapid exchange of ideas across regions and countries but also a wider sharing of findings and an intersubjective validation through a greater scrutiny and critique of scientific claims. In short, scientists and scholars could refer to and build upon the work of their predecessors, which led to a more cumulative, transparent, and systematic approach to knowledge.

Furthermore, in certain fields of learning such as geometry, architecture, medicine, and geography, print helped to advance the use of illustrations and images such as figures, maps, and charts. In the age of print, Eisenstein notes, "visual aids multiplied; signs and symbols were codified; different kinds of iconographic and nonphonetic communication were rapidly developed" (Eisenstein 1983: 42). The mass-produced printed image had a fundamental impact on the shaping of collective memory, didactics, and the role played by mnemonic aids, as the rhymes and cadences of oral culture were no longer necessary to preserve the essential knowledge content of formulas, recipes, and calculations. Print thus amplified the visual expression at the cost of the aural.

Finally, in this large ensemble of complex and interrelated changes, Eisenstein argues, print also helped the spread of individualist thought. The dissemination of diverse ideas challenged traditional religious and political authorities as the wide availability of printed materials boosted literacy rates, making it possible for people to have direct access to knowledge. This empowered literate Europeans to make their own interpretations of texts and not rely on clerics and rulers as mediators of knowledge. But individualism was not only boosted in the hands of readers, consumers, and audiences. With writers such as Michel de Montaigne, a new genre of literature entered stage – a more informal one, where the singularities and idiosyncrasies of the individual self were presented to a mass audience. In this process, personal celebrity was born. In short, as Eisenstein sees it, diversity accompanied standardization. She also makes the connection between print and the growing ideas of individual autonomy and liberties as articulated later in the seventeenth century by key Enlightenment thinkers, John Locke in particular.

Eisenstein and her critics

Print was thus, according to Eisenstein, nothing less than the key driving force of political, religious, and cultural change in the early modern era. She expressed that she found it peculiar that so little historiography had dealt with these obvious connections. According to her, print was the "unacknowledged revolution". The immediate and very mixed response to the publication of PPAC reflected this tension between, on the one hand, the existing quite substantial scholarly work on printing, book circulation, and new bibliography and, on the other hand, her rather stubborn and audacious statement that historians had not acknowledged the revolutionary force of the printing press. Looking at reviews of PPAC, one can easily detect how historians working in the field felt harmed or even offended by her treatment of the work of her peers. Librarian and book historian David Shaw noted in a review that "she often plays down insights of earlier scholars and exaggerates her own perception" (Shaw 1981: 261). A review from another colleague, Paul Needham, was even more biting. Needham simply questioned if the historical effects of printing could be "assessed accurately by someone ignorant of the history of printing" (Needham 1980: vi). According to him, the book was not only deeply flawed but basically incomprehensible.

Overviewing scholarly work on the advent of print before the publication of PPAC, Eisenstein's statement regarding the unacknowledged revolution certainly seems a bit odd. As the footnotes in her work shows, book print was indeed a popular field of research in the post-war scholarly landscape. Most well-known today is the work of Lucien Febvre and Henri-Jean Martin, *L'apparition du livre* from 1958 (English edition: *The Coming of the Book*, 1976). Eisenstein's point is however that the *effect* of the advent of print had not been sufficiently investigated, but merely hinted at. Hence, despite massive scholarship within book history, the basic question of how print affected society was left unanswered. Her carefully executed investigation of how printing "altered methods of data collection, storage and retrieval systems and communications

262 Marie Cronqvist and Kajsa Weber

networks" (PPAC 1979: xvi) remains the fruit of her work. In general, historians are not trained to ask questions of how A affects B, since there are so many factors that can have an influence on historical change, and there is no method to establish which of these factors are constitutional for the historical process at hand. Eisenstein challenged such conventional lines of thought.

Following reviews and discussions of her work, the difficulties historians had with the question of causal effect are possible to trace into communication history scholarship at the turn of the millennium. For instance, book and cultural historian Adrian Johns argued in an article 2002 that PPAC was less concerned with "how printing's historical role came to be shaped" and more with "what print culture itself is", implying that PPAC is not a proper historically investigation, but a rather ahistorical analysis of a media technology (Johns 2002: 110). Another scholar, Diederick Raven, pointed to the same thing in an article from 1999. He showed how contested standardization was in the first century of print and argued that the fixed text was not a product of the printing press, but of creative agents. His example is the "Luther rose", a graphical design device that was printed on those editions of the New Testament that Luther had overseen himself (Raven 1999).

For many historians, the question of effect appears to come from the influence of the social sciences and thus PPAC can also be seen as a product of an era when the academic discipline of history had more in common with the theories and methods of social sciences than it has today. This may explain both the, sometimes, massive criticism of her work from historians (as they usually see historical change as deeply embedded in a specific local and temporal context) and the fact that PPAC still, more than 40 years after its publication, remains relevant. Without a doubt, Eisenstein succeeded in articulating a causal relationship between print and historical change that in fact proved very useful for historical analysis – even if both historians and communication scholars over time and for different reasons have been, shall we say, a bit sceptical.

The legacy of PPAC after the cultural turn and in the digital age

Johns' already mentioned article from 2002 is but one expression indicating the curious revival of Eisenstein in the early years of the new millennium. Several scholars questioned Eisenstein's results and argued that the transition from script to print was much more complex than (they thought) she had captured in PPAC. And the complexities they identified were different from the complexities Eisenstein had talked about. This must be seen in the light of broader scholarly developments, in particular the so-called *new cultural history*. It also seems obvious that the digital condition forced historians around the year 2000 to rethink how media change interplays with social change.

Johns presented his main critique of Eisenstein in his *The Nature of the Book*, published in 1998. He argued against Eisenstein's central claim that the standardization of text enabled by the printing press was a revolutionary change in the dissemination of knowledge and hence a precondition for the Reformation, the Renaissance, and the Scientific Revolution. Johns – a historian of science – turns against the idea that print functioned as "an agent of change" and argues instead that fixity is not something that lives in the printed text itself but is something that readers attribute to the text. Especially during early modern times, Johns argues, the printed text was everything but fixed. Readers and buyers of texts could not trust that the text in front of them was what it purported to be, as misprints, bad pirated copies, and forgeries were common on the early modern book market. It is how the reader used, read, and related to the printed text that was decisive for the meaning the print acquired.

Johns also criticized Eisenstein for taking a technological determinist view, and thus for attributing agency to technology alone. Eisenstein herself found this criticism absurd, and in her introduction to the second edition of *The Printing Revolution in Early Modern Europe* in 2005, she found it necessary to underline that she sees printing as "*an* agent, not *the* agent, let alone *the only* agent, of change in Western Europe. It is necessary to draw these distinctions", she states, "because the very idea of exploring the effects produced by any particular innovation arouses suspicion that one favors a monocausal interpretation or that one is prone to reductionism and technological determinism" (Eisenstein 1983/2005: xviii).

Today, the debate can be seen in the light of the coming and establishment of social constructionism within a range of academic disciplines at the turn of the millennium. Johns and many other scholars following Eisenstein (also in less antagonistic ways than Johns) were inspired by the cultural turn within history and produced histories of print that were focused on what humans attributed to the printing press. They were interested in how people have handled, related to, interpreted, and used print, rather than the printing press itself. A central work here is David McKitterick's book *Print, Manuscript and the Search for Order* (2003), which explores the relationship between print and manuscript from the fifteenth century until the introduction of machine printing in the nineteenth century. Without the explicit attack on PPAC that characterizes Johns' work, McKitterick investigates the stability of printing and the complex interplay between manuscript and print. He argues that printing with movable types in the West during the first 350 years was not determined by fixity and stability, but rather contested instability, improvements, and adjustments. McKitterick also turns against the idea of a printing revolution and advocates a more evolutionary approach, thinking more in terms of the first hundred years of printing as a period of accommodation and linkages between old and new communication systems. Not only was the manuscript an essential part of knowledge preservation and dissemination after the advent of print, but both media were by their contemporaries seen as merely two different ways to produce text. With this view, the introduction of print was not a complete watershed in European history. As an example, McKitterick turns to library catalogues that far into the seventeenth century assembled manuscripts and prints in the same list – in contrast to modern collections management where manuscripts are singled out and form separate collections.

264   *Marie Cronqvist and Kajsa Weber*

No one can be mistaken about Eisenstein's mission – and reading her one can sometimes sense her experience of leading a crusade – to convince historians about the changing force of the printing press. On the one hand, causality and fixity were hard to swallow for cultural historians. On the other hand, Eisenstein's forceful statement in PPAC captured causal effects in ways that historians could not deny, despite having some issues with how she reached that conclusion. In the end she presented an explanation for the massive changes taking place in early modern Europe that remains highly useful for historians.

Hence, rather than having formed a particular school or a cluster of scholars being carriers of her scholarly legacy today, PPAC has contributed to a wide variety of research on early modern media systems. It has served as a catalyst for new avenues of scholarly exploration. The somewhat heated debate between Eisenstein and Johns in *American Historical Review* 2002 (Johns 2002; Eisenstein 2002) showcases this ability of her work, as both combatants give plenty of examples in their footnotes of research that springs out of her work. Even if Eisenstein sometimes is called the founding mother of book history, she was one scholar in a generation of historians interested in book print and its wider connections to the political, social, and cultural history of early modern Europe. Building on Febvre and Martin, but also the work of scholars such as McLuhan, they turned to a subject that until the 1970s and 1980s had been in the hands of literature scholars (Grafton 2002).

Eisenstein was nevertheless a key figure here and in the wake of PPAC we find other seminal works such as by Robert Darnton on the underground literature of pre-revolutionary France (Darnton 1982), Roger Chartier on print and reading (Chartier 1988; Cavallo & Chartier 2003), Anthony Grafton on scholarly practice (Grafton 1990), and Robert W. Scribner on popular culture and the Reformation in Germany (Scribner 1987). One result is that today media and communication in its different historical contexts are natural themes of investigation for historians. Before the publication of PPAC, this was not the case. Thus, Eisenstein's work bears witness to how history once widened its research object and turned to other processes than politics and social conflicts. The now flourishing fields of scholarly practices during the Renaissance, early modern translations, print and paratexts, correctors and misprinting, book trade, and book market, are offsprings of her first generation and the one that followed.

Eisenstein had an indisputable position in the emergence of print culture studies as a distinct scholarly field in the 1980s and 1990s, but her work also lingers on into the new millennium. A testament to this is the collection of twenty essays in *Agent of Change: Print Culture Studies after Elizabeth L. Eisenstein*, written by scholars from a range of disciplines (Baron, Lindquist, & Shevlin 2007). Here, the perspectives are broadened even more to tap into contemporary scholarly inquiry. Some of the essays included are exploring paratexts and the significance of the printing press not only within Europe but also beyond its borders. Others bring Eisenstein's work into the present to discuss the transition from print to digital. A new generation of communication

Elizabeth L. Eisenstein (1979)   265

historians now explore digital media as agents of change, as does for example Barbara Brannon in her essay "The Laser Printer as an Agent of Change" (Brannon 2007). Today, the history of print is a vibrant and complex field of research characterized by the possibilities and challenges of mass digitization of print. The last decades have seen the construction of large databases with printed material, and this process of remediation offers new opportunities of large-scale investigations that were unthinkable at the time of PPAC (for instance Pettegree & der Weduwen 2019).

Conclusion

Despite its very mixed reception and the fact that the book sparked some considerable controversy and even resistance among scholars, both when it first appeared and some twenty years later – or precisely because of these debates – the lingering impact of PPAC is undeniable. For contemporary scholarship about the history of late modern technologies and the emergence of digital media, in particular the transition from print to digital formats, Eisenstein's work still hovers in the background. Her seminal work prefigured our understanding of present-day transitions and the relationship between old and new media in a social setting. We find traces of her media-historical approach and her equal attention to technology and social aspects in often cited works by for example Carolyn Marvin (1988) on early electric society and Lisa Gitelman (2006) on the introduction of the phonograph. In addition, although their way of discussing media historical change is far more evolutionary than revolutionary, Eisenstein's contextual and sociological approach is an important influence and is mentioned with some degree of reverence in Asa Briggs' and Peter Burke's comprehensive media-historical overview *The Social History of the Media: From Gutenberg to the Internet* (2002 and later editions).

PPAC has also to some considerable extent sparked more recent theorizing on the materiality of texts and the relationship between scribal culture, print culture, and digital culture. Some differences are of course fundamental. In the digital world, texts no longer have a fixed link to their material inscription. Screen reading is a discontinuous and thematic activity that promotes individual search terms and keywords rather than contexts and narratives. Nevertheless, Eisenstein has something to offer contemporary discussions on the relations between page and screen taking place within fields such as digital humanities, software studies, critical code studies, and media archaeology. Furthermore, there are interesting connections or convergences between the late modern and early modern world highlighted by Eisenstein's work. One is the striking data-processing character of early modern workshops, where the printed text itself was turned into a commodity that could be quantified and measured. Another connection lies in the information search and knowledge organization aspect opened by the introduction of print.

Eisenstein's legacy is however not limited to media and communication history. For general historians concerned with the advent of the modern era and its mindset, she also demonstrated that a deeper knowledge of the printing press

266 Marie Cronqvist and Kajsa Weber

and its societal impact is essential to unlock an understanding of much wider phenomena: rationalization, modernization, centralization, and globalization, but also bureaucratization, religious divisions, urbanization, entrepreneurial organization, and commercialization. Furthermore, her work showed the links between the printing press and social hierarchies, in particular the creation and distribution of wealth and literacy, and upward social mobility.

To conclude, even though PPAC has had an unquestionable and lasting impact on the scholarship of some of the most prominent book historians of today, Eisenstein's value for the advancement of interdisciplinary research is equally important to highlight. Robert Darnton, in his obituary in *The New York Times* upon Eisenstein's death in 2016, remarked on her fearless, intellectual competitiveness and connected it to her prize-winning career as a tennis player on the senior circuit: "What I especially admired about Betty was that she thought big. She asked important questions; she challenged accepted wisdom. In a way, her history was like her tennis: It was hard hitting and intelligent" (Darnton 2016). Her work was designed to bridge the gap between history and communication studies, actively and consciously drawing insights from both fields. She discussed media forms as well as media content. In these and a myriad of other ways, her work itself serves as an inspiration for further interdisciplinary exploration and remains, much like the title of her 1979 book, an agent of change.

References

Baron, Sabrina Alcorn, Eric N. Lindquist, & Eleanor F. Shevlin (2007) (eds.), *Agent of Change: Print Culture Studies after Elizabeth L. Eisenstein* (Amherst & Boston: University of Massachusetts Press).

Brannon, Barbara (2007), "The Laser Printer as an Agent of Change", in: Baron, Sabrina Alcorn, Eric N. Lindquist, & Eleanor F. Shevlin (eds.), *Agent of Change: Print Culture Studies after Elizabeth L. Eisenstein* (Amherst: University of Massachusetts Press), p. 353–364.

Briggs, Asa, & Peter Burke, with Espen Ytreberg (2020), *A Social History of the Media: From Gutenberg to the Internet*, 4th ed. (London: Polity).

Cavallo, Guglielmo, & Roger Chartier (2003), *A History of Reading in the West* (London: Polity).

Chartier, Roger (1988), *The Cultural Uses of Print in Early Modern France* (Princeton: Princeton University Press).

Darnton, Robert (1982), *The Literary Underground of the Old Regime* (Cambridge, Mass.: Cambridge University Press).

Darnton, Robert (2016, 24 February), "Elizabeth Eisenstein, Trailblazing Historian of Movable Type, Dies at 92", *The New York Times*. https://www.nytimes.com/2016/02/24/books/elizabeth-eisenstein-historian-of-movable-type-dies-at-92.html (accessed 2023-09-21).

Eisenstein, Elizabeth L. (1969), "The Advent of Printing and the Problem of the Renaissance", *Past & Present* 45 (1), pp. 19–89.

Eisenstein, Elizabeth L. (1979), *The Printing Press as an Agent of Change: Communications and Cultural Transformations in Early-Modern Europe* (Cambridge: Cambridge University Press).

Elizabeth L. Eisenstein (1979)   267

Eisenstein, Elizabeth L. (1983/2005), *The Printing Revolution in Early Modern Europe* (Cambridge: Cambridge University Press).

Eisenstein, Elizabeth L. (2002), "An Unacknowledged Revolution Revisited", *The American Historical Review* 107 (1), pp. 87–105.

Febvre, Lucien, & Henri-Jean Martin (1976), *The Coming of the Book: The Impact of Printing 1450–1800* (London: New Left Books).

Gitelman, Lisa (2006), *Always Already New: Media, History, and the Data of Culture* (Cambridge, Mass.: MIT Press).

Goodman, Dena (1994), *The Republic of Letters: A Cultural History of the French Revolution* (Ithaca: Cornell University Press).

Goody, Jack (1986), *The Logic of Writing and the Understanding of Society* (Cambridge: Cambridge University Press).

Grafton, Anthony (1990), *Forgers and Critics: Creativity and Duplicity in Western Scholarship* (Princeton, N.J.: Princeton University Press).

Grafton, Anthony (2002), "AHR Forum: How Revolutionary Was the Printing Revolution?", *The American Historical Review* 107 (1), pp. 84–86.

Innis, Harold (1950), *Empire and Communications* (Oxford: Clarendon Press).

Johns, Adrian (1998), *The Nature of the Book: Print and Knowledge in the Making* (Chicago: University of Chicago Press).

Johns, Adrian (2002), "How to Acknowledge a Revolution", *The American Historical Review* 107 (1), pp. 106–125.

Marvin, Carolyn (1988), *When Old Technologies Were New: Thinking about Electric Communication in the Late Nineteenth Century* (New York: Oxford University Press).

McKitterick, David (2003), *Print: Manuscript and the Search for Order 1450–1830* (Cambridge: Cambridge University Press).

McLuhan, Marshall (1962), *The Gutenberg Galaxy: The Making of Typographic Man* (London: Routledge & K Paul).

McLuhan, Marshall (1964), *Understanding Media: The Extensions of Man* (London: Routledge).

Needham, Paul (1980), "Review: Eisenstein, Elizabeth L. The Printing Press as an Agent of Social Change", *Fine Print* VI (1), pp. 23–25, 32–35.

Ong, Walter J. (1982), *Orality and Literacy: The Technologizing of the Word* (London: Methuen).

Pettegree, Andrew, & Arthur der Weduwen (2019), *The Bookshop of the World: Making and Trading Books in the Dutch Golden Age* (New Haven, CT: Yale University Press).

Raven, Diederick (1999), "Elizabeth Eisenstein and the Impact of Printing", *European Review of History* 6 (2), pp. 223–234.

Scribner, Robert W. (1987), *Popular Culture and Popular Movements in Reformation Germany* (London: Hambledon).

Shaw, David (1981), "Review: Elizabeth L. Eisenstein, The Printing Press as an Agent of Change: Communications and Cultural Transformations in Early-Modern Europe. Cambridge University Press, 1979", *The Library* 6 (3), pp. 261–263.

19 Roland Barthes (1980) *Camera Lucida*

Patrik Åker

Introduction

Frenchman Roland Barthes is a prominent figure in semiotics but is just as often referred to as a philosopher, literary scholar, cultural critic, or essayist. While many of his texts are characterized by a linguistic elegance that is relatively uncommon in academic writing, *Camera Lucida (CL)* (1980/1981) stands out as a kind of stylistic pinnacle. Since it was published, there have been discussions about how to understand it. Is it a total break with his earlier semiotic studies of photography, or is it just that he is interested in different things as a result of new scientific trends such as post-structuralism and postmodernism? Or, maybe, is it not so much about photography as it is about Barthes's mourning his mother and about his personal desires and memories? Important contexts for *CL* are the death of Barthes's mother, as well as his own death just after the book was released. These circumstances both colored contemporary interpretations and continue to influence how the book is understood today.

Even though *CL* has been one of the most influential texts on what makes photography unique, the main interpretation has been that it has limited critical value; it is praised more for its literary qualities than its contribution to critical theory (Oxman, 2010: 71). Literary critic Jonathan Culler also explicitly encouraged attendees at the conference "Back to Barthes" at the beginning of the millennium to return to "the early and middle Barthes and not the late, nostalgic or sentimental Barthes" (2001: 439). However, a more general "affective turn" in critical media theory has led to a newfound interest in *CL* and has highlighted its continued relevance in the digital age through its primary focus on the bodily experience of the media user rather than on the photograph as such (Shurkus, 2014). Moreover, many of the thoughts Barthes developed in his early semiotic studies recur in *CL*. One is his insistence on the dimension of photography he calls the "message without a code". In *CL*, this dimension – with a departure in personal experiences and emotions – can offer a space for reflection around the discourses that try to frame a photograph. In Barthes's early semiotic writings, this dimension of photography was instead understood as being used *inside* language systems to conceal ideologies and power relations.

DOI: 10.4324/9781003432272-20

Roland Barthes (1980) 269

The photographic paradox

When Barthes became an academia superstar in the 1950s and 1960s, he was a part of the "linguistic turn", whose followers, inspired by Swiss structural linguist Ferdinand de Saussure (1857–1913), claimed that all forms of texts and indeed whole cultures could be understood as systems of language. From this followed a specific ontological understanding of the world – there is no reality outside language. In Saussure's theory of signs, the sign consists of two parts – the signifier (signifiant) and the signified (signifié). The signifier is the expression itself, for example a spoken word, and the signified is the mental concept this word is associated with in a particular language system. If someone says the word skyscraper, we think of a certain type of building. It is important to note that signs get their meaning in relation to each other. The word skyscraper thus acquires its meaning in relation to words like villa, mansion, house, and so on. Signs have no inherent meaning; they are arbitrary, culturally determined. To communicate with someone verbally, we select words and put them together into sentences that can be understood by those listening. What Saussure was interested in was the underlying structure (la langue) – rules and conventions – governing the use of signs in a language system (la parole). In semiotics, the set of rules that govern the use of signs are called codes. This is something we do not think about in everyday life, but according to semiotics it structures the way we think and understand the world around us.

It is this theory of signs that Barthes uses as his starting point when analyzing cultural phenomena such as fashion, food, beauty, cars and the like in *Mythologies* (1957/1991). What he discusses there exemplifies in various ways the notions he links to his definition of the concept of myth — that which is perceived as common sense and cannot be questioned. However, his semiotic approach caused certain problems for him when he turned to photography, and in his essay "The Photographic Message" (1961/1977) he suggested that photography contained two parallel messages: One with a code (that could be understood as a language) and one without a code (that is, outside language). According to Barthes, photography thereby differs from all other "analogical reproductions of reality" (1961/1977: 17) such as drawing and painting, in that these are all characterized by certain "styles" – an intention has guided the selection and combination of signs. While Barthes does not deny that photography is also marked by styles and intentions, for him there is also a dimension of direct correspondence between what we see in the photograph and what the camera has been pointed at. This goes beyond the structuralist semiotic view that photography, like other practices that produce images, is made up of culturally anchored signs and functions as a language.

One way to understand how photography differs from other media is to bring in American philosopher Charles Sanders Peirce (1839–1914). Peirce distinguished between three categories of signs depending on what the sign stands for. Indexical signs are based on a causal relationship. If I go out on the stairs, look up at the sky and see dark clouds, I put on my raincoat before I go out.

270 *Patrik Åker*

The dark clouds in the sky communicate indexically: I know there is a causal relationship between a certain type of cloud and rain. Iconic signs are instead based on similarity. The typical example is paintings and drawings depicting people and places. The third category, symbols, contains signs that are completely arbitrary but stand for something specific through their use in a given culture. Here, the typical example is the spoken and written word. The photograph complicates the categories of index and icon by being both: On the one hand, a photograph is an image that resembles what it represents; on the other, it is, by its very nature, a mechanical record of what was in front of the camera (a causal relationship).

In "The Rhetoric of the Image" (1964/1977), Barthes draws on two further semiotic concepts – syntagm and paradigm – to deepen the discussion of the paradox that he argues characterizes photography. In semiotics, syntagm stands for the whole, the combination of signs, while paradigm stands for the signs that have been chosen. Thus, to form a syntagm, different paradigmatic choices are made. A photograph can be understood as a syntagm, but what is special for Barthes is that the whole is not made up of different paradigmatic choices but rather, again, is a mechanical recording of what was in front of the camera. Barthes struggles with this "paradox" but solves it in a way that is elegant and, for someone working within the structuralist tradition, typical. For Barthes, it was precisely photography as a mechanical reproduction – a direct imprint of what the camera had been pointed at – that gave it its power to neutralize and conceal what were actually ideological messages. For Barthes, photography had the ability to transform culture into nature, to turn a particular worldview into something that was perceived as self-evident and common sense.

When Barthes returned to photography in what would be his last book, *CL*, nearly two decades had passed since his first two essays on photography were published. At this point structuralism had been abandoned for post-structuralism, and literary critic Terry Eagleton (1996: 116–123) illustrates this development with Barthes's work. The idea of a stable structure (la langue) in the early works is abandoned in favor of understanding structures as articulated in the use of language (la parole) in his later writing. With this move, the focus tends to shift towards deconstructing "texts", revealing contradictions, highlighting the polysemic nature of language, and exposing how the premises on which certain texts rest – their structures – are in fact fragile constructions.

However, if we look at Barthes's work addressing photography, this reading can be somewhat problematized. In *CL* he is not interested in deconstructing photographic realism as such. For Barthes, photography can still be understood from the binary opposition between nature and culture. His early assumption that cultural realism, or objectivity in photography, conceals its constructed nature is not contradicted in *CL*. And it is not as if he has given up on his post-structuralist project; there are ways to undermine photography's claim to realism within systems of language. But because photography does not have a "style", he wants to know more about "the message without a code" and how it can be distinguished from the way this aspect of photography has come to serve realism as a cultural construction.

Capturing the essence of photography

In *CL*, figuring out what distinguishes photography seems almost like an obsession. At the beginning of the book, Barthes writes: "I was overcome by an 'ontological' desire. I wanted to learn at all costs what Photography was 'in itself,' by what essential feature it was to be distinguished from the community of images" (1980/1981: 3). In doing this, he has to leave the structuralist semiotics he practiced in his earlier writing on photography and instead focus on the experience of photographs. He has to take departure in himself, and abandon any systems of language. The contrast to semiotics cannot be more explicit, then, when he says: "...I am a primitive, a child – or a maniac; I dismiss all knowledge, all culture, I refuse to inherit anything from another eye than my own" (1980/1981: 51). This is in line with his rejection at the beginning of the book of all forms of attempts to classify photography. For Barthes, sorting photographs based on whether they are taken by a professional or an amateur, on content, or on which genre they belong to simply becomes a way of concealing the essence of photography. In this way, rejecting attempts to classify photography is a way to "dismiss all knowledge, all culture" and find a place to experience photographs outside language. Another way is to refuse to inherit the photographer's gaze. For Barthes, the photographer ("Operator") works within the accessible cultural codes, while he instead wants to highlight the act of seeing (what he calls the role of "Spectator"). But it is a special way of seeing. Already in "The Photographic Message" Barthes had highlighted that photographs are also "...*read*, connected more or less consciously by the public that consumes it to a traditional stock of signs" (1961/1977: 19). However, in *CL*, instead of investigating different, culturally anchored, ways of reading photographs, the goal is to understand the experience of partaking of the light that has been registered by the camera (1980/1981: 10).

So, what becomes central for Barthes is the innovations that made it possible to capture the light from the reflected object in front of the camera. Accordingly, to him, it is the chemists and not the inventors of camera obscura who are the true creators of "'Photography'" (1980/1981: 80). Barthes does not mention Charles Sander Peirce or the category of signs he called indexical, but it is obvious that what we see in the photograph has a causal relationship with what has been in front of the camera: "It is as if the Photograph always carries its referent with itself, both affected by the same amorous or funereal immobility, at the very heart of the moving world: they are glued together..." (1980/1981: 5–6).

In order to approach the essence of photography, however, he takes departure from a more familiar binary thinking in line with his earlier structuralist works. In *CL* he introduces two new concepts that have a supplementary relationship – "studium" and "punctum". Studium is a general interest in certain photographs that capture his attention in some way; these are what he calls "good photographs". According to Barthes, this interest is anchored in history and culture, and thereby in systems of language. Punctum, on the other hand, is

272 *Patrik Åker*

something that is located outside history, culture, and language. Studium is necessary for Barthes to get interested in a photograph, and if he is lucky it also has a punctum, which cannot be explained or described through language (1980/1981: 26).

Curiosity and desire

With the help of these two concepts – studium and punctum – he then starts his search for the ontology of photography by discussing pictures that "prick" and "bruise" him. In the beginning he is a bit vague. Looking at a magazine, Barthes is confronted with a photograph that captures his interest. It is a news picture from the ongoing civil war in Nicaragua (from 1979), showing patrolling soldiers and two nuns in the background. In the picture by photographer Koen Wessing, Barthes finds a way to combine the co-presence of heterogenous elements that recur in Wessing's pictures, in this case the soldiers and the nuns. Barthes says that it is not really a good photograph but that, in some way, it creates a general interest in line with his definition of studium. However, a couple of pages later he returns to the photograph and says that, for him, there is also a punctum in the picture. It has to do with the same co-presence of two different worlds (soldiers and nuns) that created the general interest, but for Barthes as "Spectator" the accidental is crucial:

> It is a matter of co-presence, that is all one can say: the nuns 'happened to be there,' passing in the background, when Wessing photographed the Nicaraguan soldiers; from the viewpoint of reality (which is perhaps that of the *Operator*), a whole causality explains the presence of the 'detail': the church implanted in these Latin-American countries, the nuns allowed to circulate as nurses, etc.; but from my Spectator's viewpoint, the detail is offered by chance...
>
> (1980/1981: 42)

In the first part of this quote, "the viewpoint of reality" is the picture's studium and part of the systems of language, while what he describes as the accidental is the picture's punctum, whereby he refuses to "inherit anything from another eye".

Despite Barthes's explanation, it is a bit hard to follow his argument. Even though he explicitly says that punctum is something truly subjective and clearly distinct from the photographer's intentions, the picture from Nicaragua uses a highly common convention in photojournalism by which studium and punctum seem to merge. His perspective becomes clearer in the examples that follow. In another picture from Nicaragua (from 1979, by the same photographer), the detail that pricks Barthes is the sheet a woman is holding as she stands beside a covered body "(why this sheet?)"; and a photograph by William Klein (from 1954) shows a young boy in New York City's Little Italy with a gun pointed at his temple, but Barthes sees only the child's bad teeth. He also changes his mind about one picture: Looking at a family portrait by James van der Zee (from

1926) he first thinks the picture's punctum is one of the woman's "strapped pumps" (1980/1981: 43), but says that when he returns to the photograph a couple of pages ahead it has "worked" on him and he finally realizes that the real punctum is the necklace the woman wears (1980/1981: 53). The necklace reminds him of an old relative he had always felt sorry for. This clearly shows that punctum has nothing to do with the analysis of pictures but is rather anchored in personal memories and life experiences. As art historian Margaret Olin (2009) has pointed out, it is not even necessary for the picture to show what he starts thinking about. The necklace he describes isn't the same as the one we see in the picture. Punctum can also be about fantasy. Referring to a photograph of Queen Victoria by George W Wilson (from 1863), Barthes starts to wonder what would happen to the Queen if the man holding her horse suddenly lost control of it.

However, it is not necessarily a detail in the photograph that "pricks" him. Sometimes it is something much more diffuse, as in a photograph by Charles Clifford (ca. 1854–1856) showing a house in Alhambra. For Barthes, the picture's punctum becomes: "...it is quite simply *there* that I should like to live" (1980/1981: 38). In Robert Mapplethorpe's picture (from 1976) of Bob Wilson and Philip Glass, he can't even decide what it is in the picture that captures his interest in Wilson: "...is it the eyes, the skin, the position of the hands, the track shoes?" (1980/1981: 51). So, punctum can also be something that is "unlocatable". What is clear, at any rate, is that punctum has to do with the possibility for reflection and contemplation, anchored in the fact that the photograph shows a frozen moment. Barthes draws a comparison to film, saying that the difference is that in that medium we are constantly on our way forward: "...in front of the screen, I am not free to shut my eyes; otherwise, opening them again, I would not discover the same image..." (1980/1981: 55). What we see in a photograph does not move, does not disappear; and Barthes draws a both touching and sad comparison to framed real butterflies (1980/1981: 57). However, as soon as there is a punctum in the picture the frozen moment comes alive for Barthes, and he starts to reflect on what he sees. He dedicates his book to philosopher Jean-Paul Sartre's *The Imaginary* (*L'Imaginaire*) (1940/2004), and the first part of his investigation to find the essence of photography is close to Sartre's ideas about the imaginary. For Sartre the imaginary is what we add, based on our lived experience, when looking at an object. It takes departure in the subject's experience, not what is culturally shared, and is not based on perception or the knowledge we gain through our senses. However, the way the imaginary works for Barthes in the first part of his book is still not satisfying to him.

It is easy to agree with him. Even if he underlines the importance of coincidence in the photograph – which is an aspect of its being a mechanical registration – the punctum becomes vaguer along the way (as it moves from a specific detail to something more unspecified), and in the end it is hard to see what distinguishes the photograph from other visual media, like a painting. His use of punctum is more in line with how he writes about literature in *The*

274 *Patrik Åker*

Pleasure of the Text (1973/1975). It is characterized by a kind of playfulness that Eagleton (1996) finds so typical of post-structuralism at the time, but also by "pleasure" as a subjective exalted experience outside the culturally framed language – "jouissance" in Barthes's text. The punctum he examines in the first part of *CL* is about curiosity, desire, and fantasy; but as he says at the end of this part, he has to go even deeper within himself in order to find the essence of photography: "I had to grant that my pleasure was an imperfect mediator, and that a subjectivity reduced to its hedonist project could not recognize the universal" (1980/1981: 60). What he does not know at this stage of the book is that there are two different punctum, and that so far he has only discussed one of them. When he returns to this question, he describes punctum in the following way: "I know now that there exists another *punctum* (another 'stigmatum') than the 'detail.' This new *punctum*, which is no longer of form but of intensity, is Time, the lacerating emphasis on the *noeme* ('*that-has-been*'), its pure representation" (1980/1981: 96).

Life and death

Photography's relation to life and death is anticipated in the first part of the book. Already at the beginning, Barthes says he always feels uncomfortable when being photographed. He starts to pose and try in different ways to make himself look like what society expects of him (presumably as an intellectual). He describes this as

> ...that very subtle moment when, to tell the truth, I am neither subject nor object but a subject who feels he is becoming an object: I then experience a micro-version of death (of parenthesis): I am truly becoming a specter.
>
> (1980/1981: 14)

We are all likely familiar with the photographer who calls out "Cheese!" as a way to vivify the moment when the picture is taken. For Barthes, this is nothing but a useless struggle to fight photography's inevitable connection to death (the frozen moment). It is only when he hears the click of the camera, indicating that the picture has been taken, that he feels relieved. Another connection to death is that he somewhat surprisingly makes a connection between photography and theater:

> We know the original relation of the theater and the cult of the Dead: the first actors separated themselves from the community by playing the role of the Dead: to make oneself up was to designate oneself as a body simultaneously living and dead...
>
> (1980/1981: 31)

This presence of both life and death is what Barthes experiences in photography.

One important context for *CL* is of course the death of Barthes's mother. Nearly 30 years after *CL*, the diary he had written in parallel to it, *Mourning Diary* (2010), was published. It further strengthens that *CL* was written in a state of grief. Barthes's fragile condition is also an explanation for his own death just after the book was released. Having been hit by a truck on a street in Paris, his injuries themselves were not fatal but after some time in hospital he had become so weak that he died. These circumstances are hard to ignore when, in the second part of *CL*, he starts his search after the other punctum. He takes departure from how he goes through his mother's things after her death and, among them, her photographs. He has an intention when looking at the photographs "of 'finding' her" (1980/1981: 63) and searching "...for the truth of the face I had loved" (1980/1981: 67). It becomes obvious to him that his mother had behaved in a much more natural way in front of the camera than he does. She doesn't pose and try to live up to cultural expectations in the way he does. Despite this, however, he is unable to find a picture that truly captures how he experienced his mother; that is, not until he finally finds one of her as a child. The photograph is not included in the book, but is described as very old with faded print. Barthes tells us it shows his mother, at the age of five, beside her two-year-older brother, standing on a small bridge in a winter garden: "I studied the little girl and at last rediscovered my mother" (1980/1981: 69).

The explicit reason Barthes gives for not including the photograph is that we as readers would not find the same (or any) punctum in the picture. At best, the picture might lend itself to studium; but its quality is perhaps too poor even for this. In other words, including the photograph would counteract Barthes's ambition to go deeper within himself and let himself be guided by affect to find something general in photography. He tells us his mother had been very weak in the final years of her life, and that he had almost become like a parent to her: "...she had become my little girl, uniting for me with that essential child she was in her first photograph" (1980/1981: 72). Experiencing his mother as his child while she was ill is also a way of resolving death: "...I who had not procreated, I had, in her very illness engendered, my mother" (1980/1981: 72). It is this child whom Barthes finds in the photograph from the winter garden. In front of the camera his – to the highest degree living – mother (and she is also alive in the present for him, because that is how he really knew her (1980/1981: 99)), with her whole life ahead of her, had reflected light rays that had been registered by the camera, or in Barthes's more general words about photography: "...to know that the thing of the past, by its immediate radiations (its luminances), has really touched the surface which in its turn my gaze will touch..." (1980/1981: 81) In this punctum time is decisive, that she was there "*on that day*" (1980/1981: 82), and time opens for a spectator who "becomes the reference of every photograph" (84). With this insight, Barthes starts to wonder how many of the soldiers in an old picture are still alive, thinks about whether he was at a photographed beach that very same day, and notes that a picture of a schoolchild makes him ponder how that boy's life turned out (1980/1981: 82–84).

276 *Patrik Åker*

The fact that in a photograph of his mother as a child he finds her as he had truly experienced her also reveals photography's complex relation to memories. He naturally cannot remember his mother as she was at the age of five. For Barthes, a photograph functions almost as the opposite of memory: It "quickly becomes a counter-memory" (1980/1981: 91) that only confirms what the picture shows. However, in this way it serves a function as "a certificate of presence" (1980/1981: 87), and in front of the picture from the winter garden he cries out: "There she is! She's really there! At last, there she is!" (1980/1981: 99). In a desperate attempt to get closer to his mother's face, he even engaged a photo laboratory to enlarge the picture, with the only result that the larger it got, the more his mother's face vanished. In the end, what was left was "the grain of the paper" (1980/1981: 100). With departure from the photograph of Barthes's mother, it becomes clear that the second punctum is about life and death. She was there, alive in front of the camera with her whole life ahead of her; but she has also just died, and the photograph cannot wake her from the dead.

To convince his readers that the essence of photography – from the perspective of the spectator – is about life/death, he uses another example that we as readers can more easily relate to. It is a picture by Alexander Gardner (from 1865), showing the death by hanging of convict Lewis Payne. Payne had tried to murder the American foreign minister, and Gardner's picture is taken just before he was executed. The photograph shows a young man with his eyes directed towards the viewer, his clothes and haircut, in combination with a stripped-down environment, giving the photograph a kind of timeless impression: "The photograph is handsome, as is the boy: that is the *studium*. But the *punctum* is: *he is going to die*. I read at the same time: *This will be* and *this has been...*" (1980/1981: 96) This example also illustrates that studium and punctum are hard to separate in the second part of *CL*. In the photograph of his mother Barthes takes departure from his own life experiences, but in the picture of the young man who is sentenced to death, studium is a necessary condition for Barthes being "bruised" by it. If he had not known that the man had died immediately after the picture was taken, he would not have been captured by it in the same way.

The tamed photograph

Through these two examples – the mother as a child and the young man sentenced to death – Barthes had, with the help of the second punctum, reached the essence of photography: The co-existence of presence (the living person reflecting light rays) and absence (the moment is lost in an unreachable past). According to Barthes, it doesn't matter whether or not the person in the photograph is dead, because photography is inevitably linked to a specific moment in time and anticipates a future death (also of the spectator). For him, the cultural and societal use of photographs entails ways of taming the medium's essence and turning it into something else. The overall contexts he points at are (mass) media and art. In relation to art, it is not hard to follow Barthes's thought. Art always wants to say something more than "this-has-been". The same goes for advertising and its selling of dreams. But what about press photography? Even if it is true that the intention is to say "this-has-been", the journalistic mission is bigger than this. Here, photography becomes a collection of bricks in narratives with the ambition to tell us about the world; or, in other words, here photography is turned into cultural realism. We are then back to the language systems, the structures Barthes tries to, not deconstruct, but set aside. He is close to his theorizing about photographic objectivity as a myth in his early essays when he claims that "...when generalized, it completely de-realizes the human world of conflicts and desires, under cover of illustrating it" (1980/1981: 118).

The tamed photograph is thereby easy to relate to ideologies and power relations – the language of culture. This is also what interested the early Barthes in his semiotic studies of photography. When he finally reaches the essence of photography in *CL*, it is a purely private existential experience and the photograph cannot prove anything other than "this-has-been"; but it also has the capacity – when there is a punctum – to make the past moment come alive: "this-will-be". Barthes describes this co-existence of presence and absence as "mad" (1980/1981: 119). This is opposite to how he had previously described the "message without a code" as serving the myth of photographic objectivity, and "mythologies" (1957/1991) as being understood as common sense and unquestionable. In this way, it is possible to read his explorations about photography in *CL* as an antidote to ideas about photographic realism as a reflection of reality. Experiencing the mad photograph is an awakening from the continuous streams of images we are confronted with in today's media societies. It becomes a way to develop a critical gaze.

The mad photograph

Capturing experiences beyond language systems has been part of Barthes's thinking from the beginning. In "The Photographic Message" (1961/1977) it is called "the message without a code"; in "The Third Meaning" (1970/1977) it is called "the obtuse" and is something that disrupts the obvious meaning and opens the language system; and in *The Pleasure of the Text* (1973/1975) he argues for a playful relation to texts, rejecting all sorts of categorizations, and reading becomes a sort of hedonist rebellion that he calls "jouissance". The emphasis on reading as a private creative act is also in line with how Barthes approaches photography in *CL* from the perspective of the "Spectator" and not the "Operator". Another important essay that takes a similar departure is "The Death of the Author" (1968/1977). Art historian Geoffrey Batchen (2009) has argued that the thought about "the death of the author" can be used to understand *CL* as a history of photography. As a history, *CL* is completely different from ordinary photo history writing. It contains some of the most celebrated photographers, but Barthes's attitude is that it is amateur photographers rather than professionals who are closer to the essence of photography (1980/1981: 99).

278 *Patrik Åker*

It is the spectator's perspective on photography and its history that Barthes is interested in, and in this way it is similar to how he approached literature: It is a photo history that assumes "the death of the photographer". Like Batchen (2009: 263) says, there are as many photo histories as there are subjects looking at photographs.

Barthes's way of moving the attention from the celebrated genius – author, photographer – and his urge to open texts/pictures to different readings and experiences of course signals that he is part of the post-structuralist movement that developed during the 1960s and 1970s. However, if we take him at his word in *CL*, he seems to understand his own work as being at odds with contemporary academic tendencies: "It is the fashion, nowadays, among Photography's commentators (sociologist and semiologists), to seize upon a semantic relativity: no 'reality' (great scorn for the 'realists' who do not see that the photograph is always coded)..." (1980/1981: 88). In the same paragraph a bit further down, he develops his argument:

> The realists, of whom I am one and of whom I was already one when I asserted that Photography was an image without code – even if, obviously, certain codes do inflect our reading of it – the realists do not take the photograph for a 'copy' of reality, but for an emanation of *past reality*: a *magic*, not an art.
>
> (1980/1981: 88)

But what does Barthes really mean by a "reality" that is not "coded"? One way to understand this is to turn to psychoanalyst Jacques Lacan, to whom Barthes also refers in *CL* (for art historian Margret Iversen, *CL* is an interpretation of Lacan's psychoanalysis (2009)).

Lacan's well-known theory on the development of the human psyche and its different phases – the real, the imaginary, and the symbolic – provides keys to thinking about Barthes's struggle to experience photographs outside any language system. Even if it describes phases in the development of the human psyche, Lacan argues that these are dimensions we carry with us through life. Media scholar Sean Homer (2005: 94) has used Barthes's thoughts about photography as an illustration of how a punctum that disrupts a studium can be understood as a moment when the symbolic is disrupted by the real: "...the photograph is that fleeting glimpse, or encounter with the real..." This is a way to understand the essence of photography as being beyond language and representation. In an almost overexplicit way, we have the (of course impossible) reunion with the mother, and the photograph also marks the limit of language – we are faced with Lacan's psychological trauma of the child's separation from the mother and with it an unconscious death drive (the liquidation of the subject) to reunite with the mother. It is tempting to understand the missing photograph of Barthes's mother in *CL* as a consequence of this impossibility to reunite with the mother. Thereby, it becomes an illustration of the co-existence of presence and absence that constitutes the essence of photography.

Roland Barthes (1980) 279

For another more literal aspect of the encounter with *the real*, we can return to Jean-Paul Sartre's *The Imaginary* (1940/2004). Sartre is not really interested in the differences between various media. When he looks at a portrait painting of Charles VIII, the imaginary merges with the physical object (the painting), and in the end he only sees the subject in the picture and not the picture itself:

> It is he that we see, not the picture, and yet we posit him as not being there: we have only reached him 'as imaged,' 'by the intermediary' of the picture. One sees that the relation that consciousness posits in the imaging attitude between the portrait and its subject is magical.
>
> (Sartre, 1940/2004: 23)

It is this thought that Barthes develops in *CL* in relation to photography and that he understands as "a magic":

> The Photograph then becomes a bizarre *medium*, a new form of hallucination: false on the level of perception, true on the level of time: a temporal hallucination, so to speak, a modest, *shared* hallucination (on the one hand 'it is not there,' on the other 'but it has indeed been'): a mad image, chafed by reality.
>
> (1980/1981: 115)

In *CL* it is foremost portrait photography that creates this hallucinatory feeling for Barthes (people are missing in only three out of 25 photographs, and most of the pictures are portraits). It is also portraits that he relates to society and culture: "Photography, moreover, began, historically, as an art of the Person: of identity, civil status, of what we might call, in all senses of the term, the body's *formality*" (1980/1981: 79). It is also this use of photography that Barthes wants to problematize by discussing how it has tamed photography and reduced it to images (which can't be separated from other visual media). When he goes through the photographs of his mother it naturally looks like her in the pictures, but it is not until the photograph from the winter garden that he finds her in a way that goes beyond likeness; there, she is as he truly knew her. In regard to likeness, photography is an improvement on earlier media such as paintings or drawings, and this is why it was quickly adopted in the 19th century by institutions like the police, hospitals, and courts (Tagg, 1988). The photograph became an excellent tool in the increasingly penetrating state apparatuses that emerged at the time. These practices strived for objective representations and can, from Barthes's early perspective, be understood as serving the myth of objectivity, turning culture into nature. This way of using photographs as a surveillance tool has increased in today's digital media environments. However, if we compare it to a phenomenon such as today's selfie culture, it seems like an opposite use of photography compared to the message without a code as a myth (early Barthes), or as a hallucinatory experience of presence and absence (late Barthes). Media scholar José van Dijck (2008) describes selfies as a movement

280 *Patrik Åker*

from Barthes's "that-was" to treating photography as a communicative resource in a continuous identity-building project (we just can't get enough of pictures).

The digital photograph

For van Dijck, digital photography is oriented towards the future, in contrast to the analogue photograph's indexical relation to the past. This has to do with the ease of taking, manipulating, and circulating photography in a digital environment. Even though photographs have been manipulated and retouched throughout history, the ease of post-production today has made it the rule rather than the exception, and this goes for both professional and amateur photographers. While the premise of photography is still the registration of light rays, in the digital camera the light is converted into information, making the pictures computable. This process is what media scholar Lev Manovich (2001) (see Chapter 28 in this volume) defines as the central meaning of digitization – digital media transform existing media (for instance, the analogue registration of light) into numeric data; in other words, machine code. If the photograph of Barthes's mother in the winter garden had been a digital image, she would not have vanished when he enlarged the picture. Instead, he would have seen the smallest units, pixels, upon which the picture had been built. These units can be rearranged and substituted in infinite ways, and from this viewpoint a digital photograph is never finished. We thereby approach the photograph in a paradigmatic way and start to think about choices (of signs) that have been made to communicate a certain meaning. What we have is a photograph that is always coded.

What Barthes says about what we see in a photograph – that it can never lie about its own existence (1980/1981: 87), and that through photography "...the past is as certain as the present, what we see on paper is as certain as what we touch" (1980/1981: 88) – seems to be obsolete today. If we, as for instance philosopher Bernard Stiegler (2002) holds true, live in a general cultural mistrust of photography, we can no longer talk about it as "a message without a code". Thus, in contrast to Barthes, there is no essential difference between photography and other visual media. However, this does not have to mean that it isn't possible to find a punctum in photographs; much like what Barthes does in the first part of the book – which wasn't enough to find the essence of photography – where details open up to his imagination. Even if Barthes stresses the importance of the accidental, this is in the eye of the beholder, and even in a painting it is possible to be captured by something that goes beyond a certain intention of the painter (or something that is culturally anchored).

But what about the second punctum, regarding life/death? Van Dijck's understanding of digital photography as oriented towards the future is anchored in increased control over the pictures, but she also underlines that the new digital environment can mean a loss of control. One example she discusses is the private pictures American soldiers took of prisoners at the Abu Ghraib prison in Iraq in 2004. These pictures of torture and grave humanitarian

Roland Barthes (1980) 281

assaults, often with the American soldiers looking into the camera and posing beside their prisoners, were not intended to reach outside their own group. However, they were spread along different channels and also entered the mainstream media, generating huge international attention and anger. Don't these photographs have a dimension of a "message without a code"? The possible intention of the photographer (a total loss of humanity) makes them even more horrible. As "shock photos" they are "calculated, overconstructed" for the soldiers' own group (cf. Rabaté, 1997: 14), but for me as spectator outside their group this code doesn't work; or in other words, they do not become tamed within a language system – the experience is one of true horror. All doubts regarding "this-has-been" vanish, and one starts to wonder what happened to the prisoner after the pictures were taken. This experience is similar to how Barthes recalls a photograph from a slave market that he had kept for a long time:

> I repeat: a photograph, not a drawing or engraving; for my horror and my fascination as a child came from this: that there was a *certainty* that such a thing had existed: not a question of exactitude, but of reality: the historian was no longer a mediator, slavery was given without mediation, the fact was established *without method*.
>
> (1980/1981: 80)

The pictures from the prison in Iraq had the same effect on me, and for this the circumstances are important, much in the same way as they were for Barthes when he encountered the picture of the young man who was sentenced to death. Van Dijck highlights that it is these amateur photographers' loss of control that transforms the pictures from communicative resources to making us as spectators "certain" that this has taken place. In the case of the Abu Ghraib pictures, the loss of control meant something typical of photography, which according to Barthes is "a return of the dead" (1980/1981: 9). The idea that we have entered an era of distrust in photography is connected to the thought that the digital photograph is never fixed, and has no negative original; in other words, that it is released from being tied to a referent in a specific moment in time. However, in the pictures from the prison in Iraq, the posing in front of the camera breaks with the idea of digital photography as a performative tool in an ongoing communication. Photography can still stop time in today's endless stream of pictures. These pictures truly tell the spectator of "...*a catastrophe which has already occurred*" (1980/1981: 96). I would say that, in philosopher Jacques Derrida's words (2001: 58), it is the "supplementary" relationship between punctum and studium that makes this possible. The loss of control over the distribution of these photographs fixed them in time, and the knowledge of how they had been made "returned them to death".

Concluding remarks

If we go back to Barthes's early essay, "The Photographic Message", it is possible to understand "the message with a code" as equivalent to the studium in

282 *Patrik Åker*

CL ("The *studium* is ultimately always coded...", he says on page 51), and "the message without a code" as equivalent to the punctum. However, if the two parallel messages served the myth of the transparent photograph in the early essay, in *CL* their supplementary relation results in curiosity or an exalted pleasure experience (jouissance) in the first punctum, and for the second punctum offers an encounter with "the real". Both these experiences in *CL* take place outside language systems, and thereby outside ideologies and culture. I would say that the digitization of photography is not a serious challenge for the first punctum, but it is for the second. The similarity between analogue and digital photographs is how we – in cultural practices in different ways – tame them in continuous image streams, the difference being that the relation of digital photographs to death is more fragile. This is crucial in Barthes's understanding of how we are enclosed by language systems. In *The Pleasure of the Text*, he compares stereotypes (an example of repetitive and conventional use of language in the service of politics and ideology) with a character in a story by Edgar Allan Poe ("The Facts in the Case of M. Valdemar") who is trapped in a state of false death, "what has no end": "The stereotype is this nauseating impossibility of dying" (1973/1975: 43). The argument in *CL* is that photographs can make us confront and reflect on life/death and past moments; something that is perhaps more urgent than ever in today's era of post-truth, in which history is as uncertain as the future.

References

Barthes, R. (1957/1991). *Mythologies*. The Noonday Press.
Barthes, R. (1961/1977). The Photographic Message. In Barthes, R. (Ed.), *Image, Music, Text* (S. Heath, Trans.) (pp. 15–31). Fontana Press.
Barthes, R. (1964/1977). The Rhetoric of the Image. In Barthes, R. (Ed.), *Image, Music, Text* (S. Heath, Trans.) (pp. 32–51). Fontana Press.
Barthes, R. (1968/1977). The Death of the Author. In Barthes, R. (Ed.), *Image, Music, Text* (S. Heath, Trans.) (pp. 142–148). Fontana Press.
Barthes, R. (1970/1977). The Third Meaning. In Barthes, R. (Ed.), *Image, Music, Text* (S. Heath, Trans.) (pp. 52–68). Fontana Press.
Barthes, R. (1973/1975). *The Pleasure of the Text*. Hill and Wang.
Barthes, R. (1980/1981). *Camera Lucida: Reflections on Photography*. Hill and Wang.
Barthes, R. (2010). *Mourning Diary*. Hill and Wang.
Batchen, G. (2009). Camera Lucida: Another little history of photography. In Batchen, G. (Ed.), *Photography Degree Zero: Reflections on Roland Barthes's Camera Lucida* (pp. 259–274). MIT Press.
Culler, J. (2001). Barthes: Theorist. *The Yale Journal of Criticism* 14 (2), 439–446.
Derrida, J. (2001). The Deaths of Roland Barthes. In *The Work of Mourning* (pp. 31–69). The University of Chicago Press.
Eagleton, T. (1996). *Literary Theory. An Introduction* (2nd ed.). The University of Minnesota Press.
Homer, S. (2005). *Jacques Lacan*. Routledge.

Iversen, M. (2009). What is a Photograph? In Batchen, G. (Ed.), *Photography Degree Zero: Reflections on Roland Barthes's Camera Lucida* (pp. 57–74). MIT Press.

Manovich, L. (2001). *The Language of New Media*. MIT Press.

Olin, M. (2009). Touching Photographs: Roland Barthes's 'Mistaken' Identification. In Batchen, G. (Ed.), *Photography Degree Zero: Reflections on Roland Barthes's Camera Lucida* (pp. 75–90). MIT Press.

Oxman, E. (2010). Sensing the Image: Roland Barthes and the affect of the visual. *SubStance* 39 (2) (Issue 122), 71–90.

Rabaté, J-M. (1977). Introduction. In Rabaté, J-M. (Ed.), *Writing the Image after Roland Barthes* (pp. 1–18). University of Pennsylvania Press.

Sartre, J-P. (1940/2004). *The Imaginary. A Phenomenological Psychology of the Imagination*. Routledge.

Shurkus, M. (2014). Camera Lucida and affect: Beyond representation. *Photographies* 7 (1), 67–83.

Stiegler, B. (2002). The Discrete Image. In Derrida, J. & Stiegler, B. (Eds.), *Echographies of Television: Filmed Interviews* (pp. 145–163). Polity Press.

Tagg, J. (1988). *The Burden of Representation: Essays on Photographies and Histories*. University of Minnesota Press.

van Dijck, J. (2008). Digital photography: Communication, identity, memory. *Visual Communication* 7 (1), 57–76.

20 Benedict Anderson (1983) *Imagined Communities*

Per Ståhlberg

Introduction

Nationalism is usually associated with political conflict, social identity, or historical tradition. In the first instance, disciplines such as political science, sociology, and history attempt to explain or understand the phenomenon. However, with the publication of Benedict Anderson's *Imagined Communities* the research on nationalism was broadened to include cultural perspectives and thus to become a concern for critical media studies. In addition, the very expression "imagined community" proved increasingly useful as a designation of cultural communities of various kinds also outside the study of nationalism.

One reason Anderson's book quickly became widely read and a classic was probably its literary style and highly personal appeal. The book opens with a poem by Daniel Defoe, *The True-Born Englishman*, the first lines of which read: "Thus from a Mixture of all kinds began/ That Het'rogeneous Thing, *An Englishman:*/ In eager Rapes, and furious Lust begot,/ Betwixt a Painted *Britton* and a *Scot*" (2006[1983]: *x*).

Throughout the study, the author then quotes works of fiction from different eras and different parts of the world. Here and there, one can sense ironies, jokes, and provocations. *Imagined Communities* is rather unusual as an academic study and lacks some of the formalities one would expect, such as clearly formulated research questions, a methodology section, and conclusions. Anderson says in his autobiography, *A Life beyond Boundaries* (2016), that he did not originally consider the book as a strictly academic work. It was not published by any of the usual university publishers, but by the left-wing political publisher Verso in the UK.

Anderson's way of writing is thus not burdened by abstractions; instead, he likes to dwell on the concrete empirical details of historical, literary, or ethnographic examples. At the same time, it is precisely his way of using empirical material that makes the book theoretically interesting. Anderson brings together examples and details from completely different parts of the world and over several centuries. The parallels and contrasts that emerge reveal the theoretical level of the study. However, the common thread is not always easy to follow; each chapter makes a short essay of its own and it is only when put together

DOI: 10.4324/9781003432272-21

that the chapters form the whole that makes up the book's argument. *Imagined Communities* is very much a geographically and historically comparative study of the phenomenon of nationalism. It is also a book that has taken on a new relevance despite being written four decades ago and essentially dealing with an even older historical period.

Puzzling phenomena

Indeed, after having been briefly regarded as obsolete, the political current of nationalism seems to have returned with renewed vigour in the early decades of the 21st century. In Europe, nationalism helped to radically redraw the political map in the 19th century, and in the first half of the 20th century it was the most powerful, and often frightening, of political doctrines – with, it is sometimes argued, two world wars on its conscience. In the latter half of the same century, nationalism often played a role in the struggle for independence in the colonized world of the global South. However, in the decades just before the turn of the millennium, when the world seemed to be increasingly interconnected – with keywords such as "globalisation" or "cosmopolitanism" – political ideas about the "nation" were assumed having lost vitality. It is fair to say that this was a misjudgement. And it was not the first time that academics and intellectuals had underestimated the strength of nationalism.

Indeed, the success and popularity of nationalism has long eluded academia. The nationalist world of ideas seems to be riddled with contradictions, and the starting point for Benedict Anderson's study are three paradoxes. Firstly, for a historian the nation is clearly a modern phenomenon while the nationalists stubbornly maintain the very ancient origins of their people. Secondly, nationality is a universal socio-cultural belonging (everyone must, according to the doctrine, belong to a nation) while the nationalists always understand their people according to very specific conditions. The third paradox regards the political strength of nationalism despite its philosophical poverty and inconsistence (2006: 5). It is not possible to formulate a general definition of what a "nation" consists of, as its content varies greatly from case to case. Anderson therefore suggests that the nation is "an imagined political community – and it is imagined as both intrinsically limited and sovereign" (2006: 6).

It has puzzled (and annoyed) generations of scholars and thinkers that the doctrine of nationalism could generate such enthusiasm. In 1983, when the first edition of *Imagined Communities* was published, research on nation and nationalism, that had been intense in the preceding decades, culminated. That year two other books that tackled the problem of nationalism from similar perspectives was published: the anthropologist Ernest Gellner's study *Nations and Nationalism* and a collection edited by historians Eric Hobsbawm and Terence Ranger, *The Invention of Tradition*. All three books share a focus on the construction of the nation as a cultural and political idea (though they approach the impetus for its creation differently) and they have all become standard references in later scholarship. However, it is Benedict Anderson who

286   *Per Ståhlberg*

has most clearly inspired scholars across disciplines and left the deepest mark on academia. In addition, *Imagined Communities* is a book that often appears in undergraduate and graduate course literature – again in a variety of academic disciplines.

Media researchers often emphasise the importance that Anderson gives to media technologies in the construction of nations, especially the novel and the newspaper. Yet it is only on a few pages of the book that the author concretely develops this reasoning. There are, however, several other connections with media studies in the book, such as the description of the historical situation that preceded the emergence of nationalism. Here, Anderson's argument is close to some of the most central conceptual discussions in media studies.

Before the nation

I mentioned earlier that most historians much agree that nationalism is a modern phenomenon. The idea that humanity can be divided into distinct "nations" with specific characteristics and that these communities should be the basis for political power is hardly more than a couple of hundred years old. Before that, however, there were other strong ideas about human communities and legitimate governance. Anderson describes two such cultural beliefs that the idea of the nation would come to replace, and which had to be weakened before this could happen.

The first idea regards the transnational communities of the major religions, held together by specific privileged written languages (e.g., the Latin of Christianity and the Arabic of Islam). People of the same religion, who were culturally different in all other respects, could come together in belief in the same God, conveyed in a common script and in the same written language. This togetherness could, in the case of the major world religions, exist across vast geographical areas and connect people who would never meet each other. Religious communities gave continuity to an uncertain existence; life and death were given meaning in an eternal historical tradition. During the 18th century in Western Europe, however, religious world views began to be challenged by the secular rationalism of the Enlightenment, and the sacred cosmopolitan languages were increasingly replaced by vernacular and everyday written languages. Accordingly, Anderson argues, it is also during this period that a new form of imagined community begins to emerge. It is also emphasised throughout *Imagined Communities*, that nationalism cannot be understood as another ideological "ism", like socialism, conservatism, or liberalism. Rather, nationalism belongs to the same system of ideas as religions and, like religions, can interact with radically different political ideologies. It is also the communicative ability of the major religions (through uniform written languages) that Anderson means has a special significance in these historical communities.

The second cultural notion that precedes nationalism is the belief in the centralised and divinely given power of dynastic empires. In these empires, rulers and common people were not perceived as the same kind of human beings. They were not supposed to share a cultural community; quite the contrary. The people were subjects, not citizens, and their language and traditions were irrelevant to the ruler, nor did the subjects expect anything other than that the people in power were of a different ilk. Territorial boundaries were also unclear, and it was not considered strange that power over populations shifted between different dynastic centres, through both conquests and marriages between heirs to the dynastic thrones. Also in this context, Anderson attributes a transforming power to the ideas of the Enlightenment. When the divinity of the ruler is questioned, the legitimacy of power shifts from the ruler himself to the object of power: the territory and the population. It then becomes necessary to ask who these people are that live within a particular geographical area. It is only when a population shifts in status from subjects to citizens that the "nation" becomes a plausible notion: now it is the "ancestry" of these people that takes centre stage, and that power over a population is based on a shared sense of belonging.

For media scholars, the above reasoning about the Enlightenment's challenges to power and the church sounds familiar. It is in fact in the study of the same period, and with similar arguments about a changed notion of political legitimacy, that Jürgen Habermas takes his starting point in his writing on the transformation of the public sphere (see Chapter 7). Although, Habermas's study is not about the nation but about the emergence of a "bourgeois public sphere", where issues previously dominated by church or state authorities can be critically discussed by private individuals, both "the nation" and "the public sphere" are based on the same basic idea of the historical advent of a social community where differences in status between individuals are irrelevant. In addition, both authors describe a kind of vanguard of people who, with new experiences, take the lead in creating the institutions where ideas are articulated and disseminated to broader layers of society. It may seem strange that Anderson in *Imagined Communities* does not mention "the public" or refer to Habermas's book (which was published in 1962). The two authors do write from rather different academic traditions, but they also belong to different language spheres. Habermas's *The Structural Transformation of the Public Sphere* was written in German and was not published in English until 1989, six years after Anderson's book was published. It was not until then that the two classics began to be increasingly cross-referenced by many scholars writing on both the public sphere and the nation. The concepts of "imagined communities" and "public spheres" are intertwined. But there are also some significant differences.

One such difference is that Anderson sees a third cultural transformation that must occur before the nation can be imagined, something which is completely absent from Habermas's description of the emergence of the public sphere. This regards the perception of time, and it is something that puts forward ideas about the crucial importance of media technologies for which Anderson is perhaps best known.

288 *Per Ståhlberg*

Simultaneity

For medieval man, history and cosmology were inextricably linked, Anderson argues, drawing on Eric Auerbach and Walter Benjamin (see Chapter 1). In the Middle Ages, time was not perceived as a chain of successive events. Rather, history had a contemporary presence which could be clearly visualised in art. Anyone looking at a medieval painting with a religious theme today may find it strange that the Virgin Mary, the shepherds, and the baby Jesus are depicted in costumes and in settings from the artist's own time. However, for a medieval artist, it would have been unthinkable to depict the biblical stories as if they took place in a distant and different time, since they lived under "a simultaneity of past and future in an instantaneous present" (Anderson, 2006: 24).

People alive today probably take our own notion of "simultaneity" for granted: different events happening at the same time but in different places. But, says Anderson, this is a notion that has emerged as the older idea of simultaneity along history has lost its relevance. The modern notion of time and history is based on the logic of the calendar and the clock, where existence moves forward in a measurable but "homogeneous and empty time" (a phrase Anderson borrows from Walter Benjamin) that does not connect the present with the past. Togetherness then arises, so to speak, across time.

So, what is the link between the perception of time and imagined communities? Well, it is in this context that Anderson highlights two media forms that started to become popular in Europe in the 18th century: the novel and the newspaper. The novel introduces simultaneity as a literary technique: a series of disparate events are described, performed by actors who are embedded in a community but unaware of each other's existence. Because they are connected by the fact that the events take place at the same date and time, a fictitious affinity between the characters is evoked in the reader's mind. A modern reader or viewer is quite used to the fact that the narrative in a novel, film, or television series moves between different characters and events that take place in parallel, but in the 18th century this was a completely new way of telling a story. This depiction of society as a kind of social organism moving through time is, Anderson argues, an exact counterpart to the notion of the nation. In perhaps the most quoted lines from the book, he states:

> An American will never meet, or even know the names of more than a handful of his 240,000,000-odd fellow-Americans. He has no idea of what they are up to at any one moment. But he has complete confidence in their steady, anonymous, simultaneous activity.
>
> (Anderson, 2006: 26)

One may recall that Jürgen Habermas, in his book on the bourgeois public sphere, also gives the novel significance for a shift in the history of mentality. But interestingly, Habermas takes up a theme in early mass literature that is completely opposite to Anderson's observation. Where the latter saw an extended social community taking shape, Habermas instead emphasises the importance of the novel for the production of a subjective sphere of intimacy (1989[1962]: 51–56).

Anderson describes the newspaper as an extreme form of the book. Each day, the newspaper presents a variety of news stories about different events and geographical locations, and the only thing that ties them together is the date at the top of the page. Reading newspapers encourages readers to constantly relate themselves and others to the world around them. Moreover, as Anderson points out, this takes place in a gigantic mass ceremony in which a newspaper is consumed simultaneously, but individually, by thousands of people who do not know each other but are well aware of each other's existence.

It may be noted that Anderson is describing two kinds of "simultaneity" enabled by the novel and the newspaper (see Gupta, 2004). In the novel, a social community is constructed *in the text*, through a narrative in which unrelated events take place in different places, but simultaneously. The newspaper also provides this possibility by linking widely differing news by coinciding with the calendar, but also has an additional significance in that it creates a community through simultaneous *reading* (unlike the novel, a newspaper is usually consumed on the same day it is published). The newspaper thus gives rise to a simultaneity that is not only about a literary imagined community but rather about how a cultural technology synchronises the audience. It is at this point that the newspaper is similar to other technologies that are preconditions for the breakthrough of industrialism, such as the clock and the calendar. It is also easy to see the same potential for audience synchronisation in the mass media technologies that emerged in the 20th century. Perhaps even more so because radio and television listeners (before the era of digital content streaming) must participate in the community at the same time as everyone else – or not at all.

In his book, Anderson makes no great point about the difference between these two types of simultaneity (i.e., the techniques of representation *in the text*, and the synchronicity *of reading*), but we will return to the issue later. It can be noted, however, that Anderson's discussion of the novel and the newspaper is about the importance of *the form* of media technology for the nation to be imagined. Unlike many later cultural researchers, he does not discuss how different nations are portrayed in media content. Anderson's focus is on the morphology of the media (their form), not on their representations.

Spatiality and seriality

The novel and the newspaper are thus important for the way communities are imagined in a temporal dimension. However, in this argument Anderson does not address the conditions for how nations can be imagined in a spatial dimension. This is notable. As previously mentioned, the Enlightenment meant that the legitimisation of power shifted from the ruler to territory and population, and in the doctrine of nationalism, places and borders between people are central. A reasonable theory of the nation should include a spatial dimension,

290   *Per Ståhlberg*

but the first version of *Imagined Communities* largely lacks this. Anderson himself admits that this was one of several obvious shortcomings (2006: *xiv*) which he tried to remedy by adding two additional chapters in a revised edition of the book, one of which deals with the importance of censuses, maps, and museums in categorising and describing people and places and thus spatially imagining extended communities. In this new chapter, Anderson approaches the spatiality of the nation through an analysis of colonialism's preoccupation with mapping and classifying the territories and people it ruled (the empirical focus is primarily on Southeast Asia). This is not an obvious route to take because, as Anderson recognises, the colonial state is not actually nationalist; rather, it is violently anti-nationalist. But the institutions (i.e., censuses, maps, and museums) that were created to describe subaltern populations and geographies later became a legacy of nationalism. 20th century nationalists in the newly independent states of Asia and Africa did not need to look to America or Europe for tools, because they were already in place.

What Anderson tries to capture in this part of the book is a pattern of thought common to the map, census, and museum in the colonial context. Together they built "a totalizing classificatory grid, which could be applied with endless flexibility to anything under the state's real or contemplated control: peoples, regions, religions, languages, products, monuments, and so forth" (2006: 184). This way of thinking means that everything belongs in a specific place, everything can in principle be counted or measured and ambiguities are not tolerated – nothing and no one can belong in more than one place in this grid, mixtures do not exist. It is not difficult to see how this logic easily coincides with nationalist thinking. In a concrete way, Anderson argues, the census, the map, and the museum institutions become a precondition for the emergence of new imagined communities in the decolonised world.

In this context, Anderson also introduces the concept of "seriality" as a fundamental principle of national thinking. It is to this concept that he attaches the notion that every nation must contain several elements that constitute its core. Each nation is preoccupied with its particular elements, but on the premise that all other nations have corresponding elements, such as a language, a literature, a glorious history, and national heroes. In a later book, *The Spectre of Comparisons* (1998: 29–57), Anderson develops this idea and discusses the difference between what he calls unbounded and bounded seriality. As an example of unbounded seriality, he again highlights the newspaper, but now as a media form that creates a spatially *serialised* imaginary world (i.e., not just simultaneity). Even the most localised newspaper, Anderson argues, describes the world in categories – politics, crime, business, bureaucracies – that are assumed to exist everywhere without limitations; it is pointless to try to count them. The census, on the other hand, is an example of bounded seriality because it is always assumed to be able to determine, for example, exactly how many Swedes there are at any given time. Nationalist thinking operates with both these forms of seriality: each imagined community is part of an unbounded series of human communities, while the elements that make up each individual

Benedict Anderson (1983)   291

community (people, places, languages, religions, etc.) create bounded series. The concept of seriality introduces into Anderson's theory a dimension of spatiality and geographical comparison as, so to speak, a component of the logic of nationhood he seeks to describe.

Imagined communities

It might be appropriate to say something about the ambiguities and misunderstandings that sometimes arise around Anderson's theories of nationalism. Much of the confusion is related to the very title of the book which rather quickly took on a life of its own. Firstly, the phrase "imagined communities" is easily misunderstood to mean that Anderson regards nations as free fantasies that do not exist "in real life". But this is not how Anderson should be understood. Of course, the fact that the nation is a culturally imagined community does not mean that it lacks reality or significance; once imagined, the nation is very much a reality that has significantly shaped human societies and social affiliations around the world. Sometimes the term "imagined" is also interpreted as Anderson delivering a scathing critique of nationalism in that he seems to expose its delusions. But Anderson's book is rarely characterised by the antagonism of many other scholars. In particular, the aforementioned theorists Ernest Gellner and Eric Hobsbawm were keen to emphasise the unsympathetic aspects of nationalism, and many more scholars point to its link to racism or hatred of "the other". But Anderson is basically sympathetic, pointing out that nationalism has also had positive influences, not least as an inspiration for cultural production (2006: 141). This attitude may seem strangely uncritical, but there is an explanation for it, to which we shall return.

Another reason for this misunderstanding is that many of the scholars inspired by Anderson's book are working in the field of cultural studies, with an interest in representations. Quite reasonably, based on a reading of *Imagined Communities*, one can ask how specific nations have been constructed through representations in history books, art, literature, or the media. Ethnologist Orvar Löfgren, for example, has, in this spirit, concretely described how the press, radio, and television in the 20th century create Sweden as an imagined community by producing and disseminating a specific cultural content that all Swedes are familiar with (1989). But this type of study is rather an extension of Anderson's argument; descriptions of how different nations are represented or what kind of content national representations are filled with are not characteristic of *Imagined Communities*. The book is about how the nation, as a particular form of community, is enabled by specific media technologies and social institutions. In many ways, Anderson's theoretical perspective on the nation is close to a school of thought he does not refer to at all, namely medium theory (see Chapter 8). Curiously, relatively few studies on nationalism have built on this approach (cf. Mihelj, 2011: 11–16).

292   *Per Ståhlberg*

Print capitalism

If the title of the book, *Imagined Communities*, has become Anderson's main contribution to the academic vocabulary, there is another term coined in the study that actually says more about the author's perspective. This is the concept "print capitalism", which is introduced in Chapter 3, entitled "The Origins of National Consciousness". The presentation here takes a somewhat surprising turn. Once Anderson lifts the understanding of nationalism from the concrete political world to human consciousness (changing conceptions of cosmology, power, and time), it turns out that he sees the driving force as highly materialistic: nationalism seems to be fundamentally a notion produced by the emerging capitalism of the 18th century in search of new markets.

The main idea is that it is neither the ideas nor the technology itself that drives change. After all, the art of printing has been known since the 16th century without the emergence of nationalism. What was required was the convergence of a media technology with a mode of production that sought to make ever greater profits. As long as books in Europe were printed in the religious language of Latin, the market was soon saturated. It was only after the printing houses were transformed into capitalist companies that they began to look for new markets. Books had to be printed in languages that more people could read. But the vernacular varieties of languages and dialects spoken by people in Europe were too numerous and diverse for it to be commercially viable to print books in all these various languages and dialects. What happened was that related vernacular languages were merged and standardised into more practical "print languages"; i.e., a form of English, German, Spanish, and so on. This also creates a communicative space, and a reading community, that lies between the spoken languages and Latin. (Again, there is a striking parallel with Habermas and the bourgeois public sphere.) The book thus becomes, Anderson argues, capitalism's first modern mass-produced commodity. The implication of this historiography is that the nation emerges *before* industrialisation and not as an effect of it (as Ernest Gellner and others argued). It should be added that print capitalism must also produce a commodity that people not only can read, but also want to read. The particular forms of commodity that are emerging and reaching ever larger audiences are precisely the novel and the newspaper.

Pilgrims of bureaucracy

When it comes to "print capitalism", the presentation in *Imagined Communities* focuses almost entirely on early market capitalism in Europe. Readers are led to believe that it is obviously on this continent that nationalism first takes shape. But in the chapter that follows, Anderson takes the reader to the Americas and locates the first wave of nationalism in the initiatives of Creole pioneers. This is not only somewhat surprising to the reader, but also a presentation that challenges fundamental assumptions in the previous understanding of the emergence of nationalism. First, nationalism had obviously been understood as a

Benedict Anderson (1983)   293

phenomenon emerging from European ideas and conditions; second, national aspirations had usually been understood as intimately linked to differences in language or ethnicity. However, in the North and South American territories where demands for national independence from the European colonial powers began to emerge from the late 18th century, the leading figures (who were of Spanish, Portuguese, or British descent) shared both language and culture with the countries from which they wanted to break away. How does Anderson explain this?

Indeed, print capitalism emerged early in the American colonies and catered to a very specific audience with its goods, especially newspapers. The essential readers were the America-born Creole officials who governed and administered the vast colonial provinces. The colonial administration worked in such a way that the official was often travelling between locations in the provinces he worked with. The local bureaucrat was placed here and there to carry out his duties; he was continuously transferred to new cities and tasks. But unlike his European-born superiors, the Creole bureaucrat had no real "home" and no overall context for the geography he travelled through. However, on these missions, he meets Creole colleagues who share the same experience. Anderson describes these experiences as a kind of bureaucratic equivalent of the pilgrimages of the great religions (the inspiration from the anthropologist Victor Turner is clear). A form of secular community is created through these experiences and encounters within the colonial administration. In the provincial newspapers that emerged very quickly in both North and South America in the 18th century, this community can be confirmed and eventually leads to the formulation of independence from colonial power in national terms. Nationalism thus emerges, Anderson argues, in America, from where it soon spreads to other parts of the world. This also emphasises the thesis he wants to pursue against several other researchers: that nationalism emerges before the breakthrough of industrialism in Europe.

While it is an important point in *Imagined Communities* that nationalism first emerges outside of Europe, it was a point missed by many readers of the first version of the book. Several early critics even suggested that Anderson had a Eurocentric view of nationalism. This was a criticism that Anderson listened to and was sensitive to, in later editions renaming the America chapter from "Old Empires, New Nations" to "Creole Pioneers". But why was this so important to Anderson? The answer has a lot to do with Anderson's personal background and involvement as an academic and writer.

The author: Benedict Anderson

It is not easy to assign a national affiliation to Benedict Anderson himself. He was born in China (Kunming), educated in the UK (at Cambridge University), worked for most of his professional life in the US (at Cornell University), but after retirement lived in Thailand and died in 2015 during a visit to Indonesia. Anderson's two adopted children are from Indonesia. However, he himself was

294   *Per Ståhlberg*

an Irish citizen, a background he emphasised in the later part of his life by adding his Irish-sounding family name, O'Gorman, between Benedict and Anderson.

It is also not obvious which academic discipline Anderson belongs to; he has been labelled a historian, an anthropologist, and a political scientist. The latter is, strictly speaking, most accurate, but Anderson was a professor of political science at a centre for regional studies of Southeast Asia where disciplinary boundaries were not strict. In *Imagined Communities*, the political science influences are not the most prominent; instead, an anthropological perspective is emphasised (e.g., by considering the nation as a cultural concept). First and foremost, however, Anderson is an authority on Southeast Asia, and he has been particularly interested in Indonesia. However, he was banned from visiting this country between 1972 and 1998 because of a publication critical of the government that he had co-authored. Instead, for three decades he focused his attention on the Philippines and Thailand. In his autobiography, he himself comments that regional experts are often not highly regarded in academia and describes being somewhat surprised when, after the success of *Imagined Communities*, he began to be regarded as a "theorist" in the field of nationalism (2016: 151).

Anderson's long engagement with Southeast Asia also informs his presentation and understanding of nationalism. Firstly, his knowledge of this part of the world often takes over the presentation, which otherwise has transnational ambitions. But it is also clear that Anderson is committed to the region and sympathetic to the anti-colonial movement that emerged here in the 20th century. He fully understands that this struggle is expressed in nationalist forms, and in *Imagined Communities*, colonialism and decolonisation are given a lot of space. Here we also find a reasonable explanation for Anderson's reluctance to see only the dangers and negative aspects of nationalism, but also his insistence that it is not in Europe, but in America, against European domination, that the first nationalists are formed.

Imagined communities in the contemporary world

According to Anderson, nationalism around the world can be described in historical waves. The first wave emerged in the 18th century in the American colonies. Then, in a second wave in the 19th century, the model spread to Europe, which was transformed into nation states, first in opposition to dynastic rule and then, in a third wave, as an official nationalism where old states sought national legitimacy. The fourth and last wave emerged when new independent states were created in the post-war decolonisation, often legitimised by nationalist thinking.

It is not far-fetched to think of a fifth wave with the new nation states that emerged after the fall of the Soviet empire in 1989, and which extends to today's world where nationalist tendencies are growing stronger and are once again reshaping the political landscape in many countries, in Europe as well as in Asia and the Americas. Does *Imagined Communities* have anything to tell us about this contemporary nationalism?

The answer to this question may seem obvious: if the nation has a newfound importance in a world increasingly permeated by media technologies, then of course a classic study discussing the role of media in nationalism should be worth reading. But one could also argue that many of Anderson's arguments seem outdated. If print capitalism in the 18th century played a crucial role in the emergence of nationalism, it can hardly be this form of media technology that now supports the nation. After all, both the capitalist mode of production and the technologies of the media have changed fundamentally. It is difficult to argue that contemporary nationalism can be understood on the principles described by Anderson in *Imagined Communities*. In the global and digital media society, neither narrative nor synchronous simultaneity is as tangible as before. Reading novels and newspapers – or listening to the radio and watching television live – is a continually shrinking part of media consumption of people around the world. Rather, we increasingly live in an everyday life of asynchronous and fragmented digital media that is often not at all characterised by the qualities that Anderson sees as the prerequisites of "thinking" the nation. At least not in the way depicted in *Imagined Communities*.

Based on a reading of Benedict Anderson, it can be argued that the "fifth wave nationalism" we can discern today should not necessarily be equated with previous waves. If the basic conditions have changed, the phenomenon should probably also be understood differently. In fact, Anderson himself, in a later publication in which he discusses contemporary forms of diasporic and transnational nationalism, posed the question: "does capitalism, in its perpetual restlessness, produce new forms of nationalism?" (1998: 59). Anderson has often shown himself open to re-evaluating his own theories, and one could well imagine that today he would have seen new forms of synchronisation and serialisation emerging from the development of media technologies. Or perhaps entirely new concepts are required to describe the dimensions of time and space relevant to the latest wave of nationalism?

When we look at the resurgence of nationalism, we often try to understand its ideas, messages, and activities. What Anderson reminds us of is that the nation was created through the interaction of specific media technologies and a mode of production. Two hundred years ago, this was through "print capitalism". A key to understanding contemporary nationalism is to study the form of "media capitalism" that characterises the world today. What kind of "imagined communities" are produced from the conditions provided by the digital communication technologies and institutions that characterise our own time? It is this perspective that we can learn about by reading Benedict Anderson.

References

Anderson, B. (2006 [1983]). *Imagined Communities: Reflections on the Origin and Spread of Nationalism*. Verso.

Anderson, B. (1998). *The Spectre of Comparisons: Nationalism, Southeast Asia and the World*. Verso.

296 *Per Ståhlberg*

Anderson, B. (2016). *A Life Beyond Boundaries*. Verso.

Gellner, E. (1983). *Nations and Nationalism*. Blackwell.

Gupta, A. (2004). Imagining Nations. In D. Nugent & J. Vincent (Eds.), *Companion to the Anthropology of Politics* (pp. 267–281). Wiley.

Habermas, J. (1989 [1962]). *The Structural Transformation of the Public Sphere: An Inquiry into a Category of Bourgeois Society*. MIT Press.

Hobsbawm, E. & Ranger T. (Eds). (1983). *The Invention of Tradition*. Cambridge University Press.

Löfgren, O. (1989). The Nationalization of Culture. *Ethnologia Europaea*, XIX, 5–23.

Mihelj, S. (2011). *Media Nations: Communicating Belonging and Exclusion in the Modern World*. Palgrave Macmillan.

21 Frederic Jameson (1984) 'Postmodernism, or the Cultural Logic of Late Capitalism'

Anders Burman and Magnus Rodell

Introduction

In those parts of the academic world that systematically reflect on contemporary society, culture and media from a critical perspective, the American literary scholar Fredric Jameson's 'Postmodernism, or the Cultural Logic of Late Capitalism' was one of the most discussed texts at the end of the 20th century. The essay was published in 1984 in the left-wing journal *New Left Review* and became the introduction to Jameson's book with the same name, which was published seven years later.

One of the reasons for the impact of the essay is Jameson's consistent attempt to relate postmodern culture to broader economic, social and political developments. The cultural geographer David Harvey notes that one of Jameson's daring ideas is that 'postmodernism is nothing more than the cultural logic of late capitalism' (Harvey, 1990: 63). The anthology *Modernity and its Futures* (1992) describes how Jameson put forward the idea that 'postmodern culture logically corresponds to a certain stage of capitalist development' (Thompson, 1992: 231). In short, Jameson changed the conditions of the entire debate on postmodernism.

When Jameson published 'Postmodernism, or the Cultural Logic of Late Capitalism', he was a well-established scholar. In 1961, at the age of 27, he had defended a thesis on Jean-Paul Sartre and had subsequently written a series of acclaimed books on Marxist literary criticism, Russian formalism and French structuralism. In 1981, he published his most important work to date, *The Political Unconscious*, which explores the development of the realist novel through a series of contextualising analyses of writers such as Honoré de Balzac and Joseph Conrad. The book, which reinforced Jameson's position as one of the leading Marxist critics of the day and 'probably the most important cultural critic writing in English today' (Roberts, 2000: 1), opens with the imperative 'Always historicise!' – an exhortation Jameson followed throughout his career and that greatly informed his understanding of postmodernism (Jameson, 1981: 9).

The 1984 essay is characterised by a broad historical approach against which Jameson interprets contemporary intellectual, cultural and aesthetic phenomena. The reader is struck by the ease with which Jameson moves through the

DOI: 10.4324/9781003432272-22

298 Anders Burman and Magnus Rodell

landscape of aesthetics theory and continental philosophy, with numerous references not only to artists, architects and writers but also to some of the most well-regarded theorists of the time. In the abundant references, high culture is interspersed with allusions to popular culture, which in itself can be said to be characteristic of postmodernism as well as of the concoction of various more or less impenetrable theories labelled as 'French theory' in the United States of the 1980s. At American universities and liberal arts colleges, students read theorists such as Roland Barthes, Gilles Deleuze, Jacques Derrida, Michel Foucault and Julia Kristeva, and countless academic essays were devoted to deconstructive readings of everything from Shakespeare to Madonna and the TV series *Dallas* (Cusset, 2008).

In general, discussions of postmodernism can be traced back to at least the 1960s. The term had been used earlier, by the Spanish poet Federico de Onís and the British historian Arnold Toynbee, among others, but it was in the context of mass media changes and the vibrant art scene of the 1960s that it began to be used more frequently (Anderson, 1998). There was much talk of postmodernism in literature and architecture in the 1970s, and Jean Baudrillard began to develop his theories on media, hyperreality, simulation and simulacra, which were later interpreted in terms of postmodernism (see Chapter 10 on Baudrillard). The major breakthrough for the concept came in 1979, with the publication of Jean-François Lyotard's *The Postmodern Condition*. In this book, which was a report commissioned by the Quebec provincial government, Lyotard examined what was happening to the status of knowledge in a society that no longer believed in what he calls 'grand narratives' – that is, historical-philosophical narratives about, for instance, the development of reason or freedom – which had previously been intended to give an overall meaning to separate events (Lyotard, 1984).

Lyotard's study attracted a great deal of attention at the time, and the author gained the status of being the postmodern philosopher *par préférence*. However, Lyotard's work was far from convincing everyone. In particular, there was initially widespread scepticism on the left about the new so-called postmodern ideas. In the fall of 1980, Jürgen Habermas gave a lecture in which he attacked the relativism of the postmodern philosophers, which he politically perceived as being part of a broader right-wing project that manifested itself during that decade with Ronald Reagan, Margaret Thatcher and an emerging neoliberalism. Against the postmodern critique, Habermas defended the Enlightenment heritage and the unfinished modern project (Habermas, 1984). Although Habermas did not directly target Lyotard – among the French contemporaries, he mentioned instead Derrida and Foucault – the debate soon came to be referred to as the Lyotard-Habermas debate. With an implicit reference to Habermas, Lyotard would later describe postmodernism as 'a war on totality' (Lyotard, 1986: 132). Like many of his contemporaries, Lyotard associated postmodernism with the elusive, random, distinctive and fragmentary.

When the English translation of Lyotard's book was published in 1984, it contained a foreword signed by Jameson (Jameson, 1984a). Here, Jameson

Frederic Jameson (1984)   299

outlines the main features of the book, although he also notes that the grand narratives that the French philosopher claims have lost their legitimating power in the postmodern condition have not disappeared at all but have merely gone underground and continue to operate at a politically unconscious level (Jameson, 1984a: xii). For example, the belief in the market and constant economic growth may be understood as a still-dominant grand narrative.

Given that 'Postmodernism, or the Cultural Logic of Late Capitalism' was published in the same year as the preface to Lyotard's book, it is remarkable that the French postmodernist is not mentioned at all in the essay. An important difference between the two is that, while Lyotard speaks in the name of postmodernism, Jameson analyses postmodern culture from an outside perspective. When Jameson discuss postmodernism, he does so without claiming to be a typical postmodernist himself.

If Jameson's text initially functioned as a contemporary diagnosis, it has since been used as a way to historicise the 1980s. Opening up to both of these approaches, we would here like to clarify the main points of Jameson's overall understanding of postmodernism based on the characteristics that he highlights as the crucial features of postmodern culture, emphasising the notions of depthlessness, the death of the subject, the weakening of history and a new kind of spatiality.

Capitalism and postmodernism

In the introduction to 'Postmodernism, or the Cultural Logic of Late Capitalism', it is already clear that the author wants to diagnose and understand his time:

> The last few years have been marked by an inverted millennarianism, in which premonitions of the future, catastrophic or redemptive, have been replaced by senses of the end of this or that (the end of ideology, art, or social class; the 'crisis' of Leninism, social democracy, or the welfare state, etc., etc.).
>
> (Jameson, 1984b: 53)

As a Christian concept related to notions of the imminent millennium, millenarianism is used by Jameson in a broader sense to denote that the belief that we are on the verge of profound changes in society in the contemporary world has been reversed or cancelled. This belief can be linked to what Jameson perceives as an increasing sense of the present and a weakening of historical thinking, as well as a related inability to imagine another world. As he later noted, we now find it easier to imagine the end of the world than an alternative social order (Jameson, 2003: 76). Even more today than in 1984, contemporary capitalism tends to be presented as a part of the natural order.

However, Jameson himself argues that it is necessary to understand capitalism in a historical perspective; otherwise, postmodernism cannot be understood either. To historicise the capitalist system, he draws on the theories of Belgian economist Ernest Mandel. In *Late Capitalism* (1975), Mandel identifies three main stages in the history of modern capitalism, which he links to an equal number of 'power technology' revolutions. Under market capitalism in the mid-19th century, mechanical production was characterised by steam-powered engines. In contrast, monopoly capitalism from the late 19th century onwards was dominated by combustion engines and electric motors, while in the post-war period – the era of late capitalism – the corresponding function is played by nuclear and electronic machines.

In line with the historical narrative, both Mandel and Jameson criticise the notion of the American sociologist Daniel Bell and others that we now live in a post-industrial society that 'no longer obeys the laws of classical capitalism' (Jameson, 1984b: 55). According to them, this is not the case. Contemporary society rather represents 'a *purer* stage of capitalism than any of the moments that preceded it' (Jameson, 1984b: 55).

According to Jameson, the three periods in the history of capitalism have temporal equivalents in the aesthetic field in the form of the stages of realism, modernism and postmodernism. In his terminology, this means that realism was the cultural dominant of 19th century market capitalism, while avantgarde modernism was the cultural dominant of monopoly capitalism, just as post-modernism is the same in our own late capitalist society. However, it is important to note that postmodernism has a different social function today than modernism had at the beginning of the 20th century. Art and culture have now become an integral part of the economic cycle. Thus, Jameson concludes 'that every position on postmodernism in culture', whether defended or rejected, is also 'an implicitly or explicitly political stance on the nature of multinational capitalism today' (Jameson, 1984b: 55).

In other words, instead of being reduced to an aesthetic style, postmodernism should be understood within the context of a much wider social and cultural transformation. It is against this background that Jameson describes post-modernism as the cultural logic of late capitalism and as its cultural dominant. This does not mean that he believes that all art, architecture and literature created today is postmodern. However, he perceives postmodern art and literature as the most contemporary and dominant cultural expression in our late capitalist society. From his basic Marxist perspective, Jameson also notes that postmodern culture has a dark political underside: 'that this whole global, yet American, postmodern culture is the internal and superstructural expression of a whole new wave of American military and economic domination throughout the world: in this sense, as throughout class history, the underside of culture is blood, torture, death and horror' (Jameson, 1984b: 57).

Jameson is far from affirming everything related to postmodernism. Rather, he understands the cultural development of late capitalism in the same dialectical way that Marx understood capitalism and its associated bourgeois culture – namely, 'positively *and* negatively all at once', as both 'the best thing that has ever happened to the human race, and the worst' (Jameson, 1984b: 86).

Frederic Jameson (1984) 301

Beyond high modernism

Postmodernism is a distinctly contrastive concept. Its meaning shifts in relation to what the modernity or modernism it is set against is thought to imply. In 'Postmodernism, or the Cultural Logic of Late Capitalism', Jameson contrasts postmodern culture with what he calls 'high modernism'. More specifically, he links high modernist art, architecture, literature and music to the academisation and institutionalisation of the early 20th century modernist avantgarde in the post-war period. Teaching and research on modernism began at universities, and museums of modern art were built around the world. At the same time, the prices of canonised modernist artworks rose with the expansion of the international art market and rapid economic development in general.

In another essay from the early 1980s, 'Postmodernism and the Consumer Society', Jameson writes that high modernist art from the 1940s onwards 'conquered the university, the museum, the art gallery network and the foundations' (Jameson, 1998: 2). He exemplifies high modernism with American abstract expressionists such as Jackson Pollock and Mark Rothko; poets such as Ezra Pound, T. S. Eliot and Wallace Stevens; fiction writers such as James Joyce, Marcel Proust and Thomas Mann; architects such as Le Corbusier and Mies van der Rohe; and the composer Igor Stravinsky. While this type of modernism had previously been perceived as scandalous, it appeared to young people in the 1960s and beyond as 'dead, stifling, canonical, the reified monuments one has to destroy to do anything new' (Jameson, 1998: 2). It was in accordance with this logic that postmodern architects, artists and writers distanced themselves from and defined themselves in relation to high modernism. This contrast was most evident in the field of architecture, where the postmodernists loudly criticised the high modernist style. High modernist or international architecture was 'credited with the destruction of the fabric of the traditional city', and even the image of the charismatic architect was criticised (Jameson, 1984b: 54).

Within high modernism, there was a strong notion of a 'true' art that was thought to stand in a clear and hierarchical relationship to more superficial, popular cultural expressions. The postmodern representatives also turned against this conception in favour of what Jameson calls 'aesthetic populism'. The new aesthetic approach is already hinted at in the title of Robert Venturi, Denise Scott Brown and Steven Isenour's classic book *Learning from Las Vegas* (1972). This work of architectural theory highlighted two tendencies that would come to characterise different types of postmodern expressions: a rejection of high modernism's distinction between 'high culture and so-called mass or commercial culture'; and an affirmative interest in highlighting the features of the popular culture industry that had previously been rejected by 'all the ideologues of the modern', including Theodor W. Adorno and the other members of the Frankfurt School (Jameson, 1984b: 54). In short, postmodernism moves beyond the distinction between high culture and mass culture that was constitutive of high modernism. Postmodernism is playful and affirms much of what had previously been perceived as low and kitschy.

The new depthlessness

To identify the key differences between high modernism and postmodernism, Jameson chooses to analyse several works of art. Although he primarily associates high modernism with post-war aesthetic developments, he highlights Vincent van Gogh's painting *Peasant Shoes* from 1887 as a representative work of modernism. Jameson argues that, in the interpretation of that painting, it is possible 'to reconstruct some initial situation out of which the finished work emerges', by which he refers to the harsh living conditions of the rural population in the second half of the 19th century (Jameson, 1984b: 58). It is their conditions, brutal existence and object world that the painting relates to. In *Peasant Shoes*, as well as in some of van Gogh's landscape paintings, the contrast between the dullness of peasant life and the oil painting's use of sumptuous colours is striking. The paintings' explosions of colour can thus be interpreted as 'an act of compensation' leading to 'a whole new Utopian realm of the senses'. According to Jameson, this reading can be described as hermeneutic in that it interprets the work 'as a clue or symptom for some vaster reality which replaces it as its ultimate truth' (Jameson, 1984b: 59).

In contrast to this modernist artwork and the related hermeneutic model of interpretation, Jameson highlights Andy Warhol's *Diamond Dust Shoes* from 1980 as an artwork typical of postmodernism. Warhol's fetishistic high-heeled shoes stand for something completely different than van Gogh's peasant shoes. The misery van Gogh depicted is absent. Jameson states that Warhol's shoes do 'not really speak to us at all' (Jameson, 1984b: 59). In fact, in *Diamond Dust Shoes*, the viewer seems to encounter nothing more than 'a random collection of dead objects' that cannot be used to hermeneutically recreate an original context. What Warhol's painting shows is a crucial tendency in postmodern art and culture: namely, 'the emergence of a new kind of flatness or depthlessness' (Jameson, 1984b: 60).

In Jameson's analysis, depthlessness is closely related to what he calls the 'waning of affect'. He clarifies this feature of postmodern culture with the help of a contrasting example taken from art history: Edvard Munch's *The Scream* from 1893. Munch's painting may be viewed as a collective expression of modernism's themes 'of alienation, anomie, solitude and social fragmentation and isolation' (Jameson, 1984b: 61). While the painting conveys these feelings, it can also be interpreted as a kind of dismantling of the aesthetics of these emotional expressions and as a deconstruction of the aesthetic approaches that characterised high modernism. The anxiety-laden aesthetics of expression that *The Scream* both conveys and dismantles have little to do with emotionally muted postmodernism. 'This is not to say that the cultural products of the postmodern era are utterly devoid of feeling', Jameson explains, 'but rather that such feelings – which it may be better and more accurate to call "intensities" – are now free-floating and impersonal' (Jameson, 1984b: 64).

Jameson emphasises that postmodern depthlessness is not only an aesthetic concern; it also characterises much of contemporary theoretical thinking. He speaks of different theoretical depth models that have been challenged in different ways in the contemporary world, which he sees as a sign of a postmodern culture. More specifically, Jameson distinguishes five such models: the hermeneutic model of inside and outside; the Marxist dialectical model of essence and appearance, along with the concept of ideology; the psychoanalytic model of manifest and latent (e.g. a dream's secret content that requires interpretative work to uncover); the existential model of authenticity according to which we can live our life in either a genuine, authentic way or an inauthentic way; and, finally, the semiotic model of the signifier and the signified, an opposition that, according to Jameson, was 'rapidly unravelled and deconstructed during its brief heyday in the 1960s and 70s' (Jameson, 1984b: 62).

All these models are based on the notion that truth, in one way or another, is hidden beneath the surface and can only be revealed through some kind of interpretive work. According to Jameson, it is this basic assumption that now has been questioned. Instead, postmodernism and poststructuralism prefer to speak of practices, discourses and intertextual games – that is, a kind of surface phenomena without any depth where the truth is thought to be hidden. Indeed, as Jameson notes, the concept of truth is seen as 'part of the metaphysical baggage which poststructuralism seeks to abandon' (Jameson, 1984b: 61).

The status of the subject and history

Postmodernists and poststructuralists also question the modernist notion of the individual creative subject. Within high modernism, this concept of the subject, as well as the idea of a unique style, had been taken for granted. The notion of the sovereign subject, which had its heyday from around the middle of the 19th century until the end of the Second World War, was not only the basis for what was perceived as great art; it was also a subject that took control of nature through its scientific and technological achievements. In addition, it was an imperial Western male subject that subjugated other continents.

The treatment of the status of the subject in the context of postmodernism illustrates why the depth models discussed above have lost their validity. The alienation of the subject exemplified by Munch's painting has been replaced by a notion of the fragmentation of the subject. Jameson specifies this in the text – firstly, as a dissolution of the bourgeois individual that is paralleled by a decentring 'of that formerly centred subject or psyche' (Jameson, 1984b: 63). Secondly, he brings up the 'death of the subject' in a discussion of how the role of the film star has shifted from male actors such as Marlon Brando and Steve McQueen to the contemporary image of major stars who, according to Jameson, are almost entirely devoid of personality in the traditional sense. Rather than referring to various theories of the death of the subject, Jameson connects this empirical observation to the contemporary use of nostalgia and, more generally, to the status of history in postmodernism – a theme he dwells on much more than the death of the subject.

304 *Anders Burman and Magnus Rodell*

The literary scholar Christopher Butler argues that one of the central themes of postmodernism is a loss of realism. He links this theme to Jameson's argument that one of the defining features of postmodernism is the disappearance of a natural relationship with history. Postmodernism is characterised by a pervasive depthlessness and an ever-present now in which the memory of the tradition has been lost. Butler notes that, for many postmodernists, 'something in the actual state of society led to this' (Butler, 2002: 110).

With the collapse of high modernism and its idea of a valid ideology of style, Jameson argues, artists no longer have 'nowhere to turn to but to the past' (1984b: 65), as they typically have no actual relationship with this past. Rather, the postmodern tendency is usually an imitation of 'dead styles, speech through all the masks and voices stored up in the imaginary museum of a now global culture' (1984b: 65). This tendency is particularly evident in postmodern architecture, which arbitrarily 'cannibalises all the architectural styles of the past' (1984b: 66). 'The postmodern era is one of incessant choice', as the architect Charles Jencks succinctly puts it (Jencks, 1987: 7). The retrospective and citational dimension of postmodern culture in general and its architecture in particular can be illustrated by an example borrowed from the religious scholar Ira Chernus. A postmodern building can combine elements of Egyptian, Gothic, Victorian and modern architecture, with each element being interpreted in its own way without any overarching interpretive code explaining the style combination as such. Each element becomes, as it were, free-floating, disconnected from its original context with no meaning beyond itself (Chernus, 1992).

Something similar applies to the postmodern view of history in general. Here, too, something has been lost: the sense of an 'organic' connection with history. In the 1980s, when Jameson wrote his essay, he argued that there was no longer such an organic relationship between 'the American history we learn from the schoolbooks' and the experience of 'the current multinational, high-rise' metropolis of the newspapers and everyday life, characterised by high unemployment and high inflation (Jameson, 1984b: 69). The loss of an organic connection with history is emphasised in Jameson's analysis of the concepts of pastiche, simulacra and nostalgia.

Jameson describes pastiche as the imitation of 'a peculiar mask, speech in a dead language'. It is a 'blank parody, a statue with blind eyeballs' (Jameson, 1984b: 65). In an elaboration of Jameson's theory of postmodernism, Jonathan Clark argues that pastiche can be understood as a superficial and empty imitation of styles and as a transformation of an accumulated past into pure images, in what is commonly called 'simulacrum'. As 'an identical copy for which no original ever existed', this postmodern form of simulacrum consists of copies that have been created 'for the sole purpose of becoming mass-produced signs (such as corporate logos)' (Clark, 1996: para. 18). In postmodern culture, pastiche and simulacrum are utterly dominant, which – according to Jameson – has a 'fatal effect on what used to be historical time'. The past as a 'referent' becomes 'gradually bracketed', eventually being cancelled altogether, 'leaving us with nothing but texts' (Jameson, 1984b: 66).

The point is that we are now surrounded by a constant flow of shifting images – something that is even more relevant in the early 21st century than when Jameson wrote his essay – and that this has contributed to the loss of the ability to think historically. What Jameson highlights as a dominant 'postmodernist "nostalgia" art language', which he argues cannot be reconciled 'with genuine historicity', emerges from so-called nostalgia films, for example (Jameson, 1984b: 67). The prototype for these films was *American Graffiti* (1973), which was spun off into the popular TV series *Happy Days* (1974–1984). Other similar films include *Grease* (1978), *Back to the Future* (1985) and Lukas Moodysson's *Together* (2000) (Lindgren, 2009: 166). Such nostalgia films try to relive the past through stereotypes and cultural myths. For example, a sense of the past can be conveyed through glossy film images or through various artefacts and fashions typical of, say, the 1950s or 1980s. Just as the 1950s were fantasised through *American Graffiti*, so Oliver Stone created a simulacrum of the 1960s. 'For us', Chernus writes, referring to three films by Stone, 'the Platoon is the Vietnam War, Anthony Hopkins is Nixon, and Val Kilmer is Morrison' (Chernus, 1992).

The new spatiality – the example of the Bonaventura Hotel

The weakening of historical consciousness has gone hand in hand with an accentuation of spatial consciousness. With examples from architecture, Jameson illustrates how contemporary life is characterised by spatial rather than temporal categories. It is in the field of architecture that postmodernism as a cultural dominant and cultural logic appears most clearly, he argues, partly because the concentration of big capital and artistic expression so clearly merge in architecture. In Los Angeles, the Westin Bonaventura Hotel was built between 1974 and 1976, designed by American architect John Portman. This hotel, the largest in the city, quickly became a popular destination for tourists and locals alike. Jameson visited the hotel in connection with a conference, and his experience became central to his analysis of postmodernism and its orientation from the temporal to the spatial (Soja, 2015).

If the architectural language of high modernism was concerned with producing something different from the old, while often being charged with utopian energies, then postmodern architecture strives not only to be popular – preferably incorporating a commercial sign system – but also to follow what Jameson calls the 'vernacular of the American city fabric' (Jameson, 1984b: 80). This is evident in the Bonaventura Hotel and its relationship to its surrounding urban space. To begin with, the hotel has three entrances but none of them are easy to find – which is a clear difference from the monumental gates of high modernism that were almost impossible to miss. According to Jameson, the design of the Bonaventura Hotel creates 'a total space, a complete world, a kind of miniature city', which, through its large reflective glass façade, rejects the surrounding city (Jameson, 1984b: 81). The glass enclosure does not even function as an exterior, since what the viewer encounters is merely a reflection of the city that surrounds the hotel.

306 *Anders Burman and Magnus Rodell*

When the Bonaventure's visitors enter the hotel's atrium or vestibule, the language of volume is overridden. The size is simply not possible to appreciate. The sense of being engulfed by space, Jameson argues, can be understood as the architectural equivalent of what we perceive in other media as a repression of depth. The hotel consists of four symmetrical towers, which makes it almost impossible for the visitor in the lobby to create a functioning orientation. This can be seen as an illustration of what Jameson calls the postmodern 'hyperspace', which exceeds the human capacity for orientation. In this hyperspace, people have no overview. Jameson sees a clear parallel between this and our general inability to make sense of the multinational and global 'decentred communicational networks' in which we are trapped 'as individual subjects' (Jameson, 1984b: 84). In other words, postmodern architecture is as evasive and conceptually elusive as late capitalism.

The aesthetics of cognitive mapping

Is it then possible to identify some tools through which it would be possible to grasp the postmodern as a social and cultural condition? To answer this question, Jameson outlines an aesthetic and theoretical programme for what he calls 'cognitive mapping' at the end of the essay.

In general, Jameson's approach to history and the present is at odds in many ways with what he emphasises in the essay as the distinctive features of postmodern culture. Without ignoring the importance of spatial categories, he holds onto a rather traditional historical thinking. As discussed earlier, he assumes that a painting such as van Gogh's *Peasant Shoes* or a building such as Portman's Bonaventure Hotel manifests something beyond the work itself. In this way, Jameson politically and aesthetically interprets various past and present phenomena as signs of something with general validity. This pursuit of generality is an integral part of the aesthetics of cognitive mapping.

According to Jameson, cognitive maps 'enable a situational representation on the part of the individual subject to that vaster and properly unrepresentable totality which is the ensemble of the city's structure as a whole'. What he calls for is a social equivalent to this mapping work. Following the French Marxist Louis Althusser, Jameson uses the concept of ideology in connection with Jacques Lacan's structuralist psychoanalysis. Lacan distinguishes what he calls 'three registers' that structure human existence: the symbolic, which has to do with language in the broadest sense; the imaginary, which relates to our dreams and fantasies; and the real, which deals with the ultimate reality that we cannot really access. Based on the latter two registers, Althusser defines ideology as a 'representation of the subject's *Imaginary* relationship to his or her *Real* conditions of existence' (Jameson, 1984b: 90). In cognitive mapping, however, it is important to consider the symbolic, linguistic register as well. Only then can the social map become sufficiently complex to really contribute to our political orientation. Based on this description, it is worth asking whether this can be understood as an aesthetic parallel to Jameson's own theoretical and historical work. For is it not precisely a mapping of the contemporary cultural landscape that he offers, which helps the reader to orientate herself in late capitalist society?

In 'Postmodernism, or the Cultural Logic of Late Capitalism', Jameson gives no examples of works that respond to the aesthetics of cognitive mapping. In other texts, however, he mentions authors such as the Chinese scholar Lu Xun and the Senegalese researcher Sembene Ousmane (Kellner, 1989: 34). In addition, Jameson emphasises that cognitive mapping requires the invention of 'radically new forms' (Jameson, 1984b: 92). If such a new political art is to be possible at all, he argues, it 'will have to hold to the truth of postmodernism, that is, to say, to its fundamental object – the world space of multinational capital' (Jameson, 1984b: 92). This is a remarkable statement in many ways. Although many postmodern theorists want to put the question of truth in brackets, Jameson imagines that postmodernism itself has a truth that is not primarily related to things like fragmentation or a suspicion of grand narratives. No, the truth of postmodernism, according to Jameson, consists of the object or objects with which it is somehow concerned – that is, the elusive global space of contemporary capital that cognitive mapping is supposed to help us orient ourselves in, a context in which various spatial dimensions have become increasingly central.

Whatever one may think of this, it is clear that it was largely through Jameson's radical historicisation and broad global outlook that he contributed to postmodernism being perceived as a left-wing project in the 1980s (Anderson, 1998). In other words, it was after – if not with – the publication of 'Postmodernism, or the Cultural Logic of Late Capitalism' that the scepticism towards postmodernism previously expressed by Habermas and large parts of the left began to change. Since then, postmodernism has become increasingly associated with the left. When the term is used today – which is not nearly as often as it was in the 1980s – it usually refers to things associated with the left, whether it be identity politics or ideological cultural analyses. Instead of being understood as the cultural logic of late capitalism, postmodernism has now been reduced to what is sometimes called the 'postmodern left'.

It is also clear that some of the characteristics of postmodernism that Jameson identified in 1984 are not as relevant today. For example, the theme of the 'death of the subject' seems less relevant today than it was in the 1980s. Posthumanism has certainly emerged as a strong field in recent decades, but it problematises human beings and the subject in different ways than those Jameson focused on. But, above all, there is reason to claim that another form of subject and subjectivity gained an increasingly strong position in the early 2000s. If you want to read contemporary cultural dominance, you should no longer turn to the field of architecture, where postmodernism is now mostly used as a dirty word. The clearest expressions of the contemporary aesthetic and political unconscious can be found elsewhere – whether in the autofiction masterpieces created by authors such as Annie Ernaux and Karl Ove Knausgård or in the ways in which most of us constantly create images of ourselves on social media. These are just a few examples of contexts in which meaning-making subjects now occupy a prominent role.

308 *Anders Burman and Magnus Rodell*

Nevertheless, we would like to conclude by arguing that the cultural logic that is dominant in our (still) late capitalist society can be said to be typically postmodern in Jameson's sense. Even more so than in the 1980s, we live in an era of constant choice, with no absolute and eternally valid truths to rely on. Not least because of this, we are still in great need of the kind of orientating narratives and contemporary diagnoses that Jameson so convincingly presents in 'Postmodernism, or the Cultural Logic of Late Capitalism'.

References

Anderson, P. (1998). *The origins of postmodernity*. Verso.

Butler, C. (2002). *Postmodernism: A very short introduction*. Oxford University Press.

Chernus, I. (1992). *Fredric Jameson's interpretation of postmodernism*. University of Colorado. https://spot.colorado.edu/~chernus/NewspaperColumns/LongerEssays/JamesonPostmodernism.htm.

Clark, J. (1996). Fredric Jameson's postmodern Marxism: A politics of aesthetic representation. *Cogito*, 4.

Cusset, F. (2008). *French theory: How Foucault, Derrida, Deleuze, & co. transformed the intellectual life in the United States* (J. Fort, Trans.). University of Minnesota Press.

Habermas, J. (1984). Modernity – An incomplete project. In H. Foster (Ed.), *The anti-aesthetic: Essays on postmodern culture* (pp. 3–16). Bay Press.

Harvey, D. (1990). *The condition of postmodernity: An enquiry into the origins of cultural change*. Blackwell.

Jameson, F. (1981). *The political unconscious: Narrative as a socially symbolic act*. Methuen.

Jameson, F. (1984a). Foreword. In J.-F. Lyotard, *The postmodern condition: A report on knowledge* (G. Bennington & B. Massumi, Trans.) (pp. vii–xxi). University of Minnesota Press.

Jameson, F. (1984b). Postmodernism or the cultural logic of late capitalism. *New Left Review*, 1(146): 53–92.

Jameson, F. (1988). Cognitive mapping. In C. Nelson & L. Grossberg (Eds.), *Marxism and the interpretation of culture* (pp. 347–360). University of Illinois Press.

Jameson, F. (1991). *Postmodernism, or, the cultural logic of late capitalism*. Verso.

Jameson, F. (1998). *The cultural turn. Selected writings on the postmodern, 1983–1998*. Verso.

Jameson, F. (2003). Future city. *New Left Review* (21).

Jencks, C. (1987). *What is post-modernism?* (2nd ed.). Academy Ed.

Kellner, D. (1989). Introduction: Jameson, Marxism, and postmodernism. In D. Kellner (Ed.), *Postmodernism: Jameson critique* (pp. 1–42). Washington: Maisonneuve Press.

Lindgren, S. (2009). *Populärkultur: Teorier, metoder och analyser*. Liber.

Lyotard, J.-F. (1984). *The postmodern condition: A report on knowledge* (G. Bennington & B. Massumi, Trans.). University of Minnesota Press.

Lyotard, J.-F. (1986). Answering the question: What is postmodernism? (R. Durand, Trans.). In K. Crome & J. Williams (Eds.), *The Lyotard reader and guide* (pp. 123–132). Columbia University Press.

Roberts, A. (2000). *Fredric Jameson*. Routledge.

Soja, E. (2015). Ed Soja – The postmodern city / Bonaventure Hotel [Video]. *Archive56.org*. https://archive56dotorg.wordpress.com/2015/11/30/ed-soja-the-postmodern-city-bonaventure-hotel-2/.

Stephanson, A. (1989). Regarding postmodernism: A conversation with Fredric Jameson. In D. Kellner (Ed.), *Postmodernism/Jameson/critique* (pp. 43–74). Maisonneuve Press.

Thompson, K. (1992). Social pluralism and post-modernity. In S. Hall (Ed.), *Modernity and its futures* (pp. 221–272). Polity Press.

22 Janice Radway (1984) *Reading the Romance*

Stina Bengtsson

A book about female popular culture

Reading the Romance (RTR) is a classical text in Cultural Studies. It significantly contributed to early feminist theory and studies of popular culture (Storey, 1993/1997). Furthermore, it is an early media ethnography and a milestone in media reception theory. This chapter will contextualize and discuss the book's theoretical contributions and show how and why it is one of the classics in media theory.

RTR revolves around a significant type of popular culture: romance books, mass-produced for (mainly) female readers, that are characterized by stereotypical characters, repetitive and formulaic topics, simple crimes, one-dimensional villains, and, of course, romantic love. In the romance book genre, Canadian book publisher Harlequin's book series is one of the most well-known, but worldwide there are many romance book series reaching vast audiences.

Until about the 1960s, mass-produced culture was either harshly criticized by academic scholars or ignored. There was a fear that mass-produced culture would destroy traditional folk culture (which was considered part of everyday culture and created by the users themselves), by either accentuating subversive ideas and enflaming the "masses" to fight the power or, on the contrary, cradling them into "false consciousness" and hence obstructing the kind of change that would take them out of their oppressed position. In the post-war period, however, scholars started to develop new perspectives on mass-produced popular culture, aiming to understand it in new critical ways and in its own right. *Reading the Romance* is a central academic text in this tradition. The author, Janice Radway, is an American researcher, and her study was conducted in the United States. Despite this, the book is often discussed in relation to the British Birmingham School as it has many similarities in terms of research topics, theoretical perspectives, methods, and so on, with British Cultural Studies. However, when undertaking her study and writing her book, Radway was unaware of the research tradition that emerged in Britain during the 1960s and 1970s and the studies produced there (Radway, 1987: chapter one). Yet, the similarity between RTR and other contemporary texts, such as Stuart Hall's work on encoding-decoding (see Chapter 11 in this volume), is not surprising considering

DOI: 10.4324/9781003432272-23

the general political and theoretical developments during this time, such as the renewed interest in Marxist theory and a growing interest in feminist theory. RTR is often mentioned in overviews of classic texts in the Cultural Studies tradition (Storey, 1993/1997, 1994) and in discussions about the tension between British and American Cultural Studies (see Chapter 11 in this volume).

The book is, however, also part of a broader feminist scholarship and an often-referenced example in feminist literature. During the 1970s, feminist movements in the Western world grew on both sides of the Atlantic. In Birmingham in the UK, for example, several female Media and Cultural Studies researchers put together the book *Women Take Issue* (Women's Studies Group-Centre for Contemporary Cultural Studies, 1978), which presented analyses of contemporary culture using Feminist, Marxist, and Psychoanalytical theory. *The Female Gaze* (Gamman & Marschment, 1988) was published in the United States as part of a parallel initiative. This time saw a newly awakened and strong interest in feminist perspectives in cultural research (see also Chapter 14 in this volume).

An exemplary scientific work

Surprisingly many of the works presented in this volume are introduced as different, even unique, and not adhering to scientific norms (see, for example, the chapters on Benjamin, McLuhan, and Anderson). The opposite must be said about RTR: it is an emblematic example of how academic work is conducted and, thus, an excellent book to introduce to students. Why is that so? It asks research questions based on a theoretical framework, presents broad yet well-defined empirical material, uses established analysis models to address the empirical material, and shows well-developed sensitivity and reflexivity in interpretation and analytical conclusions. One can ask whether there is a connection between a scholar's gender and the extent to which they must adapt to the framework of scholarly work if they want to make theoretical contributions and reach analytical conclusions. Without answering that question, we can still conclude that RTR is a very good example of an academic work. Its open and curious approach to the empirical material led to the development of new empirical perspectives and theoretical contributions, beyond simply providing answers to the questions initially asked.

What makes this book not only an excellent example of the academic genre and very well executed but also unique in media research at the time, is that it analyses a whole chain of cultural processes, from production and distribution of romance books, via genre and text, to content, audience perspectives, and the situated practice of reading. Radway twists and turns the notion of romance books in many different ways over a long time. The result is that from basic questions formulated from an interest in reception studies and interpretive communities, as well as in the limits of a literary text, the study ends up in a rich Marxist-Feminist analysis that paves the way for a whole tradition of ethnographically inspired studies of women's and female culture, media culture, and popular culture.

312   *Stina Bengtsson*

What was the original question?

RTR is often put forward as one of the milestones in Cultural Studies, and as with other works considered classics, the book was part of shaping the tradition rather than being born in the middle of it. Janice Radway is a trained scholar in comparative literature and, like many other researchers at the time, turned her scientific gaze toward types of culture that previous researchers had largely overlooked, namely mass-produced culture, women's culture, and popular culture, in an attempt to understand its texts and audiences better. In so doing she also expanded the boundaries of what research is allowed to do. RTR was born from an interest in popular literature, which merged with an interest in feminist theory, nurtured in the reading circles where women in the 1970s met to delve into feminist literature, outside of the seminar rooms of the universities (see also Chapter 14 in this volume for a similar example).

During the 1960s and 1970s, new ways of thinking about literature were developed within structuralist theory and semiotics, with the meaning of a text becoming detached from its author and the text itself, and the primary focus shifting to the reader. In the semiotician Roland Barthes' famous text *The Death of the Author*, he states:

> a text is made of multiple writings, drawn from many cultures and entering into mutual relations of dialogue, parody, contestation, but there is one place where this multiplicity is focused and that place is the reader, not, as was hitherto said, the author.
>
> (Barthes, 1977: 148)

Researchers in reception theory, devoted to understanding the reception of texts, started to explore how the meaning of texts could travel through time, seeking to understand how a literary classic is made: why are certain texts meaningful to audiences across time and space while others immediately lose their magic and feel irrelevant just after a short period, or when read outside of their geographical context (cf. Iser, 1978)? The meaning of the text, contemporary theorists claimed, is born when the text and reader meet; it does not exist in the text itself.

Literary scholar Stanley Fish, in the 1960s, coined the concept of interpretive communities, which argued that the meaning of texts is shaped in cultural communities of readers, emphasizing the social and broader contextual meanings of reading (Fish, 1980). Fish's theory was developed from studies of the interpretive communities of literary scholars and reviewers, and others: educated readers who approached new literary works with an academically trained eye.

Radway instead put the theory of interpretive communities to work in a different context, with a different kind of reader and relating to a mass-produced and formulaic type of (popular) literature. The theoretical question initially asked in Radway's project had its roots in literary reception theory, a theory that also inspired the emerging fields of Cultural and Media Studies, visible in for example Stuart Hall's encoding-decoding model of communication (see Chapter 11 in this volume) and contemporary research projects such as Charlotte Brunsdon's and David Morley's Nationwide Project (Brunsdon and Morley, 1978). To answer the question, Radway combined Marxist-Feminist theory with narrative and psychoanalytic theory, studying the production and distribution of the books, the texts, and readers' interpretation and meaning-making processes.

Production and distribution of romance books

The study begins with an analysis of the books' production process, how the publisher works with authors, conducts audience analyses, and how the results of these analyses influence the production. A particular bookseller, Dot, and the distribution of the books is also included. Dot used to send newsletters to her clients with reviews, information about new books, and ratings of books, gathering a circle of readers around her. Dot is a core person in the book as a key informant who establishes contact with the readers of the books. In addition, this part of RTR is an early example of what was later discussed as participatory culture (Jenkins, 2006), fan communities (Fiske, 1992; Jenkins, 1992/2012), and so on. However, the romance readers are not organized as a network in any formal sense; they do not meet and do not discuss the books with each other but form a loose group through relationships with authors and publishers through the bookseller Dot.

Reading in a social context

With contemporary reception theory as a vantage point, Radway looked beyond traditional literary text analysis and embarked on thorough qualitative and quantitative analyses of the readers. This part of the study was initially centred around the content of the books: Radway asked questions about readers' taste preferences, the characters of the hero and heroine, the types of stories readers preferred, and so on. But the answers she got repeatedly directed her away from the texts and toward the social context of reading. The readers were all women, most of them housewives, many also mothers. They spent their days caring for the households of their husbands and children and helped them manage their lives outside the home (at work, school, activities, and so on). The women were hence dependent on others, not only economically, but also to make their everyday tasks meaningful. In the interviews, the readers frequently highlighted romance reading as an enjoyable activity as it required their full attention, creating a space only for them. In this cultural context, women's reading made an escape from the duties of family life and a way to spend time on their own needs, forming a micro-rebellion against their subordinate role in the family. Based on this, Radway concluded that reading is an ambiguous act meaningful to readers as both instruction and escape. The women continuously emphasized all that they learnt from the books, legitimizing the time they spent

314   *Stina Bengtsson*

on this activity that so many considered useless, a group of readers often looked down upon by those around them.

The escape dimension is ambiguous. The readers clearly stated that the characters in the books neither resembled them nor the people and events that made up their own lives to any significant extent. They were also open with their preferences within the genre of romance books, clearly preferring some books more than others. Their favourite books were those in which the heroine lived an exciting life in an interesting place and in which the hero adhered to a traditional masculinity yet being very tender, looking after the heroine with almost motherly care, helping her develop a strong and independent female identity. The stories and the characters in the books were interpreted in relation to the readers' own experiences, which meant constantly giving of what you have to support and care for others, but without getting the same in return, neither from husband nor child. Despite these discrepancies, Radway argued, readers identified with the heroines' exciting lives to temporarily escape their own lives, immersing themselves in the emotionally healing relationships between heroines and heroes in the books. But the act of reading also constituted a very concrete way of escaping their reality, as the act of reading created a space where the women could forget about housewifery and their focus on others and sit down and devote time to the sheer pleasures of reading.

The escape dimension is ambivalent also as the act of reading was associated with guilt. The women felt guilty because reading kept them from other more altruistic tasks and was a waste of (useful) time. They also felt guilty because books cost money, something the women did not have at their disposal. And they felt guilt (and shame) for reading books of such low-quality content, often dismissed by others as romantic drivel, drama, and "soft porn for housewives".

The interview study concluded that the act of reading can be understood as a utopian protest. A protest as the women, through the act of reading, claim their right to have fun and to spend time for sheer pleasure. The protest is utopian due to their preference for stories about conventional heterosexual relationships that bring together a man and a woman in a passionate love story in which they also care for and support each other on equal terms. Therefore, the books, according to Radway, offer a kind of compensatory literature providing its readers with emotional recovery in a situation lacking such redemption.

This sensitive and multi-layered interpretation put forward initially unpredicted conclusions in which the women's everyday lives, which formed the context of the books' content, became a core aspect of understanding how readers found the books meaningful.

The narrative structure of romance novels

The romance books as texts and their encounter with the readers were originally at the core of Radway's scholarly interest built into the study's starting point. At this time, the influences from structuralist and semiotic theory guided scholars to shift interest from the author's intentions to the text (and not least to its readers). In the 1920s, the Russian literary scholar Vladimir Propp had analyzed and formulated a narrative theory about the structure of the Russian folktale, which profoundly influenced Western cultural theorists when it was translated into English in 1968 (Propp, 1928/1968). According to Propp, the folk tale was formalized. He showed that Russian folk tales were put together of the same 31 specific and recurring elements (or, using the correct terminology, functions) such as: Departure - the hero leaves home (11); First function of the donor - the hero is tested, gets a magical agent or helper (12); Hero's reaction - the hero reacts to the agent or donor (13); Receipt of a magical agent - the hero finds a use for the agent (14), and so on. In each folk tale, how or why the hero left home, what kind of help the hero received (e.g., a rhyme, a fire device, or a magic sword), and so on varied, but the basic structure was the same for all the tales. The Italian semiotician Umberto Eco in the 1960s used Propp's theory to show that the popular novels about the British intelligence agent James Bond, written by author Ian Fleming, just like the Russian folk tales followed a fixed narrative structure (Eco, 1979: chapter 6). Even though Fleming's books (and the James Bond films that followed them) were produced in a different geographical, cultural, and historical context than the Russian folktales, their narrative structure also followed a given formula. This way of thinking about popular narratives had a significant impact and became hugely influential in the then-emerging research about popular culture.

In RTR, Propp's model of analysis is also used to study the narrative structure of the novels and the binary oppositions on which the narrative structure is built (Radway, 1987: 132). By analyzing the narrative structure of a number of the women's favourite romance books, she showed that the narrative structure of the ideal romance novel was characterized by the following elements (Radway, 1987: 134):

1   The heroine's social identity is destroyed.
2   The heroine reacts antagonistically against an aristocratic male.
3   The aristocratic male responds ambiguously to the heroine.
4   The heroine interprets the hero's behaviour as evidence of a purely sexual interest in her.
5   The heroine responds to the hero's behaviour with anger and coldness.
6   The hero retaliates by punishing the heroine.
7   The heroine and hero are physically and/or emotionally separated.
8   The hero treats the heroine tenderly.
9   The heroine responds warmly to the hero's act of tenderness.
10   The heroine reinterprets the hero's ambiguous behaviour as the product of previous hurt.
11   The hero proposes/openly declares his love for/demonstrates his unwavering commitment to the heroine with a supreme act of tenderness.
12   The heroine responds sexually and emotionally.
13   The heroine's identity is restored.

316 *Stina Bengtsson*

This narrative structure, Radway argued, confirmed, and reinforced patriarchal culture. The books followed and fulfilled the practices and ideologies that patriarchy enjoins, articulating heterosexual love with a man as the best way a woman can achieve a healthy female identity and a happy life. The heroines in the books had to be sexually confirmed by a man to mature as individuals and to develop into whole human beings.

The meanings of romance: A psychoanalytic perspective

Since Radway was interested in the reception of the books, the narrative structure of the texts needed to be understood in relation to the meaning-making of the readers. Using the narrative structure of the most popular romance books, Radway deepened the analysis by exploring the texts' meaning from a psychoanalytic perspective. This analysis was built mainly on the work of American psychoanalyst Nancy Chodorow (1978), who combined Marxist and gender perspectives to understand the relationship between mother and child better. Chodorow argued that girls and women cannot detach themselves from their mothers in the same way as boys but continue to identify with her throughout their lives. In addition, boys are part of their mother's Oedipal satisfaction and, therefore, valued more than girls and paid more attention. When boys construct a male identity, they have a deeper need and a stronger capability to disconnect from their mothers than girls. Girls keep seeking the attention of and liberation from their mothers (which boys naturally receive) but cannot obtain either. Girls consequently transform their envy of boys' privileges into heterosexual desire. Chodorow suggested that women's desire for men comes from their longing for their mother and, even more importantly, the kind of unreserved love and care a mother gives her child.

Chodorow supported her theory about the mother's essential role in both men's and women's gender identity and their need for emotional support by adding a Marxist political-economic perspective to the psychoanalytic model. She concluded that the cultural and emotional differences between girls and boys, women and men, result from capitalist society and its organized absence of fathers in children's everyday lives. Capitalist society makes men autonomous, financially, and emotionally. In contrast, women come into being in relation to others and continue to depend on others (men, children) when seeking existential meaning, even as adults.

Based on Chodorow's feminist psychoanalyst theory, the content of the books, and her interviews with readers, Radway concluded that the act of reading can be understood by the Oedipus complex, as the female readers must, in accordance with the social norm of capitalism, bond with a person of the opposite sex to become whole. However, this person (the man) does not offer her the emotional confirmation she seeks. Women give men (and children) time, support, emotional commitment, and love but do not get the same back from their men, and children grow up and become independent of their mothers. To endure this unfortunate position, women in capitalist society have three options: (1) be lesbian and establish a relationship with a woman who provides the needed emotional support, (2) build a relationship with a man and learn to live with emptiness and longing for unreserved love, or (3) find something else in life to fill the emotional void within them. The American 1970s society in which the interviews were conducted precluded the first option and the masculine norm of the same society the second option. From her combination of text analyses and interviews with readers, Radway concluded that romance reading could be understood as a third option. The reader's need to be cared for and loved found satisfaction through identification with the romance heroines who, from the male heroes, received the same attention and tenderness that women conventionally give to their husbands (and children), but which the readers had not received since they were children and objects of their own mother's love and care. This conclusion was uncovered by the narrative structure of the romance books, in which the heroines were transformed from insecure and lonely to having a solid female identity through the relationship with the motherly hero. In the interplay between narrative structure and interviews with readers, it became most evident that the element of the books that readers liked the most was that the hero offered the heroine paternal protection and maternal care in combination with passionate adult love.

When this conclusion is put in relation to the previously described analysis of the narrative structure of the books, an ambiguous picture emerges, one in which text and reading construct partly conflicting messages. The narrative structure of the books offers a simple recapitulation to patriarchy and suggests that readers adhere to the practices and ideologies of a patriarchal society. As the heroine comes into existence through her relationship with a man, the story reproduces the patriarchal order and signals to readers that a heterosexual relationship with a man helps women reach fulfilment in a patriarchal, capitalist society. However, the interviews and the analysis of reading as a socially situated act suggest, in contrast, that romance reading is oppositional to the patriarchal order and provides the reading woman with opportunities to rebel by stealing her own time, gaining emotional strength through identification with the heroine, and so on. Taken together, this makes romance reading a "utopian protest", an act that aims to change the current conditions but lacks real prospects of reaching completion.

Cultural Studies

In the chapter about Stuart Hall's encoding-decoding model of communication in this volume, Johan Fornäs describes the emergence and development of Cultural Studies. Its cradle is often connected with the researchers at the University of Birmingham and the Centre for Contemporary Cultural Studies (CCCS) or, as it is often called, the Birmingham School. The Birmingham School emerged due to the increased recruitment to British universities in the 1960s, with students from the working class now entering higher education and inhabiting

318 *Stina Bengtsson*

universities to a greater degree than before. The transition from an industrial society to a service society required a larger administrative sector followed by an increased need for a university-trained labour force. Inviting more students to universities was a way to meet this need, but it also had other unanticipated consequences. The new type of students – women and working-class men – who entered the universities reacted to the fact that their university studies did not offer them the tools to understand their own place in the world, their own backgrounds, their own taste preferences, and so on. Comparative Literature studied classical and canonized literature, and History of Arts studied artworks displayed in museums and galleries, but few academic departments spoke of adventure books, comic magazines, matinee films, and the like, that working-class kids had grown up with and that had shaped their individual development. The Cultural Studies tradition arose, among other things, as an ambition to widen the academic scope to also address other types of cultures beyond that of the elite.

Early Cultural Studies scholars used but modified the scholarly tools – theories, methods, perspectives – that they learnt within the Arts and Social Sciences and turned their gaze toward culture and communication that researchers had hitherto largely neglected, namely popular culture, play, games, and contemporary subcultures. They used structuralist, semiotic, and psychoanalytic perspectives to interpret and understand contemporary youth cultures and popular cultures of varied kinds. Cultural Studies emphasizes ideologies and dimensions of power and often explores the cultures of weak and/or marginalized groups without political and economic influence.

At the beginning of this period, men from the working class dominated the new group of university students and often brought a class perspective to the analysis of contemporary culture. As male youth cultures had higher visibility in society and were considered more threatening to the adult world, the societal "need" to understand them better (to control them) was also stronger. Girls' bedroom cultures were not considered as urgent to understand from a societal perspective as they did not create as much social debate, and they hence did not get as much scholarly attention.

But more women entering universities resulted in a similar cultural turn as when men did; they turned their gaze toward their own everyday life, experiences, and cultural forms. Cultural Studies research also began to include other cultural dimensions, such as gender and ethnicity. The development of feminist theories and a more systematic interest in the study of women's culture, therefore, began somewhat later than the initial interest in social class.

Early feminist media research was closely associated with research on popular culture as this is how women's culture has traditionally been regarded: soap operas on TV, weekly magazines, romance books, and so on. Cultural Studies researchers approached these cultures to understand them on their own terms, which was one of the tradition's important contributions.

The meaning of the text – outside the text

As we have seen, RTR has made sufficient impact on feminist studies, feminist theory, and popular culture theory. In what ways is it also an important contribution to media theory? The rich combination of theoretical approaches – reception theory, narrative theory, feminist psychoanalysis, Marxist theory, and an ethnographic approach – is unusual, as is the way the different approaches enrich and deepen each other. RTR further contributed to contemporary reception theory by addressing a formulaic genre of mass literature and a group of uneducated female readers.

The study's first contribution to media and communication theory regards the insight that the meaning of mass-produced, standardized, popular culture must be sought in the intimate relationship between text, the audience's interpretations of the text, and the specific reception context. Radway writes in the preface to the second edition (1987) that during the research project she repeatedly asked her interviewees about varied aspects of the content of the romance books but got replies that dealt with their everyday lives at large: how they needed rest, needed a place on their own, and a time in the day when they could let go of responsibilities for others and that was devoted to their own pleasures, and about the underlying dissatisfaction they felt with their lives. David Morley paid the same attention to the social context of the reception of media texts in his *Family Television* (1986), which deals with television viewing among British working-class families. However, Radway's book was published earlier and makes a significantly deeper theoretical and empirical contribution. The perspective is in line with contemporary reception theory as formulated by Roland Barthes and others, but is here addressed from a more sociological perspective in which class, gender, and socioeconomic factors enrich the understanding of the encounter between reader and text.

This conclusion also led to another important contribution: the Marxist analysis, following from the psychoanalytical text analysis in combination with the analysis of the readers' experiences. The reading of romance books – like uses of all mediated texts – must be understood beyond the individual reader's encounter with a text. A wider perspective must be adopted in which economic and cultural power structures shape how a certain meaning is constructed, right there, right then. Cultural Studies was, in the years following RTR, criticized for producing only affirmative celebrations of popular culture by putting forward "oppositional readings" and the potential for change built into cultural practices. Radway's book, however, does emphasize romance reading as a way of micro-protesting against patriarchal society. It also highlights this protest's "utopian" aspect as it simultaneously prevents the female reader from actively seeking more substantial change.

The analysis also contributes in a third important way, namely by the feminist analysis. As already mentioned, the entrance of women into the academic world and the political agenda of the 1960s and 1970s gave birth to a newly awakened theoretical interest in women's practices, women's culture, and the

320 *Stina Bengtsson*

power structures that regulate women's lives. RTR constitutes an important contribution to such feminist theory. But it is also a contribution to the study of popular culture. Based on a Marxist-Feminist perspective, the contextual understanding of romance reading shed new light on and contributed to a deeper understanding of a media audience that cultural research had mostly treated with disdain and contempt in previous decades and within other theoretical traditions.

Radway's book is an early example of and remains one of few works in Media and Communication Studies that commits to studying the entire communication process, from production, via text, to reception (and its context). Its focus on the production process, as well as the distribution of the books and the loosely cohesive distribution network that the bookseller Dot spun around her, pointed to the importance of informal distribution structures and fan communities only much later noticed by media research on a larger scale (cf. Fiske, 1992; Jenkins, 1992/2012, 2006).

Reception and resonance

As with other strong and controversial books, RTR has been criticized. One point of critique is that its epistemology is too realistic, failing to acknowledge how the study was involved in constructing its results (Ang, 1994). Feminist media researcher Ien Ang has also criticized Radway for creating "we-and-them" in the book, with the "we" referring to the author and the academic readers of RTR and with "them" referring to the women who make up the book's object of study that "we" look at from the outside and feel sorry for. "They" are not feminists like "we" are, and "they" do not get out of their oppressed situation but have to read mass-produced romance books to survive (Ang, 1994). Ang believes that implicit in Radway's book is the idea that romance readers must stop reading romances and become feminists instead and that Radway, through her Marxist analysis, focuses on the ideological significance of pleasure as part of the act of reading instead of theorizing pleasure in his own right. During the 1980s and 1990s, Feminist Media Studies, just as Cultural Studies more broadly, abandoned this overtly political power analysis in favour of just exploring the various meanings popular culture – texts and practices – could have for its audiences and the popular culture dimensions of pleasure, resistance, and rebellion. Today, the pendulum is about to swing back. Affirmative analyses of the practices of subcultural groups have given way to more power-oriented studies of the relationship between production, text, and reception, not least in light of the economic, social, and cultural, powers associated with digital and social media, data, algorithms, and Artificial Intelligence.

Today, RTR is an important source of inspiration for studies that try to seriously understand "the low" within culture with respect and an open mind, including both the audiences' voices and everyday experiences and a macro-oriented analysis of power. It is also important as a background for studies that believe the entire communication process should be considered to understand the societal implications of culture and communication.

References

Ang, I. (1994). Feminist desire and female pleasure. In John Storey (ed.). *Cultural theory and popular culture. A reader*. Harvester Wheatsheaf (pp. 554–563).

Barthes, R. (1977). *Image, music, text* (Vol. 6135). Macmillan.

Brunsdon, C., & Morley, D. G. (1978). *Everyday television: Nationwide*. British Film Institute.

Chodorow, N. J. (1978). *The reproduction of mothering: Psychoanalysis and the sociology of gender*. University of California Press.

Eco, U. (1979). *The role of the reader: Explorations in the semiotics of texts* (Vol. 318). Indiana University Press.

Fish, S. E. (1980). *Is there a text in this class? The authority of interpretive communities*. Harvard University Press.

Fiske, J. (1992). "The cultural economy of fandom". In L. S. Lewis (Ed.). *The adoring audience: Fan culture and popular media*. Routledge (pp. 33–49).

Gamman, L., & Marschment, M. (Eds.). (1988). *The female gaze: Women as viewers of popular culture*. The Women's Press.

Hall, S. (2007/1973). "Encoding and decoding in the television discourse". In A. Gray, J. Campbell, M. Erickson, S. Hanson & H. Wood (Eds.). *CCCS Selected Working Papers: Volume 2*. Routledge (pp. 386–398).Iser, W. (1978). *The act of reading. A theory of aesthetic response*. Johns Hopkins University Press.

Jenkins, H. (1992/2012). *Textual poachers. Television fans and participatory culture*. Routledge.

Jenkins, H. (2006). *Convergence culture: Where new and old media collide*. New York University Press.

Morley, D. (2005). *Family television: Cultural power and domestic leisure*. Routledge.

Propp, V. (1928/1968). *Morphology of the folktale*. USA: American Folklore Society and Indiana University. University of Texas Press.

Radway, J. A. (1984). *Reading the romance: Feminism and the representation of women in popular culture*. Chapel Hill.

Radway, J. A. (1987). *Reading the romance: Women, patriarchy, and popular literature*. Verso.

Storey, J. (1993/1997). *An introduction to popular theory and popular culture*. Harvester Wheatsheaf.

Storey, J. (red.) (1994). *Cultural theory and popular culture: A reader*. London: Harvester Wheatsheaf.

23 Neil Postman (1985) *Amusing Ourselves to Death*

Michael Forsman

Introduction

Neil Postman describes *Amusing Ourselves to Death* (AOD) as an "an inquiry into and a lamentation about the most significant American cultural fact of the second half of the twentieth century: the decline of the Age of Typography and the ascendancy of the Age of Television" (AOD: 8). The first part of his book (chapters 1–5) presents Postman's media ecological and historical principles, while the second part (chapters 6–11) is a critical discussion of television as a medium, with a focus on genres such as news, commercials, religious programs, and children's programs. In his book, Postman generally discusses how the audio-visual logics of television have deformed print culture and public conversation, turning politics, journalism, religion, and education into entertainment. Postman suggests that this transformation is irreversible and that it has had profound (and mainly negative) effects on our common systems of knowledge and our understanding of truth. Postman even suggests that "we are getting sillier by the minute" (AOD: 24).

The impact of technology on human culture is central in Postman's media ecological approach, but *Amusing Ourselves to Death* is not a media history *per se*; rather, it is a cultural history in which media are understood more as environments for human communication than in terms of their content. In other words, according to Postman's media ecological approach, technology precedes the message (cf. McLuhan's famous aphorism, "the medium is the message"), while media are the environments in which language and consciousness grow.

In accordance with this perspective, Postman suggests that the emergence of American democracy in the late 18th and early 19th centuries was enabled by an oral and printed culture that was "detached, analytical, devoted to logic, abhorring contradiction" (AOD: 57). However, this changed with the emergence of electronic media, beginning with the telegraph during the second half of the 19th century and escalating with television in the second half of the 20th century, and this process came to affect public conversation in a profound way. Hence, the full title of this well-known book is *Amusing Ourselves to Death. Public Discourse in the Age of Show Business*.

DOI: 10.4324/9781003432272-24

Amusing Ourselves to Death has been reprinted several times and translated into dozens of languages, but of course, much has changed in the media environment since this book was first published in 1985, particularly regarding the Internet and the development of social media, platform media, algorithms, datafication, and so forth. Still, I argue that *Amusing Ourselves to Death* can be read as being more relevant than ever (cf. Strate 2014). Neil Postman is also a key figure in the media ecological tradition (Strate, 2006, 2017), so do not let the somewhat conservative tone of *Amusing Ourselves to Death* discourage you from reading this classic. Postman is a well-read and original scholar, and his somewhat essayistic writing is quite amusing.

My presentation of *Amusing Ourselves to Death* starts with a brief biography of Postman, followed by a presentation of some of his media ecological principles. My reading then centers around four themes: *Amusing Ourselves to Death* as media philosophy, as media history, as media critique, and as a proposition for a media ecological approach to education. In the summary and discussion, I point out some media ecological principles, make some critical remarks, and argue for the relevance of Postman's approach to the media ecology of today.

Neil Postman

Neil Postman (1931–2003) was born in a Jewish family in which both English and Yiddish were spoken. He grew up in Brooklyn, New York, where a variety of languages were present in everyday life. Perhaps this triggered Postman's interest in linguistics and communication and led him to pursue a career as an English teacher. He received his M.A. in 1955 and became a Doctor of Education in 1958. After a stint working as a teacher in San Francisco, Postman returned to New York University and the School of Education, where he remained for the rest of his career (Strate, 2014).

Postman's original interest was in linguistics and semantics, and these disciplines clearly inform his writings. In his first book, *Television and the Teaching of English* (1961), Postman was already aiming to widen the common understanding of language; he also suggested that English teachers should use contemporary television as a material to train students' linguistic abilities and their capacity for critical thinking. Postman's early writings were pedagogically progressive and, together with Charles Weingarten (the co-author of several of Postman's books), he even proposed that the ordinary curriculum and traditional school disciplines should be replaced with a more thematic and reality-oriented arrangement (Postman & Weingarten, 1969, 1971, 1973).

Postman remained true to his ideals, but—with the growing impact of television and popular culture on public life and public education—his writings became more conservative. *Amusing Ourselves to Death* (1985) mirrors this shift in perspective. The same can be said about *The Disappearance of Childhood* (1982) and *The End of Education* (1995). In comparison, *Technopoly* (1992) is a criticism against the suggestion that, in principle, most social and

324 *Michael Forsman*

ecological problems can be solved through technological progression. However, in his last book, *Building a Bridge to the 18th Century. How the Past Can Improve Our Future* (1999), Postman argues that the only way to reclaim some balance and sense in modernity would be to reconnect to the classical ideals of the Enlightenment, which should be the main task for public education to accomplish.

Postman's publication list includes over 20 books and numerous articles. In much of his writings, Postman seems to address teachers and the public more than his fellow academics. As an often-requested public speaker and a regular guest on television, Postman loved dialogue and viewed his contact with students as the most rewarding part of his job (Strate, 2014).

Entering media ecology

The first time Postman used the term "media ecology" was in a speech in 1968, inspired by a letter Marshall McLuhan had written a few years earlier (Strate, 2014). In 1971, Postman established a department of media ecology at New York University; in 2000, he and his companion—his later successor and main interpreter, Lance Strate (2006, 2014, 2017)—formed the Media Ecology Association (MEA). This is how they described media ecology on the MEA website:

> Media ecology looks into the matter of how media of communication affect human perception, understanding, feeling, and value; and how our interaction with media facilitates or impedes our chances of survival. The word ecology implies the study of environments: their structure, content, and impact on people. An environment is, after all, a complex message system which imposes on human beings certain ways of thinking, feeling, and behaving. It structures what we can see and say and, therefore, do. It assigns roles to us and insists on our playing them. It specifies what we are permitted to do and what we are not. Sometimes, as in the case of a courtroom, or classroom, or business office, the specifications are explicit and formal. In the case of media environments (e.g., books, radio, film, television, etc.), the specifications are more often implicit and informal, half concealed by our assumption that what we are dealing with is not an environment but merely a machine. Media ecology tries to make these specifications explicit. It tries to find out what roles media force us to play, how media structure what we are seeing, why media make us feel and act as we do. Media ecology is the study of media as environments.
>
> (quoted in Islas & Bernal, 2016: 191)

The media ecological approach thus involves an understanding of media as environments and complex message systems, where each medium has its own ontology and epistemology, functions and positions, affordances and biases. Different forms of media also belong to different technological and cultural "genealogies" (i.e., telegraph to telephone to radio to television) and lines of development (i.e., radio and film became television), while they compete for their own survival and modernization (i.e., television changed radio). Media ecological research is also interested in the long-term historical transitions that take place between different orders of communication (oral, written, typographic, electronic) or different forms of literacy, which impacts on relationships between different communication cultures and the organization of time, space, and knowledge during different eras and in different civilizations (cf. Stephens, 2014).

In his writings, Postman often returned to Marshall McLuhan, whom he saw as the originator of the media ecological approach through McLuhan's books *The Gutenberg Galaxy: The Making of Typographic Man* (1962), and *Understanding Media: The Extensions of Man* (1964/1987). In *Amusing Ourselves to Death*, Postman also refers to Lewis Mumford's *Technics and Civilization* (1934), which is a history of modern media technologies, from the Middle Ages and the invention of the clock to the coal-steam factories of early industrial capitalism and on into the electronic era and the first part of the 20th century. Postman also refers to Harold Innis and his analysis in *Empire and Communication* (1950) of how media—from papyrus and clay to the Greek alphabet—have influenced different civilizations in their ways of organizing time and space, politics and trade, and knowledge and power.

The following works are other recurrent points of reference in Postman's work: *Preface to Plato* by Eric Havelock (1963), which argues that the invention of handwriting enabled Greek philosophy, which eventually laid the foundation for modern Western thinking; Elisabeth Eisenstein's exploration into the effects of moveable-type printing in the post-Gutenberg era of Western Europe, in *The Printing Press as an Agent of Change: Communications and Cultural Transformations in Early Modern Europe* (1980); and Jacques Ellul's *Technological Society* (1964) and its warnings that automation, artificiality, and rationality may transform society into a technocratic nightmare. These thinkers—as well as other names in the media ecological tradition—belong to different academic fields (e.g., literature, history, philosophy, sociology, anthropology, and linguistics). What unites them is their humanistic interest in media, which distinguishes their views from functionalistic and sociological perspectives on media.

For those who want to read more about media ecology, its traditions, and its central themes, there are numerous anthologies and overviews (Cali, 2017; Gencarelli, 2006; Islas & Bernal, 2016; Lum, 2006; Strate, 2006, 2014). It is noticeable that several of the thinkers included in the present volume (i.e., Jean Baudrillard, James Carey, Donna Haraway, Raymond Williams, and others) are also mentioned in these overviews. However, this does not necessarily make them "media ecologists"; rather, it suggests that media ecology is a complex meta-discipline (Cali, 2017; Islas & Bernal, 2016).

AOD as media philosophy

In chapter 1 of *Amusing Ourselves to Death*, Postman transforms Marshall McLuhan's famous aphorism "the medium is the message" to "the medium is the metaphor," to point out that a medium that prevails during one epoch tends to become a metaphor for the mentality of society at that time. Hence, Postman argues that images of the feather pen, the book, and the printing press came to represent print culture and thus the Enlightenment. Our own era of "digital enlightenment" can be represented by computer-generated images that—in a bluish and futuristic light—may contain something like "Unreal holographic interfaces, half-flesh half-circuit brains, lines of code waving in space, robots tapping on smart touchscreens, and at least one of the hundred variations of Michelangelo's *The Creation of Adam* in a human–robot version" (Romele, 2022: 4).

Postman's alignment with McLuhan can also be noticed in their broad understanding of the term "medium." In both Postman's (1985) and McLuhan's (1964) work, weapons, watches, money, roads, maps, and typewriters can be mentioned in the same breath as radio and television. In an article called *The Humanism of Media Ecology* (2000: 10), Postman accordingly explains his understanding of media by claiming that "a medium is a technology within which a culture grows; that is to say, it gives form to a culture's politics, social organization, and habitual ways of thinking."

Here, Postman once again suggests that media are not only communication tools and extensions of the human body but also environments that form what and how we can think. In *Amusing Ourselves to Death*, he writes: "Definitions of truth are derived, at least in part, from the character of the media of communication through which information is conveyed" (AOD: 17), this is how he describes the relation between technology and media.

> We might say that a technology is to a medium as the brain is to the mind. Like the brain, a technology is a physical apparatus. Like the mind, a medium is a use to which a physical apparatus is put. A technology becomes a medium as it employs a particular symbolic code, as it finds its place in a particular social setting, as it insinuates itself into economic and political contexts. A technology is merely a machine. A medium is the social and intellectual environment a machine creates.
>
> (AOD: 84)

In chapter 2 of *Amusing Ourselves to Death* (titled "Media as Epistemology"), Postman suggests that media helps us classify the world and understand ourselves, whether we experience the world through speech, print, a photographic lens, or a television camera. To explain this point further, he refers to Lewis Mumford's (1934) writings about how the invention of eyeglasses during the 12th century not only made it possible to improve defective vision but also "refuted the belief that anatomy is destiny by putting forward the idea that our bodies as well as our minds are improvable" (AOD: 14). In a similar fashion, it can be suggested that the telescope positioned humans as the centre of the cosmos. To summarize: media (oral, written, print, visual and electronic) enables human thinking and public debate, although few of us may reflect on this regularly. "A person who reads a book or who watches television or who glances at his watch is not usually interested in how his mind is organized and controlled by these events" (AOD: 11).

As mentioned earlier, Postman was interested in linguistics; he referred to speech as "the primal and indispensable medium" and suggested that speech "made us human, keeps us human, and in fact defines what human means" (AOD: 9). He also referred to *Amusing Ourselves to Death* as an examination of how the shift from print to electronic media transformed "conversation," which is the term Postman uses for "all technologies and techniques that permit people of a particular culture to exchange messages" (AOD: 6).

Then came typography and the printing press, which enabled the large-scale dissemination of books, paving the way for the nation state, individual rights, and democracy. Later, when America shifted from being a print-based democracy to becoming a consumerist society centred around television, the principles of public debate changed. Postman would say that it degenerated: "I will say once again that I am no relativist in this matter, and that I believe the epistemology created by television not only is inferior to a print-based epistemology but is dangerous and absurdist" (AOD: 27).

AOD as (American) media history

Postman's philosophy and approach to media can be seen to be ecological, interpretative, and normative, formed around a linear narrative about how modern print defined the early stages of the American nation before being out-performed by television. In the third chapter of *Amusing Ourselves to Death* ("Typographic America"), Postman describes how the English settlers in the 1620s brought the Bible with them across the Atlantic and then gave it a central place in their households. In the 1640s, the Bible had become a big seller and, for a long time thereafter, it remained essential for the development of literacy among ordinary people. Between 1825 and 1850, the number of subscription libraries in America tripled and print became a prerequisite for the public sphere, the public school system, and the formation of the reading public. Postman even suggests—again, with reference to Mumford—that the establishment of print as the dominant media form released people from their immediate and local context and opened their minds to more elaborated forms of thinking and debate.

The forums for public debate that grew from print culture included not only conversations about things that had been read but also different forms of oral presentations. Postman addresses this matter in chapter 4 of AOD ("The Typographic Mind"), where he tells the fascinating story of how large audiences in the late 1850s gathered to listen to a 7-hour debate between President Lincoln and one of his political opponents. In such "speaking events" (which were also common in the programs of county and state fairs), one debater could

328   Michael Forsman

argue for an hour or more before the opponent had the chance to reply. The audience was far from quiet; moreover, the length of a debate sometimes made it necessary to have a dinner break between speakers. Postman refers to another form of oral public communication as well: the tradition of revivalist preachers. He viewed these often spectacular and, in some cases, famous public speakers as cogs in an informal system of adult education and community building, which was important for newly arrived immigrants and partly challenged the religious and social establishment.

Such speeches rarely had any manuscript form, but Postman still considers them to be extensions of print culture, since they took an argumentative and analytical approach. He also suggests that this ideal of the long and coherent public conversation was challenged in the later part of the 19th century due to the growth of the newspaper industry and mass reading, in parallel with advertising and photography. According to Postman, this led to "the descent of the typographic mind, beginning, as it does, with reason, and ending, as it does, with entertainment" (AOD: 58).

In chapter 5 of *Amusing Ourselves to Death* ("The Peek-a-Boo-World"), Postman takes on electronic communication and "the age of show business." First, he focuses on the telegraph. In the late 1850s, America was a composite of regions, each with its own ways and concerns, which made it difficult to set up a continent-wide conversation. The solution to this problem was electricity and the development of the telegraph, based on Morse code and built in parallel to the expansion of the national railway system.

Postman argues that the fact that the telegram became a commodity contributed to the undermining of coherent communication, since a telegram transmits fragments and sensations. Hence, the telegraph—in combination with the mass press and photography—transformed public conversations into idiosyncratic events. For Postman, this meant the development of a discontinuous language in a system of "broken time and broken attention" (AOD: 69) that led to a "dismembering of reality" (AOD: 73ff).

This order was further confirmed by television when it became a mass medium in the 1940s and the 1960s. Many of the public meeting places where people had previously congregated disappeared, and the audience became consumers of "pseudo-events" in their homes instead (Boorstin, 1963). For example, according to Postman, an event such as a press conference, TV gala, or other form of television event is to consider it as a pseudo-event since it attracts attention and amuses but does not improve or change anything. The viewers are instead "overwhelmed by irrelevance, incoherence, and impotence" (AOD: 76).

AOD as media critique

In the second part of *Amusing Ourselves to Death*, Postman criticizes what he sees as the supra-ideology of television: "No matter what is depicted or from what point of view, the overreaching presumption is that it is there for our amusement and pleasure" (AOD: 87). In chapter 6 ("The Age of Show

Business"), Postman describes television as a speed-of-light-medium that delivers a constant flow of newscasters, TV preachers, presidential candidates, advertising, murders, weather reports, and child programming. This may sound like an elitist complaint against popular culture, however, Postman assures us that he likes television, precisely because it is rubbish; what annoys him is when television tries to be a space for serious conversations.

In chapter 7 ("Now ... This"), Postman refers to television as "anti-communication" and as something that "entertains but does not inform" (AOD: 107), and in chapter 8 ("Shuffle off to Bethlehem"), he debates evangelistic TV preaching (a common genre of local American television). Postman finds these TV sermons to be completely empty of any form of authentic religious experience and suggests that the reason for this is that television can only handle personalities and not abstractions: "There is no ritual, no dogma, no tradition, no theology, and above all, no sense of spiritual transcendence. On these shows, the preacher is tops. God comes out as second banana" (AOD: 116).

In chapter 9 ("Reach Out and Elect Someone"), Postman dismisses television debates as "pseudo therapy" (AOD: 128) and links political communication to television commercials, both of which are about image politics. He also argues that, after millions of commercials, television viewers tend to believe that any form of social or psychological problem can be solved with the help of a new product; in the long run, this makes us think that there are (or, at least, should be) quick fixes to very complex social and political problems.

AOD as an approach to education

Postman's crusade against American television in the 1980s continues in chapter 10 ("Teaching as an Amusing Activity"), where he turns his attention to educational programs for children and uses the children's program *Sesame Street* as an example. This series premiered in 1969, and is still being shown, so it has been part of the childhood experience for generations of Americans and thus has become something of an institution. *Sesame Street* is a highly acclaimed and multi-award-winning series aimed at training young (preschool) children in language and math, and directing them ethically and socially. This is done through a combination of comedy, animation, and puppetry, but what Postman sees is just "cute puppets, celebrities, catchy tunes, and rapid-fire editing [was] certain to give pleasure to the children and [would] therefore serve as adequate preparation for their entry into a fun-loving culture" (AOD: 142).

Postman's acid comments regarding the underlying, consumerist curriculum of children's television align with his criticism against the enthusiasm shown by many teachers in the 1980s toward the idea of installing computers in classrooms. Postman instead advises teachers to turn on their bullshit detector and ask: To which problem is this a solution, who will benefit from this, and what do we have to give up so as to gain the benefits that have been promised?

By comparing the school curriculum to the underlying "curriculum" of television and computers, Postman suggests that public education must take on

330 *Michael Forsman*

greater responsibility for upholding classical principles of knowledge, critical thinking, and Bildung, since this is the only way to balance contemporary culture (cf. Biesta, 2010). It would be interesting to apply Postman's thinking to the hype surrounding the digitalization of public education (Selwyn, 2016) or to insert Postman's media ecology into media and information literacy (Forsman, 2019).

The Huxleyan warning

Amusing Ourselves to Death was published at a time when "new media" was represented by rental videos, CDs, and round-the-clock satellite and cable television services (e.g., CNN, MTV), or the launch of Apple's first Macintosh computer. The traditional book culture still stood strong and many teachers, librarians, and others with a profound orientation towards print culture took Postman's book to their hearts. Around this time, America (and the world) was on the brink of the neoliberal era (in which we still remain), and former Hollywood actor Ronald Reagan had just been re-elected president. The Cold War was ongoing, and the threat of a global nuclear war was a reality. Perhaps this zeitgeist influenced the tone of *Amusing Ourselves to Death*. It is also notable that *AOD* was published a year after 1984—that is, the year referenced in George Orwell's famous novel *1984* (from 1948) as the symbol for a dystopian future. As is well known, Orwell's book revolves around a totalitarian society in which citizens are under constant surveillance by "Big Brother" while being fed propaganda, sedative drugs, and contradictory slogans ("Truth is lie. War is Peace. Freedom is Slavery."). However, *Amusing Ourselves to Death* was even more influenced by Aldous Huxley's *Brave New World* (1931) and in chapter 11 ("The Huxleyan Warning"), Postman consequently explains the lesson to be learned from Huxley's dystopian novel.

> What Huxley teaches is that in the age of advanced technology, spiritual devastation is more likely to come from an enemy with a smiling face than from one whose countenance exudes suspicion and hate. In the Huxleyan prophecy, Big Brother does not watch us, by his choice. We watch him, by ours. There is no need for wardens or gates or Ministries of Truth. When a population becomes distracted by trivia, when cultural life is redefined as a perpetual round of entertainments, when serious public conversation becomes a form of baby-talk, when, in short, a people become an audience and their public business a vaudeville act, then a nation finds itself at risk; culture-death is a clear possibility.
>
> (AOD: 155f)

Amusing Ourselves to Death can thus be read as an anticipation of and a warning against what a consumerist and short-sighted society might lead to. Postman became even more distinct on this point in one of his later books, *Technopoly: The Surrender of Culture to Technology* (1992), which was published just before the Internet and the era in which we all obtained personal computers (and then smartphones). Here, Postman argues that we are (once again) faced with a "Faustian bargain" between the speed and comfort of now computerized communication and what could be described as inalienable human values. Postman suggests that, in this era, technological progression through the enforcement of technocrats, bureaucrats, and economists has become the dominant ideology, leaving societies in a state of spiritual emptiness, with a shortage of alternative routes for the future.

Today, in the age of climate change and ongoing ecological catastrophes, when many of us live almost in symbiosis with the Internet, screens, platforms, on-demand services, and social media, we are embedded in networks where machines learn from machines, fed by the data we generate through our daily activities online. This may feel like freedom; but it can also be described as a new form of sophisticated surveillance (Zuboff, 2019).

We also hear about how Meta (the former Facebook) continues to invest heavily in the development of the "Metaverse"—a digital ecosystem based on already-existing three-dimensional (3D) technology that allows real-time collaboration in a parallel universe in which we can be present through personal avatars. The plan is for this virtual world to eventually and seamlessly merge with our physical reality (Mystakidis, 2022). At the same time, there is a growing debate about the consequences of generalized and adaptive AI, along with reports on digital divides, digital unhealth, and so forth. We can only speculate on what Neil Postman, if he still was alive, would have said about the current situation. How would he have applied his media ecological approach to Twitter, TikTok, Facebook, YouTube, Instagram, the presidential campaigns of today, disinformation and misinformation, influencers and selfies, algorithms and platform capitalism, smartphones, and biometric media?

Summary and conclusions

In this chapter, I have presented *Amusing Ourselves to Death* by Neil Postman. Although this book is a criticism of the impact television has had on American public debate and democracy, it can also be read as an example of a media ecological approach. So, what can be learned about media ecology from Postman's book?

Firstly, media ecology can be defined as the study of media as environments in which human culture grows. Moreover, the term "ecology" implies the presence of connections between the biological and symbolic habitats of humans.

Secondly, media ecology is about media evolution, relations between different media, long-term historical changes in communication culture, and the acknowledgement that a medium is never neutral; rather, it is biased in terms of its functions and epistemological principles. Thus, the implementation of a new medium will always cause both benefits and irreversible losses. This point is essential, particularly in Postman's understanding of media ecology, since he argues for the importance of balance: between humans and nature, between humans and media, and between different forms of media.

332 *Michael Forsman*

Thirdly, media ecology can be understood as an umbrella term for a complex meta-discipline consisting of different theoretical orientations and researchers from different areas (i.e., history, anthropology, linguistics, psychology, literature, art, archaeology, informatics, etc.). The connecting link is a humanistic and holistic approach to media technologies, often on a macro level, with a focus on long-term transformations and the relations between communication cultures and social organization, mentalities, and knowledge. This means that media ecology can move from pre-modern oral culture and ancient debates on the effects of writing to medieval monastic cultures or different periods of electronic media. Media ecology can also help us thematize the future.

The conclusion is that media ecology is a tradition within a continuous and multidisciplinary development, and that this perspective may very well be more relevant than ever. The examples mentioned above are just snippets of first classics then some more recent scholarly work that can be connected to the media ecological tradition. Other important examples in the media ecological tradition include Sherry Turkle's (2011, 2015) studies of interpersonal communication in the age of digital abundance, as well as her studies of the relations between humans and social robots; Katherine Hayles' (2012) research on literacy, intelligence, and memory in relation to digital changes (see Chapter 26 in this volume); and Donna Haraway's (1991) thinking about cyborgs and long engagement in studies of agency and ethics between humans, technology, nature, and animals (e.g., Haraway, 1991). Another intriguing and current example of a media ecological approach is John Durham Peters' (2015) discussion on what he refers to as elemental media (clouds, oceans, etc.) (see also Chapter 27 in this volume).

Final remarks

Of course, there are things to be criticized in *Amusing Ourselves to Death*. Postman's views on television and society are elitist, moralistic, and pessimistic, and his understanding of childhood and education is too general. He focuses on what media technology does to people but says very little about what people do with media. He is gender blind, and his view on America is idealistic and nostalgic, completely lacking any sort of multicultural or postcolonial awareness. In a book like this, one would also expect there to be a more systematic declaration of what scientific principles, sources, and methods that argumentation is based on.

Another relevant criticism is that Postman is a technological determinist. In other words, his main argument is that it is technology that influences social structures, mentalities, and value systems, rather than such constructs being influenced by politics, economics, and culture. This approach can and should be debated. At the same time, an analytical interest in media technology may be more relevant than ever if we want to develop as consumers, students, and researchers in a time when everything is mediatized, media is everywhere, and almost anything can be understood as a form of media. This means that we

Neil Postman (1985) 333

need to nourish our thoughts in order to achieve balance, find alternatives, and chart new paths. I suggest that *Amusing Ourselves to Death* could or even should be read from this perspective.

The use of the acronym AOD in this chapter stands for *Amusing Ourselves to Death*.

References

Biesta, G. (2010). *Good education in an age of measurement: Ethics, politics, democracy.* Boulder. Paradigm Publishers.

Boorstin, D.J. (1963). *The image: Or what happened to the American dream.* Penguin Books.

Cali, D.D. (2017). *Mapping media ecology: Introduction to the field.* Peter Lang.

Durham Peters, J. (2015). *The marvelous clouds: Toward a philosophy of elemental media.* The University of Chicago Press.

Eisenstein, E.L. (1980). *The printing press as an agent of change: Communications and cultural transformations in early-modern Europe: Volumes I and II.* Cambridge University Press.

Ellul, J. (1964/1954). *Technological society.* Vintage Books.

Forsman M. (2019). Rebalancing MIL: The revised Swedish curriculum and the emerging media citizen in a new media ecology. In U. Carlsson (Ed.), *Understanding media and information literacy (MIL) in the digital age: A question of democracy* (pp. 149–156). Nordicom.

Gencarelli, T.F. (2006). Neil Postman and the rise of media ecology. In C.M.K. Lum (Ed.), *Perspectives on culture, technology, and communication: The media ecology tradition* (pp. 201–253). Hampton Press.

Haraway, D.J. (1991). *Simians, cyborgs, and women: The reinvention of nature.* Free Association Books.

Havelock, E (1963). *Preface to Plato.* Harvard University Press.

Hayles, N.K. (2012). *How we think: Digital media and contemporary technogenesis.* University of Chicago Press.

Huxley, A. (1931/1989). *Brave new world revisited.* Perennial Library.

Innis, H. (1950). *Empire and Communication.* Clarendon Press.

Islas, O. & Bernal, J.D. (2016). Media ecology: A complex and systemic meta discipline. *Philosophies*, 1, 190–198. doi:10.3390/philosophies1030190.

Lum, C.M.K. (ed.) (2006). *Perspectives on culture, technology, and communication: The media ecology tradition.* Hampton Press.

McLuhan, M. (1962). *The Gutenberg Galaxy. The making of typographic man.* Toronto University Press.

McLuhan, M. (1964). *Understanding media: The extensions of man.* McGraw-Hill.

Mumford, L. (1934). *Technics and civilization.* Harcourt, Brace & World.

Mystakidis, Stylianos. (2022). Metaverse. *Encyclopedia*, 2, 468–497. doi:10.3390/encyclopedia2010031.

Orwell, G. (1948/1984). *Nineteen eighty-four.* Secker & Warburg.

Postman, N. (1961). *Television and the teaching of English.* Appleton-Century-Crofts.

Postman, N. (1979). *Teaching as a conserving activity.* Delacorte P.

Postman, N. (1982). *The disappearance of childhood.* Delacorte P.

Postman, N. (1985). *Amusing ourselves to death.* New York: Viking Penguin Inc.

334 *Michael Forsman*

Postman, N. (1992). *Technopoly: The surrender of culture to technology*. Alfred A. Knopf.

Postman, N. (1995). *The end of education: Redefining the value of school* (1st ed.). Alfred A. Knopf.

Postman, N. (1999). *Building a bridge to the 18th century: How the past can improve our future* (1st ed.). Alfred A. Knopf.

Postman, N. (2000). *The humanism of media ecology: Keynote address delivered at the inaugural Media Ecology Association Convention Fordham University*, New York, June 16–17, 2000 (pp. 10–16). Proceedings of the Media Ecology Association, Volume 1.

Postman, N. & Weingartner, C. (1969). *Teaching as a subversive activity*. Dell.

Postman, N. & Weingartner, C. (1971). *The soft revolution: A student handbook for turning schools around*. Delacorte Press.

Postman, N. & Weingartner, C. (1973). *The school book: For people who want to know what all the hollering is about*. Delacorte Press.

Romele, Alberto. (2022). Images of Artificial Intelligence: A blind spot in AI ethics. *Philosophy & Technology*, 35:4. Published online 29 January 2022. doi:10.1007/s13347–13022–00498–00493.

Selwyn, N. (2016). *Is Technology Good for Education?* Polity Press.

Stephens, N.P. (2014). Toward a more sustainable media ecology: Postman's metaphor versus posthuman futures. *International Journal of Communication*, 8:2014, 2027–2045.

Strate, L. (2006). *Echoes and reflections: On media ecology as a field of study*. Hampton Press, Inc.

Strate, L. (2014). *Amazing ourselves to death: Neil Postman's brave new world revisited*. Peter Lang.

Strate, L. (2017). *Media ecology. An approach to understanding the human condition*. Peter Lang.

Turkle, S. (2011). *Alone together: Why we expect more from technology and less from each other*. Basic Books.

Turkle, S. (2015). *Reclaiming conversation: The power of talk in a digital age*. Penguin Press.

Zuboff, S. (2019). *The age of surveillance capitalism: The fight for the future at the new frontier of power*. Profile Books.

24 Friedrich Kittler (1985) *Discourse Networks 1800/1900*

Otto Fischer

Introduction

When Friedrich A. Kittler, Professor of Aesthetics and History of Media at the Humboldt University, gave his last public lecture at the department at Sophienstraße in Berlin-Mitte on July 15, 2011, the hall was full of young, reverential and visibly moved listeners.[1] It was a master bidding farewell to his disciples. The last German master thinker, or if you like, a media-theoretically updated guru of the techno-generation, sat behind a table with an appropriate glass of red wine in front of him, clearly affected by the cancer that would take his life a few months later, and spoke about the relationship between teacher and student, about wisdom and love. But above all, he spoke of the Greeks – of the discovery of mathematics, the Greek gods and the Greek vocal alphabet; themes that largely occupied his final years, but which may not be entirely obvious to a scholar whose work, although essentially always dealing with historical materials, was characterized by his absolute contemporaneity. Few scholars embody as much as Kittler the history of post-war Germany and Western Europe, both in their life and in their research.

The author

Friedrich A. (Adolf) Kittler was born in Rochlitz, Saxony, in 1943, grew up in the GDR and, after his family's escape in the 1950s, ended up in West Germany. Already in his earliest student works from the 1960s, Kittler combines classical learning and a thorough orientation in classical German literature with a certain theoretical ferocity and a deeply felt interest in sex, drugs and rock'n'roll (especially of the pyschedelic kind: Pink Floyd, the Doors and Jimi Hendrix are recurring references in his texts) (Hron & Khaled 2015). The texts wander uncontrollably between the clever, the puerile and the downright silly, but still give some sort of indication of what was to come.

After studying philosophy and German literary history, Kittler earned his doctorate with a psychoanalytically oriented thesis on the 18th century Swiss writer Conrad Ferdinand Meyer (Kittler 1977). Together with some of his contemporaries, he was instrumental in introducing the French thinkers who

DOI: 10.4324/9781003432272-25

336 *Otto Fischer*

came to be associated with poststructuralism, in particular Jacques Derrida, Jacques Lacan and Michel Foucault. The latter two in particular were to have a major impact on Kittler's development. In Germany, poststructuralism had a clear bias towards Foucault, and the term "discourse analysis" was used rather than "deconstruction", which was otherwise common in the American version of the theory. Another distinctive feature of German discourse analysis was that it was largely characterized by a kind of re-import of German philosophy that had been removed from the domestic philosophical tradition for political reasons. Now it suddenly became possible to read Friedrich Nietzsche and Martin Heidegger again, which meant that the German discourse analysts used the French theoretical import to react against the strong left-wing tradition that with critical theory (Theodor W. Adorno, Max Horkheimer, Herbert Marcuse, Jürgen Habermas) dominated German philosophy in the 1970s. But just as much, discourse analysis offered a critical edge directed against the strong hermeneutic tradition that still strongly dominated the German humanities, especially thanks to Hans-Georg Gadamer.

Kittler's public and theoretical breakthrough came with his 1984 habilitation thesis (equivalent in the German university system to the first major study after the doctoral thesis), *Aufschreibesysteme* 1800/1900, published in 1985. The title is difficult to translate, and the English translation opts instead for "discourse networks". The latter title has the advantage of giving us a clearer idea of what is involved – different instances linked to each other in a network – while the German original, by focusing on the medium of writing itself and by emphasizing the systematic character, allows us to see this network as something almost machine-like, where texts, voices and subjects are the products of a technological system.

This technically hard-boiled way of writing literary history severely provoked the literary science establishment, and the dissertation could only be approved after an almost parodic number of deeply disagreeing experts had given their opinion on the matter (Sprenger & Pakis 2016).

In interviews, Kittler provides a personal background to the interest in media and technology expressed in the book. During his student years in Freiburg, he was deeply involved in electronic music in his spare time, spending his days in one room of his apartment analyzing Goethe and Novalis, and his nights in the other soldering circuit boards and tinkering with his synth. Eventually, this habitation in two worlds became uncomfortable, and he decided to combine the two spheres. The result of this fusion was the book entitled *Discourse Networks 1800–1900*. Such an anecdotal explanatory model definitely has elements of self-mythologization, but also contains important metaphorical points. It is a heightened awareness of the technical conditions of all communication, precisely of the kind made possible by the development of communication technology in recent decades, that makes us aware of the defining presence of technology even in earlier eras.

Reading Kittler is not easy. His writing style is characterized by a mixture of technical terminology, French philosophical jargon and countless allusions to

German classical literature and philosophy. All this in a rhetorically rigorous form, which not least comes to expression in a preference for paradoxical and sometimes rather cryptic formulations. The term "Kittlerdeutsch" – Kittler's German – has even been coined to describe his writing style (Winthrop-Young 2005). Reading Kittler can be reminiscent of reading Marshall McLuhan, but a McLuhan whose style has been shaped by Hegel, Heidegger and Lacan, rather than by English Renaissance literature and contemporary advertising.

McLuhan is also theoretically an obvious starting point when approaching Kittler's work – even though he is not cited to an extent that one would expect, given how related their ideas are. Like McLuhan, Kittler sees media as crucial not only to the development of culture and society, but also to the shaping of human perception and subjectivity. This means that for Kittler the question of media is also always a question of power. Based on Foucault, Kittler simply asks how different media, by producing certain types of subjects, have also produced and reproduced power. Above all, Kittler's work is permeated by the historical insight that all modern media development, from the telegraph system during the Napoleonic Wars to today's Internet, has taken place within the technology of war, or at least in its absolute vicinity; something that very much determines Kittler's ethical position, even though he is notoriously reluctant in his work to make normative statements, and rather more or less consistently provoked his contemporaries by taking an ironic approach to the prevailing left-wing jargon as well as to a more ideologically pronounced humanism. Additionally, there has long been a very lively discussion in Germany about the relationship between technology and various aspects of modernity: from Oswald Spengler and Walter Benjamin to Adorno, Heidegger and Günter Anders, something which has of course been of crucial importance for the penetration of the media history perspective in German research. Even if this discussion was previously conducted from other starting points, technology has always had an important position in the German discussion of cultural theory. Like few other countries, Germany has also experienced the devastating consequences of new media (film, radio) being placed in the service of political propaganda, and in the eastern parts of the country the post-war period was largely characterized by repressive surveillance, made possible by media-related practices. For Kittler, however, it is neither propaganda in itself, nor the repressive state apparatus as such, that is of interest, but rather the effects that the media as technologies have on the societies in which they are used and on the people who use them. Here his approach comes close to that usually attributed to McLuhan, and just like McLuhan, Kittler has been accused of both speculative sensationalism and reductionist technological determinism.

The work

But let's return to *Discourse Networks 1800–1900*: What exactly is Kittler doing in this book? Kittler takes his historical point of departure in the new forms of alphabetization, i.e. techniques for teaching children to read and write, that

338　*Otto Fischer*

emerged in the late 18th century. Through re-readings of the educational classics of the time such as Pestalozzi and Basedow, Kittler outlines a new educational doctrine in which the mother is given a central role in initial alphabetization. This task, which could previously have fallen to anyone, such as the father, a wet nurse or a tutor equipped with an ABC book and Luther's catechism, is now linked to a novel maternal role, and it is thus up to her to make the child literate. The result is that literacy is unambiguously and decisively linked to the intimate sphere. Initial sexualization and socialization are followed by initial alphabetization, and literacy instruction on the mother's lap in the newly invented bourgeois domestic idyll becomes something infinitely pleasurable for the child. At the same time, new pedagogical techniques are introduced, and Kittler points in particular to sounding; whereas the small child had previously had to learn whole syllables, words and even phrases by heart and gradually associate them more or less by force of habit with the written image, now each individual letter would be directly associated with a sound, and moreover this sound is perceived as immediately meaningful, precisely because it is associated with the mother's voice. We are thus dealing with a cultural technology that combines media technology with emotional and sexual energies to allow a very specific kind of subjectivity to emerge. In order to fully understand what Kittler is doing here, it is important to consider the importance of psychoanalysis: it is from there, and above all from Lacan, that Kittler draws his theories on how language and discourse are linked to psychic, emotional and sexual structures, producing readers and writers for whom writing is a completely transparent medium. From now on, reading and writing means staging the original intimate situation of alphabetization: the text is given a voice, and that voice is the mother's voice. These literacy reforms are also matched by changes in both typographic and handwriting standards – the old fracture is being replaced by modified forms that are softer on the eye, and as far as handwriting is concerned, efforts are being made to replace the old, inharmonious German style with the English cursive.

What then is the function of this new intimate approach to writing from a discourse analysis perspective? It makes it possible to put an end to textual circulation in what Foucault described as the "classical episteme" (Foucault 1966). In Foucault's description, knowledge in early modern Europe was generated by the constant circulation, reproduction and commentary of essentially the same texts. In this paradigm, knowledge was rather an effect of a certain way of relating to the amount of books; to be learned was to have read books in the right way. With the new way of reading that Kittler outlines, the book, indeed language itself, becomes a transparent container for a meaning that goes beyond both the text as a linguistic statement and the book as a material object. The text no longer remains a sacred object to be studied over and over again; it becomes a medium for immediate consumption, and thus the old-world circulation of texts in a self-reproducing and tradition-bound system can be brought to an end.

The subjects thus alphabetized will henceforth support new forms of knowledge. They themselves become the bearers of a new kind of rationality that is utterly the rationality of the modern state. Then what these novel alphabetization reforms produce is first and foremost civil servants who, unlike the functionaries of the old princely state, are animated by a humanistic pathos and work to implement a modern, rational system of administration.

However, this does not complete the system, for an important function is also fulfilled by poetry (*Dichtung*) – and I deliberately avoid the term literature here, for Kittler later makes an important point about the distinction. It is in fact poetry, primarily represented by Goethe, which is the medium of this system's self-reproduction, fulfilling a feedback function, and this feedback is in turn confirmed by philosophical hermeneutics, which, through meaning-oriented interpretation, guarantees that the texts never become visible in their crass materiality, but on the contrary remain pure and unadulterated potential for meaning. It is also now that philosophical aesthetics, and with it, aesthetic disciplines such as the history of art and literature, are gradually establishing themselves in the university system.

Dichtung is thus not an effect or a symptom of the new system, but rather plays a central role in it. All civil servants are actually poets – and all poets civil servants. That this was actually historically the case is demonstrated by a plethora of examples in the literature of the time, of course with the *Geheimrat* (approximating to court councillor) Goethe in Weimar as the prime example.

But the system also presupposes and reproduces a gender structure. The mother herself remains the silent source of all written discourse production, and the modern female reader emerges at the consumer level, identifying the lyrical egos with the writing poets and being bound to them in a desire structure that duplicates the desire structure underlying male writing. This means that the woman's function in the system is as a mother to make the men write, and as a reader to consume the texts they produce, but she herself is not allowed to write.

All this may sound more than legitimately speculative, and it is of course impossible to do justice to Kittler's often quite subtle and complicated reasoning in a short presentation like this. Kittler's strength is not least as an archival researcher with an extraordinary handling of an extensive and seemingly disparate empirical material. The basic idea of a kind of *Aufschreibesystem* – a term Kittler uses rather imprecisely, and more or less in the sense of a technical information system with source, transmitter, channel and receiver – is both a strength and a weakness. On the one hand, it gives focus and substance to Kittler's treatment of the material; on the other hand, it entails a totalizing tendency that sometimes seems too reductionist.

The second part of the book, dealing with the *Aufschreibesystem* of 1900, is not so much about a system as it is about how the old system reacts to and finally succumbs to the pressure of the new audiovisual media. The maternal voice that in the old system guaranteed a meaning beyond the materiality of writing is reduced by the phonograph to oscillations and intervals that can be recorded on a wax roll, and by photography and film the eye, the mirror of the

340 *Otto Fischer*

soul, is reduced to an interface between nerve pathways and light waves. The transcendental subject established by the technology of writing at the center of the *Aufschreibesystem* in 1800 is dissolved, and instead of the hermeneutics of idealist philosophy, it is now psychophysics, brain and nerve research that will define the human being. The Swedish author August Strindberg's *Inferno*, for instance, offers an excellent example of a reaction to this process (see e.g. Götselius 2003).

Psychoanalysis appears from this perspective as a discourse instituted to produce a form of "Ersatz" subjectivity for these modern, mechanized exsubjects reduced to their neural pathways and sensory organs. Poetry, on the other hand, which through virtual orality and virtual visuality had a monopoly on the storage and processing of sensory data, is now reduced instead, as one medium among others, to literature in the doubly literal sense of the word – that is, to what is made with letters. A typical example of such literature is Mallarmé's pure poetry, but the nonsense poetry of Morgenstern and the Dadaists, for example, also make excellent illustrations. Writing is no longer transparent, but as once upon a time at the beginning of the Gutenberg galaxy, carries meaning in and through its materiality, as for example in Apollinaire's calligraphic poetry. And in parallel with these processes, the male monopoly on writing ends: the trained hand of the scribe and poet, with which the 19th century secretary wielded the quill and shaped writing into organic forms, is around 1900 replaced by the anonymous female typist, who mechanically reproduces the same writing over and over again by technological means. What we can detect here is not only the end of the hyper-literacy that characterized the writing and reading forms of Romanticism, but also the end of the entire epoch of alphabetic media monopoly.

Discourse Networks 1800–1900 can quite rightly be described as a double epochal study of romanticism and modernism, where Kittler's analysis of modernism in many respects is quite striking: not only because it reiterates the oft-discussed thesis of the marginalization of literature under the pressure of the new media and because it interprets modernist literature as a reaction to such a process, but because it also shows how the concept of modern literature is medially conditioned, and that the position of literature in the system around 1800 is decisive for the way in which we basically still deal with literary texts. In this way, Kittler's analysis also means that literary studies itself is written into the system of writing, where it appears as a knowledge specially created to serve literature and ensure that the feedback loop between writing and subjectivity can be maintained through constantly new hermeneutic interpretations.

In the book *Grammophone, Film, Typewriter*, which followed the year after *Discourse Networks*, Kittler further develops his arguments about the media situation around 1900. In many respects, the book can be said to offer a more easily digestible version of the arguments he put forward in the second part of *Discourse Networks 1800–1900*.

The reception

When the purge of politically charged teachers at the former GDR universities in the early 1990s created a number of vacancies and triggered a veritable flood of West German researchers from the often-overcrowded humanities departments in the West, Kittler was also given the chance to swap the obsolete discipline of German studies for the more contemporary media history. Or rather: aesthetics with media history, for it was somewhat ironically one of the aesthetics professorships at the venerable Humboldt University in Berlin, the institution historically most closely associated with the 19th century writing system, that was thus updated.

If *Discourse Networks 1800–1900* was relatively infavorably received by the scholarly establishment, it had a much greater impact on younger researchers. Relatively soon, a number of researchers influenced by discourse analysis oriented themselves towards a media history perspective. This applies, for example, to Norbert Bolz, who is known as an enthusiastic spokesman for the end of the Gutenberg galaxy in the light of the new electronic media, but also to a significant number of other influential scholars in Germany in the last decades of the 20th century, as for example Jochen Hörisch, Manfred Schneider and Bernhard Siegert, to name perhaps the most important ones. The following decades saw a series of studies on such topics as the cultural and literary history of the postal system, the history of the voice from the Greek play to modern microphone technology, the literary history of the photocopier, the history of the wind tunnel and so on forth.

In accordance with his basic understanding of the crucial importance of the media, Kittler himself came to see it as a major task to promote a new humanistic research that bridges the gap between C. P. Snow's two scholarly cultures, the classical humanities, and the empirically orientated culture of modern science. The Department of Media History in Berlin consequently involved computer programming as part of its training. Kittler's vision for his professorship was to educate a new kind of humanist who would work as naturally with Goethe and Schiller as with mathematical problems, computer programming and so on.

In this respect, Kittler's approach is reminiscent of McLuhan's; perhaps it can be best described as a kind of scholarly stoicism. The researcher's task is neither to deplore nor to affirm the development of the media, but rather to try to keep up with the development and never lose sight of power. But the way to remain modern is to historicize: Foucault already teaches us that we do not have access to our own archive; that is to say, the blind spot of discourse analysis will always be the discourses in which one is embedded and which regulate the immediate present.

And it is in some sense this realization that determines the somewhat paradoxical position of media history-oriented discourse analysis today. We do not have access to our own archive, and yet it is our task as humanistic researchers to try to uncover power and the discourses it organizes. If I have understand

342   *Otto Fischer*

them correctly, the ethical implications for Kittler are that we have to fight a sustained battle to ensure, as far as possible, that our time leaves behind at least an archive that is accessible to research. It is important to warn and be aware that our devices, which control how we think and write, are not discourse-neutral, but produce a discourse of power. It is also important to realize that this discourse is no longer a discourse in the traditional sense of the word; that it does not consist of words and letters but of numbers. In short, it is a question of trying to gain access to the structures which, in the IT industry in particular, regulate our present and future thinking. And this is of course a paradoxical ambition, since we do not have access to our own archive, and consequently when we try to prepare the ground for such an archive we are largely groping in the dark. And this is where the media-historical perspective comes to the rescue: by studying past systems with respect to their media conditions, we can work our way to at least educated guesses about our own media predicament.

Today, when worrying about the effects of digitalization, the focus is very much on social media and its impact on our culture and political system. Simultaneously, we worry about the enormous possibilities of data management that enable far-reaching manipulations of our social and political behavior. Kittler had nothing to say about social media, at least not publicly. He had no website, and certainly no account on the platform formerly known as Twitter. Yet the digital is very much a prerequisite for his entire scholarship. But it is a very hard-boiled, technologically determined understanding of digitalization that he expresses. True to his media archaeology starting point, he wants to understand how the medium basically works: the medium is the message, and in the case of computers this means that we are dealing with a medium consisting of transistors and mathematics. A media science that dwells on the type of content this medium conveys will also inevitably blind itself to its profound effects. The media historian or media archaeologist must try to get as close as possible to the technological core of the medium.

During the last twenty years of his career, Kittler's influence was mainly through teaching and supervision. Given that he is one of the few German humanities scholars in recent decades to have come close to international stardom, his international involvement was limited. He spent some time as a visiting professor at Stanford, but otherwise remained loyal to Berlin. He also published relatively little in traditional monograph form in the last decades, instead publishing his lectures in book form – itself a venerable tradition intimately connected to the classical German philosophical tradition that he both criticized and felt at home in (Kittler 1999; 2000; 2013). Hegel and Heidegger, along with the perennial provocateur Nietzsche, remained essentially Kittler's recurring dialog partners to the end.

Conclusion

"The media determine our condition" is one of Kittler's most often quoted statements (Kittler 1986). The type of media history that Kittler pursued was based on this simple statement. We can only understand our current situation, as well as history, by examining what the media conditions are for each specific historical situation. This also means that Kittler's approach remained historicizing; it is always through a careful historical investigation of the open and hidden media conditions that we can approach a qualified understanding of our contemporary situation as well. But it also means that the search must go back even further - to the time that gave us not only the alphabet that came to define the culture of the West, and with whose help young men and women in Europe around 1800 created themselves as writing and reading subjects, but also the mathematics that forms the basis of the digital world we live in.

In the final decades of his life, Kittler returned to Greece – not primarily to classical philosophy, but to the pre-Socratics, Homer and the Pythagoreans. His last work, the monumental *Musik und Mathematik* (Music and Mathematics), remained a torso. In this work, Kittler takes the fact that the Greek vowel alphabet was used not only for writing, but also for counting and annotating music as his point of departure. Based on this primordial medium of the West, Kittler paints a picture of how poetry, music and mathematics developed in parallel and in constant dialogue with each other. In this pre-classical Greece, which in many ways is drawn in remarkably romantic colors, he sensed the contours of a media landscape where thoughts and feelings, voice and writing, fertilized each other in a single medium. In a way that may surprise those who have primarily seen Kittler as the interpreter of the hard material truth of culture, his thinking in these late writings increasingly revolved around religious themes; in the Greek gods he saw something more than just mythical figures symbolically embodying one or another phenomenon in the world of culture or nature. On the contrary, he envisioned Greek culture as a world in which these gods, or perhaps rather the divine aspects of phenomena, were very much a reality. Kittler – the great revealer of the technical truth behind Romantic aesthetics – thus came himself to embrace a conception of the ancient world that is astonishingly close to the ideas expressed in the Romantic conception of true symbolic art, and which resonates, for example, in Friedrich Schiller's poem "Die Götter Griechenlands" (The Gods of Greece). The basic idea of Schiller's poem is that in the pagan, ancient world the divine was actually present in the immediate world of human life; dryads actually lived in the trees and naiads in the water. And above all: we could experience the presence of the gods in our own lives and our own emotions.

There are indications that in his last years, Kittler actually became a professing pagan, and he was particularly interested in one deity: Aphrodite, the goddess of love. In the later parts of the great work on Greece, republished in the form of Kittler's collected works edited by Martin Stingelin, the theme of love plays a major role. And perhaps it is, in a sense, logical that the same thinker who once pointed to the role of love in the creation of the rational and emotional subjects required by the rationality of the modern state, returned in his last work to love as a primordial force in all human life and all human creation; a primordial force expressed in music and literature as well as in philosophy. In his interest in the Greek world, Kittler was able to immerse

344 *Otto Fischer*

himself in ecstasy and sensual pleasure, but also in philosophy, mathematics and the abstract thinking made possible by the very first medium of Western culture. In the prayer to Aphrodite to which his late thinking is shaped, themes converge that have been present in various ways throughout his life and throughout his writing. To a large extent, these thoughts still resonate in his last appearance.

According to an account confirmed by several sources, yet almost too good to be true, Kittler's last words were: "Alle Apparate abschalten" – "Turn off all appliances" (Roch 2011). The life-support apparatus to which he was attached was turned off and Friedrich Kittler died on October 18, 2011. In the video documenting his last public appearance, he leaves the wine glass untouched. But the program for the event in which this appearance took place, a moving-out party from the premises on Sophienstraße that had become so closely associated with Kittler's scientific work, states as its last item: "Bar und Tanz bis der Wachschutz kommt" – "Bar and dance until the security guards arrive".[2]

Notes

1 See "Friedrich Kittler - Abschied von der Sophienstraße", Youtube, https://www.you tube.com/watch?v=csDCdqU-DGY (accessed on February 4, 2019).
2 "ÜBERTRAGEN, PROZEDIEREN, SPEICHERN. Abschied von der Sophienstraße – Buchpräsentation'Media Archeology'", https://www.musikundmedien.hu-berlin.de/de/m edienwissenschaft/medientheorien/medien_die_wir_meinen/chronik1/ubertragen-proze dieren-speichern-abschied-von-der-sophienstrase-2013-buchprasentation-bbmedia-archa eologyab (accessed on April 4, 2019).

References

Foucault, M. (1966) *Les mots et les choses. Une archéologie des sciences humaines.* Paris: Seuil.
Götselius, T. (2003) Die Hölle ist los: Strindberg schreibt, in Baumgartner, W. & Fechner-Smarsly, T. (eds.) *August Strindberg. Der Dichter und die Medien* (pp. 113–133). München: Wilhelm Fink.
Kittler, F. (1977) *Der Traum und die Rede. Eine Analyse der Kommunikationssituation Conrad Ferdinand Meyers.* Bern: Francke.
Kittler, F. (1985) *Aufschreibesysteme 1800/1900.* München: Wilhelm Fink.
Kittler, F. (1986) *Grammophon, Film, Typewriter.* Berlin: Brinkmann & Bose.
Kittler, F. (1999) *Optische Medien. Berliner Vorlesung.* Berlin: Merve.
Kittler, F. (2000) *Eine Kulturgeschichte der Kulturwissenschaft.* München: Wilhelm Fink.
Kittler, F. (2013) *Philosophien der Literatur. Berliner Vorlesung.* Berlin: Merve.
Kittler, F. (2015) *Baggersee. Frühe Schriften aus dem Nachlaß* (T. Hron & S. Khaled, eds.). München: Wilhelm Fink.
Roch, A. (2011, November 17) Hegel is dead. *Telepolis.* https://www.heise.de/tp/features/ Hegel-isdead-3392030.html (accessed on April 2, 2019).
Sprenger, Florian & Pakis, Valentine A. (2016, Spring) Academic networks 1982/2016. The provocations of a reading, *Grey Room*, 63, pp. 71–88.
Winthrop-Young, G. (2005) *Friedrich Kittler zur Einführung.* Hamburg: Junius.

25 Daniel Dayan and Elihu Katz (1992) *Media Events: The Live Broadcasting of History*

Johanna Sumiala

Media, events and social imaginaries

'An event is something to experience, to live in for a while, and to be a part of with others', as described by media historian Espen Ytreberg (2022). The scale of events can vary from family rituals to large-scale mega-events such as the death of Queen Elizabeth II. They can be once-in-a-lifetime events, such as the landing of the first man on the moon, or recurring ritual celebrations like the Olympic Games. Following the existing literature, events can be characterised as temporally bound intensifications of social action and related moments of heightened sociality (see, e.g. Durkheim, 1912/1995; Collins, 2005; Alexander et al., 2006; Wagner-Pacifici, 2017). In short, events matter because they *do* things in society.

The intensification of the meaning and influence of mediatisation (see, e.g. Hjarvard, 2013) in modern society has led scholars to pay particular attention to the media as a site of increased sociality and associated social imaginaries (see, e.g. Shils and Young, 1956; Boorstin, 1963; Kellner, 2003). The scholarly response to 'eventisation' in modern, mediatised society has been divided. On the one hand, events have been analysed as media spectacles of modern society (Debord, 1967; Kellner, 2003; see also Scannell, 2014). They have been called 'pseudo-events' (Boorstin, 1963), and their manufactured and manipulative nature has been critically analysed (Rojek, 2013). Scholars in this strand contend that events serve to mask power in society and that their consequences are usually considered negative and alienating. In the lexicon of media scholar Paddy Scannell (2014, 179), the core of the critical response to societal events can be articulated as a distaste for the idea of public life as theatre. Scannell (2014) reflects this perspective below:

> [...] Ceremony and spectacle have always been part of public life in any society, and objections to them are as old as the events themselves. Puritanism has an iconoclastic dislike of conspicuous public display which offends its austere worldview. Utilitarianism grumbles that such things are a waste of time and money, both of which could be better spent on less idle and more practical things. By any cost-benefit analysis, ceremonial events are irrational. They are neither useful nor necessary.
>
> (Scannell, 2014, 180)

DOI: 10.4324/9781003432272-26

346 *Johanna Sumiala*

However, not all have been satisfied with such pessimism about media events. For example, inspired by the French tradition of sociology and anthropology and the work of Émile Durkheim, Victor Turner, Daniel Dayan and Elihu Katz wanted to paint a different picture of events as mediated and ritual performances in modern society (Sonnevend, 2018b). Their view of events in society is more positive, optimistic and hopeful. It draws on the 'anthropology of ceremony in mass communication' and appreciates the media's role in organising public life (see also Sonnevend, 2018b, 123).

Dayan and Katz's theory of media events also evolved throughout their writings in the 1980s, a decade of significant political change. The book's early inspiration dates back to Egyptian President Anwar el-Sadat's visit to Israel in 1977. The next decade witnessed the collapse of the Iron Curtain, symbolised by the fall of the Berlin Wall and the end of the Cold War era. Dayan (2010, 27) describes the historical undertone that guided their writing as follows:

> ...during the liminal moments we described in 1992, totality and simultaneity were unbound; organizers and broadcasters resonated together; competing channels merged into one; viewers gathered at the same time and in every place. All eyes were fixed on the ceremonial centre, through which each nuclear cell was connected to all the rest.
>
> (Dayan, 2010, 27)

Media Events: The Live Broadcasting of History was published by Harvard University Press in 1992, and the book soon became a modern classic. Its anthropological perspective was fresh to the field, as the authors emphasised the importance of rituals and the symbolic in bringing to life the 'social' in the public sphere at extraordinary occasions in history that are broadcast live.

Since its publication, the theory of media events has been the subject of lively scholarly debate – celebrated but also critiqued, reconsidered and revised (see, e.g. Couldry, Hepp and Krotz, 2010). Dayan and Katz, both together and separately, have also contributed to this debate by self-critically reflecting on the original theory and revisiting its foundations (see, e.g. Dayan, 2010; Katz and Liebes, 2010[1]; Katz and Dayan, 2018).

In this chapter, I aim to provide an overview of the theory's main developments and reflect on its relevance for current media and communication studies scholarship. First, I present the original media event theory as first formulated in the book *Media Events*. Second, I discuss the main trends of the 'critical turn' as a critical assessment against the original media event theory (see also Sonnevend, 2016b). Third, I explain how media event theory, in its revised and elaborated form, continues to live on in the literature and how the theory has been revisited in the field. Finally, I conclude this chapter by reflecting on future avenues in the study of media events and the related legacy of Dayan and Katz's original book.

Original media event theory in a nutshell

Dayan and Katz's original idea was that media events are best characterised as mediated social performances. They represent a special *genre* powerful enough to interrupt the everyday flow of news and journalism, engage the audience with society's core values, and invite them to participate in the event (Dayan and Katz, 1992, 5–9). In the authors' lexicon, media events are 'ritual media'. They have their own grammar, structure of meaning (story form or script) and practices characterised by live (television!) broadcasts, the disruption of daily media rhythms and routines, the scripting and preparation of the event, a huge audience, 'the whole world' watching, social and normative expectations attached to viewing, 'must see', the ceremonial tone of media narration and the objective of connecting people.

Furthermore, Dayan and Katz (1992, 25) classified media events into three categories: 'coronations', 'conquests' and 'contests'. These scripts constitute (i) the main narrative possibilities within the genre, (ii) the distribution of roles and (iii) the way in which these roles are enacted. In many cases, the three-story forms are closely intertwined, and historical events correspond to and resonate with each other at different levels. Moreover, the form of an event can also change and shift into another narrative form as the event unfolds.

As Dayan and Katz remind the reader, it is also important to recognise that all these scripts are embedded in deeper symbolic and ritual structures of meaning in a given culture and society (1992, 28–29). The common feature of their original 1992 work is the *ceremoniality* associated with media performance. The authors point out that the significance of media events lies in their ability to reach a larger audience than any event requiring a physical presence. The audience itself is well aware of this mediated presence, as they follow the developing media event in different locations, which can be private, semi-public or public. The shared social imaginary around the social as constitutive of society is created and maintained in these exceptional moments in time and history.

As a landmark study, the book has generated much discussion among scholars. Its value has been seen in its theoretical innovation, bringing anthropological concepts such as symbol and ritual into a new dialogue with the tradition of studying mass communication. Its methodological innovation lies in its emphasis on mediated participation and observation as a method for studying media events unfolding on screens (Hepp and Couldry, 2010, 2; see also Scannell, 1995, 2001, 2022).

The main criticisms of Dayan and Katz's original approach relate to (1) the assumed ceremonial and integrative function of media events; (2) the attempt to exclude disruptive or traumatic events from the focus of their theory; (3) the strong focus on mass media, especially television and radio; and (4) a certain presentist take on interpreting media events as 'live broadcasting of history', as the book's subtitle suggests (see, e.g. Sonnevend, 2018b; Sreberny, 2016). Media sociologist Julia Sonnevend (2016b) has called these later developments in the theorisation of media events a 'critical turn' (see also Frosh and Pinchevski, 2018). I address the main critiques below.

348   *Johanna Sumiala*

'The Critical Turn'

Perhaps the most influential critique of the original media theory stems from its supposed emphasis on ceremoniality as an affirmation of the social. Many critics maintain that Dayan and Katz's initial account of media events assumes an overly direct relationship between media coverage and audience approval, obscuring the ideological construction of the social order and the challenges and disruptive potential inherent in many media events (see, e.g. Scannell, 1995, 2001; Couldry, 2003). Second, scholars drawing on criticism have placed more emphasis on the conflictual nature of media events (Fox, 2016; Mortensen, 2015), calling for them to be analysed through a framework of terror, disaster and war rather than focusing on theoretical and empirical analyses of media events as ceremonial and ritualistic national occasions that stimulate a sense of belonging to a nation, as Dayan and Katz (1992) did. With this turn, media events are typically examined as disruptions and as endorsements of polarising performances in society (Liebes, 1998; Liebes and Blondheim, 2005; Nossek, 2008; Sumiala et al., 2018; Valaskivi et al., 2019).

A third cluster of critiques concerns the demand to consider the changing media environment as a context for media events. The original book was written in an era dominated by television and broadcast media. However, with the globalisation of communication through the Internet, mobile communication and social networks, critics have called for reconsidering the context in which media events and their theorising occur. Andreas Hepp and Nick Couldry (2010, 9) argue that in theorising media events in the digital age, we should not view them as situated in a particular national location and orchestrated primarily by national media institutions but as disembedded or even ubiquitous communicative practices. In their edited volume, *Media Events in a Global Age* (2010), Couldry and Hepp, together with Fredrich Krotz, call for the theory of media events to be further developed to identify them as translocal phenomena articulated through the digital connectivity of communication processes.

The fourth main critique relates to the assumed presentist nature (see, e.g. Sreberny, 2016; Sonnevend, 2018b; Ytreberg, 2022). The book's subtitle, 'Live Broadcasting of History', suggests that the focus on media events as they unfold 'live' in front of viewers' screens is the 'present'. According to Espen Ytreberg (2022, 9), Dayan and Katz placed more emphasis on the role of the media in contemporary events and less on events as a broader category of social and historical phenomena. One of the main criticisms of Dayan and Katz's approach to media events is therefore their alleged anachronism and unwillingness to discuss the broader (historical) frames embedded in the contemporary experience of liveness in media events (Sreberny, 2016). Barbie Zelizer (2018) indicates that these 'mnemonic schemes' are temporal interpretive frameworks that determine the way media events are produced and made sense of in 'real time'. Sonnevend (2016a) adds another important dimension by providing a time-sensitive *narrative* approach to analysing media events. Such narratives, she contends, are typically grounded in the mythical and historical story

Daniel Dayan and Elihu Katz (1992) 349

layers of society and culture and activated in the meaning-making of the event as it unfolds before the public's eyes.

Dayan and Katz's response

Dayan and Katz have responded to the above criticism by readjusting their ideas both individually and together (see, e.g. Dayan, 2010; Katz and Liebes, 2010); Katz and Dayan, 2018). One of the best-known self-critiques by the authors is an article called 'No More Peace' by Katz and Liebes (2010). In this text, Katz, together with Liebes, suggests that the focus of analysis of media events should indeed shift from conquests, contests and coronations to disaster, terror and war. In their vocabulary, ceremonial media events have been 'upstaged' by disruptive events. The authors assert:

> We believe that cynicism, disenchantment, and segregation are undermining attention to ceremonial events, while the mobility and ubiquity of television technology, together with the downgrading of scheduled programming, provide ready access to disruption. If ceremonial events may be characterized as 'co-productions' of broadcasters and establishments, then disruptive events may be characterized as 'co-productions' of broadcasters and anti-establishment agencies, i.e. the perpetrators of disruption.
>
> (Katz and Liebes, 2010, 157)

Katz and Liebes also posit that marathons of terror, natural disasters and war should be distinguished as a separate genre from ceremonial media events (see also Liebes, 1998; Liebes and Blonheim, 2005; Cottle, 2006).

In addition, Dayan (2010, 26–27) has acknowledged the 'macabre accoutrements to televised ordeals, punishments, and tortures' and the emphasis on 'stigmatisation and shaming' in today's mediated public events, whereby media events lose their potential to reduce conflict; instead, Dayan (2010, 28) argues that they 'foster rather than suspend belief'. Furthermore, Dayan claims that in the present context, media events tend to lose their distinct character and instead migrate towards other genres. This means that media events, in Dayan's self-critical conception, are no longer clearly differentiated entities but exist on a continuum. Dayan (2010, 27) states that what we see today are 'almost media events' and characterises this process as the 'banalisation of the format'. Moreover, he reminds his readers that the pragmatics of media events have changed as messages have become more diverse, audiences more selective and social networks more ubiquitous. Dayan leaves the reader in a state of doubt. For him, in today's contested territory of media events, disenchantment and the loss of the 'we' – their most critical functions – are the likeliest consequences.

In one of their later co-published pieces, Dayan and Katz rearticulate their pessimism about the future of media events. In their joint article '*L'esprit de l'escalier: 25 years of hindsight*' (Katz and Dayan, 2018, 151), the authors predict: 'We are on the verge of the Big question: will Media Events survive post

350 *Johanna Sumiala*

modernity? We think that they won't'. In their analysis, the proliferation of new media and attendant endless interruptions, the fragmentation of the public and the weakened legitimacy of authority are the main explanations for the diminishing power of this genre.

However, the theory has proved more resilient than its creators may have first estimated. Judging by a number of scholars who consider the theory relevant, the prognosis of the death of media events seems premature. Instead, many media and communication studies scholars continue to acknowledge the theory's transformative potential in the present media environment (see, e.g. Fox, 2016; Mitu and Poulakidakos, 2016). In the remainder of this chapter, I discuss the continued relevance of media event theory for understanding how major events as mediated performances are now constructed as 'shared experiences and frames of reference' in the digital context (Frandsen et al., 2022, 1–18; see also Ytreberg, 2022) and how existing critiques have influenced recent developments in media event research.

The lasting charm of media events

Sonnevend's (2016b, 2018b) work on global iconic events offers a fruitful approach to rethinking ceremoniality in today's media events. Unlike many critics, she continues to see relevance in the ceremonial aspects of media events and advocates for their resilience as a cultural form and, consequently, for their lasting charm (Sonnevend, 2018b). Sonnevend (2016a, 2) is particularly interested in what she calls 'global iconic events', that the international media cover extensively and remember ritually. In her analysis, global iconic events have the capacity to transcend national boundaries in an enduring manner. She cites the fall of the Berlin Wall in 1989 as an example of such an event. But instead of considering media events as universally integrative, Sonnevend (2016a, 2) underlines their nature as fragmented. In her vocabulary, even if media events are transported from one context to another, they are not necessarily transmitted by everyone and everywhere. This is to say that 'global iconic events touch many hearts, but they do not have the same meaning for everyone' (Sonnevend, 2016a, 2–3). Global iconic events are therefore ceremonial, but they may also be rearticulated, contested or even ignored somewhere.

Furthermore, Sonnevend (2016a, 20) is interested in rethinking how narratives in global iconic events travel (across time, space and media platforms) in the present global and digital context. She suggests that these events have five narrative dimensions: (1) foundation, the narrative prerequisites of events; (2) mythologisation, the development of their resonant message and elevated language; (3) condensation, the encapsulation of an event in a simple short narrative and recognisable visual scene; (4) counter-narration, stories that go against the prominent event narrative; and (5) remediation, the ability of the event to travel across multiple media platforms and changing social and political contexts (Sonnevend, 2016a, 3). Elsewhere, she clarifies her stance as follows:

...media events might be just as alive as they have been before. People follow them on a variety of platforms and on a multiplicity of screens. The interpretations of ceremonial events are even more fragmented than they were in the 1990s. But there are still moments that glue millions and occasionally billions to screens, there are still events that are discussed for years to come, setting a standard for future occasions.

(Sonnevend, 2018, 125)

Such a view has also been underlined by Anne Jerslev (2022), who confirmed the continuing relevance of broadcast media in bringing people together even in the era of global, digital and platform-based communication.

Conflictual media events

While Sonnevend (2016a, 2016b, 2018a) and Jerslev (2022), among others, have contributed to rethinking and reclaiming the meaning of ceremoniality and the iconic nature of media events as global and historical gatherings, Tamar Liebes (1998), James Carey (1998), Hillel Nossek (2008), Andreas Hepp and Nick Couldry (2010), Tal Morse (2018) and Mette Mortensen (2015), to name but a few scholars, have emphasised the importance of advancing research on media events as disruptive and divisive phenomena and the meaning of journalist news media in it. In this context, the early work of Tamar Liebes (1998) has been particularly influential. Liebes refers to unexpected (from the perspective of the media, not the perpetrators) violent media events as 'disaster marathons'. Terror attacks such as the Charlie Hebdo massacre in Paris, France, or the Christchurch shootings in New Zealand would be paradigmatic examples of such an event type. When a terror attack strikes, the everyday flow of news and their rhythm are suddenly interrupted, and the ritual media 'take over' and begin to build up a symbolised time-out for the disaster. When this happens, media professionals, including journalists, editors and producers, begin to follow a familiar and highly ritualised script that is also recognisable to its audience. Clearing space for a disaster puts massive pressure on the professional media to repeat, anticipate developments and create news (Liebes 1998, 76). It also creates a need in society for 'quick solves' to respond to violence. In Liebes' (1998) view, disruptive media events as ritual and symbolic intensifications thus tend to reinforce polarisation and division of society (between 'us' and 'them') instead of bringing people together in solidarity to recover from a collective trauma of terrorist violence.

Since Liebes' publication (also later developed in a co-authored piece published with Katz), considerable scholarly interest in disruptive media events has taken hold. Hillel Nossek (2008) has developed a concept of 'news media' – media event. He argues that journalists in the face of massive-scale violent events tend to move into a ritual mode of communication and 'abandon their usual normative professional frame that encompasses such activities as critical scrutiny of governmental actions, and assume a national-patriotic coverage

352 Johanna Sumiala

frame that seeks to reestablish normality and restore order' (Nossek 2008, 313) among the in-group.

Tal Morse (2018) has extended the idea to include the category of 'asynchronous continuous media events' to characterise ongoing conflicts. When writing this piece in 2023, the Russian war of aggression in Ukraine and the war between Israel and Hamas stand out as examples of this type of event. As such, these events may not have a fixed beginning (as one obvious starting point), climax or end; instead, they continue to exist in the global media in a more or less explicit and/or latent form.

Furthermore, drawing on the work of Hepp and Couldry (2010), Mette Mortensen (2015) discusses conflictual media events as yet another new subcategory of disruptive media events. In her view, conflictual media events are best described as 'major situations of conflict (terror, armed conflict, disaster) involving both mass media and connective media and drawing the attention of a wide audience, who increasingly contributes actively to the representation and communication of the event'. Following Mortensen's observation, a new dynamic between journalistic media and connective, or social, media has come to play a key role in characterising today's disruptive media events and their theoretical and empirical study.

Hybrid media events

An important debate in the re-theorisation of media events concerns their hybridisation. Building on my co-authored work on hybrid media events (see, e. g. Sumiala et al., 2018; Valaskivi et al., 2022), I argue that new, globally dispersed communication technologies play a critical role in enabling today's media events and creating complex relationships between the actors and media platforms involved in shaping and participating in these events on a global scale. These changing conditions also pose a significant challenge to rethink not only how to theorise today's media events but also what they 'do' in these global high moments of ceremony and/or disruption.

When we analyse today's media events as hybrid, it means emphasising the complex interplay between the different actors, messages and platforms that contribute to making a media event. Such hybrid interplay takes place in a complex network of mass media, internet-based and mobile communication technologies, and it creates relatively fluid social intensifications between and among different actors. Thus, hybrid constellations in contemporary media events may comprise elements of ceremonial mass media communication, but they increasingly converge with contemporary forms of vernacular mass self-communication (see also Castells, 2009).

Furthermore, we can see that the degree of connectivity between 'official' and 'viral' narratives about the event can vary greatly from case to case in hybrid media events. This means that the idea of 'the whole world' watching, as applied in the original media theory (Dayan and Katz, 1992), must be considered an experience scattered onto a multiplicity of screens. As Sonnevend

(2016a) reminds us, while people may take part in a hybrid media event on a global, iconic scale, they are connected to it in different ways. They use different communication media to follow the event, associate different – and even conflicting – narratives circulating in relation to the event, and thus feel connected to different groups and identities involved in the event. As a result, a multiplicity of shared experiences around a hybrid media event and related sociality follows.

And yet, the ubiquity of a hybrid media event by no means diminishes its social and cultural power in the present world. On the contrary, I maintain that today's hybrid media events can be perceived as more global, visible and omnipresent than ever and speak to a larger and more heterogeneous audience. Consequently, as highlighted in Dayan and Katz's (1992) original theory, the question of power embedded in social integration needs to be addressed at several levels. Multiple collective imaginations and their associated social, cultural and political implications may be in play simultaneously, and they may also conflict with each other. This state of multiple narratives and related collective imaginations, as well as the symbolic battles and uneven hierarchies between them, may paradoxically heighten the significance of simplified and condensed narratives that have far-reaching cultural, historical, political and religious resonance in communicating terror and violence in the contemporary world (Valaskivi et al., 2022; Sumiala et al., 2018; Sumiala and Korpiola, 2016).

Rethinking media events in theory and in the world

In this chapter, I have argued that in the present digitally saturated social world, the role of a media event is still crucial as a public ritual that gathers around certain extraordinary moments powerful enough to sustain shared emotions and related collective imaginaries crystallised around certain symbols. As scholars who have revisited the ceremonial, disruptive and hybrid nature of contemporary media events would suggest (see, e.g. Sonnevend, 2016a, 2016b, 2018a, 2018b; Morse, 2018; Sumiala et al., 2018), the theory and concept of media events have the potential to be adapted and adjusted to the changing media landscape and the associated dynamics of different institutions, actors and content (see also Frandsen et al., 2022).

In today's world, media events are generally best characterised as relatively fluid social intensifications, most emerging in a complex network of Internet-based and mobile communication technologies. In this context, media events are theorised as flexible and contingent projects that may include elements of ceremonial and/or disruptive communication and increasingly converge with professional journalism and contemporary forms of platform-based and vernacular social communication (Frandsen et al., 2022).

In such a theoretical framework, the element of liveness in theorising media events is seen to be intensified by the real-time circulation of texts and images of and about the event in several locations simultaneously. Moreover, the level of connectivity between the 'official' and 'viral' narratives about the event can

354 *Johanna Sumiala*

vary greatly depending on the case. Therefore, Dayan and Katz's original concept of 'the whole world' watching can be understood as an experience divided into people glued to a multitude of screens (Sonnevend, 2018b).

Even though people share the media event on a global scale, they are connected to it in different ways. That is, they use different communication media to follow the event, associate with different narratives circulating about the event, and feel connected to different groups and identities involved in the event. This condition creates a multitude of shared experiences. However, contrary to what Dayan and Katz suggest in their 2018 article, the ubiquity of a media event can in no way diminish its social and cultural power. On the contrary, I maintain that today's media events can be perceived as more global, visible and omnipresent than ever before and thus speak to larger audiences. Consequently, numerous collective and shared social imaginaries may be at play simultaneously. Following Sonnevend (2018b, 125) in her defense of future media event studies, 'events still structure our global lives and times, sometimes offering hope, other times uniting many in a feeling of despair'.

Rather than claiming that the power of media events is diminishing, I assert that media events in the current media environment in fact attract considerable attention, triggering various emotions and inviting participation among and within a range of audiences (Valaskivi et al., 2022). They promote public engagement in 'participatory liveness' (Frandsen et al., 2022, 9). While these actively participating publics may profoundly disagree in their interpretation of a media event or in their desire to shape its course, they nonetheless (and perhaps precisely *because* of this affective attachment) briefly bring the 'public to life' in these moments of heightened sociality (cf. Katz and Dayan, 2018).

The question then should not be whether media events will survive – because they do – but what does this mean if we theorise them in the footsteps originally offered by Dayan and Katz (1992)? What conceptual tools and empirical perspectives should we apply now to better understand the current relationship between media events, society and the media context in which they are made and experienced? I argue that there is an urgent need to explore how the AI and data-driven commodification of our communication environment impacts how the social is brought to life (Valaskivi et al., 2022) and how we imagine our sense of community and belonging in today's society saturated with platform-based events and communication.

Note

1 Daniel Dayan first wrote his piece in 2008 and Katz and Liebes published their article in 2007. In this chapter I refer to their articles as republished in the Couldry, Hepp and Kroz (2010) edited volume *Media events in a global age.*

References

Alexander, J. C., Giesen, B., & Mast, J. L. (eds.) (2006) *Social Performance: Symbolic Action, Cultural Pragmatics, and Ritual.* Cambridge: Cambridge University Press.

Boorstin, D. J. (1963) *The Image: Or what happened to the American Dream*. London: Pelican Books.

Carey, J. W. (1998) Political Ritual on Television. Episodes in the History of Shame, Degradation and Excommunication. In Liebes T. & Curran J. (eds.) *Media, Ritual and Identity*. Abingdon: Routledge, pp. 42–70.

Castells, M. (2009) *Communication Power*. Oxford University Press.

Collins, R. (2005) *Interaction Ritual Chains*. New Jersey: Princeton University Press.

Cottle, S. (2006) Mediatized Rituals: Beyond Manufacturing Consent. *Media, Culture & Society*, 28 (3): 411–432.

Couldry, N. (2003) *Media Rituals: A Critical Approach*. London and New York: Routledge.

Couldry, N., Hepp, A., & Krotz, F. (eds.) (2010) *Media Events in a Global Age*. Abingdon: Routledge.

Dayan, D. (2010) [2008] Beyond Media Events: Disenchantment, Derailment, and Disruption. In Couldry, N., Hepp, A. & Krotz, F. (eds.) *Media Events in a Global Age*. New York: Routledge, pp. 23–31.

Dayan, D. & Katz, E. (1992) *Media Events: The Live Broadcasting of History*. Harvard University Press.

Debord, G. (1967) *The Society of the Spectacle*. New York: Zone Books.

Durkheim, É. (1995) [1912] *The Elementary Forms of Religious Life*. (K. E. Fields, Trans.). The Free Press.

Fox, A. (eds.) (2016) *Global Perspectives on Media Events in Contemporary Society*. IGI Global.

Frandsen, K., Jerslev, A., & Mortensen, M. (2022) Media Events in the Age of Global, Digital Media: Centring, Scale, and Participatory Liveness. *Nordic Journal of Media Studies*, 4 (1): 1–18, https://doi.org/10.2478/njms-2022-0001.

Frosh, P. & Pinchevski, A. (2018) Media and Events after Media Events. *Media, Culture & Society*, 40 (1): 135–138, https://doi.org/10.1177/0163443717726007.

Hepp, A. & Couldry, N. (2010) Introduction: Media Events in Globalized Media Cultures. In: Couldry, N., Hepp, A. & Krotz, F. (eds.) *Media Events in a Global Age*. Abingdon: Routledge, pp. 1–20.

Hepp, A. & Krotz, F. (2008) Media Events, Globalization and Cultural Change: An Introduction to the Special Issue. *Communications - The Journal of European Communication Research*, 33 (3): 265–272.

Hjarvard, S. (2013) *The Mediatization of Culture and Society*. London: Routledge.

Jerslev, A. (2022) Contemporary Ceremonial Media Events – Time and Temporalities of Liveness. *Nordic Journal of Media Studies*, 4 (1): 19–36, https://doi.org/10.2478/njms-2022-0002.

Katz, E. & Dayan, D. (2018) L'esprit de l'escalier: 25 years of hindsight. *Media, Culture & Society*, 40 (1): 143–152, https://doi.org/10.1177/0163443717726015.

Katz, E. & Liebes, T. (2010) [2007] 'No more peace!' How Disaster, Terror and War Have Upstaged Media Events. In: Couldry, N., Hepp, A. & Krotz, F. (eds.) *Media Events in a Global Age*. Abingdon: Routledge, pp. 32–42.

Kellner, D. (2003) *Media Spectacle*. London and New York: Routledge.

Liebes, T. (1998) Television's Disaster Marathons. A Danger for Democratic Processes? In: Liebes, T. & Curran, J. (eds.) *Media, Ritual and Identity*. London: Routledge, pp. 71–84.

Liebes, T. & Blondheim, M. (2005) Myths to the Rescue: How Live Television Intervenes in History. In: Rothenbuhler, E. W. & Coman, M. (eds.) *Media Anthropology*. Thousand Oaks: Sage, pp. 188–198.

356 Johanna Sumiala

Mitu, B. & Poulakidakos, S. (eds.) (2016) *Media Events: A Critical Contemporary Approach*. Houndmills: Palgrave Macmillan.

Morse, T. (2018) *The Mourning News. Reporting Violent Death in a Global Age*. New York: Peter Lang.

Mortensen, M. (2015) Conflictual Media Events, Eyewitness Images, and the Boston Marathon Bombing. *Journalism Practice*, 9 (4), 536–551, https://doi.org/10.1080/17512786.2015.1030140.

Nossek, H. (2008) 'News Media'- Media Events: Terrorist Acts as Media Events. *Communications*, 33 (3): 313–330.

Rojek, C. (2013) *Event Power: How Global Events Manage and Manipulate*. London: Sage.

Scannell, P. (2022) The Life and Times of Media Events: A Tribute to Elihu Katz. *Nordic Journal of Media Studies*, 4 (1): 118–133, https://doi.org/10.2478/njms-2022-0007.

Scannell, P. (2014) *Television and the Meaning of 'Live': An Enquiry into the Human Situation*. Cambridge: Polity Press.

Scannell, P. (2001) Editorial. *Media, Culture & Society*, 23 (6): 699–705, https://doi.org/10.1177/016344301023006001.

Scannell, P. (1995) Media Events (Review). *Media, Culture & Society*, 17 (1): 151–157.

Shils, E. & Young, M. (1956) The Meaning of the Coronation. *Sociological Review*, 1 (2): 63–82.

Sonnevend, J. (2018a) Media Events Today. *Media, Culture & Society*, 40 (1): 110–113, https://doi.org/10.1177/0163443717726014.

Sonnevend, J. (2018b) The Lasting Charm of Media Events. *Media, Culture & Society*, 40 (1): 122–126, https://doi.org/10.1177/0163443717726013.

Sonnevend, J. (2016a) *Stories Without Borders: The Berlin Wall and the Making of a Global Iconic Event*. Oxford: Oxford University Press.

Sonnevend, J. (2016b) More Hope!: Ceremonial Media Events Are Still Powerful in the Twenty-First Century. In: Fox, A. (ed.) *Global Perspectives on Media Events in Contemporary Society*. IGI Global, pp. 132–140. https://doi.org/10.4018/978-1-4666-9967-0.ch010.

Sreberny, A. (2016) The 2015 Charlie Hebdo Killings, Media Event Chains, and Global Political Responses. *International Journal of Communication*, 10: 3485–3502.

Sumiala, J. (2013) *Media and Ritual - Death, Community and Everyday Life*. Abingdon: Routledge.

Sumiala, J. & Korpiola, L. (2016) Tahrir 2011: Contested Dynamics of a Media Event. In: Mitu, B. & Poulakidakos, S. (eds.) *Media Events: A Critical Contemporary Approach*. London: Palgrave Macmillan, pp. 31–52.

Sumiala, J., Valaskivi, K., Tikka, M., & Huhtamäki, J. (2018) *Hybrid Media Events: The Charlie Hebdo Attacks and Global Circulation of Terrorist Violence*. Bingley: Emerald Publishing Limited.

Turner, V. (1969) *The Ritual Process: Structure and Anti-Structure*. London: Routledge and Kegan.

Valaskivi, K. (2022) Circulation of Conspiracy Theories in the Attention Factory. *Popular Communication: The International Journal of Media and Culture*, 20 (3): 153–161, https://doi.org/10.1080/15405702.2022.2045996.

Valaskivi, Katja, Sumiala, Johanna, & Tikka, Minttu (2022) Ambivalent Rituals of Belonging: (Re)theorising Hybrid, Violent Media Events. *Nordic Journal of Media Studies*, 4 (1): 81–98, https://doi.org/10.2478/njms-2022-0005.

Valaskivi, K., Rantasila, A., Tanaka, M., & Kunelius, R. (2019) *Traces of Fukushima. Global Events, Networked Media and Circulating Emotions*. London: Palgrave Pivot.

Wagner-Pacifici, R. (2017) *What Is an Event?* Chicago: University of Chicago Press.

Ytreberg, E. (2022) *Media and Events in History*. Cambridge: Polity Press.

Zelizer, B. (2018) Seeing the Present, Remembering the Past: Terror's Representation as an Exercise in Collective Memory. *Television & New Media*, 19 (2): 136–145.

26 N. Katherine Hayles (1999) *How We Became Posthuman*

Jesper Olsson

Introduction

In the summer of 2017, the American podcast Radiolab broadcast an episode that, in the programme's own words, promised to take its listeners down 'the rabbit hole of technology'. These words alluded to the twisted and unsettling world encountered by Alice in Lewis Carroll's famous novel *Alice in Wonderland* (1865), where the homely and familiar is overturned by such things as talking animals and living playing cards. What the people behind Radiolab wanted to convey was also quite worrying. The focus in the episode was on two new pieces of software that interact with people's sensory apparatus: a video programme, Face2Face, in which a recording of one person's face – let's say the Pope's – can be controlled and manipulated by another person to make the church's leader smile gently, widen his eyes in surprise or frown in concern; and Adobe Voco, a program for voice synthesis, which makes it possible to create long, invented utterances out of a short recording of a person's voice. In both cases, reality is fabricated. We are dealing with technological transformations that raise questions about true, false and fake news to another level – a level that makes the ground shake a bit.

At the same time, we have long since become accustomed to the fact that technological innovations drive us in such reality-expanding directions. It is part of a cultural logic that has characterised modernity for hundreds of years. Furthermore, the computer programs described above were created in an age that exhibits things such as self-driving vehicles and semi-autonomous weapon systems – not to mention the latest and much-publicised developments in generative artificial intelligence (AI) – and in which some people are convinced that we will be able to download a person's consciousness to a computer in a not-too-distant future.

What characterises these objects, events and ideas is that they manifest a stronger and increasingly more intimate relationship between individuals and media. Above all, from this viewpoint, the ways of seeing and accessing a world – of communicating with it and its inhabitants – will always take place in compounds of humans, technologies and various artefacts. Undoubtedly, this may trigger fascination – as well as frustration and concerns about the loss of

DOI: 10.4324/9781003432272-27

control, agency and identity. It raises questions about how we should understand who we are and who can be accountable for what happens in the world. Ontological and epistemological, as well as political, ethical and aesthetic issues of varying density, are brought to the fore, concerning everything from how the writing of texts is affected by the interventions of auto-correct to moral dilemmas about military drone attacks.

On closer inspection, such 'anthropotechnical' compositions, as the German philosopher Peter Sloterdijk has called them, have always shaped culture and everyday life to some degree. At the same time, however, they seem to take on different traits and have different consequences today. They are embedded in a specific historical and technological context that might be designated as the 'information age', which has unfolded since World War II and has laid the foundation of the digital ecology of the 21st century – an ecology that points to the appearance of a *threshold* in the history of the media.

This threshold is the object of analysis and the intellectual engine in the work to be discussed in this chapter. The influential study by the American literary and media scholar N. Katherine Hayles (born 1943), titled *How We Became Posthuman: Virtual Bodies in Cybernetics, Literature, and Informatics* (1999), was published at another symbolically charged threshold between two millennia. The core of Hayles' book is shaped by the kinds of questions about subjectivity, communication and reality touched upon above, and by how these things have been affected by the digital media culture that has emerged in connection with the development of hardware, software, platforms and networks since the middle of the last century. As the subtitle of the book indicates, Hayles examines this problematic through a complex and in-depth reading of cybernetics, literary fiction and informatics. Her book tells a story about information, bodies and technology; about how these are linked to each other and about what it means to become and to be 'posthuman'.

Background

Although N. Katherine Hayles is a humanities researcher and theorist, her academic background is dual. As a trained chemist and literary scholar, she connects the two cultures that C. P. Snow (1959) once outlined and between which he discerned a widening gap in the decades after World War II. From the start, Hayles' activities were shaped by the ambition to build bridges across this divide. In her early books, such as *The Cosmic Web: Scientific Field Models and Literary Strategies in the Twentieth Century* (1984) and *Chaos Bound: Orderly Disorder in Contemporary Literature and Science* (1990), she approaches issues of complexity and chaos theory to explore points of contact between natural science and literature. One example is her perceptive analysis of Thomas Pynchon's novel, *The Crying of Lot 49* (1966), in which she addresses the interweaving of 19th-century thermodynamics with 20th-century information theory and cybernetics – and how these fields infiltrated both content and form, motif and metaphor in Pynchon's text.

360 *Jesper Olsson*

The Crying of Lot 49 is now considered a postmodern classic, and Hayles' thinking was inspired, in many ways, by literature and theory from the 1960s to the 1980s, often designated by the term 'postmodern'. At the same time, she has combined an interest in ideas developed by Jacques Derrida and others with insights from science, media theory and digital technology. Although she does not refer very often to media theorists such as Marshall McLuhan (see Chapter 8 in this volume), connections to his perspective on media as 'extensions of man' (McLuhan, 1964) can be observed in her work. Similarly, Hayles has been engaged in a critical exchange with German media theory and the output of its most prominent representative, Friedrich A. Kittler (see Chapter 24 in this volume) – particularly his analyses of how 'media determine our situation' (Kittler, 1986/1998). Although Hayles has been critical of what she perceives as a tendency towards technological determinism in Kittler, which she wants to supplement with an analysis of the human, phenomenological experience – that is, perception, cognition and desire – there are convergences in the shared understanding of media as directly formative for human thought and culture.

The theoretical legacy outlined above has also influenced Hayles' language and prose; perhaps especially in her early works, among which *How We Became Posthuman* can be counted today. These are impelled in part by a somewhat condensed and poetical style. Reading them can therefore be something of a balancing act, in which the reader must navigate between the two cultures and their intertwining, as well as through the surroundings of poststructuralist theory and its multiple connections to fiction and literary experimentation.

How We Became Posthuman was published in the final year of the last century and found its immediate historical prerequisites in a time that witnessed the breakthrough of personal computers in the 1980s and the spread of mobile phones, screenscapes and global digital networks in the 1990s – especially the World Wide Web, which came to define technical communication worldwide after 1989. This was a time of expansive dreams and fantasies of the digital and its potential to transform life.

Although computers had been present in society for 50 years by this time and had played an important part in everything from the building of infrastructure and industry to the cultural imagination and art, it was during these decades that 'intelligent machines' assumed a more prominent position in people's everyday lives. This was manifested through video games, websites, email and the downloading and sharing of texts, images and music. Suddenly, data could travel between people and machines across improbable distances – an entire planet – at an unprecedented speed. It may be difficult to imagine today, but when Hayles' book appeared, things such as reading newspapers online were new or unfamiliar to most people. The fictional and evocative – yet simultaneously alien and abstract – 'cyberspace' that William Gibson had outlined in his best-selling novel *Neuromancer* (1984), one of the literary works Hayles draws her readers' attention to, suddenly had tangible reality. People's experiences and understanding of time and space imploded and took on new forms. How could this come about?

N. Katherine Hayles (1999) 361

This question is answered in Hayles' book, although the book has more far-reaching and penetrating ambitions than to simply depict how digital media were developed and disseminated in society and everyday life. As already indicated, crucial existential questions are at stake, about how we understand ourselves and the world, how we can know – see and hear, think and feel – anything and share this with other beings. The book tells a story about the dissolution and reconfiguration of a certain image of the human and the autonomous 'liberal' subject that has been a philosophical anchoring point at least since the Enlightenment – a subject whose boundaries have come to be transgressed by electronically based signals and data flows.

Hayles is thorough in her investigation of these circumstances. On one level, *How We Became Posthuman* offers a chronological story that runs from the 1940s and the rise of *cybernetics* – an interdisciplinary study of communication and control that particularly emerged through the efforts of the American mathematician Norbert Wiener (1894–1964) – to the 1990s, when her study was published. 'The larger trajectory of my narrative', Hayles observes, 'arcs from the initial moments when cybernetics was formulated as a discipline, through a period of reformulation known as "second-order cybernetics", to contemporary debates swirling around an emerging discipline known as "artificial life"' (1999, p. 6). This narrative can also be divided into different layers or strata. There is a layer of theory or history of science, which contains sections on the so-called Macy conferences on cybernetics, *autopoiesis* and artificial life (chapters 3, 6 and 9 in Hayles' book); there is a layer that focuses on media technologies and applications of theory (chapters 4, 8 and 10); and, finally, there is a layer that consists of analyses of literary works (chapters 5, 7 and 10).

Hayles returns to the importance of fiction in this context several times. She emphasises early on in her book that literary texts play a 'central role' (1999, p. 21) in this setting by depicting how scientific ideas travel through society. At the same time, she contends that literature is not only shaped – it is not just a 'passive conduit' – but also *shapes* how technologies and theories gain meaning and significance in a cultural context:

> In this regard, the literary texts do more than explore the cultural implications of scientific theories and technological artifacts. Embedding ideas and artifacts in the situated specificities of narrative, the literary texts give these ideas and artifacts a local habitation and a name through discursive formulations whose effects are specific to that textual body.
>
> (Hayles, 1999: 22)

That is to say, the stories of Italo Calvino, Phillip K. Dick, William S. Burroughs, Richard Powers, Neal Stephenson and others that Hayles discusses conjoin new media technologies, along with the practices and ideas that arise in connection with them, with a particular, sensorially tangible time and place.

362 Jesper Olsson

Cybernetic variations

In the subtitle of her book, Hayles addresses two distinct topics in addition to literature: 'cybernetics' and 'informatics'. The meaning of the latter term might seem elusive at first, but after a while the reader realises that what Hayles designates as 'informatics' are phenomena that have given rise to charged concepts such as 'information age' and 'information society'. In a footnote to chapter 8, 'The Materiality of Informatics', Hayles delivers a more direct comment on the matter:

> By 'informatics', I mean the material, technological, economic, and social structures that make the information age possible. Informatics includes the following: the late capitalist mode of flexible accumulation; the hardware and software that have merged telecommunications with computer technology; the patterns of living that emerge from and depend on access to large data banks and instantaneous transmission of messages; and the physical habits – of posture, eye focus, hand motions, and neural connections – that are reconfiguring the human body in conjunction with information technologies.
>
> (Hayles, 1999: 313)

Hayles also stresses the difference between her use of the term and Donna Haraway's 'informatics of domination', which highlights issues of power, as evident in Haraway's early feminist analysis of the cyborg (Haraway, 1985). Moreover, Hayles points out that, for those who work professionally with computers, the term 'informatics' primarily refers to the design of computer technology. Some other observations in the quote above might require clarification. The late capitalist 'flexible accumulation' mentioned can be squarely equated with a capitalism that operates in a global market based on digital media and networks. The other descriptions refer to the Internet and the Web, and to the changes in lifestyle and interaction that have been triggered by digital interfaces (screen, keyboard, mouse, etc.).

If 'informatics' covers quite a wide territory in Hayles' hands, 'cybernetics' is presented within a more clear-cut historical framework. As mentioned earlier, this theory and practice emerged during the 1940s; like many scientific ideas and inventions throughout history, it was partly connected to military-driven research – in this case, during World War II. At that time, Norbert Wiener – who was a mathematician at heart, having received his doctorate in mathematics from Harvard at the early age of 17 – was engaged in engineering problems in the US Air Force. One of the most pressing challenges Wiener faced was the automation of air defence, which included both questions related to information theory and reflections on human-machine interaction.

Such questions and reflections would be further elaborated on the Macy conferences in 1946–1953, named after the Josiah Macy Foundation, which financed the activity. From the very beginning, the aim of these gatherings was clear: to develop a general theory of communication concerning animals (including humans) and machines – as stated in the subtitle of Wiener's book *Cybernetics: Control and Communication in the Animal and the Machine* (1948), a theory that would be decisive for the development of automatic systems and 'intelligent machines'.

The actual title of the conferences was longer and more complicated but captured both their content and their high degree of technical sophistication: 'Circular Causal and Feedback Mechanisms in Biological and Social Systems'. Thus, the conferences addressed the transmission of information between, for example, two persons, as well as the operation of *feedback*, which included how different systems could reuse, reflect on and learn from the information they generated. Against this background, researchers from many fields contributed to the discussions, including mathematicians, physicists, biologists, psychologists and anthropologists. The complex problems that were addressed required collaborations across disciplinary boundaries, which was not always easily achieved in practice. Differences in mindset and methods could be challenging, and a partially new conceptual apparatus was needed. Hayles describes the misunderstandings that seeped into the conversations between psychoanalyst Lawrence Kubie and neurologist Warren McCulloch regarding matters of language and consciousness:

> For experimentalists like McCulloch, concerned to give an objective account of mental processes, psychoanalysis was the devil's plaything because it collapsed the distance between speaker and language, turning what should be scientific debate into a tar baby that clung to them the more they tried to push it away.
>
> (Hayles, 1999: 71)

As Hayles points out, cybernetics needed a theory of information that circumvented questions of meaning and semantics and instead could be described mathematically and thus applied technically – as ones and zeros, and as signals – in machines. Such a theory was to be found in the work of mathematician Claude E. Shannon (see Chapter 5 in this volume), as well as in the approaches proposed by Wiener and others. In addition, a model and theory of the brain were needed that described cognitive processes in terms of information processing. Here, McCulloch's theory of *neural networks* came to play a major role. Accordingly, people could be viewed 'primarily as information-processing entities who are *essentially* similar to intelligent machines' (1999, p. 7). As a result, the differences between humans, machines and animals, along with their ways of being and communicating, were blurred. The *ontological* and *epistemological* regimes that had organised a human-centred world – anthropocentrism and humanism, in some of its guises – were shaken and at the risk of being overthrown.

How this came about, including the variations and vicissitudes of the process, supplies Hayles' story with its content – from the first phase of cybernetics, which revolved around feedback and equilibrium (*homeostasis*) between an

364 *Jesper Olsson*

actor and its environment, to the second phase, in which the question of how an observer becomes part of the observed system was central (an important problem in 20th century science, explored here through the Chilean biologists Francesco Varela's and Humberto Maturana's concepts of *autopoiesis* and *self-organising systems*), and on to the third phase, in which issues of artificial life, cellular automata and computer simulations were addressed. This last phase would later lay the foundation for various types of digital philosophy that approach reality as 'a program run on a cosmic computer' (1999, p. 11). In 2023, such an idea has gained further traction. We live today embedded in a complex media ecology, where digital operations – expressed in data mining, probability theory, targeted advertising and so on – occupy and shape our identities and behaviours, our time and our lives.

Bodies, information and 'flickering signifiers'

The development of a cybernetic perspective on humans and machines as information-processing entities had many consequences. In part, it gave rise to fictional creations, such as the famous teleporter in *Star Trek*; in part, it contributed to a philosophically problematic separation between information and materiality. It is this distinction that – in theory – makes it possible for a person in a spacesuit to step into an elevator-like construction to be disassembled and transmitted to another location and then step out in the open, wearing the same suit. The journey is based on a transformation of body and matter into 'pure' information.

Such ideas would be set in motion in the theories, ideologies and fantasies that flourished around digital media, culminating in the 1990s in what was sometimes designated as 'cyber idealism'. Since information was considered a 'disembodied flow', digital media could free us from our earthly anchoring, from the weight of the material world. On the Internet, a person could become anyone, and information could be circulated in time and space without distortion – almost without effort or waste of energy. Thus, on the very first page of her book, Hayles states that 'a defining characteristic of the present cultural moment is the belief that information can circulate unchanged among different material substrates' (1999, p. 1).

Hayles makes a key observation about this loss of body and materiality: namely, that one of the most important conceptual binaries in the history of philosophy and metaphysics is displaced in the digital information age – that of *presence/absence*. This couple loses some of its function when the significance of the body diminishes, since it is the body that situates a subject in time and space and makes it present or absent. Instead, two other concepts become more significant – that is, *pattern/randomness* – which aligns with the medial shift from the analogue reproduction of an image or a sound to the digital creation of these through the employment of code and combinations of ones and zeros.

To illustrate this media-historical and media-philosophical shift, Hayles turns to virtual reality (VR) – a technology that was still in its infancy some 25 years ago, but whose implications for the relations of subject-reality-representation had already sparked a debate. The experience of VR with the help of familiar prostheses, such as eyeglasses and gloves, induces a feeling of disorientation, Hayles writes, an 'illusion that the user is *inside* the computer', that 'subjectivity is dispersed throughout the cybernetic circuit'. Moreover, 'In these systems, the user learns, kinesthetically and proprioceptively, that the relevant boundaries for interaction are defined less by the skin than by the feedback loops connecting body and simulation in a technobio-integrated circuit' (1999, p. 27). Rather than skin and body, it is the flow of information that comes to the fore. The focus shifts from presence/absence to pattern/randomness – or, from *body* to *information.*

Hayles offers a number of examples to illustrate this shift in focus: money is transformed from bills and coins into patterns of information, production in factories is automated, criminals are linked to crimes with the help of DNA rather than testimony, sexual relationships are established through digital networks rather than through encounters in a bar, and so on. Today, all this has become commonplace. It has been naturalised to the point of invisibility through our constant connectivity – via computers, tablets and mobiles, of course, but also via sensors, surveillance cameras and smart home appliances. That just makes the process more important to examine.

For Hayles, as mentioned earlier, the role of literature in this context is essential. That the rise of digital media has affected writing, reading and the form of the book may be a trivial observation in the 21st century. But Hayles wants to show how literature itself has taken these changes into account and aesthetically investigates them at a more fundamental level. With other technologies of textual production follow other modes of signifying and embodiment, she notes, further contending that the direction 'toward pattern/randomness and away from presence/absence, affects human and textual bodies on two levels at once, as a change in the body (the material substrate) and as a change in the message (the codes of representation)' (1999, p. 29).

Consequently, in Hayles' literary analyses, she moves between *what* is represented, *how* it is done (i.e. new *forms* of representation, brought about by technology) and *the embodied experience* materialised in the interaction with new media. It is clear that this is a more complex process than writing and reading on paper. Between what is read on the screen and the machine code with which a computer operates are several layers of programming languages and software procedures. What at one level is a 'signifier' (denoting something) is transformed on the next level into a 'signified' (that which is denoted). It is this specific composition of language and machine that Hayles names 'flickering signifiers' – they flicker, and their status and function shift. This is a profound media technological shift that will also have effects on the surface, in the interfaces through which we interact with machines.

366 *Jesper Olsson*

Posthumanism and literature

While information's loss of body and materiality forms a *leitmotif* in Hayles' story, she is also clear from the beginning about the absurdity of the idea that something in the world could exist and survive without being embodied: 'Information, like humanity, cannot exist apart from the embodiment that brings it into being as a material entity in the world; and embodiment is always instantiated, local, and specific' (1999, p. 49). Information is concrete, material and situated somewhere – and such concretisations and localisations belong to the special capacities of fiction, which is precisely what grasps Hayles' attention.

In her readings of literary works, Hayles considers everything from how experiences and representations of space and time are transformed in digital contexts to how data flows permeate the boundaries between public and private, between 'they', 'you' and 'me'. Above all, the latter forms the axis around which Hayles' discussions revolve – the transformation of a subject's relationship to its surroundings. Hayles formulates this in her discussion of the data cowboy Case's entry into cyberspace in Gibson's *Neuromancer* (1984): what happens when 'data are [...] humanised, and subjectivity is computerised' (1999, p. 39)?

As mentioned at the beginning of this chapter, Hayles is particularly interested in contemplating the transformation of what she designates a 'humanist liberal subject', characterised by autonomy, self-determination and free will. Such an understanding of the individual goes back to the liberalism formulated by philosophers such as Hobbes and Locke in the 17th century. Although they approached it as a natural condition, the spread of the idea coincided with the rise of Western capitalist society, in which private ownership forms a hub. Thus, a subject is something that owns itself and is in possession of itself.

This understanding is challenged by the cybernetic concept of information and is opened up to a 'posthuman subjectivity'. The latter is characterised, in short, by the idea that information and patterns precede the body, by the view of consciousness as secondary and the body as a manipulable prosthesis and, finally, by an image of the human that makes it compatible with intelligent machines. But Hayles also stresses, as described earlier, the inescapability of materiality and embodiment, and she formulates her own vision of the posthuman:

> [...] my dream is a version of the posthuman that embraces the possibilities of information technologies without being seduced by fantasies of unlimited power and disembodied immortality, that recognises and celebrates finitude as a condition of human being, and that understands human life is embedded in a material world of great complexity, one on which we depend for our continued survival.
>
> (Hayles, 1999: 5)

How, then, might this posthuman subjectivity be represented in literature? One of the first works Hayles discusses in detail is a sci-fi novel from the early

1950s, which not only acknowledged Wiener's recently developed cybernetics but also imagined some of its potential effects. Bernard Wolfe's *Limbo* (1952) takes place 40 years into the future (i.e. in the 1990s), after a third world war has taken place. The story comes from the notebooks of a certain Dr. Martine, a brain surgeon, who has escaped to a South Sea Island where he begins experimenting with lobotomy in the service of society. Martine discovers that certain human traits always tend to appear in pairs: aggression-lust, creativity-violence and so on. This binary structure, which is organised around the hyphen and its coupling function, recurs on several levels in the novel, such as in the cyborgs who populate the island, whose artificial limbs have been attached to their bodies, directly integrating technology with the organism.

This last point is important. Rather than splitting the subject, Wolfe's cybernetic organism points to a new and improved hybrid species of humans. In the novel, this connective logic is transferred to other pairs as well, such as West and East (it is the beginning of the Cold War) and man and woman. As Hayles observes, 'No less than geopolitical ideology, sexual ideology is subverted and reconfigured by the cybernetic paradigm' (1999, p. 123). The fact that the work is haunted by misogynistic notions does not, as Hayles emphasises, prevent *Limbo* from being a thought-provoking work – in part because the cybernetic fantasy at play affects the novel's form and creates a kind of prosthetic or cyborg-like text, where different modes and expressions are linked together, such as story, drawing, non-linguistic passages and strange neologisms, defamiliarising the supposedly natural textual body. Here is the seed of a posthumanist literature and aesthetics.

Another chapter in Hayles' study is dedicated to a writer who has perhaps more than anyone else in the past half century come to be associated with androids, cyborgs and the technological infiltration of the 'human': Philip K. Dick, author of *Do Androids Dream of Electric Sheep?* (1968), which formed the basis of the famous *Blade Runner* films. Several of Dick's other stories have not only been widely read but also adapted into well-known Hollywood productions, such as *Total Recall* (1990) and *Minority Report* (2002). Early on in her discussion, Hayles points out that Dick's work demonstrates how cybernetics and the cyborg were disseminated in post-war culture. Moreover, in Dick's texts, 'androids are associated with unstable boundaries between self and world' (1999, p. 160). Her discussion focuses on precisely what characterises a posthuman subject: its porous walls towards the environment and how subjectivity and agency are thereby transformed and re-composed, so to speak – or, as Hayles terms it in the book, how a *distributed* subjectivity takes shape. For Dick, the medial and technological development that provokes this porosity is linked to capitalism: 'the landscapes of Dick's mid-sixties novels [...] are highly commercialised spaces in which the boundaries between autonomous individual and technological artifact have become increasingly permeable' (1999, p. 162). In addition, as in the work of Bernard Wolfe, there is a charged portrayal of gender at play, which Hayles discusses under the heading of the 'schizoid android'. This figure deconstructs the image of a white male subject, with its

368   *Jesper Olsson*

supposed autonomy and freedom, by blurring the differences between an inner and an outer world.

Against this background, it is perhaps no coincidence that Hayles primarily discusses male authors. The posthumanist displacement and shift of perspective brought forth by cybernetics naturally evoked anxieties in the subject with the greatest opportunity to identify itself as a free individual – that is, the Western white man from the middle and upper classes. Or, as Hayles notes towards the end of her book:

> But the posthuman does not really mean the end of humanity. It signals instead the end of a certain conception of the human, a conception that may have applied, at best, to that fraction of humanity who had wealth, power and leisure to conceptualise themselves as autonomous beings exercising their will through individual agency and choice.
>
> (Hayles, 1999: 286)

For those who have not been able to occupy such a position in any self-evident way, the posthumanist cyborg can, on the contrary, as Donna Haraway has shown, function as politically empowering and become utilised in the development of a feminist politics, aesthetics and epistemology. This reveals yet another component of *How We Became Posthuman*: its theoretical reflection on gender. Although it is not dominant, this element is present, integrated into the analysis of how the liberal individual is dissolved and how this makes room for a distributed and embodied posthumanist subjectivity.

Continuation and legacy

There are many reasons to highlight *How We Became Posthuman* as a decisive media theoretical work today. Firstly, Hayles shows how many couplings can be made and how much knowledge can be extracted from a bridging of the two cultures – in this case, by bringing together cybernetics, technology, media and literary theory and fiction. As discussed in this chapter, fiction and the study of literature can not only illustrate the social and cultural effects of new science and technology – how identities and relationships are affected, for example – but also resituate new ideas and objects in the historical context in which they were materialised and influence the form and function of technology through language, as in the case of William Gibson's notion of a 'cyberspace'.

Secondly, Hayles' analyses of how an 'autonomous liberal subject' is displaced and challenged by a more open, embodied, and distributed posthumanist subjectivity has had an impact on everything from media philosophy to feminist theorising and has also seeped out into the wider layers of culture and society. The political critique that today problematises such things as rigid gender constructions, economic injustices, anthropocentrism and environmental destruction has been able to find inspiration and energy from this discussion. Thirdly, and perhaps most importantly here, Hayles' historically grounded and media materialist analysis of digital technologies and their effects has been important for new theoretical perspectives on the contemporary media landscape.

In her subsequent works, Hayles has built on a series of observations from *How We Became Posthuman*, while simultaneously developing its lines of thought and questions much further. One important aspect is discussed in a short book published a few years later under the title *Writing Machines* (2002), which puts emphasis on how new media have influenced literary practice – both electronic works that are written, distributed and read via digital interfaces, and literature printed in books. In the next major study, *My Mother Was a Computer: Digital Subjects and Literary Texts* (2005), the focus is once again on the medial interzone where analogue and digital and page and screen meet, which is examined through the lens of a 'regime of computation' – that is, a culture in which everything can be understood as data processes. Here, a central concept is 'intermediation', signifying an exchange between language and code and man and machine, which Hayles explores in a series of readings of digital and printed literary works.

In the last decade, Hayles' research has, for instance, revolved around how reading and thinking are affected in the context of a contemporary culture of screens, networks, mobile devices and social media. In relation to the worries about reading, memory and attention that the digital has evoked (cf. Carr, 2010), Hayles has attempted to nuance the picture by discussing various types of reading, such as close reading, hyper-reading and machine reading (*How We Think*, 2012). In *Unthought: The Power of the Cognitive Nonconscious* (2017), she explores a non-conscious realm of cognition that humans share with non-human actors, including both technological and biological systems. Here, one of her aims is to highlight and deepen the understanding of the cognitive, political, ethical and aesthetic problems that intelligent machines and autonomous systems present us with today. Moreover, in *Postprint* (2021), her latest book to date, Hayles sets the task of exploring how digital technology has reconfigured the culture of print in a hands-on way, through a series of case studies.

Hayles' early investigations of the two cultures were partly connected to an emerging field of science studies in the 1990s that contained a crucial feminist component. This interdisciplinary research has grown and expanded in recent decades. Today, there is increasing talk of inter-, trans- and post-disciplinary practices, which focus on complex epistemological and societal problems that cannot be handled by established academic disciplines. Hayles' works have played and can play an important role in these areas. Her most obvious contribution may be the legacy of *How We Became Posthuman* in the field of knowledge circumscribed by the concept of 'posthumanism', which gathers a wide array of researchers, artists and activists. At the same time, there are other prominent philosophers and theorists in this context, such as Rosi Braidotti (2013), who have worked with similar questions for a long time – not least from a feminist point of view.

The thinking known as 'new materialism' is closely linked to posthumanism. Braidotti is linked to this strand, as is Jane Bennett, who has explored

370 Jesper Olsson

more-than-human agency in an inventive way (Bennett, 2009) by examining how everything from stones to spools of thread and insects can be attributed agency through their potential to influence events. Another name that must be mentioned here is Karen Barad, who has developed a philosophy based on the event and performativity and who, like Hayles, problematises a model of thought based on a stable subject facing and managing a world – a model that has legitimised political and ethical hierarchies according to which some people are assigned the roles of active agents while others are reduced to passive objects.

Perhaps most important, however, are the connections between Hayles' work and new ecological and, in particular, media ecological perspectives. Her investigations of a posthuman subjectivity and the increasingly complex alliances between human and machine have contributed to a more nuanced view of how media shape the world. Machines cannot be understood solely as isolated objects (a radio transmitter, a television set, a computer) or tools that human subjects control; rather, they must be studied as larger compositions, in which agency and affect not only emanate from a human operator but are disseminated in force fields by biological, technological and discursive actors and systems. Against this background, it has become important to analyse media in terms of *media ecologies* (Fuller, 2005; Parikka, 2010) – a perspective that can find inspiration in Hayles, as well as in older works by McLuhan (1964), in the cybernetics of Gregory Bateson (1971), and in the previously mentioned Friedrich A. Kittler's media theory (see also Chapter 23 on Neil Postman in this volume). Similarly, there is a resonance between Hayles' analyses in *How We Became Posthuman* and today's expanded understanding of environments and ecologies in general, which aims to look beyond nature in the narrower sense to incorporate cities, technological systems and artefacts into the concept. Similar concepts include Timothy Morton's (2007) influential idea of an 'ecology without nature' or German media philosopher Erich Hörl's concept of a 'general ecology' (Hörl & Burton, 2017).

Such a catalogue of philosophers and theories points in several directions and might give a fragmented impression. However, it is also a measure of the richness of Hayles' work. The various names listed above provide a hint on how to extend and further the readings of *How We Became Posthuman*; they also suggest how compounded and multifaceted the theories around media, subjectivity and reality are and must be today – that they need to be formed by the kind of interdisciplinary thinking that Hayles' posthumanist practice encourages.

References

Bateson, G. (1972). *Steps to an ecology of mind*. Ballantine Books.
Bennett, J. (2009). *Vibrant matter: A political ecology of things*. Duke University Press.
Braidotti, R. (2013). *The posthuman*. Polity Press.
Carr, N. (2010). *The shallows: What the Internet is doing to our brains*. W.W. Norton.
Fuller, M. (2005). *Media ecologies: Materialist energies in art and technoculture*. MIT Press.

Haraway, D. (1985). Manifesto for cyborgs: Science, technology and socialist feminism in the twentieth century. *Socialist Review*, 80: 65–108.

Hayles, N. K. (1984). *The cosmic web: Scientific field models and literary strategies in the twentieth century*. Cornell University Press.

Hayles, N. K. (1990). *Chaos bound: Orderly disorder in contemporary literature and science*. Cornell University Press.

Hayles, N. K. (1999). *How we became posthuman: Virtual bodies in cybernetics, literature, and informatics*. University of Chicago Press.

Hayles, N. K. (2002). *Writing machines*. MIT Press.

Hayles, N. K. (2005). *My mother was a computer: Digital subjects and literary texts*. University of Chicago Press.

Hayles, N. K. (2012). *How we think: Digital media and contemporary technogenesis*. University of Chicago Press.

Hayles, N. K. (2017). *Unthought: The power of the cognitive nonconscious*. University of Chicago Press.

Hayles, N. K. (2021). *Postprint. Books and becoming computational*. Columbia University Press.

Hörl, E., & Burton, J. (Eds.) (2017). *General ecology: The new ecological paradigm*. Bloomsbury Academic.

Kittler, F. A. (1986/1998). *Grammophon film typewriter*. Stanford University Press.

McLuhan, M. (1964). *Understanding media: The extensions of man*. McGraw Hill.

Morton, T. (2007). *Ecology without nature*. Harvard University Press.

Parikka, J. (2010). *Insect media: An archeology of animals and technology*. University of Minnesota Press.

Snow, C. P. (1959). *The two cultures*. Oxford University Press.

27 John Durham Peters (1999) *Speaking into the Air*

Johan Fredrikzon

Rethinking the problem of communication

The most important works in any enterprise or field of knowledge are arguably those that change our view of the foundations of the field itself. In rare cases, such a shift in perspective can result from the disproving of a central axiom in the natural sciences. In the humanities, such shifts come from asking new types of questions or drastically rephrasing old ones. The trick is to know where productivity is hiding, to sense which questions will get actual purchase on our collective perception of what we are doing and why. John Durham Peters' *Speaking into the Air* (1999) is a demonstration of how this can be done. Essentially, it is an achievement that comes from being disrespectful to the tradition in such a way that tradition later thanks you for it. Perhaps this is the main use of Peters' work: observing what is needed in terms of materials, arguments and creativity to direct a gentle but well-aimed kick at own's field of practice. This is the reason we keep returning to the classics, after all – they teach us how to think. Although we will never be able to do it in precisely the way they did, we can come away with a meta-level notion of the kinds of equipment needed in terms of recklessness, conviction and hard work.

Fundamentally, Peters wants his readers to think differently about communication. Communication, he suggests, has always been about failure. We cannot get through; our packages are lost, the message is warped, the line is noisy. Or, the audience is not paying attention. On this general principle, centuries of technical innovation look like a long line of efforts to repair our unsuccessful stabs at reaching one another. How, scholars and philosophers have asked, can minds truly become one? What is the path to authentic and mutual understanding? This, Peters suggests, was the wrong premise all along. It is a view predicated on an idealisation of what can be practically achieved and, more importantly, what we should strive for. The alternative Peters offers is one of humbleness. This position, it turns out, enables him to solve several problems at once. By expecting less than a perfect union of souls in our interactions with others, we might cultivate an awareness of our limits as living beings. Consequently, we will be less inclined to reach for technical fixes to our ruined anticipations of a perfect signal. Instead, we should marvel at the fact

DOI: 10.4324/9781003432272-28

that we are, occasionally, able to connect at all. Indeed, we should not even expect a reply; there may be sufficient meaning in the very attempt to be heard. The model Peters employs to substantiate his claim is grounded in the difference between dissemination and dialogue, which is a theme that runs throughout the book. The instigators of these divergent tracks of messaging are Jesus in the Gospels on the one hand and Socrates in Plato, especially *The Phaedrus*, on the other. While using these two figures to set the stage for the development of Western thought does not seem particularly original, posting them as trailblazers for communicative principles is. This is another of Peters' habits: employing a wide range of philosophers and authors to perform as media theorists. Starting a treatise on the history of the idea of communication by arguing in favour of the dissemination of Jesus over the dialogic obsessions of Socrates, Peters immediately invites his readers into an uncommon narrative. This move builds on his general perspective on how we ended up with a confused notion of what it means to connect with each other in the first place. Whereas Socratic dialogue insists on the *eros*, the closeness, the face-to-face interaction, dissemination is fundamentally a wasteful yet generous technique. The disseminator does not force the devotion of the audience, but speaks to those who have ears to hear. This is less about the sender demanding an authentic experience of true unity with the listener and more about respecting otherness. With dissemination, as in the spreading of seeds or the broadcasting of news, the information will sometimes do its work and sometimes not.

From these short observations, a few notable characteristics of Peters' work can already be identified. He aims to explore the historical conditions for communication as a cultural-technical phenomenon. Only then will he be able to explain why we ended up with the definitions and challenges we currently face. To succeed, he must turn to sources that do not already accept communication as a given discipline or even recognise it as a matter worthy of consideration. This, in turn, makes it necessary to employ a charitable attitude towards concepts and terms; they must allow for some stretching and bending to perform the analytical work required. Moreover, throughout this examination, Peters retains an ethical orientation on the topic of communication. Our methods and strategies for – but also our hopes of – connecting to others should be considered reflections of how we conduct ourselves in the world, Peters insists.

Media scholars in the 2010s and beyond will identify *Speaking into the Air* as a book that, first, adopts a broad notion of what media can be (Fuller, 2005; Starosielski, 2015); second, one which writes a deep history of media (Parikka, 2015; Zielinski, 2006); and, third, which tells the story of when old media were new (Gitelman, 2006). If those operations seem familiar, it is because they have become so in the decades since Peters' book was first published. Although Peters' work has contributed to the beneficial expansion of the field in these directions, the true value of his effort lies in how these moves are combined with a serious philosophical exploration. In the following, I will address each of these elements of his book; first, however, I want to present an overview of its parts.

374 *Johan Fredrikzon*

Chapter by chapter

Having introduced his readers to two opposing paths of communicative strategy, in his second chapter, Peters embarks on the problem of disembodiment. Being one of the rare media historians willing to dig deeper than the strata of the last two centuries, Peters begins with Augustine and the properties of angelic dispatches. He touches on Aquinas and then draws an arc to Locke via Newton, Bacon and others. If these thinkers do not immediately strike us as luminaries specifically worried about communication, Peters' attentive scholarship demonstrates that we may have been too fast in thinking so. To him, they belong to what he dubs 'the Spiritualist Tradition' – which is his way of significantly extending the more familiar 19th century leanings towards telepathy, séances, animal magnetism, mesmerism and so on. Once he arrives at these practices proper, Peters makes it clear that the fascinations and horrors of meanings undergoing journeys without bodies were simultaneously the objects of faith, philosophy and science. Rather than being distinct from one another, these collectives trafficked in similar interests, albeit dressed in different robes. 'Spiritualism', Peters asserts, 'offered a bridge between physics and metaphysics' (1999, p. 101). Lingering on the rich exchange between esoterics and engineering, he makes explicit what later studies have been able to support in numerous case studies: systems of belief and conviction are not readily separable from those of chicanery, festival and showmanship, and all are tied to the inventions of new apparatuses. Hence, we cannot understand the history of the radio without knowing the history of spiritualism.

In the third chapter of his book, the author leaves the spiritualists for a group of more grounded philosophers: Hegel, Marx and Kierkegaard. Again, Peters is not primarily concerned with communication as conceived by its common cadre of theorists; instead, he seeks to establish 'the conditions of possibility of communication' (1999, p. 109). To that end, he visits the 19th-century origins of thinking on history, society, and subject. In Hegel, he finds that there can be no self without a public; the self must be recognised by others to be real, and objects are intertwined with subjects. In the early Marx, Peters locates a theorist worried about the 'unhappy relations between subject and object' (1999, p. 119). In his reading, money, of course, is a medium of sorts that enables labour to be stored. In turn, capital can be seen as an agent that influences the binding of both time and space. Appreciative of Marx for noting that failures of communication lie more in unjust allocations of resources than in semantics, Peters ultimately remains critical of Marx for not recognising that alienation is part of our being, not something to be fixed. Distance, mediation and layering in human connections cannot always be corrected. This is an illustration of what Peters is able to do with some of the heavy fixtures of history by reading them in a light that is not powered by the expected sources of energy. In Kierkegaard, Peters finds much to agree with – not only because he is a philosopher who seriously takes on the problem of religious faith and the histories of the Word, but because he is sensitive to communication as a 'mode of revealing and

John Durham Peters (1999) 375

concealing, not of information exchange' (1999, p. 129). The Dane, as Peters sees him, has no time for naïve authenticity and straight messages. He trades in secrets, hidden meanings, irony and, above all, the necessity of misunderstanding. If these elements – which are ever-present in connections between parties – are sought to be eliminated on the understanding that all risks of breakdown must be mitigated, the result, according to Peters, will be a 'regime of falsity and chatter' (1999, p. 139).

Reasoning about the distinction between transmission and recording, Peters submits that 'the two key existential facts about modern media are these: the ease with which the living may mingle with the communicable traces of the dead, and the difficulty of distinguishing communication at a distance from communication with the dead' (1999, p. 149). The main difference, of course, is that there can be no dialogue with the dead. It must, therefore, be a question of dissemination. This, Peter argues, is the hallmark of hermeneutics. Speaking with the dead is like holding a conversation with pets or infants: you must take on both parts yourself. And let us not degrade the communication we can have with those who never reply. Peters insists that our staying in contact with Plato or the Beatles on a hermeneutic or aesthetic level should count as meaningful in its very act. Reaching out is more important than getting something back; dead letters and cut-off returns are not insignificant actions in the world, much less failures by definition. The focus of the book's fourth chapter is squarely on the new recording medium of the 19th century: the phonograph. As Peters has it, the result of a device that immortalised sound so that it could be replayed at will at any time meant that the breath of the human soul 'took up residence in a machine' (1999, p. 161). Sound was, so to speak, captured as a performance, rather than as a libretto or score. The voices of the dead were brought back into the present via a record, which shared with the telegraph a sense of disembodiment. The phonograph, too, seemed to operate in the world of spirits. Turning to the post office, Peters naturally centres on the status and handling of dead letters. The heroes of this chapter are Emerson and Melville's Bartleby: the first in his fundamental openness to the communicative acts of the environment in all its forms, with the universe both as the great broadcaster and as always embodied in rocks and bones; and the second in his non-violent refusal to engage in 'the moral tyranny of dialogue'. Peters views the latter position as Bartleby's 'nobility' – the traits of which Bartleby shares with Kierkegaard's Abraham and with Christ himself (1999, p. 159).

Peters' elegant design for this study can be difficult to discern for the richness of its scenery. As outlined above, his reader encounters the Gospels on communication policy, Augustine on angelic messaging as well as a number of Enlightenment figures on disembodied media forms. From there, Peters takes his reader to telegraphy as the ambiguous material instantiation of spiritual correspondence and on to the phonograph as a way to connect to the non-living. At this point (if not earlier), the reader might recognise Harold Innis' two axes of space and time being recast in the equally grand matrix of body and soul. To Peters, the principal problem with techniques aimed at removing

376 *Johan Fredrikzon*

the distance between parties in both space and time is their general dismissal of the body yet insistent demand for a pure and absolute coming-together of minds. In his fifth chapter, Peters compares the Spiritualist tradition with William James' psychical research and the phenomenon of human mediums. From there, he listens in on the puzzling noises in Kafka's telephone lines. The chapter ends with a section on early 20th-century US radio, typically (for Peters) introduced with a quote from the First Epistle of the Corinthians and from where the book has its title: 'For ye shall speak into the air' (1999, p. 206). If the previous chapter played back the recordings of the dead, this chapter is about transmitting the living – minus the flesh. In what is perhaps the most conventional part of the book, the narrative in this chapter delves into the difficulties of delays and the concept of liveness. Having dealt with – in his own way – the problems of space and time, body and soul for two millennia, Peters finally turns to media topics of the late 20th century which he considers as forming the outer limits of human communicative reach – or, indeed, entirely foreign forms of connectivity: namely, computers, animals and extra-terrestrials. Can machines think? What can truly be said about the minds of animals, and why are we so eager to find aliens out there? In this closing investigation, Peters makes explicit the inclusive posture which has been guiding his presentation all along when he suggests, 'Communication is something we share with animals and computers, extra-terrestrials and angels. As beings who not only speak but communicate, we reveal our mechanical, bestial, and ethereal affinities' (1999, p. 227).

Failure as an analytic approach

Throughout *Speaking into the Air*, John Durham Peters continually returns to the problem of failure – or, more accurately, to the perception of communication as a series of failures in the history of media. Writing things down, sending messages by wire, recording sound on tin foil, broadcasting by radio frequency – in their early days, all such techniques were not just hailed as smart fixes to urgent needs, as we are often told; in fact, they were disappointments. After all, they did not accomplish the joining of minds in splendid union, nor did they make messages unambiguous and understanding shared. Nor practices universally embraced. This, Peters tells us, has been the enduring mindset shaping our collective understanding of communication: a set of tactics mobilised to amend a chronic state of failure. When we say that we are not 'getting through' to one another, that a proper dialogue is missing, that we cannot reach a common ground, much less a harmony of beliefs, we are in fact blaming communication. In this attitude, we go on to invent novel devices to correct the shortcomings of previous technologies. Typically, such novelties have been designed and advertised as being truer or closer to reality than their predecessors. This is what they 'fix'. Of course, such aims are, at least in part, media's old habit of dreaming of their own transparency or even elimination – that is, the moving horizon of absolute fidelity (perhaps best incarnated in products for male contraception). But what Peters is more concerned with is the unfortunate idea that lurks behind these efforts. Thinking of communication as something broken, he argues, hinges on an (often unarticulated) notion of the possibility of a complete unity of minds or a harmonic connection of bodies through space and time, resulting in political balance, a synchronisation of struggles and a deep mutual understanding. This, Peters notes, is not only naïve but misguided. It cannot be, and we should not want it. Hence, we ought to save some of our critique of technological solutionism for the more fundamental issue of misrecognising what communication is for and what it can do.

In problematising failure as a critical concept in media studies, Peters is joined by an ever-growing community of researchers studying failure either as a deviation or a constant in the history of media and communications. Of their recent collection of essays, *Miscommunications: Errors, Mistakes, Media* (2021), editors Maria Korolkova and Timothy Barker say that the essays attempt to move beyond miscommunication as a function and instead seek to know 'what it can tell us about the entire communication system'. The point, they inform readers, is not to dwell on things that should be managed or forgotten for not working properly but rather to focus on what miscommunication can tell us about the contemporary world. Nevertheless, when closely observed, their approach is quite different from Peters', even though his 1999 book is mentioned on the second page of their introduction. While the authors of Korolkova and Barker's volume of essays are careful not to condemn mistakes as nuisances to be ignored or failures waiting to be overcome, they never engage in the interrogation of communication as an historical idea itself (with the chapters by Peter Krapp and Wolfgang Ernst as exceptions). Although the essayists largely adopt a forgiving or even approving attitude towards hiccoughs, glitches and catastrophes in technical systems and in different traditions of thought, these are still viewed as deviations from the norm in some sense. Steven Jackson's (2014) suggestion to reconsider repair studies in terms of 'broken world thinking' is an earlier example of a similar logic. What happens, he asks, 'when we take erosion, breakdown, and decay, rather than novelty, growth, and progress, as our starting points in thinking through the nature, use, and effects of information technology and new media?' (2014, p. xx). In its departure from historical ideas about something being broken and the strategies employed to restore it, Peters' work is connected to later endeavours in what is now known as 'repair studies' (Crosby & Stein, 2020).

Yet, while the embracing of failure and mistakes has given rise to several interesting studies and proved a generally productive analytical outlook for the study of media, these investigations generally work to solidify the foundation of communication as an activity aimed at achieving connections without disturbances in media free of noise, towards a communion of souls. As a subfield to communication studies, miscommunication studies, it seems, can only reinforce the edifice they seek to contest. Conversely, in Peters' work, the very idea of failure is identified as the actual ground on which communications as a concept is historically founded. Every attempt to communicate rests upon an

378 *Johan Fredrikzon*

implicit understanding of there being something broken that will be set right by improved communication. In such a narrative, miscommunication and failure as phenomena are not unrecognised and carefully tucked-away aspects of everyday operations that must be brought into critical light. Instead, they are the very pillars of communication history – and, for that reason, hiding in plain view –responsible for our perception of dialogue and interaction as imperative and impossible simultaneously. In her studies of accidents and catastrophe, Eva Horn comes closer to Peters' fundamental interrogation, when she states that 'accidents explore a technology's realm of possibility' (Horn, 2018: 141). In this vein, Horn follows Paul Virilio, who views breakdowns as the events of invention, the origin of technology (Virilio, 2007). Of course, the German philosopher Heidegger (1962) observed the breakdown of tools as an opening up of the fabric of the world, whereby a hammer would no longer appear as an extension of the arm performing its hammering work but as an object as such, the sudden focus of our attention. Still, Peters' understanding of the whole idea of communication as resting on a presumed chronic failure and let-down is even broader and deeper than isolated occurrences of accidents or breakings, however illuminating these may be.

Conceptual extensions

Speaking into the Air is a product of the late 1990s. The Web (not the Internet, a significantly older child of the military-academic complex), which presented the notion of a sea of information in which each piece (or should we say wave or raft?) is connected to others via clickable hyperlinks and 'surfed' using a program called a browser, was a novel experience at the time. Using a regular phone line, access to 'the net' was established with dial-up modems, at 14.4 Kbits per second: to see an image on the screen, a user would click on its icon, then go make coffee while it downloaded to the PC. From there, things sped up. Email emerged next to the postal address and phone number in our directories as a passageway to reach individuals and institutions. Phones lost their wires but were devoid of images and apps. The dream of online shopping energised the markets, even as the infrastructure could scarcely support it. At this point, the hype ran into a brick wall; the dot.com bubble was about to burst when Peters' book was first published. A few years prior, Manuel Castells (1996) had convinced many that the network was the topology of the 21st century. Around the same time, Brin and Page (1996) submitted their PhD thesis to the grading committee at Stanford with the following remark: 'In this paper, we present Google, a prototype of a large-scale search engine which makes heavy use of the structure present in hypertext'. To read the full version, it was necessary to consult a CD-ROM, a medium that is now accessible almost exclusively at museums of technology and in research libraries. Few spoke of the 'digital' in the mid-to late 1990s, but information technology (IT), a networked life and faster connection speeds had started to permeate the discursive atmosphere. The general anxiety and excitement about virtual worlds, cyberspace and online

John Durham Peters (1999) 379

forms of life, which had been systematically explored since the 1980s, seemed to have found a more solid footing in the emerging Web. In communication studies, databases and computers – dubbed 'new media' – came into view as cultural objects of study, making the more familiar forms of 20th century mass media 'old' (Manovich, 2001). A few years into the third millennium, theorists began to entertain the idea of connected computers as usurpers of all other media (Jenkins, 2004). At this point, the iPhone was still three years away.

It is hardly surprising, then, that scholars around the year 2000 used this interconnected world of computational devices as a point of departure to write histories of media and communication. Whatever they took as a distant form of interaction to explore – whether cuneiform, palimpsest, the printing press, radio, or television – they began and ended their analysis with the Internet (e.g. Hutchby, 2001; Scannell, 1996). Not Peters: while he does note the concurrent discourses of multimedia and microelectronics, his investigation is closer to James Carey's (1989) work on communication as culture, taken to be a symbolic process in which reality is produced, maintained, repaired and transformed. To be sure, the performative and constitutive elements of communication are important, both in *Speaking into the Air* and in Peters' later work, *The Marvelous Clouds: Toward a Philosophy of Elemental Media* (2015). Media and the communicative work they allow 'make' the world, in so far as opening and closing it by socio-technical means. While Peters' 2015 book solidified his reputation as a herald of markedly broad conceptualisations of media – minds, faces, earth, fire and so on – his means of perception were already well established in 1999. Acts of communication, as well as their enablers or hindrances, encompass not only devices such as the telegraph and the photograph but also a range of human and divine attempts to reach out and connect: the spreading of seeds, talking to spirits, the speech of angels, the transformation of labour into money, telepathy, the waving of boughs in a storm, the writing of law, the political organisation of society, unconnected telephone calls and dreams, to name just a few. In this line of thinking, Peters is clearly indebted to McLuhan (1964), who looms large in many areas of his study, although only occasionally invoked in an explicit manner. As Nicole Starosielski points out, where W. J. T. Mitchell suggested that we think of landscapes as media in the mid-1990s, Peters managed to perform operations of significant conceptual extensions in the horizontal (space) and vertical (time) direction in his 2015 book (Starosielski, 2021). The same, I will argue, is true for *Speaking into the Air*. Indeed, as different as the explorations of these two volumes are in character, Peters' insistence to follow streams to their headwaters connects these endeavours; for all their gentle manners, both works are radical projects undertaken to test the limits of the field.

Opening the analytical door to this veritable menagerie of actants, Peters must convince his readers not that every historical subject or object understood itself or was conceived by others to be about communication, but that they are willing, so to speak, to perform this service as long as they are kept from being intellectually damaged by careless handling in the process. In his introduction,

380 *Johan Fredrikzon*

Peters concedes: 'Though few of the figures examined in this book had any notion of "communication theory", our current situation allows us to find things in their texts that were never there before' (1999, p. 10). This is true for most of the sources in the treatise: Socrates, Jesus, Augustine, Locke and a range of others. It does not trouble John Durham Peters so long as 'they are good to think with'. This completely new use of well-known sources benefits the composition and purpose of the project (1999, p. 4). Still, taking aboard a company of such great variance, stubbornness and eccentricity places some burden on the helmsman. Peters must now ensure that his audience accepts his suggestion that all these texts – many of them classics in philology, the history of religion, economics, linguistics, psychology, literature, engineering, physics, philosophy, et cetera – can productively be considered as ruminations relevant to problems of communication. By engaging with all these men and women in history, whom we otherwise know as distinguished voices in quite different fields of expertise, Peters wagers that his readers will accept the invitation to see them – and, as a consequence, his own field – in a new light. This is arguably a feat that requires for its fulfilment a scholar with the impressive breadth and gifts for associative thinking found in John Durham Peters. Ultimately, however, this labour must be accomplished at the level of the smallest components of sentences.

The result is a volume that begins with Jesus and Socrates as founders of schools of communication and ends with the assertion that 'communication is something we share with animals and computers, extra-terrestrials and angels' (1999, p. 227). This generous extension of what communication can entail – including but not limited to intelligence, consciousness, meaning, contact, awareness, suffering, intention and existence – has indisputably become more widespread and acknowledged since the early 2000s. *Speaking into the Air* must therefore be counted among the pioneering efforts in this regard and, in the process, as having made media studies more ambitious and wider-reaching. Peters effectively demonstrates that we can turn anyone into whatever we need them to be for our analysis to make sense. His book is a testament to the hard work involved in convincing his readers that doing so in each individual case is reasonable and, indeed, useful. When it works – and it mostly does, or this title would not be part of the current volume – it brings to students and scholars what they seek and desire more than anything: inspiration to push their claims one bit further; it offers them intellectual courage.

Straddling romanticism and determinism

The American flavour in *Speaking into the Air* is unmistakable. For all his fine-tuning to a European canon of thought, Peters' story retains a quality that can only be made in the United States. Apart from its general religiousness, this is perhaps most obvious in the book's account of telegraphy and radio – especially in the support (not to say comfort) it finds in the American pragmatist tradition. Even so, a distinct influence from German media theory can be discerned. For one thing, the step from McLuhan to Kittler – the abandonment of literary

John Durham Peters (1999)   381

content for a close inspection of machines, relays and wires – was never very far. Moreover, Kittler's readings of the dynamic between Edison the inventor and psychoanalysis as a practice are a reflection on the overall ambition to let devices play a significant – sometimes instrumental – role in shaping culture and our collective attitudes towards love, death, sex, art and freedom. Observations to that effect form the backbone of Peter's work. Furthermore, Kittler's parade of names worthy of inclusion – whether to embrace or attack – are brought back onto the stage in Peters' book, including Nietzsche, Kafka, Freud and Eliot. Yet, the most recognisable influence on Peters from German scholarship in media is his 'anti-humanistic' emphasis. Kittler famously summarised this emphasis as '*der sogenannte Mensch*' in his *Gramophone, Film, Typewriter* (1986), which was translated into English in the same year Peters' book was published. While the correspondence between these two distinguished philosophers of media seems to have gone unnoticed in reviews at the time of publication, a closer look shows that Peters' work includes a few 'man' in quotes in a manner emphatically reminiscent of the Kittlerian idiom. Indeed, Peters wrote the introduction to the English translation of Kittler's *Optical Media* (Peters, 2002/2010). For his part, Kittler leaned heavily on Foucault's work in decentring the human as a purportedly authentic, unhistorical and (largely) unproblematic subject, making tangible objects out of Foucault's allusions to 'apparatuses', 'techniques', 'machineries', 'instrumentalities', '*dispositifs*' et cetera. At a conference in Dartmouth in 1980, Foucault observed:

> Maybe the problem of the self is not to discover what it is in its positivity, maybe the problem is not to discover a positive self or the positive foundation of the self. Maybe our problem is now to discover that the self is nothing else than the historical correlation of the technology built in our history.
>
> (Foucault, 1993, p. 222)

Yet, perhaps the notion of the face of humanity disappearing in the sand, as famously suggested at the end of *Les mots et les choses* (Foucault, 1966), was preceded by cybernetics when it compared organisms with thermometers two decades earlier (Pias, 2016, p. 15–16; see also Geoghegan, 2023).

Despite being influenced by Kittler and, by extension, Foucault, Peters' anti-humanistic position is nonetheless decidedly different from Kittler's. Unlike his German colleague, Peters is less interested in picking a fight with classical considerations of literature and cultural studies at large. Being in the United States, it seems that Peters has less of a reason to do so; however, ultimately, Peters' complaint is not so much with the departments of humanities and scholars in a *Bildung* tradition but rather with a more general questioning of what might be phrased as, 'who do we think we are?' Hence, *Speaking into the Air* is critical of the grandeur with which humanity has presented itself and its accomplishments during the last two millennia. We expect – even force – fellow humans to respect our wishes, listen to our commands, understand our needs, respond to our desires and, generally, stand by for our further instructions. We extend this

382 *Johan Fredrikzon*

attitude to colonies, animals, machines and ghosts; even to aliens, gods and to the dead. Communication, one might say, is the intellectual topic that Peters uses to make this sorry disposition obvious in all its historical nuance. In its highest ambitions, it asks of us to change the way in which we conduct ourselves in the world – more specifically, within our relationships to others, be they hominids, cephalopods or Turing machines. In this outlook, Peters is already on his way towards what would later become known as *environmental humanities* (Emmett & Nye, 2017), albeit – as is evident from Peters' 2015 book – with a manifest update of German media theory into *cultural techniques* (Siegert, 2013). The understanding of Jesus as a disseminator of messages in the act of telling the parable of the sower scattering his seeds emerges, in hindsight, as a heavenly amalgamation of Peters' patent take on the problem of communication with the perspective of cultural techniques: the simple and ancient operation that develops over time into systems of belief, critical concepts and cultural discourse. As Peters makes clear in his introduction:

> As I examine media of transmission and recording as the post office, telephone, camera, phonograph, and radio in later chapters, my focus will not be on how they affected face-to-face communication as an already constituted zone of human activity, but rather on how such media made 'communication' possible as a concept in the first place, with all its misfires, mismatches, and skewed effects.
>
> (Peters, 1999, p. 5)

True to his argument, however, Peters does not compel his readers to accept his telling uncritically but speaks, rather, to those who 'have ears to hear', as he puts it in a spin on Matthew 11:15. It is clear that there are no absolute demarcations in *Speaking into the Air* between the academic practice of media history and the invitation to ponder the kinds of calls we choose to heed as individuals.

Steering clear, on the one hand, of excessive determinism where meaning is eternally dispelled from problems of communication and, on the other, of the ostensibly romantic yet eventually hostile position that demands of interactions to result in the union of souls, Peters finds recourse in the pragmatists. Theirs is a recognition of communication neither as hopeless nor blessed but necessary and worthwhile, a 'making-do in community' and 'taking part in a collective world, not sharing the secrets of consciousness', as in his reading of Dewey. Therefore, pragmatism is always political (1999, p. 18–19). In Peters' view, the pragmatist stance seen in Peirce and Dewey includes no wish to defend humanism or 'man'. Instead, it invites all kinds of intelligences: 'children, animals, the mad, the deformed, spirits and the dead, aliens and nature' (1999, p. 259). But it does not do so on the Cartesian grounds that we can recognise an inner life of reason in them. We cannot hope to engage in Socratic dialogue, nor to establish a Habermasian ideal speech situation in our encounters with fellow creatures. Instead, we should accept their strangeness because they share our world. In sum, there is a mercy here that is lacking in other forms of anti-humanism (1999, p. 259). As finite, embodied beings with a variety of methods to make sense of our surroundings, we should not fear mediation; it is, after all, our only chance to connect. The medium will slightly warp every message, but that's okay. Hence, Peters suggests, we should follow William James in shifting 'the crux of communication from fidelity to an original to responsibility to the audience' (1999, p. 266).

Questions of authenticity and modes of being

For readers beyond the 2020s, some of Peters' concerns as presented in the 1990s seem to have become increasingly thorny since then. The concept of authenticity, for instance, cannot be brushed off as a credulous and vain aspiration for some unreal state that never was. After social media, podcasts, post-truth regimes, alternative facts and deep fakes, we should probably conceive of authenticity as an effect of deliberate media use – a set of techniques employed to obtain various modes of authentic being (Tillema, 2021). In other words, the recognition that there never was a nature before culture which created for itself an environment must be also true of authenticity. Moreover, if authenticity is less a utopian dream forever unfulfilled or a yearning for ultimate reality and more of a mask or attitude among others, our critique of it may need to change. In addition, with the media landscape fundamentally transformed in the past two decades, it is questionable whether the task of defending mass media and broadcasting against contempt from the puritan and elitist camps of critical theory still seems relevant. The platform formally known as Twitter, as well as the algorithms of Facebook and YouTube that are designed to manipulate human behaviour into addictive patterns of use (Russell, 2019), have made users (formally known as viewers) keen to seek out institutions that are high in trust and dependability. This is the reaction we should expect, with generative artificial intelligence (AI) masquerading as our fellow humans in both sound and image (e.g. by creating photo-realistic pictures of people that do not exist and extorting families for money using fake audio of relatives). In our current predicament, then, the quest for something real and true might actually amount to a simple set of tactics for making do; not as a vision of merging souls but to obtain a sensible bearing of one's direction.

Although *Speaking into the Air* was generally welcomed as a creative opening up of the field of study, some critics pointed out that the risk of promoting dissemination as a communicative strategy was playing into the hands of demagogues. More interesting, perhaps, is the observation that the book exhibits a certain blindness to the sociology of media, including the issues of power at play in questions related to ethnicity, race and gender. Still, such concerns seem less valid if the significantly wider scope of politics invoked in the book is rightly considered. Going into the 2020s, however, we might wonder whether lowering the bar to equal standing for all might not be so innocent after all. In their laudable efforts to dethrone humanity as ruler of the planetary realm,

384 *Johan Fredrikzon*

feminists and human rights scholars (along with their academic counterparts in gender and human-animal studies) have for almost half a century now prepared the ground for a more complex and diverse ecosystem of desires and needs (e.g. Bridle, 2022; Butler, 1990; Godfrey-Smith, 2016; Haraway, 1991; Singer, 1975). Along with others, Peters has played a part in bringing this movement to communication studies (e.g. Hayles, 1999; Morton, 2017). Of course, this process has taken place next to material, infrastructural and environmental turns in the humanities (e.g. Larkin, 2013; Parikka, 2012; Parks, 2015; Pritchard, 2011; Sörlin & Wormbs, 2018). With his highly influential *The Marvelous Clouds* (2015), John Durham Peters took the seeds from his 1999 book and spread them onto this enriched soil, while – as is his custom – accepting the analytical consequences of taking seriously the theoretical implications at hand by digging deeper and wider than most. By developing a philosophy of elemental media that essentially extends the capacity of mediation to the very air we breathe and the water we drink, Peters contributed to joining the concept of 'medium' in the natural sciences with that of communication studies. These transformations have been instrumental in ensuring the continued relevance of the humanities within a space-time marked by digital and Antropocenic constraints.

Yet, the recent developments in AI and with it the inclination – both in academia and among the general public – to extend reasoning, creative powers and even sentience to machines puts some of the questions raised by Peters in 1999 (long before large language models and self-driving cars) in need of rephrasing. It is one thing to embrace the cultural fantasy of the robot as it exists in film, literature or the odd syllabus in the philosophy of mind and quite another to grant personhood to the very software discussed by US Congress as a potential existential risk. With his scope of interests, Peters did note the 'booming interdisciplinary confluence' that was happening around cognitive science, which in the 1990s was only finding its form as a research field (1999, p. 24). Some quarter of a century later, this is no longer an area of theory and games. The situation has obviously changed, with algorithms operating on 10 orders of magnitude more processing power than a mere decade ago in predicting the next token in large language models encompassing some 1.76 trillion parameters. These are tools available to anyone with an Internet connection, standing ready to disrupt not only the VC bunkers in Silicon Valley but the actual work habits of people, from lawyers to high school students. When the business of extending rights to computer models goes from being a curious thought experiment to a broadly debated issue that is put on par with the more pressing – and in no sense declining – need to alleviate the suffering of other humans and fellow animals, that is arguably the place where the rubber of anti-humanism meets the road. Seen this way, the decentring of the human as the measure of all things must grapple with its own success as it is being utilised by communities of effective altruism, x-risk and transhumanism that count among their members and champions some of the world's leading AI developers. The situation is similar to the one Bruno Latour tried to address in his paper 'Why has Critique Run out of Steam?' (Latour, 2004), where he asked whether critical thinking had become so successful that it ended up contributing to a situation where masses of people are prepared to trust nothing and almost as many stand ready to trust anything, in what looked like an unfortunate and perplexing merger between critical theory and conspiracy theory. Twenty years later, hundreds of millions of users are in the process of turning away from search engines to routinely interact with the strongly anthropomorphic interfaces of AI question-answer applications. These are deliberately designed to encourage trust in systems that are functionally incapable of anything like knowledge representation, but which nevertheless present their results with supreme confidence (even when it is outright gibberish). Language, as Peters rightly observes in *Speaking into the Air*, is the most reliable means of persuasion we know of (1999, p. 21). Today, tens of billions of dollars are invested every month in technology premised on the idea that language is a matter of auto-completion. A good portion of the engineers in charge of building this technology believe that they are breeding a new type of consciousness (Levy, 2023). Their inescapable undependability notwithstanding, these same pieces of coding machinery are predicted to replace large chunks of skilled human labour – if they do not eliminate humanity first as rogue, autonomous superintelligences. In short, our present societal configuration seems to be one in which the dethroning of human values for the benefit and well-being of algorithms may, after all, not be our wisest course. Instead, the question becomes: if we need to, how do we retrieve our humanism without reversing the important achievements of 50 years of hard work in order to inject some humility into our species' self-image?

The enduring relevance of *Speaking into the Air*

The bomb and the computer, Peters tells us, share more than just an origin as the two great technologies of the Second World War. They also both deal in bits, flashes, bursts and impulses. Above all, they 'cater to a secret pleasure in possible apocalypse, the exhilaration moderns feel in contemplating self-destruction' (1999, p. 25). As noted, the world of the 2020s is decidedly no less haunted by nuclear and informational catastrophes than when *Speaking into the Air* was first published. Considering the embarrassing amounts of oxygen currently afforded to longtermism and so-called existential risk scenarios at the expense of global poverty and climate change, Peters' 1999 observations on the affinities between devices of calculation and devices of extermination are right on the money (Torres, 2023). The same people who fear death by AI are busy creating the very code that they hope will make machines conscious. The profits made from speculating in this peculiar blend of doom and bliss at the mercy of tech are poured into the prospect of maximising the potential quality of life for cyborgs thousands of years in the future.

Still, the relevance of Peters' book hardly rests on its predictive accuracy; on the contrary, while his colleagues wide and far were hard at work writing media histories that culminated in the World Wide Web (e.g. Negroponte,

386 *Johan Fredrikzon*

1995) – in so far as the past looked like it could offer the Internet era anything at all of value, which many outright doubted – Peters turned to scripture, scholastics and spiritism to rethink the entire concept of communication. Forget the media, he seems to say, and begin instead by asking: what is this need to communicate with the dead, with each other and with things in our environment? Where did it come from? In this way, techniques, operations and devices immediately re-enter the frame to carry the burden of our disappointment in souls that fail to unite in harmony. To Peters, this is the original misunderstanding: 'to think that communications will solve the problem of communication, that better wiring will eliminate the ghosts' (1999, p. 9). If this diagnosis might serve as a quasi-evolutionary explanation of technological progress in history right up to the projects of neoliberalism, for Peters it is the root of many of our collective shortcomings. Herein lies all the greed, self-centredness, preoccupation, naïveté and coercion that he associates with the arrogant part of humanity that demands our attention at every turn but has no ear for others. The capacity to listen in on foreign frequencies is especially dear to Peters. The noise found there should not deter us. In fact, 'sending clear messages', he suggests, 'might not make for better relations; we might like each other less the more we understood about one another' (1999, p. 30). This could be the truest statement about social media yet spoken. 'To think', Peters goes on in a later passage, 'of the sharing of inner life as an unmixed good rests upon a rather unrigorous account of the human heart' (1999, p. 267). While the volume is brimming with gems of this sort, they are not written with our present media topography in mind; instead, they are remarks on what Peters finds in his excavation of the deep history of what might be called 'being in the world with others'.

For all his acute perceptions of the history of spirit thinking, Peters consistently promotes groundedness and embodiment: in a nod to Melville, the last chapter is named 'A squeeze of the hand'. Of course, the concept of finitude of mind is more difficult, but other scholars have found much support in Peters' later work on media as infrastructures of Being – even beyond the grave, in the form of online cemeteries where the deceased keep receiving messages (Lagerkvist, 2022). Those interested in the training of AI on the audio and video of our dear ones who have passed away so that they may continue to communicate with us will find plenty of historical correspondents in Peters' account.

On a fundamental level, Peters refuses to choose between the illusion of shared interiority and the horror of inaccessibility, nor will he cuddle up with the canonical figures he engages. There is, he notes, no tragedy in Marx, no mystery in Socrates, and no sense of the depths of language in Habermas. He finds no cooperative elements in Heidegger's politics and no practical aspects of words in Derrida. The only middle ground in sight is with the American pragmatist tradition. What is communication? Ongoing work. Making do. Here, Peters connects with repair studies and critical infrastructure studies years before he and others helped such fields to take shape. To arrive at this superficially simplistic result – 'ongoing work' – Peters demonstrates that he is one of the rare breed of media scholars who master both history and philosophy and

John Durham Peters (1999) 387

are able to locate fountains of interesting knowledge from sources who never considered themselves to be in the business of communication. This is no small achievement of eloquence and style. Here is Peters' introduction to his chapter on phonography: 'New media, by smashing old barriers to intercourse, often enlarge eros's empire and distort its traditional shape, and hence they are often understood as sexy or perverse or both' (1999, p. 137). The prose is dense but not heavy. The book is clear about what is wrong with most thinking about the whole subject of communication, but there is no trace of hostility in it. In the end, *Speaking into the Air* is careful to practice what it preaches, down to the smallest letter. For all its wild associations, learnedness and eclecticism, the book brings its readers a simple question: what would happen if we took all this canonical thought on ghosts, sin, angels, power, faith, money, sexuality, dreams, suffering and love to be about communication? This is why *Speaking into the Air* has retained its freshness – an almost impossible feat for a book on media theory from the late 1990s. Distance and duration, transmission and recording, dialogue and dissemination – these problems are still very much with us. From the perspectives invoked by the book, very little has happened in a mere quarter century. In that sense, *Speaking into the Air* presents an invitation to the field to consider topics whose significance might reach beyond next year's conference.

Lastly, for Peters, the task of radically rethinking our view of communication is always an ethical one. 'The key question', he notes, 'for twentieth-century communication theory – a question at once philosophical, moral, and political – is how wide and deep our empathy for otherness can reach, how ready we are to see "the human as precisely what is different"' (1999, p. 230). Instead of longing for pure communication, we should accept the distance between us and practice empathy with the inhuman. After all, any success we might have in establishing contact with anyone, whether man, beast or machine is 'dumb luck' (1999, p. 30). Settling with the impossibility of contact does not mean that we do not yearn for fellowship, only that we must learn to tolerate a certain amount of ignorance. This critical lesson comes from Emerson, who – according to Peters – 'appreciates how wild affinities destroy epistemological hubris' (1999, p. 245). This radical otherness and, ultimately, realm of unknowable elements has a religious streak that shines through here and there in Peter's seminal work. It is disseminated in such a way that the reader can choose to ignore it and experience no loss for it, as when Peters writes: 'If we thought of communication as the occasional touch of otherness rather than a conjunction of consciousness, we might be less restrictive in our quest for nonearthly intelligence'. To hear the Gospels and the messages of angels, to pick up on the whispers of ghosts and the waves emitted by the spirits of the dead, to stand by to receive radio signals from distant planets or the singing of dolphins – all these activities come down to techniques of listening. In his masterpiece *Blood Meridian* (1985), the late Cormac McCarthy makes an observation on this topic:

> The kid thought him to mean birds or things that crawl but the expriest, watching, his head slightly cocked, said: No man is give leave of that voice.

388 *Johan Fredrikzon*

The kid spat into the fire and bent to his work. I aint heard no voice, he said. When it stops, said Tobin, you'll know you've heard it all your life.

(McCarthy, 1992, p. 130)

References

Bridle, J. (2022). *Ways of being: Animals, plants, machines: The search for a planetary intelligence*. Ferrar, Straus and Giroux.

Brin, S., & Page, L. (1996). *The anatomy of a large-scale hypertextual web search engine* [Doctoral dissertation, Stanford University]. http://infolab.stanford.edu/pub/papers/google.pdf.

Butler, J. (1990). *Gender trouble: Feminism and the subversion of identity*. Routledge.

Carey, J. (1989). *Communication as culture: Essays on media and society*. Unwin Hyman.

Castells, M. (1996). *The rise of the network society*. Blackwell Publishers.

Crosby, A., & Stein, J. A. (2020). Repair. *Environmental Humanities*, 12(1), 179–185.

Emmett, R. S., & Nye, D. E. (2017). *The environmental humanities. A critical introduction*. MIT Press.

Foucault, M. (1966). *Les mots et les choses*. Gallimard.

Foucault, M. (1993). About the beginning of the hermeneutics of the self: Two lectures at Dartmouth. *Political Theory*, 21(2), 203–204.

Fuller, M. (2005). *Media ecologies*. MIT Press.

Geoghegan, B. D. (2023). *Code: From information theory to French theory*. Duke University Press.

Gitelman, L. (2006). *Always already new: Media, history, and the data of culture*. MIT Press.

Godfrey-Smith, P. (2016). *Other minds: The octopus, the sea, and the deep origins of consciousness*. Ferrar, Straus and Giroux.

Haraway, D. (1991). A cyborg manifesto: Science, technology, and socialist-feminism in the late twentieth century. In D. Haraway (Ed.), *Simians, Cyborgs, and Women: The Reinvention of Nature* (pp. 149–181). Routledge.

Hayles, K. N. (1999). *How we became posthuman: Virtual bodies in cybernetics, literature and informatics*. University of Chicago Press.

Heidegger, M. (1927/1962). *Being and time* (J. Macquarrie & E. Robinson, Trans.). Harper & Row.

Horn, E. (2018). *The future as catastrophe: Imagining disaster in the modern age*. Columbia University Press.

Hutchby, I. (2001). *Conversation and technology: From the telephone to the Internet*. Polity Press.

Jackson, S. J. (2014). Rethinking repair. In T. Gillespie, P. J. Boczkowski & K. A. Foot (Eds.), *Media technologies: Essays on communication, materiality, and society* (pp. 221–239). MIT Press.

Jenkins, H. (2004). The cultural logic of media convergence. *International Journal of Cultural Studies*, 7(1), 33–43.

Kittler, F. (1986). *Grammophon film typewriter* [Gramophone, film, typewriter]. Brinkmann & Bose.

Korolkova, M., & Barker T. (Eds.). (2021). *Miscommunications: Errors, mistakes, media*. Bloomsbury.

Lagerkvist, A. (2022). *Existential media: A media theory of the limit situation.* Oxford University Press.

Larkin, B. (2013). The politics and poetics of infrastructure. *Annual Review of Anthropology, 42,* 327–343.

Latour, B. (2004). Why has critique run out of steam? From matters of fact to matters of concern. *Critical Inquiry, 30*(2), 225–248.

Levy, S. (2023, September 5). What OpenAI really wants. *Wired.* https://www.wired.com/story/what-openai-really-wants/.

Manovich, L. (2001). *The language of new media.* MIT Press.

McCarthy, C. (1985/1992). *Blood meridian: Or, the evening redness in the west.* Vintage Books.

Morton, T. (2017). *Humankind: Solidarity with nonhuman people.* Verso.

Negroponte, N. (1995). *Being digital.* Alfred A. Knopf.

Parikka, J. (2012). *What is media archaeology?* Polity Press.

Parikka, J. (2015). *A geology of media.* University of Minnesota Press.

Parks, L. (2015). "Stuff you can kick": Toward a theory of media infrastructures. In P. Svensson & D. T. Goldberg (Eds.), *Between humanities and the digital* (pp. 355–373). MIT Press.

Peters, J. D. (1999). *Speaking into the air.* University of Chicago Press.

Peters, J. D. (2002/2010). Introduction: Friedrich Kittler's light shows. In F. Kittler (Ed.), *Optical media* (A. Enns, Trans.). Polity Press.

Peters, J. D. (2015). *The marvelous clouds: Toward a philosophy of elemental media.* Chicago University Press.

Pias, C. (2016). *Cybernetics: The Macy Conferences 1946–1953. The complete transactions.* Diaphanes.

Pritchard, S. B. (2011). *Confluence: The nature of technology and the remaking of the Rhône.* Harvard University Press.

Russell, S. (2019). *Human compatible: Artificial intelligence and the problem of control.* Viking.

Scannell, P. (1996). *Radio, television and modern life.* Wiley-Blackwell.

Siegert, B. (2013). Cultural techniques: Or the end of the intellectual postwar era in German media theory. *Theory, Culture & Society, 30*(6), 48–65.

Singer, P. (1975). *Animal liberation: A new ethics for the treatment of animals.* Random House.

Sörlin, S., & Wormbs, N. (2018). Environing technologies: A theory of making environment. *History and Technology, 34*(2), 101–125.

Starosielski, N. (2015). *The undersea network.* Duke University Press.

Starosielski, N. (2021). *Media hot and cold.* Duke University Press.

Tillema, L. (2021). *Övningar i frihet: Pedagogiseringen av känslolivet och mellanmänskliga relationer i 1970-talets Sverige.* Makadam förlag.

Torres, É. (2023). *Human extinction: A history of the science and ethics of annihilation.* Routledge.

Virilio, P. (2007). *The original accident* [L'accident originel, 2005, J. Rose, Trans.]. Polity Press.

Zielinski, S. (2006). *Deep time of the media: Toward an archaeology of hearing and seeing by technical means.* MIT Press.

28 Lev Manovich (2001) *The Language of New Media*

Peter Jakobsson

Introduction

At the beginning of the 20th century, the Russian filmmaker Sergei Eisenstein developed a theory and a practice around the cinematic montage. At the same time, visual artists such as Alexander Rodchenko and El Lissitzky worked with photomontage in which images and texts were joined together to create new and innovative forms of visual effects. For a contemporary computer user, similar technologies are an everyday experience through apps and software such as Snapchat, Photoshop, and PowerPoint. What once was part of the artistic avant-garde's toolbox has become part of everyday culture. Today, more than ever, film also consists of moving image montages. Professional production environments make it possible to combine material filmed at different times with digital objects and still images to create a simulated reality. Contrary to Eisenstein's intentions – which were to create a psychological dissonance in the viewer through the montage – this kind of montage tries to hide its origin and to deny its illusory nature.

This kind of media history, where old and new meet and mix with each other, is explored by Lev Manovich in his book *The Language of New Media* (TLNM). TLNM is one of the truly seminal works in the field of digital media studies, matched by few others in its importance for shaping this research field in the 21st century. In what follows, I will discuss both the merits and short-comings of TLNM and answer the question of what we can derive from returning to this text today. Among other things, I will highlight and point to its potential contribution to theories of mediatization and of an algorithmic media logic, but in this context also point to the theoretical problems associated with the book's ambitions. I will also point to its value as a guide to the invisible history of digital media.

So how should one understand the history of montage according to Manovich? What causes old aesthetic ideals and established production practices to be replaced by new ones? Manovich does not offer a full answer to this question, but he suggests that one thing that cannot be ignored in understanding the development of new genres, formats, and stylistic ideals, as well as production practices, is the technical production environment. What Manovich examines in

DOI: 10.4324/9781003432272-29

his book is the shift from an analogue to a digital production environment and how this shift relates to shifts in cultural expressions, cultural practices, and aesthetic values. This was an interest he shared with several other authors who also, around the time of the publication of TLNM, tried to conceptualize and theorize what, with a somewhat problematic term, was called "new media". The question at the centre of the discussion among these authors was thus: What is new about digital media, compared to its analogue predecessors?

What is distinctive about how Manovich approached this question is, as already indicated, how he perceived new media both as a continuation of older media forms – above all the media that emerged during the industrial period, such as photography and film – and as something radically different from older media. Manovich argued that we cannot rely solely on the established media histories – be they the history of the novel or film history – to understand today's digital literature or digital cinema. It is also necessary to examine the industrial and scientific history behind the modern computer in order to understand today's media forms. People like Charles Babbage – who in the 1820s formulated the principles for an automatic calculating machine to be used in the insurance industry – or Alan Turing, who is usually described as the creator of the modern computer, are thus just as important for understanding today's media forms as is Sergei Eisenstein or El Lissitzky. Focusing solely on the cultural producers and the symbolic content of the media ignores the fact that the computer is fundamentally a calculating machine. Digital media may look like any other media, but only to those who study them on the surface and fail to analyze their underlying technical functioning (Manovich, 2001: 48). Manovich underlines that all digital media operate according to certain common principles that follow from their technical nature. The overarching question that Manovich attempts to answer is thus how these principles condition, but also to some extents are conditioned by, the dominant symbolic forms of a historical period.

Theoretical contextualization

Based on Manovich's privileging of technology over content, TLNM can best be understood in relation to the tradition within media and communication studies known as medium theory, even if TLNM has few explicit references to works within this tradition. Representatives of the North American medium theoretical tradition such as Harold Innis, Marshall McLuhan, and Joshua Meyrowitz are only mentioned in passing. Representatives of the German tradition of medium theory are not mentioned at all in TLNM. It is nevertheless, in my opinion, especially Friedrich Kittler who is worth comparing with if one is interested in finding similarities and parallels between medium theory and Manovich's work.

Kittler, who is the most famous theorist in the German medium theory tradition, describes in his book *Discourse Networks 1800–1900* how his project is an investigation of the "networks of techniques and institutions that allow a

392 *Peter Jakobsson*

certain culture to select, store and process relevant data" (Kittler, 1990: 523). Except for the focus on institutions, this could also serve as a description of what Manovich is aiming for with his investigation of how a medium's technical properties create the conditions for and shape a historical period's dominant forms of storytelling and representation. Another similarity between the two is how they turn to the technological inventions and inventors to understand 20th-century mass media and their digital successors (Kittler, 1999, 2010, see also Chapter 24 in this volume).

A more explicit connection between Manovich and the medium theoretical tradition goes through Sigfried Giedion, whose book *Mechanization Takes Command* (Giedion, 1948/2013) is referenced by Marshall McLuhan in *Understanding Media* (1967) as the latter's major source of inspiration. It is probably also Giedion that Manovich has in mind when he writes about his ambition to analyze the "small steps" in the development of the new medium – a description that is close to Giedion's ambition to develop an anonymous history. During the first years of a new media technology, there is often rapid technical and aesthetic development, along with changes in audience attitudes and perceptions. After that period, rapid change is replaced by conventions and habits. One of Manovich's ambitions with TLNM is to document the early period in the history of digital media and how the choices and developments of that period came to shape the digital media we know of today.

If Manovich has a lot to say about the language and cultural forms of new media, TLNM has less to offer regarding their political consequences. Both discussions about digital media's repressive potential, as a technology of control and surveillance, and discussions about the potentially liberating powers of digital media, in the form of organizational opportunities and opportunities for publishing and sharing information, are absent from the argument. This apolitical tendency of TLNM does not mean however that Manovich is uninterested in the historical and societal context of new media. On the contrary, he insists that media history must be understood in relation to social, political, and economic developments. As an example, he points to the parallels between the cinema, the assembly line, and mass consumption, which developed during the same period. He also points to how the development within Western capitalism from a Fordist to a post-Fordist economic logic – from mass society to contemporary ideals of individuality and consumer choice – is reflected in the illusion of interactivity, which is central to digital media.

The language of new media

In what follows, I will outline the main arguments of TLNM and discuss a couple of Manovich's points in more detail. This is by no means a complete account of the contents of the book. For example, I will here pass over Manovich's in-depth discussion of the ways in which film foretells the development of new media and the ways in which digital media change the conditions for cinema as a cultural expression.

The outline of TLNM is as follows. The discussion starts in what Manovich claims are the basic *principles* of new media. These are the smallest components that digital media is made of, and everything else follows from these principles. After the principles, the *interfaces* through which we take part of digital media are presented. Next, the *operations* through which we use new media, such as buttons, menus, and filters, are presented. Only after these chapters, which thus focus on the hardware and software of digital media, and on computers as work environments, is it time, according to Manovich, to approach the media *forms* and genres that dominate the new media landscape. The chapter on the forms of new media is the chapter that moves at the highest level of abstraction and is thus the furthest from the starting point in the principles of the new media. At the same time, the cultural *forms* resemble the *principles* of new media in the way that they are not only found in a certain kind of media content or genre, but reappear in many (even most) new media objects. In the same way that narrative is a cultural form common to film and literature, the *database* and *navigable space* are forms common to a range of different new media objects. In the following discussion I will focus on the principles and forms and refer the reader directly to Manovich's book for more information on the other chapters.

The principles of new media

The first principle Manovich proposes as defining new media objects is that they are *mathematically formalizable* and thus programmable. Digital media objects, such as sound and images, are, as we know, numerical, that is, they can be described either with the help of a mathematical function, for example a curve, or with discrete data points, for example, variable values that describe various properties of an object. Also, algorithms, that is the instructions that constitute a program or an operating system, can basically be described based on mathematical and logical principles. The second principle, which follows from the first, is that new media objects are *modular*. Because new media objects consist of discrete data, such as pixels or letters, they can either retain their original form and be combined with other objects, or they can be manipulated and changed individually without changing other parts of the structure of which they are part. An image can for example, be manipulated pixel by pixel and each sampled unit in an audio file can be changed with respect to the recorded amplitude. The images and audio files, or parts thereof, can in their turn be combined with other objects, on a web page or in another framework, without changing the individual objects or files, which allows them to be reused in an infinite number of contexts.

This description probably sounds familiar to most people and may appear somewhat banal. It sounds like a description of digital media that can be found on, for example, Wikipedia. The corollaries of the various principles for media production and for the symbolic forms of the media are however massive. For Manovich, for example, the modularity of new media objects means that the

394   *Peter Jakobsson*

production process for images and film changes to become primarily about selection and composition. This is most clear in how digital moving images that seemingly reproduce a seamless reality are actually composed of material from different sources and can mix moving images with still images.

Other media theorists have, following Manovich, attributed a social and political significance to the modularity of digital media. For example, Yochai Benkler (2002) has argued that the modularity of new media is one of three components that have created the new production model found in the construction of the Linux operating system and the online encyclopaedia Wikipedia. That people can come together, without financial incentives and with limited centralized control, and together create products that can compete with those produced by some of the largest companies in the world, is because everyone is able to work on their own and at their own pace, with tasks that they can choose themselves. This, in turn, is only possible due to the modular nature of new media objects.

The third principle of new media is *automation*. The fact that new media objects are mathematical and thus programmable means that it is possible to automate recurring and time-consuming tasks, such as searching, manipulating, filtering, presenting, and controlling information. In some cases, such automation takes the form of "agents", of sorts, that perform tasks for the user, and some such applications can be described as having a form of artificial intelligence. With this, Manovich argues that human intentionality is no longer necessary in the production of new media forms (2001: 32).

Automation in turn leads to the next principle, which is *variability*. This principle means that there are no technical or economic reasons for a new media object to exist in a fixed and reproducible form, but on the contrary, it can exist in many different and constantly new forms. Because a new media object is modular and its production process is automated through software, such a media object can, for example, be presented in different ways to different users. The industrial and economic logic that requires identical products to be sold to as many people as possible is thus partially turned on its head. Instead, it may be more profitable to sell variants of the same item to different consumers, who may experience them as unique items, tailored just for them. The consequences of this shift are discussed by Manovich in his analysis of the cultural forms of new media, which I will return to later.

The last of the five principles Manovich calls *transcoding*, which is a technical term for the operation of transforming an object from one format to another, such as the translation of an image file from one image format to another. However, the principle of transcoding draws attention to such translations at levels other than the purely technical. What happens, for example, when the physical artefacts in a museum collection are digitized, with the losses in materiality and tactility that this entails, but also the gains that arise in terms of accessibility and searchability? Manovich claims that when the computer becomes central to ever more human activities, working methods, concepts, and ways of understanding the world, which are associated with the computer and computer culture, will spread to other spheres, such as the museum or the physical archive. Manovich describes it as a translation between two "layers":

> [N]ew media in general can be thought of as consisting of two distinct layers: the "cultural layer" and the "computer layer". Examples of categories belonging to the cultural layer are the encyclopedia and the short story; story and plot; composition and point of view; mimesis and catharsis, comedy and tragedy. Examples of categories in the computer layer are process and packet (as in data packets transmitted through the network); sorting and matching; function and variable; computer language and data structure.
>
> (Manovich, 2001: 46)

What Manovich describes as the spread of computer culture to other social spheres is similar to what elsewhere in media studies is described as the process of mediatization. According to theories of mediatization, the increased autonomy, power, and influence of the media means that other social spheres and institutions must adapt to a media logic (Hepp et al., 2015). TLNM can be read as an early attempt to understand the digital media logic and how other social spheres adapt to the logic of digital media. This comparison also reveals however one of the drawbacks of Manovich's medium-centric approach. Mediatization research has been criticized for being media centric, but it nevertheless views the digital media logic as an institutional logic and as consisting of the entirety of "the processes, principles, and practices" through which digital media process information, news, and culture. TLNM on the other hand is often too narrowly fixed on the technical properties of digital media, which results in an understanding that is both too rigid and static of what digital media is and can be, and sometimes gives too little attention to the social dynamics of digital networks and the power dynamics of the digital media industry.

In the next section I will give an account of how TLNM describes the cultural consequences of the computer. Particularly I will discuss the alleged waning of narrative as a cultural form, as well as the spatialization of culture, exemplified by how computer games are privileging movement through space over psychologically driven storytelling.

The database

The database and navigable space are the two cultural forms that Manovich claims constitute the privileged cultural forms of the computer medium. This does not mean that they are exclusive to new media or that they lack historical antecedents. Ancient memory techniques based on the envisioning of a physical space to which you attach the information that you are trying to memorize is also a kind of a navigable information space. The Chinese *I Ching*, or Book of Changes, is a 2500-year-old book in database form, and so on. In the same way that the underlying principles of digital media also are not new or exclusive to

396   *Peter Jakobsson*

the computer medium – quantification and automation have their predecessors in Taylorism and in the industrial assembly-line – so the database and navigable space are not created by computer technology. Rather, Manovich argues, the principles underlying new media objects *privileges* certain cultural expressions and modes of expression over others.

In a computer, information is organized in a database so that it is quickly accessible to the programs that the computer runs. The information in a computer is thus arranged according to a logic adapted to the computer's needs, while the user is provided with various interfaces and tools to access the information, for example, a folder structure or a search field. The way information is stored and made available in a database thus differs from the way information is presented in, for example, a story or in a museum. The big claim in TLNM is that the database form is not only relevant for how information is structured and presented by the computer, but that increasingly this is also the way in which we structure our view of the world, of ourselves, and of our place in the world. In this, Manovich relies on art historian Ervin Panofsky's (1927/1991) discussion of how linear perspective in Renaissance visual art was not only an artistic discovery, but also gave expression to an emerging secular and scientific worldview. By analogy, Manovich claims that the overtaking of narrative by the database reflects and helps bring about a new cultural order for the computer age. In contrast to the interlocking chain of actors and events and of cause and effect, which is how the world is ordered by narrative as a cultural form, when mediated through the database the world appears "as an endless and unstructured collection of images, texts, and other data records...the database represents the world as a list of items, and it refuses to order this list" (Manovich, 2001: 219ff). In the age of the database, order and sequence is not something that exists independently of the choices of the user, and no particular order is necessarily the best or the given. The choice lies – literally, if we imagine a person in front of a keyboard or equipped with a smart phone – in the hands of the user.

In the description of the database as a cultural form, the influences of postmodern theorists such as Frederic Jameson and Jean-Francois Lyotard are evident. Jameson argued that postmodern culture lacks depth models for understanding reality (Jameson, 1985, see also Chapter 21 in this volume). Similarly, Manovich believes that the database represents the world in terms of lists rather than systems, and it does not impose any underlying explanations or patterns on reality. This does not mean that databases lack logic or structure, but that it is up to the user to identify such patterns themselves. Manovich also explicitly refers to Lyotard's idea of the demise of grand narratives, which was a diagnosis by Lyotard for the so-called postmodern condition (Lyotard, 1979). But where Lyotard was looking to analyze the diminished attractiveness of ideologies such as socialism, liberalism, and ideas of modernization and progress, Manovich is looking to describe and understand how new media objects change the conditions for traditional storytelling conveyed via a film or a novel. What new ways of storytelling emerge when the linear narrative is a choice among many, as we explore and move through the cultural database?

To describe the difference between the language of new media and the language of other media forms, Manovich turns to semiotics and to Ferdinand de Saussure's concepts of paradigm and syntagm, which describe relationships between signs in a sign system. In written language, a sentence is constructed by placing words one after the other, and stories are constructed by placing sentences one after the other. This is the syntagmatic dimension of language. However, each word in a sentence simultaneously relates to other words that are absent. For example, words that are synonyms of each other can be interchanged to produce a similar sentence with only small, albeit important, differences. This is the paradigmatic dimension of language, through which meaning is created by what is not present. The short three-word sentence "I am awake" gets its meaning through the paradigmatic relationship between "awake" and its antonym "asleep", but also through its syntagmatic structure. "Awake, am I" and "awake, I am" gives a different meaning to the same set of words. Literary and cinematic narratives are primarily syntagmatic. Meaning connects to meaning, scene follows scene. The syntagm is what is expressed explicitly. The database reverses this relationship. The paradigm is what is expressed explicitly, in the form of the various data points that are stored in the database. The different ways in which they can be linked together in a sequence is not given and depends on the user, who creates a syntagm out of the existing paradigm.

Navigable space

The founder of the discipline of art history, Manovich claims, "described his field as the history of spatial representation" (2001: 253). Before the modern psychological novel, the journey was one of the dominant ways of composing a story – from the Odyssey to the chivalric romance. Spatiality thus has a long history as an organizing principle within art and literature. Distinctive for new media objects, however, is that space becomes something that the user can move through; space becomes navigable. Navigable space is one of the dominant forms of digital media – from computer games and virtual reality environments to three-dimensional information visualizations and digital maps. It has also been common to describe the Internet in spatial terms. Norbert Wiener, the American mathematics professor who in the 1950s founded cybernetics – instrumental for the creation of digital media – took the name of his science from the Greek word for steersman. In the science-fiction author William Gibson's books from the 1980s, the concept of cyberspace was coined, implying that the digital world of databases and algorithms constituted a kind of space that computer and Internet users could navigate.

This, TLNM argues, also changes the way new media tell stories. To take part of a story in a computer game, we must move through space in some manner. We often have to explore every corner of the space to identify all the necessary clues, objects, or people, in order to advance to the next level of the game. It is not uncommon that this involves moving back and forth and for us to have to visit the same place over and over again. What is created is thus not

398 *Peter Jakobsson*

a linear journey from point A to B to C, and so on. Through this repetitive movement however, the player creates a mental model of the relevant circumstances and events – of the logic of the story – which allows the player to experience something that is largely consistent with a linear story. However, as a media theorist contemporary with Manovich, Espen Aarseth (1999) argued, the dialectic between aporia and epiphany – or impasses and sudden revelations or breakthroughs – is a basic structure of human experience and one that often gives rise to stories. But experiencing them in the first person – after spending a lot of time and work solving a puzzle, for example – is different from reading a story about it.

New media – 20 years later

In this section I will comment on some of the merits and shortcomings of TLNM's theoretical perspective. Given the rapid development of digital media technologies in the 21st century, it may seem unfair to point out the shortcomings of a twenty-year-old book that has these technologies as its main subject, but there is nevertheless a principal and theoretical point in doing so. TLNM can serve as an illustration of some theoretical problems with any theory that tries to identify, in the same spirit as Manovich, the fundamental principles of a medium, or to identify the specific "logic" of a medium. The most obvious problem is that it is almost always possible to find objections and counterexamples to the allegedly basic "principles" (I return to one such objection below). More problematic, however, is that the approach underemphasizes both the importance of context and the possibility of change (Galloway, 2012: 146). For example, it is enough to compare the role of the internet in politics and everyday life in different geographical contexts – for example, in countries with an authoritarian government and in liberal democracies – to recognize the shortcomings of underemphasizing context and focusing only on the "principles". Focusing on the "principles" also risks blinding oneself to agency, accountability, and the possibility of changing existing practices. For example, are automation, surveillance, and the development of artificial intelligence inevitable consequences of digitization or is it a matter of choices and decisions that have been made by actors in society? TLNM illustrates these theoretical limitations as today we can see with hindsight how both the medium as such has changed, but also how changed historical circumstances have made other characteristics appear more fundamental and important than the allegedly timeless principles emphasized in TLNM.

One thing that strikes a contemporary reader of TLNM, for example, is the problematic nature of the opposition between narrative and database that Manovich puts forward, or what has been described in more general terms as an opposition between linear and syntagmatic media forms and non-linear, paradigmatic media forms. Manovich certainly reserves himself against the claim that narrative media forms would disappear with digitization, but nevertheless envisages a reorganization of the media landscape in which certain elements – the syntagmatic media forms – will have a less prominent role, while the paradigmatic media forms will come to dominate. This clearly has not happened, and the developments that have taken place since the publication of TLNM have instead pointed in the opposite direction.

Almost all digital platforms and applications that have dominated the media landscape for the past twenty years have developed in a direction where users are served a seamless flow of content. Contrary to Manovich's remarks that the database as a media form presents the world in the form of a list that it refuses to order, more or less all market players – video platforms, music services, social network platforms, and providers of TV series – have invested in creating a ready-made and tailored syntagm, without giving the user reason to reflect on the selection or reasons to make their own choices. On the social networking platforms, users are presented with a constant feed that mixes news with notifications from friends and acquaintances, and the audiovisual content platforms automatically create playlists that continue to play until the user makes an active choice to turn them off. Of course, there are elements of the platforms offering users a smorgasbord of different kinds of content – based on a paradigmatic communication model – but the ultimate goal is to connect the user within a flow as soon as possible and to minimize the number of active choices on the part of the user. The reason for this is, of course, the simple commercial logic that follows from the fact that the digital platforms generate revenue by showing advertising to their users. Any opportunity for the user to make an active choice is thus problematic as such a choice could mean that the user switches off or moves to another platform. The goal is to automate the user's behaviour as much as possible in order to retain the user within the network or on the platform.

One reason why, at the time of TLNM, it appeared quite possible that paradigmatic media forms would become dominant is that the then most successful media companies had not yet understood that information about their users was their main financial asset. The possibility of tailoring flows according to user preferences was therefore still somewhat limited at this time. Internet cookies had indeed been introduced as early as 1995, but these only provided information about user patterns from a single browser. This browser was also usually installed on a desktop computer that was not infrequently shared by the members of a household. It is only in a situation in which internet users are basically online at all times and when they are primarily using their own devices to connect to the network – phones, tablets, and laptops – that it is possible for the network and platform companies to create individual profiles for all their users. Few realized in the late 1990s that this would be the future and that information about users would come, in an analogy with the era of industrialism, to be seen as "the oil" of the information age. However, the new business model that emerged gradually during the 21st century suggested that the idea of new media as a database of choices was appearing as old-fashioned and the model that all companies instead worked towards was to present linear, but individually adapted, media experiences.

400 *Peter Jakobsson*

If Manovich underestimated the automation of new media consumption, his discussions of media production are more accurate. Media production takes a paradigmatic form in digital media, but in a different and more pronounced way than before. Of course, media production is always about making choices based on a paradigm, but in digital media the paradigm is embodied in a different way, which Manovich exemplifies with how production software offers filters that recreate a certain historical genre or style. Since the publication of TLNM, that phenomenon has also spread outside of professional production software and caused even everyday communication to take the form of databases communicating with each other. A digital media user is not only offered an empty box to fill with content, but increasingly with predefined choices about what to communicate, even to loved ones. Communication is automated through algorithms that learn and adapt to our way of communicating, but also offer access to other communication styles – even ones we don't fully master personally. Some see this as a positive trend and as a democratization of the communication landscape, while others point to the problems for professional media producers when it is no longer necessary to be a graphic designer to create graphic design or a journalist to write journalistic texts.

Even though much has changed in the field of digital media since the publication of TLNM, the main impression of revisiting TLNM today is not a sense that its analyses are outdated. On the contrary, it can feel refreshing to read an analysis that is not overloaded with today's buzzwords, such as infrastructures, platforms, and algorithms. In that way, the book can even serve as a reminder that the concepts used today in digital media studies often are words and concepts that originates from within the digital media industry and are concepts that the tech business itself prefers to use. The dominant US and Chinese companies see themselves as *infrastructure* providers rather than media and communications companies; rather as *platforms* than as producers, suppliers, and employers; and rather as creators of brilliant *algorithms* than as part of one of the world's most capital-, energy-, and raw material-intensive industries. Revisiting TLNM today provides an opportunity to reflect on the conceptual toolbox and how well it serves the ambitions of a critical digital media studies.

A final thing that strikes a contemporary reader of TLNM is how some of the recurring themes in the book, such as navigable space and virtual reality, are still with us today and are discussed in a very similar fashion to how they are discussed in the book. To a reader unfamiliar with the history of digital media it might come across as though virtual reality has been a constant feature in the academic discussions about digital media as well as in the marketing hype of digital media. For someone a bit more familiar with the history of digital media the discussions about virtual reality in TLNM is rather a reminder of the boom-and-bust cycles of the digital media economy. There have been many technologies from the tech industry that has been seen as the next big thing, that a couple of years later are all but forgotten, only to re-emerge a decade later and once again hailed as the next big thing. It is thus also possible, and potentially analytically valuable, to read TLNM as it was intended – as a careful history of the small steps of technological development and of the invisible traces of digital technologies lost to memory.

The mediatization of the humanities

Manovich's work today is part of an academic field that he himself has named. In TLNM he suggests that instead of media studies we need "software studies", and as co-editor of the book series *Software Studies* at MIT Press, Manovich has been driving the establishment of that field.

Software studies is an attempt to analyze the process through which reality is increasingly being constructed through code; and what happens when nature, society, and culture increasingly are mediated through mathematical objects and algorithms. Contra Manovich however, researchers in the field have, in implicit or explicit polemics against TLNM, argued that what media theory needs is not general theories of "digitization" or "new media" but studies of specific software, programming languages, and algorithms, because each of these has its own specific way of mediating reality and of creating new realities (Fuller, 2008).

Another field in which Manovich has become a central figure is what is known as digital humanities, which is concerned with the methodological and epistemological consequences of using methods from data science to study and create new knowledge about film, literature, visual culture, and so on. Among other things, it is about using digital tools to analyze large archives of text, sound, and images, on a scale that is difficult to do with traditional and often qualitative humanities methods (see e.g. Berry, 2012). What Manovich proposed in TLNM – in dialogue with Lyotard's (1979/1984) discussion in *The Postmodern Condition* on the state of knowledge in the "computerized society" – is that when society's cultural infrastructure is digitized, culture and knowledge will be translated into a language and format adapted to the computer medium, and ultimately it is the cultural expressions and forms of knowledge that most conveniently can be translated into computer language that will come to dominate. Initiatives within the digital humanities to digitize archives and museums can thus be seen as an example of what Manovich describes in TLNM. Manovich's role in this can also be seen as an illustration of what is usually called the double hermeneutics of the social sciences – in such a way that he first created theoretical concepts to name what he, together with others, later helped to realize.

The mediatization of the humanities is however a broader phenomenon than the digital humanities. The development of the humanities can be understood as an example of the phenomenon that Manovich calls transcoding – through which established "categories and concepts are replaced [...] by ones that originate from the ontology of the computer" (Manovich, 2001: 47). The turn in continental philosophy towards *object-oriented ontology* for example, suggests a kinship with what is called object-oriented programming. Furthermore, the philosopher Bruno Latour suggests that the *object orientation* of programming languages is an appropriate metaphor for discussing the challenges of democracy in a world in which "objects" of various kinds seem to play an increasingly

402 Peter Jakobsson

important role (Latour, 2005). That the language of computer science is spreading to philosophy is a sign that our time is no different from previous eras in history, during which society's dominant technologies often have stood as models for how we understand humanity and society – from the fine-tuned universe of the watchmaker to the mechanical world of the steam engine (Galloway, 2013: 358). It also points to the fact that the fundamental questions asked by medium theory – about the interrelationship between media, culture, and society – are as relevant to ask today as ever.

References

Aarseth, E. (1999). Aporia and Epiphany in 'Doom' and 'The Speaking Clock': The Temporality of Ergodic Art. In M. Ryan (Ed.) *Cyberspace Textuality: Computer Technology and Literary Theory* (pp. 31–41). Indiana University Press.

Benkler, Y. (2002). Coase's Penguin, or, Linux and 'The Nature of the Firm'. *The Yale Law Journal*, 112(3), 369–446.

Berry, D.M. (2012). *Understanding Digital Humanities*. Palgrave Macmillan. https://doi.org/10.1057/9780230371934.

Fuller, M. (2008). *Software Studies: A Lexicon*. MIT Press. https://doi.org/10.7551/mitpress/9780262062749.001.0001.

Galloway, A.R. (2012). *The Interface Effect*. Polity Press.

Galloway, A.R. (2013). The Poverty of Philosophy: Realism and Post-Fordism. *Critical Inquiry*, 39(2), 347–366. https://doi.org/10.1086/668529.

Giedion, S. (1948/2013). *Mechanization Takes Command: A Contribution to Anonymous History*. University of Minnesota Press.

Hepp, A., Hjarvard, S. & Lundby, K. (2015). Mediatization: Theorizing the Interplay Between Media, Culture and Society. *Media, Culture & Society*, 37(2), 314–324. https://doi.org/10.1177/0163443715573835.

Jameson, F. (1985). Postmodernism and Consumer Society. In H. Foster (Ed.) *Postmodern Culture* (pp. 111–125). Pluto Press.

Kittler, F.A. (1999). *Gramophone, Film, Typewriter*. Stanford University Press.

Kittler, F.A. (2010). *Optical Media: Berlin Lectures 1999*. Polity Press.

Kittler, F.A. (1990). *Discourse Networks 1800/1900*. Stanford University Press.

Latour, B. (2005). From Realpolitik to Dingpolitik, or How to Make Things Public. In B. Latour & P. Weibel (Eds.) *Making Things Public: Atmospheres of Democracy* (pp. 14–43). MIT Press.

Lyotard, J. (1979/1984). *The Postmodern Condition: A Report on Knowledge*. Manchester University Press.

Manovich, L. (2001). *The Language of New Media*. Cambridge. MIT Press.

Panofsky, E. (1927). *Perspective as Symbolic Form*. Zone Books.

Index

administrative research 25, 27, 65; *see also* critical research
Adorno, Theodor W 4–5, 12, 17–18, 25, 30, 36, 39–52, 97, 148, 158, 160, 169, 176–7, 216, 243, 301, 336–7
aesthetics 13, 16–19, 50–1, 158, 173, 203, 298, 302, 306–7, 339, 341, 343, 367–8; media 16
algorithms 81, 384–5, 393, 397, 400–1
alphabet 119, 325, 335, 343
alphabetization 337–9
Althusser, Louis 141, 152, 156, 243, 306
Anderson, Benedict 6, 284–96
archaeology 133; *see also* media archaeology
Arendt, Hanna 12–13, 101–2
art: the work of 6, 9–23, 48, 144, 175; autonomous 39, 44
articulation 152, 154, 162–3
audience commodity 147, 218, 222–5
audience research 24–38, 54
aura 16–17, 20–1, 40–2, 50, 144
authenticity 17–18, 20–1, 40, 46, 303, 373, 383
author function 129–32
automation 325, 362, 394–400
autonomy 14, 18, 39, 43, 49–51, 80, 154, 220, 243, 366, 395
autopoiesis 361, 364

back stage 84–9; *see also* dramaturgy
Barthes, Roland 4, 142, 144, 154, 268–83, 298, 312, 319
Bateson, Gregory 79–80, 370
Baudrillard, Jean 11, 19, 139–50, 160, 169, 176, 180, 298, 325
Benjamin, Walter 6–7, 9–23, 39–47, 144–5, 148, 177, 288, 311, 337
Berger, Peter L. & Thomas Luckmann 132, 231

Birmingham School 11, 157, 310, 317; *see also* Centre for Contemporary Cultural Studies
bit (binary digit) 74–5, 77
Bolz, Norbert 12, 16, 341
Bourdieu, Pierre 6, 84, 88, 142, 157, 242–55
bourgeoisie 99–100, 103, 105
Blindspot debate 212, 216, 225
Braidotti, Rosi 369
brand image 35
Brecht, Bertolt 19, 40, 139–40, 142, 148, 177, 181
broadcasting 59, 147, 159, 168, 170, 175, 180, 213, 345, 347–8, 373, 376, 383

canalization 60
Cantril, Hadley 28
capital: cultural 244, 247–8, 250; economic 244, 247–8; social 244, 252
capitalism: late 39, 47, 51, 144, 173, 297–309; market 292, 300; monopoly 44, 212, 300; platform 108, 331; print 292–5; surveillance 108, 147
Carey, James 160, 183–95, 232, 325, 351, 379
Centre for Contemporary Cultural Studies (CCCS) 2, 151, 158–60, 311, 317; *see also* Birmingham School
Chicago school 90, 156, 188–9
Chodorow, Nancy 316
cinema 17, 40–2, 196–210, 390–2, Hollywood 196, 199–201
class 5, 99–100, 105, 203, 219, 243–53; middle 91–2, 99, 207, 245–8; social 61, 105, 244, 246–9, 251–2; upper 61, 247; working 61, 105, 157, 160–1, 176, 184–5, 245–58, 317–19
code 143, 146, 152–4, 268–71, 277–82, 326, 364–5, 369, 385, 401

404 *Index*

cognitive mapping 306–7
colonialism 294
Columbia school 28, 54–6, 63–6
commodity fetishism 49, 51
communication: cultural approach to
183–95; history of the idea of 372–89;
human 70, 72, 74, 77–80, 119, 146, 191,
322; linear 162, 217; Marxist theory of
217; mathematical theory of 70–83;
model of 4, 25, 70, 72, 77, 82, 162, 313,
317; non-communication 143, 147;
process 32, 70, 73, 78, 152, 155, 161,
215, 320, 348; as ritual 188, 232;
simulation of 143–4, 146; strategic 72,
74, 145; systems 168, 178, 187, 214, 263;
visual 16, 111; technology 70, 78, 81,
114–15, 121, 257, 295, 336, 352–3;
theory, 63, 74, 81, 380, 387; as
transmission 186
connotation 82, 142, 154
consciousness industry 139, 212, 218, 223
construction 227–41; social 132, 230,
239, 263
control mechanism 79, 128–9, 131, 134
Cooley, Charles Horton 91, 188
correspondence analysis 243, 248, 251–2
counter-publics 105
critical discourse analysis 127, 157, 236
critical research 25–6, 66, 215, 219; *see
also* administrative research
critical theory 7, 11, 25, 35, 66, 81, 97,
157–8, 160, 216–17, 220–1, 243, 269,
336, 383, 385; *see also* Frankfurt school
cult value 16–17, 20–1; *see also* exhibition
value
cultural dominant 300, 305
cultural form 4, 166–82, 350, 392–6
cultural practices 44, 161, 175, 246, 282,
319, 391
cultural production 39, 100, 244, 251, 291
cultural studies 7, 11, 26, 33, 62, 151,
156–63, 171, 177, 183, 185, 188–9, 203,
205, 242, 291, 310–12, 317–20, 381
cultural techniques 122, 382
cultural theory 2, 20, 174, 180, 337
culture: folk 310; high 298, 301; legitimate
247–8, 250; and nature 158, 270;
oral 115, 120, 256, 260, 332; participatory 96, 107, 313; print 256, 262,
264–5, 323, 326–8, 330; scribal 256, 258,
265; sociology of 43, 157, 242; Western
17, 344; as "whole way of life" 174;
youth 115, 156, 160, 203; *see also*

culture industry, popular culture, mass
culture
culture industry 12, 18, 39–52, 169,
176, 301
cybernetics 70, 79, 217, 359, 361–3, 367–8,
370, 381, 397
cyborg 332, 362, 367–8, 385

database 265, 379, 393, 395–9
datafication 147, 323
Dayan, Daniel 192, 345–57
decoding 2, 29, 73, 128, 151–65, 205, 236,
310, 313, 317; *see also* encoding
deconstruction 160, 302, 336
democracy 96–97, 104, 107–9, 173–4, 183,
220, 322, 327, 331, 401
denotation 154
depthlessness 299, 302, 304
Derrida, Jacques 160, 281, 298, 336, 386
Dewey, John 120, 184, 186–9
dialectic 18, 39, 42–3, 45–6, 50–51, 152,
236, 300, 303, 398
difference 80–1; *see also* information
theory
digital humanities 265, 401
digital media 21, 107, 115, 118, 122, 147,
180, 223–4, 265, 279–80, 295, 359,
361–2, 364–5, 390–400
digitization 6, 9–10, 170, 223–4, 265, 280,
282, 398, 401
Dijck, Jose van 279–81
Dijk, Teun van 136
disaster marathons 351
discourse: analysis 125–138, 157, 160, 236,
336, 341; network 335–44, 391; theory
127; order of 125–38; *see also* critical
discourse analysis
dissemination 27, 55, 193, 256, 258, 260,
263, 327, 373, 375, 383, 387
distraction 16–17, 21–2, 41, 45
dominant paradigm 53, 56, 63, 65–6
dramaturgy 85–6, 93; *see also* stage, role,
front-stage, back-stage
Durkheim, Émile 1, 90, 140, 192, 243,
345–6

Eco, Umberto 20, 112, 154, 315
ecology 176, 324, 33, 370; digital ecology
359; *see also* media ecology
education 21, 60, 100, 104, 112, 120–3,
141, 148, 170–1, 174, 247–8, 322–4,
329– 30, 332; media education
122–3, 206

Index   405

effects 4, 6, 31–2, 53–69,111, 114, 116, 123, 130, 148, 153, 155, 159, 161, 172–3, 177–8, 190–1, 215, 243, 258, 261, 263–4, 322, 332, 337, 343, 361, 365, 367– 9, 377, 382, 390; limited 53, 55, 58, 65–6; research 53, 65–6, 190, 191; *see also* media effects
Eisenstein, Elizabeth L. 256–267, 325
Eisenstein, Sergei 40, 390–1
Ellul, Jacques 325
encoding 2, 75, 151–165, 205, 236, 310, 313, 317; *see also* decoding
enlightenment 39–52, 129, 214, 256, 260–1, 286–7, 289, 298, 324, 326, 361, 375
entropy 76; *see also* information theory
environment 78–80, 117–18, 121–2, 324, 326, 364, 367, 375, 383, 386, 390–1; *see also* media environment
Enzensberger, Hans-Magnus 139, 142–3, 146, 148, 212, 216
ethnography 155, 160, 228, 310
exchange value 17, 45, 48, 141; *see also* use value
exhibition value 16–17, 20–1, 40; *see also* cult value

facticity 228, 231, 233–4, 240
Fairclough, Norman 127, 136, 236
feminism 6, 92, 197, 206–7; second wave 197–8, 200
feminist: analysis 87, 311, 319, 362; critique 106; film theory 203; media studies 320; post- 206–7; theory 310, 312–313, 319–20
female spectator 204–5, 208
field: social 242–55; -work 228, 235–6, 239
film 15–16, 18, 21, 30, 40, 42, 196–210, 273, 339–40, 390–2, 394; and photography 14, 39–40, 144, 139, 391; *see also* cinema
Fish, Stanley 312
flow 27, 55, 93, 153, 168–76, 178–81, 305, 329, 347, 351, 361, 364–6, 399
focus group 28–9, 31, 35
Foucault, Michel 84, 125–38, 156, 160, 236, 298, 336–8, 341, 381
frame 85, 87, 227, 230, 232, 234–5, 351, 352; analysis 87– 8, 229, 235
framing 228, 234–5
Frankfurt school 11, 301, 66, 97, 105, 148, 157–8, 176; *see also* critical theory
Fraser, Nancy 105, 137
freedom of speech 96, 231

Freud, Sigmund 24, 31, 35, 197–8, 200, 202, 381
front stage, 84, 86–9; *see also* dramaturgy
functionalism 28, 33, 56, 62, 90, 187, 325

Gadamer, Hans-Georg 163, 336
Geertz, Clifford 188–9
Gellner, Ernest 285, 291–2
gender 2, 5, 27–9, 87, 90, 94, 137, 148, 156–7, 161, 203–4, 206, 227, 229, 311, 316, 318–19, 332, 339, 367–8, 383–4
genealogy 31,127, 131, 133–5
genre 7, 15, 76, 152, 154, 192, 203, 206–7, 261, 271, 311, 314, 319, 322, 329, 347, 349–50, 390, 393, 400
German media theory 360, 380, 382
Giddens, Anthony 88, 237–8, 245
gift economies 140–1, 143
Gitelman, Lisa 265, 373
Gitlin, Todd 63–5, 88
Goffman, Erwing 6, 84–95, 188, 230–1
Grossberg, Lawrence 183, 185, 187
Gutenberg galaxy 113, 119, 257, 265, 340, 341

Habermas, Jürgen 6, 19, 81, 96–110, 160, 173, 176, 287–9, 292, 298, 307, 336, 386
habitus 242–50, 252–3
Hall, Stuart 2, 4, 33, 151–65, 188, 236
Haraway, Donna 6, 325, 332, 362, 368, 384
Hayles, Katherine N. 5, 332, 358–71, 384
hegemony 59, 154, 239
Heidegger, Martin 336–7, 342, 378, 386
hermeneutics 158, 163, 238, 302–3, 336, 339–40, 375, 401
Herzog, Herta 24–38, 54, 56
historicization 5, 172, 181, 183, 298–9, 341
Hobsbawm, Eric 285, 291
Hochschild, Arlie 93
Horkheimer, Max 11–12, 25, 39–52, 97, 158, 216, 336

identity 156, 161, 248, 284; gender, 156, 316–17; and politics 19, 307
ideology 19, 47, 154–5, 162, 211–227, 231, 236, 239, 306, 328
imagined communities 284–96
impression management 85, 92
information theory 70–83, 163, 217, 359, 362; *see also* cybernetics
infrastructures 116, 118–19, 153, 159, 386, 400
Innis, Harold 114–15, 187, 257, 325, 375
interfaces 393–6

406 *Index*

interpretation 152–4, 161–3, 205, 302–3, 312, 319–20
intersectionality 160

Jameson, Fredric 180, 297–310, 396
Jenkins, Henry 107
journalism 104, 227–41, 251–2

Katz, Elihu 27–8, 33–4, 55, 61–4, 192, 346–58
Kittler, Friedrich 5, 11, 116, 173, 335–44, 360, 380–1, 391–2
Kluge, Alexander 105

Lacan, Jacques 160, 198, 201, 278, 306, 336–8
Laclau, Ernesto 127, 136, 156
Lasswell, Harold Dwight 62, 78,177
Lazarsfeld, Paul 4, 25, 27–8, 30, 32, 36, 44, 46, 53–70, 173, 243
Liebes, Tamar 26, 349, 351
linguistic turn 132, 236, 269
Lippman, Walter 183
literacy 121, 261, 266, 325, 327, 332, 338, 340; academic 3; media and information 111, 122–3, 330
liveness 348, 353–4, 376
Luhmann, Niklas 80–1
Lyotard, Jean-Francois 298–9, 396, 401

male gaze 201–6
Manovich, Lev 280, 379, 390–403
marketing 25, 30–1, 62–3, 145, 218
Marvin, Carolyn 265
marxism 12–13, 17, 45, 59, 136–7, 139, 140, 154–5, 176–7, 185, 211–27, 243, 297, 300, 303, 311, 316
Marx, Karl 1, 13, 17, 45, 140–1, 147,152, 158, 161, 214, 219, 244, 300, 374, 386
mass audience 41, 261
mass communication 2, 32, 34, 53–69, 153, 162, 170, 188, 243, 346–7; research 7, 29, 31–2, 36, 55, 151–2, 154–5, 158–9, 163, 175, 177–8; sociology of 230
mass consumption 15, 40, 42, 219–20
mass culture 17, 39, 42, 47, 57–8, 301; *see also* culture
mass distribution 257
masses 16, 19, 41, 158, 176–8, 310; *see also* mass audience, mass communication, mass consumption, mass culture, mass distribution
materiality 74, 265, 339, 362, 364, 366, 394–5

mathematical model of communication 70, 72, 77, theory of communication 70–1
McLuhan, Marshall 6, 11, 89, 111–125, 140, 142, 145, 148, 173, 175–6, 180, 216, 257, 311, 322, 324–6, 337, 341, 360, 370, 379–80, 391–2
Mead, George Herbert 90–1, 188
media archaeology 7, 173, 265, 342
media ecology 324–6, 331–2; *see also* ecology
media effects 53, 62, 64–5; *see also* effects
media environment 116–19, 324; *see also* environment
media event 192, 345–357; ceremonial 345–7; conflictual 351; hybrid 352
media history 89, 327, 341–2, 392
media literacy 122; *see also* literacy
media use 25, 32–5,151–5, 221–2, 251
mediation 143, 384
mediatization 145–6, 395, 401
medium theory 114–16, 175–6, 391–2
Merton, Robert K. 4, 28–9, 31–3, 53–70
message 72–5,152; the medium is the 111–13, 142, 176, 326, 342; without a code 268, 270, 277, 279–80, 282
Meyrowitz, Joshua 84, 88–90, 114–15, 391
Mills, C. Wright 4, 63
mobile privatization 175–7
modernism 300–5
monopolization 60
Morley, David 33, 62, 159, 160, 162, 319
Mouffe, Chantal 127, 136, 156
Mulvey, Laura 196–211
Murdock, Graham 219–21
myth 269

narcotic dysfunction 66
narration 201, 347, 350
narrative 27, 168, 196–210, 231, 237, 288–9, 295, 299–300, 313–17, 319, 347–8, 350, 361, 393, 395–6
nationalism 284–96
Negt, Oskar 105
new media 3, 5, 7, 12, 20, 29, 41, 99, 107, 119, 139, 142, 265, 330, 337, 340, 350, 365, 369, 377, 379, 387, 391–401; culture 121; literacy 122; objects 393–4, 396–7; technology/ies 1, 15, 17, 119, 123, 142, 173, 206, 214, 361, 392
news 1, 29, 59, 61–2, 88, 103–4, 108, 129, 159, 173, 180, 227–41, 244, 246, 248, 251, 272, 289, 322, 347, 351, 359, 373, 395, 399; newspaper 29–30, 45, 98, 137, 217, 230, 232–3, 246–7, 286, 288–90, 292, 328; newsworthiness 229–31

Index 407

Nietzsche, Friedrich 336, 342, 381
non-discursive 127
nostalgia 303–5
novel 99, 103, 132, 286, 288–9, 292, 295, 297, 314–315, 330, 338, 358–360, 366–7, 391, 396–7

objectification 49, 202–4, 237
objectivity 129, 228, 231–2, 238, 270, 277, 279
Ong, Walter 115, 122, 257
otherness 373, 387

paradigm 4, 10, 53, 56, 63–6, 155, 159, 230, 238, 270, 280, 338, 367, 397–400
pastiche 304
patriarchy 316, 317, 321
Peirce, Charles Sanders 154, 269, 271, 382
performance 19, 40, 50, 85–93, 100, 103–4, 166, 172, 346–8, 350, 375
performativity 91, 207, 370
Peters, John Durham 7, 111, 193, 332, 372–388
phenomenology 41, 44, 230, 232, 239
phonograph 265, 339, 375, 382, 387
photography 14–15, 39–40, 144, 196, 268–282, 328, 339, 391
platform 10, 19, 96, 98, 107–9, 119, 170, 211–214, 223–4, 232, 331, 342, 350–4, 359, 383, 399–400
pluralization 160–1
political economy 5, 66, 140–3, 214–15, 242; critical political economy 212–14
polysemy 159
popular culture 160, 198, 201, 203, 206–8, 264, 298, 301, 310–312, 315, 318–320, 323, 329; *see also* culture
popular taste 53, 56–7, 59, 61–6, 173; *see also* taste
posthuman 7, 307, 358–371
Postman, Neil 121, 173, 322–334, 370
postmodernism 11, 169, 173, 176, 269, 297–309, 360, 396, 401
poststructuralism 160, 270, 274, 303, 336
power 2–3, 5, 6, 12, 20, 25, 29, 45–6, 48–9, 54, 57, 59, 66, 87, 90, 96, 99, 100, 103–4, 109, 116, 118–19, 125–6, 129, 131–2, 134–7, 140, 143, 145–6, 151–2, 154, 156–63, 171, 178–9, 186, 189, 191, 196, 198, 202–3, 208, 214–7, 220, 222, 234–8, 242, 244, 246, 249, 251, 270, 286–7, 289, 292–3, 299, 300, 310, 318, 320, 325, 337, 341–2, 345, 350, 353–4, 362, 366, 368–9, 374, 383–4, 387, 392,

395; biopower 135; counter-power 126–7, 134, 137; empower/ing 12, 45, 53, 204, 261, 368; -ful: 24, 57, 107, 139, 160, 186, 212, 285, 347, 353; -less 204, 213; relations 3, 103, 139, 141–2, 151–2, 154, 155, 159, 214, 253, 268, 277; structures 93, 99, 114, 319–20
pragmatism 91, 160, 382
preservation 62, 64, 66, 256, 258, 259, 253
printing press 112, 115, 120–1, 256–266, 292, 325–7, 379
print technology 121, 256
private 20, 59, 65, 98–204, 106, 108, 112, 125, 175, 177, 201, 231, 233, 237, 277, 280, 287, 347, 366
propaganda 30–31, 57, 60, 211, 330, 337
Propp, Vladimir 315
pseudoindividuality 48
psychoanalysis 15, 41, 198–200, 203, 278, 306, 319, 338, 340, 363, 381
public debate 97, 99, 103, 107, 116, 327, 331
public service 5, 21, 106, 109, 162, 170, 232
public sphere 6, 19, 96–109, 173, 176, 287–8, 292, 327, 346; alternative 19, 105
punctum 271–278, 280–282

quantitative methods 25, 30, 53–54, 65

radio 25–31, 44, 54–5, 57, 59, 88, 91–3, 115, 139, 142–3
Radway, Janice 310–321
realism 127, 154, 168, 177, 270, 277, 300, 304
reception 29, 80, 89, 105, 143, 151–2, 159, 163, 177, 204, 228, 312, 319–20; research 62, 163, 205; studies 26, 159, 311; theory 162–3, 310, 312–3, 319
redundancy 46, 76, 78; *see also* information theory
reformation 256, 260, 263–4
religion 40, 51, 56, 286, 290–1, 293, 322, 380
reproduction 6–7, 9–10, 14–8, 21, 24, 39–40, 102, 144, 152, 161, 222, 256, 259, 338–9; analogue 269, 364; digital 10; mechanical 7, 9–12, 14, 39, 144, 270; social 245; technical 14, 18, 21, 260
Riesman, David 91
ritual 16, 18, 33, 85, 128, 143, 156, 184, 186–93, 228, 232, 238, 239, 329, 345–8, 350–1, 353; model 189–90, 192; perspective 186, 188, 190–2

408 *Index*

role 27, 85–88, 91–93; *see also* dramaturgy
romanticism 18, 42, 46, 340, 380

Sartre, Jean Paul 243, 273, 279, 297
Saussure, Ferdinand de 152, 246, 269, 397
Scannell, Paddy 15, 345
Schiller, Herbert 185
Schramm, Wilbur 57, 185
Schütz, Alfred 190, 230, 239
scientific revolution 256, 260, 263
scopophilia 200
Screen 203, 205
selection 75, 77–78, 80–81, 145, 269, 394, 399; *see also* information theory
semiotics 154, 157, 163, 199, 216, 268–271, 312, 397
seriality 289–291
Shannon, Claude 4, 70–82, 151, 363
sign 142–3, 269–71, 304, 397
sign value 141–146
signified 202, 269, 303, 365
signifier 132, 269, 303, 364–5
simulacra 140, 144–5, 298, 304
simulation 11, 140, 143–4, 146, 172, 298, 364–5
simultaneity 288–290, 295, 346
Sloterdijk, Peter 359
Smythe, Dallas 185, 211–226
Snow, C.P. 341, 359
soap opera 25–7, 29, 178, 318
social construction 132, 230, 238–9, 263
social field 242, 244, 246
social imaginaries 345, 354
social interaction 62, 87–9, 91, 156
social media 21, 34, 59, 61–2, 84, 88–90, 96, 98, 107–9, 126, 146–8, 153, 162, 204, 206–7, 251, 307, 320, 323, 331, 342, 352, 369, 383, 386
social space 41, 245–251
Sonnevend, Julia 347–8, 350–4
space of lifestyles 248, 251
space of social positions 247
spatiality 186, 289–291, 299, 305, 397
stadium 271, 272, 275–6, 278, 281–2
stage 84–9, 91; *see also* dramaturgy
standardization 44, 46, 256, 258–9, 261–2

status conferral 58, 61, 66
strategic communication 72, 74, 145
structuralism 146, 160, 268, 270, 297, 303, 336
structure of feeling 175, 181
subculture 92, 156, 158, 318
subjectivity 42–4, 274, 307, 337–8, 340, 359, 365–8, 370
supplementation 60, 62; *see also* information theory
symbolic exchange 11, 140, 143–8
symbolic interactionism 90–1, 160
symbolic order 144
syntagm 270, 397, 399
systems theory 70, 80

taste 44, 46, 53, 57, 59–60, 66, 246–9, 313; *see also* popular taste
technological determinism 13, 114, 116, 172–3, 216, 263, 337, 360
technology 5–6, 12–15, 41, 43, 74, 113–116, 121, 142–3, 215–216, 256–8, 263, 289, 292, 300, 322, 326, 330, 336–341, 358–60, 367–8, 377–8, 391–3, 396
technology and cultural form 166–182
telegraph 13, 70–1, 75, 188, 214, 322, 325, 328, 337, 375, 379–380
television 2, 20, 73, 88, 115, 118, 121–2, 139, 142–3, 151–4, 166–82, 192, 206–7, 231, 251, 319, 322–34, 345–57
Thompson, John B 89
transmission 25, 32, 70–5, 77, 79, 82, 103, 121, 143, 151, 153, 155, 162–3, 186–191, 193, 232, 362–3, 375, 382, 387
Tuchman, Gaye 61, 227–240
two-step flow 56, 62

use value 17, 41, 48, 141
uses and gratification 24, 32, 62

Weaver, Warren 4, 70–83, 151
Wiener, Norbert 79, 361–3, 367, 397
Williams, Raymond 4–5, 114, 116, 157–8, 166–181, 188, 191, 219, 325
Wodak, Ruth 136
writing 132, 332, 336, 338–40, 365, 369

Printed in the United States
by Baker & Taylor Publisher Services